THE ECONOMICS OF THE LABOUR MARKET

MACMILLAN TEXTS IN ECONOMICS

This series presents a new generation of economics textbooks from Macmillan developed in conjunction with a panel of distinguished editorial advisers:

Published
Understanding the UK Economy (2nd edition): edited by Peter Curwen
Business Economics: Paul R. Ferguson, Glenys J. Ferguson and R. Rothschild
International Finance: Keith Pilbeam
The Economics of the Labour Market: David Sapsford and Zafiris Tzannatos

Future Macmillan Texts in Economics cover the core compulsory and optional courses in economics at first-degree level and will include:

Forthcoming
Environmental Economics: Nick Hanley, Ben White and Jason Shogren
Development Economics: Ian Livingstone
International Trade: Mia Mikic
Monetary Economics: Stuart Sayer
Macroeconomics: Eric Pentecost

In preparation
Introductory Principles
Comparative Economics
Development Economics
Econometrics
Financial Economics
Industrial Economics
Microeconomics
Public Sector Economics
Quantitative Methods
Welfare Economics

THE ECONOMICS OF THE LABOUR MARKET

David Sapsford

Professor of Economics
University of Lancaster

and

Zafiris Tzannatos

World Bank, Washington, DC

First published 1993 by
THE MACMILLAN PRESS LTD
Houndmills, Basingstoke, Hampshire RG21 2XS
and London
Companies and representatives
throughout the world

ISBN 0–333–53495–6 hardcover
ISBN 0–333–53496–4 paperback

A catalogue record for this book is available from the British Library.

Printed in Great Britain by
Mackays of Chatham plc
Chatham, Kent

Contents

List of Figures

List of Tables

Preface

This book is designed for advanced undergraduate and first-year graduate students taking courses in labour economics. It grew out of the first named author's earlier book entitled *Labour Market Economics* (London: Allen & Unwin, 1981). Labour economics has seen a range of important new developments since the publication more than a decade ago of this earlier book and the present book has been rewritten to fully reflect these developments. Taken together with our earlier set of edited readings, *Current Issues in Labour Economics* (London: Macmillan, 1990), the present book provides both instructors and students with a package which covers the range of topics typically encountered in such courses. Labour market issues are important to students of both macroeconomics and industrial relations and it is envisaged that this book will also prove to be a useful source of material for such programmes.

Thanks are due to Professor David Greenaway of the University of Nottingham for his detailed comments on the first draft of the manuscript and to our publisher, Stephen Rutt, for his efficient stewardship throughout this project.

Kirkby Lonsdale, Cumbria DAVID SAPSFORD
Bethesda, MD ZAFIRIS TZANNATOS

■ Chapter 1 ■

Introduction

Labour is one of the *factors of production*, and the subject matter of labour economics may be broadly defined as the study of its pricing and allocation. Individuals receive income from a variety of different sources, including employment or self-employment, from the state in the form of transfer income or as income arising from the ownership of assets of various sorts, including capital and land. However, income from employment is the major source of individual income. Indeed, as we shall see below, the proportion of the population which is either in or seeking paid employment is typically to the order of 50 per cent for member countries of the Organisation for Economic Cooperation and Development (OECD), while for the population of working age the figure typically rises to around 70 per cent. The issues considered by labour economists are clearly, therefore, of considerable importance in practice.

■ Some basic questions in labour economics

The problems and issues discussed by labour economists are many and varied and span both micro and macroeconomics. In order to provide the reader with an insight into the sorts of issues discussed in this book it is useful to list some of the questions which will be addressed. These include:

1. What determines the numbers of people in paid employment, their hours of work and their rates of pay? More generally, what determines the division of labour within households as between who works in the market, who works in the home and who participates in education? Do cuts in income taxation provide an increased or decreased incentive to work?
2. Why do people decide to join or leave trade unions? What is collective bargaining and how do unions and employers actually arrive at

an agreed level of wages by negotiation? Do unions actually raise the wages and employment conditions of their members above the levels that they would otherwise be? What, if any, influence do unions have upon efficiency: do they price their members out of jobs and result in a deterioration in productivity, or do they result in an *increase* in labour productivity?
3. Why do wages differ between different occupations and industries, between the sexes and between individuals of different ethnic backgrounds? How do education and training influence both the chances of obtaining paid employment and the level of earnings?
4. What is unemployment and what are its causes and cures? How and why does the structure of unemployment differ between different countries? Why is it that some individuals remain unemployed for only short spells of time, while others remain without work for many months or even years? Does the size of state unemployment benefits influence the incidence and/or the duration of unemployment? How do unemployed workers search for jobs?
5. Do employers and employees enter into an implicit contract designed to stabilise earnings over the cycle and if so, what effect does this have upon unemployment? Does the productivity of workers actually depend upon the wage rate which they receive and if so, how does this influence unemployment?
6. What determines the rate at which wages change between one year and the next? What, if any, role in this process is played by trade unions, by inflationary expectations and by workers' real-wage aspirations?

■ Analytical approach

The preceding list is by no means exhaustive but it nevertheless gives a flavour of the sort of issues which are discussed in this book. At the most basic level, economists see wages as the price of labour and as such, see these as being determined in analogous fashion to the prices of goods and services; namely by the interaction of supply and demand forces in the market for labour.

However, the reader will quickly become aware that there is much more to labour economics than this! It has long been recognised that the need for a 'special' theory of the labour market arises because of various 'peculiar' properties of labour which distinguish it from other commodities to which the usual theory of value may be applied (see, for example, Marshall, 1890; Hicks, 1932). It is these 'peculiar' properties of labour which give labour economics its own particular character and which establish it as a subject in its own right, as opposed to a particular application of price theory.

■ Plan of this book

Although much of the analytics of what might be called the 'basic' theory of the labour market have been around for a long time, the subject of labour economics has witnessed many important and exciting developments over the past 25 years or so. These developments are fully reflected in the subject matter and structure of this book.

□ *Labour supply and demand*

The market for labour has two sides. First, there is the demand side which is made up of producers of goods and services as employers purchasing labour services. Second, there is the supply side which is composed of individuals and households as sellers or suppliers of labour services. The basic analysis of labour supply is developed in Chapter 2. As we see there, a relatively straightforward model in which individuals maximise their utility, subject to the constraint imposed by the time and wage rates available to them, is able to shed light on a range of supply-side issues. These issues include the determinants of optimal hours of work and the influence of variations in income tax rates and overtime premia on the incentive to work. In addition, we will see that this basic model provides an explanation of why some workers become 'workaholics', while others choose instead to opt out of the workforce altogether. Having considered the basic model of labour supply we move on in Chapter 3 to some more sophisticated models. Many of these models owe their origins to Gary Becker's seminal (1965) paper, which explicitly recognised the *household* as the relevant decision-making unit regarding the related questions of labour force participation and hours-of-work decisions, on the one hand, and home production and consumption decisions on the other. The beauty of Becker's model lies in the way that it integrates the production, consumption and labour supply decisions within a unified framework. By so doing, Becker was able to demonstrate how utility-maximising behaviour by households can determine the division of each member's available time between paid work in the labour market and unpaid or non-market activities, as well as their chosen mix between home-produced and market-purchased goods and their chosen division of labour between various household members in the performance of the range of alternative tasks. Becker's model was extremely influential and provided the basic foundations upon which a large theoretical and empirical literature of more recent labour supply models was to grow. It is this literature which forms the subject matter of Chapter 3.

Chapter 4 considers a variety of questions relating to the *quality* of labour. The basic idea here is that education and training may be seen as forms of investment in the individual, which give rise, over the longer period, to the accumulation of a stock of so-called *human capital.* Although the origins of the human capital approach can be found in the writings of early economists (for example, Adam Smith, 1776) the studies by both Mincer (1958) and Becker (1964) were especially influential and paved the way for the emergence of, and rapid growth in, a literature which sees education and training as forms of investment in the individual which give rise to an improvement in the *quality* of labour supply. As we shall see at various places in this book, including Chapter 8, the human capital approach carries with it important implications for a variety of issues in labour economics relating to the structure of earnings.

The demand for labour, like that for any of the factors of production, is a *derived demand* in the sense that producers demand labour not directly for itself, but rather for the contribution which it makes, when used in conjunction with the other factors of production, to the producer's output of goods and services. The determinants of the demand for labour attracted considerable interest in the early literature, with the development and refinement of marginal productivity theory presented by such writers as Marshall (1890), Clark (1900) and Cartter (1959). The marginal productivity approach to labour demand is considered in Chapter 5, while Chapter 6 discusses a number of subsequent developments and refinements to the model. These include the effects of fixed employment costs, and the employer's choice between variations in hours of work and variations in the number of employees. This chapter also introduces the so-called employment demand function approach as an alternative framework for the analysis of labour demand.

☐ *Wages and employment*

Chapter 7 brings together the preceding material relating to the two sides of the labour market and shows how demand- and supply-side forces interact in the market for labour to determine both the wage rate, as the price of labour, and the level of employment. This chapter considers both market-clearing and disequilibrium models of the market for labour. Many important issues in labour economics centre on the structure of *differentials* in wage earnings. Chapter 8 considers these issues, while Chapter 9 develops the analysis in an investigation of the nature and extent of discrimination in the market for labour.

□ Trade unions and the labour market

Reporting the results of a survey of the contents of a wide range of professional journals in economics, Johnson (1975) concluded that the study of trade unions had become a Cinderella topic within the labour economics literature. However, as it turns out nothing could have been further from the truth as regards the post-1980 literature! Throughout the 1980s and 1990s the economic analysis of trade unions mushroomed to become one of the largest and most rapidly expanding branches of the subject. One of the most important driving forces behind this expansion appears to have been the publication of McDonald and Solow's (1981) paper in which they rediscovered the efficient-bargain model, originally formulated some three decades earlier by both Leontief (1946) and Fellner (1951). Like other good ideas in economics, the efficient-bargain model improved with the passage of time, to the extent that its rediscovery sparked the emergence of a wealth of studies, initially theoretical but subsequently also empirical, seeking to both extend and test its basic prediction that collective bargains struck between employers and trade unions will generate wage–employment combinations which satisfy the axiom of Pareto efficiency. Chapters 10 and 11 provide detailed coverage of both the theory of trade union behaviour and the determination of the level of wages in unionised labour markets.

□ Imperfect information in the market for labour

Over the postwar period considerable attention has been directed in the literature to the functioning of labour markets which are characterised by imperfect information regarding both job opportunities and labour availability. Under such circumstances it is usually argued that an amount of market *search* will be undertaken by labour market participants, the objective of which is to obtain an improvement in their information set regarding available alternatives. Search theory is concerned with the ways in which workers looking for jobs, and employers seeking to fill vacancies, will optimally gather information relating to the location and characteristics of available job offers and workers respectively. Market search is not a costless process and Chapter 12 explores the ways in which rational individuals may balance the costs of labour market search against its potential benefits in order to arrive at an optimal search strategy.

□ *Unemployment and wage inflation*

The final two chapters of this book are concerned with the topics of wage inflation and unemployment. Chapter 13 discusses the determinants of wage inflation. It begins with a discussion of the original Phillips curve model, which is then extended to encompass the Friedman–Phelps expectations-augmented formulation. The natural rate hypothesis is considered in this chapter in the context of both adaptive and rational expectations. Chapter 13 also outlines a number of alternative models of wage inflation, including both the target real wage and hysteresis hypotheses.

The final chapter of the book is concerned with unemployment: its types, its causes and the ways in which it might be lessened if not altogether 'cured'. The chapter provides a detailed discussion of a number of important recent developments in the unemployment literature, including the influential Layard–Nickell (1986) model, as well as the efficiency wage and implicit contract models of unemployment.

Chapter 2

Labour Supply: The Basic Model

The *supply of labour* is defined as the amount of labour, measured in person-hours, offered for hire during a given time-period. Taking population as given, the quantity of labour supplied depends on two main factors. First, there are the numbers engaged in or seeking paid employment, which together make up the *labour force* or the *supply of workers*. This amount can conveniently be expressed as a fraction or percentage of the total population, to give an *activity* or *labour force participation rate*. Second, there is the number of hours that each person is willing to supply once he or she is in the labour force – the *supply of hours*. The determinants of these two dimensions of labour supply are discussed in this chapter, while Chapter 3 explores a number of extensions to the basic model. First, we consider the supply of workers.

■ Who supplies labour?

It is important to recognise that the labour force, as those *economically active*, consists of two groups of people. First, there are those with paid jobs (the employed) and second, there are those who are seeking paid employment but are unable to find it under prevailing economic conditions (the unemployed). **Table 2.1** gives a breakdown of the labour force in a range of OECD member countries, as between the employed and unemployed categories.

While the official definition of the numbers employed corresponds, for most industrial economies, reasonably closely to the first component of the labour force (that is, the number engaged in paid employment), some important doubts are frequently expressed regarding the adequacy of the officially compiled unemployment statistics as a measure of its second component (that is, the numbers seeking paid employment). There are two general sorts of reasons for this. First, because the official statistics for many countries are a by-product of their social security system, they typically refer to those registered for employment with state agencies of various sorts. Since registration is generally a necessary condition for receipt of unemployment benefit, not all those officially classed as unemployed are actually seeking paid work; some are instead voluntarily unemployed. Second, the official statistics do not generally include all of those who are actually searching for paid employment. Depending on the precise system operating in the country in question, a number of people (such as some married women and pensioners) do not register as unemployed, presumably because of their non-entitlement to, or ignorance of, their eligibility for benefits. In addition, some job-seekers do not register because they prefer to conduct their own job search through channels outside the state network, such as newspaper advertisements, contacts with friends and relatives, or private employment agencies.

In the UK, for example, the estimated population in mid-1989 was 57.236 million giving an estimated labour force participation rate of 49.3 per cent, with the corresponding rates for a selection of OECD member countries being shown in **Table 2.1**. Population is important in the analysis of labour supply because its size in the period in question sets an upper limit to the supply of workers. Since each member of the population is either in or out of the labour force (the membership criterion being the actual or desired performance of paid or market work) we can usefully begin our discussion of the supply of workers by asking why it was that, in 1989, approximately half of the population of each of these countries remained outside the labour force?

Table 2.1 ***Labour force participation rates, 1989***

	Australia	*France*	*Germany*	*Japan*	*UK*	*USA*
Employment (000s)	7 725	21 484	27 208	61 280	26 457	117 342
Unemployment (000s)	509	2 281	1 651	1 433	1 770	6 523
Total population (000s)	16 833	56 160	61 990	123 120	57 236	248 762
Labour force participation rate (%)	48.9	42.3	46.5	50.9	49.3	49.8

Sources: Authors' own calculations based on data reported in OECD, *Labour Force Statistics*, *Main Economic Indicators* and country-specific sources.

Not all of the population is eligible to join the labour force, since all those under the school-leaving age are required to attend school on a full-time basis, while the majority of men over the age of 65, and women over 60, are retired. Others are prevented from joining the labour force for such reasons as physical or mental disability. In order to allow for the influence of the population's age structure it is useful to consider the labour force participation rate for those of working age. This can be evaluated by calculating the percentage of those over school-leaving age, but under retirement age, who are in the labour force. **Table 2.2** reports labour force participation rates for those of working age in a selection of OECD member countries. As may be seen from **Table 2.2**, this labour force participation rate was approximately 76 per cent for the UK but only 66.5 per cent for the USA. Notice also that the working-age participation rates for both Australia and Germany lie between the UK and US rates, while those of France and Japan are below the US rate. Most of the 24 and 34 per cent of the UK and USA population respectively in this age group who remained outside the labour force were either full-time students in schools and colleges or married women with homes to run and families to care for. While both these activities involve considerable work, neither receives payment and therefore neither qualifies its performers for membership of the labour force.

Table 2.2 ***Labour force participation rates, 1989: age and marital status***

(a) For population of working age (%)

Australia	72.8*
France	65.5
Germany	68.9*
Japan	62.9
UK	76.1
US	66.5

(b) By marital status, all ages

	Male (single)	*Female (single)*	*Male (married)*	*Female (married)*
UK	71.8	59.1	77.1	57.3
Germany	67.6	58.4	73.5	42.9
France	58.8	48.3	70.5	50.9

* Refers to 1988.

Sources: Authors' own calculations based on data reported in OECD, *Labour Force Statistics*, *Main Economic Indicators* and country-specific sources.

■ The labour force participation decision

Table 2.2 also gives a breakdown of activity rates in a number of countries according to sex and marital status. This table shows the existence of considerable variability in activity rates between the sexes and according to marital status. In order to explain such variations in activity rates it is necessary to explore the forces that influence the individual's decision on whether to enter or remain outside the labour force.

As we have seen, the concepts of the supply of labour and the labour force separate paid or *market work* for all other non-market uses of time. The traditional analysis of labour supply, which is reviewed later in this chapter in connection with the supply of hours, views the individual as a rational decision-maker who divides his or her time between two mutually exclusive uses: market work and time not paid for, with the latter generally being referred to as *leisure*. However, as has long been recognised (for example, Hunter, 1970, p. 42) this analysis is essentially one of marginal changes in the hours of work of those who are not only already in the labour force but also in employment. As such this analysis is not readily applicable to the discrete in/out labour force participation decision, which generally involves non-marginal changes in the allocation of one's time, because hours of work are typically demanded in the form of blocks of time to be supplied on a regular basis at or within certain specified times.

■ Households and participation decisions

Recent studies have sought to improve on the traditional analysis by explicitly recognising (1) that decisions about who enters the labour force, and the allied question of how many hours to work, are made in the context of the family or household as part of its decision about the optimum allocation of its members' time between alternative uses (Ashenfelter and Heckman, 1974; Gronau, 1973), and (2) that non-market activity is composed not only of leisure in the everyday sense but also of household work, which is itself one input in the production of a variety of home-produced goods and services, such as home cooking, childcare and a tidy house (Mincer, 1962). Such models are discussed in detail in Chapter 3.

To set the scene for what follows in this chapter we may consider the simple model put forward by Bowen and Finegan (1969) in their famous study of US labour force participation rates. Taking the household as the unit of analysis, Bowen and Finegan (1969) argued that the allocation of members' time between work in the market and all other non-market uses of time – such as working in the household, eating, sleeping, pursuing education and leisure – is determined by four classes of variables: its tastes, expected market earnings rate,[1] productivities in non-market activities[2] and its total resource constraint. A household's allocation of time is held to reflect its *tastes* for market goods relative to leisure and to home goods (for example, its valuation of the services of a paid childminder relative to a mother's care) and its preference about the performance of particular tasks by particular family members (for example, its attitude to the wife's performing heavy manual work during night shifts in a factory and to the customary social role in the UK and many other industrialised countries of the male as a breadwinner). The household's time-allocation decision will also reflect the *expected market earnings* of its members (net of tax, other stoppages and travelling expenses), as well as their *productivities* – or, more precisely, their *comparative advantages* – in various non-market activities. Last, the allocation decision will also reflect the household's *total available resources*. These are made up of the total time at its disposal (that is, 24 hours per member per day), its income from sources other than market work and the monetary value of its assets.

■ Effect of changes in non-labour income

In order to see how these forces interact to determine the labour force status of each family member, consider the case of a household that experiences a substantial increase in its resources, such as the inheritance of a large annuity, unaccompanied by any other change. This situation represents the familiar case of an *income effect* and on the usual assumption that for at least some family members leisure or some other non-market activity is a normal good (that is, one having a positive income elasticity or demand), we can expect the labour supplied by the household to decrease. This is because the increase in non-labour income enables family members to 'purchase' more of their preferred activity. Consequently we may see a decrease in its members' labour force participation, as either an elderly family member takes early retirement, or a working wife becomes a full-time housewife or resumes her education, or children stay on longer in, or return to, full-time education.

■ Effect of changes in market earnings

To illustrate the effect of a change in market earnings open to a household member, let us suppose that the wage rate of (say) shorthand typists increases, other things remaining equal. In households that already include a working shorthand typist this increase results, assuming that his or her hours of work remain unchanged, in an income increase for the family. This increase in family income may result in decreased participation by other family members for reasons discussed in the previous paragraph. Alternatively it may lead to other members working shorter hours in their market activity. In households where wives have left work to raise their families, some may be tempted to return to work as shorthand typists by the prospect of the increased earnings. The price of non-market activity to the worker is its *opportunity cost* (that is, the earnings foregone by using hours in non-market rather than market activity); and as we shall see below, the total effect of a change in market earnings (that is, in the price of non-market activities) can be subdivided into an income and a substitution effect. The increase in market earnings considered in the current example results in an increase in the price of non-market activities, since each hour spent in non-market activities now involves a greater opportunity cost in the form of foregone earnings. A *substitution effect* arises from the changed price of non-market relative to market activity, and this encourages the non-working wife to substitute market activity for the now more expensive non-market activities. If she actually resumes employment, the household experiences an income effect from which the possibility of decreased labour force participation by other family members now arises.

The wife's resumption of employment can be expected to bring about various changes to the household's non-market production and consumption activities. In its production of home goods, we can expect there to be some reallocation of housework to husbands and children, together with some adjustments in the household's production methods. For example, there may be increased use of hired labour and/or the adoption of more capital-intensive production methods within the household, with the increased use of various labour-saving devices. In its consumption activities the household may also decide to substitute market for home goods, with convenience meals replacing home cooking, or it may simply decide to consume less goods (for example, by tolerating a less tidy house).

■ Participation and the demand for labour

The influence of demand conditions in the labour market on labour force participation has attracted considerable interest since the 1930s, with attention centring on two conflicting hypotheses concerning the influence of variations in employment opportunities on labour force participation rates. The first of these hypotheses is known as the *added worker hypothesis*. According to this hypothesis, additional household members (principally wives and older children) enter the labour force in order to supplement family income when this suffers a transitory decline because the husband has become unemployed or is experiencing a reduction in the hours of work available to him. According to this hypothesis, labour force participation rates *rise* as unemployment increases.

The second of these hypotheses is known as the *discouraged worker hypothesis*. This holds that during periods of high unemployment, some of the unemployed become so dispirited in their job search that they withdraw from the labour force altogether, while others who would otherwise enter the labour force do not bother to do so. These workers leave or fail to enter the labour force during periods of high unemployment because the *expected wage* facing them (that is, the wage they will earn if they obtain a job, *multiplied* by the probability of finding a job) is lower because *either* the relevant wage falls *or* their assessment of the probability of finding a satisfactory job after a reasonable period of search is reduced. This hypothesis therefore suggests that labour force participation rates are negatively related to unemployment. In addition, the discouraged worker hypothesis carries the implication that a more adequate indication of the extent of unemployment is obtained if we add to those actually seeking employment under prevailing conditions those, the *hidden unemployed*, who would be in the labour force seeking employment if they did not feel job search to be hopeless.

Both added and discouraged worker effects can exist simultaneously in different households as unemployment changes, and the question of which, if either, effect is the stronger arises. As we shall see in the following section, this question regarding the direction of the net effect of these two opposing forces has been the subject of considerable empirical investigation.

■ Some empirical evidence

In the analysis of labour supply it is usual to subdivide the total potential supply of workers into two groups according to their degree of attachment to the labour force. Those who have a high degree of attachment, principally married men as the main breadwinners of the family, are likely to be permanently attached to the labour force until they reach retirement age and are referred to as *primary workers*. Others – such as married women who move into and out of the labour force in response to various family and other circumstances, and students who join the labour force at various times while completing their education – have a lower degree of labour force attachment and are termed *secondary workers*. This classification of workers as primary or secondary corresponds to a partition of the total labour force into its permanent and transitory components.

There is in existence a large number of empirical studies of the labour force participation behaviour of various sex, age and race groups, and in this section we briefly review some of the major findings of this research. A comprehensive survey of the literature is provided by Killingsworth (1983).

□ *Primary workers*

It is clear that the labour force participation rates of primary workers are higher than those of secondary workers and as we might expect, their variability is generally more easily explained. To illustrate the determinants of the labour force participation rates of primary workers, consider the case of men in the prime of their working lives or *prime-age males*, defined as those between 25 and 54 years of age (Bowen and Finegan, 1969, p. 39). In their classic study of the US experience, these authors pointed out that in 1967 the participation rate of this group as a whole was to the order of 97 per cent. In this study, Bowen and Finegan divided the factors that determine the labour force status of prime-age males into personal characteristics and variables reflecting market conditions.

From their detailed analysis of 1960 US Census data, Bowen and Finegan concluded that the most important factor in determining the labour force status of prime-age males is marital status. In the census week of 1960, the participation rate of married prime-age males (living with their wives) was found to be 97.6 per cent, compared to 79.1 per cent for the separated, 81.3 per cent for those who had never married, 83.1 per cent for widowers and 84.3 per cent for the divorced. However, Bowen and Finegan rightly pointed out that this result requires a cautious interpretation, since it is not clear exactly what marital status is proxying! On the one hand, marital status may be proxying tastes for money income brought about by the increased financial responsibilities that accompany marriage. Alternatively, it may be proxying tastes for market work, in that those who prefer regular market work may also prefer to marry and stay married, and indeed may find it easier to do so. In addition, the accepted social role in much of the industrialised world of the married man as breadwinner may mean that there are psychic costs of non-participation, which are higher for married than for unmarried men. On the other hand, labour force participation may be related to marital status via market earnings, in that a male's marital status may serve as a proxy for various personal, mental and physical characteristics that influence his prospective market earnings and thus his labour force status. According to this latter interpretation, it is higher market earnings, and therefore a higher (opportunity) cost of non-market activity, that is responsible for the higher participation rates of married men.

Other personal characteristics that were found to exert a significant influence on the labour force participation behaviour of prime-age males include race, number of years of schooling and the size of non-labour income. Rates were found to be higher for whites than for similar blacks and to rise with the number of years of education. Bowen and Finegan argued that both of these effects correspond to differences in market earnings (that is, the opportunity costs of non-participation), since these are typically higher for whites than for non-whites and tend to rise in all race groups with years of education. Participation rates were also found to be negatively related to the size of non-labour income – a result consistent with the positive income elasticity of demand for non-market activity discussed above.

Turning now to the influence of labour market conditions, the basic hypothesis that Bowen and Finegan sought to test in their regression analysis was that the participation rates of prime-age males are positively related to their expected market earnings. Since a worker's expected market earnings are influenced not only by the wages that he can earn in employment but also by the likelihood of his actually finding a job, independent variables were specified to represent both these dimensions of expected earnings. In a cross-section analysis by standard metropolitan statistical areas, Bowen and Finegan used the unemployment rate in the locality and a job mix variable (that is, the proportion of jobs that can be expected, by experience elsewhere in the economy, to be filled by males) to indicate the probability that a worker will find a job after a particular period of search, as well as a measure of average wages in the area. All three independent variables were found to exert significant influences on participation rates and to have signs consistent with the expected market-earnings hypothesis. Participation rates were found to be negatively related to unemployment and positively related to the 'maleness' of the job mix – results that suggest that unfavourable job opportunities discourage participation by lowering the probability of finding a job and hence the level of expected market earnings. In addition, the wage variable was found to exert the expected positive influence on participation rates. See Pencavel (1986) for a more detailed survey of the literature on the labour supply behaviour of men.

□ *Secondary workers*

Married women are the most important group of secondary workers, and their labour supply has attracted considerable research interest. See Killingsworth and Heckman (1986) for a detailed survey of the female labour supply literature. Studies of cross-section data by cities (for example, Mincer, 1962; Cain, 1966; Bowen and Finegan, 1969) have shown that participation rates of married women are inversely related to their husbands' incomes and positively related to female earnings. Similar findings emerged in the 1970s from studies of the British data by Greenhalgh (1977) and McNabb (1977). As Rees (1973, p. 10) points out, a husband's income affects his wife's labour force participation in much the same way as non-labour income does, with the consequence that the observed relationship corresponds to the negative (non-labour) income effect discussed above. The observed positive influence of female earnings indicates that improvements in prospective market earnings, which increase the opportunity costs of non-participation, increase married women's participation rates by encouraging some wives to begin and others to resume market work.

Other factors that have been shown to exert a significant influence on the participation rates of married women include the number and age of their children, their level of educational attainment and their colour. Not surprisingly, the presence of children, particularly those of pre-school age, has been found to inhibit married women's participation. In addition, the participation rates of married women have been found to rise with educational attainment and to be higher among non-whites. To the extent that potential earnings rise with the level of educational attainment, the observed positive relation between participation and education reflects, as in the case of prime-age males, the influence of market earnings. Because education increases a married woman's potential market earnings, it increases the value of her time in market activity relative to that in non-market activity and therefore, as we have seen, it increases, *ceteris paribus*, the probability of her being in the labour force. In addition, it is probably also true that education influences participation via tastes, in that education increases a married woman's preference for the challenges and social interactions offered by the sorts of market work now open to her.

Regarding differences in participation by ethnic group, Bowen and Finegan (1969, pp. 89–96) showed that in the USA the participation rates of black married women are higher than those of otherwise similar white women. Likewise, Greenhalgh's (1977) results suggest that in Britain participation rates are higher among foreign-born married women than among those born in the UK. While cultural differences in attitudes towards wives' roles are important in explaining this finding, various further explanations were put forward by Cain (1966). In particular, he suggested that in the USA the lower degree of job discrimination faced by black women than by men is one factor that results in a tendency for black households to substitute wives' market work for that of husbands.

Finally, it is useful to recognise the apparent conflict that exists between the labour force participation behaviour of married women in time-series and cross-section data. While cross-section analyses have shown that wives' participation rates are negatively related to their husbands' incomes, the evidence from time-series studies shows that married women's participation rates have risen dramatically over time (for example, from 8.7 and 9.0 per cent in Britain and the USA respectively in 1920/1, to 47.2 and 40.8 per cent respectively in 1980/1) despite the increasing real incomes of their husbands. This apparent contradiction attracted considerable attention in the early literature and was eventually resolved by Mincer (1962). Explicitly recognising the distinction between permanent and transitory income (Friedman, 1957, p. 21), Mincer in effect showed that over time the upward influence of rising female earnings on wives' participation rates was of such a magnitude that it outweighed the downward influence of rising husbands' (permanent) income on their wives' participation rates and hence gave rise to the observed upward trend.[3]

■ Added or discouraged workers?

As already noted, the strengths of the opposing added and discouraged worker effects have been the subject of much empirical investigation, and indeed the question of the direction of their net effect is one of some importance from a policy viewpoint. If the discouraged worker effect dominates, measured unemployment will underestimate the extent of actual unemployment, and consequently government policies designed to increase employment will, if based on the measured unemployment data, fail to provide enough jobs for all who will be looking for them once employment opportunities improve. However, if the added worker effect is the stronger, employment expansion policies based on measured unemployment data will provide too many jobs, because the added workers will drop out of the labour force as employment begins to increase.

The balance of international evidence from empirical studies of both time-series and cross-section data suggests that the discouraged worker effect predominates, thereby giving rise to an observed negative relationship between labour force participation rates and unemployment (Bowen and Finegan, 1969; Corry and Roberts, 1970; Dernburg and Strand, 1966; Killingsworth, 1983; McNabb, 1977; Tella, 1964). As can be seen from the following example, this result is a reasonable one. Suppose that the rate of unemployment doubles from 5 per cent to 10 per cent. In this case, the added worker effect will tend to operate in the 5 per cent of households with a newly unemployed member, whereas the discouraged worker effect may well apply in a large proportion of the remaining 95 per cent of households.

Analysis of the participation rates of various age–sex subgroups reveals that females as a whole, and in particular married women, are more sensitive to changes in employment opportunities than men are and that in both sexes sensitivity is higher among extreme age groups than among middle ones (Bowen and Finegan, 1969; Killingsworth and Heckman, 1986). In other words, the evidence confirms that responsiveness of participation to employment opportunities is greater among secondary than among primary workers (Mincer, 1966).

Hidden unemployment

Given the observed dominance of the discouraged worker effect, many studies of the determinants of labour force participation have gone on to estimate the extent of hidden (or disguised) unemployment (for example, Bowen and Finegan, 1969; Dernburg and Strand, 1966; Tella, 1965). As already noted, the hidden unemployed are those who, at the time in question, are not in the labour force but who would be if the prospects of finding a job were more favourable. Estimation of the amount of hidden unemployment is of particular importance from the viewpoint of providing a more adequate index of the extent to which labour is *underutilised* than is given by the official data of the numbers registered as unemployed.

The usual procedure for measuring hidden unemployment is to estimate a regression equation relating participation rates to rates of registered unemployment, or some similar variable, as an index of job opportunities. Given the estimated coefficients of this equation, one merely substitutes in some assumed full-employment rate of unemployment[4] and uses the estimated equation to predict what the participation rate would have been had the economy achieved 'full employment'. Multiplying the predicted full-employment and the observed participation rates by the population of the group in question, we obtain respectively the size of the estimated full-employment (or potential) labour force and of the recorded one. Hidden unemployment is then simply estimated as the excess of the estimated over the recorded labour force.[5]

Using this sort of method, Corry and Roberts (1970, 1974) derived estimates of the extent of hidden unemployment in the UK. However, in a subsequent study Berg and Dalton (1977) reconsidered the Corry–Roberts model and argued that their estimating equation is misspecified because of their omission of wage and price variables, with the consequence that their parameter estimates, and hence also their estimates of hidden unemployment, are biased. Using a participation equation derived from Wachter (1972, 1974), which basically differs from that used by Corry and Roberts by the inclusion of the real wage as an additional explanatory variable, Berg and Dalton derived alternative estimates of UK hidden unemployment. Reestimating the Corry–Roberts model, Berg and Dalton calculated that in 1972 108 000 men and 115 000 women remained out of the labour force who would have joined had the average 1947–73 rate of unemployment prevailed, whereas their own model gave hidden unemployment estimates of only 10 000 men, but 516 000 women.

The remainder of this chapter is concerned with the supply of hours, that is, the number of hours that workers are willing to supply once they are in the labour force. In the next section the theory of the individual worker's work/leisure choice is considered, and in the following one this analysis is used to derive the labour supply function. In subsequent sections the implications of the analysis for a variety of issues, including overtime payment and direct taxation arrangements, are considered. In addition some aspects of the relationship between actual hours of work and the supply of hours are discussed.

■ The individual's work/leisure choice

The traditional analysis of the supply of hours is concerned with the individual worker's allocation of time between (paid) work in the market and all other non-market activities. Following the usual convention, we refer for convenience, in the remainder of this chapter, to all uses of time other than market (that is, paid) activity as *leisure*.

The individual worker's *utility* is assumed to be an increasing function of the number of hours of leisure 'consumed' and the income obtained, where the latter, on the assumption of constant prices, serves as a proxy for purchases of consumer goods and services. The worker is assumed to allocate available time between the two mutually exclusive uses, market work and leisure, in such a way that utility is maximised. However, the worker faces a constraint which is imposed by the maximum time that is available (that is, 24 hours per day) and by the prevailing, assumed exogenously given, wage rate. The worker's problem is thus the familiar one of constrained utility maximisation, and it can therefore be analysed diagrammatically with the use of indifference curves.

Figure 2.1 depicts the individual's choice between work and leisure. The horizontal axis in this diagram denotes the numbers of hours of leisure that are consumed (L) and the vertical axis denotes income (Y). The maximum number of hours available for leisure in any one day is 24, and the number of hours devoted to market work (H) is given by 24 minus the number of hours of leisure consumed. Therefore, in **Figure 2.1** the horizontal axis denotes *leisure hours* when measuring to the *right* from the origin and hours of market *work* when measuring to the *left* from L'. For example, level L_0 represents 8 hours of market work and, therefore, 16 hours of leisure per day.

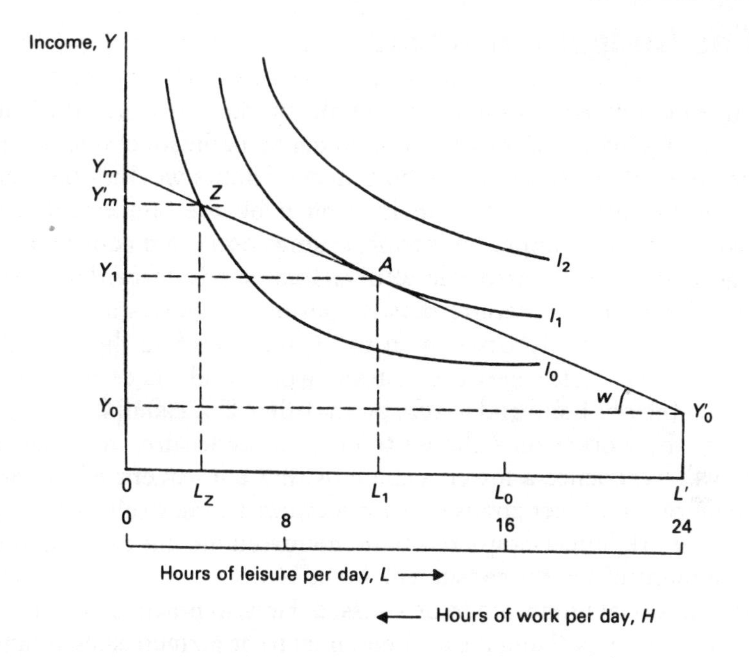

Figure 2.1 ***The individual's work/leisure choice***

■ Indifference curves

Curve I_0 is an *indifference curve*, showing the various combinations of leisure (L) and income (Y) that yield a given level of utility. Its negative slope indicates that if leisure time is sacrificed, additional income is required to maintain the individual's utility at the level in question. The *marginal rate of substitution* of leisure for income is defined as the amount of income that must be sacrificed if the worker, after consuming an additional unit of leisure, is to maintain a given level of utility. For sufficiently small changes in leisure consumption, the marginal rate of substitution is measured by the absolute value of the slope of the indifference curve at the point in question, and the convexity to the origin of the indifference curves in **Figure 2.1** represents the usual assumption of a diminishing marginal rate of substitution between the arguments of the utility function. Since more of both income and leisure is assumed to be preferable to less, the further an indifference curve lies to the north-east on the indifference map, the higher is the level of total utility that it represents.

■ The budget constraint

Turning now to the constraint faced by the worker, it is clear that given the prevailing hourly wage rate (w), which is assumed at this stage to remain constant irrespective of the number of hours worked, the worker's wage income is equal to w multiplied by the number of hours worked and that the upper limit to this sum is $24w$ (that is, the amount of wage income that is earned if *all* available time is devoted to market activity). Each hour of leisure that is consumed involves a sacrifice of income (or opportunity cost) equal to w, and therefore the individual worker faces a choice between market work, and hence income (or goods), on the one hand and leisure on the other. For example, at a given wage rate the worker may choose to enjoy more leisure, in which case he/she will experience a lower income (with a consequent reduction in consumption of market goods and services), or alternatively he/she may choose to work longer hours to obtain increased income at the expense of the amount of leisure consumed.

Two additional points are to be stressed. First, in practice, the number of hours that any individual can spend in market activity is less than 24 per day, because some minimum amount of leisure time must be devoted each day to such activities as eating and sleeping. Second, even when hours of market work are zero, income may not be zero because of the receipt of unearned (or non-labour) income accruing from the ownership of assets and from state payments such as Child Benefit in the UK in the early 1990s, which is payable to parents regardless of the number of hours worked and income received. In practice, the amount of non-labour income actually received may differ from the gross amount because of the existence of lump-sum taxes, such as a poll tax, which are payable regardless of the number of hours worked and income received.

The budget line $L'Y_0'ZY_m'$ in **Figure 2.1** illustrates the constraint faced by the worker. When zero hours are worked, income is given by the amount of non-labour income Y_0. Income in excess of this amount can only be earned by substituting work for leisure, and the budget constraint to the left of L' is linear of slope $-w$,[6] indicating that each additional hour of leisure that is foregone increases income by a constant amount equal to the hourly wage (w), which therefore represents the rate at which money income is exchanged for leisure time. In **Figure 2.1** the budget constraint is continued until it intersects the vertical axis at Y_m, which indicates the level of income that is obtained if all available time is devoted to market activity. At this point total income (Y_m) is given by $24w$ plus the amount of non-labour income. However, as already noted, there is in practice some upper limit of less than 24 hours on the total amount of time that the individual can devote to market activity, and accordingly we can terminate the budget line at some cut-off point Z, which shows the required minimum amount of leisure L_Z and the corresponding effective maximum income of Y'_m.

■ Utility maximisation

Given the worker's indifference-mapping and budget constraint, we are now able to derive the optimum income–leisure combination. The solution to the worker's constrained utility-maximisation problem lies at point A in **Figure 2.1**, where the budget line is tangential to indifference curve I_1. Assuming that the worker is free to select his/her own hours of work, he/she therefore maximises utility by choosing the combination of L_1 hours of leisure – that is, he/she works for $(24 - L_1)$ hours per day – and $(Y_1 - Y_0)$ units of wage income. At A we obtain, in the usual way, the first-order condition for constrained utility maximisation; namely, that the slope of the budget line, the wage rate in this case, is equal to the marginal rate of substitution of leisure for income.[7]

■ The individual's labour supply curve

In order to derive the individual's supply of hours as a function of their price (that is, the hourly wage rate), it is necessary to examine the way in which the optimum leisure income combination alters as the wage rate changes. This is considered in **Figure 2.2**, where point A illustrates the worker's utility-maximising income–leisure combination, given an initial hourly wage rate of w. Suppose now that the hourly wage rate is increased from its initial level w to some higher level such as w_1. This gives rise to a new, more steeply sloping, budget line $Y'_0Y'_m$ and a new utility-maximising equilibrium on the higher indifference curve I_2, as shown by point B. In this case the increase in the worker's hourly wage rate from w to w_1 results in an increase in the utility-maximising supply of hours from $(L' - L_1)$ to $(L' - L_2)$, accompanied by an increase in income from Y_1 to Y_2. The locus of utility-maximising combinations that is traced out when the wage rate is continually varied is known as the *wage–leisure curve* and is shown in **Figure 2.2** by the broken line passing through A and B. The wage–leisure curve corresponds to the price–consumption curve of consumer demand theory.

To obtain the worker's labour supply curve – the relationship between the supply of hours and the hourly wage rate as their price – it is necessary to transpose the utility-maximising positions shown by the

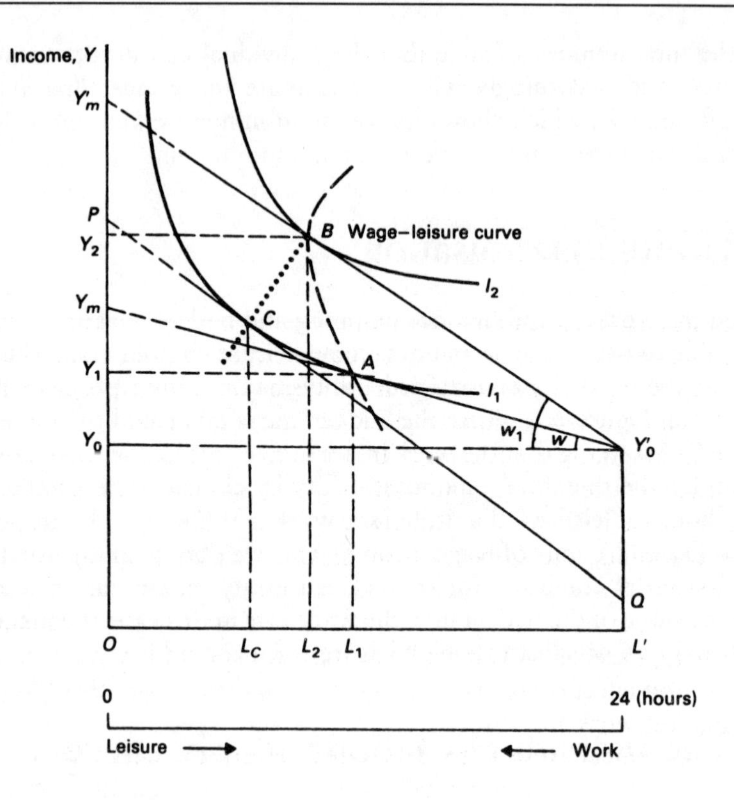

Figure 2.2 *The effect of a change in the wage rate*

wage–leisure curve on to the wage-rate versus supply-of-hours plane. Considering wage rates in the range w to w_1 and plotting the wage, as shown by the *slope* of the budget line, against the supply of hours indicated by the wage–leisure curve, we obtain the supply curve shown by the solid line L_S in **Figure 2.3**. This curve has a positive slope in the range w to w_1, indicating that, as the wage rate increases from w to w_1, the number of hours of labour offered for sale by this worker increases from $(L' - L_1)$ to $(L' - L_2)$.

■ Income and substitution effects

The effect of a change in the wage rate on the worker's supply of hours can be subdivided into an income effect and a substitution effect. In **Figure 2.2**, PQ is a hypothetical budget line, which is drawn parallel to the new budget line $Y'_0Y'_m$ and tangential to indifference curve I_1 at C. If the worker's non-labour income were reduced, through the imposition of a poll tax perhaps, by an amount or *compensating variation* equal to $Y'_m P$ (= $Y'_0 Q$) the worker would, given the new wage rate w_1, be neither better nor worse off in terms of utility than was the case before the wage rate rose.

The movement around the original indifference curve I_1 from A to C shows the *substitution effect*, which arises because of the changed price of leisure relative to market work, with utility held constant. In the current example the wage rate, and therefore the price or opportunity cost of leisure relative to market work, has risen. The substitution effect encourages the worker to decrease consumption of the now relatively more expensive good (that is, leisure) by the amount ($L_1 - L_C$) hours per day. In cases where indifference curves are convex to the origin, the substitution effect must always be *negative*; that is, it must always encourage reduced consumption of the good whose price has risen. This is easily seen from **Figure 2.2** by noting that because A and C are tangency points, the slope of I_1 at these points is given by w and w_1 respectively. Since I_1 is convex to the origin, the absolute value of its gradient increases as we move around it from right to left. Consequently, since w_1 exceeds w, C must lie to the left of A, which means that the substitution effect of a wage increase must induce the worker to substitute market work for leisure.

The movement from C to B denotes the income effect, which illustrates the worker's response to an increase in real income – or, more precisely, in utility – with relative prices held constant. If leisure is a *normal good* (that is, one having a positive income elasticity of demand), the *income–consumption* curve (CB) will have a *positive* slope. The positive slope of CB indicates that as income rises, consumption of leisure increases, in this case by the amount ($L_2 - L_C$) hours per day.

Provided that leisure is a normal good, the income and substitution effects of a wage change work in *opposite* directions, with the negative substitution effect encouraging the worker in question to substitute work for leisure, while the positive income effect encourages the worker to substitute leisure for work. In the current example the net effect of the increase in the wage rate from w to w_1 is to decrease leisure consumption (that is, to increase market work) by ($L_1 - L_2$) hours per day. This occurs because the positive income effect is of insufficient magnitude to outweigh the negative substitution effect, with the consequence that the supply curve of hours shown in **Figure 2.3** is positively sloping between wage rates w and w_1. If leisure were an inferior good, both income and substitution effects would pull in the same direction.

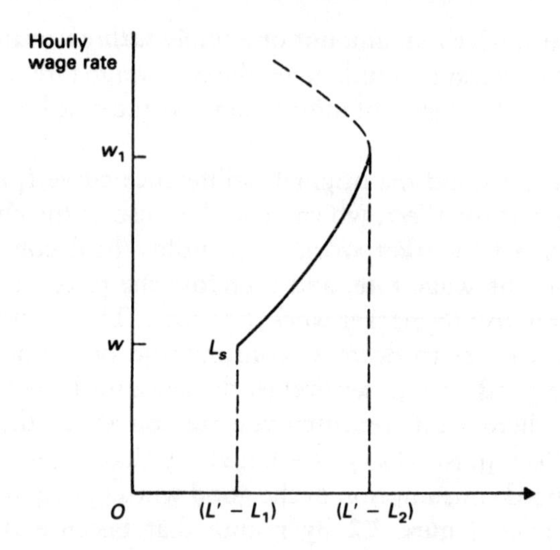

Figure 2.3 ***The individual's labour supply curve***

■ The backward-bending labour supply curve

It is reasonable to expect that for the vast majority of people leisure is a normal good, because as their income rises they have more to spend on the goods and services that enable them to enjoy their leisure. However, there is no particular reason to suppose that the relative magnitudes of the income and substitution effects are as shown in **Figure 2.2**, although it is perhaps reasonable to expect the income effect to be of relatively greater importance at high levels of income than at low ones. An important possibility which has been widely discussed in the literature is the one where the income effect of a wage increase is positive and of sufficient strength to outweigh the negative substitution effect, with the consequence that the net effect of the wage increase is an increase in the worker's consumption of leisure. In this case the worker's labour supply curve is negatively sloped, indicating that an increase in the wage rate results in a decrease in the utility-maximising supply of hours.

The possibility that the individual's labour supply curve may be backward-sloping over some range of wage rates has a long genealogy in economics.[8] The case where the income effect dominates the substitution effect at high wage levels is illustrated in **Figure 2.2.** At wage levels in excess of w_1 the wage–leisure curve becomes positively sloped, indicating that when wages are above w_1, any increase in the wage rate gives rise to increased consumption of leisure and thus calls forth a decreased supply of hours. When this section of the wage–leisure curve is mapped on to the labour supply curve of **Figure 2.3**, we obtain the backward-sloping section for wage rates above w_1, which is shown by the broken line.

Considered from the viewpoint of the amount of work demanded rather than that of leisure consumed, we see that the backward-bending labour supply curve of the individual arises from work being a *Giffen good*. If leisure is a normal good, work must be an inferior one, as it will have a negative income elasticity of demand. If we consider an increase in the wage rate as representing a decrease in the price of market work relative to leisure, it follows that if the negative income effect of the wage increase (which discourages the demand for work) is strong enough to outweigh the negative substitution effect (which encourages the substitution of work for leisure) work is by definition a Giffen good. If this is the case, the individual's supply curve of hours will be backward-sloping, because the substitution effect of a wage increase on the worker's demand for work will be more than offset by the negative income effect.

The above analysis refers to the individual worker's supply of hours, and it should be noted that whether the supply function relating aggregate hours of labour supply to the wage rate becomes backward-bending or not depends on the precise shapes of the individual labour supply curves being aggregated. The secular decline in average hours worked that has accompanied increased real wages over the twentieth century, as well as the inverse relation between wage rates and hours worked that is observed in cross-section data, is frequently put forward as evidence to suggest the dominance of income over substitution effects, with the consequence that the individual's labour supply curve will be negatively sloping at current wage levels (Douglas, 1939; Finegan, 1962). However, such evidence, which is derived from the analysis of hours actually worked, must be interpreted with caution since actual hours are determined by, and their behaviour reflects, not only supply-side forces but also (as we will see in Chapter 7) demand-side ones.[9] We return to some aspects of the relation between actual hours worked and the supply of hours in a later section of this chapter.

■ Some applications of the model

□ *Overtime working*

The analysis so far has been confined to the case where the wage rate facing the worker remains constant, regardless of the number of hours worked. In practice, it is usual for hours worked in excess of some minimum number (often eight hours in any one day) or at weekends to be paid at a higher than standard rate. In most industrialised countries payments for overtime working are generally in the range of one and a quarter times to twice the rate paid for standard hours.

The analysis of the individual's choice between work and leisure is easily extended to take account of the existence of premium payments for overtime working. Suppose that in the absence of overtime payments, our representative worker is in equilibrium at point *A* in **Figure 2.4**, supplying eight hours of labour per day. If overtime payments are introduced for hours worked in excess of eight per day, the budget line becomes kinked at *A*. The slope of section $Y_0'A$ of the budget line denotes the wage rate for standard hours (w) and the slope of the section *AE* represents that paid for overtime hours (say time and a half). In this example a new equilibrium is established at point *B*. As can be seen, the introduction of overtime payments results, assuming that the worker is free to select the number of hours of overtime actually worked, in an increase in hours of work from eight to ten per day, accompanied by an increase in both income and the level of total utility attained.[10]

Overtime payments are a form of price discrimination, because they involve the payment of a different price for different units of the same commodity. In the case where a constant wage rate is paid regardless of the number of hours worked, we have seen that an increase in the wage rate does not necessarily lead to an increase in hours of labour supplied but that the direction of the net effect of such an increase depends on the relative strengths of the income and substitution effects. However, it can be shown that the introduction of overtime payments prevents the individual's supply curve of labour hours from becoming backward-sloping.

In our discussion of income and substitution effects we have so far considered the individual's real income in terms of the ability to purchase goods yielding a certain level of utility. This constant utility notion of *real income* is referred to in the literature as Hicks real income, and on the basis of this definition we have considered the income effect that arises when the worker moves from one indifference curve (that is, level of real income) to another, with relative prices remaining constant. Alternatively, we may define real income in the Slutsky manner as the ability to buy a particular bundle of goods. In **Figure 2.4** the steeper section of the budget line (*AE*) passes through the original income–leisure bundle at *A* and therefore represents a constant level of (Slutsky) real income. The movement from *A* to *B* brought about by the introduction of overtime payments is a pure Slutsky substitution effect, because it arises from a change in relative prices, with Slutsky real income held constant.

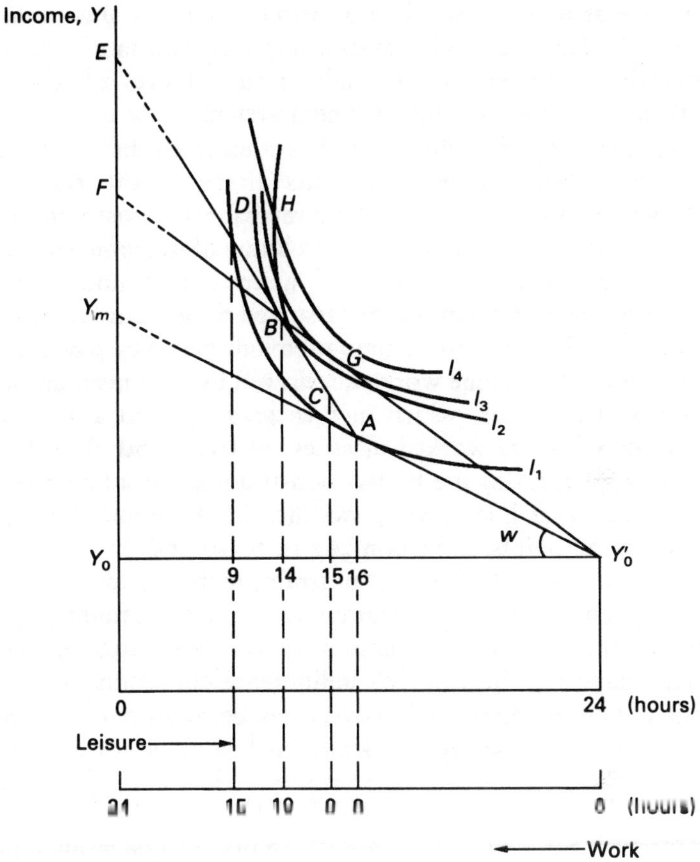

Figure 2.4 ***Overtime payments***

Provided that the worker's indifference curves are convex to the origin, it can be seen from **Figure 2.4** that the introduction of overtime payment cannot lead to a reduction in the supply of hours. By moving to the right of A, the worker would revert to the flatter section of the budget line (AY_0') because overtime payments are only made for hours worked in excess of eight per day. By reducing hours worked the worker can clearly only move to indifference curves that are below I_1. Therefore, the worker moves to the left of A, by decreasing his consumption of the more expensive good (that is, leisure), and thereby reaches successively higher indifference curves, until utility is maximised at the tangency point B. The introduction of overtime payments involves only a (Slutsky) substitution effect which, as we have seen, cannot induce an increase in leisure consumption and this therefore prevents the individual's labour supply curve from becoming backward-sloping. Note also that payment of the straight hourly wage rate that would give the worker the same income at B as the overtime payment system, as illustrated by the slope of the budget line $Y_0'BF$, results in a new equilibrium at point G. At this point the worker supplies less labour but achieves a higher level of utility than under the overtime payment system.

Although the preceding discussion has considered the situation where a single jump in hourly wage rates occurs (after say eight hours per day), it is easily extended to the case where several rates exist with overtime premia increasing progressively with the hours of overtime worked. This situation is illustrated in **Figure 2.5(a)**, where it is assumed that a wage rate (w) applies for standard hours (assumed to be eight hours per day), after which a 33 per cent overtime premium becomes payable for the first two hours of overtime worked, followed by a 50 per cent premium for the next two hours, which in turn gives way to a 100 per cent premium for all hours worked in excess of twelve per day. As can be seen from **Figure 2.5(a)** the budget constraint confronting the worker becomes *piece-wise* linear, with switches in the hourly rate payable occurring at the points corresponding to 8, 10 and 12 hours worked. Since the gradient of the budget constraint increases (discretely) as we move from right to left in this diagram, we see that the budget constraint confronting the worker in this case is (quasi-) *convex* to the origin.

By superimposing the worker's indifference curves on to this sort of diagram, the preceding sort of analysis may be conducted. For example, if the case set out in **Figure 2.4** is modified to allow for a jump in the overtime premium for hours of overtime worked in excess of two, the budget line acquires an additional kink at point B corresponding to ten hours worked per day. This state of affairs generates an additional tangency point with the higher indifference curve I_4 at point H, indicating that such an increase in the overtime premium results in additional hours of labour being supplied, with the worker thereby achieving an increase in *both* his level of income and level of utility.

□ *Income taxation*

The analysis of this chapter can easily be extended to allow for the presence of income taxation. In a number of respects, the presence of direct taxation on workers' wage income can be thought of as the opposite to the case already considered of the payment of premium rates of pay for hours of overtime. As we have seen, the existence of a premium rate of pay for overtime working results in the payment of what amounts to an *increased* hourly wage as *hours* worked rise above some appropriate threshold level. In contrast, the presence of income taxation means that the net hourly wage received by workers falls as

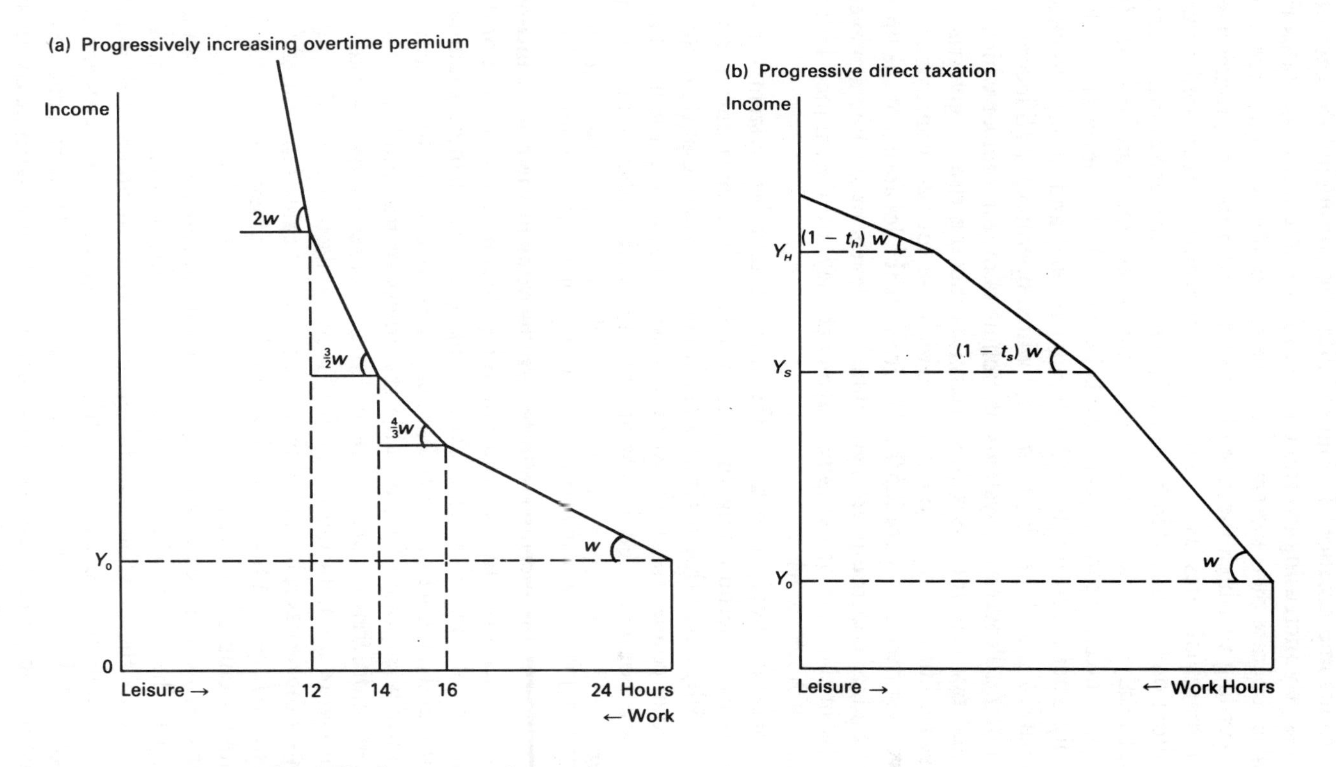

Figure 2.5 *Alternative non-linear budget constraints*

some threshold level of *income* is achieved and the worker becomes liable to income taxation. In **Figure 2.5(a)** we considered the case of a progressively increasing overtime premium. In practice, most industrial countries operate their system of income taxation in a progressive manner according to which the rate of direct taxation rises to progressively higher marginal rates as income passes appropriate threshold values. This situation is depicted in **Figure 2.5(b)** for the case of a country which operates only two bands of marginal tax rates: the *standard rate* (t_S) which operates for total income levels between Y_S (the level of which is typically determined by the individual's personal and family circumstances) and Y_H, and the *higher rate* (t_H) which operates for all incomes in excess of Y_H. Progressive systems of income taxation – under which the marginal tax rate increases (discretely) as income rises – give rise to piece-wise linear budget constraints which are (quasi-) concave to the origin, as shown in **Figure 2.5(b)**. Notice that the locations of the kinks in the budget constraint are determined by levels of *income* achieved, whereas in the case of overtime payments they are determined by the number of *hours* worked.

The labour supply effects of the income taxation system can be analysed by superimposing the individual's indifference curves on to **Figure 2.5(b)**. Since this analysis is essentially the reverse of that already discussed in connection with overtime payment systems, it is not duplicated here. For a detailed discussion the interested reader should consult Brown (1983). However, one question which has attracted particular political and economic attention in both the USA and the UK over recent years concerns the incentive effects of reductions in the rate of income taxation. This problem is considered in **Figure 2.6**, in the context of the simple case of a taxation regime consisting of two tax bands, a standard rate of t_S and a higher rate of t_h. For simplicity we assume the presence of an hourly wage rate of w, payable regardless of the number of hours worked. Indifference curve I refers to the representative worker. As drawn **Figure 2.6** indicates that utility is maximised at point A which is such that the worker, being liable to the standard rate of income tax (t_s), works for $(L' - H_A)$ hours per day and thereby achieves a *net* after-tax income for employment equal to $(Y_1 - Y_0)$.

Consider now the case where the government introduces a cut in tax rates, with the tax thresholds Y_S and Y_H remaining unchanged. This case gives rise to the new dotted budget line shown in **Figure 2.6**, which indicates an increase in the net hourly wage received by workers earning in excess of Y_S per day. Although political rhetoric during the 1980s seemed to imply that such tax reductions would necessarily result in an incentive to increase the hours of labour supplied, **Figure 2.6** shows that such an outcome is by no means guaranteed. If, for example, the

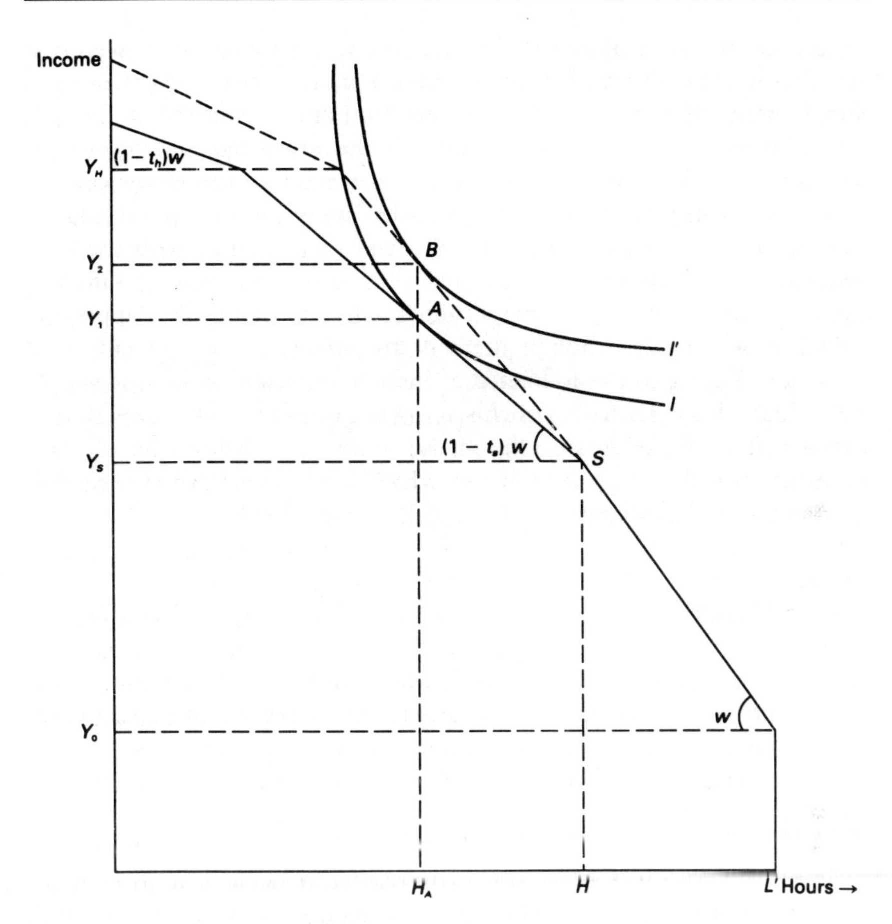

Figure 2.6 ***Reduction in direct taxes***

representative worker's indifference map is as drawn in **Figure 2.6**, the equilibrium income–work combination after the tax reduction is located at the new tangency point *B*. At *B*, the worker achieves an increase in the levels of both income and utility, without any change in the number of hours worked! As the reader may easily verify, differently drawn indifference mappings can generate different post-tax-reduction tangency points, some of which indicate an increase in the optimal hours and some of which indicate a decrease. That differences in the underlying utility function should give rise to different labour supply responses when tax rates are altered should come as no surprise. If we look at the section of the budget constraint lying to the left of point *S* in **Figure 2.6** we can immediately recognise that what we have in this case is exactly as we encountered in our earlier discussion of the income and substitution effect of a wage change (in this case, a change in the net or after-tax wage). On the basis of our earlier discussion, it is immediately seen that whether the tax cut results in an increase or a decrease in the incentive to supply hours of work hinges on the direction and strength of the income effect brought about by the increase in the net wage, relative to the substitution effect. As already noted, the weight of the empirical evidence offers support for the notion that leisure is a normal good (that is, one possessing a positive income elasticity of demand), with the consequence that the direction of the overall labour supply effect of income tax reductions hinges on its magnitude relative to that of the (opposing) substitution effect. Although there is an extensive body of empirical evidence relating to the influence of income taxation on labour supply behaviour, this is far from conclusive on the question of the direction of the net effect of tax cuts on the incentive to supply labour hours. This literature is well-surveyed by Brown (1983), Killingsworth (1983), Killingsworth and Heckman (1986) and Pencavel (1986).

□ *Payments by results and self-employment*

The preceding discussion has shown how non-linear budget constraints arise from the existence of overtime payment schemes and direct taxation. These are not the only circumstances giving rise to non-linear budget constraints, and in this section we see how non-linearity can arise from the existence of payment-by-results schemes and from self-employment.

The simplest form of payment-by-results scheme is a piece-work system, according to which the worker is paid a fixed amount for each unit of output produced. Under such a system the amount that each worker earns per hour is determined by the number of units of output which he or she produces – the marginal productivity of hours. In the particular case where the worker's output per hour is the same for each and every hour worked, the budget constraint will be linear. This is because under such circumstances, the hourly pay received will be a constant (say W), such that $W = O \times P$; where O denotes output per hour and P the amount payable for each unit produced, *both* of which are fixed. Although the preceding discussion is presented in terms of an employee working under a piece-rate payment system, an exactly analogous argument holds for the self-employed worker who sells his output at a constant price (say) in a perfectly competitive output market. For example, the hourly payment received by the self-employed window-cleaner is given by the product of the number of houses whose windows he or she cleans per hour and the price per house; where for simplicity we take the latter as fixed.

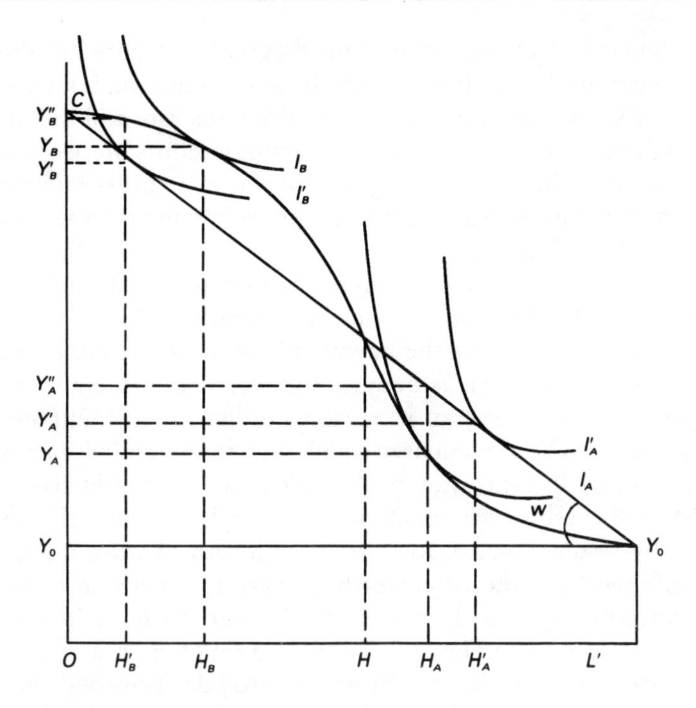

Figure 2.7 ***Payment by results***

In practice it is quite likely that the hourly productivity of both the self-employed and those paid on piece rates will vary over the working day because of both *start-up* effects at the beginning of the working day and *fatigue* effects towards the end of the working day. If we retain the assumption of a constant piece rate (P), or output price in the self-employed case, it is clear that hourly payments will vary with hourly output over the course of the working day. This situation gives rise to a non-linear budget constraint such as that shown in **Figure 2.7.** This diagram is drawn on the assumption that output per hour is low at the start of the working day but rises as workers 'warm up'. **Figure 2.7** also assumes that towards the end of the working day output per hour declines as the effects of fatigue set in and give rise to diminishing returns.

To understand the labour supply consequences of such payment schemes, we have superimposed two alternative sets of indifference curves on to **Figure 2.7.** According to the diagram worker A maximises utility by supplying $(L' - H_A)$ hours of labour, while worker B maximises utility by supplying $(L' - H_B)$ hours. In order to compare payment-by-results schemes with so-called time-rate payment systems (where each hour worked commands some constant wage) we may add the relevant linear budget constraint to the diagram. In **Figure 2.7**, the linear budget constraint $Y_0'C$ is drawn on the basis of a constant hourly wage of w, which is set in such a way that both the piece-rate and the time-rate system will yield the same income if maximum hours are worked at C. Notice also that the intersection point of the two curves indicates that both payment systems will result in the same income for a working day of length $(L' - H)$ hours.

Figure 2.7 shows how labour supply behaviour may be influenced by the nature of the payment scheme in operation. As drawn, type B workers are seen to prefer the payment-by-results scheme to the fixed hourly wage scheme. This is because the piece-rate system offers them the prospect of achieving an increase in utility via a simultaneous increase in income (Y_B as compared to Y_B') and reduction in hours worked from (H_B' to H_B). In contrast, type A workers will prefer the fixed hourly rate system since this scheme offers them a higher income (Y_A') than the payment-by-results scheme, for a reduced length of working day (H_A'). Stated differently, if the employer/firm were to switch from the fixed hourly wage-rate system of payment for its workers to the payment-by-results system shown in **Figure 2.7**, it would find type B workers opting for a shorter working day which would provide them with improved income; while type A workers would achieve a lower level of income, despite working longer hours. Regarding the employer's preferred system, it can be seen for **Figure 2.7** that firms which attract type B workers will have an incentive to opt for the fixed hourly rate system. Under this system, B's optimal hours of work are H_B' for which he receives an income equal to Y_B', which is less by the amount $(Y_B'' - Y_B')$ than that which the employer would have to pay under the payment-by-results scheme in order to induce the same daily hours of work, and therefore output. Conversely, employers attracting type A workers will prefer the piece-rate system. Under this system, the optimum hours of type A workers are $(L' - H_A)$, at which level the piece-rate system offers the employer a saving on wage costs equal to $(Y_A'' - Y_A')$ as compared to the time-rate system.

■ Supply of hours and hours actually worked

Our analysis of the work/leisure choice has so far been based on the assumption that the representative worker is free to choose his own hours of work. On this assumption the hours that the individual actually works at any particular wage rate will always equal his supply of hours. In reality, however, individual workers are rarely totally free to choose their own hours of work; rather, they must typically decide whether or

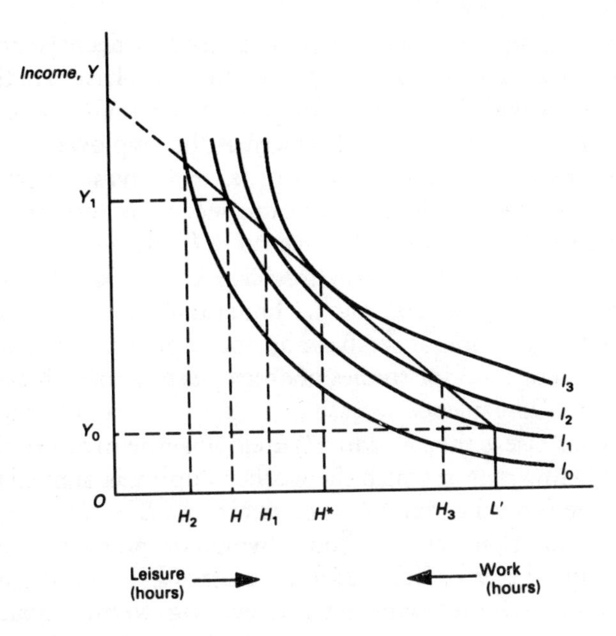

Figure 2.8 ***Employer-determined working day***

not to work some fixed number of hours at, or within, certain specified times. In such circumstances the preceding analysis of the work/leisure choice can best be thought of as one of *desired* rather than actual hours of work.[11]

At the opposite extreme to the supply-dominated case, where the worker is free to choose his own precise hours of work, is the demand-dominated one, where the employer sets the length of the working day and where the worker must decide whether to work these hours or to work none at all. This case is illustrated in **Figure 2.8**. If the employer were to fix the length of the working day at $(L' - H)$ hours then, as **Figure 2.8** is drawn, the worker in question would be indifferent between (1) not working and having an income of Y_0 (his non-labour income) and (2) working $(L' - H)$ hours and achieving income Y_1. If the length of the working day were set at some level below $(L' - H)$, such as $(L' - H_1)$, the worker would choose to work, because by so doing he would reach an indifference curve higher than the one he could achieve by not working. It should be noted that if the worker were free to choose his own hours, he would elect to work a shorter day of $(L' - H^*)$ hours and thereby maximise his utility. Such a situation arises in practice when a worker who desires to work only part-time takes a full-time job in preference to the alternative of not working.

In addition, the worker in such circumstances may decrease the effective length of the actual working week by taking extra leisure in the form of *absenteeism*, provided that the amount of such absenteeism is consistent with his retaining his job. Conversely, if the employer were to set the length of the working day in excess of $(L' - H)$ hours, at say $(L' - H_2)$ hours, the worker would choose not to work, because by so doing he would achieve the higher indifference curve I_1. However, if absenteeism is a possibility, the worker in this case can maximise utility by accepting the job (with its contractual hours of $(L' - H_2)$) and going absent for $(H^* - H_2)$ hours. See Barmby and Treble (1991) and Turnbull and Sapsford (1992) for studies of absenteeism in the UK and Allen (1981) for some US evidence.

An interesting case is the one where the employer sets the length of the working day below that at which the worker's utility is maximised. For example, if the working day were of duration $(L - H_3)$ hours, the individual in question would choose work in preference to non-participation and thereby reach indifference curve I_2. In this situation the worker, particularly if the opportunity of working overtime hours is not available, may take a second or even a third job in order to get nearer to his or her desired hours of work $(L' - H^*)$. Multiple job holders are known as *moonlighters*. The extent of moonlighting is not always easy to estimate, because in practice second jobs are often located in the cash (or black) economy and as such, often go unrecorded. However, some evidence for the UK economy in the 1970s suggested that about 3.5 per cent of men and about 2.5 per cent of women were multiple job holders.

■ Workaholics and non-participants

The possibility of corner solutions arises in cases where the indifference curves are everywhere either steeper or more shallowly sloped than the budget line. These situations are shown in **Figure 2.9**. In **Figure 2.9**(a), the indifference curves are everywhere less steep than the budget constraint, with the consequence that this individual's utility is maximised at point A, according to which the worker seeks to work every available hour. This is the case of the 'workaholic'.

Figure 2.9(b) illustrates the opposite case, where the individual's indifference curves are everywhere more steeply sloped than the budget constraint. Under such circumstances, the individual's utility is maximised at point B according to which he or she chooses not to participate in the employed labour force, but instead opts to consume 24 hours of leisure/non-market activity per day. This is the case of the non-participant.

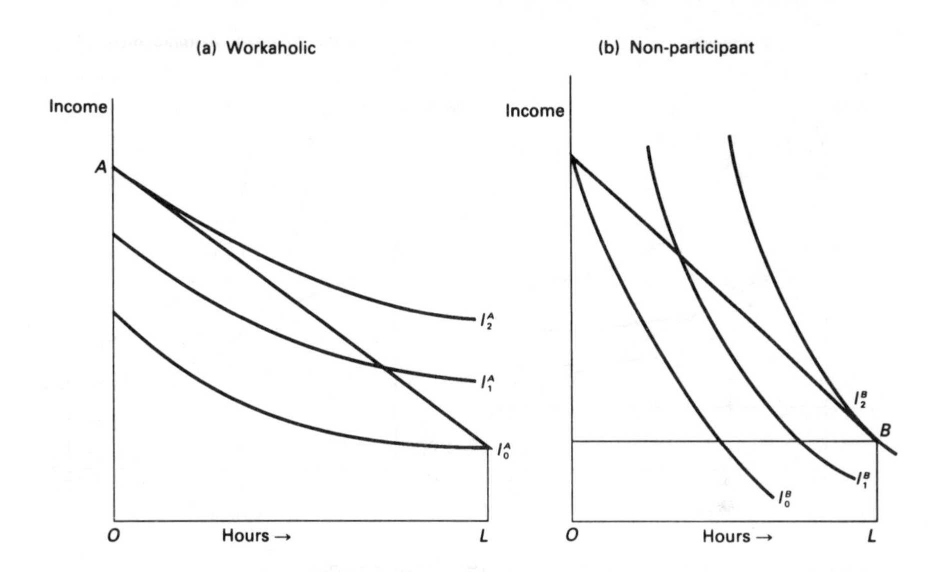

Figure 2.9 ***Workaholics and non-participants***

As we have already seen, the absolute slope of the indifference curve is the marginal rate of substitution of income for leisure. As can be seen from **Figure 2.9(a)** the workaholic case arises because the individual has a 'low' marginal rate of substitution of income for leisure (that is, one which is always lower than the wage rate as indicated by the slope of the budget constraint). The low marginal rate of substitution of the workaholic indicates that he or she is willing to forego a large amount of leisure in order to obtain even a small amount of additional income. Conversely, the non-participant possesses a high marginal rate of substitution of income for leisure, indicating that he or she is willing to sacrifice a large amount of income in order to obtain a small amount of additional leisure.

■ Unemployment benefit and labour supply

The preceding discussion may be modified to allow us to illustrate the influence of unemployment benefit upon labour supply. In order to do this it is necessary to recognise that the budget constraint in a model where the state pays unemployed workers a lump-sum benefit is of an *either/or* character. Either the worker accepts paid employment (in which case the budget constraint XY_0L in **Figure 2.10** applies in the usual way) or chooses not to participate and receives a state benefit equal to Y_0Z in addition to any other non-labour income.

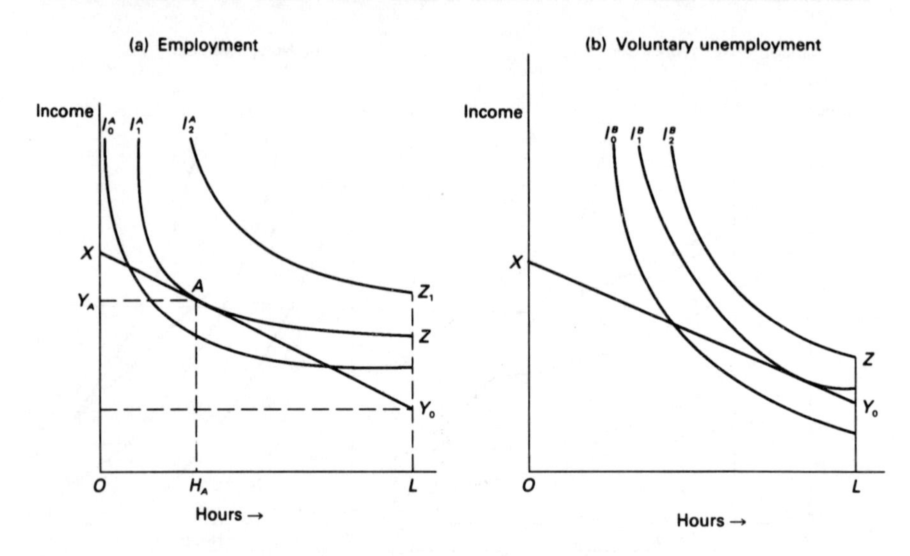

Figure 2.10 ***Unemployment benefit and labour supply***

Geometrically, the choice is between being located either somewhere along XY_0L in the case where the worker opts for employment, or at point Z if non-participation is chosen. Which of these two alternatives applies depends again on the magnitude of the individual's marginal rate of substitution between income and leisure relative to the wage rate (the slope of the budget constraint), as the price of leisure in terms of foregone earnings. In **Figure 2.10(a)** utility is maximised at the **interior** solution at point A, according to which individual A chooses to work $(L - H_A)$ hours per day and achieve a total daily income of Y_A. In contrast, the individual shown in **Figure 2.10(b)** has a higher marginal rate of substitution of income for leisure, such that utility is maximised at the corner solution at point Z. Individual B therefore chooses not to participate in the employed workforce, opting instead for $OL(= 24)$ hours of leisure per day and a total daily income of LZ, comprising non-labour income of LY_0 and unemployment benefit from the state of Y_0Z per day. Individual B may be said to be *voluntarily unemployed*, in the sense that his or her utility is maximised by remaining outside the employed labour force.

It is interesting to notice that the model predicts that a sufficiently large increase in the size of unemployment benefit may result in individuals like A in **Figure 2.10(a)** choosing non-participation in preference to participation. For example, if unemployment benefit were raised by the amount ZZ_1, individual A's utility in **Figure 2.10(a)** is maximised at point Z_1. At this *corner solution* individual A achieves a level of utility from voluntary unemployment (as indicated by indifference curve I_2^A)

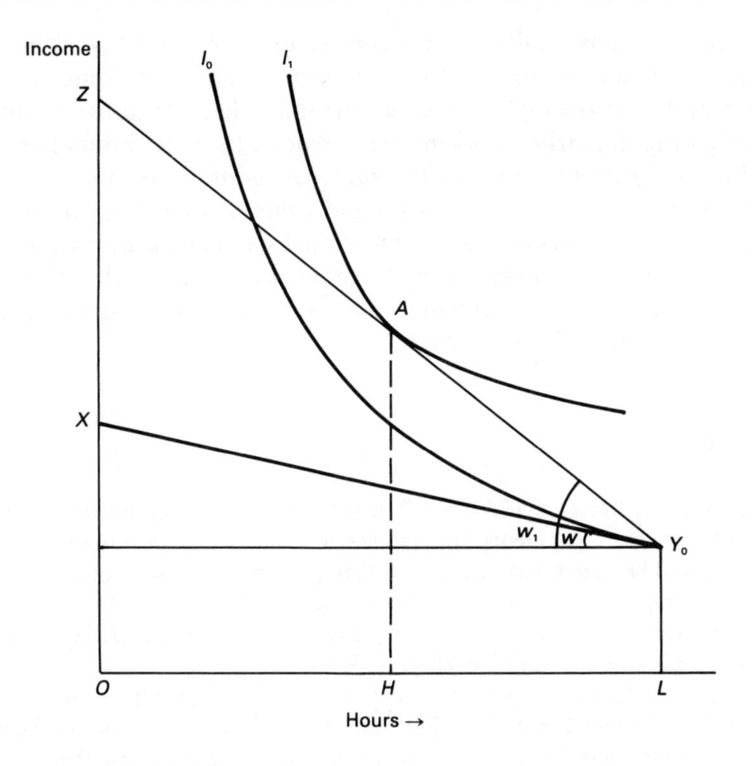

Figure 2.11 *Reservation wage*

which is greater than the maximum which is achievable from employment, as indicated by I_1^A at the interior solution point A.

■ Reservation wage

An important concept to be considered in more detail in Chapter 12 of this book is the *reservation wage*. This may be defined as that wage below which an individual is unwilling to accept a particular job offer, preferring instead to opt for non-participation. Such a decision may be made in order to allow the individual to search for a more satisfactory job offer.

Consider the situation illustrated in **Figure 2.11.** With a wage rate equal to w (such that the budget constraint is tangential to I_0 at point Y_0), the individual maximises utility by selecting the corner solution at Y_0. For all wage rates below w (that is, below the slope of I_0 at Y_0) the budget constraint becomes flatter and the utility-maximising solution remains unchanged at Y_0. However, if the wage were to rise above w to (say) w_1 the individual's budget constraint becomes LY_0Z. This new budget constraint gives rise to an interior solution at point A which indicates that at the higher wage w_1 the individual maximises utility by participating in market work to the extent of $(L - H)$ hours per day.

The wage rate w (equal to the slope of indifference curve I_0 at the corner solution Y_0) is known as the individual's *reservation wage* since for any wage in excess of w, the individual will choose participation in preference to non-participation. In other words, any job offering an hourly wage in excess of w will be accepted, while jobs offering a wage rate of w or less will be rejected.

Notcs

1. Bowen and Finegan (1969, p. 17) used the term 'earnings' to encompass not only monetary payments but also fringe benefits and working conditions.
2. It should be noted that Bowen and Finegan (1969, p. 18) dealt in terms of a set of imputed non-market earnings rates, rather than productivities.
3. For further discussion, see Hunter (1970, pp. 43–5), Byers (1976, pp. 76–7) and Killingsworth and Heckman (1986).
4. The difficulties associated with defining full employment are well-known and are discussed more fully in Chapter 14 below. In US studies a figure of 4 per cent unemployment has frequently been taken as consistent with full employment (see, for example, Dernburg and Strand, 1966). In the UK's case Corry and Roberts (1974, p. 17) derived their potential labour force estimates on the basis of a prevailing rate of unemployment equal to the average rate over their study period, 1951–70.
5. See Taylor (1974, pp. 37–9) for discussion of an alternative method of estimating hidden unemployment, referred to as the *trend through peaks* method. As its name suggests this method basically estimates the full employment level of unemployment on the basis of a trend line drawn through adjacent business cycle peaks.
6. The equation of the budget line can be written as

   $$Y = Y_0 + wH$$

   But since $H = 24 - L$ and $Y_m = Y_0 + 24w$, we obtain by substitution,

   $$Y = Y_0 + 24w - wL = Y_m - wL$$

   which is the equation of a straight line with intercept Y_m and slope of $-w$.
7. Let $u = u(Y,L)$ denote the individual's utility function and totally differentiating we obtain

   $$du = \frac{\partial u}{\partial Y} \cdot dY + \frac{\partial u}{\partial L} \cdot dL$$

   Recognising the partial derivatives of u with respect to Y and L as the marginal utilities of income and leisure respectively, we may write

$$du = mu_y \cdot dY + mu_L \cdot \mathrm{d}L$$

For movements around a given indifference curve we have du = 0, from which we may write

$$\frac{-\mathrm{d}Y}{\mathrm{d}L} = \frac{mu_L}{mu_Y} = \text{marginal rate of substitution of income for leisure}$$

By definition, the negative of the slope of the indifference curve, which equals the ratio of the two marginal utilities, is the marginal rate of substitution, which measures the rate at which the individual will trade income for leisure, with utility held constant.

Maximising $u = u(Y,L)$ subject to the budget constraint as written in the preceding endnote ($Y = Y_m - wL$) using the Lagrange multiplier technique we obtain the following augmented function and first-order conditions, where λ denotes the Lagrange multiplier.

$$v = u(Y,L) - \lambda(Y - Y_m + wL)$$

$$\frac{\partial v}{\partial L} = \frac{\partial u}{\partial L} + \lambda w = mu_L + \lambda w = 0$$

$$\frac{\partial v}{\partial Y} = \frac{\partial u}{\partial Y} + \lambda = mu_Y + \lambda = 0$$

$$\frac{\partial v}{\partial \lambda} = Y - Y_m + wL = 0$$

Rearranging the first and second conditions and dividing one by the other we obtain the familiar first-order condition for constrained utility maximisation, namely marginal rate of substitution $mu_L/mu_Y = w$, according to which utility is maximised by equating the marginal rate of substitution of income for leisure to the wage rate, as the price of leisure in terms of (foregone) income.

8. Of particular interest is Robbin's (1930) paper, which is formulated in terms of the demand for income in terms of effort, rather than the supply of hours.
9. For a discussion of the identification problems involved here, see Feldstein (1968). See also Lewis (1957) for an intuitive interpretation of the observed behaviour of hours actually worked in terms of both supply- and demand-side forces.
10. It is interesting to notice that, if the segment of indifference curve I_1 to the left of point A were everywhere more steep than the section AE of the budget line, the worker would refuse to work overtime. If the worker were unable to choose the number of hours of overtime that he actually works (for example, because the total available amount is rationed among the workforce according to seniority), he might not be able to reach his new equilibrium position at point B. For example, if only one hour of overtime were available to him, the worker would move from A to point C, and although the level of utility that he would achieve at C is less than that he would achieve if he were able to reach B, it is still in excess of that achieved

at *A* in the absence of overtime payments. If each employee is in this position, the overtime premium is set higher than is necessary to call forth the total number of overtime hours that are demanded.

11. The determination of *actual* hours of work is, however, influenced by both demand- and supply-side forces. It has long been argued that workers' preferences are likely to take effect in the long run through collective bargaining about the length of the standard working week (Hunter, 1970, p. 40) and that employers will, in any case, have an incentive to adjust offered hours to take account of workers' preferences, since by so doing an employer gains a competitive advantage in that he will be able to attract workers at a lower wage or to attract better workers, Friedman (1962, p. 205). For example, in cases where an employer finds difficulties in recruiting sufficient numbers to work his offered hours, he may choose to adjust these to workers' preferences, perhaps by introducing job-share schemes, 'twilight' shifts or working schedules for married women consistent with school times, in preference to offering increased wage rates as a possible means of attracting sufficient labour hours.

■ *Chapter 3* ■

Labour Supply: Extensions

■ Introduction

This chapter deals with two developments in the study of labour supply: the so-called theory of allocation of time and the 'second-generation' labour supply models.

The theory of allocation of time is different from the traditional income–leisure labour supply model in that it avoids the dichotomous distinction of time between work and non-work. As a consequence, it escapes the uncomfortable implication of the income–leisure model that 'goods can be consumed without time and time can be enjoyed without goods'. The theory of allocation of time has greater applicability than the traditional models of labour supply and a number of explanations emerge which could not be predicted from the income–leisure model. It should be also mentioned that the greater ability of the theory of allocation of time to explain additional aspects of labour supply comes at the cost of higher complexity.

The increase in the complexity of modelling and estimation techniques is even greater in the so-called 'second-generation models' of labour supply. The first-generation labour supply models are those which used primarily *working* persons as the basis of the empirical evidence. This practice will be properly criticised later on in this chapter but for the time being consider the following example. Assume that one used information on workers only and derived a relationship between wage rates and hours of work supplied. These results were subsequently used to simulate the response of hours supplied to a change in, say, the provisions of social security. These simulations may be totally flawed as for most practical purposes what matters in this case is the behaviour of non-participants who are the main beneficiaries of the provisions of social security but were excluded from the analysis. In contrast, the second-generation models of labour supply base their labour market analysis on the total population (rather than on a subset of it, such as those who are working). One consequence of this is that one can use models of labour supply in which all three aspects of labour supply (participation, hours and wages) are jointly analysed. As in the previous case, the incorporation of non-workers in the analysis results in additional complications compared with the models of the first generation.

Most of the applications associated with these two extensions go beyond the scope of the present book. Below we offer an exposition of the analysis involved along some general lines and more advanced treatment can be found elsewhere in the literature.[1]

■ The theory of allocation of time

As a general rule, economic models are based on the notion that something has to be maximised or minimised but this is possible only up to a point because there are constraints. The income–leisure model of labour supply explained in the previous chapter was derived from the assumption that individuals try to maximise their utility. In simple terms, utility was taken to be dependent on how much money (= goods) and how much non-working time (= leisure) the individual has. The formulation of the model in this way assumes that all that matters for the individual's welfare is (i) whatever he gets in the market – earned income in the labour market or the corresponding-to-it bundle of *market* goods, and (ii) whatever non-working time he has been left with.

As a first approximation the model is a step in the right direction. However, what has been lumped together in the 'leisure' or 'non-working time' component of time consists of an extremely diversified range of potential activities, all of which can be classified as economic ones. They are economic activities in the sense that they involve choice and constraints. They also have a relationship to labour supply. Let us explain this. 'Leisure', in the sense used so far, is the mathematical result of subtracting hours of work from total time. In this respect it includes activities such as (i) sleeping which takes place at home and is an unavoidable necessity; (ii) cooking which can be a combination of necessity and pleasure, and also a combination of market-purchased and home-produced meals; and (iii) skiing and walking which are mainly for pleasure and which are rarely consumed at home. The mix of these activities depends on the income constraint and, in the present context, the labour supply effort. For example, if the need for greater income arises, then one may decide either to work more at the expense of sleeping at least for some length of time, or to give up eating out, or to take up walking instead of skiing, or any combination of these three alternatives. Thus the labour supply effort and people's welfare depend on a combination of activities other than work and non-work, and also on a combination of market and non-market goods and services. This is missed by the income–leisure model but accommodated in the theory of allocation of time originally proposed by Becker (1965).

□ *The model*

The basic premise of the theory of allocation of time is that individuals (or households) decide not simply between work and non-work but between alternative uses of time in order to maximise consumption broadly defined to include market-purchased and home-produced goods. In this respect the labour supply decision is considered in a more general framework in which work is only one activity. In addition, the theory recognises that neither can time be consumed on its own (it requires goods) nor can goods be consumed by themselves (they require time). Consider walking. It is not simply a time-consuming exercise as it requires shoes, appropriate clothing and (at times) an umbrella, and (in a pure market economy fully covered by property rights) an entry ticket to the fields. The problem now becomes to create a model capturing these observations.

The theory of allocation of time defines the utility function over composite 'activities', Z, which are made up of goods and time. So, eating is an activity which consists of edible materials (goods) and of the time required to process and consume them. In this specification, eating embodies a decision on how to combine market goods, G, with time, t. The relationship between activities, market goods and time can be seen in the context of a production function of the general form

$$Z_i = Z_i(G_i, t_i) \qquad \text{for } i = 1, \ldots, k$$

where i is a particular activity of all k activities in which the individual can get engaged.[2] It is the utility derived from these activities that the individual is interested in maximising, that is

$$U = U(Z_1, \ldots, Z_k) \tag{3.1}$$

The maximisation of the utility function requires knowledge of the constraints. The constraint ('full income') is determined by whatever non-labour income, Y, the individual possesses and what earnings he can get in the labour market if he were to work at a wage, w, at all times, T (T is therefore the sum of all t_i's plus hours of work). The total 'money and time' value of the activities cannot exceed total income and total time. The value of a unit of a particular activity is dependent on the price of goods, P_G, and also on the price of time, w, that are required for its production. Hence, the value of all activities will at equilibrium be equal to the full income constraint, that is

$$\sum_{i=1}^{k} P_{Gi}G_i + w \sum_{i=1}^{k} t_i = wT + Y$$

For expository purposes let us assume that the production type is characterised by fixed coefficients. Let a_i and b_i be respectively the amount of goods and time that are required for the production of one unit of activity Z_i, that is

$$a_i = G_i/Z_i \text{ and } b_i = t_i/Z_i$$

From these equations one can express G_i and t_i in terms of activities and fixed coefficients and rewrite the left-hand side of the constraint as

$$\sum_{i=1}^{k} P_{Gi}Z_ia_i + w \sum_{i=1}^{k} Z_ib_i$$

Factoring Z out from the goods and time summation terms of the latter equation permits us to rewrite the constraint as

$$\sum_{i=1}^{k} (P_{Gi}a_i + wb_i)Z_i = \sum_{i=1}^{k} C_iZ_i = wT + Y \quad (3.2)$$

where $C_i = P_{Gi}a_i + wb_i$, that is, C_i is the full cost of an activity i. In other words, each activity has, first, a goods-cost component which corresponds to the amount of earnings required to purchase the goods necessary for the activity. Second, it has also a time-cost component which corresponds to the amount of earnings that one has to forego in order to purchase, prepare and consume the activity. Maximising the utility function (equation (3.1)) subject to this constraint (equation (3.2)) gives the usual equilibrium condition that the ratio of the marginal utilities derived from various activities should be equal to the ratio of costs associated with these activities

$$MU_{Zi}/MU_{Zj} = C_i/C_j \quad \text{for } i, j = 1 \ldots k \text{ and } i \neq j \quad (3.3)$$

Despite the apparent difference between this equilibrium condition and the one derived in the case of the income–leisure model, it can be easily shown that the optimising condition of the income–leisure model (see note 7, Chapter 2) is a special case of equation (3.3). To demonstrate this assume, first, that the utility function contains only two arguments, namely goods, G, and leisure, L. Second, that the production coefficients on G are $a_G = 1$ and $b_G = 0$, that is, the activity 'goods' depends only on the amount of goods one has (one unit of good gives one unit of activity) and there is no time/foregone earnings associated with it. Third, assume that the production coefficients on L are $a_L = 0$ and $b_L = 1$, that is, the activity 'leisure' consists of no goods component and is entirely made of time. Then, the ratio of marginal utility of leisure to the marginal utility of goods becomes equal to the ratio of the price of leisure (wage rate) to the price of goods

$$MU_L/MU_G = -(P_G a_L + w b_L)/(P_G a_G + w b_G) = -(w/P_G)$$

because $a_L = b_G = 0$. Thus in the case of pure goods that do not require a time input, and pure leisure that does not require a goods input, the labour supply effort depends on the ratio of the cost of leisure to the cost of goods. So the income–leisure model is a special case of the theory of allocation of time.

□ *Comparative statics*

The more general case where goods and time combine in various proportions is, of course, more interesting as it shows how a change in the wage rate will affect the labour supply effort via its effects on the allocation of time between time-intensive and goods-intensive activities. Consider a decrease in the wage rate. This will cause the two usual effects upon the demand for all activities, namely an income effect and also a substitution effect.

The income effect will be negative for all those activities that are not inferior. What will happen to the supply of labour hours (the difference between total time, T, and the sum of all t_i's)? This would depend on what happens to the t_i's, that is, the time spent on the activities included in the utility function. Is not possible to say *a priori* whether an activity is normal or inferior. If one is prepared to assume that time-intensive activities are not inferior, then the income effect from lowering the wage rate should result in fewer of them being undertaken (consumed) and this will realise more time for work. This is as far as one can go in this respect, but recall that the same ambiguity arose in the case of the income–leisure model, unless one is prepared to assume that leisure is an inferior good.

The substitution effect will decrease the cost of all activities as the time component of each activity is now multiplied by a lower wage rate. However, the decrease in the cost of particularly time-intensive activities will be greater than the decrease in the cost of goods-intensive activities. As a result, a decrease in the wage rate should result in an increase in time-intensive activities and a decrease in goods-intensive activities as the relative cost associated with time-intensive activities has decreased (this result is derived by suitably adjusting equation (3.3)). So, the individual will substitute 'time' for 'goods' (in the case of the previous illustration, when the wage rate decreases, the individual will substitute walking for skiing – assuming that skiing is a goods-intensive activity undertaken only occasionally).

The final remark can be interpreted in two equivalent ways. First, undertaking more time-intensive activities reduces the time available for work. Alternatively, giving up goods-intensive activities implies that fewer hours of work would be sufficient for purchasing whatever goods are still required. Either way, one concludes that a decrease in the wage rate has a positive (substitution) effect upon time-intensive activities and a negative effect on hours of work. Compare this result to that of the income–leisure model: in the context of the latter model a decrease in the wage rate lowers the price of leisure, causing more leisure to be demanded and less work to be offered.

To give a better insight to the complexities of the theory of allocation of time, let us examine how the income–leisure model explained in the previous chapter can be amended to incorporate work at home in addition to market work and leisure.[3]

Work at home and the income–leisure model

In **Figure 3.1** time spent outside the labour market is split into leisure and work at home. Let the horizontal axis represent time: it measures the amount of leisure, market work and work at home that can occupy a single period (say, one day; hence T corresponds to 24 hours). Let the vertical axis stand for the value equivalent of home-produced and/or market-purchased goods. Assume that a typical individual has a *home* production possibility frontier (*PPF*) with the usual property: home production increases at a decreasing rate as it is natural to assume that the first hour spent on, say, cooking, has more rewarding results than one additional hour spent on it after six or nine hours in a single day. This is shown as the concave line *T–PPF* and represents the individual's constraint in the absence of alternative uses of time. The slope of the tangent at any point along the *PPF* represents the individual's marginal productivity *at home* and becomes zero at the point where the production possibility frontier hits the vertical axis. Assume finally that the individual could fetch some positive wage in the labour market, if he were to work. Under our assumptions the benefit to time spent on home production becomes lower than the wage rate at some point to the right of *PPF*. Denote this point by *A* and note that now the constraint starts at *T*, traces *PPF* till *A* and then follows the wage line *AW*.

The model is now fully specified. The individual can be at equilibrium

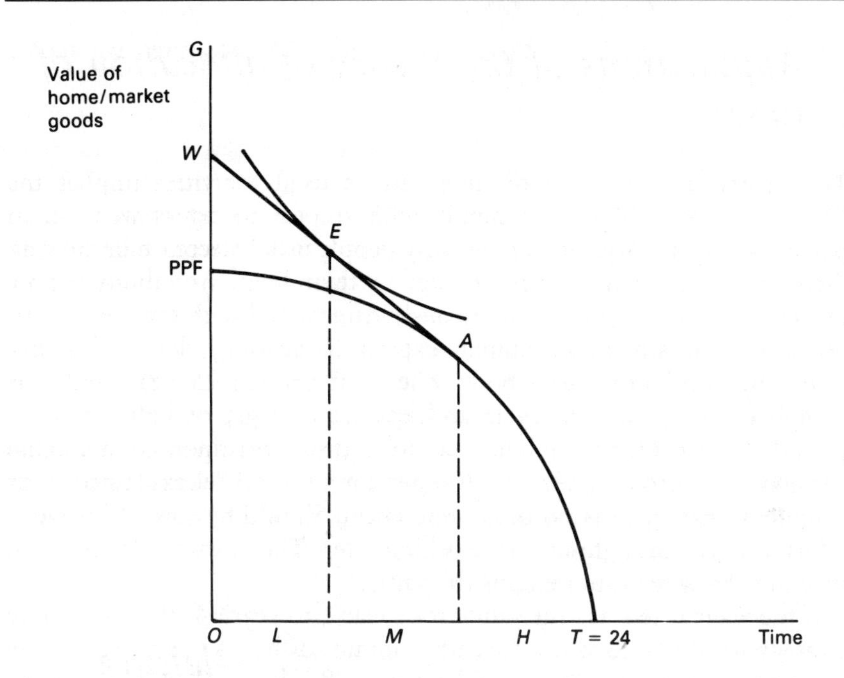

Figure 3.1 ***Allocation of time between home production, market work and leisure***

anywhere along the non-linear constraint TAW. If the equilibrium is at E, he consumes L hours of leisure while he spends M hours in the labour market and H hours on home production. If the equilibrium is to the right of point A, then he spends his time on leisure and home production and does not participate in the labour market.

The comparative statics are obvious. An increase in the wage rate makes home production less attractive and point A slides down to the right. As a result home production decreases and leisure increases. The effect on work is ambiguous depending on whether the increase in leisure was greater or smaller than the decrease in home production. This ambiguity is similar to the one derived from the simpler income–leisure model. One can introduce non-labour income into the model as a vertical shift of the budget constraint. If the individual was at equilibrium at point E, an increase in non-labour income increases leisure initially at the sole expense of work. When no work is supplied at all, further increases in non-labour income result in more leisure but at the expense of home production.

Applications of the theory of allocation of time

The theory of allocation of time can be used for the study of the life-cycle pattern of labour supply with respect to hours worked. In particular, the theory can explain why people usually work more during their prime age than earlier or later in their lives. As labour supply during the young age is simultaneously determined with the decision to undertake investment in human capital (education), let us simplify things by considering somebody who is at present 25 years old, has completed his education cycle and has set a target of half a million pounds as his lifetime labour earnings (this corresponds to annual earnings of approximately £14 300 per annum for 35 years; assume for simplicity that there is no time preference). Should he spread his work effort evenly throughout his working life? The answer depends on whether the wage rate remains the same.

If the wage rate stays the same from year 1 to year 35, then a sensible strategy would be to work the same amount of hours every year. If the wage rate varies, then he would be better off if he worked more during periods in which the wage rate is high and reduced his labour supply effort at times when the wage rate is low. This prediction is derived from the theory of allocation of time in the following way. A high wage rate causes substitution of goods-intensive activities requiring more work effort (earnings to purchase them) for time-intensive activities: as an optimising strategy one should then increase one's work effort at the expense of the time allocated to home production (consumption). By extension, a high wage rate in one period increases the cost component of consumption activities in that period and results in their substitution by future consumption. Hence, the labour supply effort should increase during periods of high wages. This is a *certain* result because it does not involve an income effect: our individual has set his income target and all he is trying to do is to achieve his goal with least work effort. So, when should he increase his work effort between now and retirement? This depends on during which periods pay will be high. Empirical evidence shows that the rate of pay increases with age up to a point; then it flattens out and it may even decline. As will be explained in the next chapter, this pattern is due to two main reasons. First, experience increases workers' productivity much at first and slowly later on in life. Second, as time passes by workers' productivity decreases for physical reasons such as ill health. Therefore, a rational individual should increase his work effort as long as the rate of pay keeps increasing and start enjoying the fruits from his work later on in life.

This is compatible with the empirical evidence, in that hours of work start increasing as people enter prime age (25 plus) but decline later in life. Ghez and Becker (1975) undertook an empirical investigation of the life-cycle pattern of hours worked by individuals of different ages. The dependent variable was annual home time, that is, total annual hours minus hours of work. The sample was men who, unlike women, typically work throughout their prime age. The price of home time was proxied by hourly earnings (a proxy for the wage rate) in the form of three-year moving averages in order to smooth out short-lived transitory variation in pay which is not sufficient to register an impact in behavioural patterns. They also included other variables to control for some obvious factors that can affect the amount of home time consumed in a year by different individuals. Such factors include age, non-labour income, family size and so on. They found that the elasticity of annual home time with respect to hourly earnings was negative and approximately equal to one-quarter. In other words, a 10 per cent increase in hourly earnings reduces annual home hours by 2.5 per cent.

The theory of allocation of time can be also used for understanding the phenomenon that has been aptly described as *The Harried Leisure Class* (Linder, 1970): with the increase in productivity over time people have been able to enjoy higher earnings and buy more goods but, given the time constraint, they have to reduce the consumption of time-intensive activities, one of which is . . . leisure! The underlying economic analysis of these series of events, amusing as they may appear, is clear and summarised in the form of an exercise at the end of the next paragraph.

The theory of allocation of time is more complex compared with the income–leisure model. Against this cost, the benefit is that it provides a better understanding of how people decide on different activities. A number of phenomena can be explained that cannot be unmasked by the simple income–leisure model. As an exercise the student can compare the explanatory power of the two theories with reference to the behaviour of the two persons who have the characteristics described below. One person lives on one side of the Atlantic while the other person lives on the other side of the Atlantic. Both are wealthy but one derives his income from his own work, while the other derives his from a substantial inheritance (for example, assume that the former is a top-paid executive while the latter has substantial holdings of land). Assume that they have the same income. Who is more likely to consume goods-intensive activities (such as having a helicopter or skiing in the Alps)? Who is more likely to enjoy time-intensive activities (such as walking leisurely in the countryside or expanding his classical education before an open fire?). Examine whether the income–leisure model or the theory of allocation of time can be used to explain the different life-styles (composition of consumption) of these two individuals.[4]

■ Sample selection bias

A typical question economic theory tries to answer may look like 'if this happens (for example, if income changes), how will something else be affected (such as the quantity of goods demanded)?'. In other words, theory tries to establish the *direction* of effects. However, in order to find out the *magnitude* of whatever change one might be interested in, one has to make use of data. It is by cranking data that one derives empirical estimates which can be then used (i) to test the validity of the underlying theory and (ii) to derive policy conclusions. If our knowledge about facts (data base) were complete, then it would be relatively easy, on the one hand, to discriminate between competing theories and, on the other hand, to design policies with certainty. In general, this is not the case on two different grounds.

First, some data (variables) are measured in practice in a different way than an economist has in mind when formulating a particular theory. Reference to data on wages makes this point clear. Economists are usually interested in net wage *rates* and gross labour *costs*. The former relates to labour supply, that is, what a prospective worker expects to obtain in the labour market if he gave up leisure. The latter relates to what the firm expects to pay from employing a worker rather than some other factor of production – such as capital equipment. However, applied work in the area of labour demand and labour supply is usually restricted to the use of published data on *earnings*, that is the pre-tax total remuneration of the worker at the end of a given period (for example, week, month or year). This practice, though unavoidable in most cases, is a deficient one as earnings (i) are the *ex post* product of the interaction of labour demand *and* labour supply; (ii) are gross of taxes, hence inappropriate for use in a labour supply framework; and (iii) are net of employers' contributions, hence inappropriate for use in a labour demand framework. One may also add that earnings also reflect the effects from matters such as absenteeism and overtime work, and this limits further their usefulness for the empirical study of labour supply and labour demand functions. Under these circumstances, one hopes that, until more relevant data become available, the applied researcher would interpret his results with some caution after examining how his results might have been affected by the use of earnings instead of whatever wage/cost measurement would have been more appropriate. Little more can be done in this respect.

Second, there may be no information at all about some variables, or the values of some available variables may be missing. How does one proceed in this case? In the first case, that is, when information is lacking, one can use a proxy variable. For example, as shown in the previous paragraph, earnings may be used as a proxy variable for wage rates or labour costs. However, such a 'proximity' need not always exist and the researcher may be eventually forced to omit the relevant variable from his analysis altogether. The second case, which refers to missing observations for a variable that is available, has been traditionally 'solved' in two different ways. The researcher either assumes a value for the missing variable or excludes altogether the cases for which information is not available. For example, in the context of labour supply, wages are observed only for workers. Hence, estimation can be restricted to those persons in the sample who have positive wages. Alternatively, the researcher can assume that non-workers' wages are zero and can include them in his estimation. Obviously, these solutions are far from satisfactory. In the case of non-workers actual (*ex post*) wages are mathematically equal to zero but had a non-worker been employed, he would have got some pay. This *ex ante* pay, which is clearly different from zero, is the concern of the economist. In short, the exclusion of cases for which information is lacking or the assumption that missing values have some particular value may lead to results whose validity is suspect. To avoid this practice one requires an alternative. The second-generation models of labour supply are such an alternative and they represent a clear improvement in this respect.

Until the 'second-generation' models of labour supply came into existence during the last decade, the usual practice ('first-generation' models) was to estimate aspects of labour supply only from samples of employed workers for which information on earnings and hours was available (non-workers work zero amount of hours and are observed to have zero earnings). In other words, rather than omitting a variable altogether, one proceeded with the 'useful' sample and omitted the observations for which there was no information. However, this practice may lead to *sample selection bias*. As the name suggests, the 'selection' of only part of the sample results in 'biased' inferences. Though the implications of this kind of selectivity are tackled in a formal context below, one may note here that, if the persons included in the estimation process are different from the persons who are excluded, then the results will reflect the characteristics and behaviour of the former but not of the latter. Obviously, there will be no sample selection bias if the included (that is, workers) are not systematically different from the excluded (that is, the non-workers).

The second-generation models of labour supply, that is, those which incorporate non-workers in their analysis, were inspired by and extensively tested in the case of women. The reason is self-evident. Most men are typically found in the labour force while this is not the case for women: for example the participation rate of prime-age men (25–55 years old) was about 95 per cent in the 12 European Community countries in 1987 compared with less than 70 per cent for women (*Labour Force Survey*, Luxembourg: EUROSTAT). Thus men appear to be more homogeneous than women and, equally important, there exists information on earnings for most of them. If selectivity is, then, an issue, then women are the first to be studied.

Below, the theoretical underpinnings of sample selection bias are outlined with the aid of a simple analogy and are subsequently explored in a labour supply context.

The theory of sample selection bias (in the context of an experiment)

The objective is to study the labour supply behaviour of *all* women. However, wages and hours are observed only for those women who are working. Hence, one cannot estimate the labour supply function of all women and has to confine oneself to the case of working women only. An interesting question is the following: Can one use the information on wages (hours) that exists for workers in order to infer what the wages (hours) of non-workers would have been, had the latter been working? If this can be done, then one can extend the empirical investigation to all women. The problem is, therefore, whether one can utilise the existing, but incomplete, information in order to predict what the whole picture on wages (hours) looks like. One expository way to show how this can be done is with the use of the following analogy to a motor car with a defective speedometer.

Assume that a driver sets off for a journey between two points. He does not know the distance between the two points and his car's trip counter is not working. He wants to find out the distance between the two points. Under normal circumstances this should present no problem. If the car travels at a constant speed of 100 kilometres per hour (kph – in line with the undergoing harmonisation across Europe) and arrives in two hours, then the distance should be 200 kilometres. If the traffic conditions are variable, then one can work out the implications. However, apart from the faulty trip counter there is another catch: the speedometer is sticky at 95kph, that is, it stays at 95kph whenever the car reaches a speed higher than this and up to the maximum of 205kph which the car is capable of doing. Fortunately, the driver is accompanied by a helpful passenger, who happens to be a statistician. They set themselves up to find out the distance in the following way: the driver will inform the passenger about the speed of the car while the passenger will monitor the time.

At the end of the journey their information consists of the following. First, the journey took one continuous hour of driving. Second, they travelled at an average of 78kph for 51 minutes, when the speedometer oscillated between 0 and 95 kilometres. On this information, they know for certain that they covered 78 kilometres. The distance covered during the remaining nine minutes of high speed (more than 95kph) is to be guessed. The driver suggests they assume that during the time that the car was driven in excess of 95kph, the speed was 150kph (half-way between 95 and 205kph). This would bring the total distance to 88.8 kilometres. The passenger considers this to be too high. In practical terms, the statistician passenger does not think that they exceeded the legal limit that often (the driver is prepared to accept this) and, utilising his knowledge of statistics, he asserts that, since the observed average was 78kph during the 51 minutes for which reliable information exists, the actual average should be around 85kph. The driver is initially mystified but, after listening to the statisticians's explanation – which is repeated in the next section – he agrees.

□ *Getting the basics*

In **Figure 3.2** a standardised normally distributed variable is depicted for which information exists up to point T (truncation) but not above. In line with the previous example, T corresponds to 95kph. The left-hand side of the distribution corresponds to the 51 minutes for which information exists. The shaded right-hand side of the distribution corresponds to the observations that have been lost for nine minutes due to the faulty speedometer. In other words, there exists information for 85 per cent of the observations but not for the remaining 15 per cent.
Denoting

μ = true mean of the distribution (unknown)
$\bar{\mu}$ = estimated mean from the sample (78kph for 51 minutes)
σ = known standard deviation (say, 25kph)
X_k = kth observation of the variable (speed in any minute)
n' = number of useful observations (51 minutes)

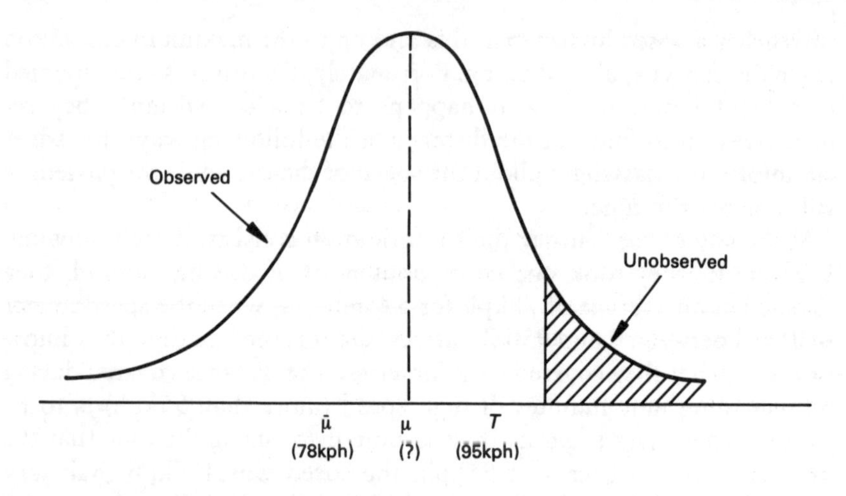

Figure 3.2 ***A truncated distribution***

$\phi(\delta)$ = height of the distribution at the standardised truncation point (95kph)
$1 - I$ = percentage of observations which are known (51/60 minutes or 85 per cent)

one can estimate the true mean using the mean calculated from the useful observations as follows. The sample mean is

$$\bar{\mu} = \Sigma X_k / n'$$

Obviously this is lower than the true mean as information on high speeds is lost. To correct for this (selectivity) bias something has to be added. The 'correction' (or 'adjustment') factor needs to take into account how *thick* the missing tail of the distribution is *at the truncation* point. The 'thickness' depends on the standard deviation of the distribution (or, equivalently, its height) at the truncation point. The truncation point determines how much information is lost (note that the truncated normal distribution is summarised completely by its mean, standard deviation and the truncation point). Hence, to calculate the correction factor one needs information on the thickness of the distribution and the location of truncation.

The derivation of the adjustment factor can be found in more advanced textbooks (see, for example, Greene, 1990, chapter 21) but, for present purposes, what has to be added to correct for the selectivity bias is the product of the standard deviation and 'lambda' (λ), that is

$$\text{correction factor} = \text{standard deviation} \times \lambda = \sigma \times [\phi(\delta)/(1 - I)]$$

and the true mean becomes

$$\mu = \bar{\mu} + \sigma[\phi(\delta)/(1 - I)]$$

Let us put some numbers into the last formula. The driver and the passenger estimated that their speed averaged 78kph during the 51 minutes for which they could check the speed of the car. They know that 15 per cent of time (observations) is lost, hence $(1 - I) = 1 - 0.15 = 0.85$. The standard deviation is assumed to be known and equal to 25kph. The final thing to calculate is the height ($\phi(\delta)$, called 'abscissa') of the distribution at the truncation point: from the standard normal tables $\phi(\delta) = 0.2323$ when $I = 0.15$. Putting these numbers together implies that the (estimated) true average speed of the car was

$$\mu = 78 + 25(0.2323/0.85) = 78 + 6.83 \approx 85\text{kph}$$

The faulty speedometer analogy and the previous exposition of selectivity bias show two things. First, when one utilises information which relates to only part of the sample, one obtains estimates which will in the general case be biased. Second, adjustment for sample selection is possible only when one is prepared to make a 'distributional assumption'. In our example, the driver assumed that the distribution of speed above 95kph had zero variance (constant speed at 150kph) while the passenger assumed a normal distribution. Though one might feel that the passenger's guess was more realistic, one has to bear in mind that selectivity correction is not something for nothing. The benefit is that one can work even with truncated distributions. The cost is the price one pays in the distributional assumption: an inappropriate assumption may result in more serious bias – consider the suggestion of the driver.

The similarity of the faulty speedometer to the study of labour supply is obvious. One can get information on wages and hours from existing workers, establish the known part of the wage/hour distribution and make an informed guess about the unknown part, that is, the *ex ante* wages and hours of the non-working. How this is done is shown in the next section.

■ Sample selection bias and labour supply

In the more relevant context of labour supply, the issue of selectivity can be highlighted with the use of the following two cases.

First, assume that we want to estimate the labour supply of men with respect to the amount of hours they are willing to work in a given week. In the sample, information on hours exists only for workers. Non-workers supply zero hours in a mathematical sense but not in an economic sense: at different wages non-working men would have supplied different hours but, given that they have decided not to participate, these *ex ante* hours are not observed *ex post*. From an economic theory point of view, the reason that hours are not observed in the case of non-working men is because their shadow wage is greater than the market wage. This observation brings us to the second case.

Second, assume that we want to estimate the labour supply behaviour of women. Wages are observed for working women but not for non-working women. Hence, a sample of working women can be taken as representative either of all (working and non-working) women, or only of those women who can attract a high offered wage, or only of women who have a low asking wage. Intuitively, it may be more reasonable to assume that women in the labour force are more likely to be a combination of women with high potential labour market rewards and low tastes for staying at home. Consequently, the sample is drawn from a self-selected group of women who are not likely to be representative of prospective female workers. As in the case of hours, what matter is not the *ex post* mathematical value of observed earnings (which includes zero values for non-participants) but their *ex ante* values. In the study of labour supply, wage *offers* is the appropriate variable that one should use, and not the *actual* wages that are, in effect, derived from the offered wage distribution *that is acceptable to job seekers* (Gronau, 1974).

One can compare the differences between first- and second-generation models with respect to either wages or hours. We prefer to show how sample selection bias arises in the case of wages because, first, the techniques involved are similar to those used in the case of hours and nothing is lost by focusing on one aspect rather than on the other. Second, the study of wages will occupy us again (i) in the next chapter in the form of 'earnings functions' within the context of the human capital theory and (ii) again in Chapter 9 when we examine pay differences between women and men in the context of pay discrimination.[5]

In terms of regression analysis, the first-generation labour supply models focused on working women only. This amounts to postulating that the observed (market) wage of a woman relates to her characteristics in the following way (omitting individual subscripts for notational simplicity):

$$W_M = \mathbf{X}\mathbf{a} + e_M \tag{3.4}$$

where W_M is the market wage, $\mathbf{X}$ refers to characteristics relevant to the labour market and $\mathbf{a}$ is the vector of their respective coefficients, and e_M is a normally distributed error term with zero mean (for simplicity we do not specify explicitly the constant term which can be assumed to be contained in vector **X**). The expected value of observed market wages thus specified is

$$E(W_M) = E(\mathbf{Xa}) + E(e_M) = \mathbf{Xa} \tag{3.5}$$

under the assumption that the error term has zero mean.

The second-generation models note that market wages are observed only for women who have already decided to work. For these women the market wage should be higher than their shadow wage at home, W_H, otherwise women would stay at home where rewards are higher than in the market. Note that this does not imply that wage offers among working women are on average necessarily greater than wage offers among non-working women. Neither does this imply that productivity at home is necessarily greater for non-working women than for working women. It is therefore possible that women who can fetch a high wage in the market do not work as they are also more productive at home than workers. In other words, the truncation point varies with *X*. This amounts to extending the car experiment to more cars whose speedometers get sticky at different speeds: we do not have a clue about which car is faster than others.

As in the case of market wages, the value of the unobserved shadow wage can be thought of as determined by women's personal characteristics, call them **Z**. The vector of personal characteristics (**Z**) which determine women's productivity at home is assumed to include all the characteristics of relevance to the labour market (**X**) plus others but not vice versa. This assumption appears to be reasonable on intuitive grounds as there are many personal characteristics which affect productivity at home but not in the market. For example, being able to drive may augment home production but very few employers would care about it. So, the home wage can be thought of as determined in the following way:

$$W_H = \mathbf{Zb} + e_H \tag{3.6}$$

where **b** is the corresponding vector of coefficients and e_H is another error term with the conventional properties. A woman's market wage is observed if the market wage rate exceeds her home wage

$$I = W_M - W_H = \mathbf{Xa} - \mathbf{Zb} + e_M - e_H > 0 \tag{3.7}$$

where *I* is the difference between the market wage and the value of work at home. *I* is a continuous variable and can be considered to be an index representing a woman's propensity to participate in the labour market. In the present formulation (equation (3.7)) when the value of the index for a particular woman is positive, the woman decides to work. In fact, the critical value of *I* at which a woman decides to join or not the labour market does not have to be zero. However, without loss of generality, one can normalise the critical value to zero as we have done in the text for expository purposes. Consequently, the expected value of a woman's market wage is dependent not only on her labour market characteristics, **X**, as was assumed in the first-generation models (equation 3.5), but on

$$E(W_M) = \mathbf{X}\mathbf{a} + E(e_M \mid I > 0) \qquad (3.8)$$

which depends also on her personal characteristics, **Z**, because equation (3.8) incorporates the arguments in the right-hand side of the inequality in (3.7). A comparison of the last equation with equation (3.4) reveals that not correcting for selectivity amounts to another omitted-variables problem, that is, we omit the second term in equation (3.8) (the 'sample selection rule') which indicates whether a woman would be in the labour market. The result from failing to take into account the effects from sample selection upon the empirical estimates can be shown with reference to **Figure 3.3**. The wages in the population are assumed to be evenly distributed within the total (shaded and unshaded) area contained in the rectangle. A regression analysis based on all observations should produce an unbiased estimate of the effect of a particular characteristic upon the wage: this is depicted as the 'population regression line' in the figure. Truncation can be taken to imply that the unshaded triangle at the bottom of the distribution is omitted from the regression analysis and the 'sample regression line' is flatter (therefore, biased) than the population regression line.

In a way similar to the car experiment illustrated earlier, the sample selection rule consists of two terms: it is the product between a scalar, σ, and λ (alternatively called the inverse Mill's ratio). The former term, σ, is a function of the standard deviations of the error terms in the market wage equation (3.4) and the home wage equation (3.6), and their correlation. In this case σ is equal to

$$\sigma = \sigma_{e(h)}(\sigma_{e(m)}/\sigma_{e(h)} - r_{e(h),\, e(m)})$$

where $\sigma(\cdot)$ stands for the standard deviation of the appropriate error term and r for the correlation between the two error terms.

The other term in the sample selection rule, λ, is the ratio of the ordinate of the standard normal density divided by the standard normal distribution both evaluated at (I). In other words, its value depends on where the critical point (truncation) lies and the height of the distribution at that particular point.[6] λ can be calculated from another regression of a woman's decision to participate in the labour market upon her personal characteristics (the participation function). The dependent variable in this case is a binary variable which takes the value of 1, if a woman is in the labour market, and the value of 0, if a woman is

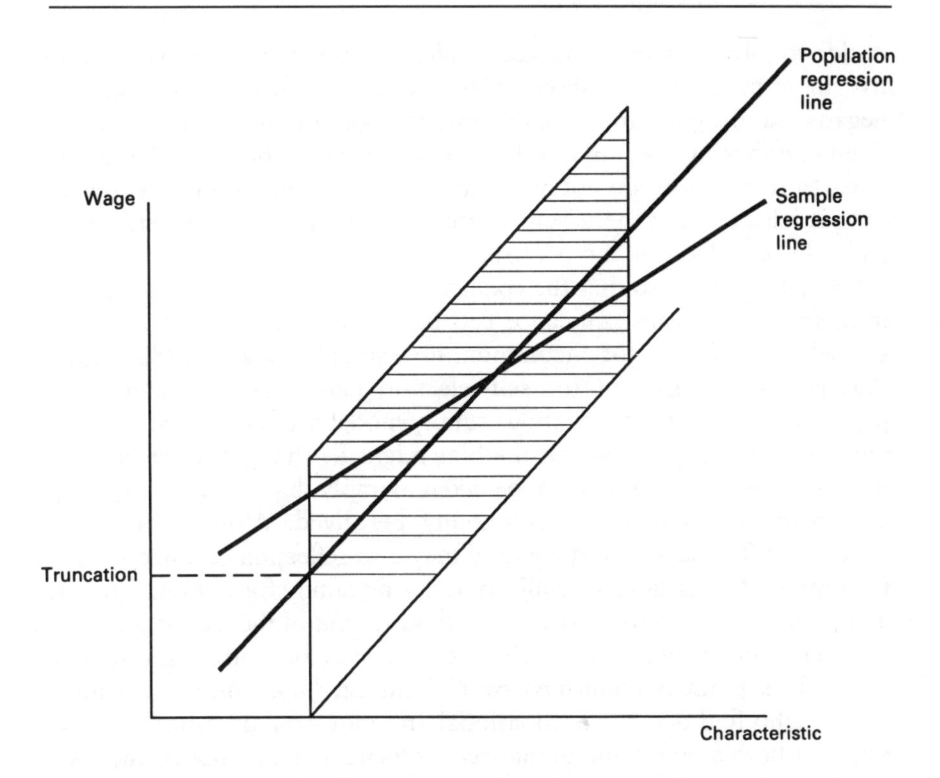

Figure 3.3 ***A comparison between sample estimates (workers only) and population estimates (workers and non-workers) of wages***

inactive. Then λ can be included in equation (3.8) in order to solve, at least in theory, the problem of omitted variables as far as selectivity is concerned and it should attract a coefficient equal to σ

$$E(W_M) = \mathbf{Xa} + \sigma\lambda \tag{3.9}$$

Equation (3.9) represents a typical 'second-generation-type' function that corresponds to the *ex ante* wages of *all* women (workers and non-workers). Two more observations need to be added.

First, the theory as presented here does not unambiguously predict the sign of σ, the coefficient on λ (that is, the outcome of the interplay between the standard deviations of and the correlation between the error terms).[7] For example, the coefficient on λ will be positive (and significant) if the unobserved factors which induce women to work are also directly related to female pay. However, rewards to home activities may be more dispersed than those in the market and unobserved variables which boost productivity at home may relate positively to returns to market work. If these two conditions are met, then women who decide to join the labour market would be those who are least productive in terms of the unobservables and the coefficient on λ will be negative (and significant). These remarks suggest that the inclusion of λ in an earnings function may solve[8] the econometric problem that arises when the error terms do not have the expected optimal properties due to sample selection, but there is no 'correct sign' or unique interpretation of its coefficient (Dolton and Makepeace, 1987).

Second, in many studies the coefficient on λ proved to be statistically insignificant. This insignificance can be interpreted as no evidence of self-selection. This is not uncommon: for example, Cogan (1980) shows that lack of adjustment for self-selection bias does not change the parameter estimates of the labour supply model for US married women, who are the group for which the bias might be thought *a priori* to be more serious. This can, in turn, be taken to imply that women as a group are more homogeneous than initially perceived. Along these lines, observed differences in participation may be a reflection of differences in the timing of household specialisation during family formation. Thus, at a point in time some women are in and others out of the labour force. At another point in time, those who were previously in are out and vice versa. This point is confirmed by Nakamura, Nakamura and Cullen (1979) who find that the occupational and industrial distribution is the same for both married and unmarried women and this supports the view that the factors affecting women are common in the two groups. These findings relate to a 'quantity' interpretation of women's labour supply and, in effect, challenge the 'qualitative' view derived from the observation that not being in the labour force at a given time is highly correlated with not being in the labour force at any time (Ben-Porath, 1973; Heckman and Willis, 1977; Keeley, 1981).[9]

One should also add that results derived only from a sample of working women may well produce biased estimates even for working women. The reason that bias creeps into the estimation is that both asking and offered wages depend on unobserved variables, as educated women may well have a lower taste for home chores. As a result, the error terms in the structural model (the decision to work, to work at what wage, and to work for how long) are correlated with other variables assumed to be exogenous to the model, and are also correlated between themselves across the different equations in the model (Killingsworth and Heckman, 1986).

The implications of selectivity are usually visualised to be more important for women, as we usually observe only a fraction of women in the labour force while male participation is taken to be nearly universal. Although economists do not address the issue of male non-participation explicitly, especially for men in their prime age, one can be reasonably sure that some selectivity bias may be present even in the estimates for men. In fact, studies that addressed the issue of selectivity bias within the context of male labour supply found that selectivity bias is in general more severe for men than for women.[10] This is not an unexpected finding. Non-working men may be less likely to be representative of all men for reasons of health or behavioural problems.

Finally, we mention in passing here that the mechanics of selectivity correction is subject to the usual reservations raised in the case of econometric applications of economic theory. For example, the participation function may not be correctly specified, or the explanatory variables may be poor proxies of the theoretical variables they are assumed to represent. (Some of these issues will be examined in some detail in the next chapter.) In addition, the estimates could be affected not only by omitted variables and measurement errors and so on, but also by optimisation errors, preference errors and budget constraint errors.[11] The net effect of these errors is as yet unknown to practitioners.

In terms of empirical applications based on second-generation models of labour supply the literature is vast. However, the findings of second-generation models of labour supply are equally as diverse as those of the first-generation models: this is not unexpected given that economic theory specifies many forms that utility functions can take but provides little, if any in most cases, guidance about which form is more appropriate for what situation. Second, the budget constraints are usually affected by many non-linearities due to various tax and social security policies. In many cases, information on how such provisions affect individuals is lacking and researchers are forced to use some *ad hoc* modifications or to assume that some average value applies to all individuals in the sample. Third, different researchers have used different sets of data. For example, some researchers have used census results while others have used household surveys or labour force surveys: there may be considerable differences with respect to coverage, methodology, definitional aspects and so on between these types of statistical sources. Fourth, the date to which the samples relate may be different: some samples were taken during periods of recession, others during periods of economic prosperity. There is no reason to assume that workers respond 'symmetrically' to downturns and upturns of the economic cycle. Finally, one may add that different researchers have different prior views on the subject they study. Theory 'impregnation' (one sees what one believes) is therefore another possible explanation for the differences in the empirical findings which range from positive to negative and by a high factor within each direction. However, these remarks do not invalidate the contribution of the second-generation labour supply models. In this respect one can argue that while they are doing no better on some empirical grounds than the first-generation models, they have definitely produced a direction of analysis which is more reliable than its predecessor.

■ Summary

This chapter showed that labour supply is a growing area of research. In theoretical terms simple models are replaced by more general ones which capture not only the distinction between work and non-work, but also the distinction between different uses of time at home. Apart from its obvious contribution to the study of behaviour in the labour market, the theory of allocation of time has attracted considerable interest from other disciplines as well – especially demography. A new term has been coined, namely 'the new home economics', which applies to models which examine marriage, fertility and marital dissolution along the lines of the theory of allocation of time (Becker, 1981; for a summary see Ermisch, 1988, or Cigno, 1990).

In terms of estimation techniques, the developments which took place in labour economics have also had an impact in other areas of economics. For example, the lending behaviour of financial institutions cannot be fully explained with reference to successful applications. These institutions do also consider applications which are unsuccessful (zero amount of lending). This results in truncation because not granting a loan is not because the 'applicant is worth nothing' but because he has not scored enough points on the credibility scale that is used by the lending organisation. The techniques developed in the context of labour supply are relevant in this respect.

In conclusion, labour economics is no longer what it used to be: an alternative to those economists who, 'horrified' by the mathematical rigour of economic theory, turned into 'softer' areas (Samuelson, 1954, p. 380; Fisher, 1971, p. ix; Addison and Siebert, 1979, p. 1). The study of labour has now been formalised to the same extent as, if not to a more sophisticated degree than, other areas in economics.

■ Notes

1. For a survey of the theory of allocation of time see Cigno (1990). For a survey of the second-generation models of labour supply see Killingsworth and Heckman (1986).

2. Some authors have used the term 'commodity' for what we call 'activity'. We prefer to use the second term as the term 'commodity' is usually used as a synonym of a 'good'. The reason for the terminology adopted here is because it is easier to understand what the 'goods component' of an activity is while the 'goods component' of a commodity may be confusing.
3. Gronau (1973).
4. You may also speculate on which side of the Atlantic each individual is more likely to be.
5. An explicit treatment of selectivity in the case of hours is provided in Fallon and Verry (1988), chapter 2.
6. Because the problem arises from the 'truncation' of the distribution of a particular characteristic, economists have habitually referred to this situation as a 'truncated' regression instead of the more accurate term 'censored'. In the present context, truncation would occur if there are observations only for working women. However, what we are presented with is censorship: there is information about the characteristics of non-working women (such as age, schooling, location, family size and so on) – though not, of course, with respect to their market wages. The correction consists in effect of predicting the missing information on the censored variable (wages) from whatever information is available in the rest of the data set.
7. In the early literature the expectation was that the coefficient on λ would be positive. In fact, studies which reported negative coefficients were more or less considered to be an 'anomalous' result (Killingsworth and Heckman, 1986). However, studies have often reported either insignificant or negative and significant coefficients on λ. See Nakamura *et al.* (1979), Heckman and MaCurdy (1980, 1982), Stelcner and Breslaw (1985), Behrman, Wolfe and Blau (1985), Wright and Ermisch (1991) and Psacharopoulos and Tzannatos (1992a, p. 211).
8. The simplified exposition of the sample selection effect and its correction adopted in our presentation masks the complexity of selection models and a number of difficult-to-resolve specification issues. More specifically, the conventional error distribution assumptions have been questioned by Lee (1982), Olsen (1980) and Duncan and Leigh (1985). In addition, problems of heteroscedasticity have not been fully resolved (Nelson, 1984). Finally, the assumed additivity in the effects of variables in the various equations in the model may not hold (Little, 1985).
9. Though there is no ambition in the present volume to pursue the 'qualitative/quantitative' interpretation of female labour supply further we note two different explanations relevant to the present discussion. One explanation is along the lines of 'persistence' and 'habit formation' (Clark and Summers, 1982; Blanchard and Summers, 1988). According to these authors, the persistence in female participation should be greater than in the working population as a whole. Cross and Allen (1988) echoed this theme at a macro level and Behrman, Wolfe and Blau (1985) confirmed that 'there is a strong serial correlation in labour force participation because of differences across individuals in tastes, needs and returns from paid labour market participation' (p. 8). The other explanation is along the lines of

'intertemporal substitution' models of labour supply (Lucas and Rapping, 1969; Altonji, 1982) and is similar to the already mentioned explanations provided by the theory of allocation of time for the observed pattern of hours worked during the life-cycle.

10. See for example the collection of papers in Psacharopoulos and Tzannatos (1992b) and references therein.
11. Optimisation errors refer to discrepancies in the measurement of optimal and actual values of the variables concerned; preference errors refer to unobservable differences in utility functions across individuals; and budget constraint errors refer to unobserved differences in the budget constraints across individuals. These issues are not pursued further in this volume since they are still at a theoretical stage (see Killingsworth and Heckman, 1986).

Chapter 4

Human Capital

Introduction

The idea that education is a form of investment is not new and traces back (at least) to Adam Smith (1776, p. 101) who noted that

> A man educated at the expense of much labour and time . . . may be compared to one . . . expensive machine . . . The work which he learns to perform . . . over and above the usual wages of common labour will replace the whole expense of his education.

In this respect the theory of human capital can be seen as an extension of investment theory in the sphere of human resources. The reason is that one may be willing to incur costs in the short run in return for higher benefits in the long run. In the present context an application of this observation is the following one: an 18-year-old may decide not to join the labour market and to stay on in the education system until he gets a university qualification because current costs (foregone earnings and education-related expenses) are lower than expected benefits (higher earnings for university graduates). As in the traditional theory of investment, the rate of discount of costs and benefits is a key determinant of the decision to invest in human capital.

Investment in 'people' (human capital) is a much broader concept than simply staying on in the formal education system at the age of 16 or 18. More precisely, investment in people occurs from the time they are born and covers their whole life. One type of such an investment is expenditure on health: the cost of preventing or treating diseases can in many cases be offset by lower labour market absenteeism rates due to ill-health and subsequently a greater level of production (for the economy) and higher earnings (for the individual). It is therefore obvious that investment in human capital can take many forms (such as in education and health) and has both a 'social' dimension and a 'private' (individual) dimension.

The improvement or the maintenance of human capital (intellectual and physical well-being) is not, of course, simply an investment decision. It can be also seen as a consumption decision: for example, individuals may prefer to pay for the sake of learning, even though the expected economic returns from such a decision are not sufficient to cover present costs. The consumption aspect of education has been traditionally labelled *social* demand for education, that is, people may want to pursue education simply because it is an activity (service) which gives them greater utility *vis-à-vis* other consumption alternatives. In contrast, the *economic* demand for education is seen as reflecting people's decision to undertake education with a view to maximising their lifetime earnings. In the western world, the economic system and the associated-with-it moral philosophy leave little room for economists to question education as a consumption good: people are free to choose between what is on offer and what their means permit. However, the literature on education as an investment has always occupied a central role in economics because of its implications for both individual and social welfare.

These observations make clear that there are potentially many approaches to the study of human capital formation and its effects. In this chapter we scale down the ambition to provide a global survey in this area which can easily extend to accommodate sociological and other interpretations. Our first concern is to show how the market for educated labour works. Then, we examine the way in which individuals decide to undertake education: a stylised example is presented which is later generalised in a formal economic model. The model and its empirical applications are subsequently examined for the relevance of the assumptions and the reliability of the derived results. Then we move from individual considerations to social policy in the sphere of education and qualified labour ('manpower'). Finally, we explore the conditions under which firms would invest in their own labour force in the form of training.

■ The market for educated labour

The market for educated labour can be represented in the following human capital model. Suppose that there is only one type and level of education. Present workers either have this education or not. And

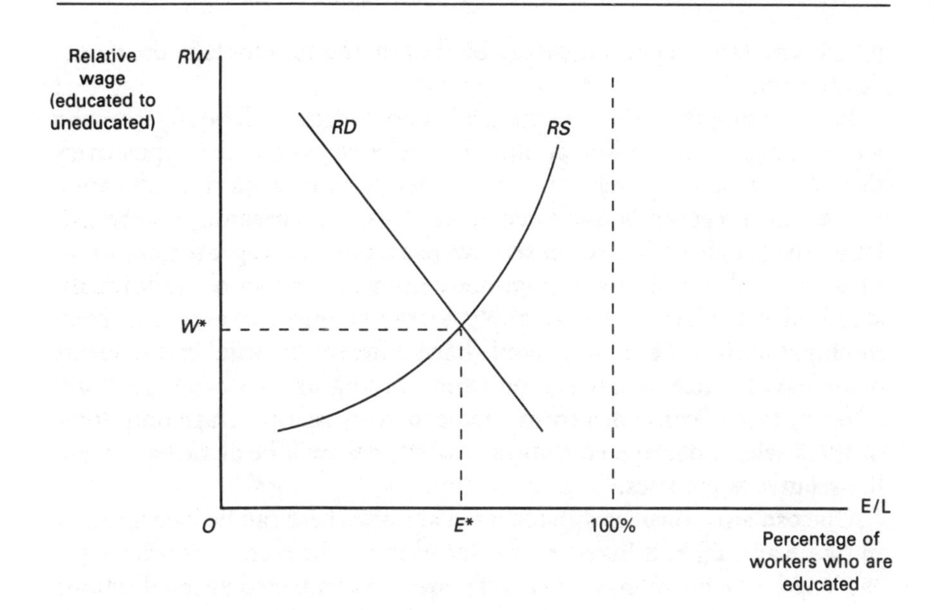

Figure 4.1 ***The market for educated labour***

prospective workers can either undertake this education or none at all.

As usual one can think of a demand for and a supply of education. It is instructive to think in terms of a *relative* demand curve and a *relative* supply curve. This means the following: denote the wage rate of the educated worker as W^e (*e* for educated) and the wage rate of the uneducated worker as W^u (*u* for uneducated). Then the *relative* wage (*RW*) becomes W^e/W^u and is depicted on the vertical axis (**Figure 4.1**). This is on the price side. On the quantity side we will use not the number of educated workers but the *percentage* of workers who are educated. This is illustrated in the following diagram where the curve *RD* is the relative demand and the curve *RS* is the relative supply.

The two curves have the usual slopes, that is, *RD* is negatively sloped while *RS* is positively sloped. It is instructive to ask why this is so. But first one should recall that *RD is not the demand for education by the individual worker* but the demand for educated labour by the firm; and also *RS* stands for the supply of educated labour (that is, it stands for the demand for education by individual workers) and it is not the supply of education, that is, the number of student places available in educational institutions (schools, polytechnics, universities and so on).

Relative demand (*RD*) indicates the education mix of the labour force at various relative wages. It is negative in slope because as the relative wage rises, firms will tend to substitute the cheap factor (uneducated labour) for the expensive factor (educated labour). This is a standard prediction of the economic theory of the demand for inputs in the theory of the firm.

Relative supply (*RS*) traces out the proportion of the labour force who would acquire education at different relative wages. It is positively sloped because the psychic and pecuniary costs of acquiring education rise as more people become educated. This is so because, on the one hand, the supply of education services has a positive slope: the provision of additional school places, teachers, libraries and so on follows the standard considerations that apply to the supply curve of any commodity. On the other hand, people have different financial endowments or time preference or satisfaction from learning or, in a catch-all word, different tastes; consequently at each and every relative wage only some of them will undertake education, and the rest will be attracted only if the relative wage rises.

One can also consider differences in ability. These can be incorporated in two ways. First, differences in education can be seen as differences in the length of education, that is, differences in completed years of schooling rather than one type and level of schooling which some undertake and others do not. This interpretation results in the negative slope of the demand for education because increases in the years of schooling decrease the marginal product of educated to uneducated labour: this prediction derives from the theory of production functions which, in our case, translates to the 'education production function' (education can be seen as another input in the production process). Second, differences in education can be seen as differences in the ability to learn: the less able find it more difficult – that is, costly in mental terms – to acquire education and need to be compensated accordingly through higher wages in order to stay on in the educational system.

So far we have firmly established that for educated labour the demand and supply curves would have the expected slopes. (In fact the demand curve can never be Giffen as it is not derived from a utility function but from a production function, in which case the income (budget) and substitution effects always operate in tandem). As a result the intersection of the two curves determines the equilibrium relative wage, W^*. This wage reflects exactly, in theory, the ratio of marginal products of educated to uneducated workers *and* the compensating differential for the last (marginal) worker who is just attracted to (that is, he is just indifferent between) becoming educated or not. Other workers earn *economic* rent while firms benefit from the difference between the sum of marginal products (total product) and the (mathematical) product of wages and employment (that is, the total wage bill paid to both educated and uneducated workers).

The comparative statics of the model are the expected ones. A shift of the demand curve to the right (for example, because the demand for more sophisticated products – which are produced by more educated workers – has increased) will result in both higher relative wages and a higher equilibrium level of the education mix of the labour force. Alternatively, a shift to right of the relative supply curve will, as before, increase the percentage of the labour force which is educated but the equilibrium wage will fall.

These remarks complete the discussion on how the market for educated labour works in aggregate and we now turn to individual considerations in the formation of human capital.

■ An illustrative example

In this section we outline a stylised (but probable) way of reasoning by somebody who is just about to leave secondary education. In this way we explain the main arguments underlying the investment aspect of human capital formation and provide a basic technique for estimating costs and benefits associated with education. In addition, the present exposition relates to a timely issue, as tertiary education in Britain may become more the financial concern of individuals than of the State (the replacement of grants by loans can be seen as a first step in this direction). To provide a more realistic picture we also indicate how the partial redemption of the tax liability of students (namely, the community/poll tax at present and whatever instrument replaces it) may affect the decision to stay on in the education system or not.

Assume that a student is now 18 years old and has the appropriate qualifications to enter a university/polytechnic for a 3-year degree. (S)he has two options: either to enter the labour market *now* and get a wage W^S which is paid to workers who have a secondary-school qualification or to join a university course, get a degree, and start work *three years later* at a wage W^T which is paid to university degree holders. To simplify the exposition, assume that both wages remain constant at their initial levels for the rest of the student's working life (this assumption is made for expository purposes and implies that there is no on-the-job training while experience does not affect earnings during the working life of an individual; unrealistic this might sound but the essence of the exposition remains unaffected). These two wages are shown as two different 'age–earnings' profiles in **Figure 4.2** where the horizontal axis measures time in years and the vertical axis measures wages and costs. According to the figure, university education will be desirable from an investment point of view, if the area marked 'benefits' is greater (or, at equilibrium, equal) to the two areas marked direct and indirect costs.

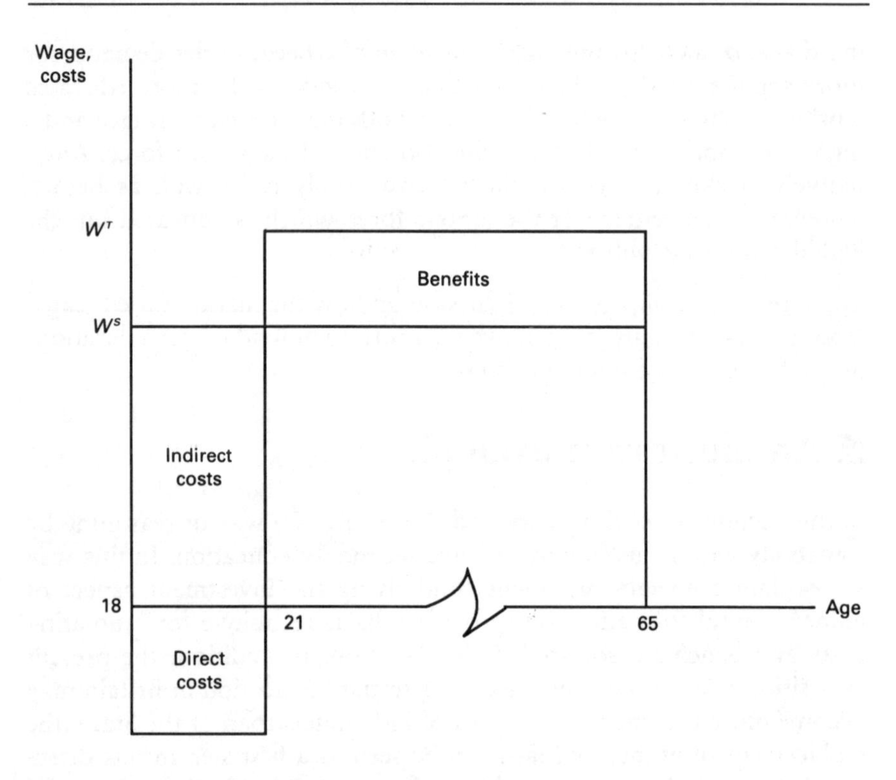

Figure 4.2 ***Costs and lifetime benefits to education***

The former is education-related expenditure (for example, fees and books). The latter is foregone wages because one stays on in the education system and does not join the labour market at the age of 18. Of course, the comparison between costs and benefits should be properly discounted as costs are paid early and benefits accrue later.

How can the prospective student decide whether staying on in the education system and getting a degree is economically worthwhile? There are many ways in which such a decision can be made but let us concentrate on one of them: we assume that the student is concerned whether the expenditure associated with acquiring a degree will fetch higher returns than an equal amount invested in the best available investment alternative. If the return to 'getting a degree' is higher than the return to alternative investment open to the student, then staying on in education would be worth undertaking. A simplified formula for estimating the return to education is as follows:

$$\begin{array}{c}\text{Rate of return}\\ \text{to}\\ \text{university education}\end{array} = \frac{\text{Difference in } \textit{annual} \text{ earnings between university and secondary-school graduates}}{\text{Net } \textit{total} \text{ cost of university education}}$$

This is a general formula and can be used for the estimation of both private and social returns to education – a difference to which we return later. For the time being note that the formula can be interpreted as the yield of a permanent constant stream of benefits (numerator) over a lump-sum cost of foregone earnings plus direct outlays (denominator). Neither the permanent benefits assumption nor the lumping of costs together are critical in this calculation, since costs occur within a period of only three years (so it does not really matter whether a cost incurs at the age of 18 or 20) and the payment of benefits (in the form of higher earnings) extends over several decades (and, perhaps, as much as 45 years) in which case discounted values even of large amounts are practically insignificant.

Let us get the numbers. The numerator requires knowledge of the difference between the two wage levels (W^T and W^S in **Figure 4.2**). It would be impractical to estimate this for the vast number of academic degrees, prospective occupational/industrial/regional employments and personal characteristics of students. Here the general case is presented by reference to the first two rows in **Table 4.1** which shows the average annual earnings by sex at the two critical levels of education in Britain in 1989.[1] The third row is their difference, that is, the figures for the numerator.

The calculation of the value of the denominator is slightly more complicated as it has, in general, four different components: first, the duration of studies; second, the indirect cost of education which is foregone earnings; third, the direct cost of education such as fees, books, stationery equipment and so on, as well as expenditure which would have not incurred had the person not been studying (for example travelling to and from the place of study or interest paid on a student loan); fourth, and finally, one should include any payment to the student (such as a grant) and any remission towards payment which would have been due had the student not been in tertiary education (such as non-payment of interest on student loans, partial relief from poll tax payment and so on). These four components enter the denominator in the following way:

$$(\text{Years of study}) \times (W^S + \text{Direct cost} - \text{Grant} \pm \text{Cost of loan} - \text{Tax remission})$$

In the lower part of **Table 4.1** we present the estimates of the returns to private education on different assumptions about the denominator. First, assuming that the only cost of education is foregone earnings, then the return to education is about 17 per cent for men and 21 per cent for women. A word of caution: one should not confuse the higher rates of return for women's education with women's actual pay. Higher rates for women do not necessarily imply that women will, on average, earn more

than men. As **Table 4.1** indicates, women in Britain have lower earnings than men with equivalent qualifications – an issue examined in the chapter discussing discrimination in the labour market. What the present estimates suggest is that a woman with a degree will earn about 20 per cent more per year than a woman without a degree. One can further qualify this finding by noting that our formula is based on the assumption that individuals work continuously after graduation till a late age. If this is not the case, then returns should be adjusted downwards and this would definitely affect women much more than men. On the other hand, since the figures in **Table 4.1** relate to the average woman, a 'dedicated' female worker, that is one who does not drop out of the labour market during some stage in her life, may be rewarded by greater than average earnings and higher returns to her education than those suggested by the table.

Second, the inclusion of £1000 per annum as a direct cost to education other than fees reduces these rates by only about 1.5 percentage points. Things do not really change much.

Third, on the assumption that the average level of poll tax (or whatever tax would replace it) would be about £333 a year, then students pursuing tertiary education would save about £800 during the three years of their studies (at present students pay only 20 per cent of the poll tax). If this is included, then the rate of return reverts practically to its initial value.

Fourth, assuming that a student gets a £6000 loan (£2000 a year) which is repaid in one instalment three years after his graduation, then (s)he benefits by about £2000 in unpaid interest (assuming further that the average commercial rate of interest is 10 per cent). This sum, if subtracted from the denominator, increases the private returns to education to about 18 per cent and 23 per cent for men and women respectively.

Fifth, and finally, it would be interesting to find out what happens if students were asked to pay full fees for tertiary education. Love and Williams (1990, Table 2) have estimated that the average cost per student full-time equivalent was £2160 in Arts, £3890 in Science and £7270 in Medical/Dentistry/Veterinary courses in 1986. These estimates are perhaps on the low side as more detailed estimates suggest that the range of costs in different departments/universities varies from about £1000 to £11 000 per student in Arts; from £1500 to £15 000 in Science; and up to £32 000 in Medicine and related subjects (ibid., Table 3). On this evidence let us assume that fees come on average to approximately £6000 a year. Then private returns drop by about one-third of their original value.

The data we used were very aggregate. Given that not all graduates

Table 4.1 ***Earnings and returns to university education in Britain***

Annual earnings (£)	*Men*	*Women*		
Degree holders	21 762	16 848		
A-level holders	14 461	10 249		
Numerator				
Difference between the two figures above	7 301	6 599		
Denominator	*Total cost of education (£)*		*Private annual returns to education*	
	Men	*Women*	*Men*	*Women*
If only foregone earnings are included	43 383	30 747	16.8%	21.1%
As above plus £1000 p.a. for books, stationery, etc.	46 383	33 747	15.4%	18.7%
As above minus 80% remission of the poll tax*	45 584	32 948	16.5%	20.6%
As above minus not-paid interest of a loan†	43 584	30 948	18.1%	23.4%
As above but the student pays full fees‡	61 584	48 948	11.3%	12.5%

* Assuming that the student ought to pay a total of £1000 in the three years of studies but he pays only £200.

† Assuming that the student receives £2000 in each year of his studies and repays it in a lump sum payment of £6000 three years after graduation (not paid interest about £2000).

‡ Assuming that fees would have been £6000 a year.

Source: Constructed from Tzannatos (1988a, Table 2) using the latest estimate for average earnings of all male employees (about £270 per week) from the New Earnings Survey, 1989.

receive the same level of pay when they start work, and also that it is harder for graduates from some disciplines to find work immediately after they complete their studies, there exists considerable variation in the rate of return to education between different disciplines. There is no need to go into this. The student now knows how the rate of return to education is calculated and all (s)he has to do is to replace the average graduate annual earnings by, say, £30 000 if (s)he becomes an accountant or £12 000 if (s)he becomes a teacher.

In conclusion, if education is seen as a *private investment* in human capital, it appears to have sizeable *real* returns. This is so to a great extent because of the benefits accruing to students from public subsidies given in the form of non-fee payments, interest-free or subsidised student loans (where applicable) and remission of the tax liability of students. This finding can be used but also qualified in a number of ways. From the point of view of 18-year-olds, it seems that going on to tertiary education, if only for the monetary benefits associated with education, is perhaps the best investment they can undertake early in their lives. It is hard to think of any other form of investment which would yield such a high return for such a long time. To this one should add that (i) there have been periods when the real interest rates have been negative while (ii) the returns to education shown in this section are economic returns and exclude consumption benefits from education. However, note that the calculation of benefits assumed that the student would have been paid the average wage during his university years. This is untrue: young people earn less than the level of average earnings and earnings in the not distant future count for more than the same amount of earnings later on in life. Therefore, some overestimation of the returns may be present. This bias can be greater if one considers that we have used pre-taxed earnings. However, neither observation should have a significant effect upon the magnitude of the present estimates.

Estimating formally the profitability of education: earnings functions

The formulation of the 'earnings function' comes from a seminal paper by Mincer (1974). At the cost of some abstraction, the basic model can be summarised as follows.

First, assume that education (i) lasts for a given number of years (denoted by S), (ii) is of a given 'type' (for example, there is no distinction between arts, humanities, science and so on) and (iii) is full-time (that is, an individual either works or studies). Thus to become educated is an all-or-nothing decision. In a more realistic setting, one can imagine S as the additional, beyond compulsory schooling, education.

Second, assume that individuals are *ex ante* identical in all respects (tastes, ability, financial endowment and access to capital markets, parental influence and socioeconomic background and so on). This and the previous assumption result in two different wages in the labour market: one for educated labour and another for uneducated labour. Then the difference between these two wage levels can be taken to be a common compensating differential for all individuals. It is immediately obvious that under the assumptions of the model the role of demand in this type of labour market is simply to determine the percentage of the labour force who are educated. Now, the question becomes 'What is the difference between these two wages in such an environment?' and this is answered below with the aid of a few more assumptions.

Third, assume that there are no direct costs to education (such as fees, expenditure on books and so on) and that the only (indirect) cost to education is foregone earnings (the cost of not being employed in the labour market).

Fourth, assume that all workers have the same total working life (T years) irrespective of whether they undertake education or not. Thus educated workers retire from the labour market S years after the uneducated ones have retired.

Fifth, assume that there is no on-the-job training and no other kind of investment in human capital takes place after the completion of formal education. In other words, the difference in the wages between educated and uneducated labour is due to differences only in formal schooling undertaken at the beginning of one's life.

Sixth, assume that with the exception of the wage rate, other characteristics of jobs requiring educated and uneducated labour are identical. As in the previous case, this assumption implies that observed wages differ because some workers have education and others have no education at all.

Seventh, and finally, assume that the market is perfect in terms of information and adjustment costs, and that there is a given rate of interest (r).

In effect, these assumptions result in **Figure 4.1** apart from the fact that the (flat) earnings profile for the educated extend till the age of 68 and there are no direct costs to education. On these assumptions, the present values (PV) of the lifetime wages (W) of uneducated and educated workers (superscripts u and e respectively) at the point they start work are respectively:

$$PV^u = (W^u/r)\,(1 - e^{-rT})$$

$$PV^e = (W^e/r)\,(1 - e^{-rT})\,e^{-rS}$$

where e is the basis of the natural logarithms (approximately equal to 2.72).

The interpretation of these two equations is as follows. The ratio of wages to the interest rate (W/r) is simply the present value of an annuity paid for ever. The term in the second parenthesis is the finite life correction factor, that is, it corrects the previous ratio for the fact that people eventually stop working for one reason or another. And the third term which appears only in the second formula is another adjustment for the fact that those who become educated will have no wage until their education stops and work starts. In other words, those who contemplate starting work immediately discount to today, while those who undertake education discount everything (in the model) to S years ahead.

With individuals *ex ante* identical, the two present values should, at a competitive equilibrium in a perfect market, be equal. Equating the right-hand sides of the two equations above, eliminating the finite life correction factor from both sides and rearranging, we obtain:

$$W^e = W^u\,e^{rS}$$

and taking the logarithms on both sides

$$\ln(W^e) = \ln(W^u) + rS$$

because $\ln(e^x)$ is simply x.

Thus the theory is compatible with the common-sense result that the educated should have greater wages than the uneducated ($W^e > W^u$). In addition, this simple model provides a convenient (semi-logarithmic) relationship between annual earnings and length of schooling (in years) which is capable of being used in econometric work. In particular, one can run a regression of the log-earnings of individual workers upon a constant term and their length of schooling. In this context, the constant term should be approximately equal to the logarithm of the wage for non-educated labour while the coefficient on schooling should be roughly equal to the rate of interest. In fact, and as the underlying assumptions necessitate, in a perfectly competitive environment the market rate of interest should be equal to the rate of time preference in the society and also to the rate of return to an additional year of schooling.

The merit of this approach is that it is derived from an explicit economic foundation that dictates the functional form (log-annual earnings on years of schooling) that econometric estimation should take. One disadvantage of the 'earnings function' derived as above is that it ignores all other aspects of human capital formation and especially

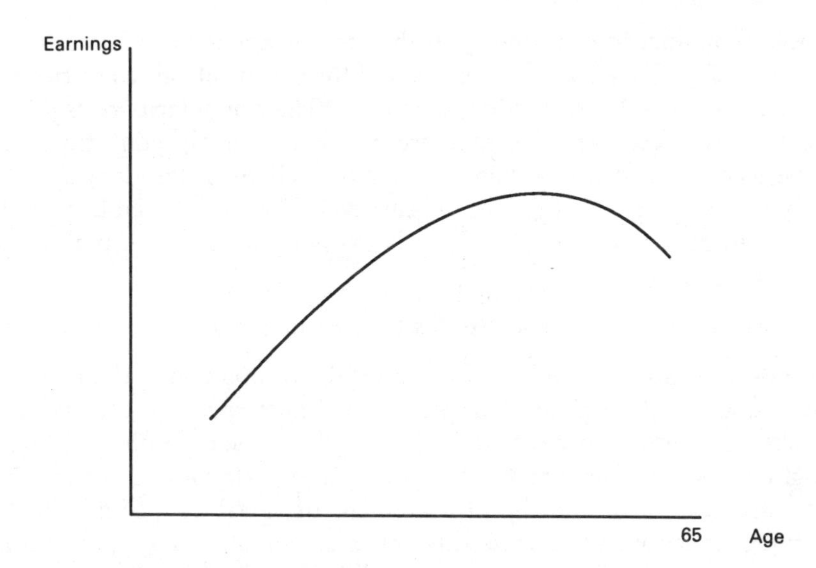

Figure 4.3 ***A typical age–earnings profile***

on-the-job training. In fact, in many jobs employer-provided training and experience may be more significant forms of human capital and more important determinants of earnings than formally acquired education. The stylised age–earnings profile for a typical individual shown in **Figure 4.3** contrasts the simplified version upon which the discussion has been based so far. Actual age–earnings profiles are increasing at first, reaching a peak sometime in the working life of an individual until they eventually start decreasing. This pattern is suggestive of the fact that other types of human capital are formed during a person's working life. These observations can be accommodated by including some proxy of post-education human capital formation on the right-hand side of the last equation. The most popular version by far of earnings functions is the following one:

$$\ln (W^e) = \text{Constant} + rS + aE + bE^2$$

where E is years of post-school work experience and a and b are coefficients. In theoretical terms the quadratic (in experience) formulation of earnings functions can be derived by assuming that investment in human capital declines linearly with time.[2] In practical terms, the inclusion of experience and its square as an explanatory variable has been found to 'belong' to the earnings functions in the sense that regression analysis returns coefficients on experience which have the correct sign, are statistically significant and are 'intuitively' of reasonable size.

The earnings functions thus specified have proved to be the most stable econometric relationship in the area of applied economics (Griliches, 1977). They have been estimated for practically all countries for which individual (cross-section) data exist. Their popularity rests partly on the very few variables that are required, namely education and experience. The former variable is usually available from many sources (labour force surveys or household surveys). The latter variable, namely labour market experience, is relatively easily proxied at least in the case of men as follows

$$\text{Experience} = \text{Age} - \text{Schooling} - (\text{school starting-age})$$

as most men are in the labour force after the completion of their formal education and throughout their prime age. Experience thus calculated is in effect *potential* experience (or, as referred to by some authors, Mincerian experience). Some methodological issues pertaining to the empirical specification of and the measurement of variables included in the earnings functions are discussed below, after we present a typical result of the by now familiar Mincerian earnings functions.

The first result was derived by Mincer (1974) and was based on annual earnings, length of schooling and potential experience for (pre-tax) annual earnings of male, urban, non-student workers below the age of 65 in the USA in 1959:

$$\ln(\text{earnings}) = 6.2 + 0.107S + 0.081E - 0.0012E^2,\ R^2 = 0.285$$

The coefficient on schooling is 10.7 per cent which is not too far off the rates of commercial investments which prevailed in the USA during the 1950s. As we are dealing with male workers, the use of potential experience is not that damaging though it assumes that people have been working without interruptions in employment since the end of their formal education: unemployment rates were not high in the early post-war era. The inclusion of experience in a quadratic form implies that experience becomes successively less important in the determination of earnings. The estimates suggest that an initial year of experience increases earnings by 8.1 per cent but the effect of additional years declines with the passage of time. The figures also suggest that the effect of experience peaks after 33.75 years in the labour market and then earnings turn down *for a given level of schooling.*[3] Given that the data are cross-sectional, this result does not mean that the typical man's earnings turn down after he has been working for 33.75 years. If earnings are growing year by year throughout the economy (as is the typical case due to capital accumulation and improvements in technology) then the peak year of annual earnings in an individual's life will occur at a *larger* number of years of experience than the cross-section peak. What the result does mean is that *at a given time* (in our case, in 1959) the highest-earning men among those who left school at the age of 18 are those aged 52.

The reasons why the people with 34 or more years of experience earn less than those with 33.75 years of experience are first, physical deterioration (such as in strength or overall health) and second, what one can call *vintage effects*. The latter simply means that in a cross-section sample the 60-year-olds who finished school 20 years before the 40-year-olds are less in touch with the modern world. For example, recent graduates in engineering know things that were not known and therefore not taught to engineers who graduated in the 1950s or, in the words of the Nobel laureate economist and main contributor to the theory of human capital, 'ask the new breed of young economists what they think of those old-fashion economists who have tenure' (Schultz, 1984). Indeed, one might argue that it is surprising that in the presence of these two effects the experience effect peaks after 33.75 years: casual observations and, indeed, an inspection of the age–earnings profiles tend to suggest that earnings peak earlier. However, similar results for the United Kingdom are derived by Psacharopoulos and Layard (1979) who give an earnings-maximising value of experience at around 30 years.

The R^2 statistic shown along the earnings function is the coefficient of determination which shows which percentage of the variance of the dependent variable (log-earnings) is explained by the variables included in the regression (in our case, schooling and experience). Its value suggests that almost 30 per cent of the variance in the natural logarithm of individual earnings is explained by these two variables. An explanation for the remaining 70 per cent should be sought in other factors – what one calls the omitted variables from the model – provided that the functional specification of the model is the correct one. An obvious candidate variable for inclusion in the earnings functions along with schooling and experience is the number of weeks and hours worked in the year to which the earnings data relate. This variable can standardise for individual differences in the work effort. Indeed, Mincer included the logarithm of weeks worked in that year and the coefficient of determination almost doubled. An interesting finding was that the elasticity of earnings with respect to weeks worked was in all cases significantly greater than unity. In other words, earnings is an increasing function of the period of work within a particular year. One can offer two explanations for this finding: first, overtime effects, that is, when normal weekly hours are already worked, then additional labour is hired at a wage premium; second, what we call a simultaneity problem. For example, those who have some characteristic (drive, from a supply point of view, or reliability, from a demand point of view) which makes them earn more than others with the same education and experience also have a lower probability of becoming unemployed. And perhaps those who earn less have poorer health or other adverse characteristics which reduce their ability to earn.

We conclude this section by noting that a substantial volume of empirical work on the determination of earnings preexisted the Mincerian formulation. However, these studies were relatively unsophisticated and relied primarily on correlation analysis between different levels of schooling and differences in earnings as evidenced by census data (Hansen, 1963). An interesting feature found in many of the pre-Mincer studies was that these gross differences were 'corrected' by reducing them by the so-called 'alpha coefficient' which was supposed to account for the influence of other variables on earnings that might be correlated with schooling attainment (Denison, 1962). Usually the value of the alpha coefficient was set at around 0.60 which is not far off the value of the unexplained part of the variance of earnings, as suggested by the R^2 of the earnings function which we have just discussed. Nevertheless, the alpha coefficient was an arbitrary device while the availability of cross-section data and Mincer's theoretical developments has led to the wide use of regression-based analysis of individual data.[4]

Econometric problems of earnings functions

A number of issues have been raised with respect to the use of earnings functions. The arguments relate to whether the parsimonious formulation of earnings functions is sufficient and appropriate for the task in hand on both theoretical and empirical grounds. The relevant literature is rich and below we summarise some main issues in the debate.[5]

□ *What is 'pay'?*

With respect to the dependent variable, the usual approach assumes by necessity that the only reward to a worker from selling his/her labour is what we observe as *reported* labour earnings at a point in time. This is deficient as, theoretically, one should use permanent earnings. In addition, one should include fringe benefits and all other aspects of pay. Needless to add that such information rarely exists. As a result the estimated rates of return to education for those workers who enjoy significant perks (for example, executives) may be seriously underestimated.

□ *Is the semi-log specification the appropriate one?*

The answer is a relatively unqualified 'yes' with respect to the dependent variable but less so in the case of what the right-hand side of the regression equation should look like. In particular, though various functional specifications have been tried, the logarithmic specification of earnings has proved to be the most successful form, on econometric criteria, that the dependent variable should take. The two main econometric criteria in this respect are first, whether the optimal properties of the error terms are satisfied (especially heteroscedasticity) and, second, the explanatory power of the regression. More specifically, the former criterion is met on the grounds that the classical assumptions of regression analysis are 'less often' violated than in alternative specifications (Dougherty and Jimenez, 1991). The relevance of the second criterion, which pertains to the regression coefficient of determination, is self-evident.[6] With respect to right-hand-side variables, some are contended with simpler earnings functions which include explanatory variables in an additive form (as the one derived earlier), while others have allowed for possible interactions between, say, schooling and experience (this can be done by including another variable defined as $S \times E$).

□ *Education*

Errors of measurement and omitted-variable problems are both common and interrelated issues in the earnings functions approach. For example, the effect of formally acquired human capital is captured by the coefficient on the education variable, the latter being usually measured as years of schooling. The shortcomings associated with this approximation are, first, that it assumes that schooling augments earnings irrespective of whether it was acquired at an elite or deprived school, or whether education relates to studies in arts, social sciences or engineering. This problem is usually overcome in practice by the inclusion of additional variables on the right-hand side of the earnings functions, which proxy these qualitative aspects of formally acquired education. Second, the regression coefficient on schooling represents the rate of return on an incremental year in excess of average schooling. However, the actual return for those who have two or 12 years of schooling should really be different. Again, this problem can be overcome by replacing schooling measured as a continuous variable by a series of 'schooling variables', each representing a different level of education. Alternatively, one can still use schooling measured in years *à la* Mincer but also include schooling-squared in a similar fashion to the inclusion of experience: when this is done, the coefficient on schooling-squared comes negative, suggesting that increases in schooling have successively a lesser impact on the growth of earnings. Third, formal schooling is not the only type of education one can have; informal education is also important (for example, adult education taken in the form of part-time evening courses).[7] This is an issue which is difficult to quantify and introduce into the regression analysis and has, as a result, evaded most econometric applications. Consequently, education may not be measured precisely, while its coefficient may be affected by the absence of variables (omitted/unobservable) which relate to the quality of education.

□ *Experience for men*

Similar considerations apply to the other typical human capital variable, 'experience', typically included in the earnings functions. Information about actual work history rarely exists in data sets. The usual strategy is to use *potential* experience (age minus schooling minus school entry age) and its square as right-hand variables in the earnings functions in order to proxy the effect of the informal acquisition of human capital. Though the inclusion of experience thus specified has been proposed on theoretical grounds (Mincer, 1974), this specification and its interpretation have been the subject of debate (Psacharopoulos and Layard, 1979; Griliches, 1977). Potential experience is still routinely assumed to be a good proxy for the labour force experience of men and is considered to be an appropriate simplification for estimating the returns to human capital (Willis and Rosen, 1979; Heckman and Hotz, 1986). However, this practice might be inappropriate for data collected in the 1980s as from the mid-1970s unemployment has increased and the assumption of a continuous work record is less accurate today than before. For example, a recent study of Britain (Main and Elias, 1987) utilising data from the *National Training Survey 1976* shows that even at that time, when the unemployment was less than half its level today, as many as 20 per cent of the men in the sample did not have continuous work histories. In addition, neither the incidence nor the duration of unemployment is distributed equally among the various groups of workers. There are some workers who do not, in practice, experience unemployment (in tenured posts) while others may have an unemployment spell only rarely (the more educated and the more skilled). The bulk of those responsible for a 5 or 10 per cent unemployment rate come from the 'bottom' 30 per cent or so of the employment distribution, the less qualified workers. A comprehensive study of the incidence and duration of unemployment among male workers of different characteristics is that of Nickell (1980), who confirms these broad patterns for the duration and incidence of unemployment in Britain. As a consequence, the regression coefficient on potential experience will be inefficient and biased downward since potential experience is greater than actual experience.

□ *Experience for women*

In the case of women, the use of potential rather than actual experience is even more problematic. Women generally leave the labour market sometime during their family cycle and, when reliable data exist, their unemployment rates are usually higher than those of men. Hence, the measurement error in the case of women is more serious than in the case of men. In fact, evidence from studies addressing this issue using cross-section or longitudinal data suggests that the estimated effect of potential experience upon female pay may be as low as 50 per cent of the effect of actual experience.[8]

□ *Proxied and unobserved human capital characteristics*

The standard human capital variables (schooling and experience) may serve only as proxies for other unobserved individual characteristics and education can be seen as a signal for these unobserved characteristics (see next section of the theoretical criticisms of the human capital theory). In addition, education and experience are not the only attributes rewarded in the labour market. There are also individual differences stemming from differences in innate ability (intelligence) and the so-called D-factor, where D represents drive, dynamism, doggedness and determination (Lydall, 1976, p. 35). In addition there may be differences that arise from environmental factors such as the family and overall socio-economic background of individuals (Lazear, 1980). These are unobserved or difficult-to-measure aspects. Consider the case of ability: it refers to the 'power to do' but this includes the 'power to do well in education', too. Hence, it is difficult to isolate the effect of ability from that of human capital variables (recall the rationale for the adjustment of earnings by the alpha coefficient). In addition, ability is a multidimensional concept: it may start with innate intelligence (IQ) but environmental effects may be more important than genetic differences between people (the 'heredity versus environment' issue is a perennially controversial one). In applied research even the use of the apparently measurable IQ has been criticised as 'there is simply no agreement about what we are supposed to be measuring' (Blaug, 1976). Hence the inclusion in or exclusion from the earnings function of these types of variables can produce biased results unless they are distributed randomly among individuals – not a very realistic scenario (Polachek, 1975).

□ *But should other variables be included?*

Earnings may vary not only by education level and experience but also by type of work or sector and region of employment. For example, somebody in industry may earn more than his civil servant counterpart, while workers in the south-east of England typically earn more than workers who have the same length of education in Wales. By omitting these differences we introduce bias in the estimated coefficients of schooling and experience. On estimation grounds one is, therefore, tempted to control for factors other than human capital ones. In fact many studies have included occupational, industrial and regional variables along with the standard human capital variables. However, this practice is objectionable on theoretical grounds because it denies the competitive framework from which earnings functions are derived. More specifically the inclusion of variables relating to the occupational status of the worker should bias the estimated effects of other variables by removing cross-occupation mobility effects (Kalachek and Raines, 1976).

Theoretical criticisms of the human capital theory

The theory of human capital is not simply a theory of earnings. It is in effect a theory of how the labour market works (recall the assumptions of the theory). Most aspects of the human capital theory have come under attack at one time or another. For example, the human capital theory implicitly makes the (false) assumption that workers get education, select jobs and decide to work and so on only to maximise their earnings (Blinder, 1976). An answer to this could be that the human capital theory is an economic theory and surely more complex models incorporating other considerations would be welcome. However, there are more fundamental criticisms than these. One of them goes as far as to challenge whether education has an effect on productivity. Alternative explanations to the human capital theory have also developed. We look at these issues below.

□ *What is the role of education?*

So far we have implicitly assumed that the prime role of education in the labour market is to augment worker's productivity. The screening and information transmission role of education has been also extensively discussed (Spence, 1974; Arrow, 1973a). The screening hypothesis has a clear bearing on the ability issue discussed earlier: is ability innate or environmental in origin? Put in strong terms, the screening hypothesis suggests that what schools produce is 'pieces of paper' helping the holder to get a better-paid job. How can such a claim be justified? The answer depends on whether schooling affects ability or not. If the former, then human capital explanations of individual earnings are relevant. If the latter, then education is a screening device which signals to prospective employers *preexisting* abilities and talents. A direct implication of the screening hypothesis is that the *social* pay-off of investment in human capital might be minimal.

The evidence for the 'education as a filter' argument is mixed. For example, an early study by Taubman and Wales (1973) suggested that perhaps as much as 50 per cent of the effect of education upon earnings comes via screening. An indirect test on the role of education in the determination of earnings is to compare the difference in education between employees and self-employed workers. If the screening hypothesis is relevant, employees would tend to acquire more education than the self-employed for reasons of signalling. In effect, the self-employed need have no education at all, if education does not change the 'power to earn'. In general, there are no substantial differences in the amount of education these two groups of workers have acquired (Wolpin, 1977). The debate is far from concluded. On intuitive grounds one may argue that 'initial' screening is likely but 'persistent' screening may not occur: it is hard to think that employers keep paying wages above the worker's productivity *after* they have had the employee under their supervision for some time.

Thus the productivity-augmenting role of education may be more relevant than its screening function. Some authors have, however, emphasised the role of education not only in economic production but in social (re)production, that is, the role of education in perpetuating established ideologies and maintaining the existing status quo (Bowles and Gintis, 1975). It is rather difficult to test this interpretation in practice though, of course, existing norms, customs and certain socio-political configurations may well dictate the contents and form that education takes in different places at different times.

□ *Alternative theories*

The neoclassical/human capital approach to the study of the labour market has been challenged by a series of alternative theories. A series of debates has taken place between, on the one hand, the 'orthodox theory' and, on the other hand, the 'alternative' theories. We first list some of these theories and then attempt to summarise their main thrust.

One alternative theory is that proposed by institutionalist economists (Doeringer and Piore, 1971; Kalachek and Raines, 1976; Piore, 1979, 1983; Sobel, 1982). The emphasis of these theories lies not on individual behaviour but on the role of 'institutions'. Relevant institutions are taken to be unions, governments, firms. It is argued that it is these institutions that have an effect on labour market processes and outcomes rather than individuals and firms interacting impersonally through markets in the context of the conventional price theory.

Another theory has been proposed by 'radical' economists (Gordon, 1972; Bluestone, Murphy and Stevenson, 1973; Gordon, Edwards and Reich, 1982). These analysts have built on Marxian criticisms of the 'orthodox approaches' and have formulated their models along the power that various organised parts of the society can exercise upon other parts. The distinction is usually made between, on the one hand, capitalists and the State and, on the other hand, workers. By focusing on the behaviour of collective agents, radical theories have much in common with institutional theories of the labour market.

Yet another group is that of 'new structuralists' whose arguments are similar to the two previous groups in that they depart from the analysis of individual behaviour and examine 'structures' (compare this to 'institutions') along sociological lines (Beck, Horan and Tolbert, 1978; Stolzenberg, 1978; Berg, 1981; Hodson, 1983; Kallenberg, 1983). This list can continue further but, given the relative similarity in the ideas involved and their common anti-human capital stance, we attempt below a synthesis, albeit heroic.

We start from the more or less common supposition among alternative theories that there are different segments in the labour market with little mobility of workers between them. Note, however, that there is little agreement as to which jobs fall into which segments (Piore, 1975; Edwards, 1979; Carnoy, 1980). The idea that the labour market is segmented, or balkanised, goes back to Kerr (1954). The argument is that there are barriers in the labour market that prevent competitive functioning. Such barriers put a limit upon, if they allow it at all, the mobility of labour and can originate from legislative, regional, occupational and similar factors. Segments in the labour market can be classified as 'structureless' or 'structured'. The former is very much what a competitive labour market implies: the only attachment between workers and firms is the wage and workers can come and go while employers can hire and fire. The structured part of the labour market is taken to have two components, an 'internal' market which is governed by certain established procedures (such as administrative rules and the principle of seniority), and an 'external' market governed by economic factors (such as wage levels and the availability of workers willing to offer their labour to the firm). The link between the two markets is provided by movements of workers from the external to the internal market ('port of entry to the internal market'). However, it is argued that there are no links between the structureless market and the internal market for reasons of custom, tradition, unionisation, managerial prerogatives and so on.

More precisely, the creation of internal markets may arise from a variety of considerations. Siebert and Addison (1991) distinguish a variety of reasons for the emergence of long-term relations between firms and their labour force: first, workers' risk aversion in that they prefer a job with stable income to riskier jobs yielding the same expected income; second, efficiency wage considerations – wages in the firm are higher than the spot market competitive wages in order to overcome monitoring, extract greater work effort and reduce turnover; third, deferred compensation – workers are initially paid less than their marginal product in return for higher wages later; fourth, various overheads in the form of initial hiring, screening and matching costs; fifth, trade unions, especially in larger firms, where monitoring costs may be important. In conclusion, the emergence of internal markets may be seen as an 'efficient' response to training and monitoring problems.

The view that the labour market is a segmented institution can degenerate to the case where there are only two segments (a dual market). Thus the labour market can be seen as consisting of two sectors, namely a primary sector and a secondary sector. The secondary sector, which can be thought of as corresponding to the structureless sectors of Kerr's classification, has jobs with low pay, employment insecurity, poor working conditions and so on. In contrast the primary sector has high wages, job security, good working conditions, prospects for advancement and well-defined administrative rules (compare these aspects with the characteristics of the structured market noted earlier as well as the internal/

external labour market). It is argued that mobility between the two sectors is limited (or, at the limit, non-existent) and this gives rise to a 'dual' labour market. The reason provided by the advocates of the theory is that mobility is limited because of institutional forces such as discrimination.

Between the 'segmented' and the 'dual' views of the labour market there are, of course, many others. For example, Althauser and Kallenberg (1981) postulate a multifold distinction between secondary labour markets, firm internal labour markets, occupational internal labour markets, and firm and occupational labour markets that do not possess the features of an internal labour market.

How can one examine whether the orthodox or the alternative theories are more relevant in practice? Of course, both theories may apply in practice to one extent or another. For example, institutional factors (say, legislation) can shape the labour market in that they can prescribe the level of pay in certain cases or exclude certain persons from some kinds of employment. At the same time firms and individuals have some flexibility with respect to whether they will hire labour or accept employment respectively. So, labour market processes and individual earnings are governed by many forces which have been summarised in the statement that work and pay is 'the intersection of societal history and individual biography' (Grandjean, 1981, p. 1057). This is a good description of *ex post* outcomes but one needs to use more precise statements in order to discriminate between competing hypotheses. In this respect, some 'tests' have developed about the validity of the competing theories along the following testable questions.

First, is schooling an avenue for higher earnings? If not, then one should observe different rates of return to schooling for different groups of workers depending on which 'segment' of the labour market they are in. For example, most women workers can be seen as employed in the lower and less privileged segments of the labour market; hence, the rates of return to female schooling should be lower than those for men. The evidence in this respect is that, if a difference exists, then rates of returns to schooling for women are greater than those for men.

Second, is there a bimodality in the distribution of jobs? This refers to whether jobs, when ranked by some criterion of 'goodness', tend to be clustered in two distinct sections with little mobility between them. Obviously, it is difficult to establish an operational definition of what is a good and what is a bad job (compare an architect with an engineer) and under what conditions (for example, being a doctor is a better job than being a ditch-digger, but few of the latter would be able to undertake or be trusted in the former job). An indirect way of ranking jobs is with reference to earnings. Then the test degenerates to whether the distribution of earnings is bimodal or not. As we will explain in Chapter 8, the distribution of earnings is continuous and unimodal.

It is hard to derive any firm conclusion from these two tests. The fact that different theoretical camps insist on their views and claim that they have evidence for them and against rival theories suggests that our answers to these two testable questions hardly constitute a conclusive proof. A discussion of the issues associated with the process of verification or falsification of economic theories will take us beyond the scope of the present volume and we refer the reader to two surveys on the 'orthodoxy versus the alternatives' debate which (i) provide additional empirical evidence on the relevance of human capital and alternative theories to the study of a wide range of phenomena in the labour market and (ii) can be used to examine how the literature developed in the course of the last two decades (see Cain, 1976, and McNabb and Ryan, 1990).

A summary of results based on earnings functions

Having examined the derivation of earnings functions, the problems associated with their estimation and a number of theoretical considerations about their relevance to the study of labour earnings, we are in a better position to interpret their empirical findings. This is the task of the present section.

Earnings functions can be used to estimate the rates of returns to education at a point in time or their movement over time. The results can be used in a number of ways. For example, one can study whether men or women have higher returns to their respective investments in education. Or one can examine whether educated labour is rewarded more in one discipline (or even in one country) relative to another discipline (or another country). Alternatively, an examination of the movement of the rates of return to education over time can help us discriminate between different theories addressing the issue of education in market economies: if returns to education are invariant over time, when everything else in the economy changes, then this may be taken as evidence against the competitive functioning of the labour market. Also, from the point of view of public policy, high rates of returns to education may be used as a signal for education expansion.

We present separately the evidence for private and social rates of returns to education. Recall that the estimation of rates of return to education involve the examination of costs and benefits associated with education. If one is interested in estimating the private rate of return, then one should include all items which affect the private profitability of investment in education. In particular, private costs include school fees, other education-related expenditure (from books to uniforms), and foregone net (after-tax) labour earnings. If the student receives any kind of support (stipends, bursaries, allowances and so on), this support should be deducted from foregone income. On the benefit side, one should include the net incremental income attributable to education, that is, total incremental income minus the tax due on it.

The estimation of social rates of return is different. For a start, school fees should not be included among the social cost of education: fees represent a transfer with a zero-sum effect in the economy. Student support (such as stipends and so on) constitutes another form of transfer and should also be excluded from the calculation of the social cost of education. What we are left with is direct expenditure on education: this includes education-related expenditure as before (books and so on) *plus* the direct public spending on education, including amortised capital costs. On the benefit side one should only include the incremental output attributable to educated workers.

Focusing on the case of private rates of returns to education, the following generalisations apply with reference to **Table 4.2.** First, rates of return to education decline with additional schooling. In other words, the rate of return to primary education is greater than the rate of return to secondary education which is in turn greater than the rate of return to tertiary education.

Second, and as a natural extension of the previous finding, rates of return to education in advanced countries are lower than rates of return to education in developing countries. Both this and the previous finding are in line with the standard predictions of the economic theory: additional investment yields lower returns at least after some point (the principle of eventually diminishing marginal productivity).

Turning now to the social returns to education, they behave very much like the private returns (see **Table 4.3**). However, social rates are, in general, lower than the private rates of return within each education level. Much of the difference between the social and private rates of returns to education is due to public subsidies. One measure of the degree of subsidisation of education is the ratio of private returns to social returns. For example, the degree of subsidisation in advanced countries is 9 per cent (12/11) for secondary education and 33 per cent (12/9) for higher education. This suggests that from a social policy point of view more is spent on higher education in which returns are lower. Apart from this efficiency consideration there are also distributional ones: university graduates who earn more in the labour market than less-

Table 4.2 ***Private returns to education by country group and level of schooling***

Country group	*Education level*		
	Primary	*Secondary*	*Higher*
Developing: Africa	45	26	32
Asia	31	15	18
Latin America	32	23	23
Middle-income	17	13	13
Advanced	–*	12	12

* Not available because of lack of control group (illiterates).

Source: Psacharopoulos, 1988.

qualified workers benefit proportionately more than the latter whose earnings are low. Hence the former benefit more from public subsidies and the assumed equity objective of public policy is called into question.

In terms of changes over time, anything can happen to rates of returns. This ambiguity rests on what has been described as the 'the race between technology and education' (Tinbergen, 1975). The former refers to technological advances which shift the relative demand curve for skilled persons to the right. The latter refers to education expansion which shifts the relative supply curve of educated persons to the right. In terms of comparative statics and with reference to **Figure 4.1**, the shift to the right of both the supply curve and the demand curve should increase the equilibrium level of quantity (educated labour/qualified manpower) while the effect on the equilibrium price (in this case, rate of return) is indeterminate.

The international evidence on movements in the rates of return to education is not uniform and much can be said about (i) the stage of development at which various countries are; (ii) differences in the quality of data used in the econometric analysis; (iii) differences in the time periods examined and (iv) differences between the exact specifications adopted by various authors. Despite these difficulties one recent survey found that in about two-thirds and perhaps in as many as four-fifths of the countries for which comparisons can be made the rates of return to education (both public and private) have declined in the last two to three decades (Psacharopoulos, 1988). However, the decline has been far from uniform and was at times small.

This result can be used in a number of ways. In terms of discriminating among competing theories one may argue that the negative response of rates of returns to education expansion is compatible with the

Table 4.3 ***Social returns to education by country group and level of schooling***

Country group	*Education level*		
	Primary	*Secondary*	*Higher*
Developing: Africa	26	17	13
Asia	27	15	13
Latin America	26	18	16
Middle-income	13	10	8
Advanced	–*	11	9

* Not available because of lack of control group (illiterates).

Source: Psacharopoulos, 1988.

competitive model. Alternatively, this finding provides evidence against theories which advocate that there are significant barriers in the labour market (such as the dual or segmented labour market theories). In other words, workers can change their 'segment' (as proxied by the earnings bracket in which they are initially found) by investing in education.

In terms of public policy, the decline in the returns to education has not been dramatic and it is perhaps still early to start talking about symptoms of 'over-education' at least as far as investment in lower levels of education is concerned: the social rates of return to education still remain high – as a general rule above the threshold of 10 per cent which is typically taken to be a reasonable measure of the opportunity cost of capital. Also the slow movement in the rates of return to education over time may be taken as suggestive that the elasticity of substitution between more and less educated workers is relatively high. This has certain implications for educational planning which is examined in the next section.

Social policy on education and manpower planning

Manpower planning is a generic term which refers to the attempt to produce the right number of persons with the right skills at the right time in order to achieve a particular objective (or objectives). This is done through policies intended to coordinate the supply and demand of different types of qualified labour. Most countries undertake some form of manpower planning. However, the most important aspect of manpower planning is the way it is implemented. The practice of manpower planning can be grouped in three philosophies (and many variants of them)[9] underlying different approaches to the utilisation of the education and training systems in the process of development and growth.

□ *The social demand approach*

The first approach, known as 'the social demand approach', assumes that the demand of households for education provides sufficient indication for an expansion or contraction of the education sector as a whole, or for sectoral changes within the education sector (HMSO: Robbins Report, 1963). This approach implies that the provision of education (such as the number of places in higher education institutions) should expand to accommodate the demand for higher education by anybody who qualifies (for example, by admitting all those who have scored two A levels and are willing to pursue further studies).

□ *The rate of return analysis*

The second approach, namely the 'rate of return analysis', is based upon our earlier discussion in this chapter. It puts less emphasis on the demand of households for education but also takes into account the demand of employers for educated labour. Costs (educational expenses) and benefits (wages that firms are prepared to pay for educated labour) are both considered in order to examine whether any expansion/contraction of education and in what disciplines is economically justified or not. This method, which presupposes some flexibility in the pattern of future requirements, evaluates the socially most cost-effective ways of meeting these requirements and relies very much on the price and quantity signals provided by the market (Blaug, 1970; Catto *et al.*, 1980).

In this respect the rate of return approach is a useful device for uncovering inefficiencies in the pattern of resource allocation within the education system (internal efficiency of education) and also between different areas of social policy (external efficiency of education). We can highlight the issue of internal efficiency with reference to two issues. First, from a given education budget, should the government spend more on higher education or on basic education? Surely a university graduate must on average be more productive than a primary-school graduate but is the difference in productivity between the two sufficient to offset the difference in the costs of their respective education? In other words it may well be more efficient to provide primary education to ten persons than university education to only one person. Second, vocational education has been conclusively found to have lower returns than general secondary education. The low return to vocational education is primarily due to high costs.

The external efficiency of education refers to the impact of educational policies on the labour market. Public expenditure on education, even if correctly allocated among different levels and types of education, may be inefficient in the sense that the returns to education are higher/lower than returns to other forms of public investment. In fact, this is a more difficult task than the one assessing the internal efficiency of education and the limits of the rate of returns analysis as a tool to guiding public policy start to show. In particular, the estimates of rates of returns indicate only orders of magnitude of the profitability of alternative investments *and not* actual amounts that should be spent on them. In addition, the estimates of rates of returns are slow to register developments in the labour markets – the previous discussion on the changes in rates of returns over time is suggestive in this respect. As a result, when problems arise in the labour market they register their impact on the rates of returns only with a lag. The implication is that other tools of analysis may be more relevant or can be used along with the rate of returns analysis. Tracer studies have been proposed for this purpose as well as some form of the manpower requirements approach.

Tracer studies, as the name suggests, 'trace' or monitor the education and work history of individuals. They are surveys which ask questions such as 'how did you learn about the programme or course you attended and why did you enter it?'; 'how did you find your present employer?'; 'how long did it take before you started working?'; 'did you have any on-the-job training?'; 'what are your salary expectations?' and so on. Obviously, tracer studies can well complement the rate of returns analysis in that they can more accurately capture developments in the labour market in the short run. On the other hand, the manpower requirements approach is primarily concerned with estimating labour market imbalances in the longer term and is explained below.

□ *The manpower requirements approach*

The third and final approach is based on 'manpower forecasting' and is called the 'manpower requirements approach'. In this approach the emphasis falls squarely on the demand for labour: desired or expected output changes are translated into occupational structures (necessary for enabling these output changes to occur) and into educational output (necessary to achieve the occupational structure). This approach ignores prices to a large extent and focuses on production and inter-industry goods flows in the economy as well as educational enrolments. Traditionally the manpower requirements approach has been associated with Leontief's fixed coefficient input–output models in socialist countries but similar techniques have been used in market economies at various times – notably in the elaboration of some French plans (Paul, 1985) and the Tinbergen model (Tinbergen and Bos, 1965).

The underlying logic behind the manpower requirements approach is that 'if the economy is to achieve a desired level/composition of production, it is necessary that the labour force possesses a particular occupational structure which corresponds to a given educational output'. Obviously what distinguishes this from a general economic forecast is the translation of production levels into numbers of people in different occupations with different educational characteristics. In this approach changing production patterns and levels do not cause a configuration of manpower. Rather, a labour force with a given occupational structure combines with the existing capital and technology in order to produce a given level of output. Bearing this logic in mind, this section outlines some basic techniques which have been used to translate output targets into manpower requirements.

Average labour–output ratios

Theoretically one can derive estimates for manpower requirements using a general production function that permits the introduction of technical change (productivity). Ignoring productivity changes, this approach can be shown in the following simplified way along the lines of the Harrod–Domar model.[10] Assume that output (Y) relates to the capital stock (K) in the following way

$$Y = (1/c)\ K \qquad (4.1)$$

where c is the capital/output ratio (or the inverse of capital productivity) and can be derived from historical associations between utilised capital and observed output. This logic can be extended to the estimation of labour requirements, if labour (L) is substituted for capital in the earlier analysis. In this case equation (4.1) becomes

$$Y = (1/b)\ L \qquad (4.1')$$

and b is the labour/output coefficient. Hence this method, which utilises average labour–output ratios, is both a logical extension of the Harrod–Domar model and also intuitively appealing. If the estimates of the labour/output coefficients are correct both at aggregate and occupational levels, then this approach will help the economy avoid (i) bottlenecks in production (via the elimination of labour shortages), (ii) unemployment (as forthcoming labour supply will be equal to demand), (iii) misemployment (as supply will match, in type, demand), and (iv) the persistence of economic rent accruing to particular groups of workers (because there would be no scarcity of skills in demand).

Despite the theoretical attraction of this approach, a number of qualifications apply. First, the *b*'s are usually estimated from historical data. However, it may not be desirable, especially in a developmental context, to 'repeat history' unless what one had in the past is good enough for the future. Otherwise, there is a real possibility of 'forcing' the economy to follow an inefficient development path. Second, in many countries, again especially in developing countries, the data are either too aggregate or too few (in terms of annual observations). As a result, estimates tend to be unreliable in that they have large standard errors.

Incremental labour–output ratios

The labour coefficients in equation (4.1′) are derived from average labour–output ratios. Ideally one would like to use incremental labour–output ratios: how much *additional* labour is required to produce that much of *additional* output. In theory this can be easily done. If equation (4.1′) is expressed in a differenced form, one can derive how much extra labour (ΔL) will be required to achieve a given increase in output (ΔY), that is

$$\Delta L = (1/b)\ \Delta Y \qquad (4.2)$$

where b is now seen as labour's marginal productivity. In this way the requirements for additional labour can be explicitly estimated for given productivity levels.

For the reasons explained in the case of average labour–output ratios, estimates of these ratios may be equally unreliable. As a matter of practice, average labour–output ratios have been used more often than incremental labour–output ratios despite the fact that the former can vary as much as four times within a period of no longer than three years (Moser and Layard, 1964, p. 296).

International comparisons

One way out of the problem (of erroneously adopting past and present imbalances as appropriate indicators for manpower expansion/contraction) is the use of international tables which provide information about the occupational structure of employment in different industries in different countries (Zymelman, 1980a). Alternatively, one can use tables which summarise (with the aid of regression analysis) the structure of employment in a wide range of countries at different stages of development (Zymelman, 1980b). The policy value of these tables is questionable because of the possibility of one country adopting patterns which were derived from imbalances in another country. These imbalances can be even more inapporiate for adoption as they apply to countries with different institutional settings. Another reason is that regression analysis, upon which the results presented in the international tables are based, allows predictions (and errors) to be made only at a chosen level of statistical (in)significance. The predictive power of many results in these international tables is uncomfortably low (coefficients of determination below 20 per cent are not uncommon). Finally, the validity of this method (called the 'international productivity approach') may be rather suspect outside the group of advanced open economies whose characteristics, production techniques and information networks are already fairly comparable and international competition ensures that convergence is relatively quick (see, for example, Loucks and Whitney, 1973, chapter 25, or Pickering and Pickering, 1985, pp. 309–11).

Onlooker forecasts

Concentrating on changes in the occupational structure, another approach to estimating requirements is the so-called 'onlooker forecasts'. These types of forecasts are based on the assumption that the variable(s) of interest (in this case, a given type of labour, say, educated labour or qualified manpower) will continue to change in the future in the same way as it did in the past in order to achieve similar growth rates. Onlooker forecasts have the advantage that they require information only about the variable in question, which is projected from its own past. In practice, onlooker forecasts can take the form of either a linear or an exponential future growth along an already established path. Manpower requirements can then be inferred from the resulting figure, if one adds the existing stock of manpower and subtracts the expected attrition. For example, one can assume that employment (L) next year ($t + 1$) will be given by either of the following two formulae:

$$\text{(linear growth)} \quad L_{t+1} = L_t + (L_t - L_{t-n})/n - A \tag{4.3}$$

$$\text{(exponential growth)} \quad L_{t+1} = L_t \times (L_t/L_{t-n})^{(1/n)} - A \tag{4.4}$$

where n is the number of years for which information is available, and A is the expected attrition (the number of present employees who will not be working next year). Linear growth implies constant absolute increases over time. Exponential growth implies a constant rate of employment growth. Which of the two is more appropriate depends on what one suspects is more relevant with respect to economies of scale. If the employment of labour is actually taking place on the production function and the rate of growth of output is expected to be the same as before, then the former formula is consistent with qualified manpower, as a factor of production, exhibiting increasing returns. In other words, the point of eventually diminishing productivity has not yet been reached, neither will it be reached during the period to which the forecasts apply. The latter formula is consistent with either constant returns to scale or the fact that labour is employed in the region of declining productivity in the production function and will be so employed during the forecast period.

The attractiveness of both types of onlooker forecasts is that their statistical requirements are as low as could be – and may be useful for countries with a limited data base. This does not, however, imply that the policy-makers' inferences based upon either type of forecast will be necessarily meaningful. For example, if a country started from a near-zero base, the rate of growth may be really high. Another reservation that was mentioned in the case of labour–output ratios also applies to onlooker forecasts. These forecasts assume that whatever has happened in the past will perpetuate in the future and the assumption that variables will follow their past pattern of behaviour is unwarranted and perhaps undesirable. One has to agree here with the comment that 'if we know that we must build a new University to increase the number of graduates by 20 percent, it is of little use to know that the demand for graduates in the future will be either 5 percent or 40 percent greater than it is now' (Ahamad and Blaug, 1973, p. 24).

□ *The occupation–education link*

The last task in manpower planning, irrespective of which of the above methods is used, is to translate occupational requirements into educational output. To establish the link between the two is a formidable task. This has long been recognised by even the most committed proponents of the output–industry–occupation link, who have not so far attempted to undertake the final and most crucial step, that from occupation to education (Zymelman, 1980b, pp. 11–18). The tip of the iceberg can be seen from the question: is the appropriate manager of a steel plant somebody with a qualification in business or management studies, engineering or economics? One can further question whether the appropriate level of studies is at degree, MSc or PhD level.

The task of identifying the educational structures which would meet the occupational requirements arising from a given growth rate and pattern of output was explicitly undertaken by the Mediterranean Regional Project in the early 1960s (Parnes, 1964). According to the methodology adopted in that project the output–education link was decided in five distinct steps: (a) from aggregate output forecasts to (b) predicted changes in the sectoral distribution of output; (c) changes in labour productivity (or its inverse, labour–output ratios); (d) the corresponding occupational requirements; and, finally, (e) the educational structure. It is obvious that only the last two steps deal with occupational and educational forecasting. Despite the initial impact of that study, experience has shown that this methodology failed to produce estimates that proved to be anywhere close to reality with the passage of time (see the collection of papers in Youdi and Hinchliffe, 1985). This is not unexpected as forecasts do not depend only on how appropriately the last two steps are formulated but also on the ability of general economic planning to anticipate correctly the growth rate of the economy, changes in the sectoral composition of output and, finally, improvements in labour productivity. The problem with any multi-step method of this sort is that the series of assumptions and data inaccuracies involved in each and every step interact in a complex way and the final results are characterised by high variances.

Where do we stand in the case of educational and manpower policy?

The manpower requirements approach gained momentum in the 1960s. One reason for this was the relatively uninterrupted growth rates that had prevailed till then from the end of the Second World War. Forecasting a 'stable' trend appeared to be an easy technical task while creating the right type of people in order to avoid bottlenecks in production was seen as the duty of a responsible State. To some extent the fact that Eastern European countries had experienced higher growth rates than their Western European counterparts till the late 1950s/early 1960s may have also created some temptation for market economies to apply some form of planning, too. However, no planning attempt undertaken in, say, 1965 or 1970 could ever anticipate the adverse developments in the early 1970s and the appearance of stagflation. The lessons are many. First, the labour market is a fast-changing institution: so, predicting the long run is a futile activity and emphasis should be placed on short-term considerations (or, if one likes it, 'short-term planning'). In this respect, tracer studies are a useful instrument.

Second, there does not seem to exist in general a given relationship between education, occupations and production. This finding has two implications. On the one hand, educational planning should be concerned with the creation of a flexible and adaptable labour force, which amounts to saying that public policy should be concerned more with the provision of general education than with specialised skills (such as vocational education or specific university courses). On the other hand, in the exceptional case when the production function is characterized by fixed-type coefficients, then manpower planning can be of some use. For example, if we know that in a year the number of births was higher than usual by 100 000, then we know that in five or six years there will be a requirement for 100 000 additional places in schools and for 'so many' teachers. Thus manpower pla ning can be relevant to some special cases (for example, ratio of doctors or policemen to population) but not to the whole labour market.

Third, and finally, education and manpower policy should not be guided by 'what we want to achieve' (that is, quantities) but 'what is efficient to achieve'. Thus benefits but also cost should be included in the calculations and in this respect the rates of return approach is at its best.

■ General and specific training

So far we have looked at human capital theory primarily from the perspective of suppliers of labour. However, the investment aspect of improving workers' human capital is not only the concern of individuals but also of firms. In many firms and organisations it is a common and established practice to 'invest' in the human capital they use. Obviously, the firm's considerations and actual choices need not be the same as those of its current workforce or its prospective employees. One aspect of the important difference between the perceptions of firms and workers can be seen with reference to 'general' training and 'specific' training.

In its pure form, general training refers to processes which improve the productivity of the worker *by the same amount* in the firm in which the worker undertakes training and in other firms. In comparison, pure specific training increases the worker's productivity only in the firm which provides the training. It is difficult to think of any actual examples for each of these two definitions, as most types of training fall anywhere between these two pure cases. However, these definitions provide a useful analytical distinction in that they can be used to examine the different standing of firms and individuals with respect to human capital

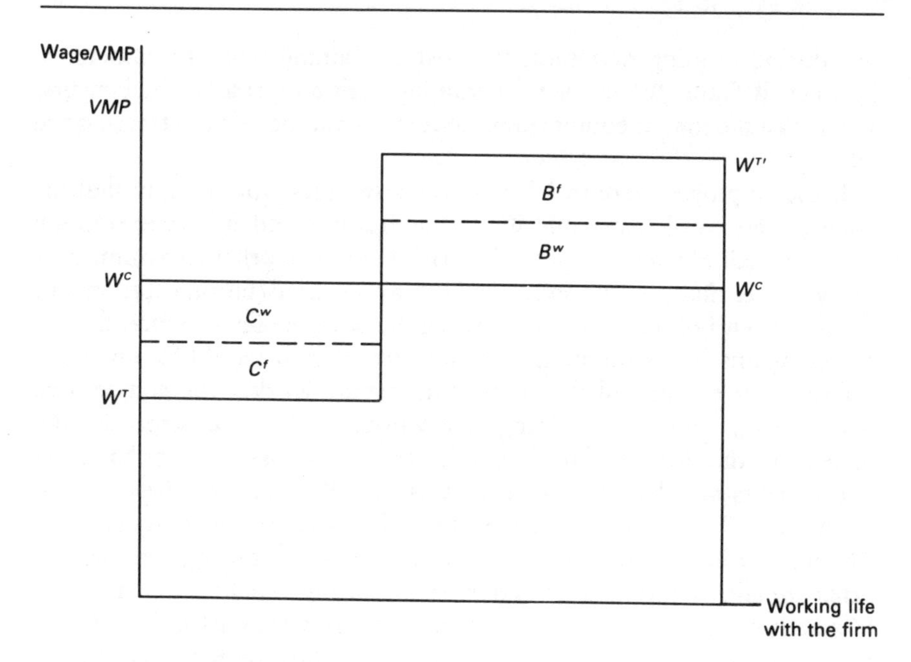

Figure 4.4 ***Specific training***

formation at the work-place. Obviously, individuals are interested in skills which can be used by different employers – this is a sensible risk-averse strategy. Firms are interested in what is going on in their own house. The question becomes who decides what and who bears the costs.

The case of general training is straightforward. Firms have no interest in it. If firms require persons with general training, they go to the open labour market and recruit workers at the ongoing wage. Thus the decision for general training is left to individual workers who also meet the costs. The case of specific training is more complicated and depends on who bears the costs and who reaps the benefits of the worker's higher productivity in the future. These considerations are shown in simple terms in **Figure 4.4** assuming that the only cost of training is foregone wages/production. The straight line W^C is the competitive wage (value of marginal product) paid throughout the worker's productive life in the absence of specific training. If specific training is undertaken for, say, four years, then some of the worker's effort during this period will be diverted from work to training. Hence his marginal product will be lower than W^C. However, after the completion of the training period, the worker's productivity will be higher than W^C. The training and post-training value of the value of marginal product is shown in the figure as the irregular line W^T to $W^{T'}$. The difference between W^C and

W^T during training represents the cost of training while the difference between $W^{T'}$ and W^C in the post-training period represents the benefits. Let us assume that at equilibrium the costs of and benefits to training are equal.

If the employee were to bear all the costs, this would imply that his wage profile would trace line W^T during training and $W^{T'}$ after training is completed. However, it would be risky for the worker to assume that he will eventually break even as he may be fired/become redundant before the end of his expected working life with the firm. Hence, he will decide against undertaking this form of training. It would also be risky for the firm to bear all the costs and pay the worker the competitive wage during and after training: the worker may leave before all the benefits to the firm are due. The only remaining possibility is that costs and benefits are shared (not necessarily equally) between the firm and the worker. The dotted line represents such a wage/productivity pattern. The worker is paid more than his product is worth during training but firms are allowed to have a stake in the resulting benefits after training. In a stylised way, the costs and benefits are shown as areas *C* and *B* in the diagram with superscripts *W* and *F* standing respectively for the workers' and firms' shares.

This argument is compatible with three patterns observed in the labour market. First, economic sectors (such as industries) which employ workers with general skills (and general education) tend to be characterised by higher quit rates. Second, we observe a positive relationship between specific training and wages. Third, the distinction between general and specific training is a useful one which can be used to explain the typical personnel policy 'last in, first out'.

It is worth noting that the previous analysis is cast within the competitive paradigm with perfect information. The problem arises from the unwillingness of firms to finance general training because of the transferability of skills (Becker, 1975). Unless there are explicit or implicit labour contracts which bond otherwise mobile workers to firms, firms will not support general training.[11] However, Katz and Ziderman (1990) argue that firms may be willing to finance even fully the cost of general training. Their argument derives from the empirical observation that workers pay few general training costs through lower wages during training. The rationale is that in the absence of perfect information recruiting firms would tend to place lower value on prospective workers' general skills than the firm that provided the training. This downgrading of general skills results in lower incentives for workers to share costs while it gives firms greater incentives to meet the costs of their own workers' general training. The key ingredient in this argument is that information asymmetry restricts the 'portability' even of general skills.

One major implication of this insight is that education and skill certification systems are socially desirable in that they signal workers' capabilities to recruiting firms, and labour is allocated where it is most productive, avoiding additional training costs.

■ Concluding remarks

Human capital has been described as inhuman in the sense that it treats peope like machines. However, this is a play with words. What human capital theory does is to examine some *economic* issues of skill formation in the labour market as perceived by individuals and firms. In this respect human capital theory is very much a supply-side story (supply of educated labour or demand for education). It incorporates aspects of demand in that it deals with equilibrium values of the variables concerned. As far as an equilibrium approach can take us into the realm of positive economics, human capital theory has improved our understanding considerably.

Of course, human capital theory is not a general theory of the labour market. Certain issues are not addressed at all by the theory of human capital while others are only explained in part. For example, recall that human capital theory does not deal with non-economic aspects of education, especially the role of education in shaping group interests. Nobody argues that these are unimportant: earnings functions are found to explain typically about one-third of the variance of earnings while the rest can be due to anything. The issue here is not to discard the theory altogether but to develop other theories which are better in one way or another than the human capital theory. Some theories which can also apply to areas studied by the human capital theory are examined in Chapters 8 and 9 where we deal respectively with the distribution of pay and discrimination.

■ Notes

1. The figures in **Table 4.1** relate to gross (pre-tax) earnings as reported by the employer. As such they are not the most appropriate ones for calculating the private return to education because individuals base their calculation on net benefits. However, our present comparison of gross earnings by level of education can still be a relatively good approximation of the magnitudes involved.
2. The proof can be found in more advanced textbooks such as Fallon and Verry (1988), pp. 149–50.
3. This is derived by finding out the maximum value the earnings function

takes with respect to experience. Based on the derivatives of the function the maximum occurs at $33.75 = 0.081/(2 \times 0.0012)$.

4. In fact, in some applied research the alpha coefficients were estimated to be in excess of unity (Griliches and Mason, 1972) and this effectively eliminated them from the literature (Psacharopoulos, 1975).
5. For surveys see Siebert (1985) and Willis (1986).
6. It is interesting to note that Sorenson (1983) argued that one can scarcely credit Mincer's model, as earnings functions explain more than half of the variance in earnings by only three variables (namely education, experience and hours).
7. Though the distinction between formal and non-formal education is far from clear (La Belle, 1986), non-formal education can be defined as the knowledge acquired outside the conventional primary/secondary/tertiary education system (Coombs, 1968).
8. Malkiel and Malkiel (1973), Mincer and Polachek (1974), and Miller (1987). These studies conclude that the earnings increment associated with *actual* labour market experience among females is comparable to that received by male workers. In fact another study (Levine and Moock, 1984) found that almost half of the wage gap between husbands and wives could be attributed to the fluctuations in the labour force attachment of wives, especially to depreciation of female skills during interruptions in employment.
9. For a survey see Debeauvais and Psacharopoulos (1985). One can also add a fourth approach along the lines of cybernetics (Dougherty, 1985).
10. Harrod (1939) and Domar (1946).
11. Firms may use 'deferred' compensation schemes, so that workers who leave the firm incur costs. Such schemes may take a variety of forms such as seniority wages and pension plans (Salop and Salop, 1976; Schiller and Weiss, 1979; Lazear, 1981).

■ Chapter 5 ■

Labour Demand: The Basic Model

Labour demand is defined as the amount of labour that employers seek to hire during a given time period at a particular wage rate. The demand for labour as a factor of production is a *derived demand*, in that labour is demanded not for its own sake but for its contribution to the production of goods and services. In this chapter we examine the theory of labour demand, which is an application of the marginal productivity theory to the particular factor of production labour.[1] In Chapter 7 we consider the interaction of demand and supply forces in the determination of the price of labour (that is, the *wage rate*).

Throughout this chapter we make the following two simplifying assumptions: first, that there are no costs other than the hourly wage associated with the employment of labour, and second, that firms purchase their labour in perfectly competitive labour markets.[2] The second of these assumptions means that the individual firm faces a perfectly elastic supply curve for its labour input, illustrating that it is a price-taker in the market for its labour, because labour's supply price (that is, the wage rate) does not vary with the quantity purchased. The case of an imperfectly competitive labour market is considered in Chapter 7.

This chapter begins by considering the individual firm's demand for labour in the short run under various product market conditions. In subsequent sections labour demand in the long run and at the industry level are considered.

The individual firm's demand for labour in the short run

□ *Perfectly competitive product markets*

In this section the short-run labour demand function of the firm is derived in the case where it *sells* its output in a perfectly competitive product market. Suppose that the firm combines inputs of two factors of production, capital and labour services, according to its production function, in order to produce a single product. In the short run capital will be a fixed factor of production, whereas labour will be a variable one. The situation is depicted in **Figure 5.1**, where curves Q_1, Q_2 and Q_3 are *isoquants*, each of which is the locus of all combinations of capital and labour inputs (measured in machine-hours and man-hours respectively) that yield a specified level of output.[3] In the long run it is possible for the firm to vary its inputs of both labour and capital, but in the short run labour is its only variable factor of production.

Denoting the level of the firm's capital inputs by K_0 and its labour input by L, we see from **Figure 5.1** that it is constrained, when altering output in the short run, with capital *fully* utilised, to move horizontally along the line K_0K_0. The further an isoquant lies to the north-east, the higher is the level of output to which it refers and consequently, by moving along K_0K_0 from left to right, the firm can increase its output in the short run. The curve that is obtained by plotting the firm's output level against its level of labour input as it moves horizontally along K_0K_0 is known as the *total physical product* (*TPP*) curve of labour and is shown in **Figure 5.2(a)**. For example, if the firm's labour input were L' man-hours, its level of output would be given by that represented by isoquant Q_2 (say q_2 units of output). This is shown as the ordinate in **Figure 5.2 (a)** corresponding to this level of labour input. It should be stressed that this curve illustrates the relationship between the firm's physical output and its labour input in the short run when its capital input is fixed (at the level K_0 in the current example). By varying the level at which the firm's capital input is fixed, a family of *TPP* curves is obtained, with a different curve corresponding to each level of capital input. The curve illustrated in **Figure 5.2(a)** shows total product as a third-order polynominal (or cubic) function of labour input, since this is a specific functional form that exhibits properties that are often assumed by economists.

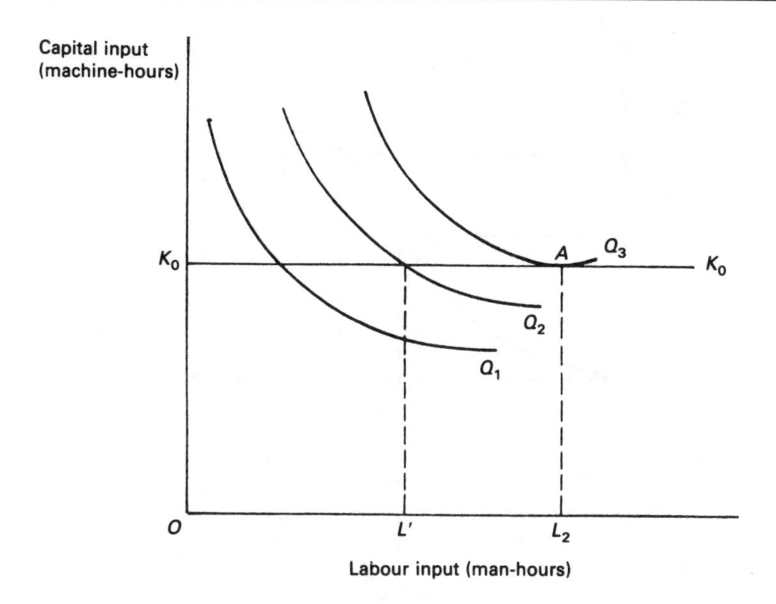

Figure 5.1 ***The firm's isoquant map***

The *average physical product* (*APP*) of labour is defined as total physical product per unit of labour input (that is, *TPP/L*). The marginal physical product (*MPP*) of labour is defined as the rate of change of total physical product with respect to the level of labour inputs (that is, $\Delta TPP/\Delta L$ for discrete changes, or $dTPP/dL$ for small changes). The *APP* and *MPP* curves that correspond to the *TPP* curve in **Figure 5.2(a)** are shown in **Figure 5.2(b)**.[4] Note that each of the *MPP* and *APP* curves displays a single maximum and that marginal physical product reaches its maximum value at the level of labour input (L_1) that corresponds to the *TPP* curve's non-stationary point of inflection at *Z*. Note also that the *MPP* curve cuts the *APP* curve at the latter's maximum value and that marginal physical product equals zero at the *TPP* curve's maximum.[5] The *MPP* curve in **Figure 5.2(b)** shows, for each level of labour input, the addition of total physical product that results when an additional unit of labour input is employed in the production process, with the capital input held constant at K_0. Its negative slope to the right of L_1 illustrates the *law of diminishing marginal returns* (or variable proportions), according to which the marginal physical product of any variable factor of production eventually begins to decline as increasing amounts of it are employed with a fixed quantity of some other factor.

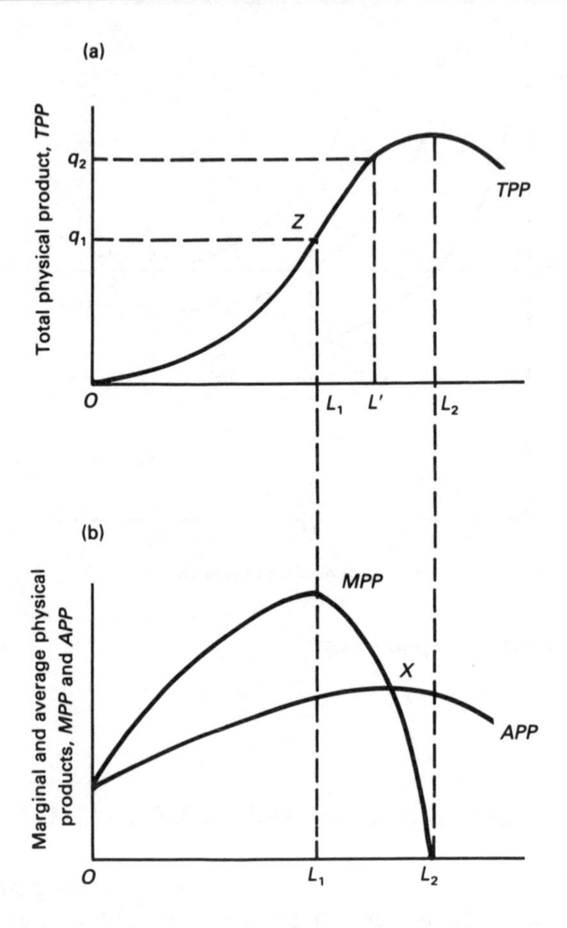

Figure 5.2 ***The firm's short-run production function***

□ *The firm's short-run labour demand curve*

If we assume that the firm's objective is the maximisation of its profits, we are now in a position to derive its short-run labour demand function. Since it is a profit-maximiser, the firm is interested not only in the physical product of its labour input but also in the contribution that this makes to revenue. More specifically, in deciding whether or not to employ an additional unit of labour, the firm must weigh the increase in revenue that would result from the employment of this unit against the resulting increase in its costs. Since the firm, by assumption, sells its output in a perfectly competitive product market, its product price is

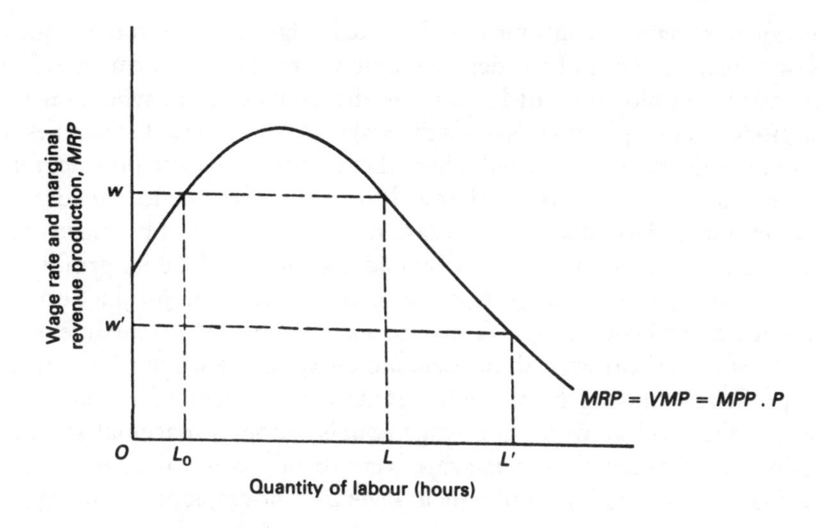

Figure 5.3 ***The firm's marginal revenue product schedule***

given as say *P*, *regardless* of its sales level. Therefore, to evaluate the contribution that the employment of an additional unit of labour would make to the firm's revenue, it is necessary to multiply the unit's contribution to total *physical* product (that is, its marginal physical product) by the contribution that each unit of output makes to revenue, which in this case is simply the given product price (*P*). The quantity *MPP.P* thus obtained is referred to as the *marginal revenue product* (*MRP*) of labour. Under perfect competition the firm's product price (*P*) is equal to its *marginal revenue* (*MR*), which means that the marginal revenue product of its labour (defined as *MPP.MR*) equals the *value of marginal product* (*VMP*) of labour (defined as *MPP.P*). **Figure 5.3** illustrates the *MRP* curve of labour, which is obtained by multiplying the marginal physical product at each level of labour input, as given in **Figure 5.2(b)**, by the constant output price (*P*).

The *MRP* curve shown in **Figure 5.3** is in fact the firm's short-run demand curve for labour. Since the firm is a profit-maximiser, it will increase its employment of labour whenever the contribution of an additional unit of labour to its revenue (that is, its marginal revenue product) exceeds the increase in costs resulting from the unit's employment. This is because under such circumstances an increase in employment and output will result in a net addition to profits. The increase in cost associated with the employment of an additional labour unit is the amount that its employment adds to the firm's wage bill and is referred to as *marginal labour cost* (*MLC*). By assumption, the firm purchases its labour inputs in an perfectly competitive labour market, with the consequence that it is confronted with a fixed wage, and therefore marginal labour cost, of say *w*. In order to maximise profits, the firm therefore expands its employment of labour, and hence its output, whenever the marginal revenue product exceeds the wage *w*. Moreover, it continues to do so until the point is reached where the marginal revenue product *falls* into equality with *w*. Beyond this level of employment, the use of another unit of labour would increase the firm's wage bill by more than it would increase its revenue and would therefore reduce its profits.

By plotting both the wage rate and marginal revenue product on the vertical axis in **Figure 5.3**, it is easy to see that the *MRP* schedule is, in fact, the firm's short-run labour demand curve. If the wage rate were *w*, the profit-maximising firm would set its employment of labour at *L* hours – the level at which the wage equals labour's marginal revenue product. If, however, the wage rate were to fall to w', the firm would find that, at the existing employment level of *L* hours, labour's marginal revenue product would exceed the prevailing wage. Under such circumstances the firm would accordingly expand its demand for labour to the new profit-maximising level of L' hours, at which point marginal revenue product equals the new lower wage w'. Because the *MRP* curve shows the amount of labour that the firm will seek to employ, in the short run at different wage rates, it is therefore the firm's short-run labour demand curve.

It should be noted that only the downward-sloping section of the *MRP* curve is the firm's short-run labour demand curve. This is because the second-order conditions for profit maximisation require the *MRP* curve to be *downward*-sloping at the point where the wage equals marginal revenue product. To illustrate this, consider the wage *w* in **Figure 5.3**. The first-order condition that the wage rate equals labour's marginal revenue product is satisfied at employment levels L_0 and *L*. However, L_0 cannot represent a profit-maximising position, because it is possible to increase profits further by expanding employment past L_0, since for additional labour hours marginal revenue product exceeds *w*. The firm therefore maximises its profits by employing *L* units of labour, because any expansion of its employment past this point would lead to a reduction in profits, as the wage paid to hire each additional person-hour of labour would exceed the value of its addition to total revenue. Strictly speaking, it is only the downward-sloping section of the *MRP* curve which lies below the point where it is intersected by the average revenue product (*APP.P*) curve which represents the firm's short-run labour demand curve. This is because this intersection point sets an upper limit to the wage rate in the sense that wages above this level would more than absorb the employer-firm's total revenue product (= *TPP.P*).

The relevant intersection point, in terms of physical rather than revenue products, is indicated by point X in **Figure 5.2**. At the labour input corresponding to this intersection point X, the firm's wage bill ($w.L$) equals its total revenue product ($APP.L$), with the consequence that it incurs a loss equal to its fixed costs. If the wage rate were to rise above this level, the rational firm will close down its operations and take a (short-run) loss equal to the level of its fixed costs: since to continue producing at the higher wage would result in a loss *greater* than the level of its fixed costs.

The area under the *MRP* curve up to a given level of employment measures the value of the total output produced, and this can be divided into payments to labour services and payments to capital services. For example, if the wage rate is w', the profit-maximising firm in **Figure 5.3** employs L' hours of labour services. The area of the rectangle below w' measures the *wage bill*, or the total payments to labour, while the area above the wage line and below the *MRP* curve measures payments to capital services.[6]

□ An alternative derivation

The equivalence of labour's *MRP* curve and the individual firm's short-run labour demand curve can alternatively be derived by straightforward application of elementary calculus.

Letting q denote the firm's output and L and K its inputs of labour and capital respectively, its production function can be written as

$$q = q\,(L, K)$$

Following usual practice, we may assume that the firm's production function is subject to the following restrictions:

$$\frac{\partial q}{\partial L} > 0, \ \frac{\partial q}{\partial K} > 0; \ \frac{\partial^2 q}{\partial L^2} < 0, \ \frac{\partial^2 q}{\partial K^2} < 0$$

according to which the marginal physical products of both labour and capital inputs are positive but diminishing. In the short run the firm's input of capital is fixed, at level K_0 in our example, and accordingly its *short-run* production function can be written as

$$q = \mathrm{f}(L)$$

subject to the restrictions:

$$\frac{\mathrm{d}q}{\mathrm{d}L} > 0, \ \frac{\mathrm{d}^2 q}{\mathrm{d}L^2} < 0$$

where dq/dL is the marginal physical product of labour, which is assumed to be non-negative. According to our assumptions, the firm purchases its labour inputs and sells its output on perfectly competitive markets. It therefore faces a given wage rate (w) and product price (P). Letting F denote the firm's fixed costs, its profits (π) can be written as the difference between its total revenue and total cost, as follows:

$$\pi = P.f(L) - wL - F$$

The firm's problem is therefore to select that level of labour usage at which profits are maximised. Differentiating the profit function with respect to L and equating to zero, we obtain

$$\frac{d\pi}{dL} = P.\frac{dq}{dL} - w = 0$$

Since $dq/dL = MPP$, this expression can be rearranged to give the first-order condition $MPP.P = w$, which requires labour to be utilised up to the point where its marginal revenue product (which in this case equals its value of marginal product) equals the wage rate (w).

The second-order condition for profit maximisation requires that

$$\frac{d^2\pi}{dL^2} = P.\frac{d^2q}{dL^2} = P.\frac{d}{dL}(MPP) < 0$$

Since $P > 0$, this requires d^2q/dL^2 (that is, the slope of the MPP curve) to be negative at the point where $w = MRP$.

□ *A note on profit maximisation*

The preceding analysis of the profit-maximising firm's behaviour has been in terms of its optimal usage of labour inputs. Implicit in the firm's decisions about input usage are decisions about its level of output, as is seen from the short-run production function, $q = f(L)$, above. It is important to recognise that the profit maximisation condition that labour be utilised up to the point where $w = MRP$ is equivalent to the condition that profits are maximised when *output* is such that the marginal cost (MC) of production equals the marginal revenue (MR) from the sale of output.

To demonstrate this equivalence in terms of our example, write the first-order condition for profit maximisation, viewed from the firm's factor market, as

$$w = MPP.P$$

from which we obtain

$$\frac{w}{MPP} = P$$

Now, given that the firm's product market is perfectly competitive, its product price (P) equals its marginal revenue (MR), and the above condition can be written as

$$\frac{w}{MPP} = MR$$

Since labour inputs are purchased in a perfectly competitive market, the employment of an additional unit of labour adds the amount w to total costs and the amount MPP to total physical output. The ratio w/MPP is therefore the extra cost that is incurred in the production of one additional unit of output (that is, the marginal cost of output). Substituting, we obtain

$$MC = MR$$

which is the familiar condition for profit maximisation in terms of the firm's output. According to this condition, the firm maximises profits by setting its output at the level where the marginal cost of output equals the marginal revenue from its sale.

□ *Non-competitive product markets*

So far we have considered the individual firm's short-run demand for labour in the case where it is a perfect competitor in both the market for its labour inputs and the market for its output. Under these conditions, as we have seen, the profit-maximising firm's labour demand curve is the marginal revenue product (MRP) of labour curve which, given the perfect product market assumption, is also labour's value of marginal product (VMP) curve. (See **Figure 5.4**(c).) In this section we retain the assumption that the firm is a perfect competitor in the market for its labour (the case of the imperfectly competitive labour market is considered in Chapter 7), but we relax the perfectly competitive product market assumption and consider the case where the firm possesses some degree of monopoly power in its product market.[7] In this case the firm faces a downward-sloping demand curve for its product, indicating that in order to sell additional units of output it must, in the absence of price discrimination, decrease the price that it charges for each unit of its output. Consequently, its marginal revenue (MR) is less than its product price (P) at each level of sales, and its marginal revenue curve is more steeply sloping than its average revenue (AR) or demand curve (D). (See **Figure 5.4** (b).)

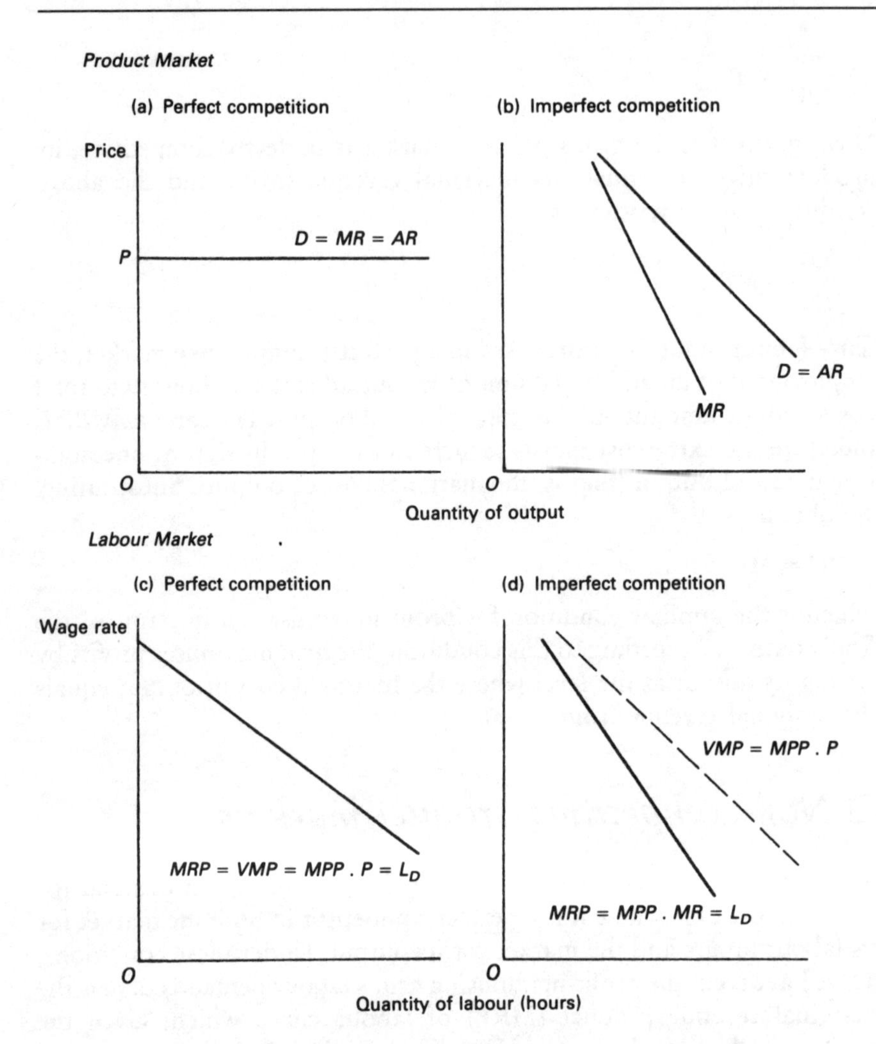

Figure 5.4 ***The firm's short-run labour demand curve and competitive condition in the product market***

Like the perfect competitor, the imperfect competitor will maximise profits by expanding its employment of labour up to the point where the cost of an additional unit of labour services equals the addition to total revenue generated by its employment. In the case of a perfect competitor, as we saw in a previous section, each additional unit of output sold increases total revenue by a constant amount equal to the product price. Accordingly in this case the marginal revenue product of labour is calculated simply by multiplying marginal physical product by the product price. In contrast to the perfect competitor, the (non-price-discriminating) imperfect competitor employing an additional unit of labour must, if he is to sell the additional output thus produced, decrease the price of *each and every* unit of his product. In this case the contribution that an additional unit of labour input makes to the firm's revenue (that is, its marginal revenue product) is equal to marginal physical product multiplied not by the product price but by the producer's marginal revenue (*MR*) at the sales level in question. (See **Figure 5.4(d)**.)

In order to maximise profits, the imperfect competitor who purchases labour inputs in a perfectly competitive labour market will employ labour up to the point where the wage rate equals labour's marginal revenue product. Therefore, this firm's short-run labour demand curve is, like that of the perfect competitor, its *MRP* schedule for labour. As we have noted, the firm's *MRP* schedule is equivalent to its *VMP* schedule in cases where product markets are perfectly competitive. However, in cases where the product market is imperfectly competitive, the value of marginal product (defined as *MPP.P*) exceeds marginal revenue product (= *MPP.MR*) at each level of employment, because at each level of sales the firm's product price exceeds its marginal revenue. In addition, since the imperfect competitor's *MR* curve slopes downwards more steeply than its *AR* curve, it follows that such a firm's short-run labour demand curve is more steeply sloped than its *VMP* curve. This can be seen from **Figures 5.4(b)**, **(c)** and **(d)**.

□ *Perfect versus imperfect competition*

Consider now the case where a given firm moves from a perfectly competitive product market situation (A) to an imperfectly competitive one (B), while all other things, including its *MPP* curve, remain unchanged. Suppose that its demand and revenue curves before and after this change in competitive structure are as shown in **Figure 5.5(a)**, and note that its marginal cost curve will remain unchanged, because by assumption both the wage at which it purchases its labour and labour's *MPP* curve remain unaltered. The firm's short-run labour demand curve for each product market structure is shown in **Figure 5.5(b)** by L_D^A and L_D^B. In both cases the firm's short-run labour demand curve is its *MRP* curve. In the perfectly competitive product market case, this curve is obtained by multiplying marginal physical product at each level of labour input by the constant market price P_A. As we have seen, the resulting labour demand curve (L_D^A) is negatively sloped, because marginal physical product declines as the level of labour input is increased. In the imperfectly competitive case the *MPP* curve is unchanged, and marginal revenue product is obtained by multiplying marginal physical product by marginal revenue (MR_B) and as can be seen from **Figure**

5.5(**b**), the resulting *MRP* or labour demand curve (L_D^B) slopes downwards more steeply than its perfectly competitive counterpart (L_D^A). The steeper slope of L_D^B for the given *MPP* curve reflects the fact that in the imperfectly competitive case marginal revenue (MR_B) as well as marginal physical product declines as employment, and hence output, is increased.

As can be seen from **Figure 5.5(b)**, the profit-maximising firm's equilibrium level of employment is lower, at each wage level, in the imperfectly competitive market situation. For example, at the wage rate *w*, on the basis of which the *MC* curve shown in **Figure 5.5(a)** is constructed, we see that imperfect competition in the firm's product market results in a level of employment which is ($L_A - L_B$) hours below the perfectly competitive level. This restriction of employment is merely the reflection in the labour market of the imperfect competitor's tendency to restrict output below the level of an otherwise identical perfect competitor. This can be seen in **Figure 5.5(a)**. The profit-maximising perfect competitor's equilibrium output is Q_A *(where* $MC = MR_A = P_A$) whereas the imperfect competitor's is only Q_B (where $MC = MR_B$). Note also that, although the wage *w* received by labour in the imperfectly competitive case equals its marginal revenue product ($= MPP.MR_B$), it is below the value of its marginal product in this market situation ($= MPP.P_B$).[8]

The firm's demand for labour in the long run

In the long run the firm is, by definition, able to alter its inputs of capital services as well as of labour. In this section we examine the firm's demand for labour when all factors may be varied. Although our analysis is confined to the case of a firm that has one fixed and one variable factor of production, it is important to recognise that the following discussion of the long-run case, in which both factors become variable, is no different from the short-run case of a firm that has two variable factors, labour and raw materials perhaps or alternatively, two different grades of labour, say skilled and unskilled.

In terms of **Figure 5.1**, the firm in the long run is no longer constrained to move along the horizontal line K_0K_0 when varying its output. To maximise its profits in the long run, the firm must – assuming that capital, like labour, is purchased in a perfectly competitive market – employ each factor up to the point where its marginal revenue product equals its price. The argument here is simply an extension of that

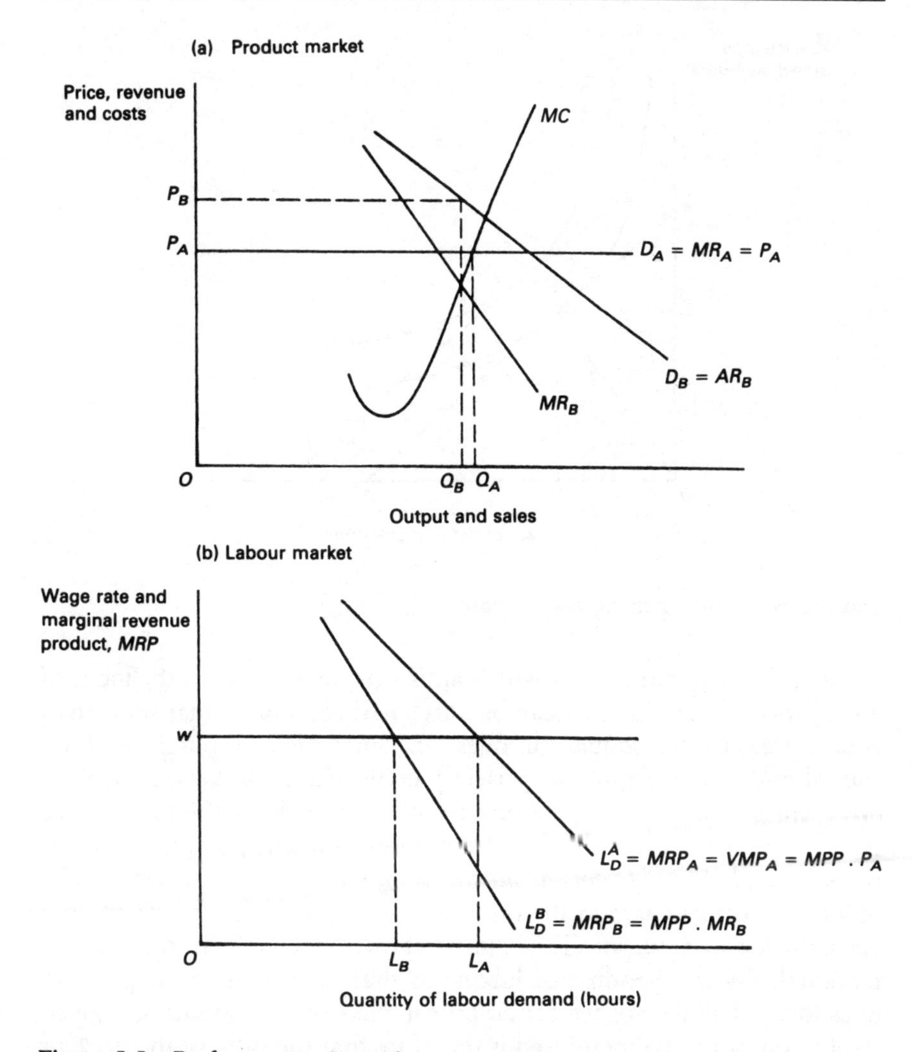

Figure 5.5 ***Perfect versus imperfect competition***

considered in the short-run case. If the marginal revenue product of either factor of production were greater than its price, the firm could increase its profit by expanding its employment of the factor in question, because the increased employment (and output) would add more to revenue than to costs. Only when the marginal revenue product of each factor *falls* into equality with its given price would it no longer be possible to increase profits further by employing additional units of inputs.[9]

If the firm were a cost-minimiser rather than a profit-maximiser, it would produce its output with the input combination represented by the

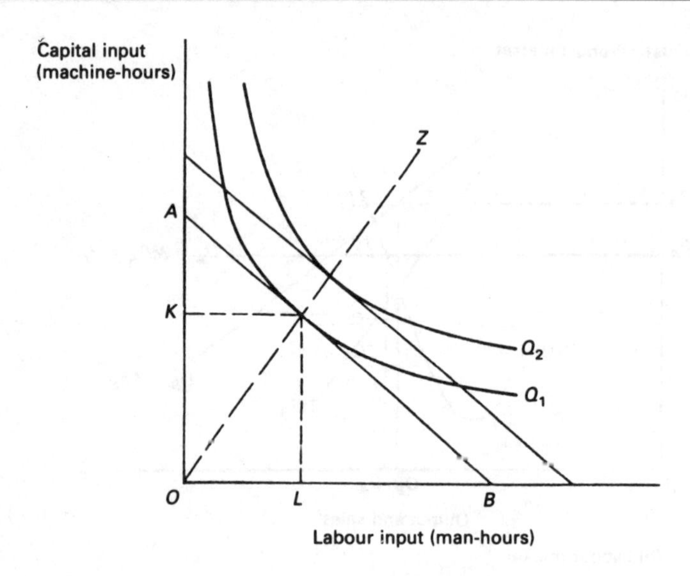

Figure 5.6 ***A long-run expansion path***

point on its isoquant map at which an *isocost* line (which is the locus of all input combinations that can be purchased for a particular total cost) is tangential to the isoquant in question. Since the firm purchases both capital and labour inputs in perfectly competitive markets, its isocost lines will be linear of slope equal to minus one times the input–price ratio.[10] The negative of the slope of an isoquant at any point is defined as the *marginal rate of technical substitution*, which is the increase in one input per unit decrease in the other that is just sufficient to maintain a constant level of output. This can be shown to equal the ratio of the marginal physical product of labour to that of capital at the point in question.[11] The first-order condition for the cost of producing a given level of output to be minimised is therefore that the ratio of the price of labour to that of capital equals the ratio of the marginal physical product of labour to that of capital.

In **Figure 5.6,** *AB* is an isocost line, and the firm minimises the cost of producing the level of output represented by isoquant Q_1 by using the input combination *K* units of capital and *L* units of labour. The locus of such tangency points (*OZ* in **Figure 5.6**) shows the firm's cost-minimising input combinations, given prevailing input prices, for each output level and is known as its (long-run) *expansion path* (which for simplicity is drawn in **Figure 5.6** as a straight line).[12] At each point along the expansion path, the input–price ratio equals the ratio of the inputs' marginal physical products. However, for long-run profit maximisation each input must be utilised up to the point where its marginal revenue product equals its price and the firm's long-run profit-maximising input combination must therefore lie at some point on its expansion path.[13]

The firm's long-run labour demand curve with perfectly competitive product markets

To derive the firm's long-run demand curve for labour, let us suppose that it is a perfect competitor in its product market and that it is initially in long-run equilibrium at point *A* in **Figure 5.7(a)**. Thus, at *A* the marginal revenue products of labour and capital equal their respective prices, say w and r. If the wage rate fell from its prevailing level w to w_1, the firm would, as we have seen, maximise its profits in the short run by expanding its employment of labour, with its capital inputs fixed, along K_0K_0 to say L' hours at point *B*, where the new lower wage equals labour's marginal revenue product. The expansion of employment that would result in the short run from this fall in the wage rate is shown by the firm's short-run labour demand curve, which is illustrated in **Figure 5.7(b)** by L_D. On the usual assumptions about the properties of production functions,[14] the employment of additional units of labour results in an increase in the marginal physical product of capital and hence also in its marginal revenue product. With the given price of capital inputs (r), the firm now finds itself in the position where the marginal revenue product of capital exceeds its price. Therefore in the long run the firm will seek to *increase* its employment of capital inputs in order to reach its new long-run equilibrium position.

This increase in the firm's employment of capital inputs results in an increase in labour's marginal physical product, with the consequence that its *MRP* curve shifts outwards, so that at each wage rate the firm will seek to expand its employment of labour. However, an increase in the employment of labour in turn raises the marginal revenue product of capital inputs, which results in a further increase in employment of capital and a further outward shift in labour's *MRP* curve, and so on! Once all these effects have occurred, labour's *MRP* curve will have shifted to, say, *MRP′* in **Figure 5.7(b)**, and long-run equilibrium will be reestablished at point *C* in **Figure 5.7(a)**,[15] where the marginal revenue products of labour and capital once again equal their respective prices. Points *E* and *F* in **Figure 5.7(b)** are both on the firm's long-run demand curve for labour, and other points can be derived in a similar manner to give the complete curve LRL_D. Note that the firm's long-run labour demand curve is not labour's *MRP* curve but an amalgam of movements along and shifts in this curve. However, at each point on the long-run

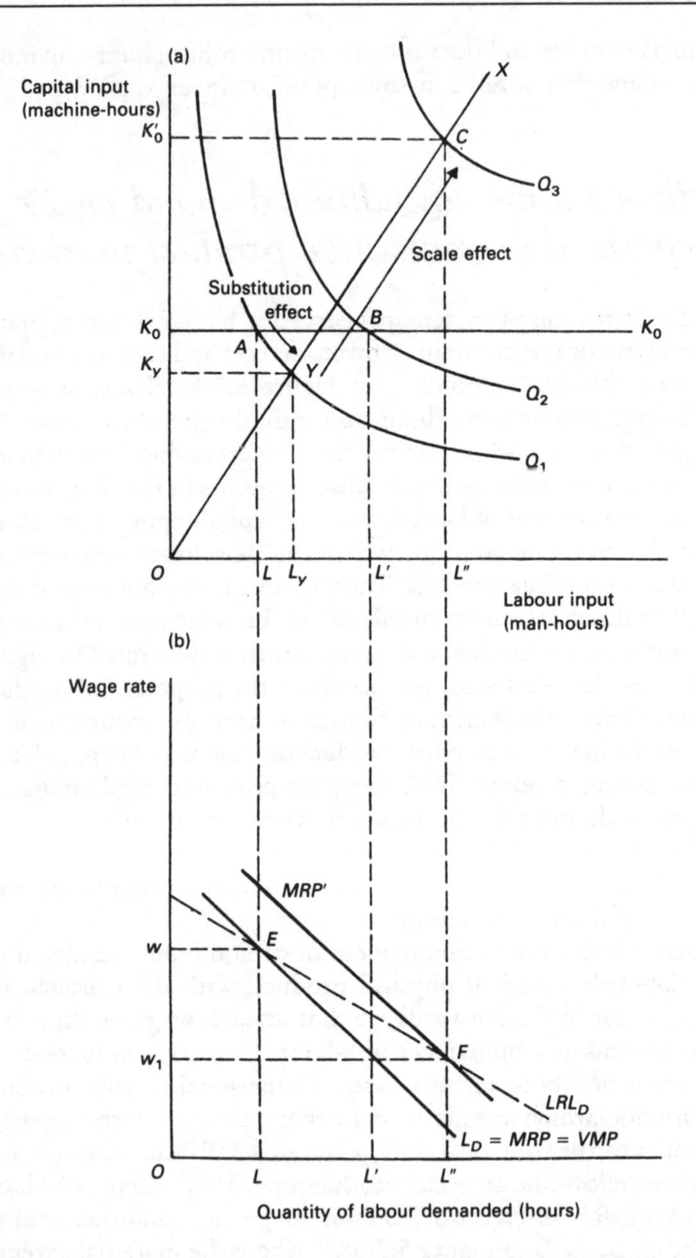

Figure 5.7 ***The firm's long-run labour demand curve***

curve the wage rate does equal labour's marginal revenue product.

As can be seen from **Figure 5.7(b)**, the firm's long-run labour demand curve is more elastic than its short-run one. The short-run effect of a decrease in the wage rate from w to w_1 is an increase in the employment of labour from L to L'. In the long run the firm is able to increase its inputs of capital services to their new optimum level K'_0, and its employment of labour increases by a further $(L'' - L')$ units.

Substitution and scale effects of a wage change

It is possible to examine the long-run effect of a wage change in more detail by subdividing the movement from the initial long-run equilibrium A to the new one C into a substitution and a scale effect. The analysis here is analogous to the subdivision in consumer theory of the effect of a price change into substitution and income effects. In **Figure 5.7(a)** OX is the firm's expansion path corresponding to the input prices w_1 and r. If the firm were a cost-minimiser, it would, as a result of the decrease in the price of its labour inputs, move around isoquant Q_1 to the new cost-minimising position at point Y, where the relevant expansion path and isoquant intersect. This movement around isoquant Q_1 between A and Y arises because the given level of output can now be produced at minimum cost with the use of a higher proportion of the now relatively cheaper input, labour. This movement is referred to as a *substitution effect* because it represents the substitution of labour for capital that would occur as a result of a reduction in the price of labour relative to capital, if the firm were constrained to maintain its original output level. Provided that the isoquants are convex to the origin (see note 3), the substitution effect of a wage decrease must always result in an increase in the firm's employment of labour. As can be seen from **Figure 5.7(a)**, the substitution effect of the decrease in the wage from w to w_1 results in an increase in the firm's employment of labour from L to L_Y units.

The movement along the expansion path OX between Y and C is termed the *scale effect* of the wage change. This represents the extent to which the firm's employment of labour increases, with relative input prices held constant at their new level, as a result of the increase in the firm's long-run equilibrium level of output that arises from the fall in the wage rate. As can be seen, the scale effect of the fall in the wage rate from w to w_1 results in an increase in the employment of labour inputs from L_Y to L'' units.[16]

Industry demand for labour

So far we have considered the individual firm's demand for labour under various conditions. When considering the industry's demand for labour it is not possible, however, merely to sum horizontally the labour demand curves of the individual firms that make up the industry without allowing for price changes. In an industry where there is a perfectly competitive product market, the individual firm is so small in relation to the size of the market that changes in its own output have no perceptible effect on the price of the product that it sells. However, when we consider the whole industry we must recognise that a decrease in the wage rate will result in each firm in the industry increasing its labour input, and hence its output, with the consequence that, for a given demand curve for the industry's product, the market price of output will fall.

Figure 5.8(a) depicts a representative firm from a perfectly competitive industry. For the initial output price this firm's short-run demand curve for labour is given by its marginal revenue product curve MRP_1. Our representative firm employs e_1 units of labour at the ruling wage w, and aggregating across all firms in the industry we see from **Figure 5.8(b)** that a total of E_1 units of labour are employed at this wage. In the analysis of the individual firm's labour demand, it was assumed that the output of all other firms in the industry, and hence the product price, remains *unchanged*. However, at the industry level we would expect the employment and output of each firm, and hence the product price, to vary when the price of labour alters. To the representative firm the decrease in output price which occurs as industry output expands in response to a fall in the wage rate results in a leftward shift in the *MRP* curve to say, MRP_2. If the product price were held constant, the representative firm confronted with a fall in its wage rate from w to w' would expand its employment of labour, along MRP_1, from e_1 to e'. Summing horizontally across firms, we see that the industry demand for labour would expand in this constant output–price case from E_1 to E'. However, when each firm in the industry expands its output the market price falls and at the lower wage rate our representative firm expands its employment to only e_2. Aggregating, we obtain the industry demand for labour in this case as E_2.

Points *a* and *b* lie on the representative firm's short-run labour demand curve in the case where market price varies, and repeating this procedure for each possible wage rate we obtain the firm's demand curve *dd'*. Points *A* and *B* lie on the industry labour demand curve, and summing horizontally each firm's demand curve *dd'* we obtain the industry's labour demand curve *DD'*. Note that in this case the individual firm's labour demand curve is steeper than the fixed product-price one and that the industry's short-run labour demand curve is more steeply sloped than the various horizontally summed (constant-price) *MRP* curves. The industry's short-run labour demand curve is more

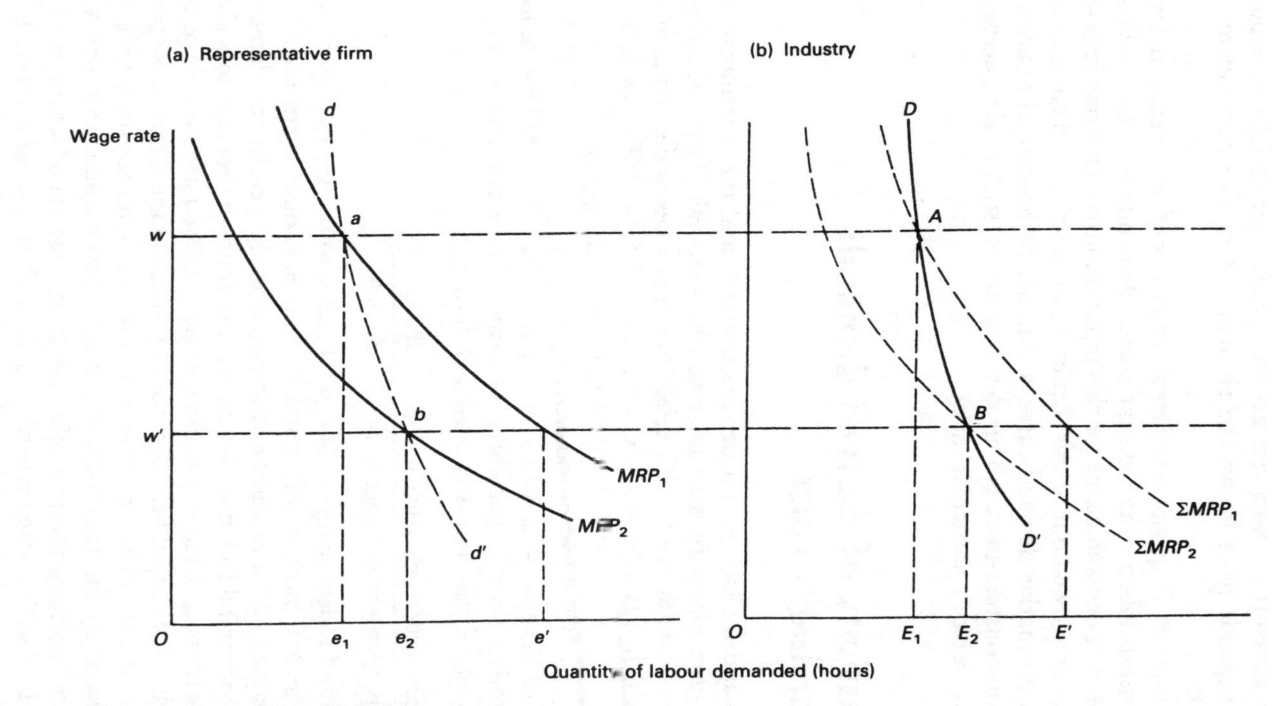

Figure 5.8 ***Industry demand for labour***

steeply sloped than the summed *MRP* curves because the latter slope downwards *solely* because of labour's diminishing marginal physical product, while the former slopes down, *in addition*, because the product price falls as industry output expands. How much steeper this demand curve is depends on how quickly the product price falls as industry output expands (that is, on the elasticity of market demand for the product).

If the industry in question is the sole employer of this particular sort of homogeneous labour, the industry labour demand curve DD' will also be the market demand curve for this input. If, however, firms in several industries employ labour of this sort in the production of their respective outputs, the market demand curve is obtained by horizontal summation of the non-constant-price labour demand curves, such as dd', across all firms that use this particular input.

Elasticity of derived demand: Marshall's rules

The demand for labour is a derived demand, and the determinants of its own price elasticity were identified by Marshall (1890, pp. 384–6, 852–3) and summarised in his celebrated four rules of derived demand, one of which was subsequently corrected by Hicks (1963, pp. 241–6).

In order to understand Marshall's rules of derived demand it is necessary to introduce the *elasticity of substitution* (σ) as providing a measure of the ease with which one input can be substituted for another in the production of a *given* level of output. In the two-factor case, the elasticity of substitution is defined as follows:

$$\sigma = \frac{\text{proportionate change in } K/L}{\text{proportionate change in } w/r} = \frac{\mathrm{dln}(K/L)}{\mathrm{dln}(w/r)}$$

where K and L denote inputs of capital and labour services respectively, r and w their respective prices and ln denotes *natural* logarithms.

The elasticity of substitution thus measures the percentage change in the ratio of capital to labour inputs which occurs in response to a given (small) percentage change (of opposite sign) in the ratio of their prices, with the level of output held constant. By virtue of the fact that output is held constant, the elasticity of substitution measures substitution possibilities faced by the firm moving around a given isoquant. Point X in **Figure 5.9** illustrates the cost-minimising equilibrium of a firm producing output Q with a wage rate of w and a capital price of r. As we have already seen, the first-order conditions for cost minimisation require that the ratio of the price of labour to that of capital (the slope of the isocost line) equals the marginal rate of technical substitution between capital and labour (the slope of the isoquant), where the latter (see note 11) is given by the ratio of the marginal physical product of labour to that of capital. The cost-minimising firm's optimal capital–labour ratio is shown by the slope of the ray OX in **Figure 5.9**. If the prices of the firm's inputs were to change to w_1 and r_1 such that labour becomes relatively more expensive, the cost-minimising producer would seek wherever possible to substitute capital for labour. In terms of **Figure 5.9** the new input–price ratio gives rise to a new more steeply sloping isocost line (CD) which generates the firm's new cost-minimising equilibrium at the tangency point Y. The capital–labour ratio at this new cost-minimising equilibrium is given by (K_1/L_1) which is greater than that pertaining at the initial position X.

As can be seen from the formula for σ, the elasticity of substitution provides a measure of the percentage change in the capital–labour ratio between X and Y, relative to the percentage change in input prices which brings the movement about. Differently shaped isoquants generate different substitution elasticities. At one extreme is the case of an 'L'-shaped isoquant, which gives rise to an elasticity of substitution equal to zero. This arises because no matter what value is taken by the input–price ratio, the firm's cost-minimising position is always at the intersection of the horizontal and vertical 'arms' of the L-shaped isoquant, indicating that no substitution is possible. At the other extreme lies the case of a linear isoquant, for which the elasticity of substitution is infinite. In such a case, the firm's two inputs are perfect substitutes for one another, with the consequence that the firm employs exclusively whichever is the cheaper input. In geometric terms we see that in such cases the cost-minimising equilibrium is always a *corner* solution except, of course, in the particular case where the input–price ratio exactly equals the slope of the linear isoquant. In this case, each and every point along the linear isoquant qualifies as a possible cost-minimising solution! In between these two limiting cases, the elasticity of substitution is positive and *finite*. In particular, it is worth noting that the Cobb–Douglas production function, regardless of its degree of homogeneity, has an elasticity of substitution equal to unity. For a proof, see Chiang (1984, pp. 425–6).

Marshall's four rules of derived demand can be stated in the two-factor case, where the price of the other factor remains constant, as follows. The elasticity of demand for labour will be greater

(1) the greater the elasticity of substitution in production,
(2) the greater the elasticity of demand for the final product,

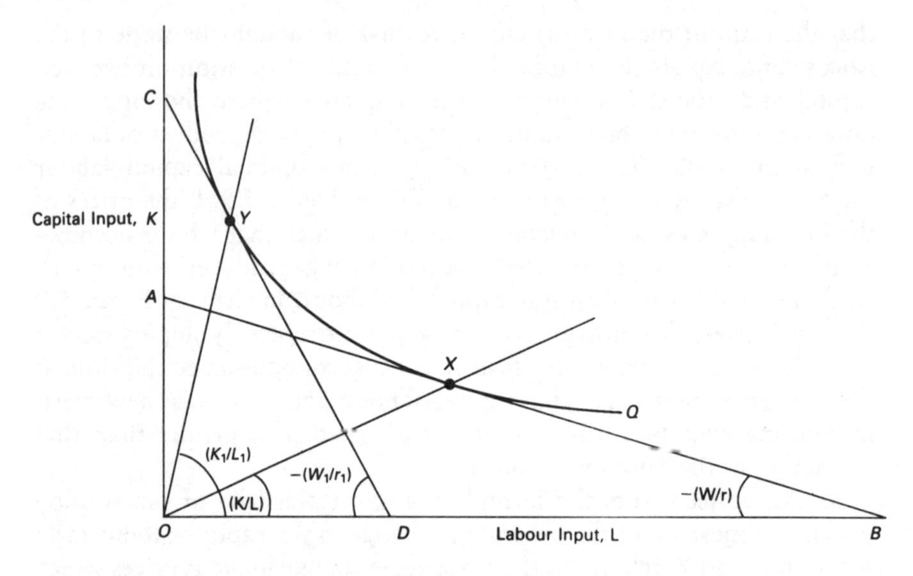

Figure 5.9 ***Elasticity of substitution***

(3) the greater the share of labour in total cost,[17] and
(4) the greater the elasticity of supply of the other factor of production.

According to rule (1), the greater the elasticity of demand for labour, *ceteris paribus*, the greater are the opportunities to substitute capital for labour in the production process. This is because the greater the firm's ability to substitute capital for labour when the price of labour increases, the larger will be the contraction in its demand for labour that results from a given wage increase. Rule (2) states that the more elastic the demand for the final product, the more elastic, *ceteris paribus*, is the firm's demand for labour. Thus, a given wage increase will, *ceteris paribus*, lead to a greater decrease in product demand, and hence also in the derived demand for labour, the more elastic is the demand for the final output produced. Rule (3) is frequently referred to as the *importance of being unimportant* and according to this rule (assuming Hicks's condition is satisfied), the demand for labour is more elastic the greater is the proportion of total costs accounted for by labour. Thus, in two firms that differ only in the ratio of their labour costs to total costs a given wage increase will, *ceteris paribus*, lead to a greater rise in product price, and hence to a greater fall in product demand and consequently in the derived demand for labour, in the firm with the higher labour-cost ratio. Finally, rule (4) states that the greater the firm's ability to attract supplies of the other factor of production (to substitute in place of labour when the wage rises) without pushing up its price, the greater, *ceteris paribus*, will be the elasticity of its demand for labour.

A cautionary note

In this chapter we have considered marginal productivity theory as applied to labour as a factor of production.[18] It is important to recognise that this analysis does not provide a theory of wages but only a theory of the demand for labour. As Rees pointed out long ago, 'to speak of the marginal productivity theory of wages is exactly analogous to speaking of the demand theory of prices' (1973, pp. 58–9). In order to construct a theory of wage and employment determination, it is necessary to consider the interaction of demand- *and* supply-side forces in the market for labour and this is the subject matter of Chapter 7 below.

Notes

1. For a useful survey of the historical origins of marginal productivity theory and a critique, see Cartter (1959, pp. 11–44).
2. A perfectly competitive labour market is one where a large number of buyers and sellers, each of whose volume of transactions is so small in relation to that of the market as a whole that its own actions have no perceptible influence on the ruling wage, negotiate the exchange of homogeneous labour. For further discussion, see Marshall *et al.* (1976, pp. 175–7).
3. The isoquants in **Figure 5.1** are drawn as continuous curves on the assumption that the firm's production function is itself continuous. Their convexity to the origin follows from the usual assumption of a diminishing marginal rate of technical substitution as one factor is substituted for the other. For further discussion, see Henderson and Quandt (1980, pp. 65–73) or Gravelle and Rees (1992, pp. 180–4).
4. In geometric terms, average physical product at any point on the *TPP* curve is given by the slope of the straight line drawn from the origin to the point, while marginal physical product is given by the slope of the tangent to the *TPP* curve at the point in question.
5. In terms of the isoquant-mapping of **Figure 5.1**, total physical product achieves its maximum at the point where the horizontal line K_0K_0 is tangential to an isoquant (that is, at point A, where the firm's labour inputs is L_2 hours). Since the slope of the isoquant at this point is zero, it must here be intersected by a ridge line.
6. For an early discussion of this point see Cartter (1959, pp. 15–18).
7. Since our analysis is confined in this section to the short-run period, it is not necessary to make a distinction between monopoly and monopolistic competition, because these two market structures essentially only differ in the long run. See, for example, Lipsey (1989, pp. 223–4).
8. For further discussion of the relationship between competitive conditions in the product market and the labour demand of firms with given *MPP* curves,

see Marshall *et al.* (1976, pp. 224–7). For discussion of the case of oligopolistic product markets, see Peel (1972).

9. More formally, if the firm sells its output in a perfectly competitive market at price P, its long-run profit function is

$$\pi = Pq - wL - rK$$

where $q = q(K, L)$ is its long-run production function and r denotes the price of capital services.

Long-run profits are a function of K and L and are maximised by setting the partial derivatives of π with respect to L and K equal to zero. Substituting and partially differentiating, we obtain

$$\frac{\partial \pi}{\partial L} = P.\frac{\partial q}{\partial L} - w = 0$$

$$\frac{\partial \pi}{\partial K} = P.\frac{\partial q}{\partial K} - r = 0$$

Noting that $\partial q/\partial L$ and $\partial q/\partial K$ equal the marginal physical products of labour (MPP_L) and capital (MPP_K) respectively, we obtain the first-order conditions

$$w = MPP_L.P = MRP_L$$

$$r = MPP_K.P = MRP_K$$

which require each input to be utilised up to the point where its marginal revenue product (which equals its value of marginal product in this case) equals its price. Second-order conditions require the marginal physical product of each input to be decreasing with respect to its own employment.

10. Letting c denote the level of total costs, we have

$$c = wL + rK$$

Rearranging, we obtain

$$K = \frac{c}{r} - \frac{wL}{r}$$

which is the equation of a straight line on the K v L plane, with slope $-w/r$. By varying c, a family of isocost lines is obtained.

11. To show this, we totally differentiate the firm's long-run production function $q = q(L, K)$ to obtain

$$dq = \frac{\partial q}{\partial L}dL + \frac{\partial q}{\partial K}dK$$

Now, the partial derivatives of q with respect to L and K are the marginal physical products of labour (MPP_L) and capital (MPP_K) respectively, and therefore

$$dq = MPP_L . dL + MPP_K dK$$

For movements along a given isoquant, $dq = 0$, so we obtain by rearrangement

$$\text{Marginal rate of technical substitution} = -\frac{dK}{dL} = \frac{MPP_L}{MPP_K}$$

12. For convenience the expansion path in **Figure 5.6** is drawn as a straight line. Expansion paths are not necessarily linear, but it is interesting to notice that a sufficient condition for linearity is that the production function is homogeneous of any degree. For a proof, see Chiang (1984, pp. 421–3).
13. At each point on the expansion path

$$\frac{MPP_L}{MPP_K} = \frac{w}{r} \tag{1}$$

and for long-run profit maximisation with perfect product markets, we have the conditions

$$\begin{aligned} w &= MPP_L . P \\ r &= MPP_K . P \end{aligned} \tag{2}$$

Since (2) is a special case of (1), the firm's long-run equilibrium must lie on its expansion path.

14. Namely, that the marginal physical product of each factor increases as the employment of the other input is increased. In terms of calculus, it is assumed that the cross partial derivatives of the production function are *positive*. Further, according to Young's theorem (see Chiang 1984, p. 313) the two cross-partial derivatives will be equal to one another providing that both are continuous. Accordingly we may write the assumption as

$$\frac{\partial^2 q}{\partial L \partial K} \equiv \frac{\partial}{\partial L}\left(\frac{\partial q}{\partial K}\right) = \frac{\partial^2 q}{\partial K \partial L} \equiv \frac{\partial}{\partial K}\left(\frac{\partial q}{\partial L}\right) > 0$$

15. Note that point C must lie on the expansion path OX pertaining to the input prices w_1 and r.
16. It is worth noting that the scale effect, Y to C, can itself be subdivided into what Ferguson and Gould (1975, pp. 372–4) termed output and profit-maximising effects. The former is the movement along the expansion path from Y to the position where output is maximised for the initial expenditure on inputs. The latter effect is the movement along the expansion path from the output-maximising position to the new long-run equilibrium point C.
17. Hicks demonstrated that Marshall's third rule only holds if the elasticity of demand for the final product exceeds the elasticity of substitution between labour and the other factor of production. If this condition does not hold

(that is, when the consumer can substitute less easily than the producer) Marshall's third rule is reversed.

The economic meaning of the Hicksian correction has generated considerable controversy over the years. See, in particular, Bronfenbrenner (1961, pp. 254–61; 1971, pp. 148–50), Hicks (1976, pp. 263–5) and, for a reconsideration of the controversy, see Maurice (1975, pp. 385–93).

18. For an interesting criticism of the marginal productivity theory as applied to labour demand, see Lester (1946) and for a well-known reply in defence of the marginal analysis see Machlup (1946). For a useful survey of the major issues here see Cartter (1959, pp. 33–44).

■ Chapter 6 ■

Labour Demand: Some Extensions

■ Introduction

In this chapter we introduce some extensions to the basic model of labour demand discussed in Chapter 5. We begin by relaxing the simplifying assumption so far adopted, according to which the *only* cost associated with the employment of labour is the hourly wage rate. Following this discussion, we explore an alternative, though related, treatment of labour demand known as the employment demand function approach. In the final section, we introduce the possibility that the position of labour's marginal physical product curve may not be independent of the level of the wage paid.

■ Fixed versus variable employment costs

In Chapter 5's analysis of the demand for labour we made the usual simplifying assumption that there are no costs, other than the hourly wage, associated with the employment of labour. This assumption allowed us to measure inputs of labour services in person-hours, without having to subdivide these into the number of workers and number of hours. It implies that an employer will be indifferent between employing one person to work (say) 16 hours per day or two people to each work eight hours per day. However, in a classic paper, Oi (1962) argued that labour is not a completely variable factor of production, in the sense that total labour costs fluctuate in direct proportion to hours worked, but that it is in fact a *quasi-fixed factor*, because the total costs associated with the employment of labour are partially fixed and partially variable.

Fixed employment costs are those which do not vary with hours worked, and these are of two basic sorts. First, there are *turnover costs*, which consist of the costs associated with *hiring* and *firing*. These include employer search and screening costs, initial training costs (which include the opportunity costs – in terms of foregone output – arising from both the person being trained and the person, or persons, involved in the supervision of the trainee) and severance payments. These costs are generally assumed to be a function of the number of new workers hired and existing ones quitting or laid off. It is also argued that these costs, as a proportion of total labour costs, are likely to rise with the skill level of the employee. As these fixed costs are, in essence, one-off set-up (or wind-up) costs, they may be termed *non-recurring* fixed costs. Second, there are those *recurring* fixed costs which are unrelated to both the number of hours worked by an individual employee and the intensity with which the individual works, but which occur throughout the period of the individual's employment. These recurring fixed costs include the administrative costs associated with a worker's employment, such as the costs of keeping employment and payroll records, of implementing the income tax and health and unemployment insurance schemes and of making wage and other payments. *Per capita* labour taxes and certain employer contributions and payroll taxes, which are of a fixed amount per employee over a specified threshold income limit, also fall into this category. Employers' pension contributions in cases where these are a certain percentage of a salary that is payable regardless of variations in hours actually worked also fall into this category. Indeed, in cases (which are commonly found in white-collar and professional occupations) where employees are paid a certain annual salary regardless of any fluctuations which may occur in their actual hours of work relative to standard hours, the whole of such salary payments may, arguably, be regarded as fixed costs. Such fringe benefits as company cars, sports and canteen facilities, subsidised housing or subsidised housing loans and the like are further examples of recurring fixed costs. An additional source of recurring fixed costs occurs in the form of holiday and sickness pay, as payments for days not actually worked.

As noted, turnover costs are usually assumed to increase as a proportion of total labour costs with the skill level of the type of labour being considered. Employer search costs are the costs of recruiting and screening new employees, and these are likely to increase with skill level for several reasons. The costs of advertising vacancies are likely to be higher in the case of skilled workers as advertising may be conducted on a national or international rather than a local basis and recruitment and personnel agency fees may be involved. In addition, interview expenses may be paid, and more expensive management time is likely to be used in interviewing prospective employees. Likewise, initial training costs are likely to increase with skill level, because the period of on-the-job training that is required before a new employee achieves full productivity may be longer at higher skill levels. While a manual worker may be able to become fully operational in a new job in a matter of days, a managerial worker taking up employment in a different company may require several months to become completely familiarised with relevant data and conditions before becoming fully operational. Firing or separation costs may include redundancy payments, and these too are likely to increase with skill level to the extent that their magnitude is determined as some fraction or multiple, generally determined by length of service, of remuneration at the time of separation.

The existence of fixed employment costs means that the costs to the firm of increasing its labour input by hiring more workers, in general, differ from the costs involved in increasing its labour input by increasing the working hours of existing employees. As we shall see in the following section, the costs of varying the number of employees relative to those costs associated with changing hours worked are important determinants of the structure of an employer's labour demand as between workers and hours. In addition, the existence of fixed employment costs helps to explain observed variations in employment stability and unemployment by skill level.

■ The size of fixed employment costs

As will be clear from the preceding discussion, the quantification of fixed employment costs is by no means straightforward. However, some recent evidence (Hart, 1984; Hart *et al.*, 1988) suggests that fixed employment costs as a percentage of total labour costs (excluding paid holidays) in 1981 varied across a sample of OECD countries from around 3 per cent in Italy to 15 per cent in Japan. When paid holidays are brought into the calculations, the ratio was found to vary from 15 per cent in the case of Italy to 26 per cent in the UK, with the USA and France only marginally behind at 25 and 24 per cent respectively. See **Table 6.1**.

□ *Hours versus workers*

To illustrate the importance of fixed costs in determining the structure of labour demand as between workers and hours, let us consider an employer's reaction to cyclical variations in the demand for his output.

Table 6.1 ***Fixed labour costs in proportion to total costs in manufacturing industry in selected OECD member countries, 1981***

	France	*Germany*	*Italy*	*Japan*	*UK*	*USA**
Measure 1 (excluding paid holidays)	0.14	0.07	0.03	0.15	0.12	0.13
Measure 2 (including paid holidays)	0.24	0.21	0.15	0.18	0.26	0.25

* All industries.

Source: Hart *et al.* (1988)

During the early stages of a recession, employers may tend to be reluctant to lay off workers, as they may be uncertain about the likely duration of the fall-off in their product demand. Fearing the costs of discharging workers, and the possibility of incurring further search and training costs in the near future should the fall-off in demand prove to be only short-lived, the employer is likely to adjust employment by reducing hours of work in preference to reducing the number of employees. This adjustment in hours may take the form of either a reduction in overtime, if this is being worked, or the introduction of short-time working.

Once the strength of the recession becomes clear, the employer may then revise downwards his output plans and begin to run down his workforce. However, the incidence of lay-offs among the workforce will be influenced by variations in fixed employment costs between different skill levels. The longer a worker remains with an employer, the longer is the timespan over which the fixed cost expenditure that the employer has invested in the worker can be spread. Consequently an employer, is likely to be more reluctant to lay off skilled than unskilled workers during a recession, for to lay off a skilled worker now in response to a current reduction in product demand may well involve incurring significant new fixed costs in the future when demand revives, as the laid-off worker may well by that time have found suitable employment elsewhere. The situation where an employer retains labour in excess of current requirements is known as *labour-hoarding* (see Taylor, 1974, pp. 26–8). Thus, the presence and nature of fixed employment costs gives one explanation for the greater employment stability and lower incidence of lay-offs which are observed among skilled as opposed to unskilled workers. In addition, such costs offer an explanation of the frequently observed tendency of changes in hours to precede changes in numbers employed at cyclical turning points.

During the initial stages of an upswing, employers are likely to be reluctant to hire extra workers and thereby incur additional fixed costs. Until they become satisfied that the recovery is likely to be sustained, employers may prefer to meet increased product demand by utilising existing employees more intensively – by initially restoring working hours back to standard hours and subsequently by offering overtime working at premium rates. Once the employer is satisfied that the recovery is likely to be prolonged, he will contemplate increasing the workforce. By so doing, additional fixed employment costs are incurred, but the costs of recruitment and initial training may be reduced if former employees who were previously laid off can be reemployed. As in the case of the downturn, we once again see adjustments in hours preceding adjustments in the same direction in numbers employed over the cycle.

□ *Voluntary quits*

An employer who lays off a worker stands, especially if the skill of the worker in question is of a general type rather than one specific to the particular employer, to lose his previous investment of fixed cost expenditure on the worker. Similar losses arise when a worker voluntarily quits employment, and in order to minimise such losses employers frequently operate various devices designed to cut down voluntary mobility among experienced workers by establishing seniority as an important characteristic. For example, up to a certain age senior employees are generally guaranteed greater employment stability, because lay-offs are typically arranged on a 'last in, first out' basis. In addition, holiday and pension entitlements are frequently tied to years of service, and seniority is often established as one criterion for promotion.

□ *Demand for overtime hours*

In Chapter 2 we examined the responses of labour-suppliers to the existence of premium rates of pay for overtime working. In this section we consider the effect of overtime payments on the employer's demand for hours relative to workers.

Consider the case of a firm whose employees are already working standard hours, and suppose that it is confronted with an increase in the demand for its product. In order to satisfy this increased demand in the short term, the employer can either increase the hours worked by the existing workforce or recruit additional workers. If the first alternative is chosen, the employer must pay premium rates of pay for the additional hours worked, and there is a possibility of decreased efficiency through increased fatigue and on-the-job leisure, particularly in cases where large amounts of overtime are worked over long periods of time. Alternatively, the hiring of additional workers involves the employer incurring fresh fixed employment costs, although, as we have seen, these can to some extent be reduced if the employer is able to rehire previously laid-off workers.

As we have noted, adjustments in hours tend to precede adjustments in numbers employed over the cycle, as employers estimate the likely duration of demand changes. If the increase in demand is *expected* to be only temporary, the employer will tend to prefer not to hire additional workers, because the overtime payments involved in meeting the increased product demand by increasing working hours will be less than the fixed costs involved in hiring additional workers now and laying them off in the near future. The longer the increase in demand is expected to last, the more likely the employer is to err towards employing additional workers in preference to additional hours. This is because he estimates that the additional fixed costs will be spread over a sufficiently long period to compare favourably with the costs of overtime working.

□ *A modified labour demand model*

It is a relatively straightforward matter to extend the basic neoclassical model of labour demand of the previous chapter to include the fixed costs discussed in the preceding section. Suppose, for simplicity, that the firm expects to employ the worker for n periods into the future and that the worker's marginal revenue product in period t is given by MRP_t, where $t = 0, 1, \ldots, n$. The present value of the return to the employer from employing the worker over the n period horizon is given by V, where

$$V = MRP_0 + \frac{MRP_1}{(1 + r)} + \frac{MRP_2}{(1 + r)^2} + \ldots + \frac{MRP_n}{(1 + r)^n} \qquad (6.1)$$

from which

$$V = \sum_{t=0}^{n} \frac{MRP_t}{(1 + r)^t} \qquad (6.2)$$

where r denotes the discount rate.

On the cost side, the employer incurs a wage cost and a recurring fixed cost during each period, which we denote by W_t and F_t respectively, for all $t = 0, 1, \ldots, n$. In contrast, the employer incurs non-recurring fixed costs (such as hiring and training costs as discussed above) only once, in period $t = 0$, and for completeness we assume that firing costs S are incurred at time $t = n$. Accordingly, the present value of the employer's labour costs, denoted by C, may be written as follows:

$$C(W_0 + F_0) + \frac{(W_1 + F_1)}{(1 + r)} + \frac{(W_2 + F_2)}{(1 + r)^2} + \ldots + \frac{(W_n + F_n)}{(1 + r)^n} + H + \frac{S}{(1 + r)^n} \tag{6.3}$$

where H denotes non-recurring fixed costs. Expression (6.3) may be rewritten as follows:

$$\begin{aligned} C &= \sum_{t=0}^{n} \frac{(W_t + F_t)}{(1 + r)^t} + H + \frac{S}{(1 + r)^n} \\ &= \sum_{t=0}^{n} \frac{W_t}{(1 + r)^t} + \sum_{t=0}^{n} \frac{F_t}{(1 + r)^t} + H + \frac{S}{(1 + r)^n} \end{aligned} \tag{6.4}$$

The employer-firm achieves equilibrium by equating V to C for the marginal worker. Given that F_t, H and S are all positive, it follows from expressions (6.2) and (6.4) that the discounted summation of the returns (the MRP_t) to the employer over the n period horizon from employing the worker (V) must exceed the discounted present value of the stream of wage payments made to the worker over this period, as given by

$$\sum_{t=0}^{n} \frac{W_t}{(1 + r)^t}.$$

In essence, what this shows is that the existence of fixed labour costs – recurring and non-recurring – serves to drive a wedge between the wage rate and the marginal revenue product of labour, and thereby to sever the equality between these two magnitudes, the condition which we saw in Chapter 5 to be central to the basic model of labour demand. This point can be shown even more clearly by making the simplifying assumption that both the wage rate and the marginal revenue product of labour remain constant over the complete n periods of the employment contract, at say W and MRP respectively. In this case, the employer's equilibrium condition is that in each of the n periods under consideration,

$$MRP = W + Z \tag{6.5}$$

where Z is that sum of money necessary to amortise the employer's investment in the worker. That is, Z is that sum which if received by the employer each period would give a discounted present value just sufficient to offset that associated with the stream of recurring fixed costs (F_t), incurred by the employer, coupled with the non-recurring fixed costs H and S incurred in the opening and closing periods of the employment contract respectively. That is, Z satisfies the following relation:

$$\sum_{t=0}^{n} \frac{Z}{(1+r)^t} = \sum_{t=0}^{n} \frac{F_t}{(1+r)^t} + H + \frac{S}{(1+r)^n} \tag{6.6}$$

Notice, from expressions (6.5) and (6.6) that within this framework the equilibrium condition of the basic model of labour demand considered in Chapter 5, requiring that the wage rate during each period be set equal to the marginal revenue product of labour, corresponds to the special case in which $H = S = F_t = 0$ (for all t) since under such circumstances $Z = 0$. When this restriction is not satisfied, $Z > 0$, and we see from expression (6.5) that in a world where non-zero fixed labour costs exist, the employer is in equilibrium, even with perfect competition in the labour market, with a level of employment in each period which is such that labour's marginal revenue product exceeds the wage rate.

The analysis of this section can be used to illustrate the hours versus workers choice discussed above. Suppose that a firm is planning to increase the size of its labour input in order to be able to meet an anticipated increase in the demand for its output. Letting k denote the overtime premium, it is seen that an additional unit of labour input from its existing employees (the 'insiders') will cost $(1 + k)W$, on the assumption that existing employees are already working standard hours. Note that $(1 + k)W$ is the marginal labour cost from hiring extra labour input internally, since for existing workers, there are no additional fixed labour costs to be incurred. In other words, the hiring and training costs (H) and potential severance costs (S) have already been met for existing employees, as have the recurring fixed costs (F_t) associated with that employment so that the marginal cost of additional units of labour input from internal sources is simply the wage rate multiplied by one plus the overtime premium. However, if the firm were to recruit new workers to meet the anticipated upturn in demand for its output, the marginal cost of 'outsider' labour will equal $W + Z$, as given by (6.5). Assuming that the productiveness of the overtime hours of insider labour does not decline due to 'fatigue' effects, the firm will opt in favour of increasing the hours of insiders rather than hiring new outsiders, whenever the following condition holds

$$(1 + k)W \leqslant W + Z$$

In practice, however, 'fatigue' effects may serve to decrease the productivity of the overtime hours of insider labour below that of their standard hours. This therefore decreases the attractiveness to the employer of extra insider hours relative to additional outside workers. Under such circumstances, the firm will err less towards internal sources of additional labour input and more towards external sources in order to equalise the marginal cost of output as between that produced with additional insider hours and that produced by newly hired outsiders.[1]

■ Employment demand functions

An alternative approach to the demand for labour is the *employment demand function* approach. The literature here is very extensive (for surveys see Berndt, 1981, 1991; Fair, 1969; Hamermesh, 1986; Hazledine, 1981) and within it there exists a variety of differing approaches. At its most basic level, this approach consists of little more than the inversion of the firm's production function in order to obtain an expression for its demand for labour services as a function of its output level, its inputs of the other factors of production, and the state of technology. As we shall see, one important advantage of this approach arises from the fact that it allows us to bring the preceding sorts of arguments regarding the existence of fixed employment costs, and their implications for the firm's optimal choice between workers and hours, explicitly into the picture.

Before looking at such models, it is useful to summarise briefly the main way in which they differ from the simple, *neoclassical*, model of labour demand considered in the preceding chapter. The labour demand models discussed in Chapter 5 focused their attention on the relationship which exists, for a profit-maximising firm, between the wage at which it hires its labour input (which is exogenously given in the case of a competitive labour market) on the one hand, and its optimal level of labour input on the other. As we saw, the relationship linking these two variables is the marginal physical product schedule, which is obtained as the partial derivative of the employer-firm's production function with respect to its labour input. The firm's production function was seen to also enter the story in another way. In the short run, with the firm's capital inputs fixed, the selection by the firm of its profit-maximising level of employment (by following the rule $W = MRP_L$) determines, via the short-run production function, its optimal level of output (that is, that at which the marginal cost of output is equal to the marginal revenue from the sale of output). In contrast, the employment demand function approach, in its simplest form, focuses attention on the latter of these two links: namely, on the influence of variations in the firm's output level upon the level of its employment of labour. The employment demand function approach, with its emphasis upon the employment–output relationship, has been widely used in the forecasting of future employment levels.

□ *A simple model*

As already noted, the most straightforward employment demand function models boil down to the simple inversion of the firm's short-run production function to give an expression for employment in terms of output. Using Q to denote the firm's output level and L and K to denote its inputs of labour and capital respectively, we may write its production function as

$$Q = Q(L, K) \tag{6.7}$$

In the short run the firm's input of capital is fixed, with the consequence that its short-run production function may be written as follows:

$$Q = Q(L, \bar{K}) = f(L) \tag{6.8}$$

Assuming invertability, (6.8) may be solved for L to give the following expression

$$L = L(Q) \tag{6.9}$$

which shows the firm's *desired* level of labour input (L) as a function of its output level (Q). Notice that the employment function (6.9) follows from the *technical* relationship between the firm's inputs and outputs as represented by its short-run production function (6.8). In this simple formulation no assumptions have been made regarding the employer-firm's behaviour, other than the usual assumption of technical efficiency which underlies the production function, in the sense that expressions (6.7) and (6.8) show the maximum output attainable for each possible input combination (Henderson and Quandt, 1980, p. 66). Notice that in consequence, the employment demand function (6.9) attributes no role to the wage rate in influencing the firm's desired level of labour input. However, as we shall see later in this chapter, more complete models, which incorporate the assumption of either cost-minimising or profit-maximising behaviour, do find a role for the price of labour (relative to that of capital) in determining the optimal level of the firm's labour input.

For purposes of further illustration, let us assume that output at time t is determined according to the Cobb–Douglas production function

$$Q_t = A.L_t^{\alpha}.K_t^{\beta}.e^{\theta.t} \qquad (6.10)$$

where t denotes time and where A, α, β and θ are positive constants. The exponential term in (6.10) is a trend term, which is included to capture shifts in the production function brought about by technical progress. Taking natural logarithms we obtain:

$$\ln Q_t = a + \alpha \ln L_t + \beta \ln K_t + \theta t \qquad (6.11)$$

where $a = \ln A$. Rearranging (6.11) we obtain the following expression for the firm's *desired* level of labour input L_t^* as

$$\ln L_t^* = a_0 + a_1 \ln Q_t + a_2 \ln K_t + a_3 t \qquad (6.12)$$

where

$$a_0 = -\frac{a}{\alpha}\ ;\ a_1 = \frac{1}{\alpha}\ ;\ a_2 = -\frac{\beta}{\alpha}\ ;\ a_3 = -\frac{\theta}{\alpha}$$

According to (6.12), the firm's desired level of labour input is positively related to the level of its output (Q_t) and negatively related to both the level of its capital input and a time trend. Given the major problems associated with attempts to measure the capital stock, it is common place in the literature – following Ball and St Cyr (1966) – to find writers asumming that growth in the firm's capital inputs, like technical progress, can be adequately represented by a time trend. In this case expression (6.12) simplifies to become

$$\ln L_t^* = \beta_0' + \beta_1 \ln Q_t + \beta_2 t \qquad (6.13)$$

where the coefficient β_2 now captures the combined effects of the growth of capital inputs and technical progress.[2] Expression (6.13) is the particular form of (6.9) which arises in the Cobb–Douglas case with a constant rate of growth of capital inputs. It is important to recognise that desired labour input in the above expressions is measured in *hours of labour*.

□ *Optimal hours–workers mix*

The employment function approach offers a convenient framework for modelling the firm's optimal mix between workers and hours of work. Letting the number of workers employed and the hours worked per employee be E and H respectively, we have the relationship

$$L = H.E$$

which indicates the possible combinations of workers (E) and hours worked (H) which can be used by the employer in order to achieve any particular level of labour input L (measured in hours). From the employer's viewpoint, we have seen that the choice of the optimal balance between workers and hours is influenced by the costs (including overtime premia) which arise when actual hours deviate from standard hours, relative to the magnitude of the various fixed costs associated with the employment of workers.

Following such writers as Brechling (1965), Wickens (1974) and Deaton (1982) we may write the employer's labour cost function as follows:

$$C = wEH + fE + cE(H - \bar{H})^2 \qquad (6.14)$$

where w denotes the wage rate for hours worked below standard hours ($\bar{H}$), and where f denotes the level of recurring fixed labour costs per worker. The last term in (6.14) captures the effects of deviations of hours per worker from the normal or standard level of hours (through progressively increasing overtime premia and short-time working compensation) assuming, in the usual way, that such costs depend on the *square* of the discrepancy between actual and standard hours, $(H - \bar{H})^2$, where c is a cost parameter.

In order to find the optimum length of the working day (say H^*) the employer minimises the labour cost function (6.14), subject to the expression $L^* = EH$. Substituting $E = L^*/H$ into (6.14) we obtain

$$C = wL^* + fL^*H^{-1} + cL^*H^{-1}(H - \bar{H})^2$$

Cost minimisation requires

$$\frac{dC}{dH} = -fL^*H^{-2} + cL^*(1 - \bar{H}^2H^{-2}) = 0$$

Dividing throughout by L^* and rearranging we obtain the optimal level of hours per worker as

$$H^* = (\bar{H}^2 + f/c)^{1/2} \qquad (6.15)$$

Notice from (6.15) that in the case where f (the level of recurring fixed labour costs) is zero, optimal hours are equal to standard hours. Conversely, the higher the level of fixed cost relative to the cost of deviating from standard hours (c), the higher is the optimal level of hours in relation to standard hours. Notice also that in cases where f, c and $\bar{H}$ remain constant through time, so also does the optimal length of working day H^*.

The employment demand function (6.13) gives an expression for the employer's desired level of labour hours and to obtain the optimal level of employment (say E^*) it is necessary to simply divide the desired level of hours given by (6.13) by H^*, to obtain $E^*_t (= L^*_t/H^*_t)$ as

$$\ln E^*_t = \beta_0 + \beta_1 \ln Q_t + \beta_2 t \tag{6.16}$$

where $\beta_0 = \beta_0' - \ln H^*$.

□ *Partial adjustment*

Equation (6.16) provides an expression describing the determinants of the firm's desired level of employment, measured in *persons*. The labour cost function (6.14) covers only employment costs, as opposed to those costs associated with the adjustment of the number of employees. These latter costs are the non-recurring fixed costs and these are typically brought into the analysis by recognising the distinction between the desired and actual levels of employment, E^*_t and E_t respectively. The transition between desired and actual employment is typically made by recognising that adjustments to actual employment involve (non-recurring fixed) costs of various sorts. When employment is increased, the employer incurs the various *hiring* costs already discussed; while a downward adjustment to the size of the workforce involves *firing* or severance costs. Because of the existence of such adjustment costs it is generally argued that only some fraction of the adjustment required to bring existing employment up to the desired level will be achieved during a single time period. This notion is captured by the well-known *partial adjustment model*, according to which only some fraction (say λ) of the desired employment change is achieved during the current time period. In its multiplicative form this process may be described by the following expression:

$$\frac{E_t}{E_{t-1}} = \left(\frac{E^*_t}{E_{t-1}}\right)^{\lambda}$$

where $0 \leqslant \lambda \leqslant 1$.

Taking logarithms this dynamic adjustment mechanism may be written as

$$\ln E_t - \ln E_{t-1} = \lambda\ (\ln E^*_t - E_{t-1}) \tag{6.17}$$

which says that starting from the previous existing level of employment, the proportional adjustment which is actually achieved is equal to some fraction of the proportional change required to achieve the desired level in the current period, E^*_t. Large values of λ imply rapid adjustment, while low values imply only slow adjustment. The adjustment speed λ is seen as being inversely related to the costs associated with adjustments in the workforce size, although in some particular formulations it is seen as being positively related to the rate of unemployment.

Substituting (6.16) into (6.17) and rearranging we obtain the following expression for the determinants of *actual* employment (E_t).

$$\ln E_t = \gamma_0 + \gamma_1 \ln Q_t + \gamma_2 t + \gamma_3 \ln E_{t-1} \quad (6.18)$$

where $\gamma_0 = \lambda\beta_0$; $\gamma_1 = \lambda\beta_1$; $\gamma_2 = \lambda\beta_2$; $\gamma_3 = (1-\lambda)$. According to (6.18) the employer's current level of actual employment is positively related to both output and its own value during the preceding period, with a negative time trend.

□ Some extensions

Although the simple approach described above provides a convenient framework within which to consider the effects of fixed labour costs upon the structure of the firm's demand for labour as between workers and hours, it is less than completely satisfactory in the sense that it finds no role for variations in input prices. This deficiency is, however, rectified in more complete formulations, which consider behaviour within either a cost-minimising or profit-maximising framework. If we opt for the less restrictive assumption of cost-minimisation, the employer's complete set of input demand functions can be derived from first-order conditions on either its production function or, via duality theory, its cost function (see Diewert, 1974). Beginning with the *duality* approach, it is necessary to simply assume that the employer-firm possesses a unit cost function of the form

$$c = c(Q{:}\mathbf{p}) = c(Q; p_1, p_2, \ldots, p_n)$$

where Q denotes output and where $\mathbf{p} = (p_1, p_2, \ldots, p_n)$ is a vector of input prices. Assuming that this function satisfies the usual regularity conditions (namely that it is positive, positive homogeneous of degree one, concave and differentiable with respect to input prices at point $\mathbf{p} = \mathbf{p}^*$) then, using Shepherd's lemma, we obtain the following expression

$$Q \frac{\partial c}{\partial p_i}(\mathbf{p}^*) = x_i\,(Q{:}\mathbf{p}^*) \qquad (i = 1, \ldots, n) \quad (6.19)$$

where $x_i\,(Q{:}\mathbf{p}^*)$ is the cost-minimising quantity of input i needed to produce Q units of output, given the vector of input prices $\mathbf{p}^*$. Equation (6.19) generates a system of cost-minimising input demand functions of the form

$$x_i = x_i\,(Q{:}\mathbf{p}) \qquad (i = 1, \ldots, n) \quad (6.20)$$

which specify the cost-minimising firm's optimal level of each of its inputs as a function of the quantity of output produced and the vector of factor input prices. For example, if the firm has only two inputs – labour and capital – with prices w and r respectively, equation (6.20) gives rise to the following pair of cost-minimising input demand functions

$$L = L(Q, w, r)$$

$$K = K(Q, r, w)$$

according to which the cost-minimising firm's optimal level of each input is given as a function of its output level, the input's own price, and the price of the other input. Comparing the first of these two expressions with the corresponding expression derived from the simple model discussed above (see equation (6.9)) for the general case, or (6.12) for the particular case of the Cobb–Douglas production function) we see that the cost minimisation approach gives rise to both the wage rate and the price of capital services as two additional determinants of the firm's optimal demand for its labour input.

The above generalises quite straightforwardly to the case where the firm employs more than two inputs – for example to the case where it employs several different types of both labour and capital. For example, if the firm employs two different types of labour – say skilled (L_s) and unskilled (L_u) at respective wage rates of w_s and w_u – its cost-minimising demand functions for labour may be written as follows

$$L_s = f(Q, w_s, w_u, r) \text{ and } L_u = g(Q, w_u, w_s, r)$$

according to which its demand for each type of labour is determined by output, its own wage, the wage of the other grade of labour and the price of its capital inputs.

An obvious advantage of the duality approach is its generality, in the sense that it allows the derivation of the employer-firm's set of factor demand equations without necessitating any more restrictive assumptions than cost minimisation and the existence of a unit cost function satisfying certain regularity conditions.

For those unfamiliar with duality theory, the same result may be obtained via the employer's production function as the dual of its unit cost function. To illustrate this approach, assume that the firm's total cost function is of the following extremely simple form,

$$C = wL + rK + F \tag{6.21}$$

with notation as above and with F denoting fixed costs.[3] Writing the firm's production function as

$$Q = Q\,(K, L) \tag{6.22}$$

with labour input L measured in person-hours, and assuming that the firm's objective is the minimisation of the costs of producing some given level of output Q, it minimises (6.21) subject to the production function constraint given by (6.22). Employing the usual Lagrange multiplier method, the firm minimises

$$Z = wL + rK + F + \lambda\, [Q - Q\,(K, L)]$$

The first-order conditions for minimisation are as follows:

$$\frac{\partial Z}{\partial L} = w - \lambda \frac{\partial Q}{\partial L} = 0$$

$$\frac{\partial Z}{\partial K} = r - \lambda \frac{\partial Q}{\partial K} - 0$$

$$\frac{\partial Z}{\partial \lambda} = Q - Q(K, L) = 0$$

Dividing the first condition by the second, recognising the partial derivatives of the production function as marginal physical products, we obtain the usual cost-minimising condition

$$\frac{\partial Q/\partial L}{\partial Q/\partial K} = \frac{MP_L}{MP_k} = \frac{w}{r} \tag{6.23}$$

Evaluating the partial derivatives of (6.22), substituting these into (6.23) and eliminating K as between the resulting expression and (6.22) we obtain the following demand for labour function

$$L = L\,(w/r,\, Q) \tag{6.24}$$

Comparing (6.24) with (6.9) above, we see that the price of labour relative to that of capital enters as an additional determinant of labour demand. If the firm's production function is of the Cobb–Douglas variety, as given by (6.10) above, then the employer's demand for labour function turns out as follows

$$\ln L_t^* = a_0 + a_1 \ln Q_t + a_2 t + a_3 \ln \left(\frac{w}{r}\right) \tag{6.25}$$

where (in terms of 6.10) $a_1 = \dfrac{1}{(\alpha+\beta)}$; $a_2 = \dfrac{-\theta}{(\alpha+\beta)}$ and $a_3 = \dfrac{-\beta}{(\alpha+\beta)}$

Comparing this to (6.13) above, we see that the hypothesis of cost-minimisation introduces the relative price of inputs as an additional determinant of the firm's desired labour input.[4] The negative sign of a_3 (given that $\alpha, \beta > 0$) indicates that, other things being equal, an increase in the price of labour relative to the price of capital results in a decrease in the firm's demand for labour input.[5]

■ Wages and productivity

The final extension to the basic model of labour demand to be discussed in this chapter concerns the possible influence of the wage rate upon the productivity of labour. The marginal productivity analysis discussed in Chapter 5 implicitly assumes that the position of labour's marginal physical product schedule is independent of the wage level. The potential implausibility of this assumption has a long track record in the labour economics literature (for example, Leibenstein, 1957) as well as business practice (see Raff and Summers, 1987). However, as we shall see in Chapter 14 below, the basic notion that labour productivity may be influenced by the wage rate paid to workers has become very fashionable of late, under the name of the *efficiency wage hypothesis*.

There are basically two routes through which a relationship between productivity and the wage rate may arise. First, there is the case where a wage increase raises the efficiency of workers, and second, there is the case where a wage increase improves the efficiency of management. The first of these mechanisms is generally referred to as the *economy of high wages* (Perlman, 1969, pp. 50–6), while the second is termed *shock theory* (King, 1990, p. 37). According to the economy of high wages argument, improved wages lead to higher levels of marginal productivity at given levels of employment through improvements in worker nutrition and health. This effect has frequently been found to be of importance in the context of less developed countries (see, for example, Todaro, 1989, pp. 35–7; Herrick and Kindleberger, 1983, p. 195). However, as we shall see later, the same sort of mechanism is sometimes seen as operating in developed economies, via the positive psychological effects thought to be associated with a higher wage. The basic argument lying behind the shock hypothesis is that the productivity of management is shocked into improving as the wage rate payable to the workforce increases. Underlying this hypothesis is the assumption that the employer-firm as an organisation is operating with a degree of slack or inefficiency, which has the potential to be reduced when the organisation becomes threatened in some way. The classic example here is that of a non-union plant which becomes unionised. If, under such circumstances, there is a sudden increase in wages from the non-union to the union level, it is often argued that special managerial emphasis will be placed upon eliminating inefficiencies in the usage of labour as the factor of production whose price has increased. As a consequence of this efficiency drive the marginal productivity of labour, at given levels of employment, is seen to increase.

Whether wages and labour productivity are linked via either economy

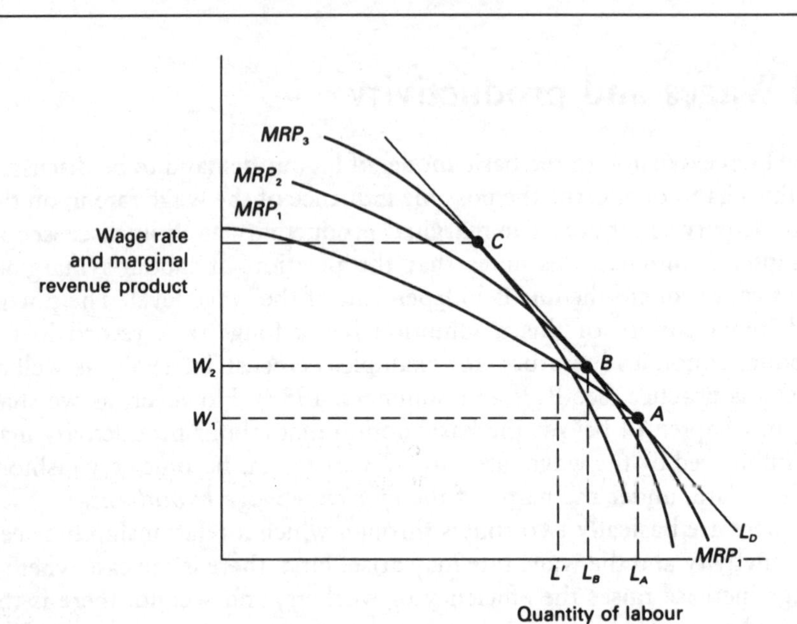

Figure 6.1 *Economics of high wages*

of high wages or shock effects, the analysis suggests that labour's marginal physical product schedule shifts upwards as the wage rate is increased. This situation is illustrated in **Figure 6.1**, where the curve marked MRP_1 denotes the firm's marginal revenue product schedule which was seen in Chapter 5 to also be the firm's short-run demand for labour curve. This equivalence, however, only applies in the case where labour's *MRP* schedule remains unmoved by variations in the wage rate. According to the above discussion, the position of the *MRP* schedule varies as the wage rate alters. For example, let us suppose that the schedule MRP_1 applies at the wage rate w_1, the schedule MRP_2 at wage w_2 and MRP_3 at w_3. **Figure 6.1** shows that in place of the single marginal revenue produce schedule of Chapter 5, we have a family of such schedules, with one corresponding to each wage rate and with higher wage rates generating higher marginal productivity schedules. The demand for labour curve under these circumstances is shown by L_D, which is the curve connecting the points *A*, *B* and *C* at which each wage rate intersects its own marginal revenue product schedule. As can be seen from **Figure 6.1**, the demand for labour curve in this case is more steeply sloped than say MRP_1 as the corresponding short-run labour demand curve in the case where productivity is unaffected by the wage level. This indicates that under conditions where productivity increases with the wage rate, the reduction in employment brought about by a wage increase will be less than would be the case on Chapter 5's assumption of a marginal productivity schedule whose position remains unchanged. For example, in the case of an increase in the wage rate from w_1 to w_2 the conventional short-run demand for labour curve (MRP_1) – based on a single marginal product schedule – indicates a fall in employment from L_A to L', whereas the demand curve L_D (which allows for the positive influence of wage rates upon productivity levels) indicates a fall of only $(L_A - L_B)$.

■ Notes

1. If $P_H(>0)$ denotes the productivity of overtime hours of existing employees *relative* to that of outside labour the corresponding condition becomes

$$\left(\frac{1+k}{P_H}\right) W \leqslant W+Z$$

According to the 'fatigue' hypothesis $P_H < 1$, from which we see that diminishing productivity of overtime hours means that employers will continue to offer overtime hours to existing workers, in preference to hiring outsiders, up until the point where the *combined* effects of overtime premia and increasing fatigue make the hiring of outsiders the more attractive alternative.

2. If the firm's inputs of capital services are growing at a constant proportional rate δ, the coefficient of the trend-term in expression (6.13) is given by

$$\beta_2 = -\frac{1}{\alpha}(\delta\beta+\theta) = a_2\delta + a_3$$

3. This formulation ignores, in the interests of simplification, both the fixed employment costs and the costs associated with deviations of hours from standard hours, as discussed above. To bring these into the picture, it is necessary to minimise (6.14), rather than (6.21), subject to the employer's production function. See Ball and St Cyr (1966) or Brechling (1965) for such an approach.
4. The analysis of the text has concentrated on cost-minimising models. If we wished to make the more restrictive assumption of profit-maximising behaviour the following analysis would apply (see Briscoe and Peel, 1975, p. 118). To maximise profits the firm must satisfy the usual condition from Chapter 5, according to which $w = (\partial Q/\partial L)P$, where both the labour market and product market are assumed to be perfectly competitive, with P denoting the price of output. Assuming that the firm possesses a short-run production function of the form $Q = Q(L, t)$, where the trend term t captures the effects of technical progress and differentiating, we obtain $\partial Q/\partial L = Q'(L, t)$ which, given the particular form of the production function (for example, the Cobb–Douglas case), we assume may be written as $Q'(L, t) = f(Q, L, t)$. Thus profit maximisation requires that $w/P = f(Q, L, t)$ and solving for L we

obtain the profit-maximising firm's desired demand for labour services (in person-hours) as

$$L^* = L(w/P, Q, t)$$

which is seen to be of the same general form as (6.9) above, except that the product real wage w/P also arises as a determinant of the firm's demand for labour.

5. An extensive literature of empirical studies of labour demand exists and much of this is well-surveyed by Hamermesh (1986). Demand for labour functions are often an important ingredient in models of macro economies. For a discussion of the treatment of labour demand in alternative models of the UK economy see Wallis *et al.* (1984).

■ Chapter 7 ■

Wage and Employment Determination

■ Introduction

At the simplest level of analysis, wages, viewed as the price of labour, are seen as being straightforwardly determined by the intersection of labour demand and supply curves in the market for labour. This view is clearly illustrated in the opening sentence of Hicks's *Theory of Wages*, first published in 1932. According to Hicks:

> The theory of the determination of wages in a free market is simply a special case of the general theory of value. Wages are the price of labour; and thus, in the absence of control, they are determined, like all prices, by supply and demand. (1932, p. 1)

This is the approach adopted in the first part of this chapter, where the models discussed in Chapters 2 and 5 are brought together in a simple analysis of the determination of the levels of wages and employment in the market for labour. It is important, however, to recognise that this approach represents a starting, and not a finishing, point. As we have already begun to see in Chapters 3, 4 and 6 above, the analogy between labour and the standard or stylised commodities analysed in price theory is far from adequate.

Although over sixty years ago Hicks himself cautioned against such a naive approach to labour market analysis, this point is all too often overlooked. As Crossley (1973, p. 213) pointed out, those who cite the above quote from Hicks all too frequently fail to quote the remainder of the paragraph which is as follows:

> The need for a special theory of wages only arises because both the supply of labour, and the demand for it, and the way demand and supply interact on the labour market, have certain peculiar properties, which make it impossible to apply to labour the ordinary theory of commodity value without some further consideration. (1932, p. 1)

Some of the peculiar properties of labour (including the fixed costs associated with the employment of labour) have already been introduced. However, the later sections of this chapter go on to highlight some of the further peculiarities associated with labour as a factor of production. Indeed, it is the special characteristics of labour (which distinguish it from the textbook notion of a commodity) to which the remaining chapters of this book are devoted.

We begin this chapter by considering the simplest of all possible cases, namely that of a firm operating in a perfectly competitive labour market. The analysis is then modified to take account of the existence of monopsony in the market for labour. The disequilibrium approach to labour market modelling is discussed in the following section.

Wages and employment determination at the level of the firm: the perfectly competitive labour market

The individual firm's demand for labour under various product market conditions and simplifying assumptions was considered in Chapter 5, where it was shown that the profit-maximising firm's short-run demand curve for labour is the schedule of its marginal revenue product. In Chapters 2 and 3 we considered the forces that determine the amount of labour supplied by individuals and households, and in order to analyse the firm's wage and employment decisions it is necessary to consider how the labour supply behaviour of individual workers and households manifests itself to the individual firm as an employer of labour.

Reference was made in Chapter 5 to the perfectly competitive labour market. Under this labour market structure there are a large number of individual, perfectly informed, buyers and sellers of homogeneous labour, and workers are assumed to be perfectly mobile. Under these

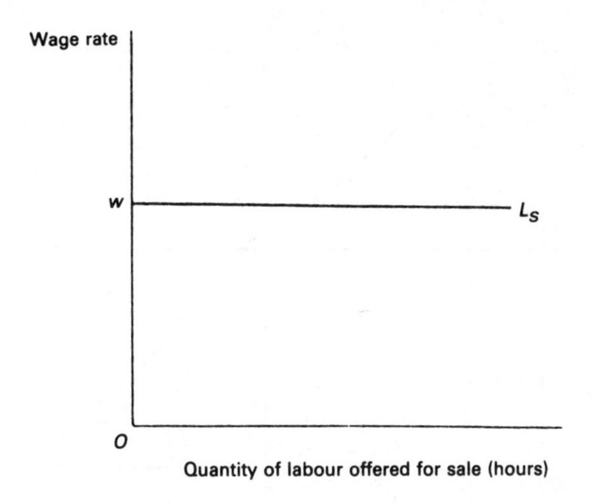

Figure 7.1 ***Perfectly elastic labour supply curve***

conditions the individual firm as a purchaser of labour is able to hire as much labour as it wishes at the prevailing market wage, which itself is determined in the broader market for the type of labour in question of which this particular firm makes up a small part. Thus, in a perfectly competitive labour market, the individual firm, like all others in the market, faces a perfectly elastic supply curve for its labour input, indicating that it is unable to exert any influence on the prevailing wage rate by varying its purchases of labour.

This situation is illustrated in **Figure 7.1**. The perfectly elastic labour supply curve (L_s) at the going wage rate (w) indicates that the individual firm is a price-taker in the market for its labour input. If it offers a wage of less than w, the firm will be unable to attract any labour, because workers will supply their labour to other firms and obtain the going wage (w). It has no incentive to offer a wage in excess of w, because it can recruit any amount of labour that it requires at wage w. The case of a single employer of a particular sort of labour (such as secretarial staff of a particular degree of word-processing competency) in a large metropolitan area is often cited as an example of a situation where an employer faces a perfectly elastic labour supply curve.

In a perfectly competitive labour market the individual firm faces a given wage rate, and its problem is to select its level of employment, and hence output, in such a way as to maximise its profits. This situation was considered in Chapter 5, where it was shown that the firm maximises its profits in the short run by employing labour up to the point where the money wage equals labour's marginal revenue product (*MRP*). Graphically, the firm's profit-maximising wage–employment combination is

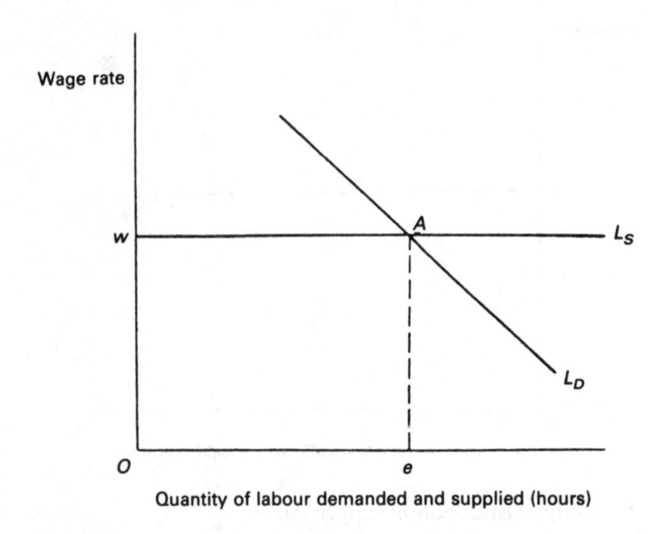

Figure 7.2 ***Wage and employment determination under perfect competition***

found at the point of intersection of its labour demand curve and its perfectly elastic labour supply curve.

In **Figure 7.2** L_D is the firm's short-run labour demand curve and L_s its labour-supply curve, and from their intersection at point *A* we see that the firm's equilibrium level of employment is *e* labour hours. The fact that a firm is a perfect competitor in the market for its labour input need not imply anything about the competitive conditions that it faces in its product market. As we have seen, the firm's short-run labour demand function (L_D) is its *MRP* curve. If it is a perfect competitor in its product market it follows that it is in equilibrium at the point where the wage rate equals the value of the marginal product. On the other hand, if the firm is an imperfect competitor in its product market, its *MRP* curve is more steeply sloping than its value of marginal product (*VMP*) curve (look again at **Figures 5.4**(**d**) and **5.5**). It therefore follows that the firm's equilibrium in this case is at the point where the money wage equals labour's marginal physical product (*MPP*) multiplied by marginal revenue (*MR*). Because the wage rate is given to the firm that hires its labour in a perfectly competitive labour market, it should be noted that in this case the marginal productivity theory of labour demand becomes in effect a theory of employment at the level of the individual firm (Cartter, 1959, p. 45).

■ Monopsony in the labour market

A case of some importance arises if we drop the assumption of perfect competition on the buyers' side of the labour market (while retaining, for the time being, the assumption of perfect competition among the sellers of labour) in favour of the assumption that the firm is the sole purchaser of the type of labour in question – the case of *monopsony*. In the case where there is perfect competition on the buyers' side of the labour market, the individual firm faces a perfectly elastic labour supply curve at the prevailing wage (w), and its marginal labour cost (MLC) (that is, the amount that the employment of an additional unit of labour adds to its wage bill) is therefore equal to w. If the firm is a large enough employer of labour for its decisions about the quantity of labour to employ to affect the wage rate, it is said to possess a degree of monopsony power. In the same way that a product market monopolist faces a downward-sloping demand curve for its product, indicating that the price of the product varies inversely with sales, so the monopsonistic purchaser of labour faces an upward-sloping labour supply curve. This indicates that the wage rate paid by the monopsonist for labour is an increasing function of the quantity that is hired.[1]

Figure 7.3 shows the upward-sloping labour supply curve (L_S) faced by a monopsonist. This curve indicates that in order to attract additional units of labour the monopsonist must offer a higher wage rate. Such a

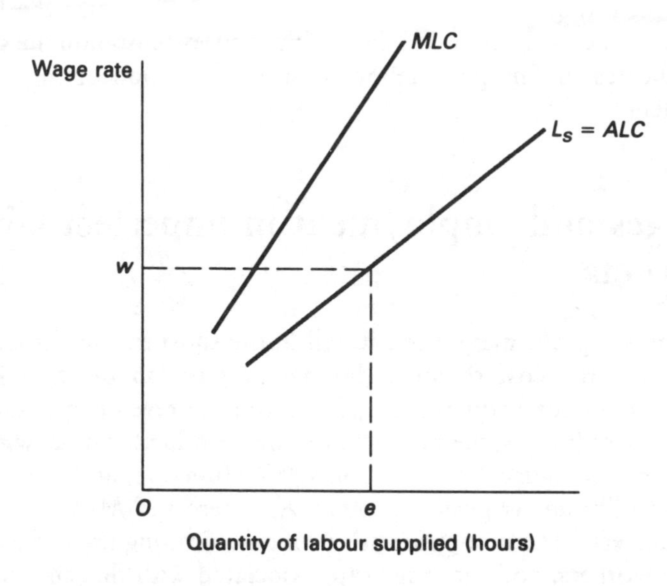

Figure 7.3 *Monopsonist's labour supply curve*

situation arises when the firm is the sole purchaser of a certain type of labour in a particular locality or *local labour market*. The upward slope of its labour supply curve indicates that in order to obtain extra units of this type of labour, it is necessary for the firm to increase the wage that it offers[2] in order to attract suitable workers from firms in other localities, to attract suitable workers who may have chosen non-participation or work in other occupations within the locality, and to encourage existing workers to increase their supply of hours (although the possibility that the individual's labour supply curve may become backward-sloping should be recalled).[3] Alternatively, monopsony may arise in practice when purchasers of labour combine to form an employers' association that acts as a single purchasing entity in the labour market – the case of *collusive monopsony*.

If the firm is a *non-discriminating monopsonist*, it pays each unit of its labour input the same wage rate, which is therefore equal to its average labour cost (*ALC*), and this means that its marginal labour cost is greater than the wage rate at each level of employment. To attract an additional worker the monopsonist must offer a wage in excess of that which he currently pays to those already in his employment, and in the absence of discrimination he must also increase the wage of each existing employee to the new level. The addition to the wage bill that results from the employment of an additional worker (that is, the marginal labour cost) is the wage that is offered to attract the marginal worker plus the extra amounts that have to be paid to existing workers to bring their wage to the new level. **Figure 7.3** illustrates the labour supply curve facing the non-discriminating monopsonist, and the steeper curve indicates the marginal labour cost as a function of the level of employment.

Wages and employment in imperfect labour markets

If the firm is a profit-maximiser, it will in the short run set its employment so that the cost of an additional unit of labour (that is, the marginal labour cost) equals the addition to total revenue generated by its employment (that is, the marginal revenue product). The downward-sloping curve in **Figure 7.4** is the firm's *MRP* function, and the monopsonist's equilibrium is given by point *A*, where the *MLC* and *MRP* curves intersect.[4] The monopsonist's profit-maximising level of employment is *e* workers, and the wage rate associated with this employment level is *w*, the ordinate of the supply curve at point *B*.[5]

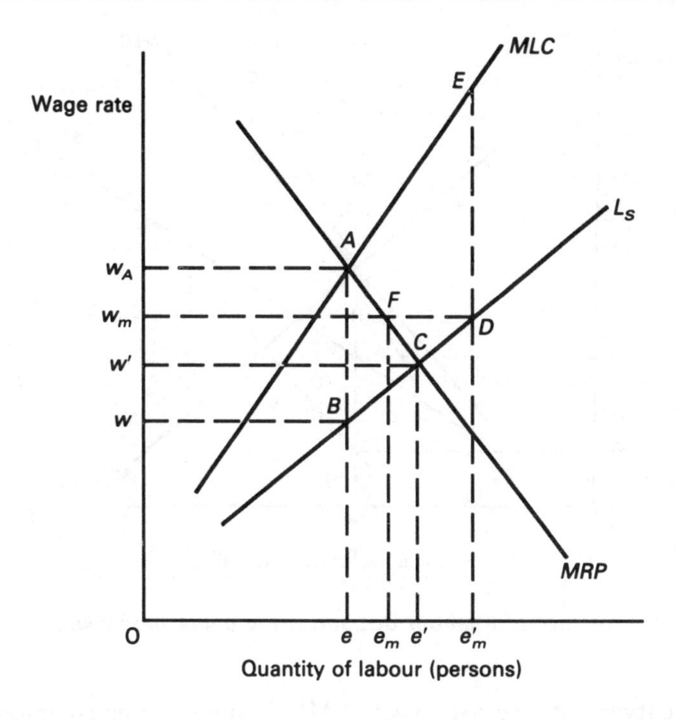

Figure 7.4 *Monopsony*

It should be noted that the monopsonist's *MRP* curve is not his short-run labour demand curve. In the same way that a monopolistic seller does not possess a supply curve for his product (see, for example, Begg, Fischer and Dornbusch, 1991, pp. 152–5), so the monopsonistic purchaser of labour has no labour demand curve. This is because there exists for a monopsonist no unique functional relationship between the quantity of labour demanded and the wage rate. As can be seen from **Figure 7.4**, the monopsonist's equilibrium employment level is determined as *e* by the intersection of the *MLC* and *MRP* curves, and the equilibrium wage rate is *w*, the ordinate of the labour supply curve corresponding to this employment level. However, the wage at which the profit-maximising monopsonist seeks to hire this quantity of labour is not uniquely determined by the *MRP* curve and its point of intersection with the *MLC* curve; it depends also on the elasticity of the labour supply curve. The absence of a labour demand curve under monopsony is illustrated in **Figure 7.5**, which shows how with a given *MRP* curve the same quantity of labour (*e*) can be demanded at different wage rates (w and w_0), according to the shape of the labour supply curve. This situation occurs under monopsony because differently shaped labour

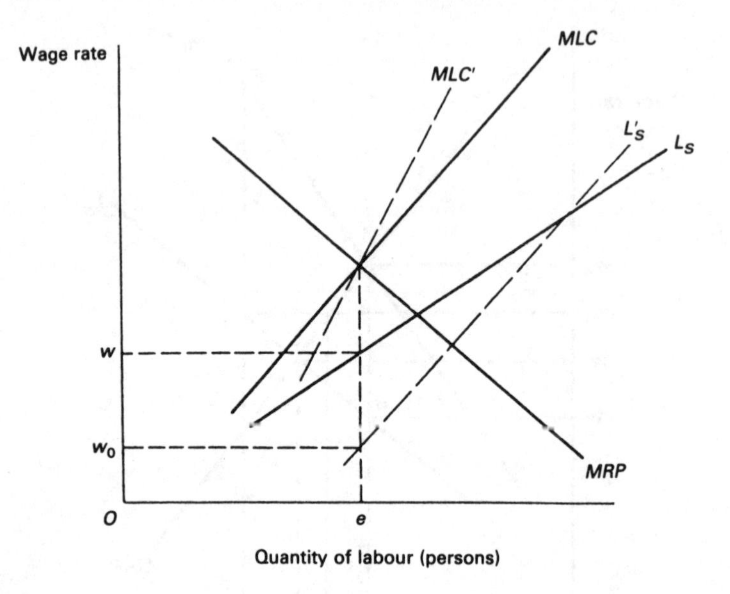

Figure 7.5 ***Absence of a labour demand curve under monopsony***

supply curves can give rise to equal *MLC* values at a given employment level.

In the same way that the existence of monopoly in the product market results in a lower level of output and a higher price than when there is perfect competition, the existence of monopsony in the labour market results in levels of employment and wages that are each lower than the corresponding perfectly competitive levels. In **Figure 7.4** the monopsonist's equilibrium position is at point *A*, where employment is *e* and the wage rate is *w*. Since the monopsonist is the *sole* purchaser of the type of labour in question in the particular labour market, the labour supply curve that he faces is in fact the market labour supply curve. If this labour market were perfectly competitive, with a market labour demand curve identical to the *MRP* curve facing the monopsonist, market equilibrium would be established at point *C*. At this point the wage rate equals the marginal revenue product of labour, giving employment e' and w', both of which are greater than the corresponding equilibrium values under monopsony. Because the monopsonist faces an upward-sloping supply curve for labour, he realises that by increasing his level of employment he will drive up the wage rate. He therefore maximises profits by expanding employment only to *A*, where marginal labour cost equals marginal revenue product, stopping short of the perfectly competitive equilibrium point at *C*. It is important to remember that the analysis so far has assumed the absence of any monopoly on the sellers' side of the labour market. This assumption will, however, be relaxed in Chapters 10 and 11 below when we consider trade unions as monopoly sellers of their members' labour services.

■ The imposition of a minimum wage

In a perfectly competitive labour market the imposition of a minimum wage, if it is set above the equilibrium level, results in a reduction of employment below its equilibrium value. However, the imposition of such a minimum wage under monopsony can, under certain circumstances, result in an *increase* in the level of employment.

If the labour market of **Figure 7.4** was perfectly competitive, with a market demand schedule equal to the monopsonist's *MRP* curve, the effective imposition (by legislation, or by a trade union perhaps) of a minimum wage of w_m would result in a contraction of employment from the competitive equilibrium level e' to e_m. At the same time the quantity of labour supplied would expand from e' to e'_m, giving rise to an excess supply of labour of $(e'_m - e_m)$ units at the minimum wage. Note that this excess supply is made up of two components: first, the $(e' - e_m)$ workers who have lost their employment as a result of the rise in the wage rate from w' to w_m and second, the $(e'_m - e')$ workers who are now attracted to offer their labour for hire by the higher wage rate.

In contrast, the imposition of a minimum wage above the equilibrium one can, under certain circumstances, lead to an *increase* in the amount of labour employed by a monopsonist. In the absence of the minimum wage, the monopsonist's equilibrium employment in **Figure 7.4** is e at wage w. If a minimum wage of w_m is imposed, *and effectively enforced*, the monopsonist's labour supply curve is no longer L_S but becomes w_mDL_S. This is because at any wage rate below w_m the firm cannot hire any labour at all, while at the wage rate w_m it can hire any amount of labour up to e'_m units. The monopsonist's marginal labour cost is no longer the *MLC* curve in **Figure 7.4** but becomes instead w_mDEMLC, which intersects its *MRP* curve at point *F*, giving rise to an equilibrium level of employment of e_m (equal to the level brought about by the same minimum wage in the perfectly competitive case). This is larger than the previous employment level (e) despite an increase in the wage rate from w to w_m. For this effect to occur, the minimum wage must lie between w and w_A. If it were set above w_A, its effect would be to reduce the level of employment, as in the perfectly competitive case.

Discriminating monopsony

So far we have considered the case where the monopsonistic employer pays each and every one of the workers whom he employs the same wage rate. In this section we consider the case of a discriminating monopsonist (that is, one who does not pay all of his employees the same wage rate). At the extreme is the case of the perfectly discriminating monopsonist, who pays each of his employees a different wage rate. However, in the absence of a piece-work or other incentive-payment system, the scope for paying different hourly wages to different workers doing the same work may in practice be fairly limited, particularly in the case of manual workers, where there is often a strong tradition of equal pay for equal work, plus a general knowledge of wage rates actually being paid. The scope for monopsonistic discrimination is somewhat larger in the case of white-collar and professional workers, where information on the earnings of others is often less than perfect and where remuneration is frequently, by tradition, confidential and often determined on an individual basis according to merit and other considerations. As we have seen, overtime payment systems are a form of discrimination in the payment of the labour hours of given workers, and other cases where monopsonistic discrimination may arise are in the payment of workers of different sexes, races and ages (but see Chapter 9 below).

In its most extreme form monopsonistic discrimination involves paying each worker only his/her supply price. In this case, which is termed *perfect discrimination*, the monopsonist must offer a higher wage to attract an additional worker, but it is not necessary to increase the wage of any existing worker to the new level. The monopsonist pays the higher wage to the marginal worker only and continues to pay those already employed only their supply prices (that is, the minimum amounts necessary to keep them in his employment). To the non-discriminating monopsonist the labour supply curve (L_s in **Figure 7.4**) shows the average labour cost as a function of the level of employment, but to the perfect discriminator this curve shows the marginal labour cost at each employment level. Therefore, the perfect discriminator's profit-maximising position is at point C in **Figure 7.4**, where the marginal labour cost equals the marginal revenue product. Notice that the perfect discriminator's equilibrium position with respect to the numbers employed is the same as that of an otherwise identical perfectly competitive market. However, although these equilibria give rise to the same wage employment combination they do differ from the distributional viewpoint. In the perfectly competitive case the area in the rectangle $Ow'Ce'$ represents the wage bill, while the remaining area under the

MRP curve represents capital's share of total revenue product. In the perfect discrimination case the wage bill comprises only that part of the rectangle $Ow'Ce'$ that lies under the labour supply curve (L_s), while the remainder of total revenue product accrues to capital.

Discrimination of a lower degree can arise when a monopsonist is able to purchase labour inputs in two different markets. For discrimination of this sort to be feasible, two conditions must be satisfied: (1) the elasticities of labour supply must differ between the two markets and (2) the markets must be separate, in the sense that it is not possible for suppliers of labour in one market to transfer their labour to the other one. This situation is depicted in **Figure 7.6**(**a**) to (**c**). Diagrams (**a**) and (**b**) show the labour supply and *MLC* functions in each separate market, and diagram (**c**) shows the monopsonist's *MRP* function and the curves ΣMLC and ΣL_S, which are obtained by horizontal summation of the *MLC* and L_S curves for each separate market. For example, at wage w the first market supplies e_1 units of labour and the second market e_2 units, so that at this wage the combined market supplies the quantity e of labour ($= e_1 + e_2$), as shown by the curve ΣL_S.

If the monopsonist were unable to discriminate, he would pay the same wage for each worker regardless of the market in which the worker is hired. As can be seen from **Figures 7.6**(**a**) and (**b**), the payment of the common wage, say w (which is equal to the non-discriminating monopsonist's profit-maximising wage rate), gives rise to a different marginal labour cost in each market (that is, C_A compared to C_B). If the monopsonist were able to discriminate by paying a different wage in each market, he would clearly be able to reduce the wage costs associated with a given level of employment by decreasing his purchases of labour in the second market and substituting in their place units of labour hired in the first market, where the marginal labour cost is lower.

In a similar way to that in which a discriminating monopolist maximises profits by equating the marginal revenue in each market to the marginal cost of the output as a whole, so the discriminating monopsonist maximises profits by equating the marginal labour cost in each market to the marginal revenue product of his labour force as a whole. The monopsonist's equilibrium level of employment is determined by the point of intersection of the *MRP* curve and the combined *MLC* curve, and the employment of the amount of labour thus determined is allocated between the two submarkets in such a way that the marginal labour cost in each market is equalised. The discriminating monopsonist's equilibrium level of employment is shown in **Figure 7.6**(**c**) as e workers, e_A of whom are hired in the first and e_B in the second market. Although the marginal labour cost is equal in each market (indeed, this is a necessary condition for profit maximisation), the wage paid in each,

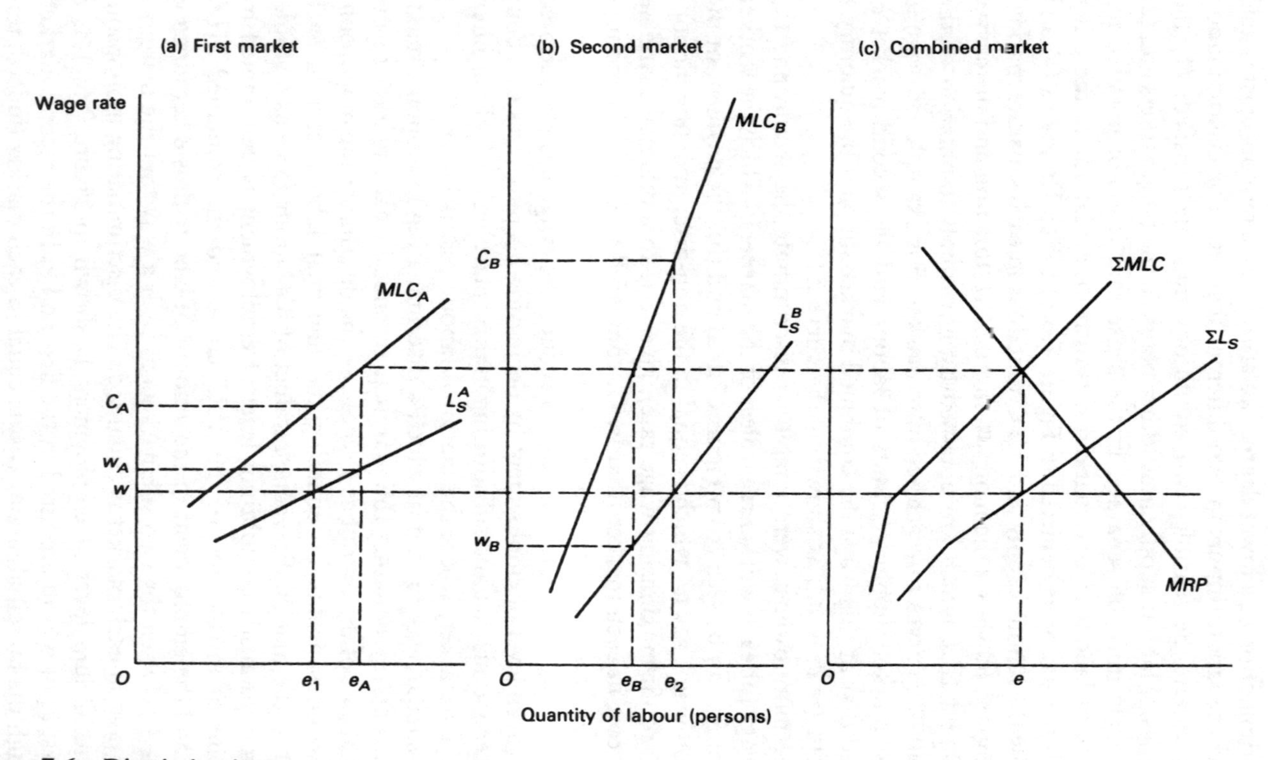

Figure 7.6 *Discriminating monopsony*

as indicated by the ordinate of the relevant supply curve at the employment level in question, differs. Labour hired in the first market is paid wage w_A, while labour hired in the second is paid only w_B. It should be noted too that discriminating monopsony results in the payment of a lower wage in the market where the elasticity of labour supply is lower.

Disequilibrium models of the labour market

One common feature of the models considered in the early part of this chapter is the assumption of market clearing, with the wage rate being determined at the intersection of demand and supply curves, as the two blades of the Marshallian scissors. There does, however, exist a body of literature which focuses its attention on the existence of disequilibrium in the labour market and it is to such models that we turn our attention in this section.

In order to illustrate this issue, consider the following model of the aggregate market for labour

$$L_t^D = \alpha_0 + \alpha_1 w_t + \alpha_2 \mathbf{Z}_t^D \tag{7.1}$$

$$L_t^S = \beta_0 + \beta_1 w_t + \beta_2 \mathbf{Z}_t^S \tag{7.2}$$

Equation (7.1) is the demand for labour function and equation (7.2) the labour supply function: both of which are assumed, for simplicity, to be linear. Subscript t denotes time and $\mathbf{Z}^D$ and $\mathbf{Z}^S$ represent the sets (vectors) of variables, apart from the money wage rate (w), which influence the employment decisions of firms and the labour supply decisions of individuals respectively. These two equations are common to a range of alternative approaches to modelling the labour market (Andrews, 1988): with the alternatives differing, amongst other things, according to their assumptions regarding what is observed and how the wage rate is determined.

The equilibrium approach adds the market clearing assumption (7.3) to the model:

$$L_t^D = L_t^S = L_t \tag{7.3}$$

according to which the wage rate is determined simply as that value which makes $L_t^D = L_t^S =$ (say) L_t, where L_t is observed. This model is illustrated in **Figure 7.7**, where w indicates the equilibrium/market-clearing wage rate. Algebraically, substituting (7.1) and (7.2) into (7.3) and solving for w_t, we obtain the following expression for the equilibrium wage

$$w_t = \frac{\beta_0 - \alpha_0}{(\alpha_1 - \beta_1)} + \frac{\beta_2 Z_t^S}{(\alpha_1 - \beta_1)} - \frac{\alpha_2 Z_t^D}{(\alpha_1 - \beta_1)} \tag{7.4}$$

Notice from (7.4) that this model gives rise to a unique value of the wage (indicated by w in **Figure** 7.7) on the assumption that other things (namely the values of $\mathbf{Z}^S$ and $\mathbf{Z}^D$) remain equal. Substituting the equilibrium wage given by (7.4) back into either (7.1) or (7.2) gives the equilibrium level of employment, shown by L in **Figure 7.7**.

In its simplest form (for example, Rosen and Quandt, 1978), the disequilibrium model differs from the equilibrium model by abandoning assumption (7.3) of market clearing in favour of the following assumption

$$L_t = \min\,(L_t^D, L_t^S) \tag{7.5}$$

The disequilibrium approach recognises that the level of employment (L_t) may under some circumstances coincide with labour demand, while under other circumstances it may coincide with labour supply. According to assumption (7.5) the level of employment is equal to whichever is the lesser of the two. The model given by (7.1), (7.2) and (7.5) is sometimes termed the *discrete disequilibrium approach* and its distinguishing feature is its assumption that the observed quantity actually traded will always be on the 'short side' of the market. Such an approach may be justified in terms of the concept of *voluntary exchange*, according to which a labour demand or supply curve may be thought of as defining the maximum amount of labour which will be voluntarily exchanged at a given wage rate. For instance, at the wage rate w_2 in **Figure** 7.7 employers are offered a greater quantity of labour than they seek to hire at the given wage. Left to their own devices employers will not seek to hire a greater quantity of labour than indicated by their demand curve L^D, with the consequence that at wages, such as w_1, in excess of w the amount of labour hired (the level of employment) will be equal to labour demand. Conversely, at wages, such as w_2, below w employers are offered a smaller quantity than they demand at the given wage, but they will nevertheless accept this trade as profitable because, as we saw in Chapter 5, the marginal revenue product of labour at this level of employment will exceed the wage rate w_2. Accordingly, at wages below w the quantity of labour hired will be equal to labour supply. Assumption (7.5) therefore implies that all possible wage rate–employment combinations lie along the *kinked frontier*, indicated by *AEB* in **Figure 7.7**. This frontier indicates that trading can take place in the labour market in question at wages other than the equilibrium wage.

In contrast to the equilibrium model, which implies the existence of a unique wage–employment combination at *E*, the disequilibrium for-

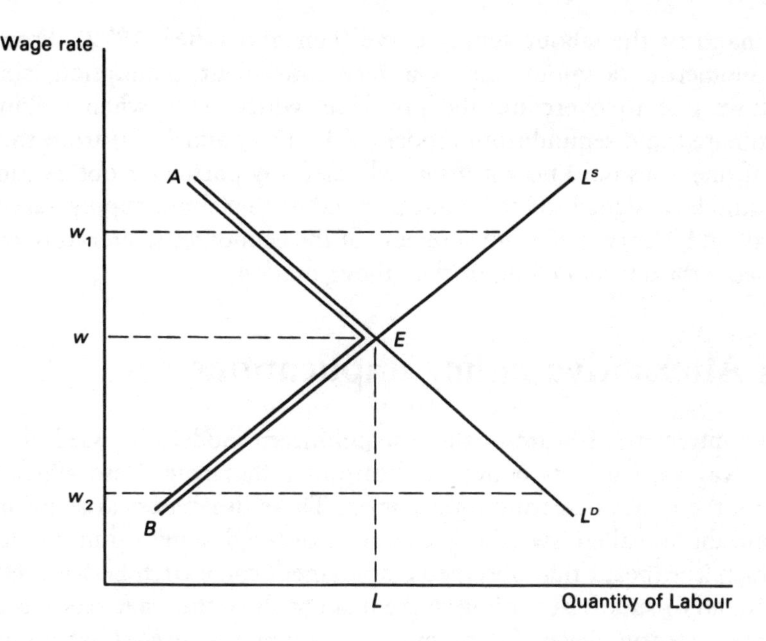

Figure 7.7 ***Equilibrium versus disequilibrium in the labour market***

mulation implies that the wage rate–employment combination can lie anywhere along the locus represented by the frontier *AEB*.

The disequilibrium model is closed by the specification of an additional assumption regarding the dynamic behaviour of wages. The usual assumption is as follows:

$$w_t = w_{t-1} + \gamma(L_t^D - L_t^S),\ \gamma > 0 \tag{7.6}$$

Equation (7.6) is a dynamic adjustment equation for wages, according to which the wage will rise if labour demand exceeds labour supply, and fall if labour supply exceeds labour demand. The speed at which the wage rate converges over time towards the market-clearing wage is determined by the size of the parameter γ. If γ is large, the disequilibrium model moves quickly towards equilibrium. Conversely, if γ is small then disequilibrium in the market for labour persists for a considerable period of time. Empirical estimates of γ are of interest because they provide us with some evidence of how closely the market-clearing formulation approximates the disequilibrium model. The adjustment mechanism (7.6) may be rewritten as

$$L_t^D - L_t^S = \frac{1}{\gamma}\,\Delta\, w_t \tag{7.7}$$

from which it is seen that the direction of wage movement serves as an exact guide as to whether any particular observation lies on the labour demand or the labour supply curve (Fair and Jaffee, 1972). From the econometric viewpoint this is a very convenient assumption, since it allows one to overcome the problems which arise when seeking to estimate the disequilibrium model ((7.1), (7.2) and (7.5)) from the fact that one does not know *a priori* whether any particular observation L_t should be assigned to the labour demand or the labour supply curve (see Hall and Henry, 1988, for a review of the econometric literature on the disequilibrium modelling of the labour market).

Alternative policy implications

One interesting feature of the disequilibrium model discussed above is the way in which its policy implications differ from those which flow from the market-clearing formulation. These differences arise primarily from the so-called 'switching' character of the disequilibrium model, by which it is meant that observed employment can switch between labour demand or supply according to the magnitude of the wage relative to the market-clearing level. At any moment in time the disequilibrium model sees the labour market as being either demand-constrained or supply-constrained. As a consequence of this, the effect of variations in one or more of the elements of the $\mathbf{Z}$ vectors in (7.1) and (7.2) will depend crucially upon the regime which is operating in the labour market at the moment in question.

Consider, for example, the shift in the labour demand curve from L^D to $L^{D'}$ shown in **Figure 7.7**. Such a shift might arise from an increase in expected output (brought about by, say, a reduction in direct taxation as an expansionary fiscal policy) if we are thinking of the sorts of labour demand functions discussed in Chapter 6. According to the market-clearing model, the effect of this increase in the conditions of labour demand, brought about by the expansionary fiscal policy, is to increase the equilibrium levels of both the wage rate and the employment level, to w' and L' respectively. However, the effects of this same policy will, according to the disequilibrium model, differ depending on whether the labour market is demand- or supply-constrained. For example, if the wage rate were fixed at w_1 ($< w$), employment is determined by the supply side of the market and we see that a policy aimed at the demand side of the labour market has no effect on the level of employment, which remains unchanged at L_1. In other words, an increase in anticipated output will be ineffective as a policy instrument when the labour market is supply-constrained. In contrast, the same policy can exert powerful employment effects when the labour market is demand-constrained. For instance, if the wage rate is fixed at w_2 ($>$ w), the

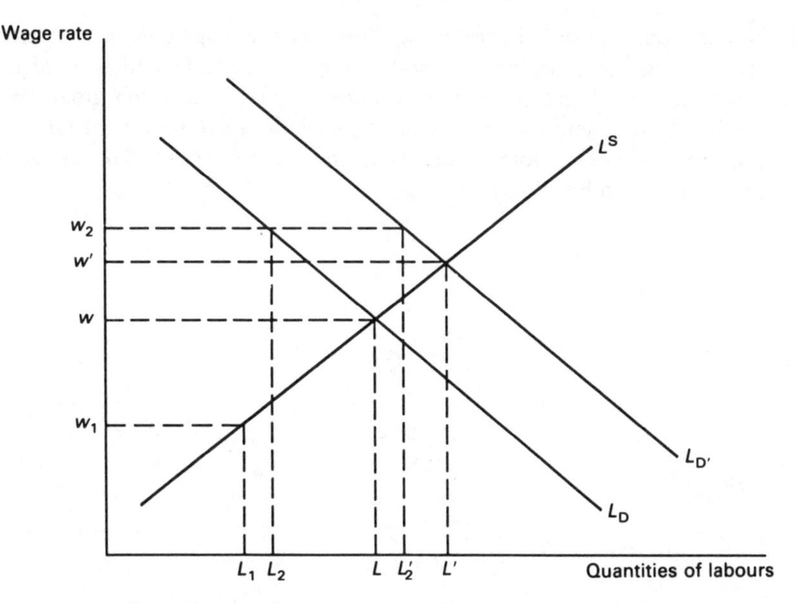

Figure 7.8 ***Policy effectiveness: equilibrium versus disequilibrium models***

labour market is dominated by the labour demand function and the policy has the effect of increasing the level of employment from L_2 to L_2'.

■ Notes

1. For further discussion, see Cartter (1959, pp. 52–6).
2. This assumes the absence of unemployed workers, of the appropriate type, in the firm's local labour market. If, however, a pool of unemployed workers exists at the prevailing wage rate, it is possible for the firm to increase its employment by the extent of the unemployment, without increasing its wage rate. Thereafter, the monopsonistic firm faces a positively sloping labour supply curve. In addition, it is sometimes argued that, if labour is not homogeneous, the employer may, in order to attract additional workers, lower employment standards. In this case, even though the wage rate per worker may remain unchanged, the wage per *efficiency unit* of labour rises, with the consequence that the employer faces an upward-sloping supply curve of labour in efficiency units. For further discussion, see Cartter (1959, pp. 52–4).
3. There is an extensive literature concerning the nature and functioning of local labour markets. See, in particular, Robinson (1970) and MacKay *et al.* (1971).
4. Notice that employment in this case is measured in numbers of workers rather than hours, on the basis of the simplifying assumption that at each wage rate all persons work a constant number of hours.

5. Notice from **Figure 7.4** that, in equilibrium, the wage paid by the monopsonist (w) is less than labour's marginal revenue product (that is, w_A). The extent to which the wage rate diverges from labour's marginal revenue product is frequently seen as a measure of the *exploitation* of labour – a concept discussed in some detail by Cartter (1959, pp. 65–70). See also the early discussion by Bloom (1941).

■ Chapter 8 ■

The Distribution of Pay

■ Introduction

Labour earnings are the benefit to a worker from selling his labour in the market and the cost to the employer for hiring the worker's labour services.[1] Thus labour earnings depend on the amount of labour supplied to and demanded in the labour market. The determination of *the level* of labour earnings in individual cases (for example within the context of individual labour supply and in representative labour markets) was discussed in the previous chapter. There the generic term 'wages' was used instead of 'labour earnings'. In this chapter we are concerned with three different aspects of how labour earnings are distributed depending on whether reference is made to the whole economy, to individual workers or to individual markets.

First, we examine the proportion of national income that constitutes labour earnings (another term that is applicable in the present discussion is 'employee compensation'). This aspect is called the *functional* distribution of income and refers basically to how national income is divided between, on the one hand, income from employment and, on the other hand, income from all other sources. This distinction is an important one as it helps us understand the position of labour earnings within the whole economy – a topic much favoured by classical economists who were concerned with the share of the nation's wealth that accrued to landlords, as a class, rather than to the rest of the population, primarily landless workers.

Second, we look at how labour earnings are distributed among individual workers. This constitutes the *size* (or frequency) distribution of labour earnings.

Third, and finally, we examine how 'pay varies' across some well-defined sectors – such as occupations, industries, regions and so on. In the last case we have avoided saying how 'pay is distributed' in order to conform with the established jargon among economists who refer in this case to occupational (or industrial, regional and so on) *pay differentials*.

Note that labour earnings are only a subset of the total income generated in an economy. Other forms of income include income from letting property (rent), lending money (interest), share-holding (dividends), entrepreneurial activity (profit), and income from transfer payments (pensions, unemployment/maternity/disability benefits and so on, as well as other income support transfers). Therefore, the study of the distribution of labour earnings falls within the more general area of economics that is concerned with the distribution of *income*. We make some reference to incomes in the concluding part of this chapter.

The distribution of income is of paramount importance to economists and those concerned with public policy. The complex systems of tax and transfer programmes which have evolved in most economies during the past two centuries clearly manifest the importance of the issue. Distribution and inequality are not the only reasons that make the study of incomes (and earnings, which constitute the greatest part of incomes) interesting. Efficiency and growth are equally important: for example, would it be better to invest more on labour (or, more precisely, on improving human capital) or on physical capital in order to enhance economic growth? This would depend on whether the former is more important in the production process than the latter. An answer to this could come from the examination of the contribution of labour and capital to economic growth, that is, the changes in their respective shares of total product.

We conclude this introductory section by noting, without pursuing further, that much of the inequality in income derives from inequality in the distribution of wealth across households and not from inequality in labour earnings across individuals. This can be verified easily. Some persons/households own assets to the order of many millions of pounds while others have practically nothing. However, most high-paid workers earn between, say, £50 000 and £100 000 a year compared to £5000–£8000 which can be thought of as the typical figure for a low-paid worker in Britain today. Thus the difference in labour earnings can be summarised as 10- to 20-fold while the difference in wealth (and the income generated from it) can be close to infinity. One of the reasons for inheritance tax being one of the heaviest taxes in most economies stems from this observation.

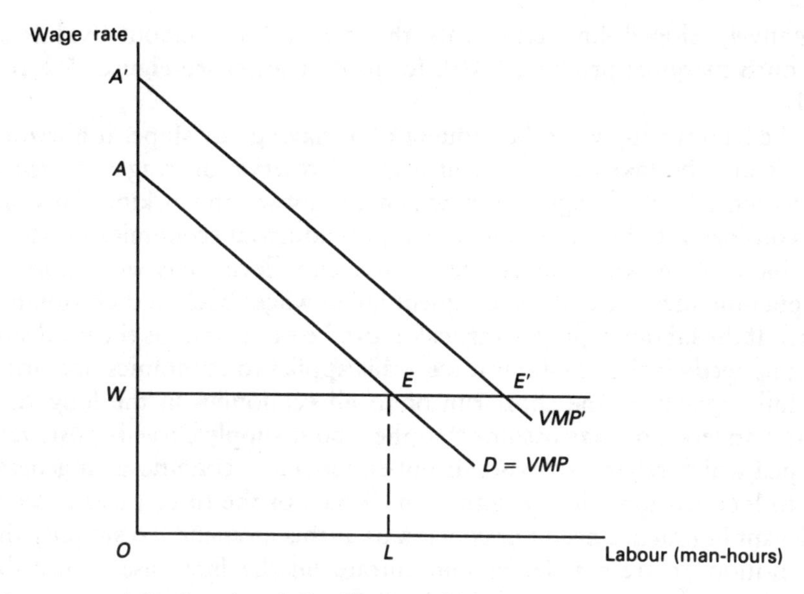

Figure 8.1 ***The functional distribution of income***

■ Relevant concepts and background theory

The functional distribution of income refers to income arising from production after depreciation and before taxes and transfer payments are taken into account. In this case income is whatever is available for consumption, saving and investment in a particular period after replacing the (physical) capital that has been used up in the process of production during the same period. In other words, the functional distribution of income refers to how total (national) income in an economy is divided among different factors of production.

A stylised exposition of the functional distribution of income in a competitive economy is shown in **Figure 8.1.** For simplicity assume that labour and capital are the only factors of production – in modern economies and, progressively, in developing economies rent constitutes a small part of national income. In addition it is hard to think of cases where rent is paid to land as such unless it relates to buildings and improved land in which case the return to 'land' can be legitimately included in the return to capital.

Assume also factor homogeneity, that is, that all labour and all capital are of the same quality and both can be conveniently aggregated and presented in a single labour market. This is in effect the labour market depicted in **Figure 8.1.** The vertical axis represents the wage rate and the horizontal axis labour measured in man-hours of a given quality. The negatively sloped line represents the demand for labour (value of labour's marginal product, *VMP*; for its derivation see **Figures 5.2** and 5.3).

The labour supply can be thought of as having any slope. If horizontal, it may be taken to represent a global reservation wage or even a subsistence level of wages below which it is not worth working. This can be considered to be a relevant case in pre-industrial economies in which an increase in wages above the subsistence level may encourage a population increase and a subsequent fall in wages back to their original level. If the labour supply is vertical, it can be thought of as the total size of a perfectly inelastic labour force – this applies to economies operating at full capacity in the short run or to all economies in the long run. Alternatively, one may assume that the labour supply curve is positively sloped which relates to less-than-full-employment conditions in general or to labour supply in the short run. Which of the three cases is more relevant in practice need not concern us at this moment. To simplify the exposition at present, let us concentrate on the first case where the labour supply curve is infinitely elastic.

The intersection of the labour demand schedule and the horizontal labour supply curve at point *E* results in an equilibrium level of employment, *L*, at the level of subsistence/reservation wage, *W*. Total income in the economy is equal to the sum of all marginal products under conditions of perfect competition, if the production function exhibits constant returns to scale (this point is explained below). Let us assume that these conditions hold. Then total output in **Figure 8.1** corresponds to the area enclosed by the *VMP* curve and the labour axis up to the equilibrium level of employment. This is the trapezium *OAEL*. The functional distribution of income in the present exposition is as follows. Total labour income is equal to the wage rate times the amount of labour employed; therefore, it is the rectangle *OWEL*. Under the assumptions of the present model, total income is fully exhausted between wages and profit. Hence, profit is the difference between total income and the wage bill, that is, it is equal to the triangle *AWE*.

□ *A digression: returns to scale*

The reason we assumed constant returns to scale is to bypass the so-called 'adding-up' problem: even if each factor is paid the value of its marginal product and under competitive conditions, the sum of all payments to factors of production (capital, labour or, in effect, all factors of production included in the analysis may not be equal to total production). If factors are paid as much as their respective marginal products are worth, their resulting shares will just exhaust total output only if constant returns to scale are present. Otherwise, if there are either decreasing or increasing returns to scale, there will be a 'residual' and the sum of all factor shares will be different from total output. One can show this in the case of a Cobb–Douglas production function as follows:

$$Q = AL^aK^b$$

where Q is total product, L and K are (strictly positive quantities of) labour and capital respectively, and A is a (positive) constant which determines how units of labour and units of capital can be transformed into units of output. The marginal products, MP, of labour and capital are respectively

$$MPL = AaL^{a-1}K^b$$
$$MPK = AbL^aK^{b-1}$$

The total payment (TP) to each factor is the mathematical product of the rate of pay (= marginal product) of each factor *times* the amount of the factor used in production. Hence, the total payments to labour and capital are (in real terms)

$$TPL = (AaL^{a-1}K^b)\,L = AaL^aK^b = a\,(AL^aK^b) = aQ$$
$$TPK = (AbL^aK^{b-1})K = AbL^aK^b = b\,(AL^aK^b) = bQ$$

and the total income, Y, paid to both factors becomes

$$Y = TPL + TPK = aQ + bQ = (a + b)Q$$

Consequently, Y, the sum of all incomes paid/received, will be equal to total product, Q, only if there are constant returns to scale, that is, $a + b = 1$. This result is called Euler's theorem: there is no adding-up problem in conditions of perfect competition and constant returns to scale. Recall that constant returns to scale imply homogeneity of degree 1 ('if inputs double, output doubles'). If $a + b < 1$, then there are decreasing returns to scale and, if both factors are paid their respective marginal products, there is a surplus (equal to $(1-a-b)Q$) after all factor payments are made. The theory tells us nothing about who appropriates this surplus – one suspects that one factor earns economic rent. If there are increasing returns to scale ($a + b > 1$), then factor payments exceed total product. In other words, there is not enough product to pay both factors – and one suspects that monopolistic conditions prevail in the product market.

The relationship between three different distributions

Let us go back to **Figure 8.1** in order to clarify the distinction between the functional distribution of income, the size distribution of labour earnings and the distribution of total income. Let us assume that the *functional distribution* of income as shown in **Figure 8.1** consists of 30 per cent in profits and 70 per cent in wages. If the ratio of capitalists to workers is also 30:70 and the economy consists of identical capitalists and identical workers, then there is no inequality in *the distribution of income* as everybody receives the same income. With respect to the size distribution of *labour earnings* there would be complete equality among workers, if all workers worked the same amount of hours. Otherwise, those who worked longer hours would have higher labour earnings. If the ratio of capitalists to workers in the population is lower than 30:70, capitalists are richer than workers and vice versa if the ratio is higher.

Let us expand on this example by assuming that the wage rate is maintained at the subsistence level but labour demand shifts to the right (VMP') due to, say, technical progress. The size distribution of labour earnings will remain as before, that is, earnings will be distributed equally among workers or they will reflect differences in hours worked. The functional distribution of income will change unless the shift of the labour demand curve to the right was parallel to its original position. The overall income distribution (capitalists versus workers) may or may not change depending on whether and by how much the functional distribution of income and the ratio of capitalists to workers in the population have changed.

These findings suggest that even in a simple expository model no firm conclusion can be drawn *a priori* about the relationship between the distribution of personal incomes, the functional distribution of total income and the size distribution of labour earnings. Therefore, one has to examine each one on its own merit.

The functional distribution of income

The analysis underlining **Figure 8.1** can be extended to the examination of the changes in the functional distribution of income. For example, one can trace the implications of various changes in the aggregate labour market. We have already shown how technical progress can affect the functional distribution of income by shifting the labour demand curve

(*VMP*) to the right (*VMP′*). In addition, the quantity of labour used in the production process may increase. This could have been shown easily had we assumed that the labour supply curve was positively sloped and it shifted, say, to the right. Finally, the price (wage rate) of labour may also increase. In reality both the quantity of labour has increased (due to population growth) as well as the level of real wages (due to improved productivity). In this and in the previous case what matters is, of course, *relative* changes to the quantity and prices of other inputs. The issue becomes how to measure these changes.

□ *Measuring capital*

Let us start with the measurement of capital. One is interested not really in the *capital stock available* for production at any time period but in the amount of *capital services used* in that period. These services have to be evaluated in monetary terms and this is a difficult task. The usual measures of the capital used in production are based on historical costs and are dependent on the market rate of return to capital. As an illustration assume that a building was purchased for £100 000 sometime in the mid-1980s and depreciation is estimated at £5000 per annum. One distortion arises from the fact that the useful life of the building may extend beyond the 20-year period implied in the depreciation rate indicated earlier. Though this is not a real problem for long-run estimates of capital utilisation, as it can be corrected after taking the value of the house into account at the end of the 20-year period, it can affect annual estimates significantly.

Another distortion in determining the flow of capital services and factor shares in a particular period arises from the fact that the value of the house may not remain constant. For example, the price of capital may change as in fact has recently happened to property values due to the recession – the acquisition price of the same building could have dropped to £75 000 by 1992. Alternatively, had this building been bought in the early 1970s, its market price could have doubled or trebled respectively by the early 1980s or the late 1980s. Consequently, historical costs may not be relevant to current values and these measurement errors affect capital's income share accordingly.

A final distortion arises from fluctuations in the market interest rate. For example, assume that the market interest rate is 10 per cent per annum and a capital asset yields a perpetual income of £1000. Given these figures, this particular capital asset is now worth £10 000. If the interest rate dropped to 5 per cent per annum, then the value of the same capital asset would increase to £20 000. Consequently, the way capital is measured and enters national account statistics is to a great extent arbitrary and far from reliable.

□ *Measuring labour*

Measuring labour may sound relatively straightforward if one concentrates on the number of workers and the amount of hours they work (the simple 'bodies times hours' or 'man-hours' case). However, the 'aggregation' problem involved is by no means a resolved issue even after a hot and continuing debate. The difficulty in approximating the overall quantity of labour input with the use of an aggregate statistic can be easily seen with reference to the composition of the labour force. Some workers are young while others are old; and some workers have little human capital while others are well-educated and/or trained. Age and human capital in this respect are worker characteristics (labour supply). Hence, the greatest difficulty is to estimate the amount of human capital embodied in the simple measure of man-hours.

The difficulty in measuring labour as an input can be seen from the attempts that have been made to estimate the contribution of education to economic growth (Schultz, 1961; Denison, 1967; Nadiri, 1972). The general consensus now is that increases in human capital have been underestimated in these early studies which were growth-accounting decompositions based on aggregate-type production functions. Later work based on econometric techniques relating inputs to output in more sophisticated analytical frameworks have emphasised that human capital may have increased faster than physical capital (Hicks, 1980; Easterlin, 1981; Marris, 1982, Psacharopoulos, 1984). If this is indeed the case, then labour's share of national income should have risen given the decline in uneducated/unskilled workers in the total labour force. Before the movement of factor shares is examined over time, we explain how technology can affect the way labour and capital combine in production.

□ *Factor substitution*

Having discussed the problem associated with the measurement of inputs used in the production (income generation) process we can examine two interrelated issues in the changes in the functional distribution of income, namely capital-deepening, and the complementarity/substitutability between labour and capital in production. Capital-deepening refers to the increase of physical capital per worker over time. If labour were homogeneous and its supply curve were perfectly elastic at a subsistence level (as shown in **Figure 8.1**), capital-deepening should reduce labour's share of income because capital's share *in the input mix* has increased. Alternatively, if the firms cannot readily substitute capital for labour, the increase in the amount of capital used in production should reduce the relative price of capital. In turn, the decrease in the price of capital due to capital-deepening should lower capital's share of income and increase labour's share. Consequently, capital-deepening as such can result in either an increase or a decrease in labour's share depending on the (relative) changes in labour used in production and the easiness of substitution between capital and labour.

The measurement of the physical amount of inputs used in production is only half of the story. The other half relates to prices. It is well-known how difficult it is to separate the effect of changes in quantities and prices over time upon a composite variable which in this case is the product of wages times employment divided by total income – compare this to the case of the statistical indices of Paasche and Laspayres. Bearing these qualifications in mind let us look at some figures.

☐ *Changes over time*

Table 8.1 shows some basic components of national income in Britain throughout the postwar period (1949–89). The first column refers to income from employment and includes wages and salaries, forces' pay and employers' contributions. Column (2) includes income from self-employment plus rent and the imputed charge for consumption of non-trading capital. Total income (column 3) is evaluated at factor cost before deducting stock appreciation. It includes columns (1) and (2) plus trading profits of companies and trading surplus of public corporations and general government enterprises. The last two columns in the table show the ratio of income from employment, and income from employment, self-employment and other sources to total income.

Two observations are already obvious. First, the difficulty one has in distinguishing factor payments by recipient in a national accounting framework. For example income from self-employment is lumped together with rent and other components of pay.

The second observation can be made with reference to what Keynes noted some time ago: 'the stability of the proportion of the national dividend accruing to labour . . . is one of the most surprising, yet best established facts in the whole range of economic statistics . . . [and this] stability . . . appears to be a long-run, not merely a short-period, phenomenon' (Keynes, 1939, p. 48). Of course Keynes referred to the

Table 8.1 ***Income from employment and other income (current prices in £ millions): Britain, 1949–89***

Year	*Income from*				
	Employment	*Self-employment and other**	*Total income*		
	(1)	(2)	(3)	(1)/(3)	[(1)+(2)]/(3)
1949	7 246	2 019	11 371	63.7%	81.5%
1959	14 107	3 266	21 262	66.3%	81.7%
1969	27 227	6 632	41 099	66.2%	82.4%
1979	115 866	29 525	180 553	64.2%	80.5%
1989	284 399	88 534	445 340	63.9%	83.7%

* Includes income from rent and the imputed charge for consumption of non-trading capital.

Source: CSO: *Economic Trends: Annual Supplement 1991*, Table 4, p. 28.

prewar period but our data do suggest that the ratio of income from employment to total income has remained remarkably stable between 1949 and 1989: on average income from employment constituted 64.9 per cent of total income with a standard deviation of only 1.2 (or a coefficient of variation of only 1.8 per cent). In addition, there is no sign of an underlying trend: the ratio was 63.7 per cent in 1949 and 63.9 per cent in 1989.

These two observations are also applicable to the combined case of income from employment and self-employment (last column of the table). These two issues will occupy most of our discussion of the functional distribution of income, that is, first, some methodological issues relating to the measurement of factor incomes and, second, the change (or not change) in factor shares over time.

□ *Qualifications*

The economists' notion of factor shares is not well-represented in the figures of the table. With respect to measuring 'labour share' in total income one should note that this term is never used in any official statistics of any country. Instead the term 'employee compensation' or 'income from employment' is more commonly used. Employee compensation is a broader term which includes wages and salaries as well as employer contributions into social insurance funds and various worker payments for pension, health, welfare and other purposes. These supplements are traditionally included in income from employment for the reasons that they are paid for and eventually used by workers, and there is no other category in the national accounts in which they could be meaningfully included.

Income from employment arises also in the case of 'independent employment'. Alternatively called 'proprietors' income', it is the income that arises from the activity of the self-employed (and, perhaps, of some members of his family) and is a mixture of labour earnings, rent, interest, and compensation to entrepreneurial risk (profit). If income from self-employment is generated in small family-based units or if it relates to highly labour-intensive activities (such as the work of barbers, lawyers and teachers), then for practical purposes one can include all such income into labour's share. However, this need not be so necessarily.

Consequently, the figures on factor incomes are derived from national *accounting* conventions which may differ at times to a significant extent from the *economic* use of the corresponding terms. The treatment of the government, as a producer, is a further example in this respect. In terms of national income accounting government activity is in effect measured in terms of labour employed (wages and salaries paid to civil servants) and pays little attention to the contributions to production arising from land-holding and the use of state-owned capital (that is, no return on government holdings is included in national income). In terms of changes over time, this accounting convention would automatically increase labour's share as it reflects the growth of the government sector over most of recent history.

A final point to be made is that the apparent constancy in labour's share, as proxied by the information from national accounts, may mask changes in the ratio of wages to profits within economic sectors, notably industries. In other words, it is possible that significant changes have occurred in the wages/profits relationship within each and every industry across the economy over time. Therefore, what we observe can be the offsetting result of highly labour-intensive industries growing at the expense of capital-intensive industries. For example, the service sector has become more important over time while the manufacturing sector has declined. Therefore, one has to take into account the changes in the structure of industry before a definitive conclusion is reached and this is a more complicated task than it may sound.

In conclusion, given (i) the discrepancy between the economic and the accounting measurement of income from employment, (ii) the errors involved in national accounting, (iii) the level of aggregation over important subsectors affected by different factors and (iv) the little or no change in the currently used measure of labour's share, one may be tempted not to challenge Keynes's observation.

A technological explanation: the production function

One can examine this empirical conclusion in the context of the Cobb–Douglas production function outlined earlier. The ratio of labour income of total income is

$$TPL/Q = AaL^aK^b/AL^aK^b = a$$

and, under constant returns to scale ($b = 1 - a$), the share of total income accruing to capital is

$$TPK/Q = A(1 - a)\ L^aK^{(1-a)}/AL^aK^{(1-a)} = 1 - a$$

This is a remarkable result: it shows that the proportion of income apportioned by the factors of production depends only on the parameter a (or b). Factor shares in this formulation are therefore independent of the amounts of factors used in production: under the present assumptions an increase in the quantity of a factor of production reduces its marginal product, and as a result its price, inversely proportional to the increase in quantity. Accordingly, technological change registers an effect only via the multiplicative constant, A. These results can be shown to hold also in the case of imperfect markets provided that market conditions do not change over time (a proof to this proposition can be found in Archibald and Lipsey, 1977, chapter 9).

A macroeconomic explanation: Kaldor

As the study of income shares refers to national income, macroeconomic approaches have also been proposed. One such attempt was undertaken by Kaldor (1956) which came to the predictable conclusion that labour's share varies inversely with the investment–income ratio. This can be shown with reference to a full-employment private economy (no government sector) whose entire income consists of wages, W, and profits, π.

If part of income is saved, S, consumption will be insufficient to purchase the entire output unless investment is sufficient to fill the gap created by saving. This is the well-known proposition in any macroeconomic textbook that, at equilibrium, savings must be equal to investment. Assume further that (i) the propensity of workers to save is

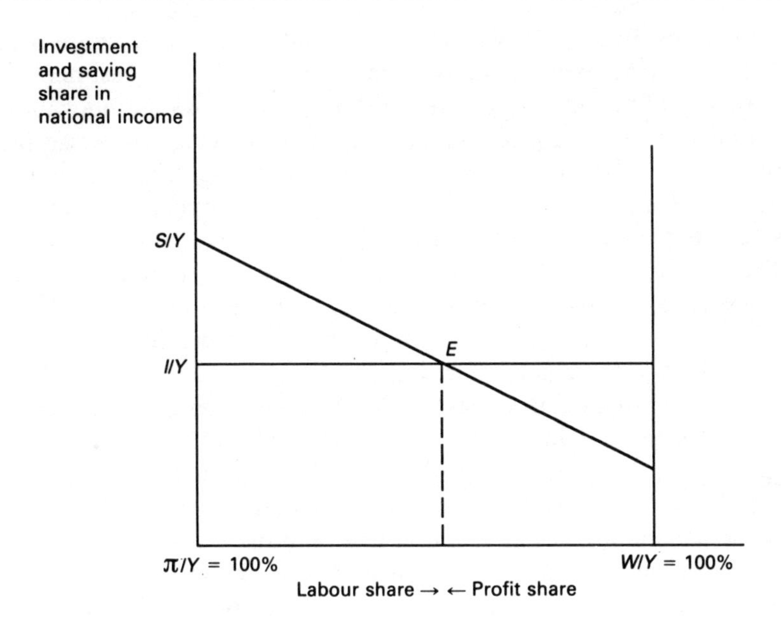

Figure 8.2 ***Kaldor's model***

smaller than the propensity of employers/capital-holders and (ii) the average propensity of each group to save does not vary with income (for example, workers save 10 per cent of their income irrespective of their income level). This model is shown in **Figure 8.2**.

The horizontal line measures labour's share of total income from left to right and the share of profits from right to left: at the origin of the axes all income takes the form of profits while on the far right all income accrues to workers. The greater the share of labour is, the lower savings (S/Y) would be as workers are assumed to have a lower propensity to save than profit-recipients. Thus the negatively sloped line depicts the ratio of savings to income as labour's share increases. Kaldor assumes that the ratio of investment to income (I/Y) is constant in that it does not vary with the level of income but depends on factors such as business expectations and technological change which are not explicitly represented in the diagram. Hence, investment is considered to be exogenous to the model and the ratio of investment to income can be represented as a horizontal line.

The economy is at equilibrium, point E in the diagram, where investment equals savings. In this diagram an increase in investment results in an upward shift of the horizontal line and alters the functional distribution of income by reducing labour's share in total output/income. The economic interpretation of this so far mechanistic exposition rests on the role of prices. Recall that we are dealing with a private economy which is at the full-employment equilibrium. The increase in investment does not create additional real income – it simply inflates total money income (or results in demand-pull inflation). *And if* product prices rise faster than wages, profits will increase more relative to wages. Savings will also increase as the recipients of profit have a greater propensity to save than workers and the new equilibrium with be to the north-west of *E*.

The analysis of factor shares even within a macroeconomic framework as presented here is not void of some problems. Though Kaldor's model is in essence a Keynesian model (by conditioning equilibrium at the savings-equal-investment point) one may argue that Keynesian theory is applicable to less-than-full-employment economies with scope for demand management policies. In addition, it is not clear why product prices increase faster than wages. One may be prepared to accept that wage adjustment follows price changes but there is no reason why the lag should be more than a few months or a single year.

By far the most damaging criticism of Kaldor's model relates to the autonomous nature of investment. In fact, it is possible that investment depends on the profits (that is output *minus* wages) that entrepreneurs expect to retain for financing it. Hence, investment is the result, not the cause, of the observed functional distribution of earnings. Nevertheless, the relative constancy in labour's share (if one wishes so to interpret the figures in **Table 8.1**) is compatible with the finding that the ratio of investment to total income has shown little tendency to vary in the longer run and the theory has had support in some quarters (see Pen, 1971, and Phelps-Brown, 1968).

In conclusion, our understanding of the functional distribution of income is limited. The reasons for this are, first, the difficulty in separating cause and effect in the observed changes in the functional distribution of income as these changes may be generated either from greater use of a particular factor in production or from higher prices paid to that factor, and second, the severity of the measurement problem in estimating the quantity/quality of factors of production which limits our ability to perceive what the real situation looks like.

■ The size distribution of labour earnings

The size distribution of labour earnings refers to the pattern of wages and salaries across individual workers. Individual labour earnings (or, for reasons of brevity, earnings from now on) is the total remuneration paid to a worker in a particular period. In other words earnings is a flow variable in that it refers to pay per hour, day, week, month, annum and so on. Earnings relate to wage rates but do not correspond exactly to them. Concentrating on weekly earnings, a simplified relationship between weekly earnings and hourly wage rates can be shown as follows:

Earnings/week = (hourly wage rate) × (weekly hours worked) + (other pay)

'Other pay' may include bonuses, pay-by-result, overtime and shift premia, *ad hoc* rewards for special duties and so on. In many cases 'other pay' relates to the hourly wage rate and sometimes it is set on a *pro rata* basis to the latter. However, this need not always be so.

□ *Statistical sources on earnings*

The first national survey on earnings in Britain was conducted in 1886. In that survey earnings were defined as 'weekly wages actually paid', 'recognised rates of weekly wages' or 'wages paid in a normal week'. It was followed by surveys undertaken in 1906, 1924, 1928, 1931, 1935, 1938 and 1960 (*British Labour Statistics, Historical Abstract: 1886–1968*, London: HMSO, 1968). These surveys focused primarily on weekly pay of manual workers. This resulted in no great loss of information as most workers at that time, especially in the earlier period, were engaged in industry – the service sector had not assumed the proportions it has today and overtime was not an important aspect of pay before the Second World War (ibid., p. 7). Shortly after its first national survey, Britain scored a European first in this area of statistics in the form of Seebohm Rowntree's pioneering work in his 1899 York survey on incomes and, indirectly, earnings.

The recession of the 1930s and the advent of Keynesian-type theories made it clear that more information on the functioning of the labour market was required for appropriate and timely demand management policies. Rowntree's 1899 work on incomes was duplicated in 1936 and provided the basis for the social policies in the 1940s and the 1942 Beveridge Report started 'from facts as revealed by [those] social surveys'. In addition, the Department of Employment introduced a biannual (April and October) series on earnings in the late 1930s which continues till today. This series covers manual workers in production industries, transport and communication and public administration. Information for other sectors is provided by the corresponding bodies (such as the National Coal Board, British Railways, the Ministry of Agriculture and so on).

Earnings of non-manual workers have been monitored on a regular basis only after the Second World War while the *Family Expenditure Survey* and the *General Household Survey* provide information on earnings based on household questionnaires. It is worth adding that currently the European Community is orchestrating the expansion and coordination of national statistics in member states, building upon the US experience with longitudinal surveys (Morgan *et al.*, 1975). Germany was the first to initiate panel designs in this area in 1984 and almost half of the other member states have already followed this example (Yfantopoulos, 1991). Britain introduced its first household panel along European lines in 1990. The study focuses on income and poverty aspects and is based at the University of Essex. The first 'wave' based on 5000 observations was conducted in 1990 and was followed up in 1992.

By far the most complete survey on earnings in Britain is the *New Earnings Survey*. It was first undertaken in a pivotal form as a 0.5 per cent sample of all employees in 1968 and has been repeated annually since 1970. Now it covers 1 per cent of employees (about 200 000) whose earnings are above a certain threshold. Information relates to pay in a particular week in April. Pay is broken down by sex, age, full- and part-time employment (for women only), age, industry, occupation, region and collective agreement. Both levels and distributions of weekly earnings are worked out. In addition, the survey provides separate information on gross and net-of-overtime-effects hourly earnings as well as on 'other aspects' of pay (such as bonuses and piece-work). An interesting feature of the survey is its 'matched' sample, that is, information about earnings of individuals who were with the same employer in two successive years. It should be noted that the results presented in the survey are based on information provided by employers. Hence, they may understate an employee's total labour earnings to the extent that this particular employee has a second job. Also, fringe benefits and non-monetary perks are not recorded – information is collected only for wages and salaries paid to the worker.

□ *The distribution of earnings*

A distribution can be usefully described if it has a particular shape (for example, the normal distribution follows a symmetric bell-shaped pattern). Then the conventional measures of central tendency and dispersion can be easily worked out and compared with other distributions or over a period of time. In this respect, the distribution of labour earnings is and has been relatively well-defined: for the most part it follows the log-normal distribution.

The normal and log-normal distributions are shown in **Figure 8.3**. Both distributions are uni-modal, that is, they have a single hump. In the

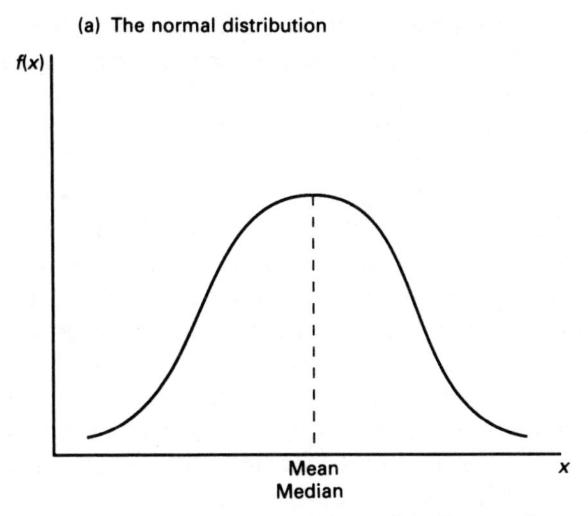

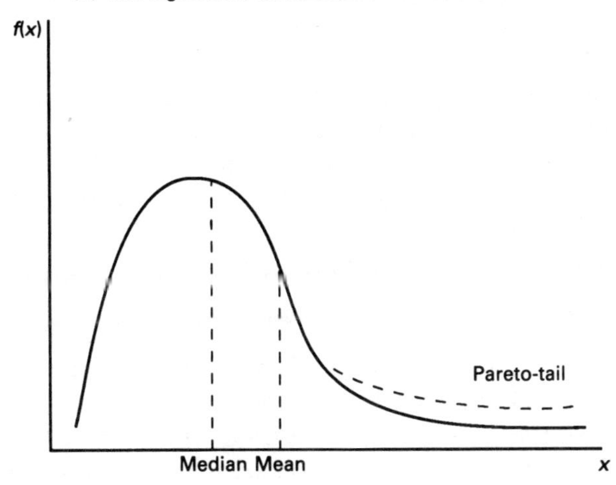

Figure 8.3 ***Normal and log-normal distributions of earnings***

normal distribution the median coincides with the mean. In the log-normal distribution the median is lower than the mean and this results in positive 'skewness': the part of the distribution around and to the left of the median is quite concentrated while the part of the distribution to the right of the median and, especially, after the mean is quite spread out in the form of a long right-hand tail. The term 'log-normality' is used because if one plots not the original values of the variable concerned (in this case, earnings) but their respective logarithms, the distribution should look like the normal distribution. In the lower panel of **Figure 8.3** we also plot the 'Pareto-tail' which, as explained below, describes better the way high earnings are distributed. In short, a fair generalisation is that the distribution of earnings follows closely the log-normal distribution for most part of it except the right-hand tail.

The observation that the distribution of earnings follows a well-defined curve, at least with respect to some large part of it, is not new. Pareto asserted, though with respect to incomes, that there is a tendency for incomes to lie on a certain curve and that this tendency appeared only weakly to depend on different economic conditions of the countries which he studied at the time, namely England (*sic*), Germany and Italy (Pareto, 1895, 1896 and 1897). In addition, Pareto attempted to compare the distribution of income in Ancient Rome with figures from Saxony and, though the evidence was scanty, he was not deterred from concluding that the distribution of income was in both cases following his favoured form which is now described as the Pareto curve. Pareto's curve is well-approximated by the formula

$$\log(N) = \log(A) - a\log(x)$$

where N is the cumulative frequency of incomes, x is income, and a and A are parameters. Pareto was striving to show that there was some law operating underneath this impressive finding. As will be argued later, this law is the 'law of proportional effect' which was put forward by the Dutch botanist Kapteyen (1903) and was eventually formalised by Gibrat (1931). As these developments came too late for Pareto, he did not have the opportunity to appreciate that there are laws which govern the outcome of chances and in his eyes 'the idea of chances and law appeared to be logically opposed and exclusive' (Brown, 1976, p. 72). We return to the relevance of Pareto's formulation later after we discuss the evidence on the distribution of earnings in Britain.

Table 8.2 presents the distribution of male manual gross weekly earnings in Britain since 1886. The figures confirm that their distribution complies with log-normality and confirms the constancy observed by Pareto. In the 1980s there was some movement away from the norm but it does not appear to be outside the boundaries established during the course of the century and may be associated with the 'sharp, short measures' introduced in the labour market and the economy around that time. In any case the changes are far from dramatic.

Before we attempt to give some reasons for the particular shape and constancy of the distribution of earnings, let us also examine the broader distribution of earnings with respect to hourly earnings, age and sex of workers and also non-manual work for reasons of completeness. These distributions can be summarised as follows:

Table 8.2 ***The distribution of male manual weekly earnings in Britain (expressed as percentage of median earnings), 1886–1987 (selected years)***

Year	*Lowest decile*	*Lower quartile*	*Upper quartile*	*Highest decile*
1886	68.6	82.8	121.7	143.1
1906	66.5	79.5	126.7	156.8
1938	67.7	82.1	118.5	139.9
1960	70.6	82.6	121.7	145.2
1968	67.3	81.0	122.3	147.8
1981	69.7	82.8	122.5	150.6
1987	63.6	79.2	125.8	156.5

Sources: 1886–1968: *British Labour Statistics, Historical Abstract 1886–1968.*
1981–7: *New Earnings Survey* (corresponding issues).

> The average earnings of manual men vary with age but the dispersion is almost the same for all age groups between 21 and 64. The dispersion of hourly earnings is not very different from the dispersion of weekly earnings . . . The distribution of non-manual men departs from log-normal because it has a long upper tail of the Pareto form . . . The distribution of annual earnings for all men is a mixture of the previous two distributions . . . The distribution of earnings of manual women is almost the same as that for manual men . . . (Thatcher, 1976, pp. 227–9)

The evidence for Britain as presented in **Table 8.2** and summarised by Thatcher is very much in line with that for other market economies. In his voluminous work, Lydall (1968) has shown that in the countries which he studied the characteristic shape of the earnings distribution is approximately log-normal but with a higher peak and a thicker tail than a strictly log-normal distribution. This amounts to saying that the distribution of earnings is leptokurtic (that is, more peaked and thicker-tailed than usual) with a Pareto-tail (that is, the right-hand end is more elongated). These observations are already familiar to the reader.

In addition, the evidence found in some Eastern European countries before the post-1989 developments confirms that these characteristics of the distribution of earnings are typical there, too. The only difference rests with the Pareto-tail in the sense that it used to be less prominent in Eastern Europe than in market economies. One explanation for this difference is that managers and high-pay personnel in Eastern Europe were not paid as highly (relative to common labourers) as their counterparts in Western Europe. However, it is well-known that Eastern

European high-level manpower enjoyed significant non-pecuniary benefits which by their nature escaped official statistics. This is also true to some extent with respect to top personnel in market economies but these economies are more monetised and the statistical problem should not be as serious as in planned economies.

To visualise better the property of the log-normality in the general area of earnings distribution, one can use Pen's (1974) analogy which transforms 'the chaotic mountain of detached figures or the tiring series of tables' into a parade of dwarfs and a few giants (note that Pen refers to incomes). Assume that every person's height is represented by his income and let those with average income have a height equal to the average height. Then, let us ask these individuals to parade in front of us within an hour and in ascending order of income and height. The result will be as follows.

For the first five minutes or so, tiny gnomes pass by who are the size of dust and up to the size of a cigarette end. For the next 25 minutes marchers eventually acquire the size of conventional dwarfs while the 'average man' appears only 10 minutes or so before the parade ends. Then things speed up and height increases rapidly. Pen expects that lawyers would be about 18 feet tall, doctors and accountants about seven to eight yards and senior executives around 20 yards or so. Perhaps the last man to parade would have been, at the time, John Paul Getty. His height might have been 20 miles and we would not have been able to see his face (he would have been three times the height of Mount Everest). This analogy gives a vivid, albeit crude, picture of the kind of distribution with which we are dealing and especially of the Pareto-tail.

This characteristic shape of the distribution of earnings is sometimes referred to as 'Pigou's paradox': if human characteristics are normally distributed, why is the earnings distribution skewed? An obvious answer to this paradox can be that workers are not paid only according to their physical characteristics but also according to non-physical characteristics which need not be normally distributed. For example, education and training are not symmetrically distributed among individuals. In Britain the majority of 16-year-olds drop out of the education system and only one in five of young persons proceed to tertiary education of some form or another. To the extent that pay depends on human capital which workers bring to the labour market, one would therefore expect that a few people command high pay and most workers are concentrated towards lower earnings. Equally, on the labour demand side (structure of occupations), if the distribution of jobs is hierarchical with a few jobs at the top and many at the bottom, then again the distribution of earnings will not be symmetric. Some of these considerations are discussed below.

Table 8.3 ***An illustration of the Gibrat's process (the law of proportional effect)***

Case											*Sum*	*Product*
A	1	6	3	5	4	6	2	3	6	4	40	311 040
B	5	3	4	2	4	6	3	2	1	5	35	86 400
C	1	5	2	3	6	1	2	4	3	1	28	4 320
D	2	6	4	5	2	4	3	5	2	1	34	57 600
E	1	2	6	3	4	2	1	3	4	5	31	17 280
F	6	3	4	1	4	4	6	1	2	3	34	41 472
G	2	4	5	3	1	5	5	3	6	4	38	216 000
Mean	2.6	4.1	4.0	3.1	3.6	4.0	3.1	3.0	3.4	3.3	34	104 873

The log-normality of the distribution of earnings

Earnings are expressed as numbers and numbers may exhibit some form of regularity, even if we are not in a position to know exactly the underlying causes which determine them. In other words there may exist a data generation process whose operation may not be readily attributed to an underlying economic explanation. One such process that generates log-normally distributed outcomes is the so-called Gibrat's process to which reference has already been made. This process is better understood with the aid of the following experiment.

Throw a die a number of times and record the outcome. **Table 8.3** is constructed along these lines. The rows record the outcome of throwing a die 10 times on seven different occasions. Take the sum of each row (last-but-one column) and you will see that the distribution of the sums is quite uniform around the mean (34). Alternatively, take the product of the outcomes in each row (last column) and, perhaps, surprisingly, you will find that there are two high products far above the rest. The other four products are concentrated around a value lower than the average of the distribution of the products of the individual outcomes (which is, in this case, 104 873).

One explanation for the results presented in **Table 8.3** is given by the Central Limit Theorem. The theorem states that the sum of a large number of independent random variables characterised by the same variance (such as the total score of a die when a die is thrown a large number of times) will have an approximately normal distribution. As a corollary the product of a large number of independent positive random variables characterised by the same coefficient of variation will have an approximately log-normal distribution.

The relevance of the theorem to the characteristic shape of the distribution of earnings should be obvious. Individual characteristics may be normally distributed at birth. However, by the time individuals enter the labour market and during their employment, they have developed and are developing different characteristics to different extents. For example, the initial distribution of innate ability in terms of physical and mental capacity develops differently for people from various socioeconomic backgrounds. This in turn shapes personal motivation as well as education performance. Then, having reached working age, individuals face different distributions of job offers which, apart from determining current earnings, also affect labour mobility later in life and subsequent earnings. If it is the additive interaction of all these characteristics and circumstances that determines earnings, then Pigou's paradox remains unanswered.

As an example assume that a person of average intelligence could earn £200 a week. In addition assume that there is a pay premium of £50 per week if the person speaks a foreign language or knows how to operate a computer or has a university degree. Additive interaction implies that a person of average intelligence who has a university degree, speaks a foreign language and can work on a computer should be paid (£200 + £50 + £50 + £50 =) £350 per week. In this case the law of proportional effect is not applicable. However, it cannot be ruled out that these characteristics interact in some multiplicative way. For example, speaking a foreign language may raise our hypothetical person's earnings to £250 a week, while knowing computers could boost earnings to £400 and possessing a university degree further to £700.

Intuitively, one may be tempted to agree that the earnings increment associated with at least certain characteristics is not the result of an additive process. If so, Gibrat's process provides an apparent explanation for Pigou's paradox. However, this explanation is not void of some methodological difficulties. In particular, some of the assumptions underlying the applicability of the Central Limit Theory are not fulfilled in the case of the distributions of earnings. First, characteristics are not randomly distributed, not even at birth. For example, well-off families have as a general rule healthier offspring and the latter have easier access both to education services (lower cost constraints) and also to better jobs (greater parental influence). Second, the distributions of these characteristics, even if they were equally distributed at birth, need not have the same variances. For example, parents' wealth is more dispersed than parents' income and it is perhaps the former (in terms of ultimate security) that allows families in greater possession of wealth to spend more on their children's welfare, even if levels of income are identical. Consequently, neither the assumption of independence or randomness nor the assumption of constant variations in earnings-related characteristics may be very relevant in practice.

In conclusion, the log-normality of earnings is compatible with the law of proportional effects but only under certain conditions. And the fact that this explanation appears to be deterministic in nature with no reference to any underlying economic relationship leaves much to be desired from an analytical point of view.

The positive skewness of the distribution of earnings

Positive skewness in a distribution implies that the average is greater than the median. In the case of the distribution of earnings this may be taken to mean (in illustrative terms) that too many people are paid too little and too few people are paid too much. This phenomenon can be explained with reference to a particular job selection process.

It is natural for individuals to choose the job which is associated with highest pay when they are faced with different job alternatives (assuming that other aspects of employment are similar across jobs). Given this preference average earnings will be greater than median earnings if certain conditions hold. Assume that there are 100 individuals and all can be employed at a wage equal to £200 a week. Assume further that these individuals have the following option: they are asked to draw a number from a hat containing an infinite pool of tickets with a number printed on them. These numbers are distributed randomly and independently between 100 and 300. The possession of a ticket enables the holder to trade off the £200-per-week job for another job where the pay will be equal to the number he drew from the hat. In theory, 50 individuals will draw a number smaller than 200, hence, they will stay with their original job at £200 per week. The remaining 50 individuals will draw a number greater than 200 and will, naturally, opt for the job that pays more than £200 per week. The average weekly wage of the 50 unfortunate individuals will be £200. For the whole sample, that is the 100 individuals, the median will also be £200. However, the average for the lucky 50 individuals will be £250. The latter will raise the overall average to £225. Thus this selection process will result in average wages being greater than median wages.

Consequently, if individuals are free to select jobs and pay is determined in the way described in the previous paragraph, the resulting distribution of earnings will have the observed property, that is, the mean will be greater than the median. However, as in the case of the law of proportional effects, this explanation is subject to certain reservations. The most important reservation is, of course, that the number of jobs and associated-with-them pay are not infinite and choice is restricted: if a high-paid job is taken by one person, this particular job is no longer available to others.

The Pareto-tail of the distribution of earnings

The Pareto-tail describes the distributional pattern of earnings of high-paid workers. In an early paper Roberts (1956) argued that the salary of the executives related to the size of the company and to virtually no other variables. He interpreted this finding as suggesting that the distribution of executive pay is not determined by conventional economic forces but is subject to some deterministic social processes, the size of company being suspected to be one of them (compare this explanation of earnings with those provided by the alternative labour market theories in Chapter 4).

The idea of company size being a determinant of the distribution of high-paid workers was explicitly incorporated in the 'hierarchical' formulation suggested by Simon (1957). Simon's explanation rests on the following three premises.

First, companies are taken to be organised in a pyramidal form, and each executive has a certain number (n) of subordinates. For example, there is a president and two vice-presidents; each vice-president has two directors and each director has two assistant directors and so on.

Second, at the lowest level of employment with respect to skill and qualifications, salaries are determined by the competitive process. This assumption is not necessary for the model, as the model goes through on ratios of salaries at different seniority levels, but it links this mechanistic model to reality.

Third, from their basic/competitive level, salaries at each successively higher level increase by a fixed proportion. Thus pay at one level is, say, b times greater than that at one level below (alternatively, assume that the president is paid £1000 per week, his vice-presidents are paid 20 per cent less, that is £800, while directors are paid £640 and assistant directors £512 and so on).

If the world were as described in this model, then the relationship between company size and remuneration will be positive and logarithmic in such a way that it 'will be in quantitative agreement with the empirical data' (Simon, 1957, p. 35) which amounts to saying that it will fit the Pareto-tail.

This result is damaging to the idea that pay is determined according to marginal productivity unless, of course, the ratio of marginal products between successive layers of organisation is fixed and equal to b. This explanation based on hierarchical structures seems to be a reasonable explanation for explaining the salaries of executives though it may be seen more as a sociological process than an economic one. However, the theory itself is not beyond criticism.

First, the empirical data upon which Roberts's and Simon's studies are based relate to executive monetary earnings but exclude fringe benefits and undetectable payments. Second, is it true that all organisations are of the same size and that they have the same steepness of hierarchical structure? Third, there are many persons with high earnings who work outside big and hierarchical organisations, such as doctors, lawyers, architects and so on. Fourth, the characteristics of the distribution of earnings are not unique to big organisations; for example, earnings classified by other criteria, such as occupations, also exhibit similar characteristics with respect to the Pareto-tail. Finally, the fact that the distribution of earnings has remained fairly constant for so long, even if not from the time of Ancient Rome to contemporary European market economies, suggests that no single theory from those outlined here can on its own help us penetrate the complexity of the issue.

This pessimistic conclusion is particularly applicable to Simon's theory as during the last 100 years, to which the data in **Table 8.2** refer, Britain has moved in effect away from small-scale competitive capitalism to large-scale corporate capitalism: organisational structures within companies and the structure of industries have undergone a radical transformation during this period but the distributional aspects of earnings seem to have evaded these developments.

Human capital and the distribution of earnings

It may sound odd that we have so far made little use of the human capital theory in the study of the distribution of earnings – after we spent some time to explain earnings along the lines of this theory in Chapter 4. In fact, the proponents of human capital theory have made attempts to apply its analytical tools to the study of the distribution of

Table 8.4 ***Average weekly earnings by sex and level of education in 1983 (as % of average all-male weekly earnings)***

Level of education	*Men*	*Women*
Degree	155	120
Other higher education	124	83
GCE A level	103	73
GCE O level	100	66
CSE	92	62
No qualifications	89	56
All levels	100	65

Note: Mean male earnings = £167.50 per week.

Source: *General Household Survey*, 1983, Table 8.15.

earnings. This seems to be an attractive extension of the theory especially since the relationship between education and individual earnings appears *prima facie* to be strong. **Table 8.4** confirms this assertion.

Hence, one may be tempted to apply human capital considerations to the size distribution of earnings. For example, will an expansion of schooling (increasing the average educational attainment of the population and the labour force) reduce the dispersion of earnings and result in a more equal distribution of earnings? This is an interesting question, but one has to be careful (i) with the way it would have to be applied and (ii) with the acceptance of the human capital theory as a general theory of the distribution of earnings. Let us examine these aspects in turn.

An increase in average schooling, as a policy instrument for greater equality, will have equitable effects only if the variance of schooling decreases. In other words the equitable effect of increasing schooling depends on which level of schooling is expanded. The equity impact of education is greatest for basic education. Recall from our discussion on human capital (Chapter 4) that returns to schooling are highest in primary education and lowest in tertiary education. Consequently, spending a 'little' on the 'many' may increase their earnings toward average earnings. But is this apparently non-controversial statement true? The empirical evidence creates some reservations. The distribution of male manual earnings has been remarkably constant during the course of the last 100 years – when the skill mix and the education mix of the workforce changed dramatically.

There is also a theoretical reservation for accepting human capital theory as relevant in the study of the distribution of earnings. The reason is that earnings differentials between, on the one hand, uneducated or less educated workers and, on the other hand, educated or more educated workers are *simultaneously* determined with the education mix of the workers. This can be shown as follows.

Denote the percentage of educated workers to all workers by L, the average wage of uneducated workers by W^u and the ratio of average wages of educated workers to the average wage of uneducated workers by W. Average earnings will therefore be equal to

$$W^u (1-L) + WW^uL$$

The ratio of average earnings of educated workers to average earnings in the economy is therefore

$$WW^uL/[W^u (1-L) + WW^uL]$$

which, if divided by W^u and simplified, becomes

$$WL/[1+L (W-1)]$$

The latter expression is in effect the algebraic formulation of the equilibrium that was shown diagrammatically in **Figure 4.1.** It implies that the distribution of earnings between educated and uneducated labour (or W, the ratio of their respective wages) is simultaneously determined with the percentage of the labour force which is educated, L, by the market. Hence, when more people become educated, the relative supply of educated labour increases and the wage of educated workers falls relative to the wages of uneducated workers. To avoid the 'chicken and egg' question one requires a reformulation of the human capital theory along the lines of a general equilibrium framework. In one case where this was done, the findings did not fit the observed distribution of earnings and schooling (Oulton, 1974).

Despite the limits of human capital theory in explaining the distribution of earnings, its contribution to our understanding of pay differentials has been significant. It is this aspect of the labour market, namely earnings differentials or differences in pay, that is examined last in this chapter.

Concluding remarks on the size distribution of earnings

The size distribution of earnings depends on many factors and in a complex way as earnings are affected by many characteristics of workers and of the production process. The age composition of the labour force, education/training, physical capital, location of employment, industrial and occupational composition of production, size and nature of firms, managerial practices, government policies, and social custom and work ethos have all undergone significant changes during the period for which reliable information on earnings exists. Yet the outcome of the interaction of all these factors has remained remarkably constant with respect to the distribution of earnings. True it may be that the *level* of earnings has increased over time and that people's material welfare is greater today than ever before. However, the *relativity* aspect of earnings has persisted.

Statistical theories seem to provide some explanations but economists tend to look at them as little more than curve-fitting exercises without much theory explaining 'why'. Statistical theories rely more on the role of chance and little on the economic factors which are known to affect individual earnings. In addition, the statistical processes outlined in this chapter were taken to work on the presumption that things happen instantaneously. Yet it has been shown that in practice the 'half-life' of some social 'matrices' (that is, the length of time required to move from the initial conditions halfway towards equilibrium) may be as long as two centuries (Adelman, 1958). We are now 200 years away from the Industrial Revolution and this observation may be given the interpretation that the social statistics matrix in Britain has only now (in the 1990s) started moving away from the characteristics established during the long reign of feudalism and before capitalism set foot in history. Clearly, this is a period longer than any economist would be prepared to accept as meaningful – though the subject may well be attractive to historians. In this respect one may have to agree reluctantly with the comment that 'Economics consists of theoretical laws which nobody has verified, and of empirical laws which nobody can explain' (Kalecki, 1954).

■ Pay differentials

Table 8.5 presents a bird's-eye view of pay differentials in Britain. Hourly pay of male workers is used because it corresponds closely to the notion of the wage rate and refers to a relatively homogeneous group of workers (female pay is discussed separately in the next chapter). Industrial differentials are presented in the form of earnings in manufacturing and non-manufacturing industries. Occupational differentials are presented in the broad aggregates of earnings of manual and non-manual workers. The table shows also the regional distribution of pay broken

Table 8.5 ***Hourly male earnings by industry, occupation and region, 1986 (as a percentage of average male earnings)***

	Manual	*Non-manual*
Industry:		
Manufacturing	82	132
Non-manufacturing	75	128
Region:		
Greater London	89	155
South-east (incl. London)	82	142
East Anglia	75	118
South-west	74	118
West Midlands	77	119
East Midlands	76	116
Yorkshire and Humberside	77	117
North-west	78	121
North	79	119
All industries/regions	78	129

Note: Average male earnings = £4.86 per hour.

Source: *New Earnings Survey, 1986*, Parts C, D, E.

down by manual and non-manual earnings. The evidence, albeit grossly summarised, suggests that there are substantial differentials across the labour market and the use of average pay as a summary statistic may be informative in certain respects but not in others.

Overall, manual workers in manufacturing are paid about 10 per cent more than manual workers in other industries. Non-manual workers are paid almost the same in these two industry groups but approximately 65 per cent more than their manual counterparts. Workers in London enjoy a pay premium of about 15 to 20 per cent compared with the national average. Some common explanations apply to these findings. For example, non-manual workers tend to be more educated than manual workers. Hence, (i) the productivity of the former can be taken to be greater than the productivity of the latter and employers are prepared to pay a premium for more productive workers and (ii) educated workers are paid a compensating differential for the costs of education they have incurred. Also, living in London is more expensive than in rural and other urban areas and higher earnings in London may simply reflect higher reservation wages.

The study of differences in occupational earnings can proceed very much along the lines of earnings functions explained in Chapter 4. In the present context the emphasis will be on why there are differences between workers employed in various industries and in particular the differences in the pay of manual workers. Below we present a summary of the arguments involved and some main results.

Most studies have included some measure capturing the extent of unionisation in the industries concerned. The variable may represent the percentage of the labour force who are union members or covered by closed-shop arrangements or benefit from collective agreements. The rationale is that unions are expected to push wages above their competitive level. In fact, this variable has been shown to have a positive and in most cases significant effect upon sectoral wages. An interesting picture emerged in studies which were able to pursue the effects of different types of collective bargaining upon pay – by including variables capturing the type of agreement under which the industry operated. In Britain most workers (about two-thirds) are covered by collective agreements though fewer than half are union members. Workers can benefit from national agreements, agreements at district and local level and company agreements as well as a variety of supplementary agreements. Thus wages can be fixed at national level or arranged in a relatively decentralised fashion. The evidence suggests that decentralised bargaining has an effect on wages but national agreements do not (Mulvey, 1976). This confirms the view that, though the ability of unions to raise the aggregate wage level and redistribute income from capital to labour is questionable, sectoral gains are possible.

Another variable included in the analysis of inter-industry was differentials is average plant size (employees per plant). There are many reasons why this may be a relevant factor. First, production in large plants requires more coordination and supervision than in small plants. Paying higher wages is a strategy for attracting better labour and, up to a point, beneficial in terms of costs (lower costs of supervision). Second, it has been alleged that workers may dislike working in large plants; hence, higher wages in large plants may constitute a compensating differential. One may also add that the organisation of labour is easier in the impersonal environment of larger plants. As a result, unions may be more effective in large plants at a given level of unionisation. However, the statistical effect of plant size upon pay differences has not been found to be conclusively significant (see, for example, Wabe and Leech, 1978). Perhaps working conditions in larger plants are better (for example, better canteens and other facilities). Also some workers may dislike the kind of direct supervision to which they are exposed in small plants. Hence the expectation that there is a positive compensating differential for working in larger plants may not hold on balance.

Working conditions, another factor giving rise to compensating differentials, are difficult to measure and include in econometric analysis. In the absence of other available indicators, the extent of shift-work has been used which can, nevertheless, stand on its own right. As expected, shift-work is associated with higher pay.

Most studies have also included in their analysis some 'human capital' variable. Obviously, industries which require a more educated labour force are willing to or should have to pay higher wages. The most common variable used in this respect is the 'skill mix' of the labour force, that is, the percentage of workers who fall in one or more categories with respect to their skill level. Indirectly, the use of this variable takes into account the occupational mix of different industries. Industries in which a high percentage of the labour force is skilled are found to pay, naturally, higher wages.

Regional effects are also important. Recall the evidence presented in **Table 8.5**: average pay varies significantly by region. Different industries may have to pay different wages depending on the labour market conditions in the region from which they have to draw their labour force. In an area with low unemployment, low wages will do. In another area where the cost of living is high (for example, because house prices are high) industries will find it more difficult to attract workers at low wages. Regional variables included in regression analysis typically perform according to expectations.

Another variable that has been included in many studies is the degree of industry concentration (Hood and Rees, 1974; Mulvey, 1976; Wabe and Leech, 1978). Concentration as a measure of (un)competitiveness has been proxied by either the volume of sales or employment accounted by the three or five largest firms in the industry or some more sophisticated measure (such as an index) of concentration. The idea is that concentrated industries can afford to pay higher wages than competitive industries because the former enjoy supernormal profits (Rees and Schultz, 1970). Why should firms give away some of their profits? First, to avoid industrial conflict over wage levels or to forestall union organisation. Second, to escape possible enforcement of competition laws. Finally, the 'bad press' associated with high profits from low wages may be another reason for higher relative wages in concentrated industries (Weiss, 1966). These reasons are more apparent than real. For example, fears of provoking the response of the competition authorities are rather hypothetical in many countries where there is little faith in competition policy and little effort is spent on enforcing it. Also, firms may get a 'better press' by spending part of their excess profits on health and safety improvements at the work-place or by donating to charities rather than by paying higher wages. In fact, higher wages is a risky strategy in the present context as wage cuts during, say, a recession may cause trouble while other forms of disposing of 'unwanted' profits are more flexible.

It is not surprising, therefore, that concentration has performed poorly as a possible explanation of industrial wage differentials. There are additional explanations to those presented in the previous paragraph. One reason is that the advantage of monopolistic industries is not over the level of profits in particular years but over the certainty of profits year after year. *Expected* profit rates (that is, after adjusting for risk) may be high in those industries but *reported* annual profits may be normal. Also, workers in these industries may be contented with greater job security, not higher wages, than in competitive industries. Another reason is the so-called 'capitalisation of rents'. This can be illustrated as follows. Assume that as a result of an innovation a monopoly situation is established. If the prospect for high profits is real, a likely course of events is for the inventor to sell the right and make a large capital gain instantaneously. Thereafter sales grow and the firm reverts to a public company. The monopoly power of the company is now reflected in the value of its shares, not in its rate of profit. It is the rate of return to the shares (in the form of dividends and capital gains) that is relevant. This is determined competitively in the stock market. Hence, the ability of the firm to hand out high wages to its labour force has gone. In other words, though prices are higher than marginal costs (the typical monopoly symptom), the high valuation of shares implies a high value of fixed costs per unit of output. It is the difference between prices and average costs (average revenue) which determines profitability – not the divergence between marginal costs and marginal revenue.

Whatever has been mentioned so far relates to an equilibrium approach in the study of industrial wage differentials. However, dynamic aspects in the labour market are also important: industries facing increases in the demand for their products want to recruit additional labour in order to produce more. These disequilibrium effects can be incorporated in the analysis by including a variable which shows the rate of growth of employment in the industry in previous period(s). The idea is that industries that want to attract labour do so by offering higher wages. However, there is no consensus on this. For example, some have argued that 'the decline of some industries and the expansion of others . . . normally occur in practice without any large inducements in the form of exceptionally higher earnings in the expanding industries. The main mechanism is simply that the expanding industries offer more vacancies than the declining industries at the going rate of pay' (Thatcher, 1976).

The important aspect in this statement is that nothing is said about what determines the 'going rate' of pay. The story would describe an economy in which inter-industry wages are determined by long-standing rules of custom – an example of this wage-setting procedure is discussed in the next chapter with reference to how female pay used to be set in Britain before equal-pay legislation was introduced. On the other hand the story would equally well describe an overall competitive labour market in which the supply curves of labour within each industry happen to be close to horizontal. In this case the ongoing rates cannot be much affected by changes in the structure of demand.

Distinguishing empirically between two such radically different views of how the labour market works is not easy. A study by Pissarides (1978) does, however, come to the conclusion that in so far as changes in relative wages are used in attracting labour from one industry to another, they are really rather effective in doing so.

What Pissarides does is to split the British labour market into 14 broad industrial sectors and use quarterly data for 1963–75. He considers the change in one quarter in the proportion of the working population in each sector *i* as a function of the following variables: (i) ratio of wage in sector *i* to all-industry average wages; (ii) notified vacancies in sector *i*; (iii) unemployment in sector *i*; (iv) the unemployment rate in all other sectors; and (v) seasonal effects. By the use of regression analysis he is able to see how net employment flows into each sector are affected by these five factors.

Pissarides finds that the relative-wage variable has significant positive effects on the flow into nine of the 14 sectors. For these nine sectors the effects of relative wages are quantitatively quite large. For example, he finds that if the wage in textiles went up by 1 per cent in one quarter relative to wages elsewhere, and if relative wages returned to their original values in the next quarter, this would induce a permanent increase of 0.2 per cent in the proportion of the working population employed in textiles. If relative wages remained constant and the one-quarter-only change took the form of a change in the number of the notified vacancies in textiles, such vacancies would have to go up by 14 per cent in the quarter to give the 0.2 per cent change in employment. Thus it appears that by temporarily raising wages in one sector relative to wages elsewhere, employers can induce quite large changes in employment structure.

This result does not necessarily deny Thatcher's point that typically intersectoral flows of labour take place via an interplay of expanding and contracting employment opportunities at very much stable rates of pay – but the point is that when employers are driven to the relatively expensive way of inducing increased employment by wage changes rather than simply by notifying vacancies, the inducements appear to work. In other words, there is a supply response in the direction predicted by simple price theory.

Instead of conclusions

This chapter discussed three aspects of labour earnings, namely, labour's share in total income, the distribution of earnings and sectoral pay differentials. Pay differentials were more successfully analysed (in terms of explanations offered) than the other two areas. This was so because by their very nature pay differentials can be examined within a partial equilibrium framework. In this respect economic analysis and the human capital theory are at their best. Some explanations for the size distribution of earnings were also offered but most of them tended to be statistical rather than economic explanations.

The functional distribution of income remains, however, a challenging issue. The difficulty associated with the study of labour share has a lot to do with the lack of informative data that relate to the economists' concepts of the variables involved. However, there may be another and more profound reason: explaining the relationship between wages and profits in the whole economy requires a general theory that goes beyond the examination of the economic component of any social system alone.

Setting aside these philosophical remarks, we present below some evidence on income inequality in an international context for empirical rather than theoretical reasons. The reason we consider the evidence on incomes is because information on the levels of individual labour earnings is not readily available across different countries. In addition, taxes, and payroll deductions and social benefits attached to earnings, are not comparable on an international basis. Ideally one would like to take into account these factors before determining the real position. At an international level the situation is more promising in the case of overall individual incomes. Nevertheless, labour earnings account for almost four-fifths of total income in advanced industrialised countries. Hence, the examination of incomes should reflect to some extent the situation with respect to labour earnings. Below, ten such countries are examined, two in North America and the rest effectively from Western Europe with the exception of Israel and Australia.

The income data come from the Luxembourg Income Study (LIS), an assemblage of micro-data sets compiled in the first half of the 1980s which (i) are based on common definitions of income sources as well as personal and family characteristics and (ii) have been adjusted by an adult equivalence scale. Incomes include all forms of cash income (such as labour earnings, income from capital and government transfers) and exclude income and payroll taxes.

The adjustment to an adult equivalence scale means that effects from different family size and different consumption patterns have been taken into account so that a more appropriate per capita income (consump-

Table 8.6 ***Percentage of persons in various adjusted income groups, early 1980s (countries ranked by % of the poor)***

	All persons				*Elderly*		
Country	*Poor*	*Middle*	*Rich*	*Country*	*Poor*	*Middle*	*Rich*
USA	24.2	53.7	22.1	UK	56.4	36.8	6.9
Israel	21.6	54.2	24.2	Australia	45.2	43.1	11.8
Australia	21.4	56.0	22.6	Israel	39.3	45.0	15.7
UK	21.4	58.5	20.2	Canada	37.1	48.6	14.2
Canada	21.0	58.5	20.6	USA	36.1	47.9	15.9
Switzerland	15.9	67.2	16.9	Norway	30.2	60.1	9.7
Netherlands	14.2	62.5	23.3	Switzerland	27.5	56.1	16.5
Norway	13.2	73.4	13.4	FR Germany	25.4	59.6	15.0
FR Germany	12.6	70.1	17.3	Sweden	11.5	85.2	3.3
Sweden	10.5	79.0	10.5	Netherlands	6.6	71.5	21.9

Source: Calculated from the Luxembourg Income Study data base.

tion) indicator is established. For example, in Britain a 'consumption unit' enjoying an income of £15 000 a year can be considered relatively wealthy, if it consists of a single individual, whereas such a unit can be well below poverty level if this income is shared between two adults and three children. These calculations lead to **Table 8.6** where a person is classified 'poor' if his/her adjusted income is below 62.5 per cent of the median income in the country concerned, 'middle-class', if income is between 62.6 and 150 per cent of the median income, and 'rich', if income is above 1.5 times the median income.[2]

In the left panel of the table the ten countries are ranked in descending order by the percentage of *all* persons who fall in the category 'poor' as defined above. Four of the top five countries are in effect non-European, the remaining one being Britain. One may also observe that these four countries are the newest ones, all formed in the last two centuries or so and Israel as late as in 1948. These countries appear to have more poverty and fewer people in the middle class than their European counterparts (except Britain) with the Scandinavian countries having the least poverty and the largest middle class.

In the right-hand panel of the table the ranking is based on the percentage of poor among the elderly (those aged 65 and over), a particularly vulnerable group that is by and large deprived of labour earnings. The same five countries which were at the top of the left-hand-side panel are again at the top, though in different order – with Britain now leading the league.

It is not surprising that despite the fact that labour earnings appear to follow some well-defined patterns (recall the discussion on the constancy of the log-normality of earnings across countries and over time and refer to the evidence provided in **Table 8.2**), the distribution of incomes varies considerably between countries. Factors such as taxation/benefit structure and the overall provisions of social policy are obvious explanations for the distribution of elderly people. Focusing on the case of Britain a more comprehensive treatment can be found elsewhere[3] but one may note that Britain has a more unequal distribution of land and of the income generated from it than many of the other countries in the table.

■ Notes

1. Of course, not all earnings are appropriated by the worker as he may have to pay taxes, social security and pension contributions, and so on. Also, workers' earnings are not necessarily equal to the total cost of hiring their services as employers may have to pay contributions and various other overheads.
2. For a description of data and a methodological exposition of the Luxembourg Income Study see Coder, Rainwater and Smeeding, 1988 and 1989.
3. See Addison and Siebert (1979), chapter 10.

■ Chapter 9 ■

Discrimination in the Labour Market

■ Introduction

This chapter has three main sections. First, it outlines the theory of discrimination. Discrimination has always proved to be a challenging topic in economics: why and how can a group of workers (such as women, ethnic or racial minorities) be systematically subjected to a different treatment than another group (such as men or white persons) in a competitive labour market driven by the pursuit of profits by employers?

Second, it examines the issues involved in measuring discrimination primarily with reference to wage differentials. Again this is a difficult empirical issue because in practice unequal pay for jobs of comparable worth is not necessarily discriminatory while equal pay for jobs of equal worth is not necessarily non-discriminatory (Killingsworth, 1990).

Third, and finally, we focus on the case of sex discrimination in Britain. It may be true that discrimination may take many forms but (i) sex discrimination may potentially affect a little more than 50 per cent of the population while, for example, race discrimination may apply to something less than 5 per cent of the population (and to a lower percentage of the labour force; see Mayhew and Addison, 1983, p. 311)[1] and (ii) Britain (as well as other European Community countries) has enacted a series of major legislative pieces in the past two decades to combat sex discrimination. It will therefore be interesting to see whether labour market 'interventions' are always distortionary.[2]

In attempting to explain discrimination reference will be made to some aspects of industrial relations. Positive economic analysis has greatly improved our understanding of how the labour market and its agents *may* operate but, at times, economists tend to forget that a whole range of theoretical abstractions become redundant, once information on real life arrangements becomes available. Let us give a slightly exaggerated analogy. As is shown below, theoreticians have put forward dozens of possible and probable reasons why women are observed to be paid less than men. However, by some coincidence women's earnings in practically all advanced countries have historically hovered at around 60 to 65 per cent of men's earnings while an early religious reference stated in effect that 'the value of a woman shall be assessed at three-fifths the value of a man' (Book of Leviticus, 27: 1–7). Therefore, one is tempted to ask whether the determination of female pay is governed by the forces of the labour market or by some institutional (cultural, even theological) arrangements.

The study of discrimination highlights the difficulty that arises in the discussion of normative issues – what can be or should be done with respect to matters such as equality. On the one hand, different people have different ideas which range from absurd theorising ('the longer the hair, the smaller the brain': Weiniger writing in 1906, p. 68) to the quasi-verifiable (the Atkin Committee, 1919, suggested that a woman working without undue strain could produce four-fifths of a man's output, something which was challenged by the Asquith Commission on Equal Pay, 1946). On the other hand, different governments have different priorities and in many cases certain issues receive only secondary priority. For example the immediate postwar governments in Britain were twice reluctant to introduce equal pay for women, despite their wartime promises which arose from appreciation of British women's heroic effort during the wars. In addition, after Britain's accession to the Common Market in 1973 (and its obligation to comply with Community policies) the provisions of the then legislation for equal pay were found to be more narrow than those that the Treaty of Rome prescribes. On the contrary, some other European governments have gone so far as to introduce measures which sound extremely egalitarian but may prove inapplicable. For example, the Dutch Equal Pay Act of 20 March 1975 makes it possible for a woman in an establishment where there is no comparable work done by a man to compare herself with a man in a similar establishment in the same trade or industry. However, in the United States 'proponents of comparable worth agree that comparable worth would not entail evaluations of jobs *across firms*' (Killingsworth, 1990, p. 13).

■ The economic theory of discrimination

□ *Early thoughts on discrimination*

The early statements on discrimination came mostly from the European side of the Atlantic and related to sex. Europeans somehow distanced themselves from other forms of discrimination at home: unequal treatment of certain groups usually took place a few thousand miles away from the homeland, namely in the land of the other groups (in the colonies). Thus, sex discrimination was the obvious candidate for a start as other forms of discrimination were associated with geographical segregation. In contrast, most American literature was spurred by racial (against black people) discrimination for the obvious reasons.

As early as the mid-nineteenth century it was argued that 'there is no natural inequality between sexes except perhaps in bodily strength . . . if nature has not made men and women unequal, still less ought the law to make them so . . . men and women ought to be perfectly coequal and a woman ought not to be dependent on a man, more than a man on a woman, except so far as their affections make them so' (John Stuart Mill and Harriet Taylor Mill in Rossi, 1970, pp. 73–4). These avant-garde statements were at the time when legislation and society made women and children the property of husbands, a woman's possessions became her husband's automatically on marriage, women could not sue for divorce on equal basis and had limited access to children in the event of separation. In addition women could not vote and participate in public life while opportunities for the education of women were practically non-existent. Compare Mill's arguments to those from another author some fifty years later: 'it is more important to have done with the senseless cry for "full equality", for even the malest [*sic*] woman is scarcely more than 50 per cent male, and it is only to that male part of her that she owes her special capacity or whatever importance she may eventually gain' (Weiniger, 1906).

The pre-neoclassical debate on the issue of women's inferior position in the labour market concentrated mostly on wage differentials. The early analysts identified potential reasons for women's low earnings to be customs and public opinion, the woman's secondary nature of employment (*vis-à-vis* that of the husband, the conventional breadwinner), lower productivity, women's lack of trade union support and lower standards of living, insufficient education and few opportunities for alternative employment (Webb, 1891; Collet, 1891; Fawcett 1892; Cannan 1914; Rathbone, 1917; Webb 1919; the Atkin War Cabinet Committee on the Employment of Women in Industry, 1919).

These observations set the stage for the debate which followed. Edgeworth (1922) and Fawcett (1917, 1918) put forward the concept of crowding. According to this hypothesis, women are over-represented in certain sectors (let them be industries or occupations) and this depresses female wages in these sectors *ceteris paribus*. This explanation, which was explicitly formalised by Bergmann some fifty years later (see below) was, nevertheless, criticised by Florence (1931) as incomplete. On the one hand, women's relative immobility in the labour market due to family and social conventions and, on the other hand, the refusal of men to work with or under the supervision of women were perceived by Florence to be more important factors for the explanation of sex wage differentials than those caused by productivity differences between men and women.

Pigou added that 'unscrupulous or unthinking employers are able to pay women less that they are worth because of the latter's strategic weakness' (1952) and this explanation was also among those considered by Florence (1931). Joan Robinson (1933) eventually put these remarks in context using the well-known theory of monopsony.

In the 'pre-Becker' era one should also mention here Myrdal's 'principle of cumulative causation' which saw the negro problem in the United States as the interaction and reinforcement of three causes moving in a vicious circle (Myrdal, 1944): first, the behaviour of whites against blacks; second, the conditions of poverty of blacks; third, the human capital and cultural characteristics of blacks. Few, if any, will challenge this view, but vicious-circle explanations, as the name suggests, tend to lead to circular arguments. What we learn from them (especially from authors in the area of development economics) is that there is a market failure and government intervention may be required to break the chain.

The pre-Becker (that is, pre-1957) literature is completed with two articles by Bronfenbrenner (1939, 1956) who examined monopsony, union and employer discrimination as sources for differential wages. An observation that should be made here is that Bronfenbrenner considered employers to be prepared to offer lower wages to the minority group (that is $w - x$, where w is the wage of the majority group and x is the expected cost of employing workers from the minority group) in anticipation for higher costs which might arise from labour conflict if the majority and minority groups were working together. This is interesting for three reasons. First, this analysis can be seen as an extension of the monopsony case (Lundahl and Wadensjo, 1984, pp. 13–14). Second, employing heterogeneous labour was seen as something which increases costs for the employer, although it could also be seen either as a form of diversification and spreading the risks or as a 'divide and conquer' tactic (Roemer, 1979). Third, the *mechanics* of Bronfenbrenner's analysis (that is, $w - x$) is, in effect, similar to that adopted by Becker who also assumed (though for different reasons) that employers will employ members from the minority group only if the latter's wages were sufficiently lower than those of the majority group.

□ *Becker*

Becker's theory of discrimination is based on physical disutility: individuals may prefer to incur costs rather than come into contact with members of certain groups. The disutility comes within the reign of tastes and in Becker's own words 'if an individual has a "taste" for discrimination, he must act *as if* he were willing to pay something, either directly or in the form of a reduced income, to be associated with some groups instead of others' (Becker, 1957, p. 14). Becker argues further that, 'when actual discrimination occurs, [the individual] must, in fact, either pay or forfeit income for this privilege. This simple way of looking at the matter gets at the essence of prejudice and discrimination' (ibid.).

Whether Becker's theory, which puts emphasis on individual behaviour (rather than group behaviour), 'gets at the essence' of discrimination may be questionable (see below). But this 'simple way of looking at the matter' has really resulted in an improvement of our understanding of the issue. Its simplicity and power can now be dissected. We adopt here a different presentation from that presented in Becker's book; nevertheless, this exposition captures the essence of the model (Arrow, 1972a, 1972b, 1973b). Define the employer's objective not as simple maximisation of profits, as is usually assumed, but as

$$\max U = f(\text{profits, percentage of men in the firm's workforce})$$

where U stands for the employer's objective (utility) function. The discriminating employer attempts to maximise his profits *and* the number of men in the firm's labour force. This reverts us to the standard two-commodity space with convex indifference curves defined over profits and the sex mix of the firm's labour force. Assume that the usual conditions hold with respect to the production function and the competitiveness in the product and labour markets. Consider **Figure 9.1** where monetary profits are depicted on the vertical axis and the sex mix of the labour force on the horizontal axis.

The representative indifference curve of the employer is shown as *IC* in **Figure 9.1**. The more an employer dislikes women, the steeper the slope of the indifference curve becomes. On the assumption that women and men are perfect substitutes in production and are paid the same

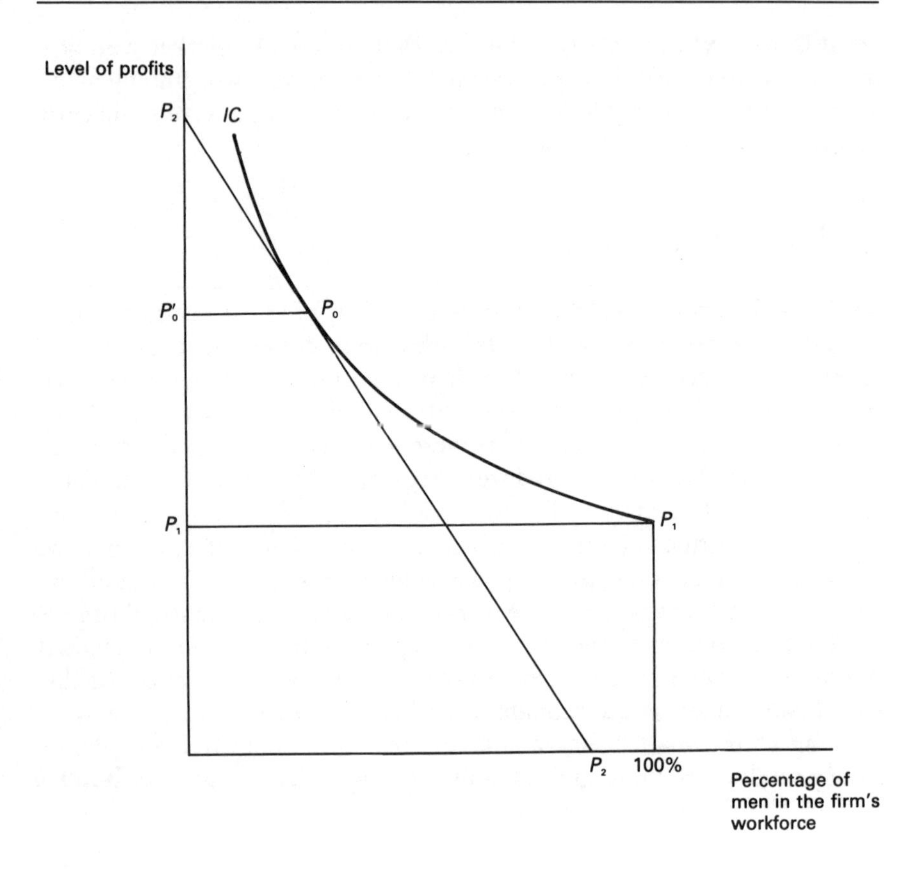

Figure 9.1 ***The equilibrium of a discriminating employer***

wage rate, total profits would be given by a horizontal line like P_1P_1. Had the employer been sex-blind, *IC* would have been horizontal too, and the equilibrium position would be indeterminate under the assumptions of the model (that is, it would depend on factors such as chance and not on the parameters of the model). As *IC* is drawn, the discriminating employer would prefer to employ only men. The reason given by the model is that the employer, due to his taste for discrimination, incurs a psychic cost from employing women. Although the monetary cost from employing women is as much as that from employing men (that is the wage rate, w), the *net* cost to him is $w(1+d)$, where d ($d>0$) is the disutility caused by the presence of women in the labour force. Becker called d the discrimination coefficient.

The value of d can be anything from minus infinity to plus infinity. Negative values of d imply nepotism, while positive values imply discrimination. When d is zero there is no distinction between different groups of workers and we are back to the conventional analysis. The term *wd* indicates the deviation of *net* costs from *monetary* costs to the employer when women are employed. It can be thought of as the exact money equivalent of the employer's psychic cost from women's employment. Thus Becker's discrimination coefficient has made it possible to incorporate explicitly the *act* (but not the cause) of discrimination into an economic model and study its *effects*. The fact that discrimination has now become potentially measurable on a continuous scale constitute the power of Becker's analysis.

Let us go back to **Figure 9.1** and examine the implications of the presence of discrimination. If the same wage rate applied to both men and women, the discriminating employer would achieve the highest level of utility by employing only men, as the monetary and net costs coincide only in the case of men. The discriminating employer's equilibrium is at the kink (point P_1). If, however, the women's wage rate were lower than that of men (and, again, under the assumption of perfect substitutability between the sexes in production), then the higher the percentage of men in the labour force, the lower the profits would be. As a matter of fact, profits will become negative before the firm's workforce becomes all-male (under the competitive conditions assumed earlier). This relationship is shown by the new profit curve P_2P_2 in **Figure 9.1**. The equilibrium position of the discriminating employer now becomes P_0 and the employer forfeits profits equal to the difference P_2P_0'.

The foregoing analysis leads to a number of predictions. First, the higher the discrimination coefficient (d), the more convex indifference curves will be and the firm will employ higher percentages of men. Second, the greater the wage differential against women, the more expensive it becomes to discriminate against women and the percentage of women in the firm's labour force will rise (though it would still be less than the non-discriminatory outcome). Third, the less substitutable women and men become in production, the higher the percentage of women in the workforce would be (as small deviations from the optimal sex mix would result in a sharp decline in profits: the profit curve in **Figure 9.1** would fall faster than P_2P_2).

One can show the implications of the model in a different way with reference to **Figure 9.2**. Assuming perfect substitutability in production between women and men, *MM* indicates the value of marginal product (and is also the demand for labour curve) for both factors in the absence of discrimination. If tastes work against women, this would result in an inward shift of the demand curve for women's labour (to *FF*) and by an amount equal to $-wd$ (to compensate for the psychic cost, namely *wd*, which derives from the discrimination coefficient). If one thinks of the inward movement as a vertical shift, this would imply that the employer

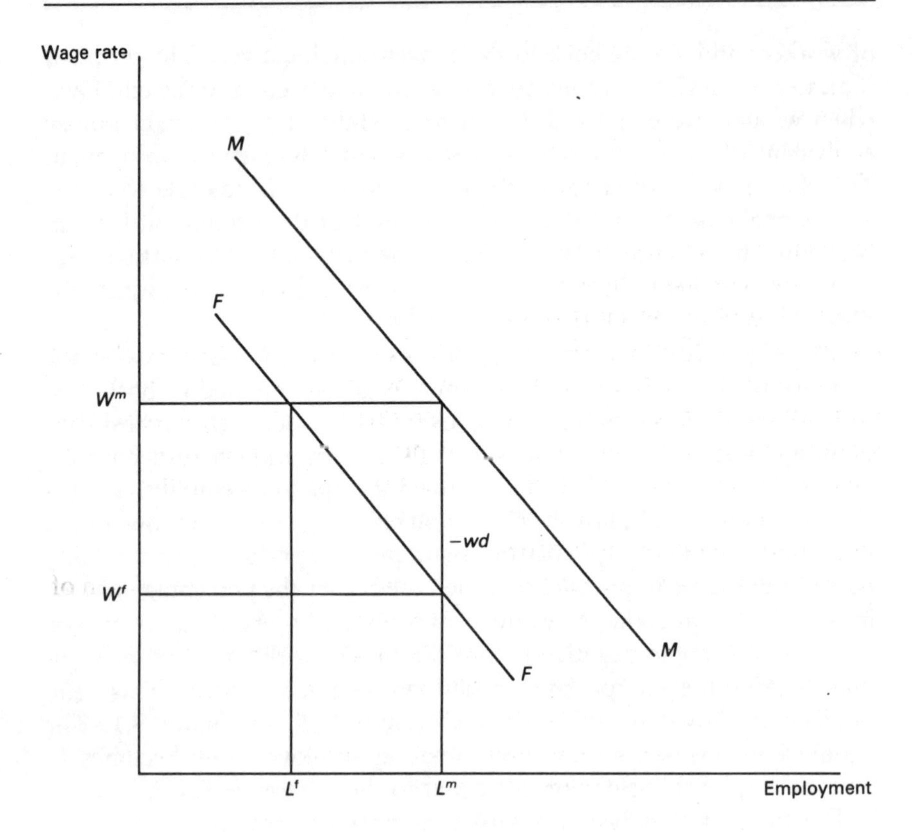

Figure 9.2 ***Employment and wages of the discriminated group***

would be prepared to hire as many women as men (point L_m) only if the female wage rate were equal to w^f. Alternatively, if one thinks of the inward movement as a horizontal shift, the employer would hire only L^f women, had the wage rate been the same for both sexes, namely w^m.

One can further derive the following predictions from the model. First, in the long run the discriminating employer will be driven out of the market by the money-cost-minimiser non-discriminating employer. Second, before the 'fittest survives', there would be both wage and employment differentials. The discriminated group will be employed in smaller proportions by the discriminating firms and will tend to join non-discriminating firms. One should place a warning here: the model is cast in terms of neoclassical full employment and does not explain differences in the unemployment or labour force participation rates between women and men. As a result, the model predicts that fewer women will be employed by discriminating firms, *not* that fewer women overall will be employed in the economy. The story takes place within a general equilibrium framework with perfectly inelastic factor supplies.

□ *Extensions and evaluation*

The foregoing presentation, albeit simple, captures the essential features of Becker's theory. The theory can be extended in various ways. Monopoly conditions in the commodity market (but competition in the capital market) result in the same predictions as before with respect to wage and employment differentials (Becker, 1959). If the discriminator is not the employer but fellow-workers, wage differences should be observed in both the short run and the long run, if the two groups are not perfect substitutes in production (or if they are complements). If they are perfect substitutes, then there will be wage differences neither in the short run nor in the long run. Under these assumptions about the substitutability of women and men in production, there will exist segregation. Finally, if consumers have a taste for discrimination, then again wage and employment differentials will prevail in the short run; the long-run outcome will depend on whether there is a possibility of segregation between different groups of consumers (for an exposition of these considerations, see Lundahl and Wadensjo, 1984).

We have examined the consequences of the existence of tastes for discrimination upon workers' wages and employment. As a general conclusion workers from the majority group benefit in terms of better wages, while members of the minority group lose. What happens to employers' profits? Of course, as far as an individual employer is concerned, his profits will depend on whether he discriminates or not and the implications of this have been already shown. However, the overall share of profits (*vis-à-vis* wages) in an economy where such discriminatory tastes are present is not easy to predict. Becker (1957, pp. 21–2) claimed that:

> There is a remarkable agreement in the literature on the proposition that [employers] . . . are the major beneficiaries of prejudice and discrimination . . . [T]he non sequitur in the mistaken analyses is the conclusion that . . . the difference between wage rates must accrue as profits to [employers] . . . These profits would only exist if this wage differential resulted from price discrimination (due to monopoly power), rather than from a taste for discrimination.

Thus, one is lead to believe that, under the assumptions of Becker's model, employers overall lose as a group (or, class?). This is hard to believe despite the fact that this is what comes out from the mathematical properties of the model.[3] That employers may lose is possible, but analyses that consider employers as benefactors from discrimination have not been proven wrong by Becker's theory. In Thurow's (1969, p. 112) words:

> if [Becker's] deduction is correct, empirical impressions are amazingly false. Do the whites of South Africa or the United States have lower standards of living as a result of their discrimination?

We pursue this point later in this chapter. In the meantime, we note that the difference between the pre- and post-Beckerian theories of discrimination may be more in appearance than in substance. In particular all possible causes of discrimination that were *formalised* by Becker (and by others who were inspired by his work) had been previously discussed and, in some cases, presented, albeit in simple diagrammatic expositions. Many have argued that Becker broke with the earlier tradition by making a 'sharp distinction between the *causes* and the *act* of discrimination' in that 'the existence of a taste for discrimination serves to explain the *act* of discrimination [and its effects]' while 'little notice is taken of the causes for discrimination' (Lundahl and Wadensjo, 1984, pp. 4 and 20). Nevertheless, it is true that the advantages of the Beckerian formulation are great as discrimination has become potentially measurable on a continuous scale rather than simply being present or absent. It is also true, however, that tastes or preferences or prejudices or whatever one wants to call d can be found implicitly in Webb as early as in 1891 and the other authors mentioned earlier. In addition d is directly equivalent to the x of Bronfenbrenner.

The important contribution of Becker is the incorporation of d into an economic model, where the mechanics of the standard optimisation procedures can apply. However, a problem appears in Becker's *'as if'* assumption in the definition of a taste for discrimination. Thus discrimination *is assumed to exist* and operate in a certain way but *its origin* still remains a 'black box' in Dex's words (Dex, 1986, p. 21). This may create little concern within positivist analysis. Theories are usually evaluated, on the one hand, on the frugality of their assumptions and, on the other hand, on the performance of their predictions. Many of Becker's results conform with common sense.

Perhaps the greatest shortcoming in Becker's analysis is the examination of discrimination not only outside a broader social context (after all the theory is an economic one) but also outside other economic aspects. The physical distance assumption may not necessarily be a relevant one in the case of sex discrimination, though possible it may be. The assumption becomes of relevance only if the firm and the owner–employer coincide; the separation of management from ownership gives little concern to the owner about the characteristics of the labour force. Also, customer discrimination can only cover a limited number of cases such as direct personal services.

Another concern relates to the fact that the model examines the effects of tastes only at the place of employment. Consider for example a discriminating employer who forfeits profits in order to satisfy his tastes at the work-place. Is it reasonable to assume that this may be his only objective? If by forfeiting profits he cannot live in a 'white' area (because house prices are higher than those in a black ghetto), or if he cannot educate his children in establishments with fewer or no blacks because of his limited income (thanks to his own discrimination at the work-place), then there are potential clashes between behaviour at work and at home which are not explored by the theory. Discrimination has to be considered in a broader context and should be examined simultaneously with consumption (demand for goods) patterns. The right analysis should be in terms of expenditure functions too, and not only in terms of *levels* of profits.

□ *Analysts other than Becker*

Becker provided an analysis based on an assumption about the act of discrimination. Nevertheless the analysis was coherent and served as a point of departure for many other studies. The level of theoretical debate was raised either by those who expanded the theory or by those who were critical.

According to Becker's theory, if there exists a taste for discrimination by some (but not all) employers there should be segregation in the short run. However, as firms which have the lowest or zero discrimination coefficients hire successively more of the members of the minority group, the non-discriminatory employers will drive out of the market the discriminating ones in the long run. As a result, Becker's theory cannot explain why discriminatory wage differentials can persist in the long run. Arrow (1972a, 1972b, 1973b) accommodated this inconsistency by taking into account adjustment costs. If there are costs of hiring and firing, it may not be cost-efficient to change the mix of the workforce as quickly as the paradigm of perfect competition suggests. The discriminatory wage differentials will be eliminated through natural wastage and/or the emergence of new firms only after a significant period of time. Arrow's extension tells us that the process of equalisation of wages and integration of the labour force will be slow but still does not explain why differentials have persisted and are with us even today after so many decades of market functioning.

Even if the market were working as postulated by neoclassical economists, economic outcomes do not depend entirely on market forces. A lot is decided by administrators who are part of central government and municipal bodies. For these agents there is no pressure to become monetary cost-minimisers. Their existence and survival does not depend on economic performance but is guaranteed by decree. Sowell (1981) highlighted this point with reference to the exclusion of blacks from certain occupations in the United States and Tzannatos (1986) made reference to the 'marriage bar' (prohibition of employment of married women) and other impediments which were utilised to exclude women from the Civil Service in Britain. Thus state monopolies may aggravate the problem. The same also applies to types of monopolies which are associated with 'no market for entrance', such as professional associations or craft unions (Demsetz, 1965). Regulating entrance to these monopolies has zero costs to those who belong to them, although there are efficiency losses associated with such actions.

Becker argued that private monopolies will be more inclined not to pursue discriminatory policies: a monopoly is worth potentially more to somebody who does not discriminate. But do monopolies (or firms in other market structures) try to maximise profits? Alchian and Kessel (1962) deny this for the case of monopolies, as such behaviour may attract either entry of other firms or government action under the provisions of competition policies. Thus it may not make it more profitable for a non-discriminating employer to possess a monopoly than for a discriminating one. As a result, the symptoms of employment segregation between the majority and minority groups of workers and wage differentials may persist, though again not in the long run.

In the models outlined so far, labour supply is assumed to be fixed at full employment. Gilman (1965) extended the analysis to include unemployment effects. If there is wage rigidity, there may be excess supply or demand in various sectors. If wage discrimination is not allowed (say, due to anti-discriminatory legislation or minimum wage provisions), the monetary cost of discrimination will be zero and there will be unemployment. Queuing for jobs in the discriminating sectors will make it possible for discriminating employers to offer lower wages in these sectors. The discriminated group will have to search for employment in the least-covered sectors and wage differentials *not within* but *across* sectors will arise. Segregation will again persist.

An early statement of how social origins and class may affect individual behaviour is found in Adam Smith (Book I, chapter 8):

> We rarely hear . . . of the combinations of masters, though frequently of those of workmen. But whoever imagines, upon this account, that masters rarely combine, is ignorant of the world as of the subject. Masters are always and everywhere in a sort of tacit, but constant and uniform, combination, not to raise the wages of labour above their actual rate.

We also mentioned earlier that the early British debate on discrimination paid due respect to the role of traditions and customs. However, Cassel's (1918) paradox had to wait a few decades before an answer was found. The paradox refers to the obvious neoclassical question 'how can one factor of production generally and permanently receive a lower wage than it is worth?'. It took time before answers were formulated into a concrete model: why should firms adhere to a given tradition and not maximise profits by employing more of the cheap factor? Akerlof (1976, 1980, 1983) showed that discrimination as a social custom is compatible with stable economic solutions as long as individuals perceive that non-adherence to social rules implies expulsion from the group to which they belong and carries certain benefits to its members. The important point here is the interdependence of the two transactions involved, namely the transaction between the employer and the worker *and* the transaction between the employer and other fellow-employers. This interdependence is overlooked by Becker. Non-discrimination in an otherwise discriminating world incurs costs as there may be 'penalties' for such a rule-breaking. Non-compliance with the rule may be *economically* profitable but it may not be *overall* advantageous.

Another line of reasoning is along imperfect information. If an employer wants to provide training to an employee of his, will he be indifferent between a woman and an otherwise identical man? Women *as a group* share disproportionately the reproduction cycle of a family and, as a result, they are less attached to the labour market than men. Recovery of the costs of training is less certain in the case of women. The inferior labour market characteristics of women as a group give rise to the so-called 'statistical discrimination'. Firms do not know in advance the precise productivity and commitment of a particular worker. Consequently sex, marital status, race, ethnicity or other characteristics become inexpensive screening devices for the firm's employment decisions (Phelps, 1972; Aigner and Cain, 1977). These considerations can explain why groups receive on average lower wages than others, or why they tend to be employed in certain sectors. However, no insight is offered into why an individual member of a minority group does not advance towards the characteristics of members in the majority group after some period of time, when the employer has had the opportunity to assess his/her individual productivity. Perhaps, one can explain some of the under-representation of women or blacks in managerial tasks today, but it is hard to offer a statistical explanation for the *total* absence of women and blacks from such ranks only a few years ago. One has to go back to Adam Smith's and Akerlof's theories to explain this phenomenon.

Finally, another group of theories come under the headings of 'dual', 'segmented', 'radical' and 'Marxist'. Their common characteristic is the emphasis on the way the firm or the labour market as a whole functions. These 'alternative' theories (Cain, 1976) which are closely identified with Piore (1975), Reich (1981) and Roemer (1979), are along the lines of the well-known 'divide and conquer' rule: the bargaining power of employees is greater the more homogeneous the labour force of the firm becomes. Firms decide on the optimal composition of their workforce so as to minimise labour disputes (compare this explanation to that of Bronfenbrenner).

The costs of discrimination

Assume that there are two identical factors of production, say men and women, which are employed separately in two identical industries. Assume for simplicity that factor supplies are equal and perfectly inelastic. This is shown in **Figure 9.3**. Under competitive conditions and assuming that there are neither costs of adjustment nor non-pecuniary differentials between the two occupations, a common wage will prevail, namely w^*. If an arbitrary wage differential ($w^m - w^*$) is imposed or if employment in the industry employing all men is artificially restricted (from M to M'), displaced male workers from industry 1 will seek employment in the industry previously employing only women, namely industry 2. This will lower wages in the later group to w^f. Thus the remaining workers in the male industry will benefit by $w^m - w^*$ while displaced male workers and all female workers will suffer a reduction in wage equal to $w^* - w^f$. The market is now characterised by wage differentials, the non-discriminated group gains, the discriminated group loses and there exists partial segregation.

These predictions are very much in line with most of the theories outlined in the previous section. Discrimination benefits some members of the society and harms others. From the point of view of an economist the analysis goes beyond sectoral gains and losses: if those who gain from discrimination do not gain enough to compensate the losers, then the discriminating economy has moved away from a potentially Pareto situation to an inferior one. As a matter of fact, all economic theories of discrimination lead to the prediction that there are welfare losses associated with any kind of discrimination, irrespective of the particular assumptions of the model. In **Figure 9.3**, the reduction in employment in industry 1 resulted in loss of output equal to the trapezoid $A + B + C$. The gain in output from the additional employment (crowding) in industry 2 is only $A + B$. Thus there has been a welfare (deadweight) loss equal to that indicated by the area of the rectangle C in industry 1. As we saw men workers gained in wages while women workers lost.

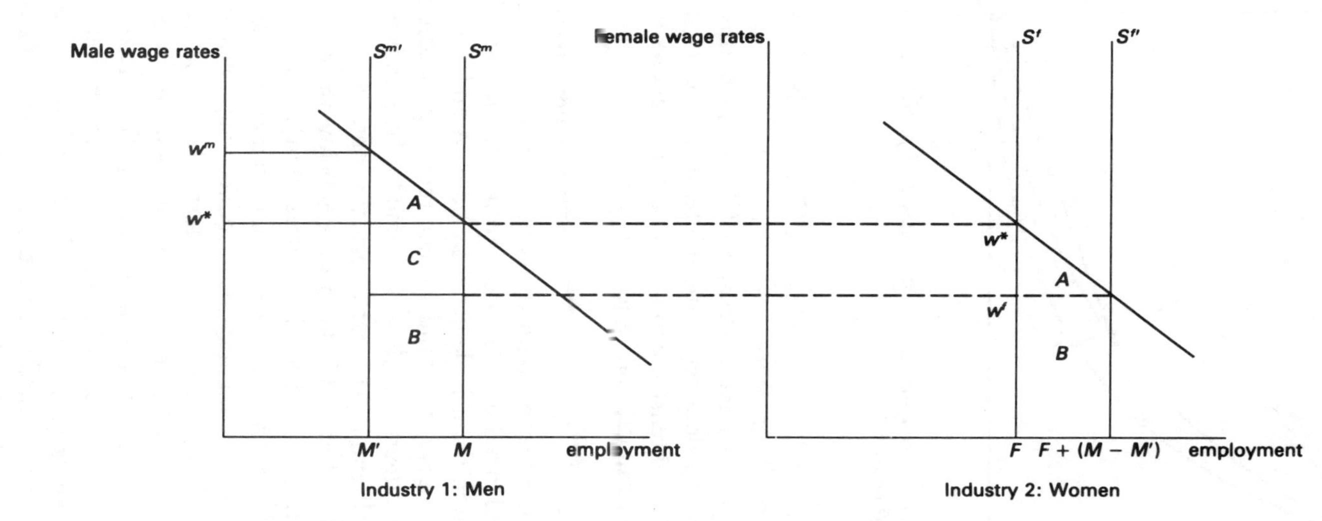

Figure 9.3 *The welfare cost of discrimination: partial equilibrium*

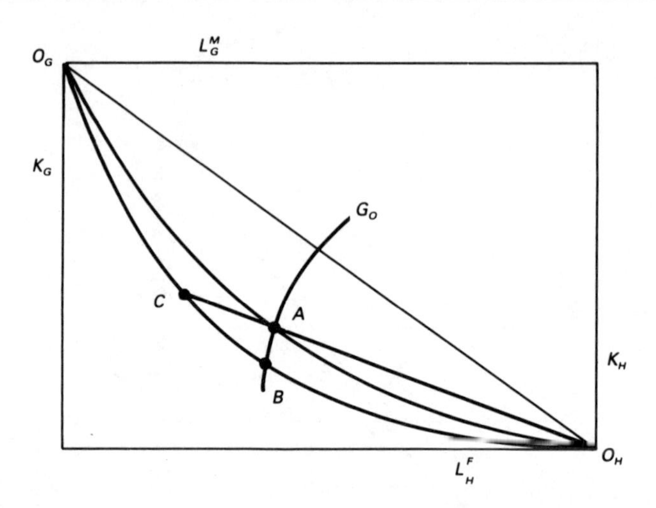

Figure 9.4 ***Effects of discrimination on wages and profits: general equilibrium***

What has happened to employers' profits? This can be shown better in a general equilibrium framework.

Figure 9.4 represents the conventional Edgeworth–Bowley box for two industries (one producing a capital intensive good, G, and the other producing a labour intensive good, *H*) and three factors of production (capital, *K*, and identical male and female labour, L^m and L^f respectively). The vertical axis measures total capital stock and the horizontal axis the labour stock. Assume, however, that labour is not randomly distributed between the two industries but that it so happens all men are initially employed in industry *G* and all women in industry *H*. The initial general equilibrium point is depicted by point *A* and is on the Pareto-efficient contract curve. Men and women receive as wages the value of their marginal products, which is the same for both industries, and the owners of capital (employers) earn normal profits.

Wages cannot be lowered in both sectors below their respective marginal products (this is ruled out by Walras's law). Neither can employment be reduced in both sectors. One can then introduce discrimination into this model either as an attempt to reduce wages below their initial marginal product in one sector (say, industry *H*) or to restrict employment in the other sector (the G industry). If the former were introduced and if the level of output in the male industry, G, were to stay initially the same as before, a new equilibrium would be reached at, say, point *B*. Point *B* lies on the original isoquant G_0 for industry *G* but on a new contract curve away from the diagonal except at its extreme points. Production is now inefficient. At point *B* women are definitely worse off (the capital–labour ratio has decreased), men are better off (the capital–labour ratio has increased) and employers may be better off or worse off depending on the quantities of goods *G* and *H* which they consumed originally (as, now, the relative price of good *H* to good *G* has changed). Notice that in the general equilibrium analysis Cassel's paradox does not arise. Women are not paid less than they are 'worth' (their marginal product): they are paid less because of the inefficiency introduced by discrimination.

Point *B* is only a temporary equilibrium. Given the income and price changes induced by changes in wages and prices in industry *H*, the production of good *G* will decrease, while the production of good *H* may increase or decrease depending on the magnitude of income and substitution effects (recall from **Figure 9.3** that an arbitrary differential results in loss of efficiency and a reduction in *total* output; hence, less production in *G* does not necessarily imply more production in *H*). Thus there will be another equilibrium point to the north-west of *B* where both men and women will be paid more relative to *B* (men will always be paid more than at point *A*). Employers will in general be better off, unless the final equilibrium point is *sufficiently* far away from point *B*. Point *C* illustrates this: if the equilibrium point moves further to the left than *C*, the capital–labour ratio in the female industry will also be higher than at *A*. In this case, female post-discrimination wages will be higher than at *A* (and male wages will be even higher). Of course, as said before, the allocation of factors as well as the allocation of production and consumption among the two industries will not be efficient. The economy is suffering a deadweight loss.

Thus, a discriminatory differential will favour the non-discriminated group while it may harm employers *or* the discriminated group depending on factor intensities, prices and initial consumption patterns. One study which addressed the question found that it is more likely that the employers' (rather than the discriminated) group gain from discrimination than vice-versa (Tzannatos, 1987a). This is more in line with Akerlof's theory than with Becker's. One thing is, however, certain: arbitrary wage or employment differentials result in net welfare losses and the winners cannot compensate the losers. The magnitude of gains and losses to individual agents and the social cost of discrimination cannot be determined by theory alone, even if the applicability of the theory were beyond doubt.

One has to resort to empirical studies to estimate the effects of discrimination on wages, employment and output. We next ask three interrelated questions. First, how much of the sex wage differential is due to discrimination. Second, how much of the employment (mis)-allocation is affected by sex wage differentials. Finally, what would the gain in output be, if both the wage and employment distributions of men and women were alike.

Measuring discrimination

To measure discrimination one has first to identify its cause. For example, women's inferior position in the labour market can be seen as the result of factors such as (i) unequal pay in the same job (wage discrimination); (ii) unequal access to some jobs (employment discrimination); and (iii) low pay in jobs undertaken by women (employment segregation). These are primarily demand factors but differences in labour supply may also be important. Hence, if discrimination against women were eliminated, one should not expect that women would be paid *equally* or would be employed on the same basis as men. This would be so only if women and men were the *same*. Notice the difference between *equal* and *same*.

Consider for example the case of a disabled person. To admit that he is *equal* to a fully able person has very few implications. The fact remains that unless he is in a position himself to restrict the effects of his disability (by means of, say, crutches or a wheelchair) and unless there are environmental provisions which allow him to exercise his potential (by special entrances and other facilities in public places), he will not be able to circumvent the effects of his disability. Think of one's own provisions to combat one's disability as the supply side of the labour market, and the environmental provisions as the demand side. To claim that a disabled person has *in general* an equal right to other people to visit public places would not eliminate differences between himself and the rest of the population. What the disabled person needs is a *special* right which will enable him to have access to improved (and costly) facilities for the disabled. Is such a right an automatic one? The answer to many is no. If this sounds strange consider another example: do slow learners have a right to receive a grant for a six-year (instead of a three-year) period for a university undergraduate course?

To the extent that women and men are *equal* but not the *same*, one would expect differences in labour market outcomes (among others) between the sexes. Some differences will be due to women's own decisions as well as those deriving from their family environment. This is the supply side and in Western societies individuals are considered to be the ultimate judges of their best interests. Other differences will be due to the environment. Some may be overt, such as discrimination. Others will be indirect; for example, lack of provision for maternity-related matters is more of an impediment for women than it is for men. In line with our previous discussion, maternity rights are special (to women) rights; the right for equal pay is a general right irrespective of sex. In order to formulate public policy on the issue, one has to find out which part of the sex wage gap is due to inequality of treatment and which is due to dissimilarity of characteristics. The usual line of argument is to relate inequalities to discrimination and dissimilarities to competitive outcomes (valuations) of the market.

Two different approaches are typically used in order to isolate which part of the pay gap is due to differences in endowments of productive characteristics and which part is due to the way these characteristics are rewarded in the labour market. First, one can examine whether there is a *fixed* premium/disadvantage associated with the sex of the worker. Second, one can investigate whether *individual characteristics* of female workers are rewarded differently in the labour market from the corresponding characteristics of men. The former approach relates to a 'shift' in the earnings function and the latter to a 'difference in the slope coefficients' of the earnings function (for a discussion on earnings functions, see Chapter 4).

The first approach consists of running a regression of earnings upon the characteristics of all (male and female) workers including a separate variable which indicates the sex of the worker (see Beller, 1984, or Killingsworth, 1990, chapter 3).[4] This can be shown as follows

$$\ln(W_i) = C + (\boldsymbol{X}_i)\boldsymbol{a} + b(F_i) + e_i \qquad (9.1)$$

where $\ln(W_i)$ is the logarithm of the ith worker's pay, C is a constant term, $\boldsymbol{X}$ is a vector denoting whatever measurable personal characteristics of relevance are utilised by the researcher, $\boldsymbol{a}$ is the vector of the estimated coefficients/effects of these characteristics upon pay, F is a (dummy) variable taking the value of 1 if the worker is female and 0 if the worker is male, and e is an error term that is assumed to be normally distributed with zero mean and refers to unobserved or unmeasurable characteristics. The interpretation of equation (9.1) is that individual earnings depend on the worker's observed characteristics ($\boldsymbol{X}$'s), the worker's sex (F), and unobserved characteristics (the error term) assuming that e is not correlated to F at given $\boldsymbol{X}$. If the error term is negatively correlated to F, then the coefficient on discrimination will be biased upwards as women will possess fewer unobservables than men with the same $\boldsymbol{X}$'s. This bias arises because the characteristics which are unobserved and affect women negatively will register an effect via the coefficient on the dummy variable measuring sex in addition to the pure effect of sex upon pay.

The coefficient of interest is that on the variable representing the sex of the worker, which shows whether women receive on average lower pay than men ($b < 0$), other things being equal (after adjusting for whatever the $\boldsymbol{X}$'s account for). This approach, however, constrains the values of the coefficients on the other explanatory variables, such as education and experience, to be the same for women and men. Given that sex-specific earnings functions have produced coefficients on female characteristics that are significantly different from those for men (Psacharopoulos, 1985; Tilak, 1987; Sahn and Alderman, 1988; Schultz, 1989; Bustillo, 1989), this approach is bound to yield, in general, biased results.

The second approach consists of running two regressions separately on women's earnings and men's earnings and comparing the two outcomes. This method requires the two regressions to have a strictly comparable specification, that is, the number and type of variables should be the same in both the female and male earnings functions. Thus the estimation can start with the following two regressions (omitting the individual subscripts $N_{i's}$ N for notational simplicity)

$$\ln(W_m) = C_m + (\boldsymbol{X_m})\boldsymbol{m} + e_m \tag{9.2}$$

$$\ln(W_f) = C_f + (\boldsymbol{X_f})\boldsymbol{f} + e_f \tag{9.3}$$

where C_s (s = male or female) is the constant term, $\boldsymbol{X_s}$ is the vector of male or female characteristics, $\boldsymbol{m}$ and $\boldsymbol{f}$ are the respective coefficients on these characteristics, and e_s is the error term. Then, the pay gap can be decomposed in the following way (Oaxaca, 1973): the difference in the *average* logarithms of male and female pay ($\ln(W_m) - \ln(W_f)$ – no subscripts) can be shown to be equal to the percentage difference of male to female average pay (W_m and W_f)

$$\ln(W_m) - \ln(W_f) = \ln[(1 + (W_m - W_f)/W_f] \tag{9.4}$$

$$= (W_m - W_f)/W_f$$

Given the previous two equations and utilising the regression property that the error term has a mean value of zero, one can rewrite equation (9.4) as

$$\ln(W_m) - \ln(W_f) = (C_m - C_f) + [(\boldsymbol{X_m})\boldsymbol{m} - (\boldsymbol{X_f})\boldsymbol{f}] \tag{9.5}$$

where the first bracket on the right-hand side refers to the respective constant terms in the male and female earnings functions, and $\boldsymbol{X_m}$ and $\boldsymbol{X_f}$ are the average values of the male and female characteristics in the sample. Adding to and subtracting from equation (9.5) the term $(\boldsymbol{X_f})\boldsymbol{m}$ or $(\boldsymbol{X_m})\boldsymbol{f}$ and rearranging produces the following two 'decompositions' of the gross differential in average pay

$$\ln(W_m) - \ln(W_f) = [(C_m - C_f) + (\boldsymbol{X_f})(\boldsymbol{m} - \boldsymbol{f})] + [(\boldsymbol{X_m} - \boldsymbol{X_f})\boldsymbol{m}] \tag{9.6}$$

$$= [(C_m - C_f) + (\boldsymbol{X_m})(\boldsymbol{m} - \boldsymbol{f})] + [(\boldsymbol{X_m} - \boldsymbol{X_f})\boldsymbol{f}] \tag{9.7}$$

Thus, the percentage difference in pay can be seen to come from two different sources, first, the differential rewards to male and female characteristics ($\boldsymbol{m} - \boldsymbol{f}$) in the labour market including the difference between the constant terms and, second, the differences in the quantities of these characteristics held by men and women ($\boldsymbol{X}_m - \boldsymbol{X}_f$). In this approach, the portion of the wage gap due to differences between the endowments of productive characteristics held by women and men can be considered to be non-discriminatory (or 'justified' discrimination (Blinder, 1974)). On the other hand, the portion of the wage gap which is due to differences in the values of the coefficients, including the constant term, can be thought of as the upper bound of 'unjustified' discrimination. Obviously, this approach (equations (9.6) and (9.7)), which utilises two separate earnings functions, encompasses the previous one (equation (9.1)) which is based on a single regression and examines, in effect, only the difference in the constant terms. This explains the popularity of the decomposition based on separate earnings functions for women and men in applied research although, in practice, the two approaches (equation (9.1) and equations (9.6) or (9.7)) may yield similar results because the constrained single equation estimation is, in effect, a matrix-weighted average of the results produced by the two-equation method (see Killingsworth, 1990, p. 96).

One should note that equations (9.6) and (9.7) do not produce the same results. The former decomposition evaluates the justified and potentially discriminatory components of the pay gap, *if women were paid as men*. The latter decomposition assumes that *men are paid like women*. This is a common problem with index numbers and is shown in **Figure 9.5.**[5] The horizontal axis measures education (schooling in years) which can be considered a typical individual characteristic. The vertical axis measures wages. The lower line represents the earnings function for women, that is, it shows that female wages increase by f (the slope of the line) for an additional year of schooling. The upper line is the earnings function for men and m is the corresponding slope coefficient. Let S_f and S_m be the average level of schooling attained by women and men respectively. The way the diagram is drawn suggests that women have on average lower wages than men ($W_f < W_m$) because (i) they are less educated ($S_f < S_m$), and (ii) their education is rewarded less than men ($f < m$) and the constant term for women is smaller in value than the constant term for men ($C_f < C_m$). Assuming that the difference in educational attainment is the result of women's free choice, one is interested in finding which part of the gross wage gap ($W_f W_m$) is justified, that is, it can be explained by the fact that women are less qualified than men in the sense that they possess a lower amount of schooling than men (that is, the difference arising from $S_f < S_m$). If 'no discrimination' is taken to mean that women should be paid as men

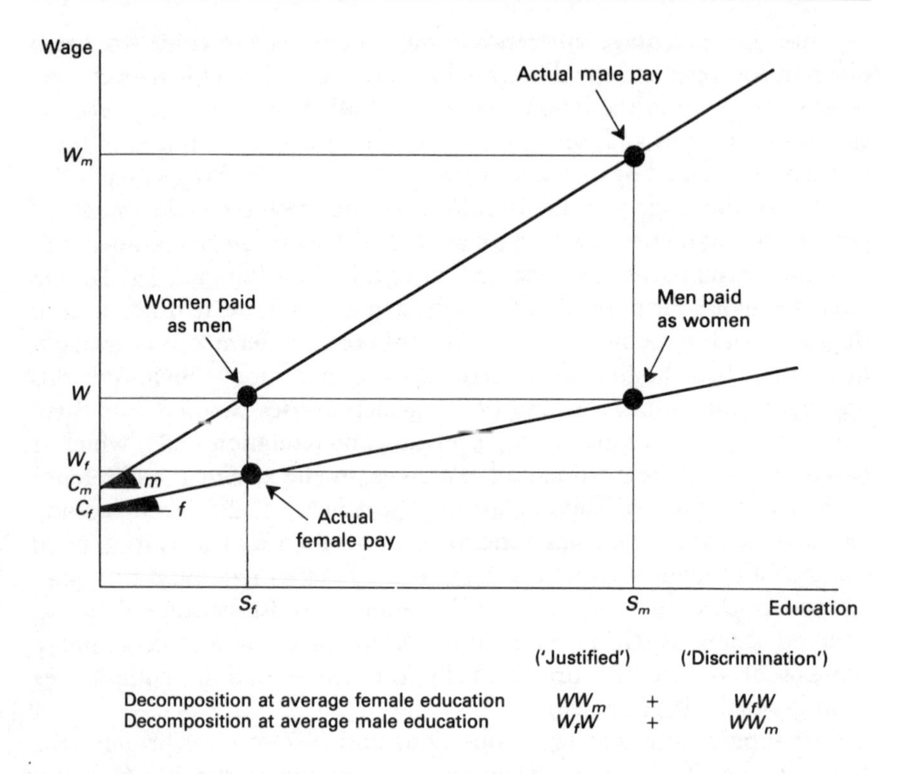

Figure 9.5 ***Decomposition of the gender wage gap***

(f should be equal to m and C_f should be equal to C_m), then women's average pay should increase to W; hence $W_f W$ is the unjustified part of the wage gap. Alternatively, if 'no discrimination' means that men should be paid as women (m equal to f and C_m equal to C_f), then the unjustified part of the wage gap becomes WW_m.

The two decompositions in **Figure 9.5** produced dramatically different results. This was purely for expository purposes. In practice, it is not certain whether a decomposition based on female means will produce a higher or a lower estimate for justified or unjustified discrimination than a decomposition based on male means. It all depends on the relative 'flatness' of the two earnings functions (that is, the curvature of the lines around the region of the average female and male characteristics) which is not captured in the simple linear specification adopted in **Figure 9.5**. However, both decompositions have produced similar results in applied research.

The role of the constant term needs further clarification as its value changes depending on how qualitative (dummy) variables are specified. Assume that a variable suggesting 'residence' (urban/rural) is included in the earnings functions to capture the fact that pay in urban areas is typically higher than pay in rural areas. If this variable takes the value of zero for rural residence and unity for urban residence, then the regression will produce a positive coefficient on residence. In this specification the constant term will have a relatively low value as it refers to the pay of rural residents. Conversely, if the variable proxying residence takes the value of unity for rural areas and zero for urban areas, it will produce a negative coefficient while the constant term will be higher as it refers to the pay of urban residents. Nothing else will change in this regression and the two specifications are formally equivalent. However, this innocuous change may have an effect on the results of the decomposition to the extent that rural/urban residence affects women's pay and men's pay in different ways. With reference to equation (9.6) or equation (9.7), the second term (difference in endowments) will remain unchanged and the percentage of the pay gap attributed to endowments will be as much as before. The first term (difference in rewards) will again be the same if considered together but the relative importance of differences in the constant terms will be different compared with differences in rewards. As a result, attempts to separate the effect of the constant term from the total effect of rewards may result in arbitrary conclusions. This point was raised by Jones (1983) who notices that up to 20 per cent of the gender wage gap may shift from the constant term component to the other rewards component when qualitative variables are specified in different forms. Despite the difficulty in the interpretation of the constant term *per se*, most modern studies on discrimination have conventionally examined the effect of the constant term separately within the 'rewards part' of the gender wage gap (see, among others, Shapiro and Stelcner, 1986; Behrman and Wolfe, 1986; Birdsall and Behrman, 1986; Birdsall and Fox, 1985; Knight and Sabot, 1982, and the collection of papers in Birdsall and Sabot, 1991).

A number of issues have been raised with respect to the use of earnings functions (equations (9.2) and (9.3)) and the previously described decomposition (equations (9.6) and (9.7)) in the attempt to identify the gender effect on pay. The arguments relate to whether the parsimonious formulation of earnings functions is sufficient and appropriate for the task in hand on both theoretical and empirical grounds. We have already covered these issues in Chapter 4. Here we concentrate on whether earnings functions can usefully apply to the study of wage differentials – not wage levels as such.

Education – There is also evidence that parents usually invest in higher-quality education for boys than for girls. Becker and Tomes (1979) suggest that parents could distribute investment among their children with different characteristics differently and empirical evidence especially from developing countries confirms that, if such differential treatment is practised (in areas such as healthcare, nutrition or expenditure on education), it favours boys (see Visaria, 1971; Chen *et al.*, 1981; Aird, 1984; Blau, 1984; Martorell *et al.*, 1984; Amin and Pebley, 1987; Schultz, 1982; and Bardhan, 1984, for an overview). Hence, the nature of the schooling variable in the men's regression may be different from that in the women's regression.

Experience – We have already explained how the inclusion of *potential*, rather than actual, experience in the earnings function can result in biased estimates. We simply remind the reader that the measurement error and bias resulting from it are more serious for women than for men. Evidence from studies that used both measures of experience suggests that the estimated effect of potential experience upon female pay may be as low as 50 per cent of the effect of actual experience.[6]

Endogeneity – Even if information on actual labour market experience for women were available, one could not use it as such in the earnings equation. The reason for this is endogeneity. Experience is nothing more than a measure of 'accumulated' participation, and participation depends on pay. For men, this is not perhaps a very important issue as the inelasticity of male labour supply to wages can be interpreted as an indication of the fact that men participate and accumulate experience independently of the earnings they can fetch (see Rosen, 1969 and 1976; Brown, Levin and Ulph, 1976; Atkinson and Stern, 1980; MaCurdy, 1981; Blundell and Walker, 1982; and for a survey, Pencavel, 1986, or Fallon and Verry, 1988). However, for women, especially married women, the elasticity of labour supply to their prospective pay has generally been found to be positive and sizeable: though the labour supply elasticities for women have been estimated to be as high as 14 or more (Heckman and MaCurdy, 1980 and 1982; Dooley, 1982), a value of around 1.5 to 3 could be considered quite typical. Therefore, by focusing on one equation only, we ignore a more extensive (multi-equation) model where past and present female pay and work exhibit strong endogeneity. In fact, the seriousness of failing to account for the endogeneity of female participation can be shown by reference to a study which reconciled the micro-evidence (cross-section data) with the observed patterns and trends in female participation (time-series data) only after correcting for (endogenising) the experience of married women (Iglesias and Riboud, 1985). This point has been forcefully made in many studies and the endogeneity problem with respect to labour market experience is clearly documented in the literature (Blinder, 1973, and Mincer and Polachek, 1974). This issue relates in part to the selectivity problem addressed below.

Selectivity – We examined the issue of selectivity in some detail in Chapter 3. Now, assuming that earnings functions have been properly corrected for selectivity bias, let us go back to the original question, that of discrimination. The correction in women's earnings functions allows us to estimate the wage offers of all women irrespective of current labour force status. However, one may argue that the kind of difference on wants to study is that arising, *in* the labour market from *demand* factors. Under these circumstances, one needs to know what is paid in the labour market to those who work. Even if working women are a self-selected group with better than average characteristics than the whole group of women, these are the ones whose productive characteristics are evaluated in the labour market. Can or should the market pay non-working women with inferior attributes as much as women who are better-qualified and actually working? In this respect, the appropriate decomposition of the pay gap should apply to the coefficients of the female wage equation uncorrected for selectivity and to the average value of characteristics held by working women only. This is, however, a procedure that practically all studies of discrimination have bypassed and they have routinely used selectivity-corrected wages for the sample characteristics of working women. If one wants to expand the notion of discrimination to include the pay potential of non-working women, one should use the selectivity-corrected wage estimates and evaluate the adjusted pay gap at the value of the average characteristics of *all* women in the sample, both working and non-working. Which mean values of variables to use in what type of decomposition is a point which has been very much missed in most studies though some recent studies have taken account of it (see Psacharopoulos and Tzannatos, 1992a).

The 'chicken and egg' question – Even if the functional form of the earnings function is the appropriate one, and there are neither specification errors nor omitted or poorly measured variables, one cannot be certain that the decomposition results accurately reflect a properly standardised difference between female and male pay. This is because it is hard to distinguish to what extent endowments are the effect of past or expected discriminatory practices, something which can be said to constitute indirect discrimination. In this case one has a different kind of endogeneity, that is, in the earnings function (earnings versus investment in human capital) compared with endogeneity in the participation function (employment versus wages). However, Griliches (1977) argues that accounting for the endogeneity of schooling typically does not alter significantly the coefficients in the estimated earnings functions. Nevertheless, if women suspect or know that they are less likely to enter a high-wage and/or senior position, they may be discouraged from acquiring human capital of the size and/or type they would have opted for had they perceived equality of opportunity in the labour market (England, 1982; Weiss and Gronau, 1981; Gronau, 1982). In this respect, the measured wage discrimination would be underestimated more often than not by the present decomposition.

What are 'comparable characteristics?' – The attempt to make the two groups homogenous before the gross wage differential is broken down into its constituent components can go beyond controlling for differences in the amount of labour supplied by women and men. For example, men could be paid more because they work in certain occupations and industries rather than because they are paid more than women who may also work in those sectors (in fact, the evidence suggests that women are predominantly found in low-pay sectors and are also paid less than men within these sectors). Consequently, one may be tempted to include explanatory variables relating to employment status in order to adjust for the effect on pay of the different employment distributions of women and men. To ask an employer to pay women in one industry or occupation as much as men in another industry or occupation may not sound immediately obvious. The same considerations apply to the effect upon pay of differences arising from the regional employment distribution of women and men. Therefore, the standardisation of certain differences in the earnings equation before one attempts to establish the discriminatory part appears *prima facie* necessary. However, it makes a lot of difference if women choose to become nurses (instead of doctors) or employers do not promote women to managers and let them stay in junior administrative tasks. If restriction of entry is a determinant factor for the employment distributions of the sexes, the inclusion of employment variables will result in more standardisation than is needed for establishing the unjustified wage gap between women and men. This will be so because that part of the wage differential which is due to employment status would be attributed to differences in characteristics although it is really due to discrimination in the form of unequal opportunities in employment. On the other hand, if occupational choice is unconstrained and the occupational wage structure reflects compensating differentials, ignoring the occupational structure would lead to an exaggeration of the extent of discrimination.

□ *Empirical findings*

A study which specifically addressed the issue for Britain along the lines of the Oaxaca decomposition is that of Zabalza and Arrufat (1985). The characteristics of interest in the study of Zabalza and Arrufat were years of schooling, labour market experience, race, health, occupation and industry. Using regression analysis and data for married women from the *General Household Survey* for 1975, they estimated the increase in female earnings which would be necessary to make m equal to f in equations (9.2) and (9.3) and in **Figure 9.5**. And an interesting feature of their study was to estimate which part of the earnings differential was due to women's breaks in their labour force participation due to family and other commitments. One can summarise their results as follows.

In their sample the ratio of female to male pay was 62 per cent and men had, on average, 24.5 years of labour market experience while women had only 15.9. Correcting for labour market experience would increase female relative to male pay to almost 80 per cent. Put it alternatively, almost 50 per cent of the earnings differential was due to women's less experience in the labour market. Differences between the sexes with respect to other attributes (such as schooling) explained another 8 percentage points (or another 20 per cent of the gross sex wage differential). Finally the remaining 12 percentage points (or 30 per cent of the differential) were unaccounted for by the model and, as a result, were seen as the upper bound of wage discrimination against women in Britain at the time.

There are two interpretations to these results. According to a narrow interpretation, the elimination of wage discrimination in Britain should result in an increase of the average female relative to male pay to 74 per cent (62 + 12). According to a broader interpretation, part if not all of the depreciation of effect on women's human capital due to breaks in labour force participation may be discriminatory. For this argument to be valid employers must use women's labour market interruptions as a reason for paying women less that otherwise equivalent men. Thus, according to the broad interpretation, non-discrimination should result in an increase in the ratio of average female to average male earnings to around 90 per cent. As a matter of fact, this figure is close to the ratio of female to male earnings in Sweden which is, perhaps, the most advanced country with respect to egalitarian public policies between the sexes both in the family and the work-place.

These results have been confirmed by a more recent study which examined the pay characteristics of a much more homogeneous group of workers than those of the *General Household Survey* utilised by Zabalza and Arrufat. Joshi and Newell (1987) used data from the *MRC*

National Survey of Health and Development and estimated that, again, 30 per cent of the sex wage gap for the 1946 cohort of women was unexplained by human capital variables or job characteristics in 1977. This is in line with the study of Zabalza and Arrufat as far as inequality is concerned. In another study, Stewart and Greenhalgh (1984) examined the work patterns history and occupational attainment of women using data for 1975–6 from the *National Training Survey*. They concluded that if women's work patterns did not suffer from less attachment to the labour force, female earnings could increase by at least 40 per cent.

Another study which addressed the issue of wage discrimination among married persons in Britain is that of Wright and Ermisch (1991). The two authors used potential and actual experience in their earnings functions for women and this makes their results particularly valuable (recall that using potential experience amounts to assuming that women work continuously after completion of their education). Their data came from the *Women and Employment Survey 1980* and suggest that married women's hourly pay was 67 per cent of married men's hourly pay in 1980 (£1.69 and £2.52 per hour respectively). Their results can be summarised as follows. If potential experience is used, the unexplained part of the sex wage gap is 88 per cent, if there is no correction for selectivity, and 77 per cent after correcting for selectivity. If actual experience is used, then discrimination is reduced by 25 percentage points in both cases. In other words, about one-quarter of the observed wage gap can be attributed to women's intermittent work histories while another one-tenth is due to women's self-selection in the labour market. Differences in endowments explain only a small part of the remaining 65 per cent of the total wage gap and the upper bound of discrimination may be as high as 50 per cent of the total wage difference. The importance of this study is that it finds the upper bound of discrimination to be higher than in previous studies, despite the fact that the inclusion of actual (rather than potential experience) explains almost one-quarter of the total wage gap primarily at the expense of the 'difference in rewards' part of the decomposition rather than at the expense of the 'difference in endowments' part.

A related issue is the importance of occupational status in determining average pay for women and men. As mentioned earlier, whether women chose for or are 'forced' into certain occupations is difficult to know. Despite this difficulty, there have been studies which have addressed the wage effect of different occupational attainments between women and men (see Brown, Moon and Zoloth, 1980, for the United States, and Miller, 1987, for Britain). Both studies concluded that the reasons for women's apparent underpayment should be sought in women's low relative pay in the sectors in which they are employed.

In conclusion, women in Britain would be paid less than men even if demand for labour were sex-blind. However, the empirical evidence suggests that still a lot of the difference between female and male wages is unaccounted for by differences in the productive characteristics of the two sexes. The potential welfare implications of the 'upper bound of discrimination' are traced in the following section.

How much is the misallocation of employment due to discrimination?

This is even more difficult to answer than the previous question. Here one has to identify not only the extent of unjustified underpayment of female labour but also the extent of 'exclusion' of women from employment in certain sectors. One way to proceed is to assume that the sex wage differentials are due to over-representation of women in a few sectors either because of direct wage discrimination or because women are effectively excluded from some sectors.

Researchers in Britain have followed the job-crowding model shown in **Figure 9.3** in order to tackle this question (Bergmann, 1971). The approach is as follows. Consider an industry, for example, the car industry. The industry employs both men and women but, as usual, not within the same occupations. Men do a wide range of masculine jobs (such as tasks relating to mechanical and electrical engineering). Assume, perhaps not unreasonably, that men are paid more than women who tend to be crowded into a few feminine tasks (such as upholstery). Recall from our discussion on the general equilibrium theory of discrimination that workers in both sectors were paid their respective marginal products. Under conditions of crowding women are, of course, paid less, than the competitive wage. However, at the non-discrimination equilibrium workers were paid the same. Go back to our example of the car industry and ask the question 'how many women should leave their occupations and join male occupations so that wages across occupations are equalised?'. The answer will be valid only if, of course, the wage differentials are due to crowding and apply to otherwise identical workers.

Two studies have addressed the problem using different data, namely Pike (1982) and Tzannatos (1988a). The difference in the two studies is that the former allowed for labour supply responses due to changing wages, while the latter introduced adjustment in the capital stock again due to changes in factor prices. Nevertheless, the results are fairly comparable and indicate that employment in male-dominated occupations should increase by up to around one-third to achieve equality of wages. What is an interesting finding in both studies is that wages in the previously female-dominated occupations will increase significantly (on average by around 50 per cent), while this need not be accompanied by a reduction in wages of more than a few percentage points in the previously male-dominated industries. This happens because there are efficiency gains from the elimination of crowding.

These estimates are only upper-bound estimates of the possible effects of discrimination. To the extent that human capital investment and employment decisions are dependent on women's preferences and their own prospects prior to their entry into the labour market and there is no discrimination after they join the labour market, then over-employment in some sectors does not indicate misallocation but simply that some workers prefer to work in some sectors more than in others (Mincer and Polachek, 1974).

□ *What is the welfare cost of discrimination?*

The analyses of Pike (1982) and Tzannatos (1988) provide as a by-product changes in total output (efficiency gains) which result from the hypothetical reallocation of female labour towards male-dominated occupations. A key parameter for this simulation is the elasticity of substitution between male and female labour. There are no direct estimates for this elasticity. Therefore, both authors estimated the effect upon output (welfare gain) using a range of values for the elasticity of substitution.

Pike experimented with elasticities up to the value of 3 and found welfare gains of up to 3 percentage points. Tzannatos extended the analysis to cases where the elasticity of substitution took a value of up to 10, as empirical evidence suggests that the elasticity is substantially greater than unity, ranging usually between 3 and 9 (see, for example, Bowles, 1970; Dougherty, 1972; Dougherty and Selowsky, 1973). As a matter of fact such a hypothetical exercise can safely assume an elasticity of substitution equal to infinity as it rests on the assumption of identical factors. However, it may be wise to allow for a smaller value of the elasticity of substitution as there is bound to be some degree of complementarity or discontinuity between the employment of men and women in production. Tzannatos found that potential gains may be up to 10 percentage points, if the use of capital is ignored, or around 5 to 6 percentage points if changes to capital utilisation are taken into account.

Concluding the issue of measuring discrimination, all the evidence presented in this section is unavoidably tentative. There is no clear winner among the competing theories of discrimination and the quality of empirical estimates are constrained by the availability of data. Nevertheless, the picture points to the fact that a good part of the wage and employment differentials between men and women in Britain are, from an economist's point of view, unjustified. The emerging picture is that the discriminated group loses while the majority group gains a little and employers benefit. The welfare cost of discrimination is, thus, disproportionately borne by workers rather than employers. This perhaps conforms to reality more than does the Beckerian analysis.

British sex anti-discriminatory legislation and its effects

Despite the fact that the women's question was first and most profoundly analysed in Britain, the introduction of legislation has been extremely slow and piecemeal. Nevertheless, the effect of sex anti-discriminatory legislation in Britain has been striking at least on the wage front. Employment effects are more difficult to establish. Let us examine these issues in turn.

□ *History*

In 1888 the Trades Union Congress unanimously passed a motion that 'where women and men do the same work as men, they shall receive the same payment'. This was reiterated by Congress on more than 40 occasions in the following 75 years, but it was not until 1963 that Congress called for legislation to enact equal pay. In the meantime, the issue was examined by three Royal Commissions (in 1912–16, 1929–31 and 1944–6), three governmental comittees (1918, 1919 and 1923) and was also raised on numerous occasions in Parliament and extra-parliamentary circles (Hepple, 1984). The introduction of equal opportunities legislation was delayed usually on the grounds that employers could not afford it.

Equality of pay in the Civil Service was achieved in 1961 and the Labour Government elected in 1964 set up the appropriate motions for equality of pay in the private sector, too. As a result, the Equal Pay Act was enacted in 1970 with the aim to eliminate differences between pay *for the same or broadly similar work or for work rated as equivalent under a job evaluation study*. The Act stipulated that the adjustment of pay differentials should take the following form: wages in low-pay jobs (usually performed by women) should be raised to the level of high-pay comparable jobs. This practice is similar to that adopted elsewhere. For example, in the USA legislation specifies that the implementation of the principle of comparable worth shall not result in a reduction in pay of any job while local governments have prohibited cuts in the pay for employees of certain job categories (Orazem and Mattila, 1989, p. 180). Adjustment of wage differentials that provide for increases only can be also found in other countries, such as Australia and Greece (Gregory and Duncan, 1981; Tzannatos, 1987a, 1987c).

The Equal Pay Act provided for gradual 5-year implementation (to 29 December 1975) in order to avoid the disruptive consequences of a sharp reduction in the long-established sex differentials. In addition, the Sex Discrimination Act 1975 outlawed unequal treatment on the grounds of sex and marital status in aspects of employment other than pay. The latter Act became operative on the same day as the Equal Pay Act 1970. In the meantime the United Kingdom had become a member of the EEC and Article 119 of the Treaty of Rome sets forth the principle that 'men and women should receive equal pay for *equal* work'. In the mid-1970s it was clarified that 'equal work' in the Treaty means 'equal value' (EEC Directive 75/117). The wording of the British legislation was then successfully challenged before the European Court as too restrictive. Recall that the *letter* of the original British law provided for cases where women and men do the same or like work and *in practice* very few women and men are actually doing the same type of work in the same establishment. As a result a new legislative piece came into force in January 1983 under the title 'Equal Pay (Amendment) Regulations', which consolidated and broadened the previous two Acts of 1970 and 1975. However, there was considerable scope for improvement in female pay prior to 1970 under the provisions of the 1970 Act, despite the narrow wording of the earlier legislation, as the way female pay was then determined was anachronistic, arbitrary and overtly discriminatory. We examine these issues in the following section.

□ *The effect of legislation on relative pay*

It is too early to assess the effects of broadening the scope of legislation in 1983. Nevertheless the effects of the original legislation are both clear-cut and impressive. Female relative to male hourly earnings in-

Table 9.1 ***Female relative pay, 1886–1987 (%)***

	1886	*1960*	*1970*	*1976*	*1987*	*Source*
Adult manual workers						
Weekly earnings	51.5*	51.4	49.9	60.6	61.1†	Department of Employment
Hourly earnings	—	60.5	60.1	71.4	69.5†	
Adult full-time workers, hourly earnings excluding overtime						
Manual	—	—	61.7	71.1	70.7	*New Earning Survey*
Non-manual	—	—	52.5	62.6	62.1	
All	—	—	63.7	73.5	74.1	

* From *British Labour Statistics, Historical Abstract 1886–1968*, Table 35.
† It refers to 1984, the latest available.

Source: Zabalza and Tzannatos, 1988.

creased from around 60 per cent to 70 per cent in the 5-year transitory period which started in the early 1970s. Up to 1970 female relative pay had been remarkably stable for the whole recorded history of wages in Britain (since 1886) and has also been equally stable post-Equal Pay (since 1976), albeit at a higher level (**Table 9.1**). The gradual implementation of Equal Pay started in 1970 and was completed by 1976. Was this a coincidence?

Early researchers on the effects of legislation upon female pay in Britain gave more emphasis to the egalitarian flat-rate provisions of the incomes policies of the early and mid-1970s (Chiplin, Curran and Parsley, 1980; Pike, 1982). These studies unavoidably suffered from lack of post-Equal Pay observations and they were undertaken more or less at the same time as the incomes policies were in operation. However, later studies observed that the increase in female wages in the early 1970s was permanent (**Table 9.1**) and the effect of incomes policies was, on the one hand, negligible and, on the other hand, short-lived (Ashenfelter and Layard, 1983). The once-for-all improvement in female relative pay was found to be attributable neither to incomes policies, nor to a deterioration in male pay, nor to changes in female employment from low-pay to high-pay sectors, nor to sudden changes in the demand for female relative to male labour (Tzannatos and Zabalza, 1984; Zabalza and Tzannatos, 1985a). The only explanation for the increase in female relative pay during the 1970–6 period remained, in a residual way, the Equal Pay Act 1970.

A characteristic of British legislation on the issue of discrimination is the lack of penalties for those who are found in breach of the law. On the contrary, penalties in the United States often reach six-figure sums; yet there is no discernible change in female pay in the United States post-Equal Pay (Dex and Shaw, 1986). The claim that legislation is responsible for the increase in female wages in Britain would be difficult to sustain unless one could show *how* the provisions of the law became operative, especially in the absence of infringement procedures. Tzannatos and Zabalza (1984) examined the system of wage determination in Britain and found that prior to 1970 collective agreements as a general rule prescribed female pay either *pro rata* to male pay, or as a differential to male pay or, if a single rate were prescribed, it was meant to apply to an activity almost solely undertaken by one sex only. Under the circumstances, enforcement took the form of a 'stroke of a pen' and affected the pay of at least 70 per cent of women workers covered by collective agreements. A corroborative argument to this explanation is that the pay of female teachers and other women employed in the narrowly or broadly defined public sector was the only one which did not experience any change in the 1970–5 period (or immediately before or after). A near-identical story can be found in the case of Australia (Gregory and Duncan, 1981) and, to a lesser extent, in the case of Greece (Tzannatos, 1989). Both countries used to have the same kind of wage determination as that which used to apply in Britain prior to 1970.

This story also explains the constancy of female relative pay for a century before Equal Pay. Why female relative wages have shown little variation after 1976 is something that no study has yet addressed. An explanation could be along the lines suggested by Arrow (1972a) and Phelps (1972): imperfect information and market imperfections make quick adjustments costly and established patterns may prevail in the short run and the 'longer' run. Perhaps the answer is that changes in wage differentials from causes that arise 'within the market' are slow and gradual, as in the American case. This intensifies the thesis that sudden disruptions of wage differentials should be sought outside the labour market.

The effect of legislation on relative employment

The employment response to legislation is difficult to predict theoretically and estimate empirically. In theory there are two offsetting effects. On the one hand, if legislation (the Equal Pay Act) is successful in raising female wages and making female labour dearer, then there will be substitution of other than female labour for the now expensive women workers. On the other hand, if legislation (the Sex Discrimination Act) is successful, employers need not be able to respond negatively to higher pay for women as they should treat men and women equally. Thus the net effect of legislation can be anything.

There are a number of alternative theories which may apply and make the employment response to legislation tilt towards the positive side. One is the possibility of relative monopsonised labour markets for female labour, a factor often discussed but rarely found relevant. Another is efficiency wage aspects: when women's pay becomes unconstrained from norms and female labour becomes more expensive to hire, employers may find better use of female labour, on the demand side, and women may become more productive in response to better wage and employment prospects, on the supply side.

There is only a limited number of studies which have undertaken to examine the employment response to legislation. There have been only a few years since legislation was fully implemented and it is always difficult to proxy a qualitative variable (such as legislation) in regression analysis of the demand for inputs. Given these limitations, Pike (1985) concluded that equal opportunities legislation has been unable to play a substantial role in halting the decline of relative employment in manufacturing during the 1973–82 period. However, Zabalza and Tzannatos (1985b) estimated for both the whole economy and the private sector separately that there was little evidence to suggest that the response to equal pay was detrimental to female employment. In another study (Tzannatos and Zabalza, 1985) the authors estimated that the variability of female employment after the introduction of legislation was somewhat lower than before. This finding applies to estimates for the whole economy as well as for the manufacturing and non-manufacturing sectors separately. Clearly, this is an issue which has to receive more attention in the future before any firm conclusions are drawn.

■ Concluding remarks

The issue of discrimination has haunted economists for a long time. Discrimination is not only an economic issue. Societal preferences and political interventions do play an important role in shaping outcomes. In addition, discrimination is a qualitative issue and its incorporation in the neoclassical theory did not formally occur until Becker's doctoral thesis in 1957. Yet Becker's theory proved more useful for a fresh look at the issue than his original model as such. The *act* of discrimination needs to be more than an assumption in order to enable the theory to explain the long-run persistence of differentials.

On the issue of policy, it is not easy to provide answers. To the extent that discrimination could not be accommodated in theory (Cassel's paradox), the orthodoxy denied its existence and avoided to prescribe policies, if not solutions. With Becker it became part of tastes, that is, part of the individual's preferences whose formation and consequences are considered to fall within the reign of individual freedom in market economies.

One thing is for sure: legislation (that is, government intervention) in Britain did not prevent the competitive functioning of the labour market. On the contrary, wage-setting is now more competitive than before. The market prior to Equal Pay was subjected to an unjustified wage differential whose origins go back in history. Here one has a concrete case that interventions are not always undesirable. This chapter showed that it is probable that policies and actions which improve the position of women in the labour market will be self-financed in that there will be substantial efficiency gains as a result of these policies. In simple arithmetic, half of the nation's intelligence is in the heads of women and women still contribute less than a third to the country's recorded output.

■ Notes

1. There are a number of useful surveys which cover additional aspects of discrimination or extend the present analysis. An early attempt is that of Marshall (1974) who almost exclusively focused on the case of race discrimination. Sex and marital status have been dealt by, among others, Chiplin and Sloane (1976), Amsden (1980) and Mayhew and Addison (1983). Lundahl and Wadensjo (1984) surveyed and extended the neoclassical theory of discrimination and Sloane (1985) provided one of the most pedagogical introductions to the subject. Dex (1986) reviewed the literature of the costs of discrimination and Cain (1986) upgraded the earlier survey by Marshall for the United States by extending his analysis to discrimination other than that of race. Finally, Dex and Sloane (1988) provide yet another survey on detecting and removing discrimination from the market-place.
2. Tzannatos (1986).
3. Madden (1973) originally argued that Becker's conclusion rests on a mathematical error but Addison and Siebert (1979, p. 235) reaffirmed Becker's derivation of his proposition.
4. For applications and extensions of this approach to measuring wage differentials in other areas of research see Smith (1977), Oswald (1985) and Ehrenberg and Schwarz (1986).
5. Some authors have taken the average of the estimates of the two approaches (Greenhalgh, 1980) but, as explained later in the text, this makes practically no difference to the results as the 'slope' effect typically dominates the 'endowment' effect.

Chapter 10

The Economics of Trade Unions

In Chapter 7 the determination of the levels of wages and employment was considered in cases where there is perfect competition among sellers of labour, as well as in the case of monopsony. An important characteristic of the labour market in industrialised countries is the existence of trade unions as organisations of sellers of labour. Trade unions are complex institutions, which can be analysed from social and political as well as economic viewpoints, but in this chapter we concentrate exclusively on the economic analysis of trade unions. In 1975 Johnson conducted a survey of the contents of a wide selection of professional journals in economics, on the basis of which he concluded that the study of trade unions had become a 'Cinderella' topic within economics (Johnson, 1975). However, as we shall see in this and the subsequent chapter this state of affairs was quickly to change, to the extent that a number of significant advances occurred during the 1980s and early 1990s in the economic analysis of trade unions.

The present chapter begins with a brief history of trade unions which is followed by a discussion of the economic theory of union growth together with a summary of the available empirical evidence relating to the theory. In the next section the questions of union objectives and the specification of a model of union behaviour are considered. In the following chapter we consider the determination of wages under collective bargaining and discuss the relative wage effect of trade unions (that is, their impact on the wages of their members relative to those of non-members) and their effect on the allocation of resources. In Chapter 13 the role of trade unions in wage inflation is considered.

Trade unions: a brief history

A trade union was defined by the Royal Commission on Trade Unions and Employers' Association set up in the UK during the 1960s as 'any combination of employees the principal activity of which is the regulation of relations between employees and employers' (Donovan, 1968, p. 207), and these unions have existed in various forms in the UK since the early nineteenth century, if not earlier. **Table 10.1** shows the number of trade unions that existed in the UK in various years between 1892 and 1980, together with details of their membership and that of their US counterparts in absolute terms and expressed as a percentage of potential membership to give what is termed *union density*. As can be seen from **Table 10.1** the organisation of sellers of labour in the UK and USA into trade unions is by no means a new phenomenon. By 1892 there were some 1233 unions in existence in the United Kingdom with a total membership of over 1.5 million workers, constituting 10.6 per cent of potential membership. However, by 1980 the number of unions had fallen to 454 while the size of their membership had risen to 12.9 million workers, equivalent to a little under 54 per cent of potential membership. Throughout the period considered in **Table 10.1** the level of union density in the US is less than that in the UK with the ratio of US to UK density varying since the turn of the century for the years shown in **Table 10.1** within the range 0.35 (in 1930) to 0.635 (in 1950). **Figure 10.1** provides a more detailed picture in the form of a plot of US and UK union density over the period 1897 to 1970.

The wider perspective: unionisation in the OECD

It is important to recognise that marked variations also exist in the extent of unionisation across other countries. **Table 10.2** documents trade union membership, expressed as a percentage of all employees, in a range of OECD member countries over the period 1970 to 1985. The figures reported in **Table 10.2** indicate a range of alternative experiences

Table 10.1 ***Trade unions in the UK and USA: selected years 1892–1980***

	United Kingdom			*USA*	
Year	*Number of trade unions at end of year*	*Membership (millions)*	*Union density (%)*	*Membership (millions)*	*Union density (%)*
1892	1233	1.576	10.6	0.477*	3.02*
1900	1323	2.022	12.7	0.869	5.54
1910	1269	2.565	14.6	2.102	9.0
1920	1384	8.348	42.2	4.775	16.66
1930	1121	4.842	25.4	3.162	8.9
1940	1004	6.613	33.1	7.055	16.45
1950	732	9.289	44.1	14.09	28.02
1960	664	9.835	43.1	15.539	26.32
1970	543	11.187	47.7	18.136	24.28
1980	454†	12.947	53.6	20.246†	19.6

* These US figures relate to 1897 not 1892.
† This figure relates to the end of 1979 in the UK case, and to 1978 in the US case.

Sources:
(1) Sapsford (1981, Table 5.1).
(2) Union density is defined as

$$\frac{\text{Actual union membership}}{\text{Potential union membership}} \times 100$$

Note:
The data series on potential membership for the period 1892–1970 was obtained from Bain and Elsheikh (1976, pp. 134–9), who defined potential union membership as the total number of employees (that is, employed plus unemployed). UK data for 1980 were defined in the same way and obtained from the *Department of Employment Gazette*. The figure for US union density for 1980 was obtained from Reder (1988).

since 1970. Of the eleven member countries considered in **Table 10.2**, Sweden has by far and away the highest percentage of unionised employees. In 1985 almost nine out of every ten employees in Sweden were union members. Another noteworthy feature to emerge from **Table 10.2** concerns the direction of the trend in union membership over the period since 1970. Comparing membership in 1970 with that in 1985 we see that in every country except Italy, Sweden, Australia and Germany the 1970s and 1980s were decades of falling union membership. Notice, however, that despite rising in the 1970s Germany's rate of unionisation had fallen back by 1985 to its 1970 level (see also Freeman, 1988).

The development of trade unionism in the industrialised economies of the world has been a complex process influenced not only by economic forces but also by political and legal factors, and there is a well-

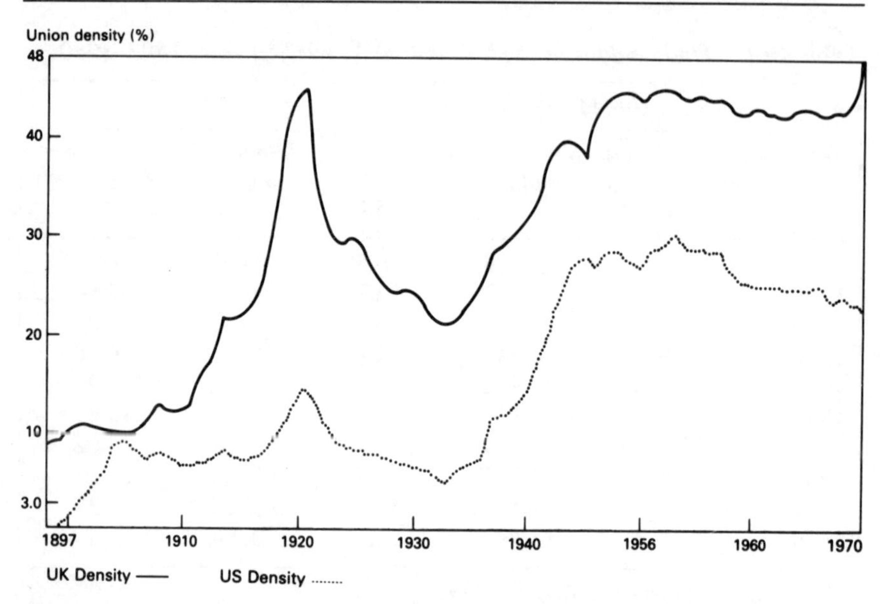

Figure 10.1 *Union density in the UK and the USA, 1897–1970*

developed literature covering these influences. (See, for example, Pelling, 1971, and Clegg, 1972.) Nevertheless, a number of important features do emerge from an inspection of the aggregate data set out in **Table 10.1**. Throughout the period covered by the table, there was a marked downward trend in the number of unions in existence in the UK, and this was accompanied by an upward trend in union membership and union density, a pattern also evident in the US membership and density data. Over and above these trends there was a cyclical pattern in membership and as we shall see in a following section, the relationship between this and the level of economic activity has attracted considerable research interest.[1]

■ Craft unions

The first trade unions to emerge were *craft unions* of skilled workers in the UK, and throughout most of the nineteenth century unionism was largely confined to skilled workers, with the consequence that unionisation covered only a small proportion of the total labour force.[2] Prior to the industrial revolution the acquisition of a craftsman's skills typically provided the passport to self-employment or employer status. However, after the emergence of the industrial society, a significant proportion of craftsmen found themselves effectively forced to remain as employees (rather than employers or self-employed) throughout their

Table 10.2 *Union membership in the OECD (percentage of all employees 1970–85)*

Country	*1970*	*1975*	*1980*	*1985*
United Kingdom	48	51	53	43
Australia	50	54	52	51
Canada	36	34	30	30[(a)]
France	23	23	19	18[(b)]
Germany (FR)	37	39	39	37
Holland	37	38	37	29
Ireland	52	53	55	46
Italy	33	42	43	40
Japan	35	34	31	29
Sweden	74	79	88	88
United States	27	25	23	16

Notes:
(a) Break in continuity of measurement in Canadian data in 1978 causes approx 4 percentage points fall.
(b) 1982.

Sources: R. Price in R. Bean (ed.) *International Labour Statistics* (London: Routledge, 1989); and Brown and Wadhwani (1990).

working lives, with a consequent lessening in their ability to represent their own interests. It has been argued that this factor provided an important impetus to the formation of craft unions by skilled workers. Historically, the wages of skilled craftsmen had exceeded those of the unskilled (see Phelps-Brown, 1977, pp. 68–81, for some evidence on the size of this skill differential), and the formation of craft unions represented a largely successful attempt by skilled workers to maintain their favourable relative wage position. A rapid growth in the demand for the services of skilled workers accompanied the process of industrialisation and it has been argued that, faced with this, craft unions restricted entry into the crafts in order to prevent an influx of new entrants, attracted by craftsmen's wages, from increasing the conditions of labour supply to the craft and thereby depressing their relative wage position. The principal instrument by which the craft unions restricted entry was the apprenticeship system which, although ostensibly designed to ensure proper standards of training and qualifications, was often used as a barrier to entry against new entrants to the craft.

The determinants of the elasticity of demand for labour (the Marshall rules) were considered in Chapter 5. It is important to notice that according to these rules the demand for craft union labour will be

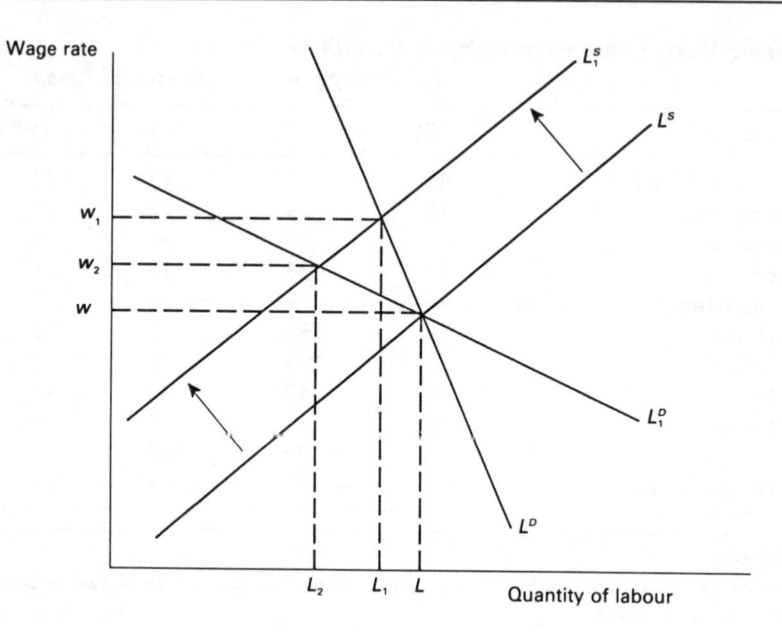

Figure 10.2 ***Craft union wage policy***

inelastic (Friedman, 1951, pp. 207–15). This is because the possession by craft union members alone of the skill in question limits, particularly in the short term, the possibilities of substituting non-craft union labour or other factors of production for craft union labour when its wage rate is increased. In addition, the demand for craft union labour will, subject to the Hicksian condition, be inelastic because the fraction of total costs accounted for by craft labour is normally small.[3] Given the inelastic demand for their members' services, the main method by which the craft unions were able to achieve their objective of maintaining their favourable wage position relative to unskilled labour was through the manipulation of the supply of labour. By controlling entry to the craft, these unions were able to shift the supply curve of craft labour to the left and thereby, given the inelastic demand curve for their members' labour, to achieve a high wage in relation to that of non-craft union labour, with little contraction in employment. This situation is illustrated in **Figure 10.2**. Given the inelasticity of the demand curve for its members' labour, the craft union is able to push wages up from w to w_1 at the cost of a reduction in the employment of its members of only LL_1. The union achieves this by shifting the supply function of its members' labour from L^s to L_1^s through exercising its ability to control entry to the craft. If the demand curve for labour were more elastic, say L_1^D, the union would be able to secure a smaller increase in its members' wages (ww_2), from the given supply shift, and only then at the cost of a greater contraction in employment (LL_2).

In the longer term, when employers can substitute other factors of production for craft union labour, demand tends to become more elastic, and to counter this, craft unions have frequently attempted to restrict the substitution of other, non-union or less skilled, labour and/or capital for their members' services, by employing such devices as manning and demarcation rules or even a straightforward refusal to accept new technologies. The hostility among the craft unions in the UK newspaper-printing industry in the 1980s towards the introduction of new technology is a clear example of this point.

■ Unskilled labour and the 'new unionism'

Until the final decade of the nineteenth century, unionism in the UK and the USA was still on a fairly limited scale and in the UK still largely confined to skilled workers. As can be seen from **Table 10.1**, only about 10 per cent of potential membership was actually unionised in the UK by the 1890s with the corresponding figure for the USA being to the order of 3 per cent. During the 1890s unionism in the UK took off into its second phase of growth – a phase characterised by the growth of the so-called *new unionism*. The spread of unionism in the London area in 1889 and during the year immediately following is generally regarded as the take-off phase of the new unionism, which, in contrast to the old (craft) unionism, catered mainly for unskilled, poorly-paid workers.

This phase of UK union growth lasted about until the outbreak of the First World War and was characterised by the formation of *general unions*, which opened their doors to all comers, regardless of their industry of employment and which charged only low subscriptions. The years immediately preceding the outbreak of the First World War saw a particularly rapid growth in the UK's union membership. Between 1910 and 1913 total membership rose by 61 per cent, from about 2.5 million to over 4.1 million. This was due in large part to the integration of unions' benefit functions into the state health and unemployment insurance schemes.

As we have seen, craft unions were able, given the inelastic nature of the demand for their members' labour services, to increase their members' wages relative to those of other workers by manipulating the supply of labour. However, general union labour was non-essential (in the sense that there existed adequate substitutes for union labour in the form of non-union labour with the consequence that there was a high elasticity of substitution between these two types of labour input), and it generally accounted for a fairly high proportion of total costs. In addition, in the late nineteenth and early twentieth centuries there was frequently a highly elastic supply of non-union labour from the sometimes massive pool of available unskilled labour made up of those shifting out of agriculture and the unemployed. Given the combination of these factors, it follows from the Marshall rules that the demand for general union labour was likely to have been highly elastic. Consequently, the general unions of the new unionism era had little opportunity to increase their members' wages by restricting the supply of union labour (compare the wage and employment effects of the given supply shift in **Figure 10.2** with the labour demand curve L_1^D opposed to L^D), except in periods when a high level of economic activity increased employment by an amount sufficient to drain the pool of available non-union labour and in cases where substitution by non-union labour could be prevented. Being generally unable to capitalise on the demand-and-supply situation, general unions therefore sought, as far as possible, to organise all sellers of labour and thereby minimise substitution by non-union labour.

■ Industrial and white collar unionism

The depressed economic conditions of the interwar years had their effect on trade unionism in the UK and USA alike. In the UK, membership reached its interwar peak in 1920 at 8.35 million, but declined quickly with the rapidly rising level of unemployment, as those losing their jobs tended to stop their union subscriptions and withdraw from membership. Between December 1920 and December 1921 unemployment among insured workers in the UK rose from 7.9 per cent to 18 per cent, and union membership declined by one-fifth to only 6.6 million. This decline continued until membership reached only 4.4 million, or just over half of its 1920 level, in the depths of the depression in 1932, when unemployment rose to 22.1 per cent of insured workers. A similar picture is evident in the US data. In 1920 US membership stood at 4.775 million, but despite a doubling in the US unemployment rate from 5.2 per cent in 1920 to 11.7 per cent in 1921, membership fell to only 4.553 million in 1921. However, union membership in the USA subsequently fell steadily to a low of 2.805 million (giving a union density figure of 7.35 per cent) in 1933 when the US unemployment rate stood at 25.2 per cent).

The economic climate of the interwar period had two main effects on trade unionism in the UK. First, there was a marked decline in the number of unions in existence (which fell between 1920 and 1940 from

1384 to 1004; see **Table 10.1**), as falling membership forced many smaller unions to merge with the larger ones. Indeed, a number or today's best-known unions had their origins in the amalgamations of this period. For example, in 1921 a merger between the Amalgamated Society of Engineers and six smaller craft unions gave rise to the Amalgamated Engineering Union (AEU). The Transport and General Workers' Union (TGWU) was formed in 1922 from an amalgamation of unions of dockers and transport workers, which in turn swiftly absorbed a number of other smaller unions. Similarly, the National Union of General and Municipal Workers, (NUGMW) arose at this time from an amalgamation of the Gas Workers' Union and other general unions.

Second, faced with falling membership, unions sought to offset this by making inroads into new areas. In an attempt to recruit new members the AEU, for example, opened membership for the first time to semi-skilled and unskilled workers in 1929, and both the TGWU and the NUGMW sought during the interwar period to recuit new members from among clerical workers and from the new and expanding mass-production sectors within the economy, including automobile-manufacturing and the electrical industries.

Industrial unions, which sought to organise all workers in a particular industry (usually defined by reference to its product market) irrespective of their individual skill or status, emerged in the USA in the 1920s in an attempt to organise fully the mass production industries. Although this type of union also became common in mainland Europe, it did not become widespread in the UK, principally because of the existence of a well-established system of craft and general unions by this time. However, a number of industrial unions did arise as a result of mergers between several unions operating in the same industry, the National Union of Mineworkers (NUM) being a case in point.

During the Second World War period there was a marked change in the occupational structure of the UK labour force with a shift in employment away from manufacturing towards the service sector, and this resulted in the UK, as in a number of other industrialised countries, in the latest phase of union growth: the emergence of large-scale and quickly growing *white-collar unions*. The process of trade union amalgamation continued in the UK during the postwar period, so that by 1977 the number of unions had fallen to under half of its 1940 level, while membership, boosted by white-collar unionisation, had amost doubled.

In the UK, white-collar unions have made significant inroads into both the public and private sectors, and union membership is now a common feature of various white-collar employments with, for example, the Association of Scientific, Technical and Managerial Staffs

(ASTMS) – recently renamed as Manufacturing Science Finance (MSF) – organising, among others, some supervisory and managerial grades in industry and commerce and the National Association of Local Government Officers (NALGO) organising salaried local government employees. In addition, unionisation is now common in many professional employments with various unions, the largest of which is the National Union of Teachers, organising school-teachers, and the Association of University Teachers and the Australian University Staff Association representing university teaching staff in the UK and Australia respectively. It is, however, important to recognise that not all trade unions include the term 'union' in their title (MSF and NALGO are examples) and as we see in the following section, various professional bodies – including the British and American Medical Associations, as well as Britain's Law Society and its US counterpart, the American Legal Association – conform very closely in their behaviour to the craft unions described above.

■ Trade union structure

The above fourfold classification of unions as craft, general, industrial or white-collar corresponds broadly to their historical development. However, Turner (1962) argued that in practice it is not easy to find unions that conform closely to this classification, since they frequently possess characteristics and behave in ways that resemble more than one of the above union types, and that in any case a union's characteristics and behaviour vary over its life-cycle. Turner therefore proposed an alternative threefold classification of unions as being either closed, open or intermediate unions.

Closed unions are those characterised by the existence of restrictive membership policies and entry controls of the sort employed by the traditional craft unions considered above. In contrast, *open unions* are those which pursue expansionist policies, designed to increase their membership. These unions correspond closely to the general and industrial unions already considered, particularly in cases where the latter's expansionist aspirations spill over to recruitment outside its industrial boundaries, as in the case of the UK's National Union of Railwaymen, which has recruited into its membership some road transport workers. Finally, there are *intermediate unions*, which contain both closed and open compartments. These comprise those closed unions which have expanded to embrace groups of workers previously excluded. While the nineteenth-century UK craft unions fit well into the closed union model, craft unions can and do become intermediate ones, as we saw in the example of the AEU's recruitment of semi-skilled and unskilled workers, which began in 1929.

In the UK and USA, as elsewhere, various professional bodies, such as those of the legal and medical professions, fit closely the traditional craft or closed union model, restricting supply or entry via their control of the training of prospective entrants. However, it is not entirely clear to what extent these entry restrictions are necessary, as these bodies often vociferously claim, to maintain standards and to what extent they represent barriers to entry designed to maintain or increase the wages of existing practitioners (see Friedman and Kuznets, 1945).

The preceding discussion, which has been designed to set the scene for what follows, provides little more than a brief introduction to the nature and structure of the trade union movement. A more detailed analysis of the structure and functioning of the trade union movement would take us into the realms of the industrial relations analyst and is therefore outside the scope of the present book. It is, however, important to notice that the development of trade unions in the UK along craft, general and white-collar rather than industrial lines has resulted in the characterisation of many bargaining units, at both industry and work-place levels, by a situation of *multiunionism*. Throughout the 1980s the UK railways, for example, had three main unions: the Associated Society of Locomotive Engineers and Firemen with membership drawn from drivers and firemen; the Transport Salaried Staffs' Association, with a membership drawn from clerical workers; and the National Union of Railwaymen, whose members are principally porters, ticket-collectors and workers in similar work.

■ The determinants of trade union growth

A brief description of the trends and fluctuations that occurred in union membership in the UK and the USA was given above. However, a more detailed analysis of the union membership data relating to a range of countries shows that the growth of aggregate union membership is typically characterised by cyclical fluctuations of varying amplitude and duration. Early writers saw fluctuations in aggregate membership as being related to fluctuations in the level of economic activity or the business cycle. (See Bain and Elsheikh, 1976, pp. 5–25, for a literature survey.) More recently, however, researchers have employed econometric techniques to explain observed fluctuations in aggregate trade union membership in various countries in terms of a vector of explanatory variables that is specified to represent various individual components of the business cycle.

In a series of publications Bain and Elsheikh (see in particular their 1976 study) have investigated the determinants of the rate of growth of trade union membership in Australia, Sweden, the UK and the USA and found a considerable degree of support for a simple model of trade union growth. This model sees the annual percentage rate of change of union membership as depending on the following four factors: (a) the rate of price inflation, (b) the rate of wage inflation, (c) unemployment and (d) union density defined, as in **Table 10.1**, as the ratio of actual to potential union membership. While Bain and Elsheikh's model is not without its critics (see the debate between Richardson, 1977 and 1978, and Elsheikh and Bain, 1978) it has nevertheless become something of a focal point in the union growth literature.[4] For example, in a recent study Bain and Elsheikh (1982) have applied this model to industry-level UK data, while Sapsford (1984, 1986) has investigated the applicability of this model to union growth in postwar Ireland. In their analysis, Bain and Elsheikh see changes in trade union membership as being determined by changes in both the propensity and opportunity to unionise and on the basis of the reasoning sketched out below, they suggest that the rate of union growth is expected to be *positively* related to the rates of changes of retail prices and wages and *negatively* related to both union density and the level and/or rate of change of unemployment.

Bain and Elsheikh argue that workers are more likely to enter and to seek to remain in trade union membership during periods of rapid price inflation as they attempt to achieve money wage improvements of sufficient magnitude to protect their real standard of living from being eroded by rising prices. This they term a 'threat effect'. In addition, they suggest that if price rises are seen as an index of the general 'prosperity of industry' they may also influence the opportunity to unionise. Employers may be more willing to concede demands for improvements in wages and other conditions of work during periods of rising prices partly because the opportunities for passing on increased costs may be more favourable and partly because they may fear the disruption of profitable production by industrial action in the cause of furthering unionisation. This is referred to as a 'prosperity effect'. Both threat and prosperity effects work in the same direction and suggest a positive relationship between union growth and the rate of price inflation.

They also suggest that workers are more likely to join and remain in unions during periods when money wages are rising rapidly, as during such periods workers tend to credit increased money wages to unions and hope that by joining or remaining with them they will do at least as well in the future. This is termed the 'credit effect'.

It is also argued that union growth can be expected to be negatively related to union density, primarily because of the presence of a 'saturation effect' which arises because the higher the density, the greater will be the difficulties of increasing membership further since there will be fewer workers left to recruit and because those who remain are likely to have a lower propensity and/or ability to unionise.

Last, it is suggested that membership can be expected to grow more slowly, or to fall, when unemployment is high or rising because the opportunities for extending union membership are less favourable during such periods. There are several lines of reasoning giving rise to this hypothesis. Bain and Elsheikh argue that given the low level of aggregate demand prevailing at such times, employers are more able to resist the spread of unionism as the (opportunity) costs in terms of foregone output resulting from disruptions of production in the cause of extending unionism tend to be lower. From the employees' viewpoint, it is also suggested that unemployment influences the propensity of workers to become and remain union members via its effects on the expected benefits of membership relative to its costs. Those becoming unemployed tend to withdraw from the union (possibly after some time lag, as many unions permit members to be in arrears for a number of months before withdrawing their membership) as they may feel that, being unemployed, membership has little benefit to offer them and, in addition, as membership costs typically rise in relation to their incomes. Some employed workers may also become reluctant to join unions during periods of high unemployment for fear of antagonising their employers to the extent of losing their job in a period of excess labour supply. Furthermore, it is also argued that employed members may also tend to withdraw from membership during periods of high and rising unemployment as they estimate that under prevailing economic conditions the scope for union-won collective-bargaining advances is limited, to the extent that the expected benefits from membership (in the form of union-won improvements in wages and conditions of work) are no longer sufficient to outweigh membership costs.

The Bain and Elsheikh model can therefore be summarised algebraically by the following expression

$$\Delta T_t = \alpha_1 + \alpha_2 \, \Delta P_t + \alpha_3 \, \Delta W_t + \alpha_4 \, U_t + \alpha_5 \, D_{t-1} \qquad (10.1)$$

where subscripts denote time and where ΔT = the annual proportional rate of change of trade union membership, ΔP = rate of price inflation, ΔW = rate of wage inflation, U = the level (and/or rate of change) of the unemployment rate and D = union density. On the basis of the above arguments, the expected signs of the coefficients are as follows:

$$\alpha_2, \alpha_3 > 0 \text{ and } \alpha_4, \alpha_5 < 0$$

Bain and Elsheikh (1976) analyse the evidence covering the period from about 1900 through to 1970 for each of the four countries mentioned above and find in this a considerable degree of support for their suggested model.

One additional hypothesis which has recently been tested for both the UK and Irish cases (see Burkitt and Bowers, 1978, and Sapsford, 1986, respectively) concerns the influence of profits on the rate of union growth. The argument here is quite simply that workers may be more likely to join unions during periods of high or rising profits because they judge that the scope for union-won gains is increased at such times. The evidence from both the UK and Irish economies reported in the above two papers seems to strongly support this notion, but for an alternative view and some further evidence regarding profits and union growth in the UK see Elsheikh and Bain (1979).

An alternative model of US union growth

Seen by many as a rival to the Bain and Elsheikh model when it comes to explaining the rate of US union growth is the model proposed by Ashenfelter and Pencavel (1969). This model sees the workers' decisions about whether to join a trade union or not as the outcome of a decision-making process in which rational workers seek to balance the marginal costs of union membership against the expected marginal benefits arising from membership. Within this framework, the benefits of union membership are seen to include not only improved wages, but also improvements in employment security and working conditions. Set against these benefits are the costs of union membership, which embrace not only union membership dues, but also the potential of job loss and other retaliation (including victimisation) from employers hostile to the spread of unionisation.

The Ashenfelter and Pencavel model may be written as follows:

$$\Delta T_t = \beta_0 + \beta_1 \Delta P_t + \beta_2 (L) \Delta E_t + \beta_3 g\{U_t^P, t-\theta\} + \beta_4 D_{t-1} + \beta_5 POL_t \qquad (10.2)$$

where ΔT_t, ΔP_t and D_{t-1} are defined, as above, as union membership growth, price inflation and lagged density respectively. The additional terms are defined as follows:

ΔE = the rate of change of employment in the unionised sector of the economy

$g\{U_t^P, t-\theta\}$ = some function of the extent of unemployment in the preceding business cycle trough, which occurred $(t-\theta)$ periods ago

POL = an index of the political climate

(L) = a distributed lag operator, defined in such a way that the term

$$\beta_2 (L) \Delta E_t = \sum_{i=0}^{n} \beta_{2i} \Delta E_{t-i}$$

The arguments for the inclusion of both the rate of price inflation and the level of union density in (10.2) are essentially the same as those already discussed in connection with the Bain and Elsheikh model. The variable POL is included as an explanatory variable in the model to capture pro-labour sentiments in the political arena, sentiments which Ashenfelter and Pencavel argue can influence both worker's responses to union recruitment activities and the amount of legislation conducive to union growth. In their study of the US experience Ashenfelter and Pencavel proxy this variable by the proportion of democrats in the US House of Representatives.

Next, there is the unemployment term $g\{U_t^P, t - \theta\}$ which differs from the more straightforward unemployment variable included in the Bain and Elsheikh model (10.1). In the specification of their model, Ashenfelter and Pencavel see workers as possessing a 'stock' of grievances, which give rise to discontent which in turn results in their seeking to join a trade union as a form of protest. They argue that the size of the grievance stock is determined by the extent of unemployment which prevailed at the previous business cycle trough, denoted by U_t^P. It is also argued that the pool of grievances decays over time and these ideas are captured by their specification of the function $g\{U_t^P, t - \theta\}$. For purposes of estimation they adopt the following specification.

$$\lambda^{(t-\theta)} U_t^P \text{ where } 0 \leqslant \lambda \leqslant 1 \qquad (10.3)$$

according to which the grievance stock declines geometrically as the length of time since the preceding trough increases. Lastly there is the distributed lag term in employment growth in the union sector. The basic argument for the inclusion of this variable as an additional determinant of membership growth is threefold; first, that employers are less likely to retaliate against workers seeking to unionise as the labour market tightens; second, the existence of closed-shop agreements (according to which union membership is a necessary condition for employment) means that membership tends to rise 'automatically' as employment increases and third, because the costs incurred in organising membership recruitment campaigns are likely to fall as employment growth rises. The employment growth term is specified in a distributed lag form to allow for the fact that workers may be reluctant to leave union membership immediately employment declines because of social and political ties, as well as in light of such economic considerations as union assistance with job search and the fact that current membership data may include some unemployed workers who have temporarily stopped paying membership dues.

In light of the preceding arguments the hypotheses of this model may be written as follows:

$$\beta_1, \beta_{2i}\ (i = 0, 1 \ldots, n), \beta_3, \beta_5 > 0; \beta_4 < 0$$

The evidence

Ashenfelter and Pencavel (1969) tested (10.2) against US data spanning the period from 1904 to 1960 and found what they took to be a considerable degree of support for their model. In particular, they found the coefficient of the political climate variable (*POL*) to be both positive, as expected, and significantly different from zero; thus indicating that, other things being equal, US unions grow more rapidly during those periods when the Democrats were the dominant force in the House of Representatives. In addition, it is interesting to notice that their findings suggested that the value of λ in expression (10.3) lay somewhere in the range 0.95 to 1.0, a result implying that the workers' stock of grievances decays only slowly with the elapse of time.

As mentioned above, models (10.1) and (10.2) are sometimes seen as rivals when it comes to the explanation of US union growth. In this context it is interesting to notice that in a study of the adequacy of these two alternative explanations of US union growth, Sheflin, Troy and Koeller (1981) found evidence to suggest that *both* models suffer from problems of structural instability (that is, that the parameters of both (10.1) and (10.2) appear to change within the period being studied), with such instabilities appearing to be associated with certain items of US labour market legislation. This finding throws the adequacy of each model, at least without further modification, into some doubt.

The 1980s: a decade of declining union membership?

As we saw from **Table 10.2** above, one notable feature of the recent experience of many OECD member countries (including both the UK and the USA) has been a rapid fall in trade union membership. For example, UK union membership declined from 13.3 million in 1979 to 11.3 million in 1982, to about 10.5 million in 1986. Carruth and Disney (1988) develop a model of UK trade union membership over the period

1896 to 1984, which they find is well able to forecast the observed decline of over 2 million members since 1979. This study makes a clear separation between short- and long-run influences and finds that the post-1979 decline in UK union membership is largely accounted for by cyclical factors (such as variations in unemployment and wage and price inflation) rather than trend or secular influences (such as changes in employment). It is, however, interesting to notice that this study also reveals some evidence to support the US finding noted above to the effect that the political climate exerts a significant influence on the rate of union membership growth, with the rate of membership growth in the UK being found to be higher, other things being equal, under non-Conservative than under Conservative governments. Much political and popular discussion (for example, Minford, 1983) has attributed the observed decline in UK union membership since 1979 to the Conservative Government's industrial relations legislation which was designed, in part, to curb what it saw as the excessive power of unions to push up the earnings of those they represent. However, in a detailed investigation of the nature and effects of this legislation, Brown and Wadhwani (1990) could find little, if any, evidence to support the argument that decline in union membership in the UK in the 1980s was a consequence of such legislative changes. Given that the UK was far from alone in experiencing a substantial decline in union membership in the 1980s they were led to conclude that such factors as the high unemployment levels prevailing over the period were the root cause of the membership decline. This conclusion is broadly consistent with Bain and Elsheikh's (1976) evidence, discussed above, regarding the influence of the business cycle on union growth. In contrast, Bean and Holden (1992) investigated the determinants of *cross-national* differences in the extent of unionisation (as measured by the ratio of union membership to the size of the labour force) in 16 OECD countries in the 1980s. Higher unionisation in this sample of countries was found to be associated with a higher degree of centralisation of wage bargaining and a higher percentage of employees covered by collective bargaining. It was also found to be positively associated with the size of the (highly unionised) public sector and by the existence of governments favourably disposed towards unions.

Trade unions: economic or political institutions?

The question of whether it is valid to analyse trade unions as economic institutions has excited considerable controversy and gave rise to the so-called Ross–Dunlop debate of the late 1940s and early 1950s.

Conventionally, economists have analysed questions of trade union wage policy by drawing analogies with the rational firms and households of microeconomic theory, which are typically assumed to maximise (or minimise) some clearly defined objective function.

The classic pronouncement of this viewpoint is due to Dunlop, who argued that an

> economic theory of a trade union requires that the organisation be assumed to maximise (or minimise) something. (1944, p. 4)

However, considerable difficulties arise in the specification of precisely what this something is that the union is supposed to be maximising and, as we shall see, a wide variety of union maximands have been suggested.

Over and above the difficulties inherent in the specification of the precise form and arguments of a union objective function, Ross (1948) challenged the economic approach to the analysis of trade union behaviour on the grounds that unions are oganisations composed of a heterogeneous set of members with heterogeneous interests and goals. Ross argued that union policies are formulated not on the basis of any simple maximising process but on the basis of a political decision-making mechanism, whereby the union leaders, given their own objectives, reconcile the pressures brought to bear on them both internally (by the various factions within the union) and externally (by employers, other unions and governments). Because of their personal professional ambitions and their identification with the union, Ross saw the central objective of union leaders and decision-makers as being *organisational survival* and viewed economic factors as being of only secondary importance, to the extent that they generate political pressures that have to be dealt with. In short, Ross argued that unions behave in ways that appear irrational by the criterion of orthodox economic analysis but that their behaviour is rational when viewed within a political framework. He therefore concluded that union objectives and behaviour could not be properly understood by conventional economic analysis and appealed instead for a political approach.

In response to this challenge, Dunlop argued that, while unions do have political dimensions, these are by no means as significant as Ross would lead us to believe and that, on the basis of the US evidence, the dominance of political factors is in fact a characteristic of the behaviour of only a small number of new unions. Dunlop went on to argue that, despite the existence of political forces, union leaders are aware of economic, particularly long-run, realities, as is evidenced by the fact that the behaviour of wages can be well-explained by market variables.

In broad terms, the divergence of opinion between Ross and Dunlop as to the appropriate method by which to approach the analysis of unions boiled down to a disagreement over the relative weights to be attached to political and economic factors.[5] While it is perhaps true that the policy-making mechanisms internal to the union could only be fully understood within a wider framework than was offered by the conventional economic analysis of that time, it was, and still is, nevertheless true that union policies, once formulated, are typically expressed in terms of economic variables, such as changes in the level of wages and conditions of employment. These policies and the economic activities of the union are therefore subject to the workings and constraints of the economic system and are consequently amenable to economic analysis regardless of the precise way in which the policies themselves are formulated. In short, if we take the union's internal decision-making process and resulting economic objectives and policies as given, it is perfectly legitimate to employ the tools of economics to analyse the consequences and outcomes of these policies and of the union's economic activities.

Over and above the preceding defence of the economists' approach it is important to recognise that during the last decade or so a range of economic models of union behaviour have been constructed which explicitly consider the mechanisms by which union objectives are formulated. These models will be considered later in this chapter.

■ Union objectives

□ *The neutralisation of monopsony power*

Considerable attention has been devoted over many years to the construction of theories of union objectives and behaviour. Perhaps the simplest view of the objectives and role of trade unions is that they exist primarily to neutralise the monopsony power of employers (Burkitt, 1975, pp. 8–22; Mulvey, 1978, pp. 51–2). The perfectly competitive labour market, which we considered in previous chapters, is *atomistic*, in the sense that there exist large numbers of unorganised individuals on both the buyers' and sellers' sides of the market. The case of monopsony was considered in Chapter 7, and we noted that this situation can arise through labour-purchasers combining to form an employers' association to act as a single purchasing unit in the labour market. Alternatively, monopsony can occur on a local basis when a firm is the sole purchaser of the type of labour in question in a local labour market. As we have seen, the monopsonist faces an upward-sloping labour supply curve and maximises profits by equating marginal labour cost (*MLC*) to marginal revenue product (*MRP*), with the consequence that the equilibrium levels of employment and wages are each lower than the corresponding, perfectly competitive values. Look again at **Figure 7.4**, and recall that the monopsonist's equilibrium level of employment is e workers, which falls short of the competitive equilibrium employment level by $(e' - e)$ workers, at wage w, which is $(w' - w)$ units below the competitive wage.

When discussing monopsony, we saw how the imposition of a minimum wage above the monopsonist's equilibrium level can, over a certain range of wages, result in an increase in employment. Accordingly, this *neutralisation of monopsony power* view sees the objectives of trade unions as the establishment of a union minimum wage above the monopsonist's equilibrium value in order to achieve increases simultaneously in members' wages and employment. The analysis here is exactly the same as that of minimum wage imposition considered in Chapter 7. In so far as the union membership supports the minimum wage policy, the union establishes a perfectly elastic section to the labour supply curve at the official union wage rate, and the monopsonist can hire any amount of union labour at this rate up to the point where this section meets the original labour supply curve. If, for example, the union were able to set the wage rate in **Figure 7.4** at w', the labour supply curve facing the monopsonist would be $w'CL_S$. The monopsonist would maximise profits at point C by employing e' workers at wage w'. Therefore, by following such a policy the union will have succeeded in increasing both wages and employment to their perfectly competitive levels. Notice that a union wage in excess of w' can only be achieved at the expense of contracting employment below its perfectly competitive level. However, provided that the union wage is set at a level no greater than w_A in **Figure 7.4**, employment will still be higher than in the absence of union action. If, for example, the union wage were set at w_m, the resulting equilibrium level of employment would be e_m workers as compared to the e workers that would be employed in the absence of union action.

□ *Early maximising models*

In the early literature there was, as we have seen, a marked tendency for economists to view unions as being economic agents analogous to firms. It was frequently argued that in the same way that a rational firm seeks to maximise a single variable, its profits, so too a rational union must possess some single maximand. Various suggestions were put forward in this early literature as to precisely which variable trade unions could reasonably be assumed to be seeking to maximise. A number of these are summarised below.

(a) Wages

A very simple view of the objectives of trade union wage policies is that these aim to maximise wage income per member. Given the existence of a downward-sloping demand curve for union labour, this objective clearly implies that the union will seek to raise wages to such a level that the bulk of its members will be forced out of employment.[6] As we have seen, workers tend to withdraw from unions on becoming unemployed, and so the pursuit of this objective implies in addition that the bulk of existing members will subsequently leave the union. According to this specification, the union's objective is actually achieved by pushing the wage rate so high that only one member remains in employment and by implication remains in the union – clearly a highly implausible prediction. If this objective is reformulated to be the maximisation of the average wage income of the original members, the prediction is ultimately the same, except that employment and membership are contracted more slowly (that is, at the rate at which members retire, resign or die). If one views the union as an institution, with goals of its own, the prediction of this particular model of union wage policy becomes even more implausible, for it implies that the union has no interest in either the employment of its members or the size of its membership and hence, by implication, no interest in its own survival.

(b) Employment

At the other extreme is the view that unions aim to maximise the employment of their members. This specification implies that the union will seek to move down the demand curve for union labour, trading lower wages for increased employment of its members. Given the existence of a downward-sloping demand curve for union labour, this objective will be achieved when the union has succeeded in pushing its members' wages as low as possible.

Consider the case of an individual firm (with no monopsony power) employing only union labour, and assume the existence of a negatively sloping demand curve for union labour. Assume also that all workers hired by the firm are accepted into union membership and that all workers leave the union on becoming unemployed, so that we can talk of changes in employment and changes in union membership as being synonymous. This situation is shown in **Figure 10.3**, where L_s denotes

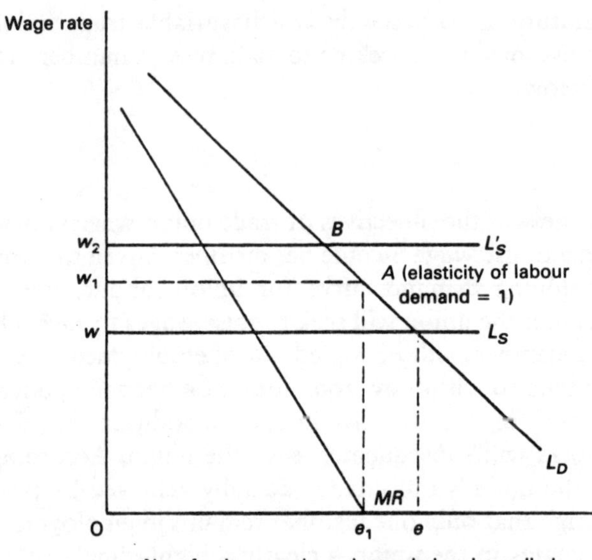

Figure 10.3 ***Union objectives***

the perfectly elastic labour supply curve that it is assumed the firm would face in the absence of the union. In this figure L_D is the firm's demand (*MRP*) curve for union labour, measured for simplicity in this and subsequent figures in terms of numbers of members employed.

If the union in this example were an employment-maximiser, it would achieve its objective by setting wages at the level *w*, to give employment of *e* members. This wage is the competitive one that would prevail in the absence of unionisation, and the employment of *e* members is the maximum attainable, as presumably workers would withdraw from the union if membership required them to take a wage less than that which they could obtain without unionisation. Under this latter condition the labour supply curve represents a constraint that sets a lower limit on the wage rate (equal to *w*) at any particular employment level (Cartter, 1959, p. 82).[7] In the absence of any such supply constraint, the employment-maximising model of union wage policy implies that the union will seek to push its members' wage down to zero.

The wage-maximising formulation gives the implausible prediction that the union has no concern about its members becoming unemployed and subsequently leaving the union and, therefore, about its remaining in existence as an organisation. The employment-maximising formulation, however, gives the equally implausible prediction that the union seeks the lowest wage possible, by aiming to increase its members' employment up to the point where they are no better off than they would be without a union! In addition, if one adopts a Ross-type (1948) view of the union as an institution, it is difficult to see how such a membership maximisation policy can survive. To the extent that existing members are able to exert greater pressure than potential members on the union leadership, it is not easy to see how the leadership can continue to pursue such a maximisation policy, which sacrifices the wages of existing members in the cause of increasing the numbers of members employed. In a nutshell, this model fails to provide any answer to the question as to why existing members should support a policy designed to sacrifice their own wages in order to increase the employment prospects of others.

(c) The wage bill

Clearly, it is more satisfactory to argue that unions are concerned both with their members' wages and the size of their membership, and as a consequence the product of the members' wage rate and employment (that is, the *wage bill*) has been put forward as a likely union maximand.[8] At any point on the union labour demand curve the wage bill is given by the area of the wage–employment rectangle lying under the curve at the point in question. The wage bill is maximised at the point where the elasticity of the union labour demand curve is equal to unity. This is shown in **Figure 10.3** by point *A*, where employment is e_1 members and the wage is w_1. If we think of the union in **Figure 10.3** as a seller of labour facing the downward-sloping demand curve L_D, we can draw the marginal revenue (*MR*) curve corresponding to this labour demand curve to show the addition to the total union wage bill that arises when the wage is lowered by an amount sufficient to allow employment to be increased by one member. Notice in the usual way that the wage bill, as the union's 'total revenue', is maximised at the point where marginal revenue equals zero. Notice also from **Figure 10.3** that, if the wage that would prevail in the absence of the union were above w_1, at say, w_2 (that is, if the labour supply curve that the firm would face in the absence of unionisation were L_S') then by the reasoning of the previous section it follows, because of supply constraints, that the maximum wage bill actually achievable is at the non-unionised wage–employment combination at point *B*.

Although the wage bill maximisation hypothesis has the attraction of combining both wage and employment dimensions into a single maximand, it is unsatisfactory because it gives the unrealistic prediction that in cases where the demand for union labour is elastic (that is, to the left of employment e_1 in **Figure 10.3**) the union will seek to achieve wage cuts! However, in cases where the wage is initially low, this hypothesis can simply be interpreted as not seeking to raise it above w_1 in **Figure 10.3**. As under the employment maximisation hypothesis, the union in this model sacrifices the wages of its already employed members in order, in this case, to increase the wage bill. As in the employment maximisation specification, it is not easy to see how such a policy, if pursued, could survive as existing members would be unlikely to be willing to continue to subscribe to a union policy that persistently sacrifices their own interests. In addition, the plausibility of the wage bill maximisation model can be further questioned, because it implies that the wage of a given type of union labour will differ both within and between relevant employments according to the elasticity of labour demand – a prediction that does not appear to be borne out in practice, since uniform rather than varied union wage rates are typically observed (Mulvey, 1978, pp. 31–2).

(d) The monopoly analogy

In the search for a union objective function it has been suggested that the union can be viewed as a monopoly seller of the labour services of its members and that it can therefore be assumed to behave in a manner analogous to a product market monopolist.[9] It has therefore been argued that, in the same way as a product market monopolist is assumed to set sales so as to equate marginal cost to marginal revenue, it is reasonable to assume that the trade union as a monopoly seller of labour seeks to equate the marginal revenue from the sale of its members' labour to their supply price. This situation is shown in **Figure 10.4** where L_D is the firm's downward-sloping demand curve for union labour and L_S is the upward-sloping supply curve for labour that it is assumed the firm would face in the absence of unionisation. The union's demand curve for its 'product' (L_D) is its average revenue (*AR*) curve. Since this is downward-sloping, the union monopoly can (in the absence of price discrimination) only gain additional units of employment at the expense of a lower wage rate. The curve *MR* in **Figure 10.4** is the marginal revenue curve corresponding to the labour demand curve (L_D).

Acting as a monopolistic seller of labour the union, according to this model of its wage policy, seeks to equate the marginal revenue from the sale of its members' labour services (or, as it is sometimes called, the marginal demand for labour: Marshall *et al.*, 1976 p. 330) with its supply price at employment *e* in **Figure 10.4** demanding a wage of *w*. Notice that this wage is above the level (w_c) that would prevail in a perfectly competitive market with the same labour demand and supply curves, but that this gain in wages is achieved only at the expense of

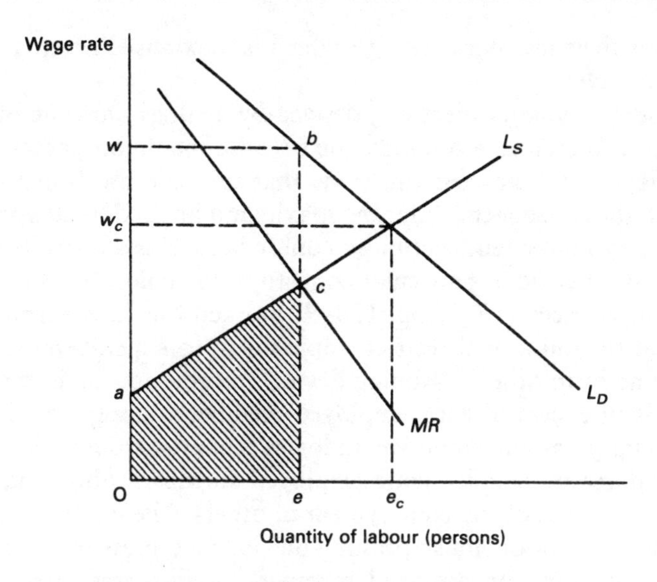

Figure 10.4 ***The union–monopoly analogy***

$(e_c - e)$ units of employment. Notice also from **Figure 10.4** that in the case where there is a perfectly elastic labour supply curve, at a wage of zero (that is, the analogue of a monopolistic firm with zero marginal cost) this formulation reduces to the wage bill maximisation model considered above.

The problem with the monopoly analogy arises on the supply side. In discussing the behaviour of monopolistic firms, it is usually assumed that they aim to maximise their profits and, therefore, that they equate their marginal cost to the marginal revenue from the sale of their output. The union, however, does not *produce* the labour services of its members but acts instead as their agent. Therefore, unlike a firm, the union does not incur production costs. The labour supply function (L_S in **Figure 10.4**) is not a marginal cost function analogous to that of a monopolistic producer but illustrates, as we saw in Chapter 2, members' work–leisure preferences at various wage rates. Therefore, according to the monopoly analogy, the union is seen as attempting to maximise an *economic rent*; namely, the surplus of its members' total wage income over and above the total of their individual marginal supply prices or their transfer earnings. The latter is shown by the area lying under the labour supply curve at the employment level in question. In **Figure 10.4** the union–monopoly's equilibrium level of employment is *e* members. At this point the membership's total transfer earnings are given by the shaded area under L_S; the surplus of the membership's total wage income over their transfer earnings, which is maximised here, is shown by the area *awbc*.

This model of union objectives, derived by analogy with the monopolistic firm, is therefore a dubious one because the union possesses nothing analogous to the cost functions that underlie the firm's supply curve, with the consequence that the maximand implied by this analogy (that is, the economic rent accruing to union labour) is a quantity that is unlikely in itself to be of particular concern to the union (Reder, 1952). In addition, as Rees (1973, pp. 128–9) pointed out, this formulation implies that the union will restrict employment to *e* members (presumably by some form of job-rationing device) in order to obtain the wage *w*, which is in excess of each employed member's supply price. However, the wage gains and employment losses that arise from such a policy accrue to different people, with employed members obtaining wage gains at the expense of the employment of others. The union leadership in its policy formation must presumably balance pressures for work from any remaining unemployed members against pressures for improved wages from employed workers. Therefore it is, in the absence of any mechanism for redistributing the gains from the pursuit of such a policy from employed to unemployed members, only by mere chance that this political balancing exercise will lead to the maximising solution predicted by this model.

(c) The membership function

A variant of the employment maximisation model considered above was put forward by Dunlop (1944). Suggesting that unions attempt to maximise their membership, Dunlop argued that the number of workers who will be allied to the union will be a function of the wage rate. Accordingly, Dunlop constructed a *membership function* showing union membership as an increasing function of the union wage rate and suggested that this should be substituted in place of the conventional labour supply curve, which as we have seen, reflects the income–leisure preferences of workers rather than their allegiance to the union. In cases where union membership is required in order to work (that is, the *closed* or *union shop*[10]), the labour supply and membership functions will be identical for any unionised firm. Notice however that these need not necessarily coincide with the labour supply curve that the firm would face in the absence of unionisation as some workers may choose to work or to search for employment elsewhere rather than join the union. In other cases the membership function will lie to the left of the conventional labour supply schedule, with its displacement to the left of the latter

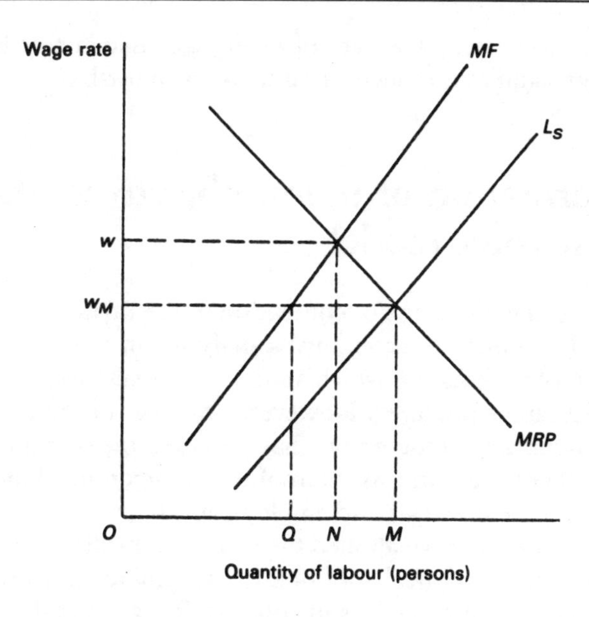

Figure 10.5 *Union membership function*

indicating the number of workers who will not be union members at the wage rate in question.

In **Figure 10.5** L_S is the labour supply curve, assumed to be upward-sloping, faced by a unionised employer, and the curve *MF* is the membership function, showing the number of employees who will be union members at any given wage rate. If the union's objective is to maximise its membership (the analogy in the theory of the firm being the sales-maximising producer), it will seek the wage rate w (where the membership function intersects its *MRP* curve[11]) in order to achieve its maximum membership level of *N* workers. In the case shown in **Figure 10.5** the union membership function lies to the left of the labour supply curve, with the consequence that the maximisation of membership is not synonymous with the maximisation of employment. The union would have maximised employment at the competitive wage rate of w_M, but in so doing it would have lost $(N - Q)$ members.

Although the membership function approach has the advantage of explicitly recognising the distinction between employment and the size of union membership, it suffers from the same sort of defect as the other simple maximising formulations, in that it implies that the union is willing and able to sacrifice the wages of its employed members in order to maximise its membership. In addition, the specification of union membership as a function of only the union wage rate is an oversimplification because, as we have seen, a variety of other economic factors have been shown to exert significant influences on union membership.

The formation of union objectives: the median voter model

As noted above, a major bone of contention in the Ross–Dunlop debate was the extent to which the economist's analysis can adequately capture the internal mechanisms by which union objectives over wages, and other variables, are formulated. However, a number of recent studies of the microeconomics of trade unions have focused their attention explicitly on the role of mechanisms internal to the union in shaping union policies regarding both wages and employment. In particular, a number of recent contributions have applied the so-called 'median voter model', borrowed from the analytical tool-box of the political scientist, to the determination of union objectives in collective bargaining (for example, Farber, 1978; Booth, 1984). The basic idea of these models is quite straightforward; namely, that the union's objectives in bargaining are determined by a ballot in which the rank and file membership of the union vote for the policy which they wish the leadership to follow in future negotiations with the employer over their wages and employment. More specifically, such models typically consider the situation where the union rank and file membership is electing, in a simple first-past-the-post ballot, their leadership from amongst a range of candidates, each of whom offers a different 'package' of wage and employment demands which he or she intends to take into future negotiations with the employer throughout the elected term of office.

For simplicity, consider the situation where bargaining takes place over *only* wages and in which the union rank and file are voting in an election to select a single leader from a field of only two candidates; one candidate (A) is running on a ticket of pushing for high wages in negotiations with the employer, while the other (B) is offering a policy of moderate wage demands. Which of these candidates will win the election, or stated alternatively, which policy will emerge as the membership's choice in future negotiations? To answer this question it is common to make the assumption that there exists an (inverse) *seniority rule* of the 'last in, first out' variety to be operated in the event that lay-offs occur. Under such circumstances it is argued that the more senior workers will tend to support the candidate offering the high-wage policy, because they personally stand to gain more from this than from the alternative low-wage strategy. This occurs because the strategy

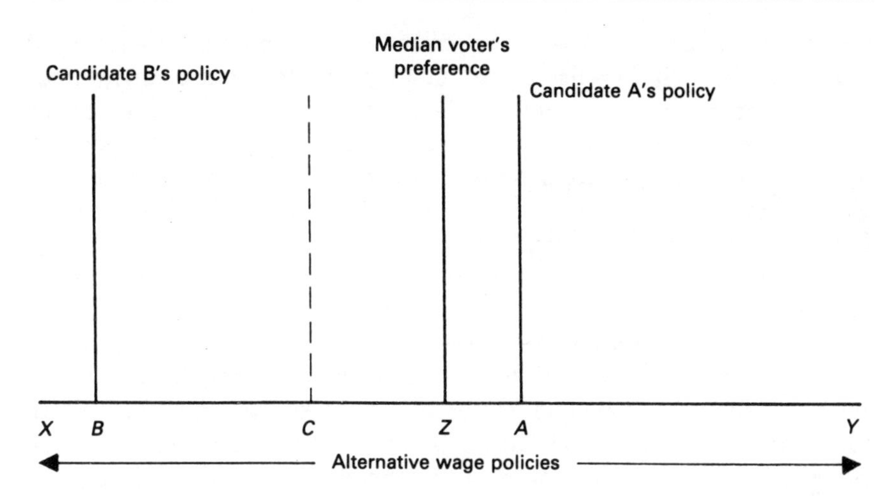

Figure 10.6 ***Median voter model of union preferences***

proposed by candidate A offers senior workers the prospect of high wages with little, if any, risk to their employment, since in the event that the employer were to shed labour (by moving up the labour demand curve) as a result of a high-wage settlement, it would be junior workers (the 'last in') who would lose their jobs under the seniority rule. Notice that this model effectively assumes that the utility of senior workers is not influenced by the employment prospects or job security of their junior colleagues, but is determined only by their own wage rate. Conversely, junior workers will tend to support candidate B, whose more moderate wage policy offers them the prospects of job security by minimising the likelihood of lay-offs occurring. The standard result or prediction to emerge from the median voter model is that the candidate to be elected (that is, in our framework, the wage policy to be adopted) will be that which corresponds (most closely) to the preferences of the *median* voter. This result can be seen very straightforwardly from **Figure 10.6** which plots the range of possible wage policies, varying from point X (representing, say, a policy of keeping wages unchanged[12] at their present level, which would thereby minimise the likelihood of any job losses occurring amongst union members) to point Y (representing a policy of going for such a high wage that the wage bill exhausts the employer's total revenue, with the consequence that at any higher wage the employer ultimately goes out of business).

Suppose for simplicity that the union has a total membership of $(2n + 1)$ persons, and that their preferences in relation to wage policies are evenly (or uniformly) distributed along the line XY according to the inverse of their seniority. Thus the most junior (that is, recently recruited) worker's preferred wage policy is at X (representing unchanged wages and little, if any, risk of redundancy), while the next most junior worker's preference is one unit to the right of X and so forth, up to the most senior worker's preferred strategy which is represented by point Y. The median of any distribution is, by definition, that entity which is at the distribution's centre in the sense of having an equal number of entities with values below and above its own value. In other words, the median value in a ranked set of data is that value below and above which there is an equal number of observations. The wage policy preferred by the median union member according to seniority is indicated by point Z in **Figure 10.6.** Since we assumed that the total membership of the union is $(2n + 1)$ people, the preferred wage policies of the n more junior members lie to the left of point Z in **Figure 10.6**, while the preferred policies of the n more senior members lie to the right of Z.

Suppose now that the wage policy proposed by candidate B (the low-wage candidate) is represented by point B in **Figure 10.6** while that proposed by candidate A is indicated by point A. It is now easy to see that candidate A will win the election and, accordingly, that the wage policy represented by point A will emerge as the union's policy objective in future wage negotiations with the employer. Candidate A will win the election because he/she will receive the votes of all the members whose preferences lie to the right of point A *plus* the votes of all of the members whose preferences lie to the right of C (the mid-point of AB), since the proposed wage policy at A corresponds more closely to the preference of each of these voters than does the strategy proposed by B. Candidate B will win the votes of all members whose preferences lie along XC. Since we have assumed that members' preferences are evenly distributed along XY, it is clear that A will gain more votes than B and will accordingly be elected in the simple majority ballot being considered. A moment's reflection reveals that the reason why A emerges as the winner is that his proposed policy more closely approximates the preferences of the median voter than does the policy proposed by his rival B. This conclusion can be easily verified by the reader by simply altering the positions of A and B in **Figure 10.6**, from which it will quickly be seen that the policy located nearest to Z will always emerge as the winner. Stated differently, we see that in order to win this sort of election a candidate should pitch his or her manifesto at the preferences of the median voter. Interestingly, it might also be noted that if points A and B are located the same distance either side of Z the result will be a tie, and the median voter will have the deciding vote in a situation where he or she is likely to be indifferent between the two alternatives on offer!

The preceding discussion is obviously a considerable simplification of what goes on in practice, but it does, nevertheless, serve to illustrate how the preferences of one particular group within a union (theoretically the preferences of the median voter) can, through democratic processes internal to the union, exert a major influence upon union policies and behaviour in collective-bargaining situations (Farber, 1978).

Although the particular scenario considered above referred to the situation where union members were electing their leadership according to the wage policies offered by alternative candidates, the analysis could equally well have been presented in terms of the membership selecting via a ballot (at its annual conference perhaps) the wage policy to be followed by its existing leadership over, say, the coming year. In this version of the model, one would merely substitute the words policy A and policy B in place of candidates A and B, in which case the preceding discussion would apply unaltered. The median voter model of union preferences is important because it directs attention to the role of mechanisms internal to the union in determining its policies regarding both wages and employment. In particular, it illustrates the way in which the wage policies pursued by union members may be interpreted as reflecting the preferences of their membership, as communicated via the ballot box.

Utility-maximising models of the trade union

During the 1980s a number of important developments in the micro-economic theory of the trade union occurred. Central to much of this recent work is a rejection of the simple maximising models suggested in the earlier literature, in favour of a utility-maximising approach. The notion that the union possesses a utility function defined over such variables as the levels of wages and employment of their membership is by no means a new one. Accordingly, we begin this section with a discussion of the early literature, before proceeding to examine the more recent contributions. As we shall see in Chapter 11, the notion that the union possesses such a utility function underpins much of the recent literature addressing the way in which wages are fixed in unionised labour markets.

□ *Union preference functions*

In view of the difficulties encountered in the specification of a single union maximand, it is perhaps most reasonable to argue that trade unions are concerned at least with increasing both the wages and employment of their members, but to accept that the precise weights attached to these two objectives differ both between unions and over a given union's life-cycle. Presumably, closed (or craft) unions place relatively large weight on the wage-increase objective, while open (or industrial and general) unions attach particular weight in their policies to employment, because of the influence that this has on the size of their membership. As a development of this sort of approach to trade union wage policy Cartter (1959), developing Fellner's (1951) earlier analysis, specified a utility function according to which a trade union's utility is assumed to be an increasing function of two variables: its members' wage rate and their level of employment. Given this utility function, it is possible to employ the standard techniques of indifference curve (or, as these are often called in the present context, preference function) analysis to study the union's wage–employment objectives. Although unions in practice may be concerned with a variety of issues (including safety in the work-place, the amount of paid holidays and other factors relating to the conditions of work), this simple two-variable formulation serves to illustrate the nature of the trade-offs and constraints faced by the union.

In the extreme case where the union's utility is a function of only its member's wage rate (that is, the wage maximisation case considered above), the union's indifference-mapping will consist of a series of horizontal lines on the usual wage–employment diagram (with the wage on the vertical axis and the level of employment on the horizontal one). In this case utility-maximising behaviour, given the existence of a downward-sloping demand curve for union labour, implies that the union will seek to move to the top point of the labour demand curve in order to reach the highest possible indifference curve. At the other extreme is the case where the union's utility is a function of only the level of its members' employment (that is, the employment maximisation case considered above). In this case the union's indifference map is a series of vertical lines, and utility-maximising behaviour implies that the union will seek to increase employment to the maximum level possible, given the constraints imposed by the labour supply schedule. These two extreme cases are discussed in more detail in Cartter (1959, pp. 86–8). The wage bill maximisation hypothesis was considered above and in this case, the union's indifference map is a series of rectangular hyperbole. At every point along any particular rectangular hyperbolic indifference curve the wage bill (the product of the wage rate and the level of employment) is constant, with the consequence that utility-maximising behaviour implies that the union will seek to reach the highest indifference curve consistent with the constraints to which it is subject.

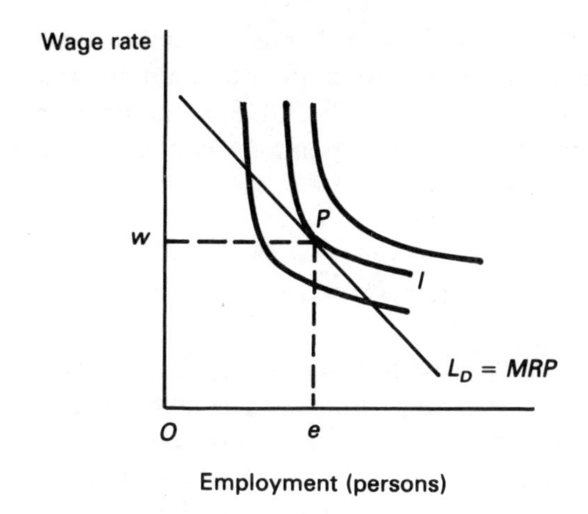

Figure 10.7 ***Union indifference map***

As already noted, it is much more plausible to argue that unions are concerned with *both* the wages and employment of their members and therefore to specify union utility as an increasing function of both these arguments. Given such a utility function we can construct, in the usual way, a mapping of union indifference curves, each of which is the locus of combinations of wage rates and employment levels that yield a given level of utility to the union. **Figure 10.7** shows an example of such an indifference map of a union for which wages and employment are the only arguments entering its utility function. Since wages and employment are unlikely to be perfect substitutes for one another, the union's indifference curves are drawn convex to the origin on the basis of the usual assumption of a diminishing marginal rate of substitution between them.

The precise form of the union's indifference map, in terms of both the shape and the configuration of its indifference curves, will vary from case to case according to its utility function. However, it is generally argued that the union attaches a special significance to the prevailing wage–employment combination, with the consequence that its indifference curve is likely to be sharply *kinked* about this combination, indicating that once a union is enjoying a particular wage–employment combination, it will take a considerable increase in wages to compensate for even a small decrease in employment to compensate for any wage reduction. The argument here, which is in the spirit of Ross's political view of the union, is that any worsening of the situation relative to the status quo will generate internal political pressures within the union. Such pressures threaten its existence, with the consequence that any reduction in wages (or employment) must be accompanied by a large increase in employment (or wages) in order to maintain union utility at a constant level (Cartter, 1959, pp. 89–90). Such an indifference curve is shown by I in **Figure 10.7** where point P denotes the existing wage–employment combination.

□ *The union's equilibrium*

Assuming that the employer has no monopsony power the demand (*MRP*) curve for union labour imposes a constraint upon the union, since it shows the quantity of union labour that the employer will seek to hire at each particular wage rate. In the same way that the consumer's equilibrium is found by superimposing the budget constraint on to the indifference map it follows with a given labour demand curve that the union's utility is maximised at the wage–employment combination where this curve is tangential to an indifference curve. In **Figure 10.7** the union is in equilibrium at point P, where the slope of its indifference curve (that is, the marginal rate of substitution of wages for employment) is equal to the slope of the labour demand curve. This straightforward utility-maximising model of union objectives therefore predicts that the union will seek to achieve the wage w accompanied by an employment level of e.

The equilibrium condition for the utility-maximising union is easily derived as follows. Assume that the union's utility function is of the form

$$U = U(w, N) \tag{10.4}$$

where w, denotes the (nominal) wage and N the level of employment. Further, let us assume that this utility function is 'well-behaved' in the usual sense that it possesses positive, but diminishing, marginal utilities. Writing the demand for labour function as

$$N = N(w, \eta) \tag{10.5}$$

where η is a shift parameter, the union's optimisation problem of maximising (10.4) subject to (10.5) may be solved by application of the conventional Lagrange multiplier method. Forming the augmented function z and maximising we obtain the following first-order conditions, where λ denotes the Lagrange multiplier and with notation

$$U_w = \frac{\partial u}{\partial w}, U_N = \frac{\partial U}{\partial N}, N_w = \frac{\partial N}{\partial w}.$$

$$z = U(w, N) + \lambda\,[N - N(w, \eta)]$$

$$\frac{\partial z}{\partial w} = U_w - \lambda N_w = 0$$

$$\frac{\partial z}{\partial N} = U_N + \lambda = 0$$

$$\frac{\partial z}{\partial \lambda} = N - N(w, \eta) = 0$$

Dividing the first of these conditions by the second and rearranging we obtain

$$-\frac{U_w}{U_N} = N_w$$

according to which the union maximises utility subject to the labour demand curve constraint by equating its marginal rate of substitution between wages and employment to the slope of the labour demand curve.

Dynamic considerations: the wage preference path

The utility maximisation approach can be extended to allow analysis of the union's reaction to the shifts which may occur over time in the position of its short-run demand for labour curve. It has been recognised over many years (for example, Lewis, 1963) that trade unions do not typically react in a symmetrical manner to increases and decreases in the conditions of demand for their members' labour. Confronted with an increase in the conditions of labour demand, unions are frequently observed to attach a higher order of preference for improvements in wages than for increases in employment, but when confronted with a decrease in labour demand conditions, they are often observed to resist any reduction in money wages despite the resulting contraction in employment. Notice that such downward rigidity in the money wage is a feature central to the supply side of the labour market in the Keynesian macromodel.

In **Figure 10.8** point *P* denotes the union's equilibrium position, given an initial demand curve for union labour (L_D). In this diagram various levels of labour demand both greater than and less than the initial level are shown, and given these we are able to trace out the locus of utility-maximising wage–employment combinations or tangency points between labour demand and indifference curves. This path, which can

Figure 10.8 ***The wage preference path***

be thought of as analogous to a firm's expansion path or a consumer's income–consumption curve, indicates the path that the utility-maximising union would seek to follow if the conditions of labour demand were to change from their initial level at L_D, and it is known as the union's *wage preference path*.

The wage preference path shown in **Figure 10.8** illustrates the observed asymmetrical response of unions to upward and downward changes in the conditions of labour demand. The path is sharply kinked at the prevailing equilibrium (P), and its shape indicates the different weights attached by the union to improvements in wages and employment for potential increases or decreases in the conditions of labour demand. As shown in **Figure 10.8** the union uses an increase in labour demand conditions primarily to secure wage increases and only accepts increased employment for substantial upward shifts in labour demand. When there is a decrease in the conditions of labour demand, the union resists money wage cuts, despite the resulting inroads into its members' employment. It continues to do so until the decrease in labour demand becomes so substantial that it becomes willing to accept wage cuts in order to stave off further reductions in the employment of its members.[13]

Some recent microeconomics of the trade union

The preceding utility-maximising approach is by no means new. However, over recent years it has attracted considerable attention from at least two viewpoints; first, the likely form taken by the union's utility function (10.4) and second, the way in which the range of alternative hypotheses regarding union preference discussed above may be put to the empirical test. The first of these orientations is well-discussed by Oswald (1982, 1985); while the second is fully set out in Dertouzos and Pencavel (1981) and Pencavel (1984).

□ *Utilitarian approach to union preferences*

The particular form of union utility function proposed by Oswald (1982) is what may be termed a ***utilitarian*** formulation, which assumes that union utility is simply the sum of the utilities of each of its individual members. Such a utility function may be written as follows:

$$U = Nu(w) + (M - N)\, u(b) \tag{10.6}$$

where $u(\cdot)$ denotes the utility function of an individual worker. The total membership of the union is M workers, N of whom are employed and in receipt of the union-negotiated wage (w), while the remaining $(M - N)$ are unemployed and in receipt of state unemployment benefit (b). Although (10.6) assumes that the only alternative to employment at the union wage is unemployment, this formulation is easily amended to allow employment outside the union sector to be the alternative, in which case b simply becomes the wage in the alternative sector. In essence, (10.6) assumes that the union is utilitarian, in the sense that it attempts to maximise the sum of its members' utilities.

Notice that the utilitarian formulation of the union utility function (10.6) may be rewritten in a slightly different way by dividing both sides of the expression by union membership, M. By doing so we obtain

$$u = \frac{N}{M}\, u(w) + \frac{M - N}{M}\, u(b) \tag{10.7}$$

where u $(= U/M)$ denotes utility per member. Expression (10.7), known as the *expected utility* formulation, says that the utility of the representative member (u) is equal to a weighted average of the utility derived from employment, $u(w)$, and unemployment, $u(b)$; with weights given by the probability of having a job N/M and the probability of being unemployed $(M - N)/M$ respectively. Rewriting the union's objective function as (10.7) shows that the assumption that the union seeks to maximise (10.6) is equivalent to assuming that the union aims to maximise the representative member's expected utility.

We will encounter the utilitarian model of union preference again in Chapter 11 when we consider the way in which wages are fixed in unionised labour markets. However, it is interesting to notice that (10.6) and (10.7) can be thought of as representing 'special cases' of the following more general utility function (Mayhew and Turnbull, 1989).

$$U = \alpha\,[Nu(w)] + (1 - \alpha)\,[(M - N)\,u(b)]$$

where $0 \leqslant \alpha \leqslant 1$. In this formulation α is a constant, the magnitude of which indicates the relative influence or weight exerted on the union's policy by employed and unemployed union members. The utilitarian formulation thus assumes that $\alpha = 0.5$. As Mayhew and Turnbull point out, the kinked union indifference curve hypothesis discussed above assumes a value of α approaching unity, indicating that union policy is largely determined by the currently employed and largely self-interested members of the union (1989, p. 107).

□ *The Stone–Geary utility function*

The final recent development to be considered under the utility-maximising approach to union behaviour utilises the well-known Stone–Geary utility function. The basic idea here is that the union's utility function (10.4) takes the following form

$$U = U(w, N) = (w - \gamma)^{\theta}\,(N - \delta)^{1-\theta} \tag{10.8}$$

As before, w denotes the wage rate and N the level of employment and γ and δ in (10.8) denote so-called 'reference values' for these two variables. The bracketed terms $(w - \gamma)$ and $(N - \delta)$ represent *supernumerary* wages and employment respectively. The parameter θ shows the relative importance attached by the union to each of these magnitudes. The beauty of (10.8) is that it *encompasses*, as special cases, a number of the models of union objectives which are encountered in the literature. For example, in the case of a closed-shop situation where $\theta = 0.5$ and $\gamma = \delta = 0$, expression (10.8) reduces to the wage bill maximisation hypothesis discussed above. Setting $\gamma = \delta = 0$, we obtain the wage maximisation hypothesis in the case where $\theta = 1$ and the employment maximisation hypothesis in the case of $\theta = 0$. In our earlier discussion we considered the union–monopoly analogy and saw this to imply a form of economic rent-maximising behaviour. Several other examples of rent maximising-type models may be found in the literature. For example, in a study of the US experience, de Menil (1971) specified union utility as an increasing function of the surplus of the actual wage bill over and above the wage bill that would apply if its members received only the competitive wage. A similar rent maximisation hypothesis may be found in Rosen (1970). Such a formulation arises from (10.8) in the particular case where $\theta = 0.5$, $\delta = 0$ and γ equals the competitive wage.

The great advantage of the Stone–Geary approach to the analysis of union objectives is the opportunity which it offers for empirically discriminating between a number of the alternative hypotheses which have been widely discussed in the literature. As we have seen, a range of alternative models of union objectives are *nested* within (10.8), with the consequence that in principle, if we are able to satisfactorily estimate the values of the parameters θ, γ and δ we have the possibility of ascertaining exactly what the union in question appears to be seeking to maximise.

Such empirical investigations of the activities of the US International Typographical (ITU) Union over the period 1945–65 were undertaken by Dertouzos and Pencavel (1981) and Pencavel (1984). For this approach to be valid it is necessary to assume that the union holds a dominant position in bargaining with the employer, so that the observed values of wages and employment can reasonably be taken as reflecting the union's preferences; a condition which Dertouzos and Pencavel (1981) and Pencavel (1984) see as being satisfied in the case of the ITU. While the evidence does seem to suggest that the ITU takes the employment consequences of its wage policies into account, it fails to support the wage bill maximisation hypothesis. However, these studies do provide some tentative evidence to suggest that the larger ITU locals seek to maximise the rents for unionisation. In addition, the evidence appears to offer some support to the kinked indifference curve hypothesis discussed above.

Notes

1. Early analysis showed the existence of a number of fairly distinct phases in the growth of trade unions in the UK, with international comparisons suggesting that such behaviour was mirrored in the experiences of other countries (Davis, 1941).
2. The origins of craft unions have been traced back to the medieval craft guilds. For a detailed historical analysis of the forerunners and origins of trade unionism in Britain, see Webb and Webb (1920, pp. 1–64). Notice, in particular, that the Combination Acts of 1799 and 1800 (subsequently repealed in 1824) made combinations of workers illegal.
3. For early discussion of this point see Ulman (1955) and Reder (1960).
4. For a recent reappraisal of the UK evidence, see Booth (1983). For a detailed survey of the US literature, see Fiorito and Greer (1982). For a survey of the earlier literature in the four countries studied by Bain and Elsheikh, see their 1976 publication.
5. For an attempt to reconcile these two views by explicitly recognising the uncertainties associated with union–employer bargaining, see Mitchell (1972).

6. Marshall *et al.* (1976, p. 332) cite the behaviour of the US United Mine Worker's union between 1930 and about 1950 as an example lending support to this wage-maximising model of union behaviour.
7. If one allows for the existence of union membership subscriptions, it is perhaps plausible to argue that workers will leave the union if their wage does not exceed that prevailing in the union's absence by an amount sufficient to outweigh membership subscriptions. In this case the maximum employment that the union can achieve will be below *e* members by the amount necessary to give a wage sufficiently in excess of *w* to just outweigh membership subscriptions.
8. For a generalisation of the wage bill maximisation hypothesis to take account of the existence of unemployment compensation, see Cartter (1959, pp. 82–3).
9. The monopoly *analogy* in the analysis of union wage policy objectives should not be confused with the related monopoly model of wage determination in unionised labour markets, which is discussed in Chapter 11 below.
10. In a closed shop only those workers who are already members of the union can be hired by the employer, but a union shop allows the employer to select workers according to his own criteria, provided that the new employees join the union within some specified time period.
11. Although it is usual to refer to the *MRP* curve in this diagram as the firm's labour demand curve (see, for example, Cartter, 1959, p. 84), it should be recalled that, strictly speaking, because the firm faces an upward-sloping labour supply curve, it is a monopsonist and therefore does not possess a labour demand curve. (See Chapter 7 above.)
12. Although this example considers policies regarding the level of wages, the analysis applies equally to situations where policies are specified in terms of rates of change of wages. In such cases, point *X* may be taken as representing a zero rate of change of wages, while *Y* represents some suitably specified upper limit of wage increases.
13. As already noted, closed unions attach greatest weight in their policies to wages, while open unions place particular emphasis on their members' employment. To the extent that closed unions place greater weight than open unions on increasing wages when labour demand increases and on resisting cuts in wages when labour demand decreases, one can expect the wage preference path in the case of a closed union to be more steeply sloped above the current equilibrium (*P*), and more shallowly sloped below it, than in the case of an open union.

■ *Chapter 11* ■

Wage Determination under Collective Bargaining

The analysis of the previous chapter was concerned with the union's *objectives* in respect of the wage rate and employment of its membership. In order to analyse wage determination in the presence of trade unions, it is also necessary to consider the employer's equilibrium levels of wages and employment. Since these will, as we shall see, typically differ from those of the union, it is also necessary to consider the negotiating or *collective-bargaining* process which takes place between the union and the employer in order to determine the wage that will actually be paid within the limits set by the preferences of these two parties.

Wage determination under trade unionism: the bilateral monopoly model

Traditional neoclassical analysis treats the problem of wage determination in the presence of trade unions as a particular case of *bilateral monopoly*. According to this formulation, the union is assumed to behave as a monopolistic seller of labour, while the employer is assumed to be a monopsonistic purchaser of labour. The monopoly view of union behaviour was considered in the previous chapter (see pp. 268–70) and the case of a monopsonistic purchaser of labour was considered in Chapter 7 (see pp. 154–63) **Figure 11.1** brings together the models of the union–monopoly seller and the employer–monopoly purchaser (considered above in **Figures 10.4** and **7.4** respectively) in order to illustrate the bilateral monopoly formulation.

As we have seen, the monopsonistic purchaser of labour faces an upward-sloping labour supply curve, and in order to maximise profits the monopsonist equates the marginal labour cost (*MLC*) to the marginal revenue product (*MRP*), seeking to employ e_1 units of labour at the wage w_1. According to the union–monopoly analogy (the limitations of which were discussed above; see p. 269), the union is assumed to aim to equate the marginal revenue (*MR*) from the sale of its members' labour services to their supply price, and therefore to seek to have e_2 members employed at w_2.

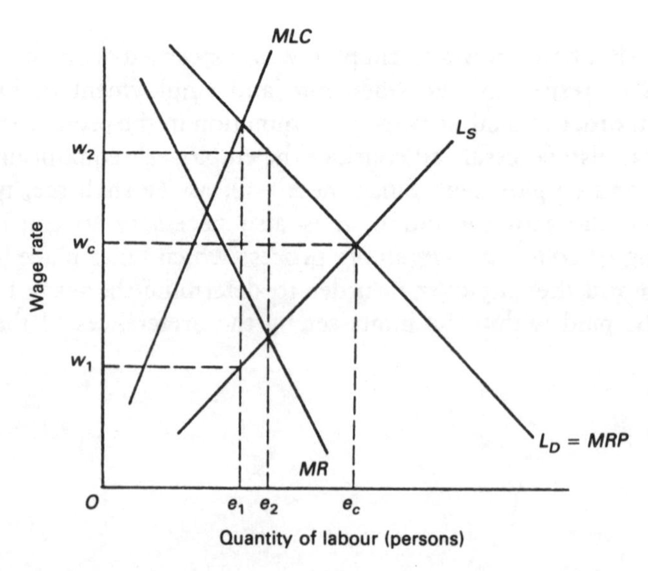

Figure 11.1 ***Bilateral monopoly formulation***

According to the bilateral monopoly model, the employer attempts to restrict employment below the competitive level e_c in order to maximise profits, while the union likewise seeks to restrict the sale of its members' labour services in order to maximise the collective rent of its membership. It is important to recognise that the bilateral monopoly model, which is based on the usual assumptions of rational maximising behaviour, is unable to yield a unique prediction of the wage settlement that will be established; rather, it is only able to delineate a *range of indeterminacy* within which the outcome can be expected to lie. In **Figure 11.1** the union seeks the wage w_2 and the employer the lower wage w_1, but the actual wage rate is left *indeterminate* meaning that, while it can be argued that the wage rate will lie somewhere between w_1 and w_2 the analysis is unable to predict the actual wage that will be established within these limits. Given that this analysis predicts that the actual wage will lie somewhere in the *range of indeterminacy* (w_1 to w_2), it is usually argued that its precise value within this range will be determined as the outcome of some process of collective bargaining which takes place between the union and the employer.

The bilateral monopoly model does not, however, provide any theory of the bargaining process that is presumed to operate these limits and therefore offers no prediction as to its outcome. Notice from **Figure 11.1** that the competitive wage (w_c) lies between the employer's and the union's desired wage levels and that this can conceivably arise as the outcome of the union–employer collective-bargaining process.

The wage preference path and the wage bargain

The bilateral monopoly model can be criticised for the reasons considered above in our discussions of the union–monopoly analogy, principally because of the questionable nature of the maximand implied by the analogy, plus the fact that the union does not possess cost functions analogous to those underlying the firm's supply function. The absence of such cost curves was one of the reasons that led Cartter (1959, pp. 92–4), in his development of Fellner's (1951) earlier analysis, to put forward the union's wage preference path as being a more appropriate concept than a labour supply curve of the conventional sort in the analysis of unionised labour markets.[1] In cases where wages are determined by collective bargaining, the wage preference path (*WPP*) analysis gives us much the same conclusion as the bilateral monopoly model; namely, that market forces are primarily important in establishing

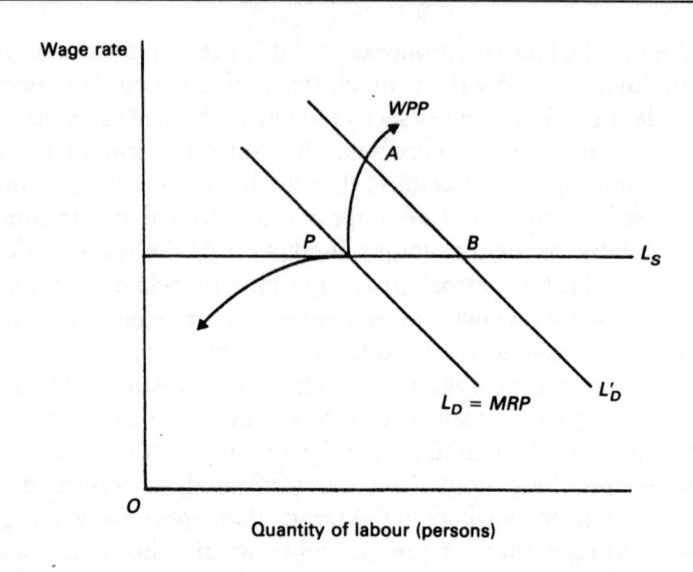

Figure 11.2 ***The union's wage preference path and the bargained wage***

boundaries within which the levels of wages and employment can be expected to lie.

In order to illustrate the determination of the union wage within the utility-maximising framework offered by the *WPP* analysis, let us assume for simplicity that there is perfect competition among purchasers of labour, so that the individual purchaser of labour faces a perfectly elastic labour supply curve. Assume also that the initial wage–employment combination coincides with the perfectly competitive equilibrium. This situation is shown in **Figure 11.2** where L_S denotes the labour supply curve faced by the employer in question, L_D is the employer's short-run labour demand curve and *P* denotes the initial wage–employment combination.

At point *P* the firm is maximising its profits, given initial conditions, because the wage is equated to labour's marginal revenue product. In addition, we assume that the union is maximising its utility subject to the constraint imposed by the initial labour demand curve at this point, so that point *P* lies on the *WPP* path. Suppose now that there is an increase in the conditions of labour demand, such that the labour demand curve shifts from L_D to L'_D. Given the shift, the union will seek to move along its wage preference path from *P* to its new utility-maximising position at point *A*, while the employer will seek to move along the perfectly elastic labour supply curve to point *B*, where profits will be maximised given the new labour demand conditions. In this case the employer seeks to absorb the increased conditions of labour demand *solely* in the form of increased employment, while the union seeks to absorb this mostly in the form of a wage increase.

According to this formulation, the union seeks the wage–employment combination shown by *A*, while the employer seeks that at *B*, so that as in the case of the bilateral monopoly model we are left with a range of indeterminacy. Since the labour demand curve shows the quantity of labour that the profit-maximising firm will seek to employ at any given wage, the new wage–employment combination will, in the case where the employer is free to adjust employment once a wage is agreed, lie somewhere along the new labour demand curve between *A* and *B*.

Therefore, this analysis, like the bilateral monopoly model, does not provide a determinate solution; instead, it is only able to predict a range within which the agreed wage can be expected to lie. Once again it is argued that the actual wage–employment combination within this range will be determined by a process of collective bargaining, within which the conflicting preferences of the union and employer are resolved. However, the analysis gives no theory of the collective-bargaining process which operates between these limits and therefore offers no prediction as to where the final outcome will lie. While the *WPP* analysis is easily generalised to cases where the initial wage–employment combination does not coincide with the perfectly competitive equilibrium, and to cases where there is a decrease rather than an increase in the conditions of labour demand, its conclusion that the wage is indeterminate within some range remains unaltered (see Cartter, 1959, pp. 92–4 for details).

■ Indeterminacy and the bargaining process

As we have seen above, the traditional tools of intermediate microeconomic analysis have, as far as the above approaches are concerned, proved unable to provide a unique prediction of the wage that will be determined in unionised labour markets. Instead they have only been able to delineate a range of indeterminacy within which the outcome is predicted as lying. Faced with this indeterminacy, many writers have been content to follow the spirit of Edgeworth's famous pronouncement of the so-called classical view that

> contract without competition is indeterminate' (1881, p. 20)

and to dismiss the determination of the precise outcome of the bargaining process within the range of indeterminacy as being beyond the realms of economic analysis.[2]

Monopoly-union and efficient-bargain models

During the 1980s considerable attention was directed towards the construction of models designed to overcome the indeterminacy of earlier approaches. This literature is dominated by two particular approaches to the determination of wages and employment in unionised labour markets: the monopoly-union model and the efficient-bargain model.

□ *Monopoly-union model*

This model is extremely simple: it assumes that the wage is set unilaterally by the union so as to maximise its utility, subject to the constraint that employment must lie on the labour demand curve. The *monopoly-union model* is a special case of the wider class of models, known as *right-to-manage models*. The essential feature of the right-to-manage model is the assumption that while the union may bargain over the wage rate, the employer retains the right to unilaterally decide upon the number of workers to hire. In right-to-manage models (see Nickell and Andrews, 1983) the wage is determined as the outcome of a bargaining process between the employer and the union. Once the wage is set by the bargain, the employer exercises the 'right-to-manage' by unilaterally selecting the number of workers to hire so as to maximise profits: with the consequence that employment will, for the reasons discussed in Chapter 5, always lie on the demand curve for labour. The monopoly-union model arises as the special case of the right-to-manage model in which the union unilaterally chooses the wage rate.

The utility-maximising approach to union preference was considered in the previous chapter, where we saw that the union's utility-maximising wage–employment combination is given by the tangency point between the demand for labour function and an indifference curve. By assumption, the union in the monopoly model is able to set the wage rate, knowing that the employer will respond by setting the employment level so as to maximise profit subject to the union-determined wage. Profit maximisation on the part of the employer implies that employment must lie on the labour demand curve, at the point corresponding to the union-determined wage. We can therefore see from **Figure 11.3** that the union maximises its utility by setting the wage equal to w^u, as the employer will respond by setting employment at n^u, thus allowing the union to reach its utility-maximising wage–employment combination at point E.[3]

Isoprofit curves

The discussion which follows requires us to introduce employer indifference, or *isoprofit*, curves. The assumption here is simply that the employer-firm's utility is an increasing function of profits. We may therefore write the employer's utility function as follows

$$U = U(\pi),\ U' > 0 \tag{11.1}$$

where π denotes profits. Since a given level of profits may be achieved with alternative wage–employment combinations, we can simply plot all such combinations associated with the profit level in question to obtain an isoprofit contour as the employer-firm's indifference curve.

The geometry of the union-monopoly model is seen more clearly by the introduction of the employer's isoprofit contour, or profit indifference curves, into the picture. As we have seen, these indifference curves illustrate the various different wage and employment combinations which give rise to any given level of profits. Three such curves (denoted by π_0, π_1, and π_2) are shown in **Figure 11.3**, from which it can be seen that each isoprofit contour is of an inverted 'u' shape and has its turning-point at the point where it intersects the firm's labour demand curve.

The shape of the employer's isoprofit curves in wage–employment space is easily demonstrated by writing the employer's profit function as

$$\pi = p \cdot f(L) - wL - k \tag{11.2}$$

where it is assumed that the firm sells its output in a perfectly competitive product market at price p, with short-run production function $q = f(L)$ and with fixed costs equal to k. Setting profits (π) equal to some fixed value (say π^0) and solving for w we obtain the following expression for the employer's isoprofit curve

$$w = p \cdot f\frac{(L)}{L} - \frac{(k + \pi^0)}{L} \tag{11.3}$$

Totally differentiating the employer's profit function with respect to labour input L and equating to zero we obtain

$$\frac{d\pi}{dL} = 0 = p \cdot f'(L) - L\frac{dw}{dL} - w \tag{11.4}$$

Recognising $f'(L)$ as the marginal physical product of labour and re-arranging we obtain the following expression for the gradient of the isoprofit curves

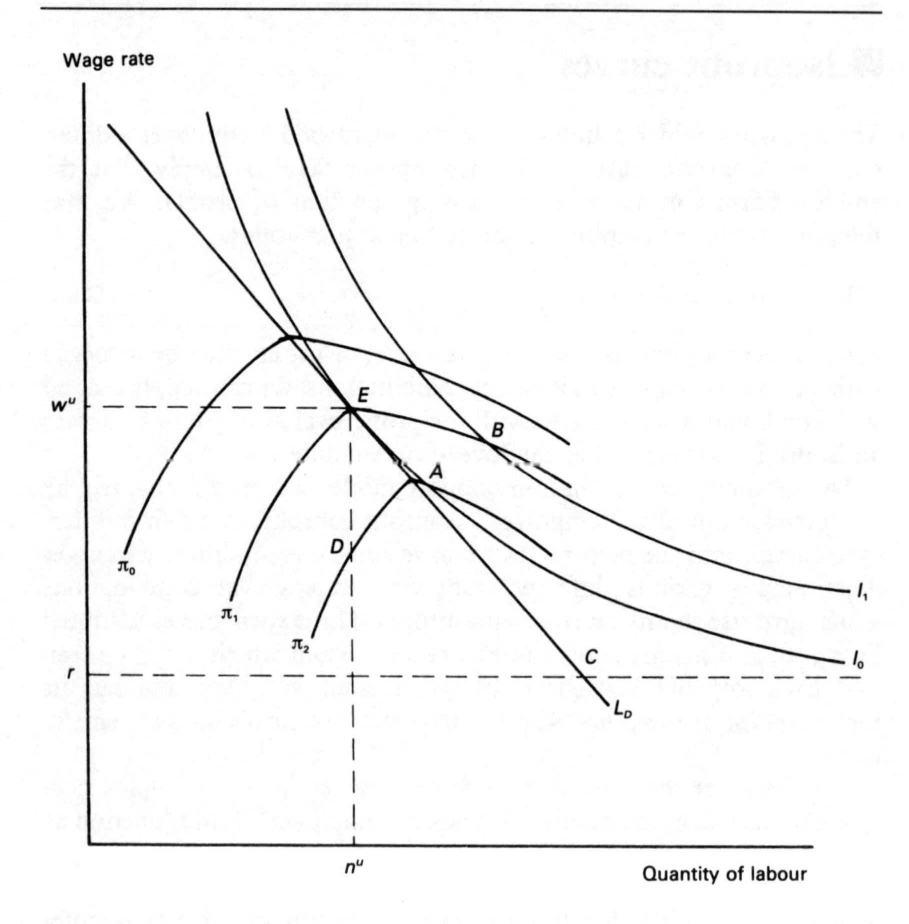

Figure 11.3 ***The monopoly-union model***

$$\frac{dw}{dL} = \frac{[MRP - w]}{L} \tag{11.5}$$

Using (11.5) we may therefore write

$$\frac{dw}{dL} > 0, \text{ when } MRP > w$$

$$\frac{dw}{dL} = 0, \text{ when } MRP = w$$

$$\frac{dw}{dL} < 0, \text{ when } w > MRP$$

These conditions indicate that to the left of the labour demand/*MRP* curve (that is, when $MRP > w$) the isoprofit curves will be positively sloped. To the right of the demand curve $w > MRP$ and the isoprofit curves will be negatively sloped. At the point where the isoprofit curve intersects the labour demand curve $w = MRP$ and the slope of the isoprofit curve is zero, indicating that the turning-point in the isoprofit curve is situated at its point of intersection with the labour demand curve.

It should also be noted that the further south an isoprofit contour lies the higher is the level of profits which it represents; from which we may, for **Figure 11.3**, write $\pi_2 > \pi_1 > \pi_0$. The intuition here is quite straightforward; for any given level of employment, profits will, other things being equal, be higher the lower is the wage rate. Thus, for example, with employment equal to (say) n^u, profits will be higher at D (on isoprofit countour π_2) than at E (on isoprofit curve π_1) because D corresponds to a wage rate below w^u. However, with the wage set by the union in this model at w^u, the best the employer can do, as we have seen, is to employ n^u union members at point E. It is clear from **Figure 11.3** that profits are maximised at E, given w^u, since at any other level of employment given a wage of w^u the employer would be on a more northerly isoprofit contour (such as π_0), which represents a level of profits lower than π_1 which is achieved at E. It is important to notice that in this model, the tangency point at E represents an equilibrium from the viewpoints of *both* the union and the employer. The union maximises utility at tangency point E, and the employer, given the union determined wage w^u, maximises profits at this point. For obvious reasons, this model is sometimes referred to as the *labour demand model*.

□ *Efficient-bargain model*

Although the monopoly-union model has the appealing feature that its solution (point E in **Figure 11.3**) lies on the employer's labour demand curve, it suffers from one major drawback, in that its solution is *inefficient* in the Paretian sense. That is, it is possible by moving away from the equilibrium E to increase the utility of one party above that at E without decreasing the utility of the other party. This is easily seen from **Figure 11.3** by comparing points E and A. Thus, if the agreed outcome were to shift from E to A the union's utility would remain unchanged (because E and A both lie on the same indifference curve, I_0) while, as a result of this move, the utility of the employer would increase because profits are higher at A than at E, as point A is situated on a more southerly isoprofit contour. Likewise, comparison of points E and B in **Figure 11.3** shows that a move away from the monopoly-union model's equilibrium to *B* would offer an increase in utility to the union (from I_0 to I_1), while leaving the employer's profits (utility) unchanged. Wage and employment combinations like those represented by *A* and *B* are therefore said to be Pareto superior to the combination represented by point *E*.

The second model to attract particular attention in the recent literature is the *efficient-bargain* model. The basic notion of the efficient-bargain model is that, whatever solution is reached, it seems reasonable to expect it to satisfy the requirement of Pareto efficiency, in the sense that it is not possible to make one party better off in utility terms without making the other worse off. The efficient-bargain model is by no means new, and indeed it can be traced back to the writings of Leontief (1946), Fellner (1951) and Cartter (1959). However, following McDonald and Solow's (1981) 'rediscovery' of this model, considerable attention has been directed in the 1980s towards extending and developing it, both theoretically and empirically (for example, Ashenfelter and Brown, 1986; MaCurdy and Pencavel, 1986), relative to other models of union behaviour, especially the monopoly-union model described above.

Figure 11.4 illustrates the basic idea of the efficient-bargain model in a little more detail. Once again point *E*, corresponding to the wage rate w^u and employment level n^u, represents the equilibrium solution of the monopoly-union model. A movement away from *E* to *G* would result in an increase in the union's utility (from I_1 to I_2), while leaving the employer neither better nor worse off. Notice that point *G* corresponds to a 'back-to-back' tangency point between the union's indifference curve I_2 and the employer's isoprofit curve π_1, with the consequence that this point represents the highest level of utility which the union can achieve, subject to the employer's utility/profit remaining unchanged at π_1. Similarly, the back-to-back tangency point at *F* represents the maximum level of profits which the employer can achieve, subject to the requirement that the union is neither better nor worse off in utility terms than at *E*. If we think of a situation where wages and employment are being renegotiated from an initial solution at *E*, then points *F* and *G* correspond to what Pigou (1905) termed *maximum concession points*.

The dotted line *CC′* in **Figure 11.4** joins together all of the back-to-back tangency points which exist between union indifference curves and employer's isoprofit curves and is known as the *contract curve*. At all points along the contract curve *CC′* the utility of one party is maximised subject to the value of the other's utility. Consequently, all of the outcomes lying on the contract curve satisfy the requirement of Pareto optimality and are, therefore, said to be Pareto *efficient* outcomes. The union would obviously prefer to move to point *G* (in order to appropriate for itself all of the 'gains from trade'), while the employer would likewise prefer the outcome to lie at point *F*. The section of the contract

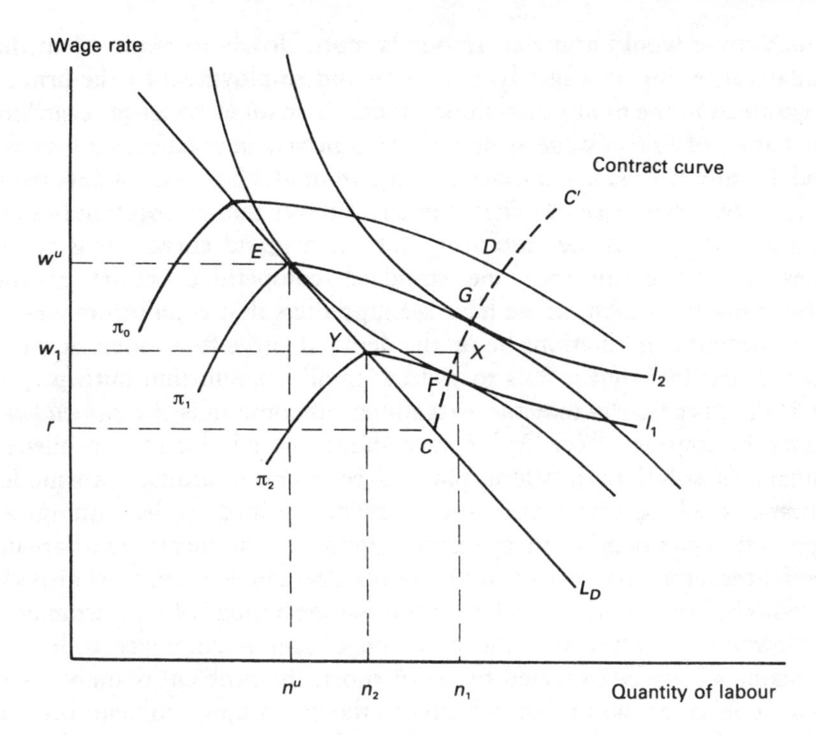

Figure 11.4 ***The efficient-bargain model***

curve lying between the maximum concession points G and F is sometimes referred to, following Pigou (1905), as the *range of practicable bargains*. There are however an infinite number of possible wage–employment combinations lying within the range of practicable bargains (GF), all of which offer utility gains to *both* the employer and the union over and above the monopoly-union equilibrium at point E. In consequence both parties would be better off, in utility terms, by moving from the monopoly-union equilibrium at E to some point along the contract curve betwen the limits set by points G and F. The efficient-bargain model requires that the outcome of the union–employer bargaining must satisfy the requirement of Pareto efficiency and therefore predicts quite simply that it must lie *somewhere* along the contract curve. But where?

As proponents of the efficient-bargain model are quick to point out, the model has the advantage over the monopoly-union model of explaining the occurrence of so-called 'all or nothing' bargaining, in the sense that it considers negotiations which take place over *both* wages and employment (where the latter may in practice take the form of negotiations over manning agreements or 'feather-bedding'); a situation which some would argue corresponds more closely to reality than the unilateral setting of wages by the union and employment by the firm as is assumed in the monopoly-union model. (For some evidence regarding the nature of British wage–employment contracts in practice, see Oswald and Turnbull, 1985). The efficient-bargain model however, suffers from at least two main defects. First, there is the fact that its solution lies off and to the right of the employer's labour demand curve.[4] This result does not fit easily into the standard competitive model of the labour market which, as we have seen, predicts that equilibrium wage–employment combinations lie on the demand curve for labour. Second, there is the fact that it fails to yield a unique equilibrium outcome, in that all it predicts is that the bargaining outcome must lie *somewhere* along the contract curve. As we have already noted, this sort of indeterminacy of solutions has long plagued economists' attempts to model situations where prices and wages are determined by bargaining, as opposed to competitive, mechanisms. Opponents of the efficient-bargain model therefore argue that all the model does, in essence, is to provide yet another theory which yields as its outcome a range of indeterminacy, somewhere within which the outcome of union–employer collective bargaining may be expected to lie. In short, the problem is simply that this model offers no unique solution to the bargaining problem; instead what it offers is an infinity of possible solutions, as represented by the infinite number of possible outcomes indicated by the (relevant section of) the contract curve. However, as Pen points out, it is important to be clear that it is *not* the outcome of the bargaining process in practice which is indeterminate (as any reader who has recently bought or sold a used car will confirm!) but the theory (1959, p. 95).

■ The Nash solution

In order to narrow the infinity of possible solutions represented by the contract curve in the efficient-bargain model down to a single unique predicted outcome, a number of analysts have invoked ideas developed elsewhere in the theory of bargaining (see, for example, Coddington, 1968; Sapsford, 1982). The best-known formal solution to the bargaining problem is due to Nash (1950, 1953). As we shall see in more detail below Nash's solution to the bargaining problem is that point on the contract curve which maximises the *product* of the parties' utility gains over and above the outcome which would apply if no agreement were reached. Oddly enough, it can be shown (McDonald and Solow, 1981, p. 905) that in the context of the efficient-bargain model the Nash solution is that point on the contract curve at which the wage is equal to the arithmetic mean of the average and marginal revenue products of labour, as indicated by, say, point X on CC' in **Figure 11.4**. The efficient-bargain model, with the aid of Nash's solution, therefore predicts that point X, corresponding to a wage rate of w_1 and employment n_1 will emerge as the outcome of union–employer collective bargaining.

One interesting feature of the efficient-bargain model is that once agreement is reached (say at the Nash solution at point X in **Figure 11.4**), it is always in the employer's interests to renege on the deal by cutting down employment below the agreed level (n_1) in order to revert to the labour demand curve. Thus, by breaking the employment dimensions of the agreed package, the employer can increase profits by moving horizontally from X to Y, decreasing employment from n_1 to n_2 since by so doing he is able to move to the more southerly isoprofit curve π_2.[5]

Finally, it is important to recognise that the (simple) Nash solution discussed above is not the only solution concept which may be invoked in order to achieve a determinacy of solution in the efficient-bargain model. In particular, a number of recent studies (for example, Ulph and Ulph, 1990) have employed a generalised version of Nash's solution concept which sees the solution as occurring at that point on the contract curve at which the following *weighted* product of the parties' utility gains is maximised

$$Z = [U_u(w, n) - \bar{U}_u]^s \, [U_e(w, n) - \bar{U}_e]^{(1-s)}$$

where the subscripts u and e denote the union and employer respectively, where $U_i(w, n)$ denotes the utility which the party in question ($i = u, e$) achieves from the wage–employment combination (w, n) and where $\bar{U}_i$ denotes the utilities that would apply in the no-agreement case. The parameter s in this expression represents the relative bargaining strength of the union. The larger the value of s the more powerful is the union relative to the employer, and the smaller is s the less powerful is the union. Notice that in the particular case where $s = 0.5$, both parties are equally powerful, and the generalised version of Nash's solution reduces to the simple (unweighted) version discussed above. Notice also that in the extreme case where $s = 1$, the wage is determined so as to maximise the utility gain solely to the union, and the solution is consequently that point on the contract curve which corresponds to the firm earning profits just sufficient to keep it in business. For example, if the entrepreneur's transfer earnings, or shut-down level of profits, were π_0, the union's gain would be maximised at point D in **Figure 11.4**.[6] At the other extreme is the situation where $s = 0$, in which case the wage selected will be the reservation wage r (as shown by point C in **Figure**

11.4) which maximises the gain to the firm. For values of s lying between 0 and 1, the agreed settlement varies along the contract curve between point C (which pays only the reservation wage r) and the employer's shut-down point at D.

■ Some extensions

The preceding models may be extended in a variety of directions: for example, to include income taxes payable by workers, as well as employment and income subsidies payable to employers and workers respectively. Oswald (1982, 1985) uses the utilitarian utility function discussed in Chapter 10 (see equations (10.6) and (10.7)) to derive a number of predictions regarding the comparative static properties of the monopoly-union and efficient-bargain models. His major results are summarised in **Table 11.1**.

Our discussion of the monopoly-union and efficient-bargain models sees these as offering alternative explanations of the determination of wages and employment in unionised labour markets. While this is the approach adopted in much of the current literature, it is important to notice that in a recent study Manning (1987) has developed a general model of the trade union, which encompasses both the monopoly-union and efficient-bargain models. Manning models collective bargaining as a two-stage process, in the first stage of which wages are determined, with employment being determined in the second stage. The key feature of this sequential bargaining model is that the ability (or 'power') of the union to obtain an outcome which is favourable to itself may differ in the two stages of the process. Within this framework, it is easy to see that the monopoly-union model arises in the case where the union is all-powerful in the first stage of the bargaining process (in which the wage is determined); while the employer is all-powerful in the second (that is, employment determination) stage of the proceedings. If we use p ($0 \leqslant p \leqslant 1$) to denote the bargaining 'power' of the union in the wage determination stage and q ($0 \leqslant q \leqslant 1$) to denote its power in the employment determination stage, (with the power of the employer in the wage and employment stages being $(1 - p)$ and $(1 - q)$ respectively), we see that the monopoly union model is the case where $p = 1$ and $q = 0$. Notice that the right-to-manage model is the case where $q = 0$. Within this framework, Manning demonstrates that the efficient-bargain model arises in the case where $p = q$.

As we have seen, the monopoly-union model implies that the wage–employment outcome will lie on the labour demand curve, while the efficient-bargain model implies that outcomes will lie on the contract

Table 11.1 ***Comparative static predictions***

Monopoly-union model	
Change	*Predicted effect on union's desired wage* (w^u *in* ***Figure 11.3***)
1. An increase in unemployment benefit (b)	Raises the union's desired wage rate *providing* that the elasticity of labour demand is constant
2. A rise in the price of the employer's product	No effect on union's desired wage rate *providing* that the elasticity of labour demand is constant
3. A change in union membership (M)	No effect on union's desired wage rate
4. A change in the marginal rate of income tax paid by workers	Ambiguous effect on union's desired wage rate
5. A rise in flat-rate income subsidy to workers from government	Lowers union's desired wage rate
6. An increase in employer's employment subsidy from government	Increases union's desired wage rate
7. General	Wage is higher and employment lower than the competitive equilibrium. This is seen by setting $r = b =$ the competitive wage, and comparing points E and C in Figure 11.3

Efficient-bargain model	
Change	*Predicted effect on contract curve* (CC' *in* ***Figure 11.4***)
1. A rise in either unemployment benefit (b) or the reservation wage (r)	Shifts the contract curve up and to the left
2. An increase in the price of the employer's product	Shifts the contract curve down and to the right
3. General	The contract curve slopes upwards in wage–employment space, and equilibrium employment is higher than in an equivalent competitive labour market. The latter result may be seen by setting $r = b =$ the competitive wage in **Figure 11.4** and comparing point C (the competitive outcome) with the contract curve *CC'*

curve as the locus of tangency points between employer isoprofit and union indifference curves. One particularly attractive feature of Manning's sequential approach is the fact that it allows other outcomes to occur, especially since it is not uncommon for the empirical evidence (see below) to suggest that actual wage–employment outcomes lie off *both* the labour demand curve and the contract curve.

Flat indifference curve model

A particularly interesting model of union behaviour proposed in the recent literature is the so-called flat indifference curve model, which is typically justified in terms of the 'last in, first out'-type of seniority mechanism discussed on page 272. As already noted, one of the drawbacks of the efficient-bargain model is the fact that it predicts that bargaining outcomes will lie off the labour demand curve and advocates of the flat indifference curve model or, as it is sometimes alternatively called, the seniority model (for example, Oswald, 1987), see it as a means of reconciling the efficient-bargain model with the 'conventional wisdom' of labour economics by demonstrating that efficient wage–employment combinations may in fact lie on the employer's labour demand curve. The basic idea of this model is illustrated in **Figure 11.5**, in which the curve L_D denotes the employer's labour demand curve. The central notion of this model is that the union's indifference curves are horizontal lines in wage–employment space, indicating that union utility is an increasing function of the wage rate only (that is, that the union is indifferent to the level of its members' employment). As can be seen from **Figure 11.5**, the back-to-back tangency points between the unions (flat) indifference curves and the employer's isoprofit curves in this model all occur on the labour demand curve, which is therefore also the contract curve!

The logic behind the flat indifference curves of this model is that in situations where, as frequently occurs in practice, lay-offs are by inverse seniority (that is, last in, first out), senior workers in a union with majority voting know themselves to be well-insulated from the risk of redundancy and might therefore be expected to set wage demands with little, if any, concern for the potential employment consequences of their actions. Accordingly such a union is seen as having flat indifference curves (Oswald, 1987). In other words, the average union member in this model, being secure in his employment, is seen as caring only about his own wage rate. It is thus assumed (as in the median voter model considered in Chapter 10 above) that senior workers attach no weight to the welfare of those amongst their junior colleagues who are threatened

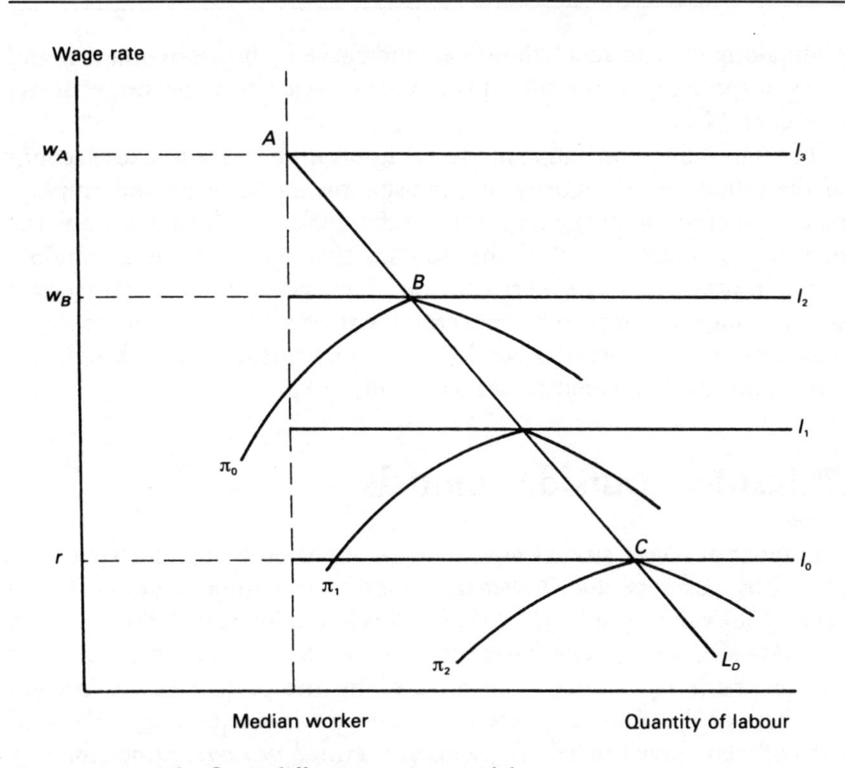

Figure 11.5 ***The flat indifference curve model***

with redundancy. Notice from **Figure 11.5** that the indifference curves are flat until employment falls to the point at which the member with median seniority is laid off.

The precise predictions of this model vary according to the additional assumptions made. For example, if the monopoly-union approach is adopted, where the union seeks to maximise utility subject to the constraint imposed by the employer's labour demand curve, then the implication is that the union would seek to maximise utility at *A* in **Figure 11.5** by seeking the wage w_A. That is, the union literally pushes wages as high as possible subject to L_D while leaving the employer to decide on the level of employment (which in this case will be such that the median worker *just* keeps his or her job). More precisely, the employer's shut-down point mentioned above may form an additional constraint by imposing an upper limit, wages above which would drive the employer out of business. If the minimum level of profits necessary to keep the employer operating in this particular line of business were, say π_0, then the utility-maximising wage sought by the union would be w_B corresponding to point *B* in **Figure 11.5**. Alternatively, if one adopted the efficient-bargain framework, then the solution would lie at some point along the contract/labour demand curve L_D between points *B* and *C* (corresponding to the shut-down and reservation wages respectively) in **Figure 11.5.**

The flat indifference curve model is important because it takes account of the influence of seniority mechanisms on union wage and employment policies. In particular, the model seeks to illustrate how the presence of mechanisms of the 'last in, first out' sort, as commonly found in practice, may give rise to situations where unions, at least over certain ranges, appear to be concerned with the maximisation of wages regardless of the potential employment consequences of such policies. For a critique of this model see Turnbull, 1988.

■ Insider–outsider models

A number of recent studies have focused attention on the differing roles played by 'insiders' and 'outsiders' in the formulation of union preferences (for example, Solow, 1985; Lindbeck and Snower, 1986; Carruth and Oswald, 1986). The basic idea here is that the utility of, and the choices made by, a union are affected by the preferences of current members of the union (or perhaps in certain circumstances by those of currently employed members), who are termed *insiders*, rather than by the preferences and objectives of others (known as *outsiders*), who are not currently members of the union in question. This framework implies that union utility functions of the sort discussed above are only applicable for a particular range of employment levels; namely, only when employment is less than or equal to union membership. Insider–outsider models assume that once all members of a labour group or trade union are employed, the union no longer attaches any importance to increasing employment, with the consequence that it then becomes exclusively concerned with raising the wage rate earned by its members. This model therefore generates union indifference curves which are kinked at an employment level equal to current union membership. To the left of this point the union's indifference curves have the conventional negative slope, indicating the presence of a trade-off in union preferences between wages and employment, while to the right of this point they are horizontal. A family of such union indifference curves is shown in **Figure 11.6**, where current union membership is denoted by *M*. Notice, in particular, that for employment levels in excess of *M*, the flat indifference curve analysis applies in exactly the manner described above, so that in consequence, to the right of point *M* in **Figure 11.6** efficient contracts lie on the labour demand curve.

Models of the insider–outsider variety constitute an important new

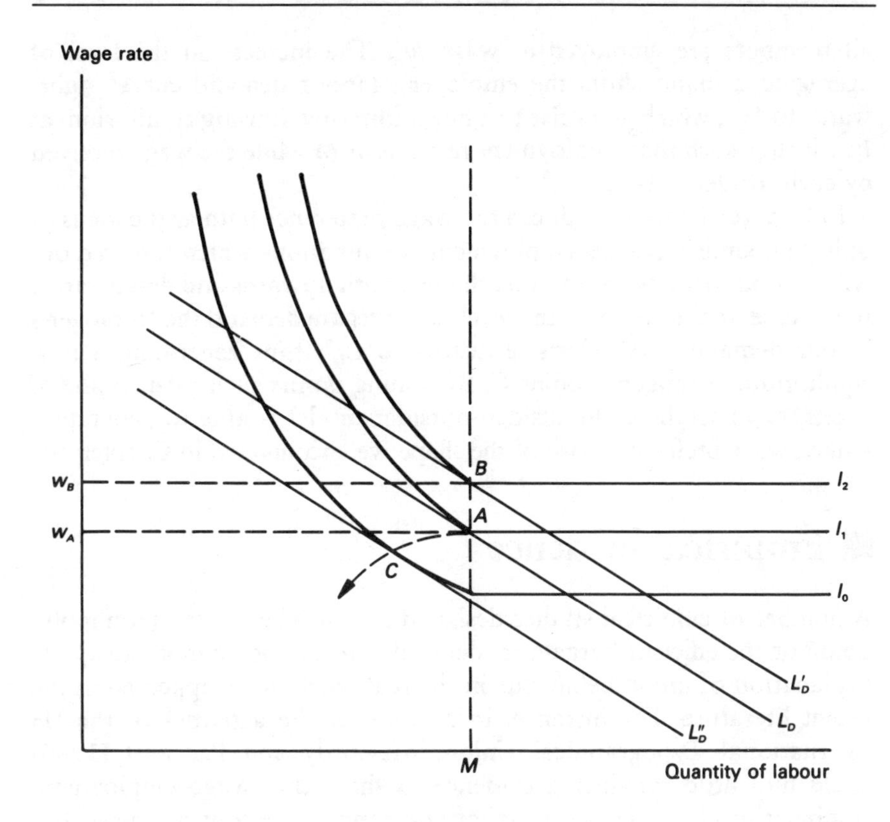

Figure 11.6 *The insider–outsider model*

area of research in labour economics and work so far has shown how such models can throw useful light on a number of important issues. For example, this model provides a reasonably plausible explanation for the fact that unions sometimes appear to prefer to respond to an increase in the level of aggregate demand in the economy by seeking mainly to push up wages rather than employment. If union wage policies are determined by insiders (for example, employed members) it seems plausible perhaps to argue that insiders have little incentive to allow in outsiders, but would rather prefer to go for higher pay for themselves. This need not always be the case, since it can be shown (see Carruth and Oswald, 1986) that sufficiently high product prices may make it feasible for both insiders and the employers to benefit from an expansion in employment above current membership (M). The simple case, where the union responds to an increase in aggregate demand entirely by pushing up the wages of existing members/insiders is shown in **Figure 11.6.** In the initial situation the employer's labour demand curve is L_D which gives rise to the union's utility-maximising equilibrium at, say, point A, where all members are employed at wage w_A. The increase in the level of aggregate demand shifts the employer's labour demand curve[7] rightwards to L_D', which gives rise to a new utility-maximising equilibrium at *B*, which is such that employment remains at *M* while the wage received by each insider rises to w_B.[8]

In Chapter 10 we introduced the wage preference path as the locus of utility-maximising wage–employment combinations which is traced out when labour demand conditions change, both upwards and downwards. In the case of a decrease in the level of aggregate demand the employer's labour demand curve shifts leftwards to L_D'', thus generating a new equilibrium at tangency point *C*. By joining points such as *A*, *B* and *C* together we see how the insider–outsider model is able to generate a kinked wage preference path of the shape we encountered in Chapter 10.

■ Empirical evidence

A number of empirical studies designed to test whether the monopoly-union or the efficient-bargain model is able to provide a more adequate explanation of union behaviour in the real world have appeared in the recent literature. For instance, in a study of the activities of the US International Typographical Union, MaCurdy and Pencavel (1986) could find little convincing evidence to show that wage–employment combinations lie on either the labour demand or the contract curve, but concluded that the efficient-bargain model appears to come closer to providing a satisfactory explanation than the monopoly-union model, especially in newspaper-composing rooms. However, in a study of negotiated contracts in the same industry Ashenfelter and Brown (1986) could find little evidence of contract efficiency. Other studies have considered US airline mechanics (Card, 1986), New York's public school teachers (Eberts and Stone, 1986) and British coalminers (Bean and Turnbull, 1988). The results of all of these studies reject the monopoly-union/labour demand model.[9] However, as Mayhew and Turnbull (1989) caution, there is a danger in interpreting rejection of the labour demand model as necessarily offering evidence in favour of the efficient-bargain model.

As noted above, one advantage of the sequential bargaining model proposed by Manning (1987) arises from the fact that it allows for a menu of possibilities which is wider than the monopoly-union versus efficient-bargain model choice which is posed in most previous studies. Alogoskoufis and Manning (1991) test this sequential model against UK data at both the aggregate and manufacturing level and find both the monopoly-union and efficient-bargain models to be generally rejected in favour of the general alternative. In other words, these findings (in line with the earlier US work of both MaCurdy and Pencavel (1986) and Card (1986)) suggest that actual wage–employment combinations lie neither on the labour demand curve nor on the contract curve, but instead appear to lie somewhere in between the two. However, as Alogoskoufis and Manning acknowledge, aggregate data are far from ideal when it comes to testing microeconomic theories of union behaviour, with the consequence that more concrete conclusions must await the analysis of industry- or establishment-level data.

The evidence so far mentioned has referred to the monopoly-union versus efficient-bargain issue. However, in a recent study Carruth, Oswald and Findlay (1986) tested the flat indifference curve model against the postwar experience of the British coal and steel industries. This study revealed little, if any, support for the model, with the consequence that the authors were led to reject the flat indifference curve model's prediction that unions typically place all of their emphasis on the goal of achieving high wages for their membership, to the exclusion of employment considerations. A similar conclusion emerged from Farber's (1978) study of the US bituminous coal industry.

Some theories of the collective-bargaining process

The monopoly-union model overcomes the classical conclusion that the outcome of the bargaining process is indeterminate within some range by adopting particular assumptions regarding prevailing wage- and employment-fixing arrangements: namely, that the union sets the wage unilaterally, while the employer unilaterally sets the level of employment, given the union-determined wage. The efficient-bargain model says nothing about the bargaining process itself, or how a solution is achieved. Instead, it merely *imposes* the requirement that the eventual solution, however reached, must satisfy the condition of Pareto efficiency. As we have seen, the axiom of efficiency is insufficient *in itself* to close the range of indeterminacy characteristic of earlier approaches.

The classical conclusion that the outcome of the bargaining process is indeterminate was first challenged in the late 1920s, and since that date an extensive literature of theories offering determinate solutions has evolved. The characteristic which distinguishes this literature from that discussed above under the monopoly-union versus efficient-bargain heading, is the emphasis which it places upon explaining the *behaviour* of unions and employers in bargaining situations. In this section we consider the contribution of this literature to the analysis of collective bargaining, as the process by which the union and the employer resolve their conflicting preferences and reach agreement on the actual value of the union wage within the range of indeterminacy bounded by their respective preferences.

■ Basic concepts

It is usual to model the bargaining process within the distributional framework as a problem of the determination of the quantities of fixed initial endowments of some homogeneous good that will be exchanged between isolated individuals. While bargaining situations can involve any number of parties, it is usual to treat union–employer negotiations as a case of two-party exchange, on the implicit assumption that each involved party behaves in the manner of a perfectly coordinated individual.[10]

Basic to the theory of bargaining is the concept of a *threat*, which is defined as a commitment to a definite course of action that is conditional on the demand associated with the threat not being met. Bargaining situations can be subdivided into fixed and variable threat cases. In *fixed threat bargaining* a failure to reach agreement has the unique consequence of no trade, so that each bargainer has only one possible (fixed) threat, namely, a refusal to trade. In the more general case of *variable threat bargaining*, each bargainer possesses a choice of several possible threats, each characterised by varying degrees of non-participation, so that there are various possible states of conflict. Obvious examples on the union side are overtime bans, work-to-rules, go-slows, one-day strikes and indefinite strikes.

It is, however, usual to treat union–employer bargaining as a case of fixed threat bargaining, on the basis of the (often implicit) assumption that, from among the various threats open to them, the union and the employer each elects to adopt a single (or pure) threat, these being respectively the threat of an indefinite strike and the threat of an indefinite lock-out.[11]

To formalise things, let bargainer 1 be the union and bargainer 2 the employer, and let w denote the wage rate. Assume that the union's utility is an increasing function of only the wage rate and that the employer's is a decreasing function of the wage. We can therefore write the bargainer's respective utility functions as

$$u_1 = u_1(w) \quad \text{and} \quad u_2 = u_2(w)$$

where $du_1/dw > 0$ and $du_2/dw < 0$.

Bargaining theorists focus attention on the *utility frontier*, which is the mapping on to the utility space of the contract curve.[12] This frontier is generally assumed to be concave to the origin.[13] The point with coordinates that are the utilities of the two bargainers when fixed threats are implemented is defined as the *threat point*. The utility frontier that is obtained by placing the origin at the threat point (that is, by adjusting the bargainers' utility functions so that the utility that each obtains in the event of disagreement is zero) is termed the *utility increments frontier*. (In technical terms, this frontier represents the boundary of the first quadrant of the outcome set when the origin is placed at the utility combination corresponding to disagreement.)

■ Zeuthen's theory

The first determinate theory of the bargaining process was proposed by Zeuthen in 1928 and first published in English in 1930. Zeuthen's is a theory of two-person bargaining, which is cast in terms of union–employer wage negotiations. Recognising the sequential nature of the bargaining process, Zeuthen treated it as a problem of *risk*. In his initial analysis Zeuthen made the assumption, which was later relaxed, that the demand for union labour is perfectly inelastic, so that bargaining over the wage rate is equivalent to bargaining over the wage bill, and although his own exposition is in money terms, we follow Harsanyi's (1956) reformulation, which is basically a straightforward translation of Zeuthen's analysis from money into utility terms.[14]

The essence of Zeuthen's theory is that at each stage of the bargaining process, both players compare the alternative of holding out for their own current demand, at the risk of causing a conflict, with that of immediately accepting their opponent's latest offer.

To illustrate Zeuthen's theory, recall that bargainer 1 is the union and bargainer 2 the employer. Let u_{ij} denote the utility to the ith bargainer of the outcome demanded by the jth and transform the bargainers' utility functions, so that the utility that each obtains at the threat point is zero. Consider the utility increments frontier shown in **Figure 11.7** and assume that bargainer 1 opens the negotiations with the demand shown at P_1, which would give him u_{11} and offer his opponent u_{21}. Assume also that bargainer 2 opens with the demand at P_2, which would give him u_{22} and offer his opponent u_{12}.

If bargainer 1, for example, were to accept his opponent's offer, he would obtain the outcome u_{12} with certainty. However, if he were to hold out for his own current demand at P_1, he would expect to achieve the higher utility u_{11} with some probability. If r_1 denotes bargainer 1's

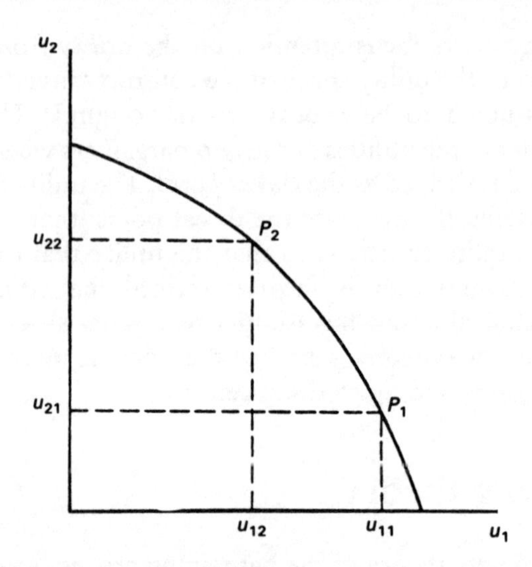

Figure 11.7 ***Zeuthen's theory of bargaining***

estimate of the probability that his insistence on this outcome will result in conflict,[15] his expected utility from pursuing this course of action is given by $(1 - r_1)u_{22}$.[16] According to Zeuthen, bargainer 1 compares this expected utility with that which he could obtain with certainty by settling on the terms of his opponent's current offer at P_2 (that is, u_{12}). Zeuthen argued that it is rational for bargainer 1 to hold out for his own current demand (that is, to insist on his opponent's *complete capitulation*) and to incur any risk of disagreement (r_1) such that

$$(1 - r_1)u_{11} \geqslant u_{12} \tag{11.6}$$

since the net expected utility gain from so doing is, say,

$$\Delta u_1 = (1 - r_1)u_{11} - u_{12} \geqslant 0$$

By a parallel route Zeuthen argued that bargainer 2 will incur any risk of disagreement (r_2) such that

$$(1 - r_2)u_{22} \geqslant u_{21} \tag{11.7}$$

Rearranging these conditions we obtain

$$r_1 \leqslant \frac{u_{11} - u_{12}}{u_{11}} \tag{11.8}$$

$$r_2 \leqslant \frac{u_{22} - u_{21}}{u_{22}} \tag{11.9}$$

Therefore, Zeuthen argued, the highest risk of disagreement to which bargainer 1 will rationally expose himself in holding out for his preferred outcome is that value of r_1 for which the net expected utility gain from this course of action is zero (that is, the value at which bargainer 1 is indifferent between pressing for his own claim at P_1 and accepting his opponent's offer at P_2). This probability, denoted by r_1^{max}, is termed that *risk-willingness* of bargainer 1 and is obtained by solving condition (11.8) an equation, giving

$$r_1^{max} = \frac{u_{11} - u_{12}}{u_{11}} \qquad (11.10)$$

Similarly, bargainer 2's risk-willingness is given by

$$r_2^{max} = \frac{u_{22} - u_{21}}{u_{22}} \qquad (11.11)$$

Crucial to Zeuthen's theory is the behavioural assumption that, at each stage of the bargaining process, the bargainer with the smallest risk-willingness (that is, the one who will rationally expose himself to a smaller maximum probability of conflict) will make some concession. From (11.10) and (11.11) the condition for bargainer 1 to make a concession is

$$\frac{u_{11} - u_{12}}{u_{11}} < \frac{u_{22} - u_{21}}{u_{22}} \qquad (11.12)$$

which can be rearranged to give

$$u_{11}u_{21} < u_{22}u_{12} \qquad (11.13)$$

Conversely, bargainer 2 will make a concession if $r_2^{max} < r_1^{max}$, that is, if

$$u_{11}u_{21} > u_{22}u_{12} \qquad (11.14)$$

Finally, in cases where $r_1^{max} = r_2^{max} > 0$, Zeuthen assumed that both bargainers will make concessions, as conflict in such a case would be 'the greater evil to each' (1930, p. 119).

Noting that $u_{11}u_{21}$ is the value of the utility product u_1u_2 proposed by bargainer 1 and that $u_{12}u_{22}$ is the value proposed by bargainer 2, it follows, given the usually assumed non-convexity to the origin of the utility increments frontier, that each concession raises the utility product proposed by the conceding player. Such a concession need not be total, in the sense of a complete acceptance of the opponent's last offer; rather, it must be large enough to reverse the inequality sign in the relevant expression (11.13) or (11.14). It then becomes the other bargainer's turn to concede, and thus this process of *successive concessions* proceeds until further concessions can no longer increase the utility product u_1u_2, so that agreement is reached at the point where u_1u_2 assumes its maximum value. Harsanyi (1956, p. 148) argued that because indivisibilities (of the smallest monetary unit and of a psychological nature) set a lower limit to the size of admissible concessions, this point will be reached after a finite number of steps. At the point where u_1u_2 is maximised, $u_{11} = u_{12}$ and $u_{22} = u_{21}$, and we see from (11.10) and (11.11) that $r_1^{max} = r_2^{max} = 0$.

Zeuthen's conception of, and solution to, the bargaining problem are easily illustrated by superimposing on to **Figure 11.7** a family of *rectangular hyperbole* given by

$$u_1u_2 = nK$$

where K denotes the Harsanyi lower limit of the admissible size of concession (say £1 when a weekly wage is being negotiated) and $n = 1, 2, 3, \ldots$ **Figure 11.8** shows a number of such hyperbole and from this we see that, for demands at P_1 and P_2, inequality (11.13) is satisfied. Therefore bargainer 1 concedes, moving around the frontier to a hyperbola above that passing through P_2 (say to point P_1'). Since inequality (11.14) is now satisfied, it becomes bargainer 2's turn to concede, and so on. Settlement is achieved (in the next step in this simple example) at point Q, where a hyperbola is tangential to the utility increments frontier.

It is important to recognise that Zeuthen's solution to the bargaining problem is the point on the utility increments frontier at which its elasticity equals −1. To show this, write the frontier as

$$u_2 = g(u_1)$$

and notice that the utility (increments) product is maximised when[17]

$$\frac{d}{du_1}(u_1u_2) = \frac{d}{du_1}[u_1g(u_1)] = u_1\frac{du_2}{du_1} + u_2 = 0$$

At this point the frontier's elasticity is

$$\frac{du_2}{du_1} \cdot \frac{u_1}{u_2} = -1 \qquad (11.15)$$

Although a detailed critique of Zeuthen's theory is outside the scope of the present section, it is nevertheless useful to notice that most existing criticisms fall into two groups. First, there are the criticisms that centre on the plausibility of Zeuthen's crucial behavioural assumption that the bargainer with the lower risk-willingness is the one to concede.[18] Second, there are the criticisms of what Saraydar (1965, p. 805) termed

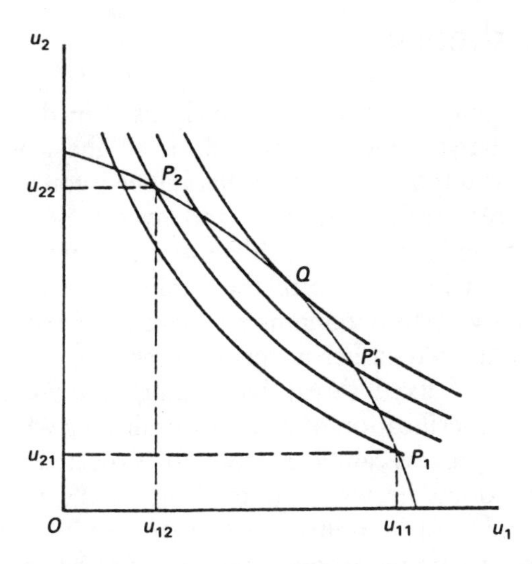

Figure 11.8 ***Zeuthen's solution to the collective-bargaining problem***

Zeuthen's *full concessions assumption*. According to this assumption, both bargainers' expected utility and risk-willingness calculations are based on the expectation of their opponent's *total* capitulation (that is, they involve the assignment of zero probabilities to all offers involving less than total concession). Yet in Zeuthen's theory these calculations provide the basis for determining the bargainer who is to make a concession that itself is not total but merely of sufficient magnitude to make it the opponent's turn to concede.[19] Since expected utility and maximum risk calculations continue to be made at each round of the collective-bargaining process on the basis of expectations that are limited to the opponent's full concession, even though modified offers have occurred in previous rounds, Saraydar argued that Zeuthen's theory also involves the questionable implicit assumption of 'ineducable bargainers'. To these we can add a third criticism, namely, that neither Zeuthen nor Harsanyi offered any explanation as to how the respective bargainers arrive at their subjective conflict probabilities.

However, despite these criticisms Zeuthen's theory is important, because it explicitly recognises the sequential nature of, and uncertainty inherent in, collective bargaining. By so doing it is able to yield a unique prediction as to the wage rate that will result from the collective-bargaining process, namely, that wage at which the utility increments product is maximised.[20]

Nash's theory

The theory of games has been extensively used in the construction of theories of the bargaining process.[21] Basic to the game-theoretic approach is the assumption that each bargainer possesses a von Neumann–Morgenstern utility function,[22] and given these utility functions it is usual to treat the bargaining problem as a non-zero sum cooperative game.[23] Of special importance in the game-theoretic literature is the determinate theory of the bargaining problem proposed by Nash (1950), which was encountered earlier in this chapter.

Nash's theory of fixed threat bargaining is *axiomatic* in nature, consisting of the specification of a set of conditions which the outcome of the bargaining process can be 'reasonably' expected to satisfy. On the basis of these axioms he was able to demonstrate the existence of a unique solution.[24] Nash argued that there are four axioms that a solution of the bargaining problem can be expected to satisfy.[25]

Axiom 1: Pareto optimality – The solution lies on the utility increments frontier.

Axiom 2: Symmetry – If the outcome set is symmetric with respect to the line $u_1 = u_2$, the solution gives equal utility increments to each party, so that the solution does not depend on the labelling of the bargainers.

Axiom 3: Transformation invariance – The solution is invariant with respect to any order preserving linear transformation of either player's utility function; that is, the solution is independent of the units and origins of the utility functions.

Axiom 4: Independence of irrelevant alternatives – If the outcome set of a bargaining game is restricted (that is, unfavourably altered) in such a way that the threat point remains unaltered and the new set contains the solution point of the original game, this point will also be the solution of the new game.

Nash proved that the only solution that satisfies these four axioms is the one at which the product of the player's utility increments from the threat point is a maximum. Although Nash's proof is set-theoretic, it is possible to derive his solution by simple geometry.[26]

Placing the origin at the threat point, let us consider the straight-line utility increments frontier with slope of -1, shown by *AB* in **Figure 11.9.** Axiom 1 requires the solution to lie on *AB*, and axiom 2 requires it to be on the line $u_1 = u_2$; so that in this case these first two axioms are

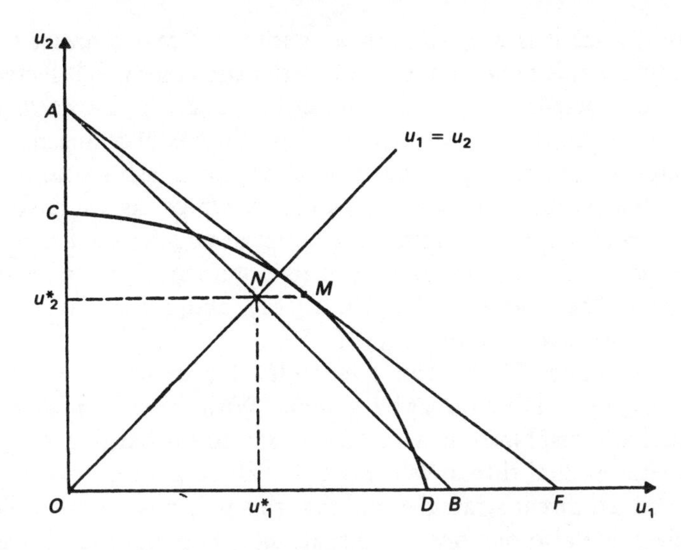

Figure 11.9 ***Nash's theory of bargaining***

sufficient to determine a unique solution at *N* (that is, the midpoint of the frontier *AB*). This solution yields the respective bargainer's utility pay-offs u_1^* and u_2^*, where $u_1^* = u_2^*$.

Now, any straight-line boundary in the utility space, such as *AF* in **Figure 11.9**, can be transformed into one with a slope of −1 by a suitable adjustment to the units in which one bargainer's utility is measured, with the origin unchanged. According to axiom 3, the solution is invariant with respect to such a transformation; therefore, since the other bargainer's utility scale is unaltered, he must obtain the same utility (u_2^*) from the solution point on the original frontier as from that on the transformed one (*AB*). Consequently, by projecting the line u_2^*N leftwards, we see that the solution on the original frontier must be at its midpoint (*M*). Therefore, in all cases where the utility increments frontier is linear, the solution lies at its midpoint. Since the maximum area of a rectangle that can be inscribed within a right-angled triangle bisects its hypotenuse, this solution is immediately recognisable as being the point at which the utility increments product is maximised.

Finally, axiom 4 allows transition to appropriately shaped non-linear frontiers. According to this axiom, any restriction on the outcome set of the bargaining game that leaves the threat point unchanged, and is such that the original solution is a possible outcome of the restricted game, leaves the solution unchanged. For example, if the bargaining game that has the linear frontier *AF* in **Figure 11.9** is restricted in such a way that the curve *CMD*, which is everywhere concave to the origin, becomes its utility increments frontier, the solution remains unchanged at point *M*.

Therefore, since it is always possible with a concave frontier to find a straight line that is tangential to the frontier such that it is bisected at the point of contact, it follows that Nash's solution is the point on this frontier at which the utility increments product is maximised.

Despite its different approach it is clear that Nash's solution is the same as that predicted by Zeuthen's theory which, as we have seen, is that point on the utility increments frontier at which its elasticity equals -1. But notice that, by the nature of its argument, Nash's fixed threat formulation has nothing whatever to say about the passage of the bargaining process to settlement.

In a later paper Nash (1953) extended his treatment to the more general case of variable threat bargaining. With the specification of two additional axioms, Nash provided a solution to the bargainer's problem of selecting optimal threats (showing that these always consist of pure and not mixed threat strategies and that this pair possesses saddle-point properties). He also demonstrated that once these optimal threats have been selected, and therefore the threat point determined, the solution is given exactly in the manner of his fixed threat theory as the point where the utility increments product is maximised.

A large number of alternative theories of the bargaining process exist in the literature. Amongst the best-known of these in the labour economics literature are Hicks's (1932) theory and Cartter's (1959) development of Chamberlain's (1951) theory.

■ Hicks's theory

Hicks's theory of collective wage bargaining appeared only shortly after Zeuthen's, being first published in 1932 (see Hicks, 1963, pp. 136–58). Perhaps the most important feature of this theory is its explicit recognition of the role of the strike threat in collective bargaining as a weapon by which pressure can be put upon the employer to pay a higher wage than would otherwise be the case. Hicks saw the union's ability to obtain such improvements in wages and other conditions as being derived from the threat of imposing on the employer a cost even greater than that associated with such a settlement and saw this as providing the compulsion towards agreement. The essence of Hicks's theory is that both the employer's tendency to concede and the union's to resist are functions of the *expected* length of the threatened strike.

According to Hicks, the employer chooses between the two alternatives confronting him (namely, pay the higher wage or take the strike) in light of his assessment of the costs involved in each. Accordingly, Hicks constructed the 'employer's concession curve' shown in **Figure 11.10**,

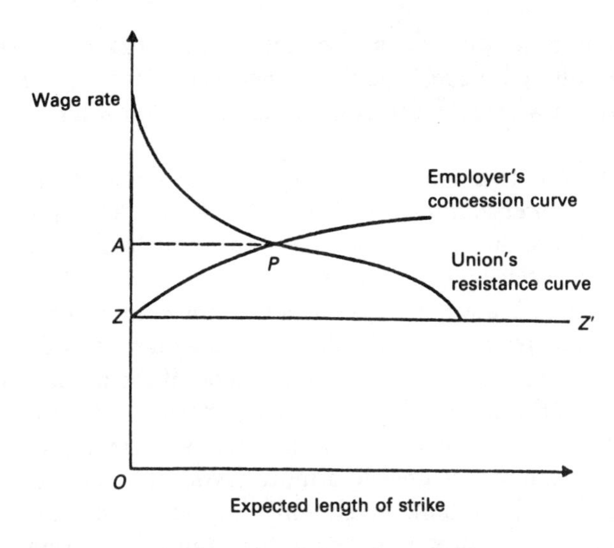

Figure 11.10 ***Hicks's theory of collective bargaining***

which relates the highest wage that the employer will be willing to pay in order to avoid a strike to the expected length of the threatened strike. At points on this curve, the expected cost of the strike and the expected cost of concession, suitably discounted, are equal, so that at any lower wage demand the employer will prefer to settle and avoid a strike whereas at any higher wage demand he will prefer a strike to take place.

The intercept of this curve on the vertical axis (OZ) is the wage that the employer would pay in the absence of union pressure, and the curve is assumed to have a positive slope, because the expected cost of the threatened strike is positively related to its expected length and the expected cost of concession is positively related to the wage demanded. Finally, Hicks argued that this curve cannot rise above some upper limit imposed by the wage at which the employer will prefer to close down, so that the slope of the employer's curve must eventually become a decreasing function of expected strike length.

Similarly, Hicks constructed the 'union's resistance curve', which shows the minimum wage that the union will accept rather than undergo a strike as a function of the expected length of the strike. Since this curve shows the length of time for which the union members will be willing to stand out rather than allow their wage rate to fall below any particular level, Hicks argued that it will have a negative slope, because the 'temporary privations' (1963, p. 142) that they will be willing to endure to prevent the wage rate falling below a particular level are a decreasing function of the wage level in question. Finally, Hicks points out that the resistance curve must cut ZZ' at some finite distance along it, indicating the maximum time for which the union can organise a stoppage, whatever the offered wage, and that it generally intersects the vertical axis, indicating a wage sufficiently high that the union will not seek to go beyond it.

Given that these two functions have opposite slopes, there will be a unique point of intersection (*P* in **Figure 11.10**) and Hicks argued that the wage corresponding to this intersection point 'is the highest wage which skilful negotiation can extract from the employer' (1963, p. 144). If the union demands a wage in excess of *OA*, the employer will refuse it, because he calculates that a strike designed to achieve this demand will not last long enough to compel him to concede. If the union demands a wage below *OA*, the employer will concede, offering little resistance, but the union will have done badly for its members since more 'skilful' negotiating could have resulted in a more favourable settlement. Hicks then argued that the union, given only imperfect knowledge of the employer's curve, will prefer to begin bargaining by setting its initial claims high, to be subsequently modified once some indication of the employer's attitude has begun to emerge during bargaining.

Although a detailed critique of Hicks's theory is outside the scope of the present discussion, it is important to notice that there exists something of a confusion in the literature as to whether or not Hicks's theory is determinate (that is, whether it predicts the wage *OA* as the outcome of the bargaining process).[27] The truth of the matter is that Hicks's own exposition seems in effect to embody two versions of his theory. In the first there is the assumption of perfect knowledge, the presence of which 'will always make a settlement possible' (1963, p. 147) – a settlement that Hicks's theory predicts will be at the wage corresponding to the intersection of his curves. Relaxing the assumption of perfect knowledge on the part of the union but not the employer,[28] Hicks presented the indeterminate version of his theory, in which he conceived of negotiations as the process by which a 'skilful' bargainer extracts information about his opponent's (curve's) position. In discussing this version Hicks considered what happens to the curves during a strike, should one occur, arguing that the union's resistance curve is likely to shift to the left as the strike proceeds and its budget constraint becomes eroded and that the employer's concession curve may also shift in response to alterations in the 'prospects of trade'.[29]

In view of the uncertainties associated with the shape and position of one's opponent's Hicksian curve and the volatility of the curves in the event of a strike occurring, it is advisable to regard Hicks's formulation from the viewpoint of bargaining *ex ante* (Bronfenbrenner, 1971, p. 240) and to interpret Hicks's curves not as the loci of the bargainers' positions but rather as the boundaries of the sets of combinations of wage rates and expected strike lengths that are acceptable to the respective parties (Cross, 1969, p. 33).[30]

■ The Cartter–Chamberlain theory

It is frequently argued that the precise outcome of the collective-bargaining process within the range of indeterminacy depends on the *bargaining power* of the union relative to that of the employer. However, the concept of *bargaining power* is not always explicitly defined. An exception here is Chamberlain, who provided a definition of the bargaining power of a bargainer (say A) as 'the cost to B of disagreeing on A's terms relative to the cost of agreeing on A's term' (1951, pp. 220–1). In his reformulation of Chamberlain's analysis, Cartter (1959, p. 117), however, preferred to interpret the above definition in terms of B's *bargaining attitude* rather then A's bargaining power. Thus, according to these definitions we have:

$$\begin{array}{l}\text{Union's bargaining power}\\ \text{(or employer's bargaining}\\ \text{attitude)}\end{array} = \frac{\text{Cost to employer of disagreeing with union's terms}}{\text{Cost to employer of agreeing with union}}$$

$$\begin{array}{l}\text{Employer's bargaining}\\ \text{power (or union's}\\ \text{bargaining attitude)}\end{array} = \frac{\text{Cost to union of disagreeing with employer's terms}}{\text{Cost to union of agreeing with employer}}$$

For each party the cost of disagreeing with its opponent's current offer at any stage of the bargaining process is the income loss that would arise from the work stoppage that would follow the opponent's implementation of his fixed threat. Within this framework the costs of disagreement to the union and the employer are, respectively, the wage income and profits foregone during a strike or lock-out. It is important to notice that neither the employer's profit loss nor the workers' wage income loss during a work stoppage is likely to correspond exactly to the value of lost production and wage payments respectively. As a number of writers have pointed out, an employer's foregone profits during a strike will diverge from lost production for a number of reasons. These include savings in variable cost expenditures and sales from stocks while the stoppage is in progress and the possibility of recouping sales once a settlement has been reached. Similarly, from the workers' viewpoint receipts of a variety of benefits result in a divergence between foregone wages (net of tax and other deductions) and actual income foregone. Examples of such receipts are union strike pay, earnings from temporary alternative employment during the stoppage and entitlements to state social security and other benefits, particularly tax rebates.

To each party the cost of agreeing to its opponent's current offer at any stage of the collective-bargaining process is the difference between the present values of its future income flows on its own and its opponent's current terms. The union's cost of agreement is therefore the difference between the wage income flows, suitably discounted, that would arise from agreement on its own and the employer's current terms. Similarly, the employer's agreement cost is the difference between the present values of the profit flows that would arise on the basis of the wage that it is currently offering and the wage that the union is currently demanding.

It is important to notice that given the absence of perfect knowledge each party's assessment of its own and its opponent's bargaining power must be based on some estimates of the relevant cost components. Each party's estimate of agreement costs will be influenced by the length of time for which it expects agreement, once reached, to last (that is, the *contract duration*), while each bargainer's calculations of disagreement costs will be based on its expectations regarding both the disagreement costs per unit of time and the likely length of stoppage necessary to make its opponent accept its own terms (Cartter, 1959, pp. 117–20).

According to this theory, each bargainer evaluates its bargaining attitude at each stage of negotations as the ratio of the cost of disagreement with its opponent's current offer by holding out for its own, to the cost of agreeing by immediate acceptance of this offer. The attitude ratio of each party will undergo change as negotiations proceed, according to each party's demands, and the bargainers are assumed to be cost-minimisers. Each bargainer will therefore accept the current offer when its attitude ratio is greater than, or equal, to unity and otherwise reject it in favour of continued pursuit of its own objective. In cases where both bargainers' ratios are less than unity, a strike will occur. Within this framework collective wage bargaining is seen as the process in which each party adopts tactics designed to raise its opponent's ratio to unity or above, while simultaneously adopting tactics of a defensive nature that are designed to keep its own ratio less than unity.[31] This process continues, through a strike should one occur, until the point where the ratio of one or both parties rises to unity and an agreement is reached.

Some comments

It is important to notice the similarity between the solutions predicted by the various theories of the collective-bargaining process reviewed above. Despite the considerable differences in the reasoning and hypotheses underlying the Nash and Zeuthen theories, we have seen that they both predict that the outcome of the collective-bargaining process will be such that the utility increments product is maximised. In addition, it has been shown (Cross, 1969, p. 29–31) that if one looks beyond the interplay of the two ratios in the Cartter–Chamberlain formulation, this model too predicts the Nash–Zeuthen solution. Indeed it can also be shown that Hicks's theory, with its still different underlying reasoning, converges under certain conditions on the Nash–Zeuthen solution (Crossley, 1973, p. 216).

While there is a danger of imputing too much significance to this result by overestimating the importance of what Pen called 'an affinity of form' (1959, p. xii), it should also be noted that the majority of the large number of theories of the bargaining process that exist in the literature in addition to those considered above can also be shown to predict outcomes that are always identical, or are identical in special cases, to the Nash solution (see de Menil, 1971, p. 15, and Sapsford, 1979, pp. 36–9). This solution equivalence result has elevated the Nash solution (that is, the maximisation of the utility increments product) to a position of special importance in the theoretical literature, and although further important theoretical work is still appearing in this area, (for example, Rubinstein, 1982), it is relevant to notice that formal models of the bargaining process have made some significant contributions in a number of areas (see Binmore and Dasgupta, 1986, 1987).

Unions and relative wages

A question that has attracted particular research interest over many years is the extent to which trade unions are able to raise the wages of their members relative to those of comparable non-union workers. In estimating the impact of unions on wages, one would ideally like observations on what the earnings of a union member would have been in the absence of unionisation. However, since this is clearly not possible, it is necessary to compare the wages of union and non-union workers who are as much alike as possible. Notice, however, that in cases where the union affects the wage paid to non-union labour the impact of unions on the wages of union relative to non-union labour will differ from their impact on union wages relative to those prevailing in the absence of unions altogether. There are two main union ways in which unions can influence the non-union wage and cause it to diverge from the wage that would prevail in the absence of all unions. First, there is the *threat effect*, which raises the non-union wage, as non-union employers raise the wages of their employees in order to reduce the probability of their becoming unionised (Rosen, 1969). Second, there is what can be called a *displacement effect*, according to which the non-union wage may fall if, in response to the higher wage paid in the union sector, less union labour is demanded and if those losing their jobs in the unionised sector seek employment in the non-union sector, thereby increasing the supply of non-union labour and depressing the non-union wage.

Theoretical framework

The usual methodology for estimating the influence of unions on relative wages was initially developed by Lewis (1963). Following his analysis we may express the observed average wage in industry or occupation $i(W_i)$ as a geometric weighted average of the wage rates prevailing in the unionised and non-unionised sectors of this market (denoted by W_i^u and W_i^n respectively). Thus we have

$$\ln W_i = U_i \ln W_i^u + (1-U_i) \ln W_i^n$$

where U_i denotes the proportion of the labour force in i that is unionised. Rearranging this expression, we obtain[32]

$$\ln W_i = \ln W_i^n + U_i \ln(1+r_i) \tag{11.16}$$

where

$$r_i = \frac{W_i^u - W_i^n}{W_i^n}$$

measures the relative wage effect of trade unions or the *union/non-union differential.*

Equation (11.16) is the basic equation employed in estimating the size of the union/non-union differential from cross-section data by industry or occupational groups. However in some studies estimates are made from a sample of individual workers, in which case the subscript i stands for the ith individual and U_i takes the value 1 if the individual is a union member and zero otherwise.

Expression (11.16) is an identity that must hold by construction, and if W_i^n as well as W_i and U_i were direcly observable, it would be a matter of simple algebra to calculate the union/non-union differential. However, although we can generally observe W_i and U_i from published sources, W_i^n is not directly observable. Therefore it is necessary when estimating the union/non-union differential to replace the non-union wage term in (11.16) by a vector of variables that are hypothesised as determining it. Let $\mathbf{X}_i$ denote a vector of the observable determinants of the non-union wage. Then, writing

$$\ln W_i^n = f(\mathbf{X}_i) + e_i'$$

and letting

$$\ln (1+r_i) = \ln (1+r) + e_i''$$

where r is the mean union/non-union differential and e_i' and e_i'' are stochastic disturbance terms, equation (11.16) can be written as

$$\ln W_i = f(\mathbf{X}_i) + \beta U_i + e_i$$

where

$$e_i = e_i' + e_i''$$

$$\beta = \ln(1+r)$$

Given observations on W_i, $\mathbf{X}_i$ and U_i, estimates of the magnitude of the union/non-union differential can be obtained by applying standard regression methods to this form of expression. However, it is important to notice that various statistical problems do arise when estimating the union/non-union differential in this way, and these are discussed in some depth in Lewis (1963, 1983, 1986), Parsley (1980) and Treble (1984) and at a more elementary level in Pencavel (1974) and Metcalf (1977). Notice that particular problems arise if union wage levels and membership are simultaneously determined (see Reder, 1965; Johnson, 1975; Schmidt and Strauss, 1976; Lee, 1978; Schmidt, 1978).

Determinants of the non-union wage

So far we have distinguished between the wages paid to union and non-union workers and noted that those of the latter can deviate from the wage rate that would prevail in the industry or occupation or for the individual in question in the absence of all unions because of the threat and displacement effects. Consider first the wages that would prevail in the absence of unions throughout the economy. The theory of wage differentials (which was discussed in Chapter 8) predicts a number of economic variables as influencing the structure of wages between industries, occupations and individuals. When estimating the relative wage effects of trade unions researchers have typically included such variables as components of the so-called *adjustment vector*, which is specified to incorporate all other variables besides unionism that influence wages. The precise specification of the set of independent variables included in the vector varies from study to study and according to whether industry, occupational or individual data are being analysed. (For a tabular survey of the explanatory variables employed in some of the early UK studies, see Metcalf, 1977, p. 160.) However, these typically include such variables as measures of skill mix (on the grounds that the inter-industry structure of wages will vary with the occupational composition of the industry's labour force), a measure of industrial concentration (on the grounds that monopolies tend, other things being equal, to pay their workers more than competitors do), sex- and age-mix variables (on the grounds that average wages will tend to be lower the higher is the proportion of women and young workers, because as we saw in Chapters 8 and 9 these workers tend, *ceteris paribus*, to be paid less than males and older workers), educational variables (on the grounds that an individual's earnings tend, as we saw in Chapter 4, to rise with the level of his/her educational achievement), and so on.

Having specified the variables hypothesised as determining the wage rates that would prevail in the complete absence of unions, it is necessary when estimating the size of the union/non-union differential to allow for differences between these and the wages actually paid to non-union members.[33]

An alternative approach is to use, when available, data that relate not to union membership but rather to *union coverage* (that is, to the numbers of workers, both union members and non-union members, who are covered by collective agreements, under which they are paid the union rate). The use of coverage rather than membership data is preferable because these data directly measure the proportion of workers (both members and non-members) in receipt of the union wage in the industry or occupation in question. In order to obtain some indication of the extent of the divergence between these two series it should be noted that one early study estimated that in 1973 at least one-quarter of the manual workforce in UK manufacturing was paid at the union rate despite not being union members (Metcalf, 1977, p. 159).

Estimates of the union/non-union differential

The earliest estimates of the impact of trade unions on relative wages were made in the USA between 1950 and 1960, and these studies were reviewed in considerable depth by Lewis (1963); his conclusion that unions had raised the average wage rate of union workers by 10–15 per cent above that of their non-union counterparts has served as a benchmark for further study. Some of these early studies provided estimates of the union relative-wage effect for particular industries and occupations, while others provided economy-wide estimates. Although the precise estimates obtained in these early studies varied quite considerably, the general order of magnitude of union relative-wage effects for particular industries and occupations in the USA during the interwar period that emerged was something under 25 per cent. Economy-wide estimates placed the union/non-union differential in the USA during the immediate postwar years in the range of 4–25 per cent. Lewis (1963) provided his own estimates of the impact of unions on relative wages in the USA between 1920 and 1958, and these implied a union/non-union differential that varied considerably over time in response to the level of economic activity, ranging from 2 per cent in the period between 1945 and 1949 to 46 per cent between 1930 and 1934. Economy-wide studies subsequent to Lewis's work estimated the US differential for the early 1960s at around 30 per cent (Throop, 1968; Rosen, 1969), while later studies based on individual data provided somewhat lower estimates. Weiss (1966), for example, estimated the 1960 US differential as 20 per cent, while Stafford (1968) provided estimates of the US differential in 1966 that showed an inverse relation between skill level and the differential and placed the differential in the range of 24–52 per cent.

The more recent US evidence is well surveyed by Freeman and Medoff (1984), who cite evidence to indicate that by the late 1970s the US union differential was to the order of 30 per cent. In addition, Freeman and Medoff also report evidence showing marked differences in the size of the union wage differential or gap, as between differing types of union members. In particular, black and less well-educated union members appear to enjoy a higher union wage differential than other categories of union members (1984, p. 49).

British research on the size of the union/non-union differential began to appear much later. The first study of the impact of unions on relative wages in the UK was due to Pencavel (1974), who analysed data covering 29 industries in 1964. Using union membership data, Pencavel estimated that for manual workers unions raised the hourly earnings of their members relative to those received by non-members by amounts ranging from zero (in industries that did not engage in a significant degree of bargaining at the plant level) to 14 per cent (in industries that did engage in a significant degree of plant bargaining). More recently, data on the coverage of collective agreements in Britain has become available from the *New Earnings Surveys*, which first appeared in 1973, and a number of estimates of the union/non-union differential have been

Table 11.2 ***Union/non-union differentials in Britain, 1980 (%)***

	Manual		*Non-manual*	
	Semi-skilled	*Skilled*	*Clerical workers*	*Middle managers*
Great Britain	10.2*	−0.4	0.7	4.0*
Manufacturing	2.0	−0.7	3.0	2.6
Non-manufacturing	14.0*	−0.9	−0.5	3.5*
Private sector	7.8*	−1.0	1.3	2.3
Public sector	25.5*	6.7	12.4*	3.5

Note: An asterisk denotes an estimated differential which is significantly different from zero at the 5 per cent level or better.

Source: Blanchflower (1986), Table 1, p. 200.

made using these data. These British studies analysed samples that variously included male, female, manual and non-manual labour, and with few exceptions their results seemed to suggest that the 1973 differential was in the range of 16–27 per cent. However, using individual data Stewart (1983) estimated the average union/non-union differential at 7.7 per cent in 1975, but his results also indicated large discrepancies across different industries and unions. For example, the differential to semi-skilled male workers was estimated at about 8 per cent, falling to only 3 per cent for skilled workers.

In a more recent study of British union/non-union differentials, Blanchflower (1986) provided separate estimates for a range of different occupational groups, as well as distinguishing between public and private sector employments and between manufacturing and non-manufacturing industry. **Table 11.2**, which summarises Blanchflower's findings, indicates the absence of significant differentials for various occupational/employment combinations. However, for those combinations yielding significant values, differentials appear to vary from 3.5 per cent for middle managers outside the manufacturing sector, up to 25.5 per cent for semi-skilled manual workers employed in the public sector.

A finding of particular importance that emerged from the early US work of Lewis (1963) and others was the existence of a significant inverse relationship between the size of the union/non-union differential and the level of economic activity as this affects the state of the labour market. Lewis interpreted this result as giving support to what he termed the Rees–Friedman *wage-rigidity hypothesis*. According to this hypothesis non-union wages are relatively more sensitive to changes in demand conditions than are union wages. This effect is suggested as arising because while trade unions are able to prevent union wages from falling during periods of depressed product and labour demand conditions (giving rise to a high differential during depressed periods), they actually prevent wages from rising during upswings as rapidly as they would otherwise do (thus giving rise to a low differential during boom periods). This wage-rigidity effect is seen as arising because of the frictions and lags that are introduced into the wage adjustment process by the existence of collective bargaining. Thus, since collective agreements typically last for a year or more, unionised workers may be at a disadvantage during periods of rapid cyclical upswing and inflation. This is because non-union employers who are not 'locked in' to collective agreements may raise wages more frequently than union employers. In addition union employers making agreements during such periods may become reluctant to make unusually large wage increases in case the period of buoyant demand turns out to be only short-lived.

In a study of the British experience Demery and McNabb (1978) reestimated Pencavel's (1974) model and introduced into this the role of demand factors in order to measure the impact of non-zero excess demand on the effects of unions on relative wages in the UK. By so doing they found evidence to suggest the presence of a wage-rigidity effect of the above sort in UK industries characterised by widespread plant bargaining.

The experience of both the USA and the UK during the mid-1970s seemed to confirm the previously observed *counter-cyclical* behaviour of the union wage differential: with the differential in both countries being seen to grow as the unemployment rate rose. However, while this behaviour seemed to continue in the UK as unemployment rates continued to rise in the early 1980s, the US evidence is less conclusive (Raisian, 1983), with the US union/non-union differential appearing to barely change during the recession of the early 1980s. During this period there was much discussion in the USA of 'concession bargaining' in the unionised sector of the economy. However, for reasons not yet fully understood, it appears that such concessions in the union sector were broadly matched by a roughly equivalent reduction in average wages in the non-unionised sector of the US economy.

■ Unions and resource allocation

The extent to which unions, via their influence on relative wages, affect the allocation of resources within the economy is a question of some importance. This problem was considered by Rees (1963), whose analysis

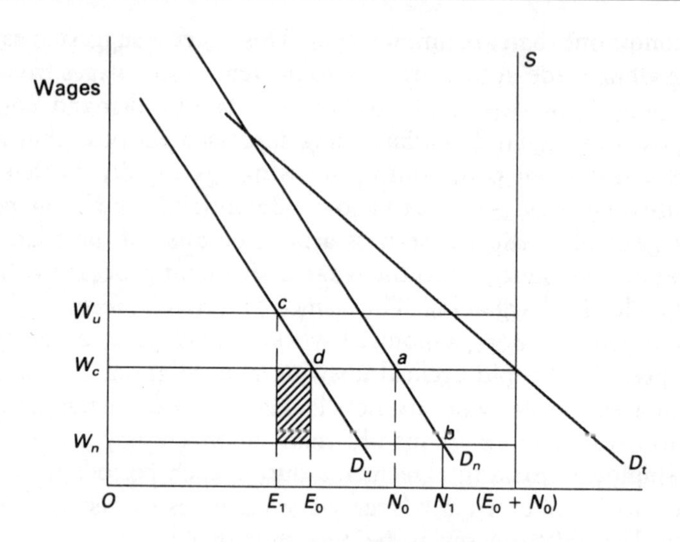

Figure 11.11 ***The effects of union wage differentials on resource allocation***

is discussed below, but shortly afterwards it was approached at a more advanced level by Johnson and Mieszkowski (1970) within a general equilibrium framework.

Rees considered an economy with a perfectly inelastic supply of homogeneous labour and assumed that the economy is divided into two sectors, say N and U; both of which are initially non-unionised. This situation is shown in **Figure 11.11** where S is the supply curve of homogeneous labour, and D_u and D_n are the labour demand curves in sectors U and N respectively. D_t is the total demand for labour, obtained by horizontal summation of D_u and D_n. In the initial situation there is no unionisation, and it is assumed that the wage in both sectors is set competitively at W_c. At this wage, employment in sector U is E_0 and in sector N it is N_0, giving total employment of $(E_0 + N_0)$.

Assume now that the union enters the stage and organises sector U. If through collective bargaining the union succeeds in raising the wage in its sector to W_u, employment in this sector declines from E_0 to E_1 as employers and consumers substitute against union labour and union-made products. On the assumption that the workers who have lost their jobs in sector U prefer to work in sector N at the non-union wage in preference to remaining unemployed, the supply of labour to the non-union sector is increased by the amount $(E_0 - E_1)$ to, say, N_1. This displacement of workers from the unionised to the non-unionised sector increases employment in N from N_0 to N_1 and depresses the non-union wage (which is still competitively determined) from W_c to W_n.

A welfare or output loss arises from this displacement of workers from the union to the non-union sector, because workers are now being employed where their marginal productivity is lower than before. Since the labour demand curve for each sector is its marginal revenue product (*MRP*) schedule, the area below each curve up to the employment level in question measures the total product or output of the sector. In order to measure the decrease in the total output of the economy that arises because the union wage is raised above the competitive level, it is necessary to measure the difference between the area under D_u from E_0 to E_1 and the area under D_n from N_0 to N_1. In the non-union sector output increases by the amount aN_0N_1b, and in the union sector output decreases by cE_1E_0d. The difference between these two areas (that is, the output loss due to the union wage increase) is the area of the shaded rectangle between E_0 and E_1. In the particular case where the demand schedules are parallel, it is easy to show by elementary geometry that

$$\text{Output loss} = \tfrac{1}{2}\,(W_n - W_u)(E_0 - E_1)$$

or one-half of the absolute union/non-union wage differential times the difference in employment.

On the basis of Lewis's (1963a) estimate of the size of the elasticity of union employment relative to non-union employment with respect to the union/non-union wage differential of approximately −1, Rees (1963) made a rough estimate of the size of the welfare loss caused by the effects of unions on earnings and employment in the USA in 1957 as being approximately 0.14 per cent of that year's gross national product. Although the findings of some more recent studies suggest that Lewis's estimates of the effects of unions on relative wages may be on the low side, Rees's analysis does suggest that the losses caused by the misallocative effects of unions are very small indeed – a general conclusion that is supported by the findings of the Johnson and Mieszkowski (1970) study, and more recent work. For example the general equilibrium study of the allocative effects of US unions by DeFina (1983) reports estimates around half the size of those reported by Rees, while Freeman and Medoff (1984, pp. 57–8) judge the effect of unions to have been no more than 0.2 to 0.4 per cent of US gross national product in 1980.

Notice, however, that Rees's analysis takes as its initial situation the case of a perfectly competitive labour market. If instead, as may well occur in practice, the initial situation is one characterised by monopsonic imperfections, the analysis might overstate the output losses due to unionisation, which may even prove to be negative in such circumstances, in the sense that unionisation may result in a structure of relative wages that conforms more closely than the initial situation to those which would be found in a competitive market (King, 1972, p. 48).

■ The other face of unionism

In a series of influential publications, Freeman and Medoff (for example, 1984) have argued that there are *two* faces to unionism. First, there is the *monopoly* face as set out in the monopoly-union model discussed earlier in this chapter, and developed in Rees's (1963) analysis of union allocative effects. Second, there is the institutional or *collective-voice* model of unions, via which it is argued that unions may exert a positive influence on productivity. One way of thinking about this distinction is to recognise the assumption, implicit in Rees's (1963) analysis of union allocative effects, that the position of the labour demand (*MRP*) schedules are unaffected by unionisation. According to the collective-voice view the advent of unionisation may for various reasons result in an increase in the marginal productivity of the unionised labour. This results, other things being equal, in a rightward shift in the position of the demand for labour curve in the unionised sector of the economy. If this hypothesis is true, the validity of the preceding analysis of the misallocative effects of monopoly unions is thrown into doubt.

According to Freeman and Medoff, the alternative face of unionism arises because unions are institutions of collective voice operating within internal labour markets. The union's role within this framework is seen as the communication of the preferences of workers on a range of issues *directly* to management, plus participation in the establishment of work rules and seniority provisions in the internal labour market. In so doing unions can contribute to increased productivity in three principal ways. First, there is the so-called *exit-voice trade-off* (Freeman, 1980; Freeman and Medoff, 1979). According to this argument the union leads to enhanced productivity amongst its members by providing them with a direct channel through which to voice their discontent to management and by establishing job rights according to seniority; both of which serve to reduce voluntary turnover (or quit rates). In short, by providing a channel through which workers' voices may be heard, it is argued that exits (or quits) as the alternative means by which workers may express their views ('voting with their feet') will be correspondingly reduced. According to Freeman and Medoff, such reductions in job turnover increases the incentives to employers to provide firm-specific training which may lead to increased productivity. The incentive to provide firm-specific training is increased because lower turnover implies a decreased likelihood of the employer losing the employee in whom he has invested. In addition, it is also argued that unions help to establish seniority provisions, one effect of which is to lessen rivalry between experienced and inexperienced workers, one consequence of which will be to increase the amount of informal on-the-job training which the former are willing to provide to the latter.

Second, trade unions may increase productivity by providing a channel through which labour can draw to management's attention changes in working methods or production techniques that may be beneficial to both parties. This channel also offers a mechanism by which the union can 'shock' management into adopting better practices or, more generally, into 'keeping on its toes'. Third, by increasing the economic rewards from employment and by providing mechanisms for grievance expression, unions may directly improve the productivity of their members by increasing their morale, motivation and effort.

Over the last decade an extensive literature of studies designed to test the net effect of unions on productivity has arisen. Although the results reported in this literature are by no means unanimous in their conclusion (see Addison and Barnett, 1982; Hirsch and Addison, 1986, for surveys; and Turnbull, 1989, for a critique), the weight of the evidence currently available seems to support the conclusion that union workers are more productive than their non-union counterparts in manufacturing. Moreover the size of the union/non-union productivity differential appears to be sufficiently large to offset the estimated union/non-union wage differential (Ehrenberg and Smith, 1991, pp. 483–4).

Notes

1. For an excellent concise summary of Fellner's classic analysis, see Bronfenbrenner (1971, pp. 235–8).
2. Ferguson, for example, argued that the 'precise result is determined by factors beyond the purview of economic analysis' (1972, p. 315). See Pen (1959, pp. 91–4) for a short history of economic thought on bilateral monopoly and the bargaining problem.
3. On the basis of the usual assumptions, the union's indifference curves in **Figure 11.3** are only defined for values of the wage rate (w) which are greater than or equal to the workers' reservation wage (r), which represents the wage which members would earn in some relevant alternative sector of the economy (or indeed as benefits in unemployment, if this constitutes the relevant alternative) should they not achieve employment in the firm in question.
4. Note that the contract curve's lowest point (C), in **Figure 11.4**, occurs at the point on the employer's labour demand curve which corresponds to the reservation wage (r). For a proof, see McDonald and Solow (1981).
5. This mechanism provides one possible interpretation of the circumstances underlying the protracted industrial dispute which occurred in the United

Kingdom coal-mining industry over the period 1984–5. According to this interpretation, the dispute appeared to be an attempt by the National Union of Mineworkers to prevent the employer, the then National Coal Board, from moving horizontally from the agreed settlement on the contract curve (at say point X in **Figure 11.4**) to the labour demand curve at point Y in order to increase profits by contracting employment in the industry by the amount $(n_1 - n_2)$.

6. As we saw in Chapter 5 the firm will, in the short run, stay in business providing that it earns either a profit, or a loss no greater than the level of its fixed costs. Therefore in the short-run context, the firm's fall-back profits position π_0 equals minus one times the level of its fixed costs. In the long run, however, π_0 may be thought of as normal profits.
7. As we saw in Chapter 5, the profit-maximising firm's labour demand curve is its marginal revenue product (*MRP*) schedule. Since *MRP* is, in the case of a competitive firm, given by marginal physical product multiplied by output price, the rightward shift in the position of the firm's labour demand curve in response to the increase in aggregate demand follows from the assumption that an increase in aggregate demand results, *ceteris paribus*, in an increase in the firm's output price. In terms of macroeconomics, the assumption here is simply that the aggregate supply curve is upward-sloping.
8. Notice that the tangency points A and B in **Figure 11.6** are drawn such that equilibrium occurs in both cases at the kink in the union indifference curves (and are therefore referred to for obvious reasons as 'corner solutions'). Although such tangency points need not necessarily occur at the kinks, advocates of the model (for example, Carruth and Oswald, 1986, p. 5) point out that such corner solutions may be important in practice, since many unions in the real world run a 'union shop', where each new worker must join the union, with the consequence that under such circumstances membership will tend to be close, if not equal to, employment.
9. But see Carruth and Oswald (1985) for slightly less negative results relating to the UK coal industry.
10. Hence, questions of the internal consensus of either organisation and intra-organisational bargaining are not considered. For a discussion of these issues, see Walton and McKersie (1965).
11. For further discussion of these and related issues, see de Menil (1971, p. 6). See also Bishop (1963, pp. 559–60) and Bacharach (1976, pp. 105–6).
12. This is defined in the usual manner as the locus of points such that, for any given attainable utility for one bargainer, the other's utility is maximised.
13. In cases where the frontier is, perhaps over a certain range, convex to the origin or discontinuous, these sections are usually eliminated by linear combinations representing expected utilities from probability deals. For further discussion, see de Menil (1971, p. 7).
14. As both Bishop (1963, p. 567) and Saraydar (1965, p. 804) pointed out, the alternative of a utility-based approach is explicit in Zeuthen's own exposition (Zeuthen, 1930, pp. 113, 115, 135) and as Harsanyi (1956, p. 148)

noted, Zeuthen's money formulation is merely the special case in which the marginal utility of money is constant (although not necessarily equal) for both parties.

15. Bishop (1964, p. 411) termed this the bargainer's *subjective probability of conflict.*
16. Plus an implicit term of $r_1.0$, since by definition the union, like the employer, receives zero utility in the event of disagreement (that is, when threats are implemented).
17. The same result is obtained on differentiation with respect to u_2. Second-order conditions require

$$\frac{d^2(u_1u_2)}{du_1^2} = u_1\frac{d^2u_2}{du_1^2} + \frac{2du_2}{du_1} < 0$$

which is satisfied for all u_1 given the usually assumed concavity of the frontier to the origin. The conditions under which the bargaining process converges to settlement at point Q in **Figure 11.8** are given in Sapsford (1982, pp. 13–15), but it should be noted that a sufficient condition for convergence is that the utility increments frontier is everywhere concave to the origin or linear.

18. See, for example, Pen (1959, pp. 117–27) and Cross (1969, pp. 25–6). However, Harsanyi (1956, pp. 149–51) provided an explicit derivation of Zeuthen's assumption by considering five 'more general postulates'. See also Bishop (1964, pp. 412) and Cross (1969, p. 25) for critiques of Harsanyi's approach.
19. See Saraydar (1965, pp. 806–13) and Cross (1969, p. 127) for two suggested modifications designed to overcome this feature of Zeuthen's own exposition.
20. For an attempt to improve on Zeuthen's theory by taking account of various psychological and subjective dimensions of bargaining and by explicitly considering the way in which the bargainers arrive at their subjective conflict probabilities, see Pen (1952, 1959).
21. For useful surveys, see Shubik (1959, pp. 38–56), Bishop (1963, pp. 559–602) and Binmore and Dasgupta (1986). See also Coddington (1968, pp. 71–80) for a discussion of the limitations of this approach to the bargaining process.
22. Briefly, the von Neumann–Morgenstern utility theory is concerned with situations characterised by uncertainty and assumes the maximisation of expected utility. The utility functions thus derived are unique up to an order preserving linear transformation. For further discussion see Henderson and Quandt (1980, pp. 52–6) or Varian (1978, pp. 104–11).
23. It is non-zero sum because there are gains from trade. However, as Coddington (1968, p. 72) pointed out, its treatment as cooperative is not inherent in the situation but depends on the way in which it is modelled.
24. Following Nash's (1950, p. 158) apparent intention, we interpret his theory as a positive description of the bargaining outcome. See Harsanyi (1956,

p. 147) and de Menil (1971, p. 7) for a similar interpretation, but see Luce and Raiffa (1957, pp. 124–34) and Shubik (1959, pp. 48–50) for an alternative normative interpretation. See Binmore (1987) and Binmore, Rubinstein and Wolinksy (1985) for recent detailed interpretations of the Nash solution.

25. For a critical discussion of Nash's axioms, see Bishop (1963, pp. 574–82), but see also Cross's (1969, pp. 20–2) defence.
26. The following proof is a modification of that given by Cross (1969, pp. 38–9).
27. For example, Cross (1969, p. 33) argued that Hicks's theory is not determinate, Comay *et al.* (1974, p. 304) and Swidinsky (1976, p. 209) argued that it is, whereas Shackle abstained, noting that the 'whole meaning of Professor Hicks' construction is very elusive' (1957, p. 301).

    Various criticisms of Hicks's theory have been put forward, a number of which stem from a determinate interpretation. Pen (1959, pp. 114–7), for example, argued that Hicks offered no explanation of disequilibrium behaviour or convergence, and Cartter (1959, pp. 127–8) argued that he failed to consider the interactive characteristics of bargaining and that, in cases where each bargainer holds different expectations about strike length, the analysis merely delineates a range of indeterminacy. Bishop (1964, p. 413) further criticised Hicks for his implicit asymmetrical treatment of union and employer, and Shackle (1957, p. 301) questioned the shape of Hicks's union resistance curve and replaced it with a *union inducement* curve, although the validity of this has in turn been questioned by Hicks (1963, pp. 353–4).
28. See Bishop (1964, p. 413) and Sapsford (1990, pp. 143–8), for a detailed discussion of this implicit asymmetry in Hicks's exposition.
29. In a number of empirical studies, Hicks's theory has been reinterpreted, with the respective curves being specified as the actual paths of offers and counter-offers during strikes rather than as functions relating wage rates to expected strike length evaluated *ex ante* in advance of any strike (see Melnik and Comay, 1972; Comay *et al.*, 1974; Swidinsky, 1976). However, it is clear from the above discussion that severe *identification problems* result from the shifts in the Hicksian curves that occur during the strike, with the consequence that the estimated curves presented in such studies bear in general little meaningful resemblance to those specified by Hicks.
30. Both Foldes (1964) and Bishop (1964) extended the Hicksian type of analysis by emphasising the time dependence of the bargaining process. Although their theoretical constructions differ, they both demonstrated that a static solution to the bargaining problem can be obtained by the formulation of a principle of compromise based on the time preferences of the bargainers. Notice also that Bishop presented his theory as a composite one, designed to incorporate the main characteristics of both Zeuthen's and Hicks's.
31. These tactics are many and varied and are catalogued in depth in Cartter

(1959, pp. 119–22). Tactics discussed include the adoption by bargainers of confident attitudes, which can be interpreted as attempts to convince the opponent of one's propensity to hold out in order to achieve one's own demand and thereby to increase his expected disagreement costs. At the same time a bargainer may try to raise his opponent's attitude ratio further by trying to convince the opponent that he has overestimated the costs of agreeing with the current offer. The union may, for example, present arguments to the employer to suggest that he has overestimated the effect of its current demand on profits, by failing to take full account of the improvements in productivity that will follow from the improved morale and living standards that will result from his conceding the claim, and so on. In addition, pre-negotiation build-ups of inventories by employers and financial reserves by the union can be interpreted as attempts by each to lower their own attitude ratios by decreasing their respective disagreement costs.
Especially important within this formulation is the compromise, the offer of which constitutes an attempt to increase the opponent's bargaining attitude through a lowering of his agreement costs, while also possibly decreasing one's own disagreement costs through a downward revision of the expected length of stoppage necessary to achieve one's own demand. Notice, however, that the offered party may take the compromise offer as a sign of its opponent's weakness, with the consequence that its attitude ratio will tend to decrease, because its estimated disagreement costs fall as it revises downwards its assessment of the length of work stoppage necessary to obtain its own demand.

32. $$\begin{aligned} \ln W_i &= U_i \ln W_i^u + (1-U_i) \ln W_i^n \\ &= U_i(\ln W_i^u - \ln W_i^n) + \ln W_i^n \\ &= U_i \ln \frac{W_i^u}{W_i^n} + \ln W_i^n \end{aligned}$$

Denoting the proportionate union/non-union wage differential $(W_i^u - W_i^n)/W_i^n$ by r_i and substituting, we obtain

$$\ln W_i = U_i \ln (1+r_i) + \ln W_i^n$$

33. Different writers have approached this question in different ways. Pencavel (1974, pp. 195–6) treated movements in the difference between the wage paid to non-unionists and the wage that would prevail in the complete absence of unions as part of the variations in the disturbance term of his regression equation, whereas Metcalf (1977, p. 173) and Nickell (1977, p. 195) specified this discrepancy as depending only on the extent of unionism within the industry or occupation in question.

■ Chapter 12 ■

Search in the Labour Market*

■ Introduction

Over the postwar period economists have devoted considerable attention to the analysis of markets characterised by *imperfect information* regarding trading opportunities. It has been argued that under such circumstances it is rational for the individual market participant to undertake an amount of market search, the objective of which is to obtain an improvement in the extent of their information or knowledge regarding the various alternatives which are available. For example, in the labour market context, individual workers will, in general, possess less than perfect information regarding available job opportunities, while individual employers will likewise be imperfectly knowledgeable regarding labour availability. Thus, it is argued by search theorists, when confronted with such imperfect information it is rational for both the worker when looking for a job, and the employer when seeking to fill a vacancy, to engage in some form of information-gathering or search exercise. Clearly there are both costs and benefits involved in the pursuit of such search activity and as we shall see, search theory considers the ways in which the rational individual searcher balances one against the other in the design of an optimal search strategy. Although our own discussion of search will concentrate exclusively upon labour market search it is important to realise that the principles involved apply equally and analogously to the case of consumer search in the market for goods when confronted with uncertainty regarding both price and qualities.

* This chapter draws freely upon Sapsford (1991).

Modelling search behaviour

It has long been recognised by economists that the problem of the selection by the individual agent of the optimal amount of search is essentially a capital and investment theoretic problem (Pissarides, 1985). However, it was not until developments in both the theory of human capital and the theory of choice under uncertainty had progressed sufficiently far that formal models of the search process began to appear. Naturally enough, interest in search processes increased in the early 1960s with the emergence of the economics of information (Stigler, 1961, 1962). The literature on search theory is an extremely large (and still growing) one and in order to provide insight into its main results we focus our attention in this section on a highly simplified model, the assumptions of which are gradually relaxed in subsequent sections.[1] To set the scene for what follows we begin our discussion with a consideration of the various costs and benefits involved in the search process.

Basic concepts

Consider the case of a worker who is looking for a job, while in possession of less than perfect information regarding the set of available job opportunities. For simplicity, we assume that all workers in the labour market in question are homogeneous and that the worker faces *not* a single market wage offer (as would be the case in simple models of the labour market which invariably unrealistically assume complete knowledge on the part of labour buyers and sellers) but a variety of wage offers summarised by some *known* frequency distribution.[2] More precisely, the wage offer is assumed to be a random drawing for some distribution of wage offers which has a known probability density function denoted by $f(\cdot)$ and a distribution function $F(\cdot)$. Denoting the wage offer by w it follows immediately that

$$\frac{dF(w)}{dw} = f(w)$$

For simplicity, we assume that all characteristics of the jobs other than wages are known and are identical across different jobs. Under this set-up, uncertainty arises because although the worker knows both the form and parameters of $F(.)$ he does not know which particular employer is offering which particular wage. Confronted with this situation the individual can begin to discover which firms are offering which wages by canvassing various firms – this phenomenon being referred to as search (Stigler, 1961, p. 213).

In practice, a wide variety of alternative methods of searching out information regarding job offers exist (including visits to employment agencies, both state and private, browsing through newspapers and trade publications, enquiries through personal contacts and so forth) each of which may be used either individually or in combination with other methods. However, for purposes of the current discussion we assume that the search process takes the form where the worker selects a firm at random and submits a job application to it.[3] Quite literally, we may think of a worker as selecting a firm at random (from the telephone book perhaps) and then enquiring as to the magnitude of its wage offer via its personnel office.

If search were a costless activity we would expect the worker to carry on searching across different firms until he discovers the maximum wage on offer, regardless of the time it takes. In such a case, high-wage firms would be be inundated with applicants, while low-wage firms would have none and a 'law of one price'-type mechanism would operate, with high-wage firms lowering their offers and low-wage firms raising theirs, until all firms eventually offer the same wage. Under such circumstances the wage offer distribution becomes degenerate, with the consequence that the problem of uncertainty regarding wage offers disappears, as does the problem of how best to search. Crucial to the theory is the assumption that each time a worker canvasses a potential employer he incurs a cost. The costs of search include not only such direct costs as the travel expenses incurred in visiting firms (to attend for interview perhaps) but also various opportunity costs (including foregone leisure, or earnings, from the time spent writing letters, filling in application forms, visiting firms and so on). For purposes of the current discussion we make the usual assumption that search costs are known and fixed and take the form of some constant lump sum expense (denoted by c) which is incurred each and every time an offer is sampled from the distribution (that is, each time an approach is made to a firm) regardless of whether the offer is rejected or accepted.

Turning now to the benefits of search, it is clear that the more search the worker undertakes the more likely it is that he will discover a high-wage firm. However, each additional unit of search undertaken imposes an additional cost (c) upon the worker. It therefore follows that a rational worker will only continue searching as long as the marginal benefit of search exceeds its marginal cost. In order to derive the *optimal* amount of search it is simply necessary for the worker to continue searching up to the point where the marginal benefit of search falls into equality with its marginal cost. Given that information is imperfect, the worker is assumed to evaluate the expected benefit from search as the mean (or expected value) of the wage distribution $f(w)$:

$$E(w) = \int_0^\infty wf(w)dw \tag{12.1}$$

Having sketched out the nature of the costs and benefits encountered in the search process we now ask the question: according to what principles might the individual worker conduct his or her search? Two of the most commonly offered answers to this question to be found in the literature are that before setting out on his search, the individual worker decides on either (a) the number of firms to approach before calling off the search or (b) upon some minimum acceptable wage offer (termed the reservation wage) which is such that a wage offer will be accepted if it is greater than or equal to the reservation wage, but rejected in favour of continued search if it falls short of the reservation wage. According to view (a), the individual worker follows the following search rule: canvass a sample of firms of a predetermined size (say n^*) and accept the largest wage offer from the n^* received if this constitutes an improvement over his present situation. However, according to view (b) the individual follows the *sequential rule*: according to which he embarks on search with a predetermined reservation wage in mind and continues searching until a wage offer greater than or equal to this is received.

Case (a), which was first considered by Stigler (1962), is referred to in the literature as the fixed (or optimal) sample size rule, while case (b) is termed the sequential decision rule.

■ Fixed sample size rule

Equation (12.1) gives the expected value of the benefit from search which may be thought of as representing the highest wage offer likely to be encountered after visiting one firm (that is, after undertaking one unit of search), which may be rewritten as

$$E(w) = E[\max w|n = 1] \tag{12.2}$$

given that with a sample of size 1, the only wage in the sample is the maximum. When deciding on the optimal number of firms to visit, the searcher must compare the expected benefits for samples of different sizes. So for instance, setting n = 2 and assuming sampling with replacement, there are various *pairs* of wage offers which the searcher may expect to encounter, the probability associated with each of which is simply, given the assumption of replacement, the product of their respective individual probabilities. Taking the product of the larger of the two wages in each sample and the probability of that sample and integrating across all such samples the searcher arrives at the expected maximum wage offer from samples of size 2, which is denoted by $E[\max w|n = 2]$.[4] Proceeding in the same manner for samples of size 3, 4 and so on[5] the individual is able to chart the maximum expected wage from all possible sample sizes. Clearly as the size of n increases $E[\max w|n]$ approaches the highest wage available. **Figure 12.1** plots the usually assumed shape of the $E[\max w|n]$ function against the sample size n, which reveals that although the expected benefits from search increase with the number of firms sampled, the additional expected return to a unit increase in the number of sampled firms decreases with n, with the consequence that there are diminishing marginal returns to search.

In order to determine the optimal sample size, the individual worker equates the marginal expected benefit of search to its marginal cost. Recalling our assumption that the unit costs of search are constant (at c per firm sampled) the cost associated with sampling n firms is simply cn, as indicated by the straight line of slope c passing through the origin in **Figure 13.1.** Since the marginal cost of search is c, while the expected marginal benefit is the gradient of the $E[\max w|n]$ function, we see that the optimum size of sample is n^* firms, which is obtained at the point at which the gradient of the $E[\max w|n]$ equals c. Clearly, the optimal value of sample size maximises the distance between the expected return and cost curves.

The preceding analysis therefore gives rise to the fixed sample size (or Stigler) rule for the conduct of search. According to this rule, the individual, prior to commencing job search, determines the optimal number of firms to approach (n^*), such that the expected marginal benefit of search is equated to its marginal cost. Having canvassed or applied to each of these n^* firms, the worker accepts the largest wage offer from the n^* received, providing that this exceeds the wage currently being earned (say $\bar{w}$). Notice that if the individual is already employed and engaging in 'on-the-job' search, then $\bar{w}$ is the wage in his or her existing employment, whereas in the case of an unemployed worker, $\bar{w}$ may be taken to represent the level of unemployment and related benefits, after due allowance for the various non-monetary disbenefits and benefits associated with unemployment.

Despite its extreme simplicity, the fixed sample size model of search has been found to yield a number of entirely reasonable predictions regarding individual search behaviour. In particular, the model predicts that an increase in the gradient of the total cost curve **Figure 12.1** results, other things being equal, in a decrease in the optimal size of the sample of firms to be approached. In other words, the model predicts quite reasonably that as search costs rise (fall), the amount of search undertaken will fall (rise). Another possibility concerns a deterioration in

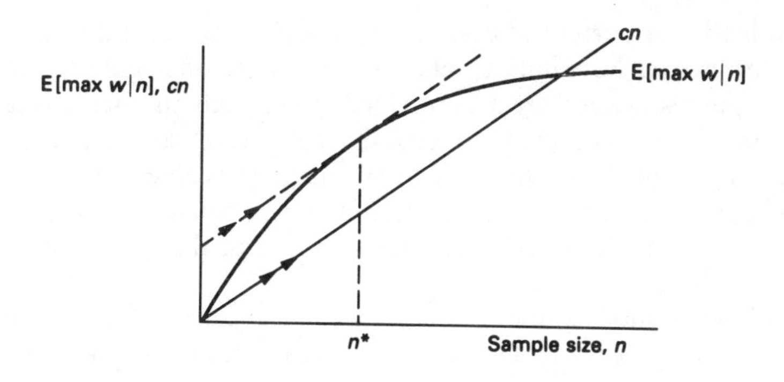

Figure 12.1 *Fixed sample size rule*

wage offers. Such a deterioration will lead to a decrease in the value of $E[\max w|n]$ for each value of n and will therefore give rise to a downward shift in the $E[\max w|n]$ curve in **Figure 12.1** resulting, other things being equal, in a decrease in the optimal amount of search.

Despite the plausibility of this model's predictions, plus the fact that these have typically been found to be fairly robust to variations in the model's assumptions, the plausibility of the underlying behaviour assumed in the model has been widely questioned. Specifically, while it is perhaps reasonable to argue that searchers set out with some notion of the maximum number of firms which it would be worthwhile to approach, it is, however, probably true that in practice most of us would stop short of submitting this number of job applications if we came across a sufficiently high wage offer in our searches. This view is widely taken in the literature and it is to models of this complexion that we now turn.

Reservation wages and sequential search models

The basic idea of sequential decision rule, or reservation wage, models of job search is that the individual does not decide prior to commencing search on the number of searches to be undertaken, but instead decides prior to search upon some minimum acceptable wage offer termed the *reservation wage*. Accordingly the individual in such models is assumed to evaluate, prior to embarking on job search, the *optimal* value of the reservation wage. If this exceeds the value of the wage associated with that individual's current situation ($\bar{w}$), search is undertaken and continues, no matter how long it takes, until a wage offer greater than or equal to the reservation wage is received. Once such an offer is received it is immediately accepted. In simple versions of such models it is frequently assumed that the individual, having accepted this offer, remains in employment forever, in which case it is convenient to interpret the wage offer as the discounted present value of the lifetime earnings from the job in question.

Clearly such models may be characterised in terms of the following *stopping rule*, where w denotes the current wage offer and w^* the individual's reservation wage:

$$\left.\begin{array}{l}\text{If } w < w^* \text{ reject } w \text{ and keep on searching} \\ \text{If } w \geqslant w^* \text{ accept wage offer } w\end{array}\right\} \quad (12.3)$$

Any search strategy taking this form is said to possess the *reservation wage property*.

Consider now the determination of the optimal value of the reservation wage. Assume as above that the individual knows the distribution of wage offers $f(w)$ and that unit search costs are constant at c. Assume also that the individual searcher is risk-neutral and seeks to maximise the expected net benefit of search. On the basis of these assumptions it can be shown that the optimal policy for the job-searcher is to follow stopping rule of form (12.3) above and that the value of the reservation wage itself may be derived by setting the marginal cost of obtaining an additional job offer equal to the expected marginal return to one more offer.

To illustrate the simplest version of the sequential search model, let us envisage the case where the individual job-seeker ventures out each and every day in search of work. We assume that each day the searcher generates exactly one wage offer which he accepts or rejects according to rule (12.3), recalling that days when no offer is received are treated as cases where the sampled firm offers a zero wage. On the assumption that the searcher retains the highest job offer[6] the return from ceasing search after the nth day is given by

$$Y_n = \max\,[w_1, w_2, \ldots., w_n] - nc \quad (12.4)$$

where w_t denotes the wage offer received on day $t(= 1, \ldots, n)$. The searcher's objective is to evaluate the reservation wage which maximises the value of $E(Y_n)$. Considering the first wage offer (w_1), this will only be accepted, by (12.3), if $w_1 \geqslant w^*$. The expected return from the optimal policy is simply $\max[w_1, w^*] - c$. Given that w^* is, by definition, the expected return from pursuing the optimal stopping rule we see that the optimal expected return from the optimal stopping rule satisfies

$$w^* = E \max [w_1, w^*] - c \qquad (12.5)$$

Writing $E \max [w_1, w^*]$ as

$$E \max [w_1, w^*] = w^* \int_0^{w^*} dF(w) + \int_{w^*}^{\infty} w dF(w)$$

$$= w^* \int_0^{w^*} dF(w) + w^* \int_{w^*}^{\infty} dF(w) + \int_{w^*}^{\infty} w dF(w) - w^* \int_{w^*}^{\infty} dF(w)$$

$$= w^* + \int_{w^*}^{\infty} (w - w^*) \,.\, dF(w)$$

it follows from (12.5) that

$$c = \int_{w^*}^{\infty} (w - w^*) \, dF(w) = H(w^*) \qquad (12.6)$$

where $H(\tilde{w}) \equiv \int_{\tilde{w}}^{\infty} (w - \tilde{w}) \, dF(w)$.

Expression (12.6) is an important result and by plotting the $H(\tilde{w})$ function, which is convex, non-negative and strictly decreasing, on a graph of search costs versus wage offers we are able to read off the optimal value of the reservation wage (denoted by w^*), associated with the given level of unit search costs c.[7] From **Figure 12.2** it is immediately seen that the lower the unit cost of search, the higher is the optimal value of the reservation wage, and hence (see below) the longer will be the duration of search. The economic interpretation of condition (12.6) is quite straightforward: namely, that the critical value w^* associated with the optimal stopping rule is selected so as to equate the marginal cost of obtaining one more job offer (c) with the expected marginal return from one further observation, $H(w^*)$. Notice also that in order to evaluate the optimal reservation wage w^* it is only necessary for the job-searcher to behave in a *myopic* fashion, in the sense that he or she need only compare the return from accepting employment with the expected return from exactly one further unit of search.

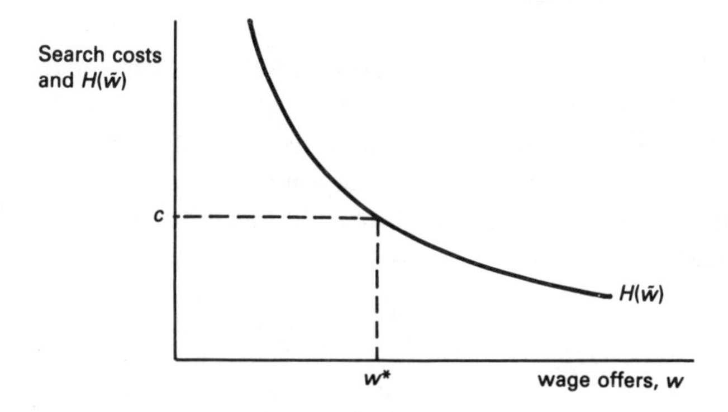

Figure 12.2 ***The optimal reservation wage***

Search duration

Further insight into this simple sequential search model may be obtained by recognising that the number of offers needed until w^* is exceeded is itself a random variable which has a geometric distribution. Denoting this random variable by N and by $p = 1 - F(w^*)$, the probability of receiving a wage offer greater than the reservation wage w^*, it follows immediately that $Pr(N = k) = p(1 - p)^{k-1}$ for $k = 1, 2 \ldots$ and that the expected search duration is given by

$$E(N) = \frac{1}{p} = \frac{1}{1 - F(w^*)} \tag{12.7}$$

indicating that the greater is w^*, the greater is the expected time spent searching.

Using this result we may write the expected gain from following the policy embodied in rule (12.3) as

$$V = \frac{-c}{1 - F(w^*)} + \int_{w^*}^{\infty} \frac{w\mathrm{d}F(w)}{1 - F(w^*)} \tag{12.8}$$

Given that the expected duration of search is $1/1 - F(w^*)$ the first term in expression (12.8) is simply the costs incurred in searching out an offer of at least w^*, while the second term is the conditional expected value of an offer given that it is at least w^*. Rearrangement of (12.8) gives

$$c = \int_{w^*}^{\infty} (w - v)\, \mathrm{d}F(w)$$

which on comparison with expression (12.6) shows that $v = w^*$, that is, that the total expected gain (net of search costs) from following the optimal strategy is precisely equal to the reservation wage w^*.

Some extensions

The two models described in the preceding section form the basis of the wide range of alternative and more advanced approaches to be found in the literature. To give the reader some insights into the wide range of alternative models which exist we explore in this section the consequences of relaxing some of the restrictive assumptions on which these simple models are based.

Discounting

One obvious extension to the sequential search model arises if we introduce discounting into the picture. Although, as already mentioned, it is common in the literature to find the wage offer interpreted as some discounted present value of future wages, the model is easily extended to include discounting explicitly. In the simplest expositions it is assumed that both search costs are incurred and wage offers received at the end of the period in question so that the present value of some wage offer w is simply βw (where $\beta \equiv 1/(1 + r)$ denotes the discount factor and r the 'appropriate' rate of discount), while the discounted cost of the first period's search is likewise βc. Writing $\beta\{E \max [w_1, w^*] - c\}$ as the analogue of (12.4) above and repeating the analysis we obtain

$$c = H(w^*) - rw^* \tag{12.9}$$

as the analogous condition to (12.5) in the no-discounting case. Condition (12.9) illustrates that the reservation wage w^* is negatively related to the rate of discount r. Thus we now have the additional and entirely plausible prediction that the higher the discount rate, the lower is the reservation wage and, using (12.7), the shorter is the duration of search.

□ *Random job offers*

Thus far in our discussion of the sequential search model we have assumed that the individual receives exactly one job offer in each period. This assumption may be relaxed in a variety of different ways and two specific versions of the case where the number of job offers received per period is a random variable are considered by Lippman and McCall (1976). In the first case, it is assumed that at most one offer is received each period, and letting q denote the probability of receiving no offer in a given period we obtain, on the assumption that the search cost is incurred at the beginning of the period in question, the following as analogous to (12.4) in the simple case already considered

$$w^* = - E\left(\sum_{k=0}^{\tau} c\beta^{k-1}\right) + E(\beta^{\tau})E \max [w_1, w^*] \tag{12.10}$$

Recognising τ as a geometrically distributed random variable with parameter q and using $E(\beta^{\tau}) = q/(q + r)$ we obtain, after some rearrangement, the following expression which represents the generalisation of (12.6) above.

$$c = \frac{q}{1 + r} H(w^*) - \frac{r}{1 + r} w^* \tag{12.11}$$

It follows from expression (12.11), given the properties of the $H(\cdot)$ function, that the reservation wage declines as q (the probability of receiving a job offer) decreases; indicating that when the chances of being offered a job decrease, the individual becomes less choosy.

In the second case considered by Lippman and McCall (1976) it is assumed that the number of offers received in a given period is a non-negative random variable with expected value equal to one. Although the proof is not presented here it is interesting to note that in this case, it may be shown that the reservation wage will be *lower* than in the situation where exactly one offer is received in each period.

■ Non-constant reservation wages

The various versions of the sequential search model so far discussed have been based on the assumptions that the distribution of wage offers, $f(w)$, is known with certainty and that the individual possesses and infinite time horizon, and in each case the reservation wage was found to be *invariant* over time. Consequently, in such models, if an offer is refused once it will continue to be refused for all time. Accordingly, it has been immaterial in the context of the models thus far considered whether or not the job-searcher is allowed the possibility of recalling previously received offers. However, the body of empirical evidence seems to suggest quite clearly that individuals' reservation wages do *not* remain constant as predicted by the models so far considered (for example, Kiefer and Neumann, 1979). Two main reasons for fluctuating reservation wages may be found in the literature. These are first, the existence of a finite time horizon and second, informational changes regarding the wage offer distribution. It is to these issues which we now turn, but it is clear that once one moves away from the constant reservation wage idea, the question of *recall* becomes of considerable importance.

□ *Finite-horizon models*

Consider now the case where the individual possesses a finite time horizon assuming, as before, a known distribution of wage offers. Assume also that recall is not permitted, so that any offer must be accepted immediately, otherwise it is lost. Let $V_n(w)$ be the maximum benefit (earnings) net of search costs which is attainable as viewed from a position n periods before the horizon date, which can conveniently be thought of as retirement. Ignoring discounting it follows that

$$V_n(w) = \max \left[w, \; -c + \int_0^\infty V_{n-1}(x)\, f(x)\, dx\right] \qquad (12.12)$$

where the x's denote future wage offers. The corresponding expression in the case of sampling with recall is

$$V_n(w) = \max\,[w, -c + \int_w^\infty V_{n-1}(x)\, f(x)\, dx] \qquad (12.12a)$$

The reservation wage in the no-recall case when n periods remain (denoted by w^*_n) is the value of w which equates the two terms on the right-hand side of expression (12.12), that is

$$w^*_n = -c + \int_0^\infty V_{n-1}(x)\, f(x)\, dx \qquad (12.13)$$

The individual's optimal search strategy, given that n periods remain, is therefore of the usual sort: namely, to continue searching if $w < w^*_n$ and to stop searching and accept w if $w > w^*_n$. Expression (12.13) holds for $n \geqslant 1$. In the final period it pays the individual to accept any positive offer so that $w^*_0 = 0$. Therefore given that $v_0(w) = w$ it follows that

$$w^*_1 = -c + \int_0^\infty x\, f(x)\, dx \geqslant w^*_0$$

and a straightforward induction argument (Hey, 1979, p. 110) reveals that

$$w^*_n \geqslant w^*_{n-1} \text{ (for all } n) \qquad (12.14)$$

Expression (12.14) reveals the important result that in this finite-horizon/no-recall model the reservation wage is *not* constant. Instead, it is seen to decline (or more correctly to not increase) as the number of periods left before the horizon falls. In other words, we see that the introduction into the model of a finite time horizon results in the additional prediction that the individual's reservation wage falls as time passes and retirement approaches.

The analysis, however, becomes considerably more complicated if we allow for the possibility of recall. Although this case is not discussed here, it is interesting to notice that with recall it is not clear whether or not the reservation wage declines over time. Indeed, in some formulations the very existence of a reservation wage is thrown into doubt (for further discussion, see Lippman and McCall, 1976, pp. 168–71).

□ *Adaptive search*

The second situation generating the reservation wages as a function of time, namely the case where the individual possesses imperfect knowledge regarding the distribution of wage offers $f(\cdot)$, gives rise to what is termed adaptive search. The basic idea in such models is that each wage offer which the searcher receives provides some *information* with which he may update his assessment of the wage distribution and thereby recalculate the reservation wage. In such models, each wage offer not only represents an employment opportunity but also constitutes a piece of information which may be used to update the prior distribution of offers. In all of the models so far considered the distribution of wage offers has been assumed known and in consequence, the reservation wage was found to be either constant or to decline through time. The incorporation of adaptive or learning mechanisms into search models is by no means a straightforward matter, although it is easy to see intuitively that such mechanisms give rise to the possibility that reservation wages may increase as search proceeds if, for instance, the searcher learns that his skills are more highly prized than he originally estimated. Although various schemes updating the prior distribution are considered in the literature, the general flavour of these models may be illustrated by considering the simple case in which the searcher is assumed to update his prior distribution in Bayesian manner, recalculate the reservation wage, and then in light of this decide whether to accept the wage or to continue searching. In this model there is assumed to be no recall and it is further assumed that while the form of the wage offer distribution is known, one or more of its parameters are only known up to a prior probability distribution.

Assume that the searcher has only imperfect knowledge regarding the k parameters $\boldsymbol{\gamma} = (\gamma_1, \ldots, \gamma_k)$ of the wage offer distribution $\phi(w)$ and that he has a prior distribution $h(\boldsymbol{\gamma}|\boldsymbol{\theta})$ over the unknown parameters summarising all the information he possesses about the moments of the wage distribution, where $\boldsymbol{\theta}$ is a vector of parameters of the prior. As offers are received, $\boldsymbol{\theta}$ is revised in a Bayesian manner and a new value is computed as say $\boldsymbol{\theta}' = T(\boldsymbol{\theta}, w_1, w_2 \ldots\ldots, w_n)$. After each observation the prior distribution $h(\boldsymbol{\gamma}|\theta)$ is revised, and then a decision is made regarding whether to either accept the offer or continue searching. Let $V_n(w, \boldsymbol{\theta})$ denote the maximum expected return when an offer of w has just been received, where $\boldsymbol{\theta}$ incorporates the information contained in the offer w, and a total of n further offers will be forthcoming. Now $V_0(w, \boldsymbol{\theta}) = w$ and

$$V_n(w, \boldsymbol{\theta}) = \max \left[w, -c + \int_0^\infty \int_0^\infty V_{n-1}(x, T(\boldsymbol{\theta}, x))\, \phi(x|\boldsymbol{\gamma})\, h(\boldsymbol{\gamma}|\phi)\, dx d\boldsymbol{\gamma}\right] \quad (12.15)$$

Letting $Z_{n-1}(\boldsymbol{\theta})$ denote the second term on the right-hand side of this expression we once again see that the optimal search policy possesses the reservation wage property since it is of the following form: accept employment if $w \geqslant Z_{n-1}(\boldsymbol{\theta})$, but continue searching if $w < Z_{n-1}(\boldsymbol{\theta})$. Clearly the precise pattern taken by reservation wages over time in this model depends on the way in which the various components of $Z_{n-1}(\boldsymbol{\theta})$ in (12.15) vary across time.

Employer search

Although our dicussion has so far focused on job search by workers it is of interest to notice that the same basic ideas have also been employed to model situations where employers search for workers to fill their vacancies. To illustrate the flavour of this branch of the literature we consider briefly in this section what is perhaps the simplest model of sequential employer search. This model is exactly analogous to the simple case of worker sequential search considered above: except that while workers face a distribution of wage offers, employers searching for new employees face a distribution of marginal products. In the employer search literature it is generally recognised that, unlike wage rates, which form a fairly clear signal to the job-searcher, the productivities of job-searchers are less easy for the searching employer to assess. Hence it is argued that the employer has an incentive to seek out information about the characteristics of job-searchers which may be positively correlated with their productivity in the job in question: most obviously via performance in aptitude tests, their previous educational achievements and so forth. The costs, including the opportunity cost of time, of such screening constitute employer search costs and the following simple model of employer search corresponds to the simple job search model discussed above, but with marginal products replacing wages.

For a given wage offer, let the employer's search cost be k (assumed constant) and the marginal product and the distribution of marginal products be m and $\phi(\cdot)$ respectively. Repeating the analysis embodied in equations (12.4) to (12.6) above we find that the optimal search strategy for the employer is one involving a reservation level of productivity: namely

accept applicant if $m \geqslant \eta^*$

reject applicant if $m < \eta^*$

where η^*, the minimum acceptable or reservation productivity, is obtained as the solution of

$$k = \int_{\eta^*}^{\infty} (m - \eta^*)\, d\phi(m) = G(\eta^*)$$

which is analogous to expression (12.6) above for the case of the employee.

Empirical evidence

Before proceeding to look at the empirical evidence relating to models of job search it is useful to summarise the predictions of the basic model and the various extensions considered above. In the case of the fixed sample size model we saw that prior to commencing search the individual decides on the optimal number of firms to approach, such that the expected marginal benefit of search is equated to its marginal cost. Having applied to each of these firms, the searcher accepts the largest of the offers received. In contrast, the central feature of sequential models of job search is the reservation wage property. In the basic version of the sequential search model we saw that the optimal value of the individual's reservation wage and the expected duration of his search are each inversely related to the magnitude of search costs. Thus the model predicts that, other things being equal, the lower the cost of the search, the higher is the reservation wage and the longer is the expected duration of search. We also saw that in such models the reservation wage is negatively related to the discount rate and positively related to the probability of receiving a job offer in a given period. Finally, we saw how the incorporation of both finite horizons on the part of workers and imperfect information regarding the distribution of wage offers can result in reservation wages which vary as time passes.[8]

Search theory is exceedingly rich in theoretical predictions and in consequence has generated a large empirical literature concerned with testing such predictions. Within the confines of the present chapter we consider only the empirical literature relating to labour market search.[9] Although the topic of unemployment is considered in its own right in Chapter 14, it should be noted that the economics of search carries a number of very important implications for the analysis and understanding of unemployment. An unemployed worker is one who is unable to find employment under prevailing economic conditions and as we shall see in Chapter 14, unemployment is a topic which abounds with alternative definitions and classifications. Of particular importance in the current context is the concept of *frictional unemployment*, according to which a worker is said to be frictionally unemployed if he or she is temporarily unemployed between jobs. Frictional unemployment is that which results from workers moving between jobs and as long as people change jobs, and as long as it takes a non-zero time to move from one job to another, some positive amount of frictional unemployment will exist. Frictional unemployment may therefore be seen as a consequence of the short-run changes which constantly occur in a dynamic economy in response to changes in the patterns of the demand for and the supply of goods and services. In short, frictional unemployment arises because the supply of labour does not adjust instantaneously to changes in the pattern of labour demand, with the consequences that unemployed workers and unfilled vacancies exist side by side. Frictional unemployment (or as it is sometimes alternatively called, search unemployment) arises because the process of matching unfilled vacancies with unemployed workers is non-instantaneous. Search theory has shed considerable light on the factors which determine the time it takes a frictionally unemployed worker to find an unacceptable job offer and by the same token, the factors which determine the time it takes employers to locate suitable workers to fill their vacancies. In particular, the marked increase in the levels of unemployment experienced in the UK, USA and other industrialised countries during the 1970s and 1980s relative to the early 1960s has led many economists to explore the extent to which such increases can be explained in terms of job search behaviour.

The pool of unemployment workers is a *stock*, the size of which at any moment is determined by two factors: the rate of *flow* into unemployment, and the *duration* of the unemployment spells experienced by individual workers. Subdivision of the UK's unemployment stock into its flow and duration components (Sapsford, 1981; Metcalf and Richardson, 1986) reveals that the rate of inflow into unemployment has remained remarkably stable (at almost 4 million per year) since the late 1960s, indicating that the increase in unemployment through the 1970s and 80s is largely attributable to increases in the duration of unemployment spells. Naturally enough, economists faced with this increase in the duration of unemployment spells turned their attention to the theory of job search for an explanation. As we saw in (12.7) above, job search theory predicts that the expected duration of a period of search unemployment is simply

$$E(N) = \frac{1}{1 - F(w^*)}$$

which indicates that the greater the value of the reservation wage (w^*) the longer is the expected duration of search. Expression (12.7) therefore suggests that an explanation of why unemployment in the industrialised countries rose requires an understanding of the behaviour of reservation wages over the period in question.

Considering the case of an unemployed worker searching for a job and making the assumption that $q(n, h)$, the probability that the individual searcher will receive n offers during a period of duration h, is distributed as Poisson, such that

$$q(n, h) = e^{-\lambda h} (\lambda h)^n / n!$$

then given a constant reservation wage w^*, the probabilistic rate at which a worker escapes unemployment is given by

$$\phi = \lambda[1 - F(w^*)] \tag{12.16}$$

which is simply the rate at which job offers arrive (γ) multiplied by the probability that a random offer is acceptable.[10] Alternatively we might adopt a probabilistic approach. If we allow the escape rate ϕ, the probability $p(t)$ that a job offer is received at time t and the reservation wage each to vary with time, we obtain

$$\phi(t) = p(t)\ [1 - F(w^*_t)] \tag{12.17}$$

according to which the probability of escaping unemployment at time t is the product of the probability of receiving a job offer and the probability that this offer is acceptable.

Expression (12.17) forms the backbone of empirical work on the duration of spells of search unemployment. It illustrates that the probability of escaping unemployment is influenced by two sets of factors, first, those which affect the value of the reservation wage, and second, those which affect the probability of locating a vacancy $p(t)$. We have already explored the determinants of the reservation wage, but turning now to those of $p(t)$, it is often argued (for example, Bean *et al.*, 1987) that its value will be determined primarily by demand conditions since it seems reasonable to argue that the probability of locating a vacancy will rise with the number of vacancies in existence. However, $p(t)$ will also depend on the intensity of search, since the more firms which the worker samples in any time period, the more likely it is that he will locate a vacancy. One particular issue which has attracted considerable attention in the empirical literature concerns the influence of unemployment (and related) benefits upon the extent of unemployment. Higher unemployment benefits are seen as reducing the cost of search, in terms of foregone earnings, and therefore (from **Figure 12.2**) as giving rise to an increase in the reservation wage which, other things being equal, results from (12.17) in a decline in the rate of escape from unemployment. The extent to which the rising unemployment levels observed during the 1970s and 1980s can be accounted for by the levels of state unemployment benefits, or insurance, is a question which has generated a large and sometimes highly charged debate. For example, Maki and Spindler (1975) and Minford (1983) concluded that the level of unemployment benefit exerted a large and significant effect on British unemployment over the postwar period, while Benjamin and Kochin (1979) concluded that the increase in Britain's unemployment in the interwar years was largely induced by the operation of the benefit system prevailing at the time. However, it is apparent that the results of such studies are highly sensitive to the particular assumptions adopted regarding both the form and magnitude of benefits actually received (Nickell, 1984) and in a whole range of further studies (Cubbin and Foley, 1977; Sawyer, 1979; Lancaster, 1979; Nickell, 1979, 1979a; Junankar, 1981), although generally still significant, the effect of benefits on unemployment was found to be much less marked than in the studies previously cited. Such studies typically take the replacement ratio (that is, the ratio of benefits received when unemployed to income earned when employed) as their measure of the extent of subsidy offered to search. In one of the most authoritative studies to date, Nickell (1979) concluded that unemployment duration is significantly affected by the replacement ratio, with an estimated elasticity, defined in household terms, of between 0.6 and 1.0. Between 1964 and 1973 actual unemployment in Britain rose by 92 per cent and Nickell's analysis suggested that only about one-seventh of this may be attributed to benefits. Atkinson *et al.* (1984) also found a weak positive association between benefits and unemployment and report estimated elasticities for different subsamples which range from around 0.1 to less than 1.0. One further interesting feature of these latter studies is that the long-term unemployed (defined as those out of work for 26 weeks or more) seem to be much less sensitive to variations in the replacement ratio than those only recently unemployed.[11] Although we have considered only the influence of unemployment benefits, via search, on unemployment, it is interesting to notice that some recent evidence for the various member countries of the OECD (Bean *et al.*, 1987) seems to suggest, at least as far as the UK is concerned, that the rise in unemployment observed through the 1970s and 1980s was in large part attributable to the influence of demand upon $p(t)$ in expression (12.17) rather than to the influence of the reservation wage, via the term $[1-F(w_t^*)]$.

Notes

1. More detailed surveys of search theory may be found, for example, in Lippman and McCall (1976), McKenna (1986, 1987) and Mortensen (1986).
2. Stigler, for example, cites as 'a tolerably pure estimator of the dispersion of wage offers to homogeneous labour' data relating to job offers received by Chicago business graduates which revealed a coefficient of variation of 7.9 per cent, which he notes is approximately equal to the coefficients revealed in national surveys of wage offers received by graduates.
3. The case where no offer is received may be treated as a zero wage offer.
4. See McKenna (1990) for some illustrative calculations.
5. With obvious notation we may write

$$E\,[\max w|n = 2] = E[\max\{w_i, w_j\}|n = 2]$$

$$= \int_0^\infty \int_0^\infty \max\,\{w_i, w_j\} f(w_i) f(w_j) \mathrm{d}w_i \mathrm{d}w_j$$

where max $\{w_i, w_j\}$ denotes whichever is the larger of the two wage offers w_i and w_j. Similarly

$$E\,[\max w|n = 3] = E\,[\max\{w_i, w_j, w_k\}|n = 3]$$

$$= \int_0^\infty \int_0^\infty \int_0^\infty \max\,\{w_i, w_j, w_k\}\, f(w_i)\, f(w_j)\, f(w_k)\, \mathrm{d}w_i\, \mathrm{d}w_j\, \mathrm{d}w_k$$

and so on for larger values of n.

6. Given (12.3) it is immaterial in the present context whether retention of the highest previous offer or retention of only the most recent one is assumed, since search continues until the reservation wage is exceeded. In more complex models, however, these assumptions do give alternative results (see Lippman and McCall, 1976).
7. In the context of the general expression $H(\cdot)$, w and $\tilde{w}$ may be thought of as denoting the value of the wage offer and reservation wage respectively, recalling that the *optimal* value of $\tilde{w}$ is denoted by w^*.
8. An alternative explanation of a reservation wage which declines with the period of search arises if one allows the job-searcher to be liquidity-constrained, for example, by an inability to borrow in the official credit market (see Mortensen, 1986, pp. 859–61).
9. However, those interested in such further issues as the determination of quits, the extent of on-the-job search, and the like, can find useful surveys in both Mortensen (1986) and McKenna (1987).
10. In the case where the reservation wage varies with the duration of search, through the existence of a finite horizon perhaps, the distribution of completed spells of search is given by

    $$\Omega(t) = 1 - \exp\,(-\int_0^t \phi\,(\tau)\,\mathrm{d}\tau), \text{ where } \phi(t) = \lambda[1 - F(w_t^*)]$$

    In the case where the reservation wage declines with search duration, $\phi'(t) > 0$ and the escape rate is said to display positive time dependence.
11. See also Narendranathan *et al.* (1985).

Chapter 13

Wage Inflation

The Phillips curve
Lipsey's theory of the Phillips curve
Some subsequent developments
Cost push or demand pull?
Policy implications for wage and price inflation
The disappearing Phillips curve
The expectations-augmented Phillips curve
The natural rate hypothesis
Adaptive and rational expectations
Some recent developments

In this chapter we consider the forces that determine the rate of increase in the level of money wages or *wage inflation*. This is a topic of long-standing interest to both labour economist and macroeconomists alike and we begin this chapter by reviewing the important early work of Phillips (1958) which to this day still occupies a pivotal role in the literature. After discussing this model we move on to consider a range of more recent developments regarding the determinants of the rate of wage inflation.

The Phillips curve

In 1958 A. W. Phillips (then at the London School of Economics) published a paper which quickly became a focal point in the study of wage inflation. The principal finding to emerge from Phillips's study was the existence of a *stable, inverse and non-linear* relationship between the rate of change of money wage rates ($\dot{w}$) and the unemployment rate (u) in the UK between 1861 and 1957.[1] This inverse relationship became known as the *Phillips curve* and it is shown as **Figure 13.1.**[2]

Phillips's basic argument was demand pull in nature. It was that excess demand in the labour market is the triggering force of wage inflation and the factor that determines its speed. Phillips argued that the extent of excess demand in the labour market can be proxied by the percentage of the labour force that is unemployed, and he interpreted his findings as supporting the hypothesis that excess demand pressure in the labour market determines the rate of wage inflation. The argument underlying the hypothesised relation between excess labour demand and

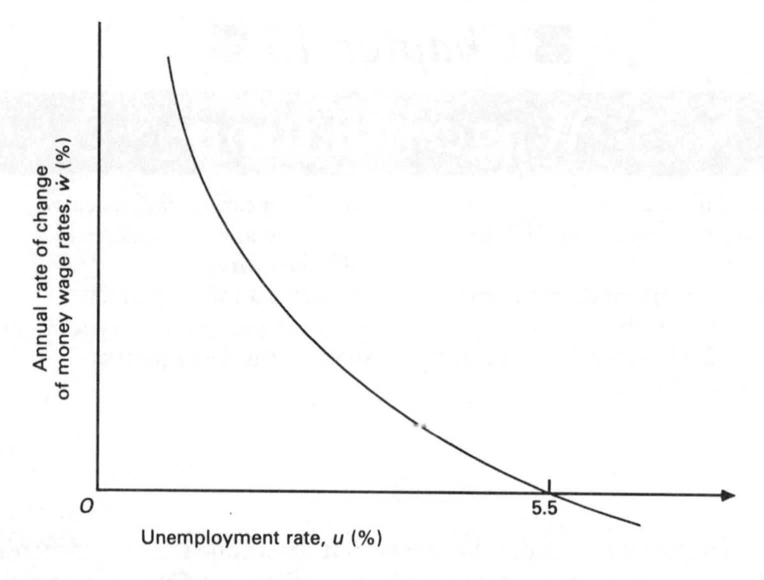

Figure 13.1 ***The Phillips curve***

wage inflation is derived from a straightforward application of traditional price theory to the perfectly competitive labour market.

Consider the competitive labour market shown in **Figure 13.2.** The equilibrium wage or price of labour is w_e, given by the point where the labour demand and supply curves intersect. At wages above w_e there is an excess of labour supply over demand, while for wages below w_e there is an excess demand for labour. If the wage is below equilibrium at, say, w_1 (because this was an equilibrium wage in the previous period perhaps), there will be excess demand for labour equal to *cd*, and there will accordingly be a tendency for wages to rise from this disequilibrium level towards the equilibrium wage w_e, as employers bid up money wages in order to attract relatively scarce labour. In addition, it is usual to assume that the speed with which the wage rate converges on the equilibrium value is greater the larger is the excess demand for labour. Conversely, at wages above equilibrium there will be an excess supply of labour (equal, for example, to *ab* at wage w_2) and a resulting tendency for wages to fall towards equilibrium, with the speed of adjustment towards equilibrium being greater the larger is the excess of labour supply over demand.

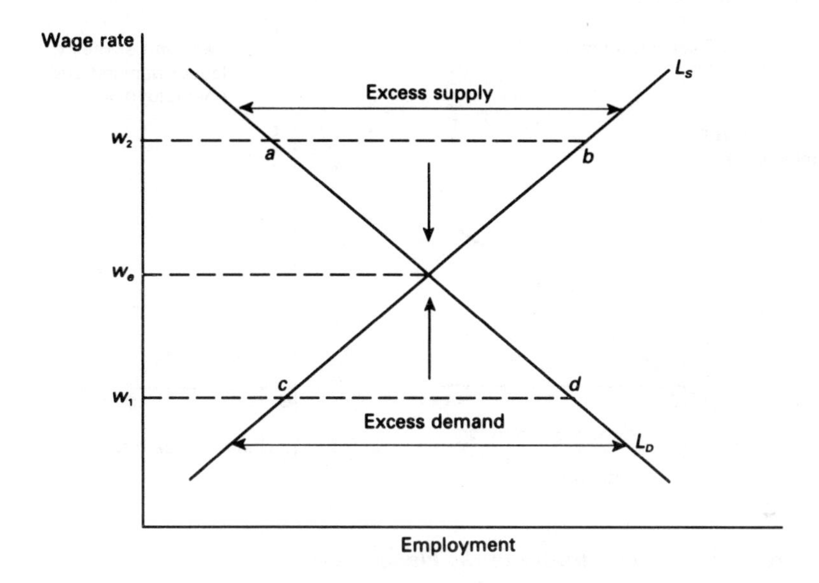

Figure 13.2 ***Wage adjustment and the labour market***

■ Lipsey's theory of the Phillips curve

While the existence of an inverse relationship between inflation and unemployment was not a new discovery, with Chicago economists claiming that Irving Fisher had discovered the Phillips curve in 1926 (see Fisher, 1926), Phillips's findings quickly attracted considerable interest. In a particularly important development of Phillips's analysis Lipsey (1960) sought to provide a sound theoretical basis for the statistical relation observed by Phillips. Lipsey explicitly considered the proxy-taking assumptions of Phillips's analysis and argued that the observed inverse relation between wage inflation and unemployment derived from the *two* separate behavioural relations shown in **Figure 13.3.** These relations refer to a single *micro* labour market. The first illustrates a positive relation between the rate of money wage change and the magnitude of excess demand for labour, and the second illustrates an inverse non-linear relation between excess labour demand and unemployment.

Lipsey assumed that the rate at which the wage level rises during any period is positively related to the proportionate excess demand for labour, that is, the greater is the proportionate excess demand for labour the more rapid is the adjustment towards the equilibrium wage level. Denoting the quantities of labour demanded and supplied by L_D and L_S respectively, we can write this relation or *reaction function* as

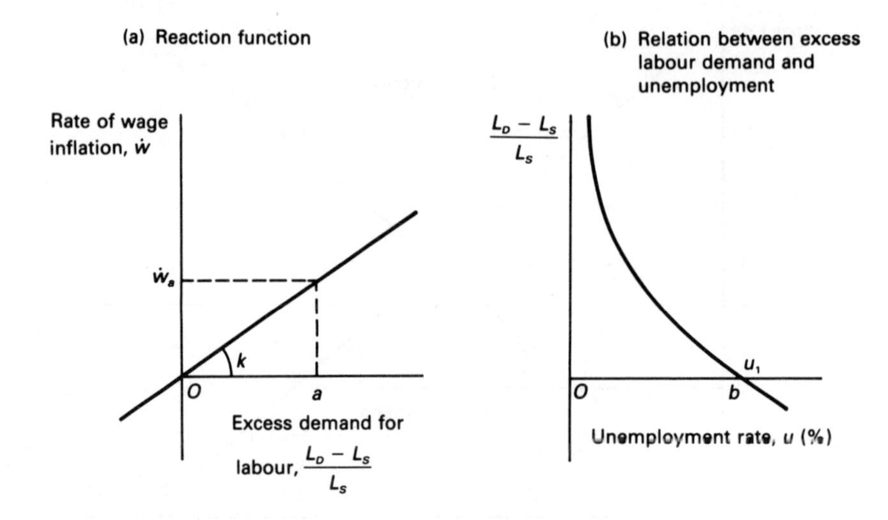

Figure 13.3 ***Lipsey's theory of the Phillips curve***

$$\dot{w} = f\left(\frac{L_D - L_S}{L_S}\right)$$

where $f' > 0$, or, adopting Lipsey's assumption of linearity,

$$\dot{w} = k\left(\frac{L_D - L_S}{L_S}\right)$$

where k is some positive constant. This reaction function is shown in **Figure 13.3(a)** by the straight line with slope k passing through the origin. At the origin, excess demand is zero and the money wage is at its equilibrium level (w_e in **Figure 13.2**), so that $\dot{w} = 0$. To the right of the origin there is positive excess demand for labour (that is, the wage is below its equilibrium level of w_e), so that money wages are rising, while to the left of the origin there is a negative excess demand (or an excess supply) of labour, with the consequence that money wages are falling. For example, if the level of excess demand were a, wages would increase at the rate $\dot{w}_a$ ($= ka$).

Because the excess demand for labour is *not* directly observable, it is necessary to select an appropriate proxy variable for purposes of testing the wage inflation–excess demand hypothesis. With this objective in mind, Lipsey examined the relation between the excess demand for labour and the unemployment rate and assumed that this will be negative and non-linear, as shown in **Figure 13.3(b)**. The negative slope of this relationship reflects the assumption that the higher is the level of excess demand for labour the lower is the level of unemployment. When excess demand for labour is zero, the labour market is in equilibrium (at wage w_e in Figure 13.2), but we cannot infer from this the absence of unemployment; rather, we can infer that the number of job vacancies equals the number of job-seekers. In a given labour market the demand for labour comprises the sum of two components: the number of workers employed (say E) and the number of vacancies that employers are unable to fill (denoted by V), while the supply of labour is likewise given by the sum of the numbers of workers actually in employment and the numbers searching for employment (that is, the unemployed, denoted by U). The labour market will be in equilibrium when the demand for labour (L_D) equals the supply of labour (L_S), that is, when

$$L_D = E + V = L_S = E + U$$

or when

$$V = U$$

The unemployed compatible with zero excess demand (that is, with equilibrium in the individual labour market) is termed *frictional unemployment*, and this is shown by rate u_f in **Figure 13.3(b)**. As we have already seen in Chapter 12, frictional unemployment arises because the process of matching unfilled vacancies with unemployed workers is not instantaneous.

Lipsey argued that the unemployment–excess demand relation will be negatively sloped to the left of point b. This is because an increase in excess demand means that jobs will become easier to find and that less time will therefore be taken in moving between jobs. Accordingly an increase in excess demand will reduce u, provided that there is not a completely offsetting increase in the number of persons moving between jobs.[3] Lipsey argued that this relation will be non-linear to the left of point b, because, while positive excess demand for labour will decrease the unemployment rate below the frictional level (u_f), it can never fall below zero however high is the level of excess demand. Consequently, he assumed that, as excess labour demand increases, u approaches zero, or some small positive value, asymptotically.

Combining the two relations shown in **Figure 13.3**, Lipsey obtained a Phillips curve of the form shown in **Figure 13.1** for a representative individual micro labour market.[4] The aggregate Phillips curve is derived by aggregation of the individual curves, and Lipsey showed that the dispersion of aggregate unemployment between the individual micro labour markets determines the position of the aggregate Phillips curve.

Some subsequent developments

The publication of both Phillips's (1958) original article and Lipsey's (1960) subsequent analysis attracted considerable international interest. Within a short space of time, numerous other investigators began searching data relating to other countries, time periods and levels of aggregation for the existence of Phillips-type relationships. This activity led rapidly to the emergence of a substantial body of empirical evidence showing the existence of inverse wage inflation versus unemployment relationships in a wide range of countries. In this literature, Phillips's original relationship has been modified in a number of ways. Its functional form has been simplified, variables have been added to the original specification for a number of purposes (including, as we shall see below, the representation of inflationary expectations), more adequate proxies for excess demand for labour than the rate of unemployment have been sought, and additional equations have been specified in order to render Phillips's wage equation part of a simultaneous equation model explaining price as well as wage inflation. This literature is well-surveyed by Goldstein (1972), Gordon (1975), Frisch (1977) and Santomero and Seater (1978).

Cost push or demand pull?

The demand pull/cost push distinction is a well-known one in the analysis of inflation. The *demand pull* school sees inflation as being initially triggered by the emergence of excess demand in the product market at the ruling price level. This results in an increase in the general level of product prices, which subsequently leads to an increase in the conditions of derived demand for labour (that is, to a rightward shift in the labour demand or marginal revenue product curve). This shift gives rise to excess demand for labour at the prevailing wage rate, with the result that money wages tend to increase. In short, the demand pull school sees inflation as arising initially from forces operating on the demand side of the product market, with feedback effects on the labour market. Notice that the initial excess demand in the goods market can arise in either the *Keynesian* inflationary-gap manner or the *monetarist* manner from too few goods being chased by too much money.

In contrast, the *cost push* school sees the reverse causal chain, with the initial inflationary push or 'shock' emanating from the supply side in the form of increased import prices, greater profit margins or higher wage costs, forced up perhaps by the actions of monopolistic trade unions. These increased costs, given the assumption of mark-up pricing (according to which prices are set by applying a mark-up factor to unit production costs), subsequently feed into the general level of prices, as producers pass them on in the form of higher product prices. Particular attention is often placed on so called *wage push inflation*, where, in its most extreme form, unions are assumed to be able to push up money wages *irrespective* of the level of excess demand in the labour market. Less extreme is the so-called *bargaining-power approach*, which sees a union's ability to influence money wages as being determined by various economic conditions, such as the pressure of excess demand in the labour market. While this variant of the cost push hypothesis, like the demand pull model, predicts that the pace of wage inflation will be positively related to the pressure of excess demand in the labour market, it offers very different explanations of the underlying mechanisms involved. The bargaining power approach sees wages as being determined as the outcome of a collective-bargaining process of the sort considered in Chapter 11, whereas the demand pull formulation sees wages as being determined by supply and demand adjustments in a competitive labour market.

Phillips interpreted his findings as providing strong support for the demand pull hypothesis, essentially on the grounds that the existence of a significant inverse relation between wage inflation and unemployment refutes the cost push hypothesis in its extreme form where the role of excess labour demand is ignored. However, as Lipsey (1960) was quick to point out, the existence of a Phillips curve is perfectly consistent with the less extreme bargaining-power type of cost push theory, according to which the wage rate is determined by some process of collective bargaining, the outcome of which is influenced by the pressure of excess labour demand.

Policy implications for wage and price inflation

The discovery of the Phillips curve attracted considerable interest from the policy viewpoint, primarily because of the implications of the relationship for price inflation. The existence of a significant inverse relationship between the rate of wage inflation and the unemployment rate appeared to present policy-makers with a *trade-off* (that is, less wage inflation at the cost of higher unemployment, or lower unemployment but only at the cost of higher wage inflation). Given the linkage which exists between fluctuations in wages and fluctuations in the prices of goods and services, the existence of the Phillips relation appeared to provide policy-makers with a similar trade-off (or 'menu' of policy choices) between price inflation on the one hand and unemployment on the other.

In order to consider the implications of the Phillips curve for policy decisions regarding the rate of price inflation, it is necessary to make certain assumptions regarding the influence of wages upon prices. The simplest assumptions to make are: first, that average productivity (or output per man-hour) is growing at some constant proportional rate; and second, that prices are set by firms applying a constant mark-up on unit labour costs. On the basis of these two assumptions, the rate of price inflation (say $\dot{p}$) equals the difference between the rates of growth of money wages ($\dot{w}$) and labour productivity (say $\dot{q}$).[5] For each value of the unemployment rate we can therefore, given the mark-up pricing assumption, calculate the rate of price inflation ($\dot{p}$) by merely subtracting the rate of productivity growth ($\dot{q}$) from the rate of wage inflation ($\dot{w}$) given by the Phillips curve. Diagrammatically, we simply transform the Phillips curve to show the relation between the rate of price inflation and unemployment by merely displacing downwards the original Phillips curve by a vertical distance equivalent to the (assumed) constant rate of productivity growth. In **Figure 13.4** curve *WW* denotes the Phillips trade-off between wage inflation and unemployment, and the curve *PP* shows the corresponding relation between the rate of price inflation and the unemployment rate, on the assumption that labour productivity is growing at the rate of 2.5 per cent per year.[6] Phillips's own estimates implied that a zero rate of wage inflation was consistent with an unemployment rate of just under 5.5 per cent (see **Figure 13.1**). With productivity rising at 2.5 per cent per year these estimates imply that a zero rate of price inflation was attainable with an unemployment rate of 2.1 per cent. This is illustrated by the point at which *PP* intersects the horizontal axis.

As can be seen from **Figure 13.4** a productivity growth rate ($\dot{q}$) equal to 2.5 per cent per year allows wages to rise at the same rate with prices remaining stable. Curve *PP* shows that a reduction in the rate of unemployment below 2.1 per cent can only be achieved by sacrificing price stability, while a decreasing price level can only be achieved at the cost of an increase in the unemployment rate above 2.1 per cent. Curve *PP* therefore shows combinations of u and $\dot{p}$ that can be attained by varying the level of aggregate demand and can be thought of as a *constraint* facing government policy-makers. While combinations of price inflation and unemployment lying on curve *PP* are attainable, those represented by points lying below the curve (signifying lower rates of both unemployment and inflation) are not.

The problems faced by policy-makers in selecting the optimum

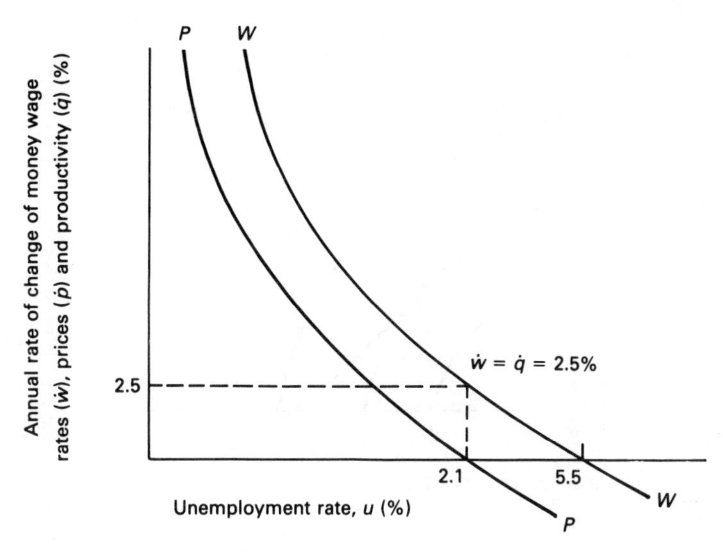

Figure 13.4 ***Wage and price inflation***

inflation–unemployment combination can be analysed with the aid of the standard techniques of indifference curve analysis. Consider the case where the policy-maker is prepared to trade some increase in the rate of inflation in return for a reduction in the unemployment rate, and assume that he or she possesses a preference function that gives rise to a set of indifference curves that are ordered in such a way that higher utility is attained by moving towards the origin. Since both inflation and unemployment are *bads* (that is, undesirables) as opposed to goods, it is usual to assume these indifference curves to be *concave* to the origin as shown in **Figure 13.5**.

Assuming that policy-makers are utility-maximisers, they will select the inflation–unemployment combination represented by point *A* in **Figure 13.5**, since at that point the trade-off curve *PP* is tangential to an indifference curve. Point *A* denotes the policy-makers' optimum inflation–unemployment combination and indicates the point at which aggregate demand policies will be aimed. If the initial position on *PP* were, say, point *R*, the reduction in the unemployment rate below *R* to its optimal level u_0 is achieved at the cost of an inflation rate of $\dot{p}_0$: a cost that is acceptable to the policy-makers, given their preference function.

■ The disappearing Phillips curve

The relationship that Phillips discovered in 1958 appeared to have remained stable as far back as the data went, for nearly a century.

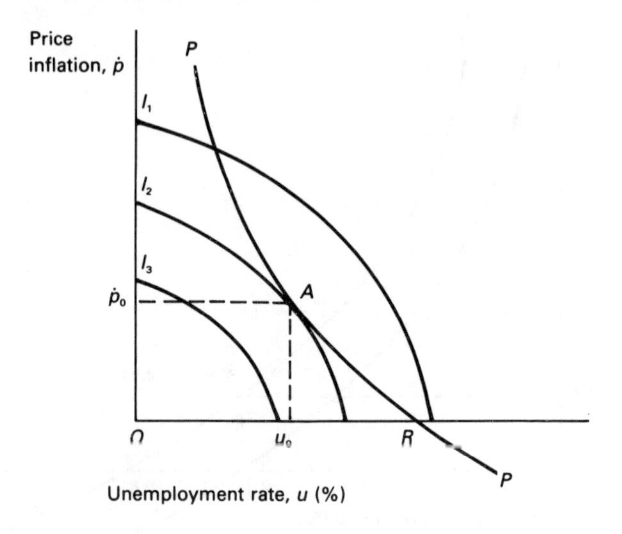

Figure 13.5 ***Inflation–unemployment trade-off and government policy***

However, from about 1967 onwards the UK Phillips curve (like those of the other major industrialised countries) was observed to break down and lose its explanatory power. Contrary to the prediction of the Phillips curve the UK experience, like that of much of the rest of the industrialised world, over most of the period since the late of 1960s was one of high rates of wage and price inflation accompanied by a *high* rate of unemployment. This state of affairs became known as *stagflation*. Comparison of the observed rates of UK wage inflation over the postwar period with the rates predicted by Phillips's own estimates, conditional on the observed unemployment rates, shows that there was a marked tendency from 1967 onwards for the Phillips curve to *underpredict* the actual percentage change in money wages. Diagrammatically, the post-1967 breakdown of the Phillips curve took the form of a rightward shift (or shifts) in the relationship, illustrating that a given rate of unemployment appears to have become associated with a higher, or rising, rate of wage inflation.

There have been a number of explanations put forward to explain this shift in what appeared, prior to the late 1960s, to rank amongst the stablest of economic relations. Such explanations fall into two main categories. First, there are those which see the instability as arising from shifts in one or both of the relations underpinning the Phillips curve (namely, the reaction function and the excess labour demand versus unemployment relation). Second there are explanations which follow from the argument that the Phillips's curve is *misspecified* in the sense that its dependent variable should be the rate of change of *real* wages and not money (or nominal) wages.

Unemployment as an index of excess demand for labour

The possibility that the Phillips curve became unstable as a consequence of shifts in the reaction function brought about by the implementation of the prices and incomes policies which were fashionable in the late 1960s and the 1970s was widely discussed at the time and this literature is surveyed by Sapsford (1981, pp. 156–62). A number of other investigators sought to rescue the Phillips curve by arguing that the underlying relationship between the rate of wage inflation and the extent of excess demand in the labour market (that is, the reaction function) still held good and that what had happened was, in fact, some form of change in the relation between the excess demand for labour and the rate of unemployment, which meant that unemployment ceased to be an adequate indicator of the level of excess demand for labour. As we saw above, the demand for labour in a particular labour market is equal to the sum of the numbers employed (E) and the number of unfilled vacancies (V), while the supply of labour is given by the sum of numbers employed and the numbers of job-seekers (that is, the unemployed, U). Therefore, the excess demand for labour, $(L_D - L_S)/L_S$, may be written as follows:

$$\frac{(E + V) - (E + U)}{E + U} = \frac{V - U}{E + U} = v - u$$

where v and u denote the *rates* of unfilled vacancies and unemployment respectively, where each is expressed as a proportion of the labour force.

From this expression we see that a direct measure of excess demand for labour is given by the difference between the rates of unfilled vacancies and unemployment. However, since data series on unfilled vacancies are generally thought to be unreliable, because many vacancies are simply not notified to official agencies and hence go unrecorded, Phillips, Lipsey and the majority of subsequent investigators took the aggregate unemployment rate (or some transformation of this) as a proxy for the excess demand for labour. However, if there exists a stable relationship between the rates of unemployment and unfilled vacancies, their difference can be reduced to a function of the unemployment rate only (Hansen, 1970), and this function of the unemployment rate can be used as an alternative measure with which to proxy excess labour demand.

However, while such a stable relationship between the unemployment rate and the rate of unfilled vacancies did exist in the UK it too became highly unstable in late 1966. After this date it began to move rightwards on the *u/v* plane, indicating that a given rate of vacancies became associated with a higher rate of unemployment. While a number of competing explanations of this shift in the unemployment vacancies relation were been put forward at the time (see Sapsford, 1981, pp. 180–5, for a survey), what is of relevance here is that, because of this shift, there occurred an outward movement in the relation between excess demand and unemployment. According to this line of argument this movement in turn gave rise to an outward movement in the Phillips curve, even though there had been no change in the underlying reaction function relating wage inflation to the level of excess labour demand.[7]

■ The expectations-augmented Phillips curve

□ *Friedman's theory*

The second class of explanation offered for the instability of the Phillips curve is attributed principally to Friedman (see, for example, Friedman, 1968), although a closely related analysis was presented by Phelps (1968). The essence of Friedman's argument is that the Phillips curve, relating the rate of change of *money wages* to the unemployment rate as a proxy of excess labour demand, is incorrectly specified, because it is the *real wage* and not the money wage that responds to disequilibrium in the labour market. During periods when prices are changing, these two concepts are not interchangeable, and so it is argued that it is necessary to introduce the rate of price inflation into the analysis. Further, since money wages are typically fixed on a discrete rather than a continuous basis, it follows that it is not the current price level that is important when money wages are being fixed but the price level that is *expected* to prevail for the duration of the agreement. It is therefore argued that it is necessary to introduce the expected rate of price inflation into the analysis.

In the interest of simplicity, let us assume that labour productivity remains unchanged, so that, given the assumption of a constant mark-up pricing policy by firms, the rate of price inflation in any period ($\dot{p}_t$) will equal the rate of wage inflation ($\dot{w}_t$). Friedman assumed that neither employers nor employees suffer from money illusion and argued that expected or anticipated changes in the price level will be *fully* incorporated into money wage settlements, with the consequence that the rate of change of money wages will be a function of both the unemployment rate (in Phillips curve manner) and the anticipated rate of change of prices. Thus, with an additional assumption about the formation of expectations regarding the rate of price inflation, we can summarise Friedman's model by the following three-equation system:

$$\dot{w}_t = f(u_t) + \alpha \dot{p}_t^e \tag{13.1}$$

$$\dot{p}_t = \dot{w}_t \tag{13.2}$$

$$\dot{p}_t^e = \dot{p}_{t-1} \tag{13.3}$$

where $\dot{p}_t^e$ is the expected rate of price inflation in period t.

Equation (13.1) became known as the ***expectations-augmented Phillips curve***, and this says that the rate of change of money wages is equal to the sum of some function, $f(u_t)$, of the current rate of unemployment (that is, the original Phillips relation) plus some proportion (α) of the expected rate of change of prices. Friedman's hypothesis that there is full compensation for expected inflation implies that α enters this equation with a value of one, while Phillips's original relation implied a value of α equal to zero. If there is only partial adjustment for expected inflation, with people perhaps subject to some degree of money illusion, then $0 < \alpha < 1$.

Equation (13.2) follows from the assumption of zero productivity, growth and mark-up pricing and states that in any period the rate of price inflation will be equal to the rate of wage inflation. If, however, productivity were growing at some constant proportional rate (say $\dot{q}_t$), we would simply replace equation (13.2) with the following equation

$$\dot{p}_t = \dot{w}_t - \dot{q}_t \tag{13.4}$$

Equation (13.3) concerns the formation of expectations regarding the rate of price inflation and represents what is perhaps the simplest possible hypothesis; namely, that the expected rate of price inflation in period t is equal to the actual rate that occurred in period $(t - 1)$. Subsequent developments in the literature have shown that the nature of the mechanism generating inflationary expectations is extremely important. We return to this issue below.

□ *A long-run trade-off?*

Friedman's theory of the Phillips curve can be demonstrated in this simple case represented by (13.1)–(13.3) by setting α in equation (13.1) equal to one. If the expected rate of inflation is zero, equation (13.1)

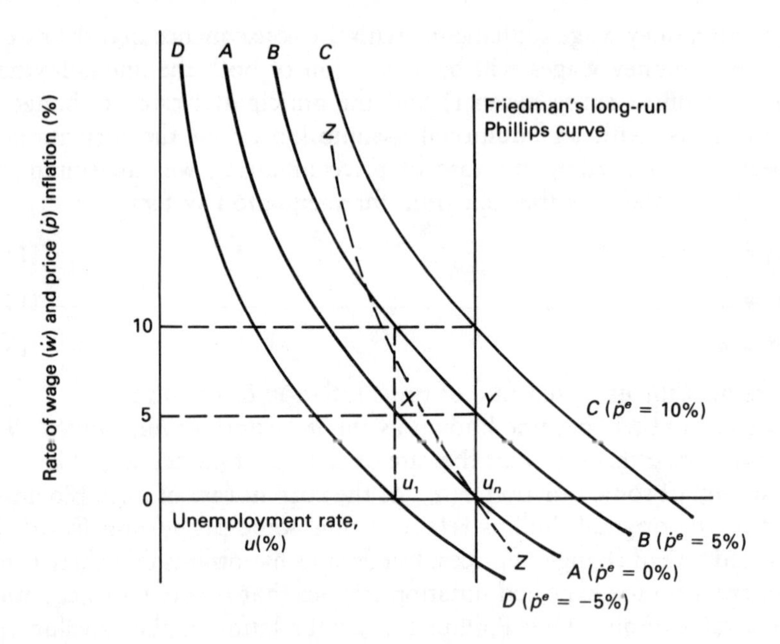

Figure 13.6 ***Expectations-augmented Phillips curve***

reduces to the original Phillips curve, where the rate of wage inflation is a function of *only* the unemployment rate; this is shown by curve *AA* in **Figure 13.6.** Suppose now that the expected rate of inflation ($\dot{p}^e$) is equal to some positive value (say 5 per cent). Then, according to equation (13.1), the rate of wage inflation corresponding to any particular value of the unemployment rate will equal that given by the zero expected-inflation Phillips curve, plus the anticipated rate of price inflation of 5 per cent. For example, if the unemployment rate were equal to u_n in **Figure 13.6,** there would be zero wage inflation (and by our assumptions zero price inflation) in the case where $\dot{p}^e = 0$. However, in the case where the anticipated rate of price inflation equals 5 per cent, the rate of inflation corresponding to unemployment of u_n will be 5 per cent, because according to equation (13.1) with α set equal to unity, there will be full compensation in current wage changes for expected inflation. Similarly, for any other rate of unemployment, the rate of inflation will equal that shown by the zero expected-inflation Phillips curve, plus the full 5 per cent expected inflation rate. Therefore, an anticipated inflation rate of 5 per cent gives rise to the new Phillips curve shown by *BB* in **Figure 13.6,** which lies above the zero expectations curve by a vertical distance equal to the 5 per cent expected inflation rate. If the expected rate of inflation were 10 per cent, we would obtain the curve *CC*, while an expected fall in the price level at a rate of 5 per cent would give rise to curve *DD*, which lies below the original zero expectations curve by a vertical distance equal to 5 per cent. Thus, according to Friedman's theory we obtain not a single Phillips curve but a whole family of Phillips curves, with one corresponding to each expected inflation rate.

Consider now the case where the expected rate of inflation in the initial period (t) equals zero, so that curve *AA* in **Figure 13.6** applies, and suppose that the initial rate of unemployment equals u_n and that the government, by either fiscal and/or monetary means, seeks to achieve and maintain a rate of unemployment below u_n. Curve *AA* shows the unemployment–inflation trade-off that applies in period t, and from this we see that the consequence of a policy designed to reduce the rate of unemployment below u_n to, say, u_1 is an increase in the inflation rate in the first period from zero to 5 per cent. However, the story does not end here, because the current period's inflation will influence the next period's expected rate of price inflation, which will in turn influence next period's rates of wage and price inflation, and so on.

□ *Wage–price dynamics*

The dynamic implications of Friedman's theory can be illustrated by considering equations (13.1) to (13.3). In our example the expected rate of price inflation in the initial period ($\dot{p}^e_t$) equals zero, and with an unemployment rate of u_1, money wages and (from equation (13.2)) prices increase at a rate of 5 per cent. Consider now what happens in the following period if unemployment is held at u_1. Equation (13.3) shows that the rate of price inflation expected in period ($t + 1$) is equal to the actual rate of the previous period (that is, 5 per cent), and so in this period, with $\dot{p}^e_{t+1} = 5$ per cent, the Phillips curve *BB* in **Figure 13.6** becomes applicable. According to (13.1), the rate of wage inflation during this period equals the rate shown by the zero expected-inflation curve *AA* (that is, 5 per cent) plus the rate of price inflation expected during this period (that is, 5 per cent), giving a total rate of growth of money wages during this period ($\dot{w}_{t+1}$) equal to 10 per cent. According to (13.2), prices rise during this period at a rate of 10 per cent, so that (from (13.3)) the expected rate of inflation in the following period ($t + 2$) rises to 10 per cent, giving rise to wage and price inflation during period ($t + 2$) of 15 per cent. So the process continues, with an ever increasing rate of inflation: 5 per cent in the initial period, 10 per cent in the second period, 15 per cent in the third, and so on.

The preceding argument predicts that any policy that holds the unemployment rate permanently below u_n will result in an ever *accelerating* inflation. Conversely, if the government were to keep the unemployment rate above u_n, the process would operate in reverse and result in the price level falling at an ever increasing rate. In short, Friedman's theory predicts that the only way in which unemployment can be permanently held below u_n is by an ever accelerating inflation rate.

Notice that, if the government were to implement policies in the second period to hold the inflation rate constant at 5 per cent (in preference to holding the unemployment rate at u_1 at the expense of a continually increasing inflation rate), the expected rate of inflation would, according to (13.3), turn out to be equal to the actual rate and the economy would revert to the original unemployment rate (u_n), but with an inflation rate of 5 per cent (at point *Y* on curve *BB* in **Figure 13.6**) as compared with the original zero inflation rate at this same level of unemployment. Therefore, in this case Friedman's theory predicts that the only consequence of the initial attempt to decrease unemployment below u_n is an inflation rate of 5 per cent.[8]

□ *No long-run trade-off*

Friedman's theory predicts that there is no trade-off between steady inflation and unemployment in the long run. What we have instead is a whole series of short-run Phillips unemployment–inflation trade-offs, each corresponding to a different expected rate of inflation, but with only one unemployment rate (u_n in **Figure 13.6**) being consistent with a constant rate of inflation.

Notice that the unemployment rate u_n is compatible not only with a zero rate of inflation but also with any constant rate. If the expected rate of inflation were, say, *x* per cent and the unemployment rate were equal to u_n, the actual rate of price inflation would turn out to be equal to the expected rate of *x* per cent. This is because unemployment of u_n would result in a zero rate of wage inflation in the case where the expected rate of price inflation was zero, so that, with expected price inflation of *x* per cent, the rate of wage inflation would be equal simply to *x* per cent. In terms of equation (13.1), the term $f(u)$ represents the original Phillips or zero expected-inflation relation (curve *AA* in **Figure 13.6**), and its intercept on the unemployment axis shows that, with a zero expected rate of price inflation, an unemployment rate of u_n results in zero wage inflation. Using (13.1) and (13.2) we see, since $f(u_n) = 0$, and given the assumption $\alpha = 1$, that

$$\dot{w}_t = \dot{p}_t^e = \dot{p}_t$$

when the unemployment rate equals u_n. This shows that at this unemployment rate the actual rates of price and wage inflation are equal to the expected rate of price inflation of x per cent. Because inflationary expectations have turned out to be correct (that is, because inflation has been perfectly anticipated), they remain unchanged in the next period at x per cent (from equation (13.3)), so that in this as in each subsequent period the rates of wage and price inflation remain constant at x per cent, giving rise to a long-run equilibrium position of a constant x per cent inflation at the unemployment rate u_n.

Since the argument applies for any value of expected rate of inflation, we see that long-run equilibrium can be established at the unemployment rate u_n with any constant actual rate of inflation, the value of which will be equal to the expected rate of price inflation. The locus of these possible equilibrium points gives rise to a *vertical* long-run Phillips curve, as shown in **Figure 13.6**. Friedman's analysis therefore predicts that in the long run, when the actual rate of inflation is equal to the expected rate, the inflation–unemployment trade-off vanishes, and the Phillips curve becomes vertical.

□ *The natural rate of unemployment*

The rate of unemployment that is compatible with any constant, as distinct from varying, rate of inflation (u_n in **Figure 13.6**) was termed the *natural rate of unemployment* by Friedman. This is the unemployment rate that corresponds to the level of aggregate demand at which there is neither upward nor downward pressure on the rate of inflation. Friedman defined the natural rate of unemployment as that ground out by the solution of a system of general equilibrium equations that accurately describe the structure and imperfections of all labour and commodity markets (1968, p. 8). In terms of the labour market, the natural rate of unemployment is that present when labour demand and labour supply, both expressed as functions of the real wage, are in equilibrium (Friedman, 1975, pp. 13–20).

Friedman argued that the natural rate's magnitude will be determined independently of the expected rate of inflation by existing real conditions in the labour market, principally the existence of *frictions* (or obstacles) of various forms, including the institutional structure of labor markets, which taken together determine the speed of adjustment of supply to demand in the labour market. The factors that determine the natural rate of unemployment include the extent to which the geographical distribution of the unemployed is matched to that of job vacancies, the efficiency of labor market institutions and the way in which the skill mix required to fill vacancies is matched by that of the unemployed. It is therefore influenced by such things as the educational characteristics of the labour force and the presence of barriers to geographical mobility of labour and jobs as well as barriers to the acquisitions of new skills. Friedman stressed that the natural unemployment rate is not some irreducible minimum of unemployment; rather, it is the rate that is consistent with existing real conditions in the labour market, and it can be lowered by removing obstacles in the labour market (that is, by reducing frictions) and increased by introducing additional obstacles.

In essence, Friedman sees the natural rate of unemployment as that rate which, given all the imperfections and institutions of the market, will prevail in equilibrium. Nowadays the unemployment rate u_n in **Figure 13.6** is frequently alternatively termed the 'non-accelerating inflation rate of unemployment' (or NAIRU). The relationship between Friedman's natural rate concept and the NAIRU is considered in the following chapter.

The natural rate hypothesis

The properties of Friedman's expectations-augmented Phillips curve model can be conveniently summarised by reparameterising expression (13.1) in the following manner. First, assume *linearity* and rewrite (13.1), with time subscripts dropped, as follows:

$$\dot{w} = \alpha_0 - \alpha_1 u + \alpha_2 \dot{p}^e \tag{13.5}$$

where the parameters α_0 and α_1 are both positive and the parameter α_2, according to Friedman's argument that there is no money illusion, is equal to one. Second, setting $\dot{p}^e = 0$ (so that the linearised version of Phillips curve *AA* in **Figure 13.6** applies) it follows that the unemployment rate corresponding to zero wage inflation is u_n. Therefore, setting $\dot{w} = 0$ in (13.5) and rearranging we obtain the following expression for the natural rate: $u_n = \alpha_0/\alpha_1$. Substituting $\alpha_0 = \alpha_1 u_n$ into (13.5) and rearranging we obtain the following reparameterised version of the expectations-augmented Phillips curve model:

$$\dot{w} = -\alpha_1(u - u_n) + \alpha_2 \dot{p}^e \tag{13.6}$$

In geometric terms, all that we have, in essence, done in moving to version (13.6) from version (13.1) is to shift the origin of measurement on the unemployment axis from zero to the natural rate. Expression (13.6) says that the rate of wage inflation is negatively related to the extent to which the actual rate of unemployment *diverges* from the natural rate, and positively related to the expected rate of price inflation.

As we have seen, long-run equilibrium in this model requires that actual inflation is equal to expected inflation ($\dot{p} = \dot{p}^e$). If we add to this assumption (13.4) of mark-up pricing with a given growth in labour productivity ($\dot{p} = \dot{w} - \dot{q}$) equation (13.6) may be rewritten as follows:

$$\dot{w} = -\alpha_1(u - u_n) + \alpha_2(\dot{w} - \dot{q})$$

from which we obtain

$$\dot{w} = \frac{-\alpha_1 u}{1 - \alpha_2} + \frac{(\alpha_1 u_n - \alpha_2 \dot{q})}{1 - \alpha_2}$$

Differentiating this expression, with u_n treated as a constant, we see that

$$\frac{d\dot{w}}{du} = \frac{-\alpha_1}{1 - \alpha_2} \qquad (13.7)$$

If α_2 is unity (indicating that expected inflation is fully incorporated into current money wage changes) as claimed by Friedman we see from (13.7) that no trade-off exists in the long run; with the consequence that the long-run Phillips curve becomes a vertical line at a value of unemployment equal to the natural rate. If $\alpha_2 = 0$, as in Phillips's own formulation, the trade-off is fully reinstated. In this case there is only one curve (*AA* in **Figure 13.6**) regardless of price expectations. Values of α_2 between zero and one, implying that there is partial but not complete compensation for inflationary expectations, give rise to an intermediate trade-off. This intermediate case generates a long-run Phillips curve such as *ZZ* in **Figure 13.6.** Although more steeply sloped than the short-run curves, *ZZ* is not vertical which means that in this intermediate case there is some trade-off between inflation and unemployment in the long run.

□ *Formation of expectations*

Clearly the size of α_2, the coefficient of the price expectations term, is of central importance to the analysis and much empirical energy has been devoted to estimating its value. We have so far said nothing about the mechanisms according to which inflationary expectations might be generated. It was common in early empirical studies to assume that expectations are generated according to the *adaptive expectations mechanism.* According to this view, expectations are updated each period by some fraction (known as the expectations coefficient) of the discrepancy between last period's actual and expected rates of inflation. The adaptive expectations hypothesis may be written as follows, where λ denotes the expectations coefficient:

$$\dot{p}_t^e - \dot{p}_{t-1}^e = \lambda\,(\dot{p}_{t-1} - \dot{p}_{t-1}^e) \tag{13.8}$$

where $0 \leqslant \lambda \leqslant 1$.

As we shall see below, the assumption that inflationary expectations are generated according to this scheme is equivalent to assuming that the current expected rate of inflation is a *geometrically* declining weighted average of all previous actual values of the inflation rate. As we will see in the following section, the adaptive expectations hypothesis is not without its problems. However, we shall accept it for the moment and consider the three equation systems made up of Friedman's expectations-augmented Phillips curve (equation (13.1) with the restriction that $\alpha = 1$ imposed), equation (13.2) (according to which $\dot{w}_t = \dot{p}_t$), and the adaptive expectations hypothesis, (13.8). Consider now the situation where the government selects its mix of fiscal and monetary policies in order to achieve some *target* unemployment rate, denoted by u^*. Substituting (13.8) into (13.1) and eliminating both $\dot{p}^e$ and $\dot{p}$ we obtain the following expression for the rate of money wage inflation.[9]

$$\dot{w}_t = f(u^*)\,\lambda + \dot{w}_{t-1} \tag{13.9}$$

Expression (13.9) may be recognised as a first-order difference equation, the solution to which (Chiang, 1984, pp. 554–5) is as follows:

$$\dot{w}_t = f(u^*)\,\lambda_t + \dot{w}_0 \tag{13.10}$$

where $\dot{w}_0$ is the given initial period's rate of wage inflation. Expression (13.10) demonstrates the central proposition of Friedman's 'no long-run trade-off' view. If u^* is chosen to be less than the natural rate (u_n) then $f(u^*)$ is *positive* and according to (13.10) the rate of wage inflation will increase for ever. Conversely, if the target rate of unemployment were set above the natural rate, $f(u^*)$ is *negative* and the rate of wage inflation will be ever declining. It is only in the case where the government sets its target rate of unemployment equal to the natural rate (so that $f(u^*) = f(u_n) = 0$) that a steady-state rate of wage inflation emerges. Notice that with the target unemployment rate equal to the natural rate, the first term on the right-hand side of (13.10) reduces to zero, indicating that in this case the steady-state rate of wage inflation is constant at $\dot{w}_0$, which may be any value, including zero.

■ Adaptive and rational expectations

The adaptive expectations hypothesis (13.8) was widely used in early empirical studies of the expectations-augmented Phillips curve. As we have seen, the basic idea of this hypothesis is that agents learn from their previous errors and adjust their current expectations in light of these. Rearranging (13.8) we obtain the following expression, which says that under adaptive expectations the current period's expected inflation rate is a weighted average of last period's expected and actual rates of inflation.

$$\dot{p}_t^e = \lambda\, \dot{p}_{t-1} + (1 - \lambda)\, \dot{p}_{t-1}^e \tag{13.11}$$

Lagging expression (13.11) by one period, substituting the resulting expression back into (13.11), and repeating this process of *backward substitution*, we obtain the following equation, which shows that the adaptive expectations hypothesis implies that the current period's expected inflation rate is a weighted average of *all* previous actual rates of inflation, with weights which decay geometrically as one goes further back in time.[10] Expression (13.12) may be conveniently rewritten using summation notation as (13.13). It is easy to show that the weights in expression (13.12) sum to one.[11]

$$\dot{p}_t^e = \lambda\, \dot{p}_{t-1} + \lambda(1 - \lambda)\, \dot{p}_{t-2} + \lambda\, (1 - \lambda)^2\, \dot{p}_{t-3} + \ldots \tag{13.12}$$

$$\dot{p}_t^e = \sum_{i=0}^{\infty} \lambda\, (1 - \lambda)^i\, \dot{p}_{t-i-1} \tag{13.13}$$

□ *Limitations of adaptive expectations*

As a hypothesis describing economic behaviour, adaptive expectations – with its basic notion that agents learn from their previous mistakes, and adjust their current behaviour in light of these – seems at first sight to be entirely reasonable. However, it suffers from at least two serious deficiencies. To illustrate the first of these, consider how inflationary expectations adjust in a world where the actual rate of inflation becomes and remains constant at some steady-state value. Denoting the steady-state inflation rate by $\dot{p}^*$ and substituting this into (13.13) we obtain the following expression:

$$\dot{p}_t^e = \dot{p}^* \sum_{i=0}^{\infty} \lambda\, (1 - \lambda)^i \tag{13.14}$$

Since the sum to infinity of the second component on the right-hand side of (13.14) is unity, we see that the expected rate of inflation ($\dot{p}_t^e$) converges upon the steady-state rate ($\dot{p}^*$) in the limit as time goes to infinity. While even moderate values of the expectations coefficient may be sufficient to ensure that convergence occurs reasonably rapidly in practice,[12] the fact that it takes agents an *infinite* period of time to adjust fully to the new circumstances is something of a problem for the adaptive expectations hypothesis. Consider now a world where the actual rate of inflation exhibits some systematic trend, either upward or downward. Under such circumstances, agents who form their expectations adaptively will be systematically wrong, and will continue to be wrong unless they change the way in which they arrive at their forecasts. For example, if the inflation rate is rising, (13.8) shows that agents will adapt their expectations in each period towards the level of actual inflation observed in the *previous* period. However, inflation in the current period is always above that in the previous period, with the consequence that expectations in the current period will inevitably fall short of actual inflation. During periods of rising inflation adaptive expectations will therefore consistently *underpredict* the actual inflation rate, with a prediction error which continually increases. By the same token, adaptive expectations persistently overpredicts the actual rate of inflation, again with an increasing error, when the actual rate is subject to a declining trend.

The second problem with the adaptive expectations hypothesis is that it assumes that agents take no notice of any information relating to the future rate of inflation other than their own past errors. This, it is argued, is unduly restrictive since it assumes that individuals are either unaware of, or choose to totally ignore, the considerable amount of information relating to the likely future rate of inflation which surrounds them in their everyday lives. This information takes various forms, ranging from publicly available forecasts of inflation produced by governments, professional forecasters and other gurus, through to information relating to variables which might reasonably be assumed to influence the inflation rate. As may be seen from (13.8), the adaptive expectations hypothesis rests on the assumption that all such information is ignored by agents in evaluating their own forecasts of inflation.

□ *Rational expectations*

In view of the above deficiencies, much recent work on wage inflation abandons the notion of adaptive expectations in favour of the hypothesis of *rational expectations*. The hypothesis of rational expectations, originally proposed by Muth (1961), has generated a vast literature since it found its way into macroeconomics in the early 1970s. Our discussion of the hypothesis will, by necessity, be confined to its implications for models of wage inflation. However, detailed surveys of the wider literature can be found in Begg (1982), Holden, Peel and Thompson (1985), Shaw (1984), and Sheffrin (1983).

The basic notion of rational expectations is delightfully simple. As we have seen, adaptive expectations is unsatisfactory as a scheme of expectation formation. Its 'backward-looking' nature will never lead agents to expect a rate of inflation outside the range of historical experience, with the consequence that adaptively generated inflationary expectations will be subject to systematic errors when the rate of inflation is subject to a persistent trend, either up or down. Since such errors will impose costs on agents, it seems reasonable to expect them to search for a more satisfactory forecasting scheme.

Enter the rational expectations school, with the argument that the only forecasting scheme which agents will not be tempted to reject in favour of some other scheme is the one with the smallest error. The scheme which satisfies this criterion is one based on the true underlying data-generating mechanism. This is the central notion of the rational expectations hypothesis: that individuals understand the economic forces at work and form their expectations in the light of this understanding. While this is a strong assumption – some would argue too strong – it overcomes the deficiency of backward-looking mechanisms such as adaptive expectations in that it assumes that individuals do not rely solely on their previous experiences when forming expectations but also take account of currently available information should they find it worthwhile to do so. Indeed, given that much relevant information is available at zero or minimal cost (for example, government forecasts, perhaps at the cost of a newspaper) it would be rather surprising if individuals in practice failed to incorporate at least some such information into their calculations.

The version of the rational expectations hypothesis described above is termed the *weak* version by Shaw (1989, p. 35); in contrast to this there is the *strong* version which follows from Muth's (1961) original exposition. To quote Muth: 'Expectations . . . tend to be distributed for the same information set, about the prediction of the theory' (1961, p. 316). According to this statement the agent's subjective forecast of the variable in question (say, the inflation rate, $\dot{p}_t$), denoted by $\dot{p}^e$, will be equal to the 'objective' mathematical expectation of $\dot{p}$, *conditional* on the available information set. The information set is assumed to include the structure of the true economic model, the values of the exogenous variables, the rules controlling government policy behaviour, and the past values of the endogenous variables. Muth's model therefore states that

$$\dot{p}_t^e = E(\dot{p}_t|\Omega_{t-1}) \tag{13.15}$$

where $\dot{p}_t^e$ denotes the value of the inflation rate ($\dot{p}_t$) which the rational agent expects to prevail in period t and $E(\dot{p}_t|\Omega_{t-1})$ is the mathematical expectation of $\dot{p}$ conditional on the information available to the agent at the time the forecast was made, Ω_{t-1}. An alternative way of stating this version of the hypothesis is that the discrepancy between the subjective expectation of the inflation rate and its out-turn is given by a random error term (ε_t) with zero mean. That is:

$$\dot{p}_t - \dot{p}_t^e = \varepsilon_t \tag{13.16}$$

The important thing to notice about the error term ε_t is that it is a random variable, and as such its realisation is inherently unpredictable. According to Muth's model, the forecast error ε_t in (13.16) has a zero mean (indicating that expectations are on average correct), is *not* correlated with the information set available at time $t - 1$ when the forecast was made, and is devoid of serial-correlation (Pesaran, 1991).

Rational expectations and the wage equation

As we have seen, the basic idea of Muth's rational expectations model is that agents make use of all relevant information which is available to them when generating their expectations of the future values of relevant variables from the true underlying economic model which generates these variables. It follows, therefore, that individuals' subjective probability distributions regarding future outcomes will be the same as the actual probability distributions, conditional on the information set available to them. As a glance at any intermediate macroeconomics text will reveal, the rational expectations hypothesis carries some far-reaching conclusions for macroeconomics, in general, and for macroeconomic policy in particular. The following simple example will illustrate the implications of the rational expectations hypothesis for the Phillips curve trade-off between inflation and unemployment.

Setting $\alpha_2 = 1$ in (13.6) we obtain the following expectations-augmented Phillips curve

$$\dot{w} = -\alpha_1 (u - u_n) + \dot{p}_t^e \tag{13.17}$$

The general character of the rational expectations solution to this model can be illustrated by rewriting (13.16) to give

$$\dot{p}_t^e = \dot{p}_t - \varepsilon_t.$$

Substituting this expression into the Phillips curve (13.17) we obtain

$$\dot{w}_t = -\alpha_1 (u - u_n) + \dot{p}_t - \varepsilon_t$$

Invoking assumption (13.2), according to which $\dot{w}_t = \dot{p}_t$, and rearranging the preceding equation we arrive at the following expression:

$$(u - u_n) = -\frac{1}{\alpha_1}\varepsilon_t \tag{13.18}$$

Equation (13.18) shows that under rational expectations the *short-run* inflation–unemployment trade-off disappears. According to (13.18) unemployment differs from the natural rate only to the extent of a zero-mean error term. Equation (13.8) implies that the actual rate of unemployment can only differ from its natural rate because of the occurrence of some unpredictable shock or surprise.

To be a little more concrete let us look at the way in which agents arrive at their expectations of the inflation rate. Suppose that the agent is aware of the existence of a systematic relationship between the rate of growth of the money supply ($\dot{m}_t$) and the inflation rate of the following form:

$$\dot{p}_t = \dot{m}_t + \sigma_t \tag{13.19}$$

where σ_t is some random error term. The agent will exploit this knowledge in arriving at his expected inflation rate such that

$$\dot{p}_t^e = \dot{m}_t^e \tag{13.20}$$

However, as period t's expected inflation rate is evaluated at time $(t - 1)$, information on monetary growth in period t is not available to the agent. Suppose that the individual is aware that the monetary authority follows the following simple rule in its monetary policy

$$\dot{m}_t - \dot{m}_{t-1} = \gamma \tag{13.21}$$

then he can predict $\dot{m}_t$ with perfect accuracy as follows:

$$\dot{m}_t^e = \dot{m}_{t-1} + \gamma = \dot{m}_t \tag{13.22}$$

Subtracting (13.20) from (13.21), using (13.22), we obtain

$$\dot{p}_t - \dot{p}_t^e = \sigma_t \tag{13.23}$$

Solving (13.23) for $\dot{p}_t^e$ and substituting into the Phillips curve (13.17) we obtain, given assumption (13.2), the following equation:

$$(u - u_n) = -\frac{1}{\alpha_1}\sigma_t \tag{13.24}$$

This expression, like (13.18), demonstrates the basic conclusion to follow from the incorporation of the rational expectations hypothesis into the model: namely, that there is no unemployment–inflation trade-off even in the short run, and that the only factor which can cause the actual rate of unemployment to diverge from the natural rate is the occurrence of some unexpected shock to the system.

Some recent developments

In this final section we outline a number of recent developments in the wage inflation literature. Although the previous section began by noting the apparent demise of the Phillips curve, and discussed a range of explanations offered for this, it is interesting to notice that a number of writers have reported, for the UK at least, some evidence of its reappearance during the 1980s (for example, Sumner and Ward, 1983; Varoufakis and Sapsford, 1990). Recent research on wage inflation has proceeded along a number of fronts. Some of these studies seek to enhance the basic augmented Phillips curve model, while others seek to offer alternatives of various sorts which are thought to correspond more closely to the actual structure and functioning of the labour market in the country in question. One of the more important alternatives offered in the recent literature has become known as the *real wage resistance* or *target real wage* model.

The target real wage model

The basic hypothesis here, which can be traced back to Sargan (1964), though see also Sargan (1980) for further refinement of the hypothesis, is extremely straightforward: namely, that although workers bargain for *money* wages, their bargaining strategy reflects some underlying target level of *real wage*, coupled with a profile of beliefs or expectations regarding the future path of price inflation. Sargan's model may be summarised as follows:

$$\frac{w_t}{w_{t-1}} = k\left[\frac{p_t^e}{p_{t-i}}\right]^{\theta}\left[\frac{(w/p)^*}{(w/p)_{t-i}}\right]^{\lambda} \quad \text{where } \theta, \lambda > 0 \qquad (13.25)$$

where w is the nominal wage, p the price level, p^e the expected price level, k some constant of proportionality and $(w/p)^*$ the target *real* wage. Taking natural logs of expression (13.25), noting that the first-difference of log w is the proportional rate of change of the nominal wage, and setting $i = 1$ for annual data, we can write the model in the following form:

$$\dot{w}_t = \alpha + \theta\,[\ln p_t^e - \ln p_{t-1}] + \lambda\,[\ln(w/p)^* - \ln(w/p)_{t-1}] \qquad (13.26)$$

where $\alpha = \ln k$.

According to this expression we see that the target real wage model views the rate of wage inflation as being positively related to both the extent to which the real wage actually received deviates from the target level, and the extent to which price expectations turned out to be incorrect. The last term on the right-hand side of expression (13.26) indicates the gap which exists between the target and the going real wage and this model basically sees wage inflation as arising from the frustration of workers' real wage aspirations as measured by the size of this gap. In essence, this model boils down to a kind of *error-correction* mechanism.

This basic model has been refined in a number of ways. First, the size of the real-wage gap has been evaluated in terms of real after-tax income (for example, Jackson, Turner and Wilkinson, 1972; Johnston and Timbrell, 1973; Apps, 1982). Second, the size of the real-wage gap has itself been modelled as depending on various economic factors, such as unemployment or profits – although it was common in the early studies (for example, Henry, Sawyer and Smith, 1976) to find the target real wage specified as a simple linear trend. Third, the extent to which the real-wage gap is translated into money-wage inflation (as indicated by the size of λ in (13.26)) has been modelled in terms of both the unemployment rate and a measure of union militancy (Varoufakis and Sapsford, 1990). One limitation of the target real-wage model is the fact that it sees things largely from the workers' side of the bargain and accordingly, has little to say about the employers' role in the wage-fixing process.

In the 1970s the target model was seen very much as a competitor to the augmented Phillips curve model. In this spirit Henry, Sawyer and Smith (1976) ran an empirical tournament between alternative models of wage inflation and found that the target real-wage model outperformed its rivals, including the Phillips curve, in explaining UK wage inflation. More recent work, however, increasingly sees these two approaches less as rivals and rather more as complements, with the consequence that a number of 'hybrid' models incorporating elements of both the Phillips curve and real-wage resistance approaches have appeared (Artis, 1989, pp. 100–1). Especially important in such models are various refinements to Sargan's (1964) notion of *error correction*. Indeed, the concept of error correction has now become established as a central plank of applied econometric practice.

One such hybrid model is obtained by combining the real-wage gap term of (13.26) with an inflationary expectations term of the augmented Phillips curve sort to give a model of the following kind:

$$\dot{w} = \alpha + \gamma \dot{p}^e + \beta\,[(w/p)^* - (w/p)] \tag{13.27}$$

where, for estimation purposes $(w/p)^*$ may be replaced by the factors determining it (such as unemployment). Model (13.27) can be solved for the *stationary state* by setting $\dot{w} = \dot{p}^e = 0$ to obtain

$$(w/p) = (\alpha/\beta) + (w/p)^* \tag{13.28}$$

which shows that model (13.27) can be altenatively estimated, in its stationary form, as a *real-wage* equation. In this form, the real wage (w/p) is explained by the determinants of the real-wage target $(w/p)^*$. If the target real wage is a linear function of some set of determinants z, denoted by say $\alpha_1 z$, substitution into (13.28) after writing $\alpha/\beta = \alpha_0$ gives the following model:

$$(w/p) = \alpha_0 + \alpha_1 z \tag{13.29}$$

which captures the spirit of much recent work on wage inflation (for example, Hall and Henry, 1987; Nickell, 1987). In such models the factors seen as determining the real wage, that is, the ingredients of the z vector, typically include such variables as the unemployment rate (current and lagged), trend labour productivity, plus various 'wage push' factors, such as the extent of unionisation and the unemployment benefit to wage ratio.

□ *Staggered wage setting*

One additional factor considered to be important in explaining the behaviour of wage inflation is the spread of multiperiod wage contracts, the existence of which may give rise to a phenomenon referred to as *staggered wage setting*. This effect is generally seen as especially significant in the context of the US economy, where multiperiod (frequently of three years' duration) wage contracts are not uncommon. This is in contrast to the UK where the typical wage contract is of one year's duration. However, the basic ideas of such models may also carry special significance for economies such as the Japanese, where there is a high degree of synchronisation of wage contracts.

The basic notion here (Taylor, 1979, 1980) is that the *current* rate of growth of money wages may be rather insensitive to variations in the current rate of unemployment because of the fact that only some fraction of wage contracts come up for renewal during the current time period, the remainder having renegotiation dates set at sometime in the future. Moreover, those contracts not falling due for renegotiation in the current period will typically contain clauses calling for wage increases under certain conditions (such as 'cost of living' adjustments in response to price movements). This means that the behaviour of the wages of a significant proportion of the workforce – the majority perhaps – whose contracts are not up for renegotiation in the current period will be unaffected by the current actual rate of unemployment. Instead, their wage adjustments will be determined by unions' and employers' *expectations* of the unemployment rate, expectations which were formed in the past at the time when the existing contract was negotiated. However, while the evidence seems to suggest that the wage increases embodied in the *initial* year of multi-year contracts seem to be no less sensitive to the unemployment rate than settlements in the non-union sector of the economy, wage adjustments in the subsequent years of the contract do not seem to be sensitive to the rate of unemployment prevailing during these years (Mitchell, 1980). In essence, the existence of such staggered wage-setting behaviour introduces an element of inertia into the wage-setting process, the consequence of which is the injection of a degree of insensitivity into the relationship between the rate of wage inflation and the rate of unemployment.

□ *Hysteresis effects*

A number of studies of the wage inflation–unemployment relation in a range of European and other economies (for example, Bean, Layard and Nickell, 1987) has suggested that what have been christened 'hysteresis' effects may be of some importance. The basic idea here is that the current level of the equilibrium or natural rate of unemployment may itself depend on past levels of unemployment. This view suggests that demand management policies may be able to influence the future values of the natural rate. In simple terms, a hysteresis effect means that 'the position of the economy today depends not only on what is happening today, but on where it was yesterday' (Nickell, 1990, p. 419). In terms of wage inflation equations, the existence of hysteresis effects suggests the inclusion of the *change* in the unemployment rate as an additional explanatory variable. Such effects can arise for a variety of reasons. Possible reasons include discouraged worker influences (which result in marginal workers quitting the labour force), the depreciation of human capital amongst the unemployed (which increases the difficulty of finding a suitable match by job search), the loss of work-place contacts (which serve for some workers as an important source of information on new job opportunities) on becoming unemployed, plus the operation of insider–outsider mechanisms of the sort discussed in Chapter 11, and the fact that employers may use unemployment experience as a screening device with which to identify low-productivity workers.

We will consider the implications of the hysteresis hypothesis for the behaviour of unemployment in the next chapter. However, since our current focus of attention is the determinants of the rate of wage inflation we can illustrate the hypothesis's implications by adding a term in the change in the unemployment rate ($\Delta u = u - u_{-1}$) to a hybrid real-wage-resistance/expectations-augmented Phillips curve model of the sort which would arise from (13.27) with the additional assumption that the target real wage is a linear function of the extent to which the actual unemployment rate differs from the natural rate. Such a model may be written as follows:

$$\dot{w} = \beta_0 + \dot{p}^e - \beta_1 \Delta u - \beta_2(u - u_n) - \beta_3(w/p)_{-1} \qquad (13.30)$$

Equation (13.30) illustrates the importance of the distinction between the *level* of unemployment rate and its *change*. If the coefficient attached to the unemployment *change* term (β_1) is large, then as the economy goes into recession wage inflation will be sharply slowed down as unemployment rises. However, once the unemployment rate has stabilised this short-term influence will disappear leaving only the unemployment *level* effect (β_2) which may be rather small in practice. It has been argued (Nickell, 1987; Artis, 1989) that newly unemployed workers joining the unemployment register add little to the downward pressure on wage inflation once they have lost their employment. In consequence we may well expect the size of the coefficient β_2 in (13.30) to be quite small, and perhaps to tend to zero as these newly unemployed drift into *long-term* unemployment where they may exert little perceptible downward pressure on the wages of those with jobs. As already mentioned, there are several hypotheses which can give rise to this sort of story. One is that the human capital of unemployed workers depreciates so rapidly that they quickly cease to become adequate substitutes from the firm's viewpoint for existing employees. Another possibility is that unemployed workers radiate signals of inferior quality if they express a willingness to accept a reduced wage. A third possibility is that those who have remained in employment ('the insiders') take steps to make it difficult for their employers to hire lower-cost unemployed workers ('the outsiders') via such channels as threats of harassment.

Notes

1. In addition, Phillips observed a positive relation between changes in the cost of living and the rate of wage inflation and found the existence of anticlockwise loops around the estimated equation during the pre-Second World War period. These loops imply that, for any given level of unemployment, the rate of wage change is higher if unemployment is falling and lower if unemployment is rising.
2. The equation that Phillips fitted to the data was of the form

   $$\dot{w} = a + bu^{-c}$$

   which is *non-linear in parameters as well as variables*. To estimate the parameters of this equation, Phillips developed a novel iterative technique, and this is discussed in some depth by both Desai (1975) and Gilbert (1976). Phillips's estimated equation was as follows:

$$\dot{w} + 0.9 = 9.638u^{-1.394}$$

implying an intercept on the unemployment axis of approximately 5.5 per cent as shown in **Figure 13.1.**

3. When excess demand is high, frictional unemployment is subject to two opposing forces. On the one hand, the duration of job search will decline as unfilled vacancies become plentiful and it becomes easier to find jobs. On the other hand, the voluntary quit rate rises as workers become optimistic, given the tight labour market conditions, about finding more satisfactory alternative employment (Corry and Laidler, 1967). The downward-sloping excess demand unemployment relation is therefore based on the assumption that the former tendency outweighs the latter.
4. The equation of the reaction function shown in **Figure 13.3(a)** is as follows:

$$\dot{w} = k\left(\frac{L_D - L_S}{L_S}\right)$$

Writing the equation of the excess demand–unemployment function as

$$\frac{L_D - L_S}{L_S} = g\,(u)$$

we obtain by substitution

$$\dot{w} = k[g(u)] = f(u)$$

which is the Phillips curve for the representative individual labour market.

5. An alternative approach is to specify a *simultaneous equation model* of the wage–price system, in which the rates of wage and price inflation are both endogenously determined. In such models the rate of price inflation is modelled as a function of the rate of wage inflation and other variables, while the rate of wage inflation is itself modelled a function of the rates of unemployment and price inflation and other variables. See, for example, Ashenfelter *et al.* (1972).
6. Studies of the underlying trend rate of growth of labour productivity in the UK have typically given estimates to the order of 2.5 per cent per year (Sapsford, 1981).
7. Since the shift in the unemployment–vacancies relation in the UK meant that a given rate of unemployment became associated with a higher rate of unfilled vacancies, it follows that at each value of the unemployment rate (u) the excess demand for labour ($v - u$) had increased. This is shown as an outward movement in the excess demand–unemployment relation (**Figure 13.3 (b)**). With an unchanged reaction function the Phillips curve will, as a consequence of this u/v curve shift, move outwards. This occurs because although a given value of $\dot{w}$ is associated with an unchanged level of excess demand for labour, the latter is now associated with a higher rate of unemployment. Alternatively, because a given rate of unemployment now

represents a higher level of excess demand for labour, it gives rise to a higher rate of inflation.

8. In the second period in the example of the text, the expected rate of price inflation is equal to the first period's actual rate (that is, 5 per cent), and from (13.1) and (13.2) we see that Friedman's model predicts that a government policy that succeeds in holding the rates of wage and price inflation at 5 per cent implies a rise in the unemployment rate sufficient to make $f(u)$ become zero. Since $f(u)$ is the original Phillips or zero price-expectations curve (*AA* in **Figure 13.6**), we see that the unemployment rate in question is u_n, the intercept of curve *AA* on the unemployment axis.

   The process by which convergence to steady-state equilibrium at u_n occurs in Friedman's model involves both employers and employees eventually becoming completely aware of the actual rate of inflation (that is, the disappearance of money illusion in the long run). Once inflation becomes fully anticipated and adjusted to, both parties revert to their original positions on the labour demand and supply curves respectively, thus reestablishing the initial unemployment rate u_n. See Friedman (1976, pp. 223–6).
9. To arrive at expression (13.9), first substitute (13.8) into (13.1) after setting $\alpha = 1$. Second, lag the resulting expression by one period and multiply both sides by $(1 - \lambda)$. Third, subtract the resulting expression from the equation obtained by substituting (13.8) into (13.1) and simplify using (13.2) and (13.8). The algebra here amounts to the well-known Koyck transformation.
10. In the particular case where $\lambda = 1$ we see that only the previous period's rate of inflation counts and expression (13.3) of the text reduces to $\dot{p}_t^e = \dot{p}_{t-1}$, according to which current expected inflation is equal to last period's observed rate. This was the case assumed in (13.2) above.
11. The pattern of weights in (13.12) constitutes a *geometric progression.* Using the result that the sum to infinity of a geometric progression is given by the product of its first term and the reciprocal of one minus its common factor, we obtain the sum to infinity of the weights as $\lambda/[1 - (1 - \lambda)] = 1$.
12. Suppose that some *shock*, which has the effect of pushing the rate of inflation up from say 10 per cent to a steady-state value of 15 per cent, occurs. If the expectations coefficient (λ) equals 0.5 and we assume that the initial period's expected rate of inflation rate is 10 per cent, expression (13.11) shows that next period's expected inflation rate is 12.5 per cent. In the next period, expected inflation rises to 13.75 per cent, then in the next period to 14.375 per cent and then to 14.6875 per cent and so on; with the steady-state rate of 15 per cent only being reached after an infinite number of time periods have elapsed. Clearly, lower (higher) values of λ result in less (more) rapid convergence.

Chapter 14

Unemployment

An unemployed worker is one who is unable to find employment under prevailing economic conditions. Although any factor of production can be unemployed, economists have placed particular emphasis on unemployment of labour, primarily because of the mental (and sometimes physical) sufferings and hardships experienced by the unemployed and their dependents.

A distinction is sometimes drawn between voluntary and involuntary unemployment. *Involuntary unemployment* occurs when workers who are willing to work at current wage levels are unable to find jobs. *Voluntary unemployment* refers to those workers who are thought to be capable of taking a job but prefer to remain unemployed, perhaps (as we saw in Chapter 12) to enable themselves to continue their search for a better-paid or otherwise more desirable job than those currently on offer. In cases where the wage ruling in a particular labour market is for some reason above the equilibrium or market-clearing level, there will be an excess of labour supply over labour demand, and the workers comprising this excess supply are said to be involuntarily unemployed, as they are seeking but are unable to attain employment at the prevailing wage rate.

■ Types of unemployment

Unemployment is a topic which abounds with alternative definitions and classifications. For example, in one survey Hughes and Perlman (1984, p. 26) cite the existence of no fewer than *seventy* different types of unemployment! However, for the purpose of tne current chapter we will place particular emphasis (at least initially) on one of the most widely discussed classifications to be found in the literature. This approach, discussed by Beveridge (1944), identifies the following four types of unemployment: frictional, structural, seasonal and cyclical.

Frictional unemployment is the unemployment that results from workers moving between jobs. As long as people change jobs, and as long as it takes a finite time to move from one job to another, some positive amount of frictional unemployment will exist at any moment in time. Frictional unemployment is a consequence of the short-run changes in the labour market that constantly occur in a dynamic economy in response to changes in the pattern of demand for, and supply of, goods and services, and it arises because labour supply does not adjust instantaneously to changes the pattern of labour demand, with the consequence that unemployed workers and unfilled vacancies may exist side by side. Frictional unemployment arises because the process of matching unfilled vacancies and unemployed workers is not instantaneous. The search processes undertaken by both workers and employers in order to bring about such matching were discussed in some detail in Chapter 12.

Structural unemployment is caused by long-run changes in the structure of the economy, which give rise to changes in the demand for labour in particular, industries, regions and occupations, and it arises because, although workers are available for employment, their skill or locations do not match those of unfilled vacancies. The distinction between frictional and structural unemployment is by no means a clear-cut one. While most writers see the distinction as being one of degree rather than kind, with structural unemployment being essentially a longer-term or more stubborn form of frictional unemployment, others have sought to clarify the distinction by explicitly considering the nature of unfilled job vacancies. Perlman (1969, p. 168), for example, defined a worker as structurally unemployed if a job vacancy exists that he is not qualified to fill and as frictionally unemployed if a vacancy that he is qualified to fill exists and remains unfilled.

Seasonal unemployment is that which results from the lower level of economic activity that occurs in certain sectors of the economy at particular times of the year. Agricultural and building workers, as well as those involved in the tourism industry, who are out of work during the winter months, are said to be seasonally unemployed. However, the most significant group of seasonally unemployed workers in recent times in the industrialised countries has probably been unemployed school-leavers, who join the unemployment register at particular times of the year. Since seasonal unemployment is often viewed as reflecting 'normal' seasonal variations, unemployment data are frequently presented in a seasonally adjusted form, sometimes with school-leavers excluded.

Cyclical or demand-deficient unemployment is that which is associated with a lack of aggregate demand. This type of unemployment was discussed by Keynes (1936) in the *General Theory*, and its cure lies in policies that succeed in increasing the level of aggregate demand. Some more recent writers (for example, Reynolds, 1978, p. 126) have differentiated between this and *growth gap unemployment*, which they see as a longer-term secular version of demand-deficient unemployment that occurs not so much due to cyclical factors but when the economy's growth potential exceeds its actual rate of growth, so that part of its productive capacity remains unutilised.

■ Factual background: OECD unemployment

Table 14.1 provides a summary of unemployment rates in a number of OECD member countries over the period 1960–90. As we saw in Chapter 2, the measurement of unemployment is an exercise which is not without its own difficulties. Accordingly, the data reported in **Table 14.1** are based on what are known as OECD standardised unemployment rates. As is usual, unemployment rates are defined as the numbers unemployed, expressed as a percentage of the labour force. **Figure 14.1** shows the time-path of the aggregate OECD unemployment rate over the period since 1955. However, as can be seen from both **Table 14.1** and **Figure 14.2** (which plots separate profiles for the USA, the UK, Japan and West Germany), the experiences of individual member countries were by no means uniform. The US unemployment rate exhibits a fairly clear cyclical pattern about a reasonably stable trend. After the mid-1960s, variations in both the UK and German rates took the form of a series of upward jumps, followed by less than complete recoveries. The time-path of Japanese unemployment is strikingly different to that of the other countries displayed in **Figure 14.2**. However, as Bean (1992) notes, the time profile of Japan's unemployment is markedly similar to that experienced by the smaller European (non-EEC) economies of Austria, Switzerland and the Nordic countries.

Table 14.1 ***Unemployment in OECD countries, 1960–90 (%)***

	1960–8	*1969–73*	*1974–9*	*1980–5*	*1986–90*
Belgium	2.35	2.38	6.32	11.28	10.27
Denmark	1.46	0.95	6.02	10.00	9.33
France	1.69	2.52	4.52	8.32	10.2
W. Germany	0.71	0.84	3.20	5.95	6.04
Ireland	4.98	5.76	6.77	11.64	15.50
Italy	3.64	3.95	4.37	6.15	7.63
Netherlands	1.14	2.05	5.05	10.05	9.46
Spain	2.42	2.74	5.27	16.58	19.00
United Kingdom	2.62	3.39	5.04	10.48	8.80
Australia	2.17	2.04	5.02	7.64	7.40
New Zealand	0.16	0.28	0.67	4.17	6.06
Canada	4.71	5.56	7.17	9.88	8.26
United States	4.74	4.86	6.68	8.00	5.79
Japan	1.36	1.22	1.93	2.42	2.52
Austria	1.96	1.40	1.78	3.23	3.33
Finland	1.83	2.34	4.53	5.60	5.10
Norway	2.01	1.66	1.82	2.55	3.11
Sweden	1.64	2.22	1.88	2.83	1.89
Switzerland	0.06	0.01	1.08	1.92	2.37

Note: These are OECD standardised rates, with the exception of Italy which is taken from the statistics prepared by the United States Department of Labor.

Source: Nickell (1990, p. 393).

■ Unemployment: stocks and flows

The pool of unemployed workers is a *stock*, the size of which at any moment of time is determined by two factors: the rate of *flow* into unemployment, and the duration of the unemployment spells experienced by individual workers. On the basis of some simplifying assumptions (principally that unemployment is constant, giving rise to what is usually termed a *stationary* register (Cripps and Tarling, 1974; Knight, 1987)) we can write the following expression which allows us to subdivide the size of the unemployment *stock* into an *inflow* component and a *duration* component:

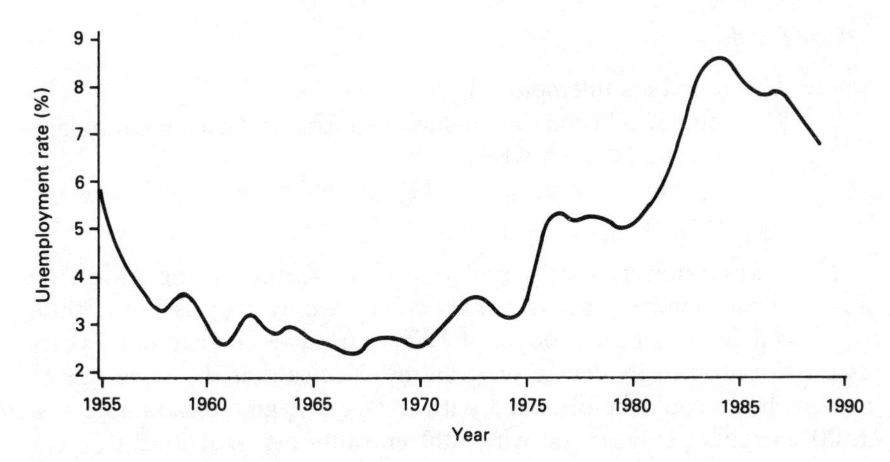

Figure 14.1 ***OECD unemployment rate***

Note: The rate presented is the OECD labour force weighted average of the individual country rates (i.e., the OECD aggregate rate).

Source: OECD, *Labour Force Statistics* and *Main Economic Indicators*.

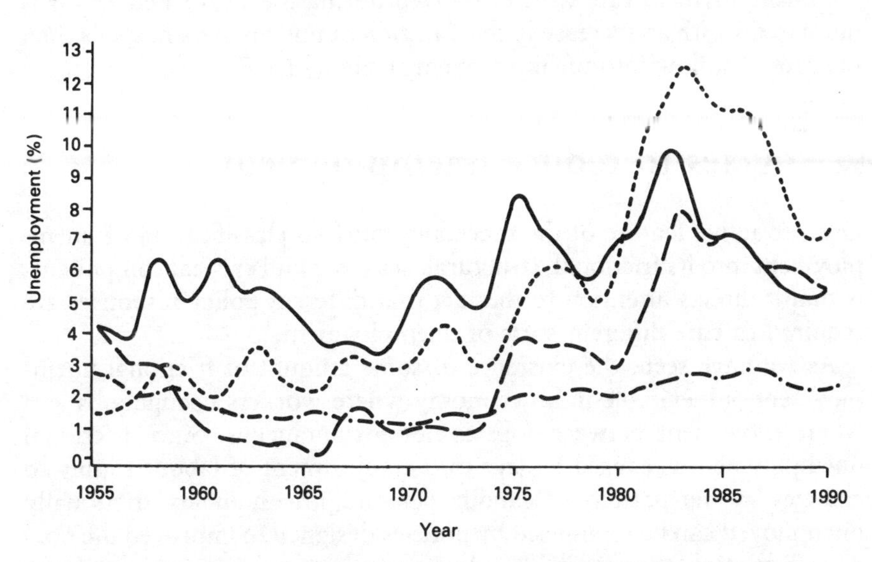

Figure 14.2 ***Percentage of unemployment from 1955 to 1990***

Note: —— United States; ---- United Kingdom; -·—·- Japan;
——— West Germany.

Source: OECD, *Labour Force Statistics* and *Main Economic Indicators*.

$$U = f \times d$$

where U = numbers unemployed,
f = numbers becoming unemployed (that is, flowing into unemployment) each week,
d = average number of weeks for which they remain unemployed.

This expression is easily understood in terms of the following analogy: the number of students attending a university is (say) 3000, which is made up of the product of 1000 entrants each year and 3 years as the duration of its degree programme. Notice that the same size of student body could be obtained with a 2-year degree programme and 1500 entrants per year, or with 600 entrants per year and a 5-year programme.

This expression is extremely useful because it allows us, in principle, to distinguish whether (say) an increase in unemployment is attributable to an increase in the numbers becoming newly unemployed (f), or to an increase in the duration of unemployment (d), or some combination of both. As far as the unemployment experience of the UK economy is concerned, most research has indicated that the upward movement in the unemployment rate which occurred during the 1970s and 1980s is more to do with an increase in the *duration* of unemployment spells than the rate of inflow into unemployment (Knight, 1987).

■ Policies to reduce unemployment

One attractive feature of the preceding fourfold classification of unemployment into its frictional, structural, seasonal and cyclical components is that it directs attention to the fact that different policy responses are required to cure different sorts of unemployment.[1]

As we have seen, the existence of some amount of frictional unemployment is inevitable in an economy where workers change jobs and where movement between jobs is not instantaneous. Since frictional unemployment is caused by lags in the adjustment of labour supply to changes in the pattern of labour demand, the numbers frictionally unemployed can be minimised by policies designed to improved the *flow of information* about unfilled job vacancies and thereby to cut down adjustment lags by decreasing the time spent in job search. The provision by the governments of most industrialised countries of employment services of various sorts, where vacancies are advertised and counselling is available for the unemployed, is an example of one such policy measure.

Structural unemployment, however, is characterised by a *mismatch* between available workers and unfilled job vacancies, and it arises because workers are neither occupationally nor geographically perfectly mobile. Long-run changes in the structure of demand and production occur in response to changes in the comparative cost position of different regions and countries, to technical progress, and to changes in tastes and preferences, and they mean that some sectors of the economy will be expanding while others will be contracting. Structural unemployment arises because workers displaced from declining sectors do not have the requisite skills or locations for job-openings provided by the expanding sectors. Examples of structural changes giving rise to structural unemployment include the decline of the shipbuilding and steel-producing industries in many of the older industrialised countries of the world economy. Notice that in both these cases the historic concentration of these industries in particular geographical regions has given rise to a corresponding geographical concentration of structural unemployment.

Since structural unemployment has its roots in the occupational and geographical immobility of labour, it can be reduced by manpower and regional policies. Such policies, which have been widely used in the industrialised economies are designed to assist workers to obtain the skills required by available vacancies (by providing retraining schemes and offering grants to participants), to improve geographical mobility (by providing financial assistance towards relocation expenses and assistance in finding accommodation) and to encourage the movement of vacancies to available workers (by offering employers various financial incentives in the form of grants, tax concessions or low-cost premises to move to certain specified areas). In addition, employment subsidies of varying sorts have been introduced at various times in order to provide firms with a sum of money for each job that they maintained, as an attempt to reduce the numbers of workers becoming displaced by declining industries.

Demand-deficient versus non-demand-deficient unemployment

Although it is often difficult in practice to distinguish between different types of unemployment, it is nevertheless very important from the policy viewpoint. If the principal cause of unemployment is identified as being demand deficiency, the cure is to be found in appropriate monetary and fiscal policies that increase the level of aggregate demand. If unemployment is diagnosed as being structural and frictional in nature, policies that increase the level of aggregate demand can have serious inflationary consequences (see Chapter 13). The solution to structural unemployment lies in manpower and regional policies that encourage mobility of labour (both occupational and geographic) and of jobs, and that improve training and retraining possibilities. As we have seen, as long as people change jobs, and as long as it takes a finite time to move from one job to another, some amount of frictional unemployment will exist. However, as we have also seen, the amount of frictional unemployment may be reduced, although not entirely eliminated, by policies designed to improve information flows regarding unfilled job vacancies and thereby to cut down lags in the matching of unemployed workers and unfilled job vacancies (that is, by cutting down the time spent in job search). Therefore, in order to prescribe the correct policies for curing unemployment, it is necessary to know at least two things: first, how the total quantity of unemployment is split as between *demand-deficient unemployment and non-demand-deficient unemployment* (that is, structural, frictional and seasonal unemployment), and second, how far it is possible to decrease non-demand-deficient unemployment without generating inflationary consequences that are in some sense unacceptable (that is, to define what can be termed the *full employment level of unemployment*). The following model, originally proposed by Lipsey (1965) seeks to clarify the important distinction between demand- and non-demand-deficient employment.

In this analysis Lipsey stressed the relevance of the Phillips curve trade-off between inflation and unemployment, and his argument can be illustrated by considering **Figure 14.3** which shows the utility-maximising approach to the policy-makers' selection of the optimal inflation–unemployment combination, as considered in the last chapter. Curve *PP* is the Phillips curve relating the rate of *price* inflation to the rate of unemployment, and utility is maximised at point *A*, where *PP* is tangential to indifference curve *I*. If the present rate of unemployment is *b*, unemployment can be reduced to *a* by demand expansion without causing the price level to rise, although clearly any reduction of unemployment below *a* can be achieved only at the cost of a positive rate of inflation. However, utility-maximising policy-makers will aim their aggregate demand policies at point *A*, and since they are willing to accept an inflation rate of $\dot{p}_0$ in order to secure a reduction in unemployment to u_0, Lipsey defined $\dot{p}_0$ as the *acceptable rate of inflation*. With a present unemployment rate of *b*, Lipsey defined the amount $(b - u_0)$ as demand-deficient unemployment, because it is the amount of unemployment that can be removed by increasing aggregate demand without creating unacceptable conflicts with other policy goals.

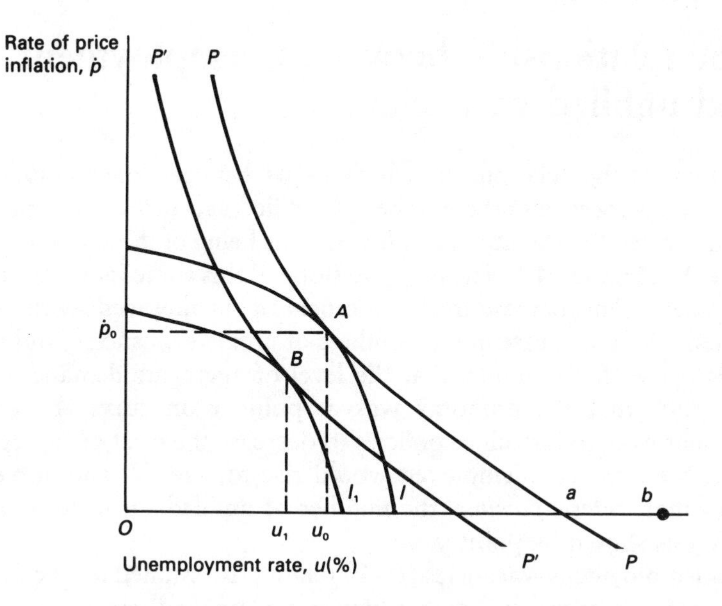

Figure 14.3 ***Demand-deficient versus structural unemployment: Lipsey's analysis***

The only way in which unemployment can be reduced below u_0 without incurring an *unacceptable rate of inflation*, as defined by Lipsey, is for the Phillips curve to be shifted to the left. In situations where the terms of the Phillips curve trade-off have been considered unacceptable, policy-makers have sought to shift the whole Phillips curve leftwards, so that each particular rate of unemployment becomes available at a lower rate of inflation. Regional and manpower policies of the sort discussed above may be seen as measures by which such a shift may be brought about.[2] However, such policies are *not* costless. If we assume that curve $P'P'$ represents the furthest shift in the Phillips curve that is justified on a social *cost–benefit analysis*, a new equilibrium position is established at B with lower levels of both inflation and unemployment. Lipsey defined the reduction in unemployment of $(u_0 - u_1)$ that can be thus secured as structural unemployment, because it is that which can be removed by structural measures that can be justified on cost–benefit grounds. The remaining amount of unemployment (u_1) was defined by Lipsey as frictional unemployment, because it is that which rational policy-makers do not wish to remove, given the costs and benefits of so doing. In view of this, Lipsey defined unemployment of u_1 as the *full-employment level of unemployment*.

The relationship between unemployment and unfilled vacancies

The nature of the relationship which exists between the number of unemployed workers and the number of unfilled vacancies has attracted particular interest in the literature. It is seen as being of the shape shown by curve A in **Figure 14.4**. The negative slope of this curve indicates that, *ceteris paribus*, an increase in the numbers of unemployed workers is associated with a decrease in the numbers of unfilled vacancies, and vice versa. Suppose, for example, that the level of aggregate demand were initially such that the economy was at point x on curve A. If the government were to introduce policies to decrease the level of aggregate demand, the number unemployed would rise to, say, U_2 and curve A indicates that, *ceteris paribus*, the number of unfilled vacancies would fall to V_2, as shown by point y.

The unemployment–vacancies (U–V) relation is assumed to be convex to the origin, because, no matter how many unfilled vacancies exist, unemployment will not fall to zero. As we have seen, as long as people change jobs and as long as job changes are not instantaneous, some frictional unemployment will exist. While the average duration of unemployment tends to fall in tight labour markets as satisfactory jobs become easier to find, the plentiful supply of job vacancies encourages some workers voluntarily to quit their jobs in such circumstances to search for better ones. This factor, together with any structural unemployment that arises because the available unemployed workers do not match the requirements of available vacancies, limits the decline in unemployment as vacancies increase. At the opposite extreme, in situations where unemployment is very high, unfilled vacancies will not fall to zero, because some undesirable jobs will remain unfilled and because some vacancies will remain unfilled for structural reasons (that is, because they require skills or are in locations that differ from those possessed by unemployed workers). In addition, some vacancies remain unfilled for frictional reasons, because, even though there are unemployed workers qualified and available to fill them, these workers have not yet, given the scarcity of job vacancies, found a suitable one. These considerations imply that the curve does not touch either axis, and it is therefore usual to assume that it is everywhere convex to the origin, as shown in **Figure 14.4**.[3]

As we have seen, changes in the level of aggregate demand result, *ceteris paribus*, in movements around a given U–V curve: leftwards when aggregate demand increases, and rightwards when it decreases. However, if policies that improved the functioning of the labour market

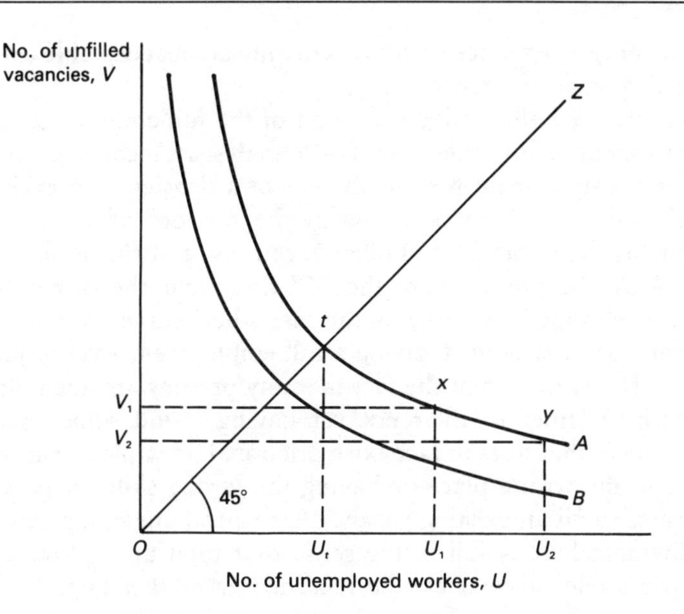

Figure 14.4 ***The relation between unemployment and unfilled vacancies***

(in the sense of reducing the adjustment lags of labour demand to changes in supply, thereby reducing frictional unemployment) and/or reduced structural unemployment were introduced, the *U–V* curve would move leftwards to, say, curve *B* in **Figure 14.4.** This occurs because, each time that an unemployed worker finds a job, there is a simultaneous unit decrease in both the number unemployed and the number of unfilled vacancies, so that such policies give rise to lower numbers of both unemployed workers and unfilled vacancies at each level of aggregate demand. Conversely, any factors that impede the functioning of the labour market and increase frictional unemployment, or that give rise to an increase in structural unemployment, result in a rightward movement of the *U–V* curve. Thus, the nearer the *U–V* to the origin, the more effective or, in a broad sense, *perfect* (Brown, 1976, pp. 137–8) are the structure and functioning of the labour market in matching unemployed workers to unfilled vacancies.

□ *A definition of full employment*

We have already considered Lipsey's definition of the distinction between demand-deficient and non-demand-deficient unemployment and the associated definition of the full-employment level of unemployment. Lipsey's definition sees full employment in terms of the extent to which unemployment can be reduced *without* creating an unacceptable conflict with the policy goal of price stability.

A commonly used alternative definition of the full-employment level of unemployment is provided by *U–V* analysis. According to this approach, full employment (or the absence of a deficiency or excess of labour demand) is said to occur when the number of unemployed workers equals the number of unfilled vacancies, and this is shown in **Figure 14.4** by the point where the 45° line from the origin (*OZ*) intersects the relevant *U–V* curve. In the case where curve *A* applies, full employment occurs at point *t*, giving a full-employment level of unemployment of U_t. At this point the fact that any persons are unemployed can be ascribed either to their not yet having found some vacancy suitable for them that does in fact exist (frictional unemployment) or to their being in the wrong place or having the wrong skills or personal characteristics to fill an existing vacancy (structural unemployment), so that employment here is full in the sense that total unemployment is wholly attributable to what can be regarded as market imperfections rather than to an excess of the supply of labour over demand.

As we saw in the previous chapter, the labour market under consideration is in equilibrium, with labour demand equal to labour supply and the level of money wages remaining stable, when unemployment equals unfilled vacancies (see above, pp. 35–7). At points along the *U–V* curve to the left of *t*, *V* exceeds *U*, and there is therefore an excess demand for labour, so that money wages tend to rise; conversely, at points to the right of *t*, *U* exceeds *V*, and there is an excess supply of labour, with a resulting tendency for money wages to fall. At points to the right of *t*, there is said to be demand deficiency, because the number unemployed exceeds the number of unfilled vacancies, while to the left of point *t* there is said to be *overfull employment*. If, for example, the level of aggregate demand were such that we were located at point *x* on the original curve *A*, the level of unemployment would be U_1, which exceeds the full employment level by the amount ($U_1 - U_t$), and according to the current definition this amount can be termed demand-deficient unemployment. The above definition of full employment corresponds to equilibrium and, therefore (on the usual assumptions), to money-wage stability in the relevant labour market, whereas Lipsey's definition is cast in terms of the level of unemployment consistent with the attainment of some *acceptable* rate of price of inflation. Notice that *U–V* analysis yields not one but a number of possible full-employment positions, with a different one corresponding to each *U–V* curve (that is, to each possible structure of the labour market) and curves representing a greater degree of market imperfection (and thus being further from the origin) yielding higher full-employment levels of unemployment.

U–V analysis allows total unemployment in a given labour-market structure to be subdivided into demand-deficient and non-demand-deficient components, but it does not provide a subdivision of non-demand-deficient unemployment into its constituent structural and frictional components. If the labour market were at its full employment position at point t on curve A, the total number of unemployed workers (U_t) would be made up of structural and frictional components. Notice that the composition of the full-employment level of unemployment as between structural and frictional elements can depend on the definition of the labour market in question. If we define frictional unemployment as that matched in skill and location by unfilled vacancies and structural unemployment as that not so matched, then it follows that, if a labour market were defined in terms of homogeneous labour in a particular locality, all of full-employment unemployment would be frictional. However, if the labour market were more widely defined (for example, covering a certain geographical region), the skills and locations required by unfilled vacancies might not match those of unemployed workers with the consequence that some proportion of full-employment unemployment would be structural.

Classical or Keynesian unemployment? the wage-gap model

Another classification of unemployment which is of interest from the policy standpoint arises from the distinction between what we have referred to as Keynesian (or demand-deficient) unemployment on the one hand, and so-called Classical unemployment on the other. The basic idea of 'Classical' unemployment is simply that if the labour market were in equilibrium, with labour demand equalling labour supply, the labour market would clear at the prevailing wage with the consequence that there would be no unemployment. According to this view, therefore, any unemployment which does exist must be due to wages deviating from the market-clearing level.

This basic idea is at the heart of the *real wage gap* model proposed by Bruno and Sachs (1985), the object of which is to provide a means of distinguishing whether unemployment is primarily Keynesian or Classical in its origin. The model is conveniently illustrated by reference to **Figure 14.5**, in which the curve NN is a conventional competitive demand curve for labour[4] and the vertical line at L denotes the size of the labour force, net perhaps of some 'normal' amount of frictional unemployment. In essence, L may be thought of as a perfectly inelastic

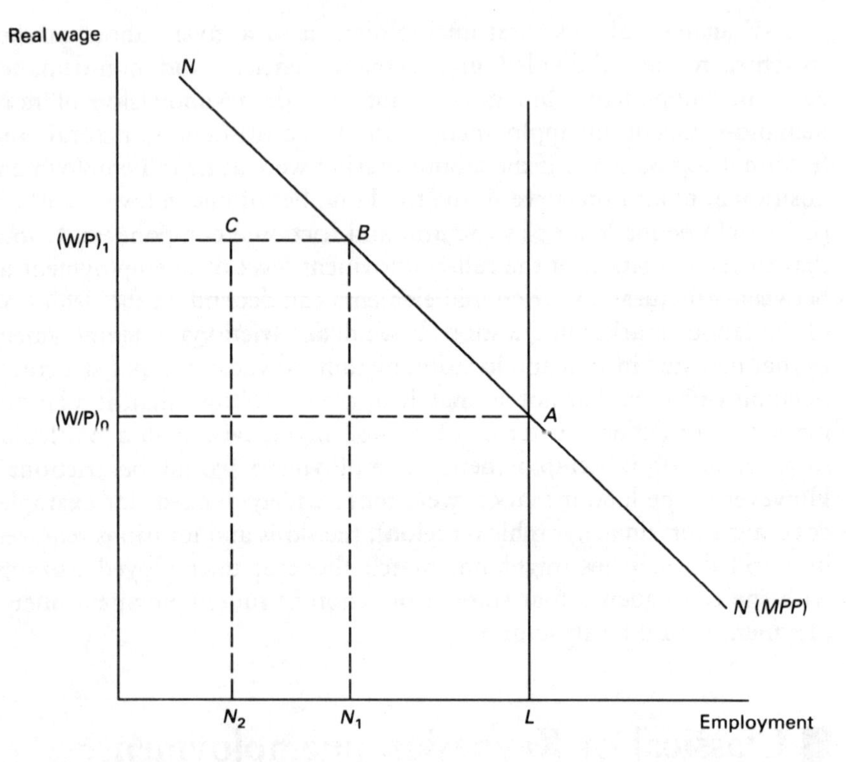

Figure 14.5 ***The wage-gap model***

labour supply function. If, for example, the economy is initially at point *A*, with the real wage equal to $(W/P)_0$, we will have full employment, provided that the level of nominal demand in the economy is sufficient to absorb the level of output which firms wish to sell. Consider now the effect of an increase in the real wage to $(W/P)_1$ at point *B*. The profit-maximising firm will react to the emergence of the *real wage gap* $(W/P)_1 - (W/P)_0$ by contracting the level of its employment to N_1. Under such circumstances we see the emergence of an amount of 'Classical' unemployment equal to $(L - N_1)$. However, in a world with inflexible prices and wages there is no guarantee that the resulting level of nominal output demand will be sufficient to absorb all of the output which firms wish to sell. If this occurs firms will find themselves rationed as to how much output they will be able to sell in the goods market, with the result that actual employment will lie to the left of the labour demand curve *NN*, at say point *C*. At point *C* the total level of unemployment is $(L - N_2)$, which comprises two elements: Classical unemployment of $(L - N_1)$, and a Keynesian element equal to $(N_1 - N_2)$. According to this model, while expansionary macroeconomic policies which succeed in increasing the level of aggregate demand can eliminate the Keynesian component of total unemployment ($N_1 - N_2$), supply-side-oriented policies are necessary to reduce the real wage in order to wipe out the Classical component equal to ($L - N_1$).

According to this model, the size of the real wage gap, taken together with the gradient of the labour demand function NN, determines the extent of Classical unemployment. The difference between the observed unemployment rate and Classical unemployment thus determined then gives the amount of Keynesian unemployment. On the basis of some simplifying assumptions regarding the firm's production function, both Bruno (1986) and Gordon (1987) estimate the size of the wage gap for a selection of OECD member countries at various dates during the 1970s and 1980s by estimating the marginal product of labour at full employment $(W/P)_0$ and subtracting it from the actual real wage.[5] The results of these exercises indicated that there was a tendency for the real wage gap to increase in the sample of countries considered to a peak in the mid- to late 1970s and to tail off thereafter. These results imply that while Classical unemployment may have been a characteristic of the mid- to late 1970s, the unemployment of the 1980s has been largely Keynesian in character. These results would seem to suggest that continued emphasis on the application of supply-side policies may not prove to be very effective in the 1990s as a means of reducing unemployment since these results imply that unemployment is more to do with the insufficiency of aggregate demand. Interestingly, the evidence revealed by these two studies for both Japan and Sweden as low-unemployment economies (see **Table 14.1**) does not seem to be appreciably different in this respect to that of other European countries.

■ Equilibrium unemployment

In the previous chapter we introduced Friedman's natural-rate-of-unemployment concept and the so-called non-accelerating inflation rate of unemployment (the NAIRU). Both of these are notions of *equilibrium unemployment*. While elementary expositions frequently treat these two concepts as synonymous, it is important to recognise that they are not (always) the same thing (see Hughes and Perlman, 1984, pp. 96–7). The basic point to notice here is that the concepts themselves are different. As Carlin and Soskice (1990, pp. 157–9) point out, the natural rate model and the NAIRU model differ fundamentally in terms of their *microfoundations*. As we have already seen, Friedman's natural rate model sees the world through competitive eyes and stresses the behaviour of individual atomistic agents in competitive labour and product markets.

Within this framework Friedman, as we have already seen, visualises the natural rate of unemployment as the rate that 'ground out by the Walrasian system of general equilibrium equations' (Friedman, 1968, p. 8). In contrast, what we might refer to as the NAIRU model rejects the Friedman-type notion of competitive market clearing with complete information in favour of the assumption that there exists *imperfect competition* in the labour and product markets. The NAIRU model is most widely associated with the work of Layard and Nickell (1985, 1986) and their basic model may be summarised as follows.

□ *The Layard–Nickell model*

The Layard–Nickell (hereafter L–N) model[6] comprises the following four major ingredients: a labour demand equation, a price-setting equation, a wage-setting equation and an aggregate demand equation. These may be summarised as follows:

Labour demand

$$\left(\frac{N}{K}\right) = \phi\left(\underset{(-)}{\frac{W}{P}}, \underset{(?)}{A}, \underset{(+)}{s}\right) \tag{14.1}$$

Price setting

$$\left(\frac{P}{W}\right) = \psi\left(\underset{(-)}{\frac{K}{L}}, \underset{(?)}{A}, \underset{(+)}{s}, \underset{(-)}{\frac{W}{W^e}}\right) \tag{14.2}$$

Wage setting

$$\left(\frac{W}{P}\right) = \Omega\left(\underset{(+)}{\frac{N}{L}}, \underset{(+)}{\frac{K}{L}}, \underset{(?)}{A}, \underset{(-)}{\frac{P}{P^e}}, \underset{(+)}{Z^s}\right) \tag{14.3}$$

Aggregate demand

$$s = \mu\left(\underset{(+)}{\frac{M}{P}}, \underset{(+)}{\frac{P^*}{P}}, \underset{(+)}{Z^D}\right) \tag{14.4}$$

where N = employment
L = labour force

K = capital stock
W = nominal wage
P = GDP deflator
A = technical progress index
s = index of real aggregate demand relative to potential input
M = money stock
P^* = overseas competitors' prices expressed in domestic currency terms
Z^S = a set of 'wage push' or shift factors (such as benefit levels, employment legislation, unemployment–vacancies mismatch, taxation and the real price of imports)
Z^D = a set of aggregate demand shift factors, such as fiscal variables.

The superscript 'e' denotes an expected variable and the signs in brackets indicate the predicted sign of the variable in question. Equation (14.1) is easily recognised as a labour demand function, while (14.4) sees real aggregate demand as being determined by the real money stock and the domestic price of output relative to that of the country's overseas competitors. Equations (14.2) and (14.3) most clearly indicate this model's imperfectly competitive character. The model rejects the competitive price-taking model of the product market which is adopted in Friedman's natural rate model and replaces this with the assumption that product prices are set as a mark-up over marginal (here wage) costs. The size of the mark-up in equation (14.2) is specified as a function of the labour–capital ratio, technical progress, real aggregate demand and the hourly wage in relation to its expectation. This latter term captures what is termed 'wage surprise', meaning that in practice some prices may well be set before the outcome of wage negotiations is fully known. Equation (14.3), describing wage-setting behaviour, is sufficiently general to encompass a wide range of possible scenarios. For example, it allows for wages to be set either by firms or by unions or as the outcome of some process of negotiation between the two parties. Indeed, the formulation is sufficiently general to also encompass the possibility that wages are set by the interaction of supply and demand in a competitive labour market. One particular point to note about the price- and wage-formation equations of this model is that it recognises firms' mark-up of prices over wages (P/W) as the inverse of the real wage (W/P), seen as labour's mark-up of the nominal wage over the price level.

As Layard and Nickell (1986, p. 121) point out, the planned mark-up of wages over prices in wage settlements must, over the medium term, be consistent with the mark-up of prices over wage costs in employers' pricing decisions. Accordingly, the model sees the behaviour of wage-setters in the medium term as providing the key to understanding unemployment, since if wage-setters attempt to set real (product) wages at a level which is higher than that which is consistent with employers' pricing behaviour, the result will be an ever increasing inflation. Unemployment, according to the model, has therefore got to rise to offset this effect if events occur which push wage-setters towards too high real wages. Such influences are the wage push factors denoted by Z^s.

The model may be solved to provide either the NAIRU itself or to provide an expression describing the determinants of the actual unemployment rate. To derive the former, it is necessary to eliminate the real wage as between expression (14.1) and (14.3) to obtain expression (14.5) below. Eliminating the real wage between equations (14.2) and (14.3) likewise gives expression (14.6).

$$\left(\frac{N}{L}\right) = f\left(\frac{K}{L}, A, \frac{P}{P^e}, s, Z^S\right) \tag{14.5}$$

$$\left(\frac{N}{L}\right) = g\left(\frac{N}{L}, A, \frac{P}{P^e}, \frac{W}{W^e}, s, Z^S\right) \tag{14.6}$$

Expressions (14.5) and (14.6) may now be jointly solved, making use of the fact that unemployment rate $u = 1 - N/L$, and setting $P = P^e$ and $W = W^e$ to give an expression for the equilibrium unemployment rate, the NAIRU (denoted by u^*), in terms of the capital–labour ratio, technical progress and the shift variables. There are, however, reasons for believing that in the long run the coefficient of the capital–labour ratio in this solution will be zero (Nickell, 1990, p. 423) and invoking this restriction, the character of this solution may be summarised as (14.7).

$$\text{NAIRU} = u^* = f(A, Z^S) \tag{14.7}$$

One particular point to notice from (14.7) is that despite the model's departure from the assumption of competitive labour and product markets its equilibrium unemployment rate is unaffected by either fiscal or monetary policy.

To derive an expression describing the determinants of the actual unemployment rate it is necessary to combine the employment equation (14.1) with the wage-setting equation (14.3). After grafting some dynamics on to each of these two equations and obtaining their long-run solutions Layard and Nickell (1986, p. 148) arrive at the following sort of expression, according to which the unemployment rate is determined by the capital–labour ratio, the technical progress index (A), the accuracy of price expectations (as indicated by the price 'surprise' term P/P^e), wage push factors (Z^S), output price competitiveness (PC, as measured by the ratio of output price in the world market to output price in the domestic market) and aggregate demand (s).

$$u = f\left(\frac{K}{L}, A, \frac{P}{P^e}, Z^S, PC, s\right) \tag{14.8}$$

□ *Model performance*

As is clear from the preceding discussion, the L–N model is important in at least two respects: first, it provides in expression (14.7) an explanation of the forces which determine the NAIRU and second, it provides in the form of equation (14.7) an expression which explains the determination of the actual rate of unemployment prevailing at any particular time. In empirical terms the model seems to perform reasonably well in explaining the unemployment experiences of a wide range of countries (see, in particular, the collection of papers contained in Bean, Layard and Nickell, 1987).

Table 14.2 reports some estimates of the British NAIRU which were obtained by Layard and Nickell (1986, p. 158) on the assumption of a zero balance of trade. One interesting feature of these results is the fact that they suggest that the rise which took place in Britain's actual unemployment rate since the 1950s was closely shadowed by the behaviour of the NAIRU.

A second major use to which the L–N model has been put is to provide a historical breakdown of the causes of the increases in unemployment which have occurred in the industrialised economies since the 1960s. **Table 14.3** summarises the results which were obtained by Bean, Layard and Nickell (1987, p. 11) for 18 OECD member countries. The results set out in **Table 14.3** are based on a number of simplifying assumptions and extensions to the basic model set out in (14.8) above. In essence, **Table 14.3**'s results are based on the assumption of no surprises (on either the wage or the price front), and involve the construction of a 'catch-all' variable – referred to as search intensity – the purpose of which is to capture the outward shift in the unemployment–vacancies relation which occurred in many of the OECD member countries, possibly in response to variations in such factors as unemployment benefit levels, search intensity and so forth. The final extension to the model utilised in deriving **Table 14.3**'s results concerns what is known as the real wage *wedge*. From the employers' perspective, the real wage which is relevant in determining the demand for labour is the real product wage, which is its nominal labour cost deflated by the GDP deflator as a value-added price index. However, the real wage which is

Table 14.2 ***Estimated NAIRU, British males, 1956–83 (percentage)***

	1956–66	*1967–74*	*1975–9*	*1980–3*
Estimated NAIRU (conditional on trade balance)	1.96	4.19	7.63	9.07
Actual unemployment rate	1.96	3.78	6.79	13.79

Source: Layard and Nickell (1986, p. 158).

relevant from the workers' perspective is the nominal wage, net of income and social security tax deductions, deflated by the *consumer* price index. Therefore the *wedge* which exists between the real product wage and the real consumption wage is an increasing function of both the tax rate on labour and the factors which determine the difference between the GDP deflator and the consumer price index: primarily the rates of excise and consumption taxes and the price of imports relative to GDP. The elements of the wedge between the consumption and product real wages are included, along with the search intensity variable discussed above, in the set of shift factors, Z^s (see Layard and Nickell, 1986, p. 139).

The results shown in **Table 14.3** appear to confirm the importance of demand factors in accounting for increased unemployment, especially in the European Community countries. Although import prices appear to play only a small role, the results do suggest that in most countries both reduced search intensity and higher tax burdens contributed towards rising unemployment rates.

■ Hysteresis effects in unemployment

In the previous chapter we introduced the notion of hysteresis, the basic idea of which is that the current level of the natural rate of unemployment depends on past levels of actual unemployment. As we saw, the presence of hysteresis effects boils down to the inclusion in the wage equation of an additional explanatory variable measuring the *change* in the unemployment rate (look again at equation (13.30)). Although our discussion of hysteresis effects in the previous chapter was conducted in the context of a hybrid real-wage-resistance/expectations-augmented Phillips curve framework, it is important to notice that the notion is equally applicable to more general formulations, such as that provided by the wage-formation equation given in (14.3). In this case, the pre-

Table 14.3 ***Breakdown of the change in unemployment, 1956–66 to 1980–3***

(percentage points)

	Taxes	*Import prices*	*Search*	*Demand*	*Total*	*Actual*
Australia	2.56	0.03	2.44	0.28	4.69	4.98
Austria	—	—	—	0.09	0.09	0.57
Belgium	1.41	0.04	5.28	2.53	9.15	8.93
Canada	1.34	0.02	—	4.59	5.95	4.56
Denmark	—	—	0.00	5.40	5.40	7.56
Finland	1.02	0.13	1.04	1.48	3.66	3.79
France	0.46	0.04	3.27	2.39	6.08	5.98
Germany	—	—	3.68	0.03	3.65	4.02
Ireland	3.73	0.38	—	2.29	5.65	4.33
Italy	1.12	0.02	—	–1.68	0.58	2.09
Japan	—	—	0.59	0.06	0.65	0.63
Netherlands	2.93	1.38	3.41	9.68	7.84	8.77
New Zealand	0.08	0.01	0.00	2.28	2.38	3.48
Norway	—	—	—	0.50	0.50	0.11
Sweden	1.70	0.12	0.47	0.49	0.85	1.04
Switzerland	—	—	0.18	0.29	0.48	0.41
United Kingdom	2.06	–0.05	2.25	5.33	9.60	8.33
United States	1.30	0.19	—	0.48	1.97	3.35

Note: Australia, Belgium, Canada, Denmark, France and New Zealand: independent variables lagged once; Italy, Netherlands, United Kingdom, United States: independent variables lagged twice.

Source: Bean, Layard and Nickell (1987, p. 11).

sence of hysteresis effects likewise boils down to the inclusion of the change in unemployment (Δu) as an additional right-hand-side variable in expression (14.3). Solving the model as described above, we likewise end up with the change in the unemployment rate entering equation (14.8) as an additional determinant of the actual unemployment rate (Nickell, 1990, pp. 423–4).

The implications of hysteresis effects for the behaviour of the actual and natural rates of unemployment may be conveniently illustrated with reference to **Figure 14.6**, which is due to Artis (1989). Refer back to wage equation (13.30) and treat, for simplicity, both the expected rate of inflation ($\dot{p}^e$) and the lagged real wage $(w/p)_{-1}$ as given. In the absence of hysteresis effects (that is, when $\beta_1 = 0$) the resulting Phillips curve is line *PP* in **Figure 14.6** which has a slope equal to $-\beta_2$. With hysteresis effects present we have $\beta_1 > 0$ and the Phillips curve becomes steeper, as

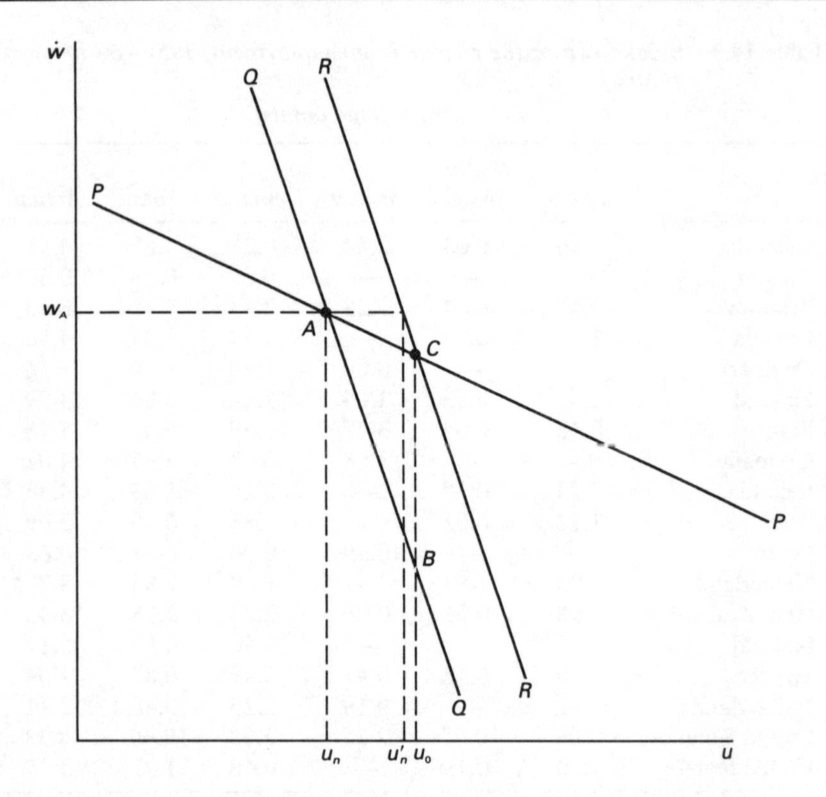

Figure 14.6 ***Hysteresis and the natural rate of unemployment***

shown by line *QQ* which has a gradient equal to $-(\beta_1 + \beta_2)$. Assume that the economy is initially at point *A*, with unemployment equal to the natural rate u_n and that hysteresis effects exist (that is, that $\beta_1 > 0$). Consider now the following sequence of events which unfolds as the economy moves into recession, with unemployment increasing to (say) u_0. With hysteresis effects present the relevant Phillips curve is *QQ* and the economy moves to point *B*. However, once point *B* is reached unemployment *stops* rising, with the consequence that $\Delta u = 0$. Therefore the β_1 effect ceases to operate and the relevant Phillips curve, given that the level of unemployment is *constant* (at u_0) is the flatter line *PP*. Accordingly, inflation resumes at the rate corresponding to point C on curve *PP*.

Failure to distinguish between these two different sorts of unemployment effects (the u and the Δu effects) can lead to the misleading conclusion that the natural rate has risen. For instance, if an investigator fails to distinguish between these two different types of unemployment effects and instead treats their joint influence as a conventional unemployment level effect, then he or she will be led to conclude that the Phillips curve is *QQ*, which has a gradient equal to $-(\beta_1 + \beta_2)$. Given this conclusion, the movement from *A* to *C* which occurs as the economy turns down implies that the Phillips curve trade-off must have shifted *outwards* from *QQ* to *RR*. Since the natural rate of unemployment is, by definition, that rate which is consistent with a constant rate of inflation this unwary investigator is forced to conclude incorrectly that the natural rate (as that necessary to hold the inflation rate constant at $\dot{w}_A$) has *risen* from its initial level u_n to the higher level u_n'. In essence, what we have here is a failure to distinguish correctly between movements along a given Phillips curve and shifts in the position of the curve itself. In cases where the hysteresis effect is strong (as evidenced by a large value of β_1) this problem can be particularly acute and can give rise to continual reestimation of the natural rate in the direction of the actual rate.[7] In a nutshell, hysteresis effects can give rise to the impression that the natural rate of unemployment chases the actual rate of unemployment!

■ Some other theories of unemployment

The imperfectly competitive framework discussed above is sufficiently flexible to accommodate a range of alternative theories of unemployment. We conclude this chapter by including three such theories which have established themselves as important in the recent literature. These are as follows: efficiency wage models, implicit contract models and insider–outsider models.

■ Efficiency wage models of unemployment

As we saw in Chapter 6 the basic idea lying behind efficiency wages is a simple one: namely, that the marginal product of labour may not be independent of the wage. Efficiency wage models of the labour market became very popular in the 1980s (see, for example, the collection of papers contained in Akerlof and Yellen, 1986) and provided insight into a range of issues, including unemployment. The common feature of these models is that they predict that, in equilibrium, an individual firm's production costs are reduced if it pays a wage in excess of the market-clearing level. Accordingly these models predict that in equilibrium there will be involuntary unemployment as the excess of labour supply over labour demand (Yellen, 1984).

The basic idea in efficiency wage models is that firms set wages and that for some reason, an increase in the wage paid generates a benefit to the firm which offsets the consequent increase in direct costs. How do firms benefit from paying higher wages? There are four main answers to this question to be found in the literature and we summarise each in turn.

□ *The shirking model*

The so-called shirking model rests on the observation that in practice most workers have some degree of discretion over their performance at the work-place. Piece-rate payment systems may not be viable in practice because monitoring is too costly or too inaccurate. Under such circumstances, the payment of a wage which is greater than the market-clearing level may offer firms an effective way of providing workers with the incentive to work rather than shirk (Calvo, 1979; Shapiro and Stiglitz, 1984).

□ *The labour turnover model*

According to this view, firms may offer wages in excess of the market-clearing level in order to discourage labour turnover which is costly to them (Stiglitz, 1974, 1985; Salop, 1979). The turnover model predicts that workers will become less likely to quit their jobs the higher is the wage paid by their employer relative to the market-clearing level and the higher is the aggregate rate of unemployment.

□ *Adverse selection*

If the ability or quality of workers is imperfectly observable, then higher wages may enable the firm to attract a higher-quality pool of job applicants. If the ability of workers is positively correlated with their reservation wages, firms which offer higher wages will attract more able job-applicants (Weiss, 1980; Malcomson, 1981). In such models firms typically pay an efficiency wage and optimally turn away candidates offering to work for a lower wage.

□ *Sociological models*

The last group of explanations leading to the efficiency wage hypothesis to be found in the literature are what might be termed sociological models (Akerlof, 1982, 1984). The basic idea here is that each worker's effort depends on the work norms of the work-group to which he belongs. In what is usually referred to as the partial gift exchange model (Akerlof, 1982), the firm may succeed in raising group-work norms and average effort by group members by paying a 'gift' in the form of wages above the minimum required, in return for the worker's 'gift' of effort in excess of the minimum required from them. In essence, high wages serve to improve morale and increase labour productivity.

■ Efficiency wages and unemployment

In order to see how the above ideas provide an explanation for unemployment consider an economy with identical, perfectly competitive firms. Assume that labour is the only factor of production and that each firm has a production function of the form

$$q = f(E) \tag{14.9}$$

which specifies its output (q) as a function of what may be termed its *effective* labour force, denoted by E. Assume also that the *effort* per worker, denoted by e, is an *increasing* function of the real wage w. The effort–real wage relation may be written as follows:

$$e = e(w), \text{ where } e'(w) > 0$$

Denoting the number of employees by L, the firm's effective labour force (E) can therefore be written as

$$E = e(w)L \tag{14.10}$$

and substituting (14.10) into (14.9) we obtain the production function as

$$q = f(e(w)\ L) \tag{14.11}$$

Solow (1979) showed that within this framework, a firm that can hire all of the labour it wants at the wage it chooses to offer will maximise its profits by offering the real wage (w^*) which satisfies the condition that the elasticity of effort with respect to the real wage equals unity. This condition has become known as the *Solow condition* and the wage w^* is referred to as the *efficiency wage* since it minimises labour costs per efficiency unit. The Solow condition can be written as follows:[8]

$$we'(w)/e(w) = 1 \tag{14.12}$$

Rewriting (14.12) in the following form we see that the Solow condition has a particularly straightforward geometric interpretation.

$$e'(w) = e(w)/w \tag{14.13}$$

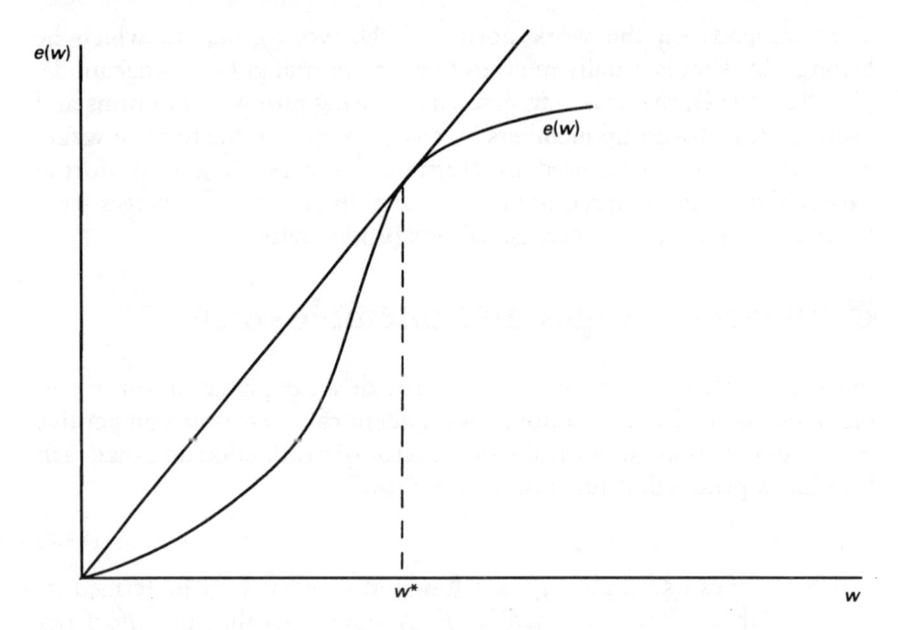

Figure 14.7 *The Solow condition and the efficiency wage*

Figure 14.7 plots the effort–real wage relation on the basis of its usually assumed shape. According to condition (14.13), the efficiency wage is that which equates the gradient of the effort function ($e'(w)$) to the ratio of effort per worker to the real wage ($e(w)/w$). Since the latter is the gradient of a ray from the origin in **Figure 14.7** and the former is the gradient of the effort function itself, we see that the efficiency wage w^* is that at which such a ray is tangential to the effort curve.

One interesting thing to notice from (14.12) is that the efficiency wage depends only on the function $e(w)$ and is otherwise unaffected by conditions in either the product or the labour market. In essence, what condition (14.12) says is that, other things being equal, the only thing which will induce the firm to vary the wage it offers is a change in the functional form of $e(w)$.

According to the above model each firm will optimally hire labour up to the point where its marginal product[9] is equal to the real wage w^*. Provided that the aggregate demand for labour falls short of its aggregate supply (and that the efficiency wage w^* exceeds labour's reservation wage) the firm will not be constrained by labour market conditions in pursuing its optimal (that is, profit-maximising) policy, so that the equilibrium will be characterised by the existence of involuntary unemployment. Although unemployed workers would prefer to work at the real wage w^* than to be unemployed, firms will be unwilling to hire

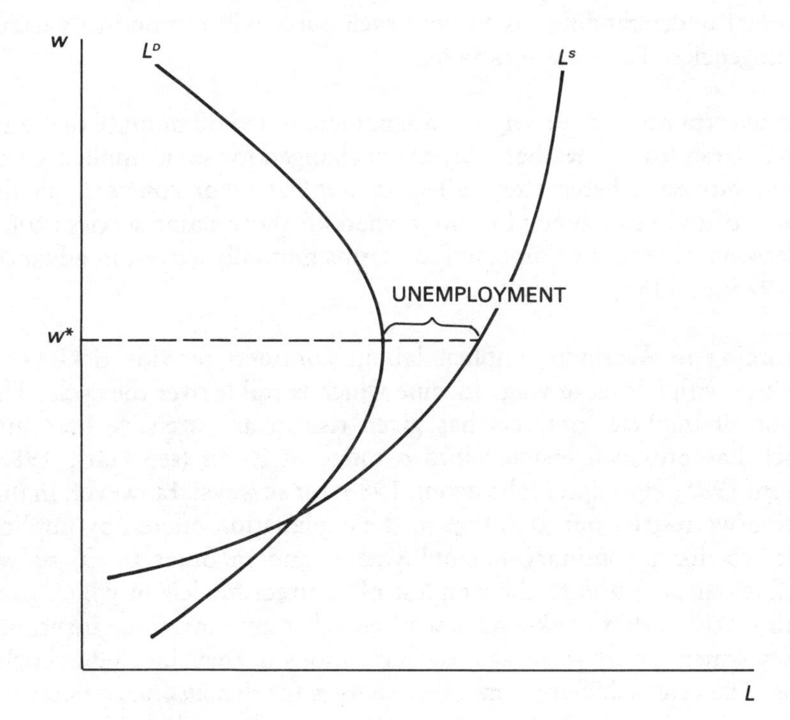

Figure 14.8 *The efficiency wage and unemployment*

them at either that, or at some lower, wage. The reason for this is simply that any reduction in the wage paid would lower the productivity of all existing employees. **Figure 14.8**, suggested by Weiss (1990), provides a convenient summary of the efficiency wage model of unemployment.[10]

■ Implicit contract theory and unemployment

Implicit contract theory provides another possible explanation for the occurrence of unemployment. Implicit contract models were initially developed in the 1970s (Baily, 1974; Gordon, 1974; Azariadis, 1975) to focus attention on the nature of optimal labour contracts between risk-adverse workers and risk-neutral employers. The principal ingredient of such models is their recognition of the role of uncertainty regarding the future course of events. Implicit contract models recognise that the labour market in practice is *not* a spot auction market. Instead, the contracts which are agreed between employers and workers typically carry with them an implicit agreement in the form of a set of shared informal understandings as to how each party will respond to various contingencies. To quote Azariadis,

> in uncertainty, labour services are not auctioned off in quite the same way fresh fruit is. Rather, they are exchanged for some implicit set of commitments, hereinafter called an *implicit labor contract*, on the part of the firm to employ the owners of those labor services for a reasonable period of time, and on terms mutually agreed in advance. (1975, p. 1183)

According to Azariadis, implicit labour contracts provide risk-averse workers with a level of wage income which is stable over the cycle. The notion of implicit contracts has given rise to an extensive literature which has provided insights into a range of issues (see Hart, 1983; Rosen, 1985; Hart and Holmstrom, 1986, for surveys). However, in this section we restrict our attention to the explanation offered by implicit contracts for involuntary unemployment, and in order to do so we confine our attention to the simplest of contract models in which risk-neutral firms 'sell' to risk-averse workers what amounts to an insurance policy which covers them against fluctuations in their income over the cycle. The price which the employer charges for this insurance takes the form of a reduction in the average wage over the cycle below what it would otherwise have been. In short, workers receive higher wages in the 'bad times' in exchange for lower wages in the 'good times'. As we shall see, such a model leads to the prediction that money wages will optimally remain unchanged over the cycle.

To outline implicit contract theory one has, first, to explain what such a contract is; second, how it arises; third, why it is undertaken between the worker and the employer instead of between the worker and a third party (it will soon become obvious that an implicit contract is in effect an insurance policy, hence it could be offered by an insurance company); fourth, and finally, how it is enforced. After this is done, we consider the implications of the analysis for unemployment.

What is, then, an implicit contract? In modern economics an implicit contract is typically viewed as an insurance policy between a worker and his employer in the form of some security offered by the employer against the worker's employment status (hence labour income) in the uncertain economic environment within which the firm operates. Though such an arrangement is rarely observed in practice, it can be justified (or suspected to exist) on theoretical grounds. This observation brings us in effect to the second question, that is, how such a contract arises: the answer lies on the supposition that a worker may be more risk-averse than the employer. The asymmetry in the perception of risk can arise as follows. On the one hand, a worker has usually just one type of (human) capital and his income is either the wage, if he is employed, or nothing, if he loses his job (omitting for simplicity social insurance benefits and non-labour income). Consequently, it is not easy for the worker to 'spread the risks' and, if adverse economic conditions prevail, the implications for the worker's welfare are severe (loss of income, at least in the short run, and subsequent loss of experience with adverse consequences for reemployment in the longer run). On the other hand, employers or owners of capital can be less risk-averse because (i) they can diversify between different assets or activities; (ii) the loss from a worker separation is not that severe for them as there is usually some degree of substitution between different types of labour and, in theory, employers should be able to replace the worker even at a somewhat higher wage than the one previously paid. Hence, the worker may have a higher probability of an adversity happening to him (more workers become unemployed than firms go bankrupt) and the implications may also be more severe to him compared with the employer. This brings us to the third point, why this insurance is not undertaken by a third party. The answer is information. A third party, such as an insurance company, can hardly know whether a worker's services are no longer demanded because his skills are no longer relevant or his work effort is below par. On the contrary, such information is available to the employer.

The final question, that is, how implicit contracts are enforced, can be answered only in an indirect way as by their very nature such contracts are difficult to be detected by outsiders and even more difficult to be enforced by a court or an industrial tribunal. In short, the problem of enforcement arises from two different considerations (recall that an implicit contract amounts to workers paying an insurance premium to their employers during good times in return for employment security during bad times). First, if wages elsewhere rise above those paid by the firm, the worker can quit, leaving the employer with a cost (that is, the cost of retaining the worker when the firm was facing adverse conditions). Second, if wages elsewhere are lower than those currently received by the worker, the firm can replace the worker with another worker from the open market and the worker would have to bear the cost of a protection which did not materialise (the cost to the worker is the lower wage he accepted during the 'good' period).

The theory attempts to answer this dilemma in three different ways. First, and least successfully, if adjustment is not costless for the worker and the firm (for example, if a separation involves the cost of moving house, costs of hiring/training and so on), the contract wage would be enforced as long as such costs are sufficiently high to make a separation undesirable (Baily, 1974). One may note that the firm can still lay off the worker, if the marginal product of the worker falls sufficiently below the wage. One may alternatively argue that in the presence of workers' adjustment costs, the underpayment of the worker in the first instance is not really the result of an implicit undertaking on behalf of the firm to insure the worker's employment status but a wage policy which pays the worker the minimum he would accept to stay in his present job, given his constrained mobility. A second way of enforcing an implicit contract is by asking the worker to accept a low wage initially (in the first contract) on the understanding that his wage will increase in future contracts: this ensures that the worker will not leave in the second (or successive) period(s) and the theory goes through as long as the firm has committed itself to honour the contract. Finally, one can appeal to reputation effects: whichever party acquires the reputation of dishonouring the contract would find it difficult to contract with other parties in the future (Holmstrom, 1981).

Let us now introduce a stylised presentation of implicit contracts. Recall that risk is a crucial ingredient of the model. Workers are assumed to be risk-averse in that they do not like fluctuation in their wage/employment status while employers are risk-neutral in that they care only about the average wage bill. One can show that both parties can be made better off (compared with an 'always on the demand curve' spot equilibrium), if the wage is lower than that in the conventional marginal productivity framework *and* does not vary over time. Consider the case where the firm's demand for labour changes because the value of production or the production function as such changes. For example, the demand for agricultural labour can be affected by adverse weather while workers in the hospitality industry may be affected by a change in the exchange rate or events abroad. In a catch-all way assume, therefore, that uncertainty exists about the price of the product the firm supplies. For simplicity let us further assume that the future price of the product can be either 'low' or 'high'. The probability of a high price occurring in the future is known to all parties and is equal to p_1. The probability of a low price is therefore equal to $p_2 = 1 - p_1$. Under the conventional marginal productivity analysis and other things being constant, these two prices would result in either a low wage or a high wage (W_1 or W_2 respectively). Now suppose that the employer has decided to employ the worker, so uncertainty relates only to the level of wage that will be paid to the worker in the two different price outcomes ('states'). The expected utility, $\bar{V}$, of the worker is

$$\bar{V} = p_1 U(W_1) + p_2 U(W_2) \tag{14.14}$$

where $U(W_i)$, $i = 1$ or 2, is the utility the worker derives from a particular wage level. Equation (14.14) can be thought of as an indifference curve representing the trade-off between different levels of wages for given probabilities.

Assume that the employer wants to minimise the expected average wage bill, C, of employing the worker, which is given by

$$C = p_1 W_1 + (1 - p_1) W_2 \tag{14.15}$$

which gives rise to a family of isocost curves. Equations (14.14) and (14.15) provide the basics for the determination of an optimal contract between the worker and the employer, that is, a solution that leaves the worker in his original utility level while it minimises the costs to the employer. It is easy to show that under these conditions the optimal contract would be one which specifies that the worker's wage would be the same ($W_1 = W_2$) *irrespective* of which of the two prices is realised. This is so because the slope of the indifference curve is

$$\text{slope of indifference curve} = [-p_1/(1 - p_1)][(U'(W_1)/(U'(W_2)] \tag{14.16}$$

where U' stands for the change in utility of the worker due to a change in the wage (marginal utility). The slope of the firm's isocost line is

$$\text{slope of isocost} = -p_1/(1 - p_1) \tag{14.17}$$

The equilibrium condition requires that the indifference curve is tangential to an isocost curve in the wage employment space, which amounts to saying that the slope of the worker's indifference curve should be equal to the slope of the employer's isocost curve. This requires that the second term in equation (14.17) is equal to one ($U'(W_1) = U'(W_2)$) which is possible only if $W_1 = W_2$. This solution is shown in **Figure 14.9.**

This analysis shows that combining uncertainty in the (risk-neutral) employer's and the (risk-averse) worker's maximisation problems, the optimal contract will be one which provides for wages which do not vary with the price of output (if employers are also risk-averse, then wages will vary with the firm's output price as in the conventional marginal productivity model). Therefore, the observed wage stickiness has been explained.

The model presented in this section was a basic one and can be extended in a number of ways. For example, one can incorporate variable hours or even allow for employers to pay unemployment compensation. Nevertheless, the basic message of the theory of implicit contracts has come through in that wage rigidity and, even, unemployment may be efficient given, on the one hand, the desire of workers to get some form of insurance against future variability of their work status/conditions and, on the other hand, the existence of less than perfect information and the inability of insurance markets to offer such security to workers.

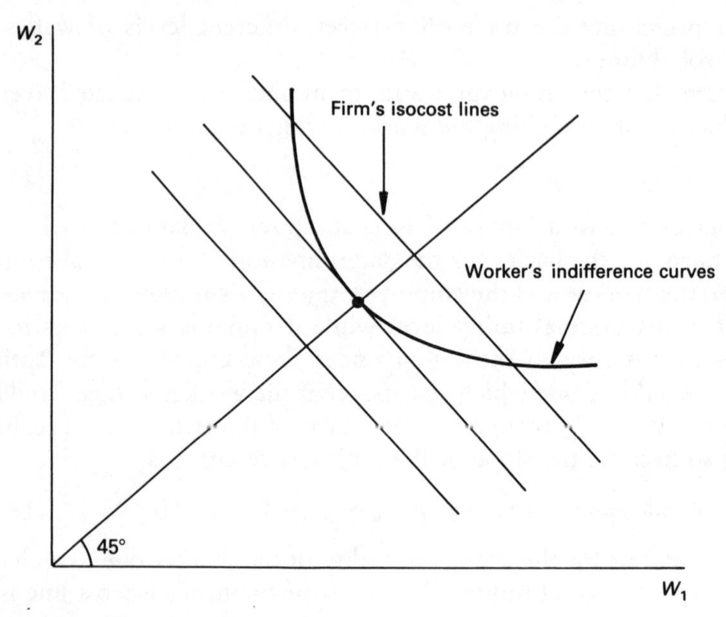

Figure 14.9 ***The optimal contract***

Implicit contracts and involuntary unemployment

As can be seen from **Figure 14.10** this rigid wage result provides an intuitively appealing explanation for the occurrence of involuntary unemployment. **Figure 14.10** captures the essential spirit of the preceding model. It shows the demand curve for labour shifting leftwards as the economy goes into recession and the price of output falls from p_1 to p_2, with labour's marginal physical product assumed to remain unchanged. The preceding discussion has shown that the optimal wage is such that $W_1 = W_2 =$ (say) W.[11] As can be seen from **Figure 14.10**, the rigidity of the money wage, coupled with the leftward shift in the labour demand curve which occurs as the economy goes into recession, results in the opening up of an excess of labour supply over labour demand equal to $(n_1 - n_2)$. This is involuntary unemployment and it occurs because of the rigidity of the money wage.

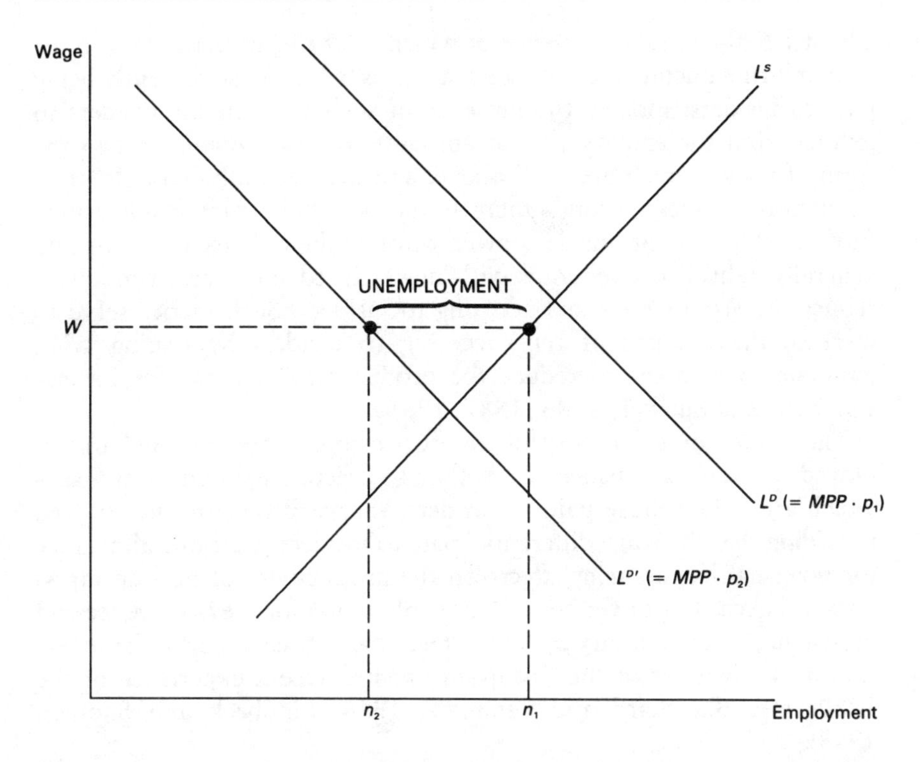

Figure 14.10 *Implicit contracts and unemployment*

Insider–outsider models of unemployment

The final explanation of unemployment to be considered stems from the insider–outsider model of the trade union which was discussed in Chapter 11.[12] As we saw there, the basic idea of this model (which is primarily associated with the work of Lindbeck and Snower (1988)) is that the interests of employed (and perhaps also temporarily laid-off) union members (the *insiders*) figure more heavily in the formulation and pursuit of union wage policies than do the interests of the unemployed and non-members as *outsiders*. The central feature of such models is their assumption that the present workforce can not easily be replaced by new workers hired from the ranks of the unemployed. In short, such models allow for the possibility that insiders and outsiders are *imperfect substitutes* for one another. Two main sorts of reasons are suggested for this in the literature. The first stems from the existence of various turnover costs (such as hiring, firing and training costs of the sort discussed in

Chapter 6 above), the existence of which limit the attractiveness to the firm of hiring unemployed workers at wages below those currently being paid to insiders. Indeed, the presence of such costs enable insiders to extract from the employer what amounts to an *economic rent* in the form of wages which are both above, and less cyclically variable, than competitive wages. Second, there is the possibility that insiders may further enhance their 'insider power' through their ability to harass and generally refuse to cooperate with newly hired outsiders who might reduce the size of the rents accruing to insiders. Such tactics serve to increase the amount of rent accruing to insiders by issuing what amounts to a threat to reduce the productivity of new recruits (see Lindbeck and Snower, 1986, 1987, 1988a).

The insider outsider model therefore predicts that even though unemployed workers as outsiders are willing to accept employment at wages which are below those paid to insiders, they will remain unemployed providing that the wage differential paid to insiders (after due allowance for potential harrassment effects on the productivity of new entrants) does not exceed turnover costs. This explanation for the occurrence and persistence of involuntary unemployment has attracted particular attention in the context of the European unemployment experience of the 1980s (see Blanchard and Summers, 1986; Lindbeck and Snower, 1988).

Notes

1. The extent to which the unemployment rate is influenced by the level of unemployment benefit (see pp. 39–41 above for a discussion of the influence of benefits on labour force participation behaviour) is a topic which attracted much attention in the 1970s. For a review of the early UK literature, see Sapsford (1981, pp. 175–6). The more recent evidence has already been discussed in Chapter 12 in the context of search unemployment. For a more detailed review see Atkinson and Micklewright (1991).
2. By transferring excess demand for labour to areas of excess supply, and vice versa, and by improving geographical and occupational mobility and the flow of information regarding unfilled vacancies, such policies can reduce the length of adjustment lags by reducing market frictions and periods spent in job search. If successful in achieving these objectives, such policies result in a lower unemployment rate at each level of excess labour demand. This brings about a leftward shift in the relationship between excess labour demand and unemployment – see **Figure 13.3 (b)** – and thereby leads to a leftward shift in the position of the Phillips curve.
3. It is often assumed that the *U–V* relation can be adequately represented by a *rectangular hyperbola*, that is, by the equation

$$UV = K$$

where U and V denote the numbers of unemployed workers and unfilled vacancies respectively and K is some constant (see Hansen, 1970). However, in cases where the observations on U and V are confined within a narrow range, a local linear approximation may prove adequate (Thirlwall, 1969).

4. The vertical axis in **Figure 14.5** refers to the real product wage. In Chapter 5 we saw that the profit-maximisation condition for the firm which both hires its labour and sells its output in perfectly competitive markets is that it hires its labour up to the point where the nominal wage (say W) equals the value of its marginal product, that is, $W = MPP.P$, where P denotes the product price. Cross-multiplying we see that this condition may be written as $(W/P) = MPP$, where W/P denotes the real product wage. This version of the profit maximisation condition defines the labour demand schedule – line NN – in **Figure 14.5**.
5. In such studies the full-employment marginal product of labour is typically evaluated using either the 'peak to peak' approach or by regressing labour productivity on a polynomial time-trend, plus some cyclical indicator (most commonly unemployment). According to the latter approach, one uses the results from such a regression to predict the level of productivity conditional on some definition of full employment, most commonly in the sense of a particular rate of unemployment. Both Bruno (1986) and Gordon (1987) take the late 1960s as their full-employment benchmark.
6. The following discussion of the L–N model is highly (over) simplified. For more detailed discussion the interested reader should consult Layard and Nickell (1985, 1986).
7. The process described in the text is sometimes referred to as *partial* hysteresis in order to differentiate it from the case of *complete* hysteresis, where the natural rate of unemployment equals the current rate.
8. The Solow condition may be derived as follows. With the price of the firm's output normalised to one, its optimisation problem is to maximise its profit function with respect to both w and L, subject to the condition that the wage rate is not less than some minimum real wage W which the firm must pay to hire employees. W will be the reservation wage of individuals if some are involuntarily unemployed. If none are involuntarily unemployed then W is the wage offered by other firms. Although the firm may not pay a wage below W it is free to pay a wage in excess of W. The firm's choice problem is therefore to

$$\max_{L,w} \{f[e(w)L] - wL\} \text{ subject to } w \geqslant W \qquad (1)$$

This gives rise to the following necessary conditions

$$f'[e(w)L]\, e(w) - w = 0 \qquad (2)$$

$$\left.\begin{aligned} f'[e(w)L]\, e'(w) - 1 \leqslant 0 \\ w \geqslant W \end{aligned}\right\} \qquad (3)$$

where the bracketed inequalities are complementary. Combining (2) and (3) we obtain the required solution for w, which is as follows:

$$we'(w)/e(w) = 1$$

which is immediately recognisable as Solow's condition, as given by expression (14.12) in the text.

9. Differentiating expression (14.11) with respect to L using the function of a function rule we obtain the marginal product of labour as:

$$e(w^*)f'(e(w^*)\ L^*)$$

10. The peculiar shape of the labour demand curve in **Figure 14.8** arises because of the distinction between labour inputs measured in terms of employees and efficiency units. As we have seen wage costs per efficiency unit are minimised at the efficiency wage w^*. The horizontal axis in **Figure 14.8** refers to the number of *employees* and the backward-bending character of the labour demand curve at wages below w^* reflects the fact as wages fall below the efficiency wage, the number of efficiency units embodied in each worker falls. To take Weiss's own example: if the average worker hired at $8 per hour is more than twice as productive as the average worker hired at $4 per hour, then the $8 workers are cheaper in terms of cost per efficiency unit than the $4 workers (1990, p. 19).
11. The difference between the contract wage W shown in **Figure 14.10** and that which would be given by labour demand–supply intersection represents the price which workers pay for their income stability insurance; it is the lower wage that they accept during the 'good times' in return for the more favourable wage which they receive during the 'bad times'.
12. The role of insider–outsider models in the generation of hysteresis effects was also mentioned in Chapter 13.

References

Addison, J. T. and Barnett, A. H. (1982) 'The Impact of Unions on Productivity', *British Journal of Industrial Relations*, vol. 20, no. 2, pp. 145–62.

Addison, J. and Siebert, W. S. (1979) *The Market for Labor: An Analytical Treatment* (Santa Monica, Calif.: Goodyear).

Adelman, I. (1958) 'A Stochastic Analysis of the Size Distribution of Firms', *Journal of the American Statistical Association*, vol. 53, no. 284, pp. 893–904.

Ahamad, B. and Blaug, M. (eds) (1973) *The Practice of Manpower Forecasting: A Collection of Case Studies* (Amsterdam: Elsevier).

Aigner, D. J. and Cain, G. G. (1977) 'Statistical Theories of Discrimination in the Labor Market', *Industrial and Labor Relations Review*, pp. 175–87.

Aird, J. S. (1984) 'The Preliminary Results of China's 1982 Census', *China Quarterly*, vol. 96, pp. 613–40.

Akerlof, G. A. (1976) 'The Economics of Caste and of the Rat Race and Other Woeful Tales', *Quarterly Journal of Economics*, vol. 90, pp. 599–617.

Akerlof, G. A. (1980) 'The Theory of Social Custom, of Which Unemployment May Be One Consequence', *Quarterly Journal of Economics*, vol. 94, pp. 749–75.

Akerlof, G. A. (1982) 'Labor Contracts as Partial Gift Exchange', *Quarterly Journal of Economics*, vol. 47, no. 4, pp. 543–69.

Akerlof, G. A. (1983) 'Loyalty Filters', *American Economic Review*, vol. 73, pp. 54–63.

Akerlof, G. A. (1984) 'Gift Exchange and Efficiency Wage Theory: Four Views', *American Economic Review (Papers and Proceedings)*, vol. 74, no. 2, pp. 79–83.

Akerlof, G. and Yellen, J. (eds) (1986) *Efficiency Wage Models of Labour Markets* (Cambridge: Cambridge University Press).

Alchian, A. A. and Kessel, R. A. (1962) 'Competition, Monopoly and the Pursuit of Money', in *Aspects of Labor Economics* (Princeton, NJ: National Bureau of Economic Research), pp. 157–83.

Allen, S. G. (1981) 'An Empirical Model of Work Attendance', *Review of Economics and Statistics*, vol. 63, no. 1, pp. 77–87.

Alogoskoufis, G. and Manning, A. (1991) 'Tests of Alternative Wage Employment Bargaining Models with an Application to the UK Aggregate Labour Market', *European Economic Review*, vol. 35, no. 1, pp. 23–37.

Althauser, R. P. and Kallenberg, A. L. (1981) 'Firms, Occupations and the Structure of Labor Markets: A Conceptual Analysis', in I. Berg (ed.) *Sociological Perspectives on Labor Markets* (New York: Academic Press), pp. 119–49.

Altonji, J. G. (1982) 'The Intertemporal Substitution Model of Labor Market Fluctuations: An Empirical Analysis', *Review of Economic Studies*, vol. 49, no. 5 (Special Issue), pp. 783–824.
Amsden, A. H. (ed.) (1980) *The Economics of Women and Work* (Harmondsworth: Penguin).
Amin, S. and Pebley, A. R. (1987) 'The Impact of a Public Health Intervention on Excess Female Mortality in Punjab', mimeograph (Princeton, NJ).
Andrews, M. (1988) 'Some Formal Models of the Aggregate Labour Market', in M. Beenstock (ed.), *Modelling the Labour Market* (London: Chapman & Hall), pp. 25–48.
Anker, R., Buvinic, M. and Youssef, N. (eds) (1982) *Women's Roles and Population Trends in the Third World* (London: Croom Helm).
Apps, R. J. (1982) 'The Real Wage Hypothesis: Some Results for the UK', in M. Artis, C. J. Green, D. Leslie and G. W. Smith (eds), *Demand Management, Supply Constraints and Inflation* (Manchester: Manchester University Press), pp. 170–89.
Archibald, G. C. and Lipsey, R. G. (1977) *An Introduction to a Mathematical Treatment of Economics* (London: Weidenfeld & Nicolson).
Arrow, K. J. (1972a) 'Models of Job Discrimination', in A. H. Pascal (ed.), *Racial Discrimination in Economic Life* (Lexington, Mass.: D. C. Heath), pp. 83–102.
Arrow, K. J. (1972b) 'Some Mathematical Models of Race in the Labor Market', in A. H. Pascal (ed.), *Racial Discrimination in Economic Life* (Lexington, Mass.: D. C. Heath), pp. 187–203.
Arrow, K. J. (1973a) 'Higher Education as a Filter', *Journal of Public Economics*, vol. 2 (July), pp. 193–216.
Arrow, K. J. (1973b) 'The Theory of Discrimination', in O. Ashenfelter and A. Rees (eds), *Discrimination in Labor Markets* (Princeton, NJ: Princeton University Press), pp. 3–33.
Artis, M. (1989) 'Wage Inflation', in D. Greenaway (ed.), *Current Issues in Macroeconomics* (London: Macmillan), pp. 91–109.
Ashenfelter, O. and Brown, J. N. (1986) 'Testing the Efficiency of Employment Contracts', *Journal of Political Economy*, vol. 94 (Supplement), pp. S41–87.
Ashenfelter, O. and Heckman, J. (1974) 'The Estimation of Income and Substitution Effects in a Model of Family Labour Supply', *Econometrica*, vol. 42, no. 1, pp. 73–85.
Ashenfelter, O. and Layard, R. (1983) 'The Effects of Incomes Policies Upon Wage Differentials', *Economica*, vol. 50, pp. 127–44.
Ashenfelter, O. and Layard, R. (eds) (1986) *Handbook of Labor Economics* (Amsterdam: North-Holland).
Ashenfelter, O. and Pencavel, J. H. (1969) 'American Trade Union Growth, 1900–1960', *Quarterly Journal of Economics*, vol. 83, no. 3, pp. 434–48.
Ashenfelter, O., Johnson, G. E. and Pencavel, J. H. (1972) 'Trade Unions and the Rate of Change of Money Wage Rates in United States Manufacturing Industry', *Review of Economic Studies*, vol. 39, no. 117, pp. 27–54.
Asquith Commission on Equal Pay (1946) *Report* (London: HMSO).

Atkin War Cabinet Committee on the Employment of Women in Industry (1919) *Report* (London: HMSO).

Atkinson, A. B. and Micklewright, J. (1991) 'Unemployment Compensation and Labor Market Transitions: A Critical Review', *Journal of Economic Literature*, vol. 29, no. 4, pp. 1679–1727.

Atkinson, A. B. and Stern, N. H. (1980) 'On the Switch from Direct to Indirect Taxation', *Journal of Public Economics*, vol. 14, no. 2, pp. 195–224.

Atkinson, A., Gomulka, J., Micklewright, J. and Rau, N. (1984) 'Unemployment Benefit, Duration and Incentives in Britain: How Robust is the Evidence?', *Journal of Public Economics*, vol. 23, no. 1, pp. 3–26.

Azariadis, C. (1975) 'Implicit Contracts and Underemployment Equilibria', *Journal of Political Economy*, vol. 83, no. 6, pp. 1183–1202.

Bacharach, M. (1976) *Economics and the Theory of Games* (London: Macmillan).

Baily, M. N. (1974) 'Wages and Employment under Uncertain Demand', *Review of Economic Studies*, vol. 41, no. 1, pp. 37–50.

Bain, G. S. and Elsheikh, F. (1976) *Union Growth and the Business Cycle: An Econometric Analysis* (Oxford: Blackwell).

Bain, G. S. and Elsheikh, F. (1982) 'Union Growth and the Business Cycle: A Disaggregated Study', *British Journal of Industrial Relations*, vol. 20, no. 1, pp. 34–43.

Ball, R. J. and St Cyr, E. B. A. (1966) 'Short Term Employment Functions in British Manufacturing Industry', *Review of Economic Studies*, vol. 33, no. 3, pp. 179–207.

Bardhan, P. K. (1984) *Land, Labor and Rural Poverty: Essays in Development Economics* (New York: Columbia University Press).

Barmby, T. A. and Treble, J. G. (1991) 'Absenteeism in a Medium-Sized Manufacturing Plant', *Applied Economics*, vol. 23, no. 2, pp. 161–6.

Bean, C. (1992) *European Unemployment: A Survey* (London: London School of Economics, Centre for Economic Performance), Discussion Paper no. 71 (March).

Bean, R. and Holden, K. (1992) 'Cross-National Differences in Trade Union Membership in OECD Countries', *Industrial Relations Journal*, vol. 23, no. 1, pp. 52–9.

Bean, C. and Turnbull, P. (1988) 'Employment in the British Coal Industry: A Test of the Labour Demand Model', *Economic Journal*, vol. 97, no. 393, pp. 1092–1104.

Bean, C., Layard, R. and Nickell, S. (1987) 'The Rise in Unemployment: A Multi-Country Study', in C. Bean, R. Layard and S. Nickell (eds), *The Rise in Unemployment* (Oxford: Basil Blackwell), pp. 1–22. Also published in *Economica*, vol. 53 (Supplement), pp. S1–S22.

Beck, E. M., Horan, P. M. and Tolbert, C. M. (1978) 'Stratification in a Dual Economy: A Sectoral Model of Earnings Determination', *American Sociological Review*, vol. 45, pp. 712–19.

Becker, G. S. (1957) *The Economics of Discrimination* (quotations from the 2nd edition, 1971) (Chicago: The University of Chicago Press).

Becker, G. S. (1959) 'Union Restrictions on Entry', in P. Bradley (ed.), *The Public State in Union Power* (Charlottesville, Va.: The University of Chicago Press).

Becker, G. S. (1964) *Human Capital: A Theoretical and Empirical Analysis* (New York: National Bureau of Economic Research).

Becker, G. S. (1965) 'A Theory of the Allocation of Time', *Economic Journal*, vol. 75, no. 299, pp. 493–517.

Becker, G. S. (1975) *Human Capital*, 2nd edn (Columbia University Press).

Becker, G. S. (1981) *A Treatise on the Family* (Cambridge, Mass.: Harvard University Press).

Becker, G. S. and Tomes, N. (1979) 'An Equilibrium Theory of the Distribution of Income and Intergenerational Mortality', *Journal of Political Economy*, vol. 87, no. 6, pp. 1141–87.

Begg, D. (1982) *The Rational Expectations Revolution in Macroeconomics* (Oxford: Philip Allen).

Begg, D., Fischer, S. and Dornbusch, R. (1991) *Economics*, 3rd edn (London: McGraw-Hill).

Behrman, J. R. and Birdsall, N. (1983) 'The Quality of Schooling: Quantity Alone is Misleading', *American Economic Review*, vol. 73, no. 5. pp. 928–46.

Behrman, J. R. and Wolfe, B. L. (1985) 'Labor Force Participation and Earnings Determinants for Women in the Special Conditions of Developing Countries', *Journal of Development Economics*, vol. 15, pp. 259–88.

Behrman, J. R., Wolfe, B. L. and Blau, D. M. (1985) 'Human Capital and Earnings Distribution in a Developing Country: The Case of Prerevolutionary Nicaragua', *Economic Development and Cultural Change*, vol. 34, no. 1, pp. 1–29.

Beller, A. H. (1984) 'Trends in Occupational Segregation by Sex and Race, 1960–1981', in B. F. Reskin (ed.), *Sex Segregation in the Workplace: Trends, Explanations, Remedies* (Washington, DC: National Academy Press) pp. 11–26.

Benjamin, D. and Kochin, L. (1979), 'Searching for an Explanation of Unemployment in Inter-War Britain', *Journal of Political Economy*, vol. 89, no. 3, pp. 441–78.

Ben-Porath, Y. (1973) 'Economic Analysis of Fertility in Israel: Point and Counterpoint', *Journal of Political Economy*, vol. 81, no. 2 (part 2), pp. S202–S233.

Berg, I. (ed.) (1981) *Sociological Perspectives on Labor Markets* (New York: Academic Press).

Berg, S. V. and Dalton, T. R. (1977) 'United Kingdom Labour Force Activity Rates: Unemployment and Real Wages', *Applied Economics*, vol. 9, no. 3, pp. 265–70.

Bergmann, B. (1971) 'The Effect on White Incomes of Discrimination in Employment', *Journal of Political Economy*, vol. 79, no. 2, pp. 294–313.

Berndt, E. R. (1981) 'Modelling the Simultaneous Demand for Factors of Production', in Z. Hornstein, J. Grice and A. Webb (eds), *The Economics of the Labour Market* (London: HMSO), pp. 125–42.

Berndt, E. R. (1991) *The Practice of Econometrics* (New York: Addison-Wesley).

Beveridge, W. H. (1944) *Full Employment in a Free Society* (London: Allen & Unwin).

Binmore, K. (1987) 'Nash Bargaining Theory I–III', in K. Binmore and P. Dasgupta (eds) *The Economics of Bargaining* (Oxford: Basil Blackwell), pp. 1–76 and 239–56.

Binmore, K. and Dasgupta, P. (eds) (1986) *Economic Organisations as Games* (Oxford: Basil Blackwell).

Binmore, K. and Dasgupta, P. (eds) (1987) *The Economics of Bargaining* (Oxford: Basil Blackwell).

Binmore, K., Rubinstein, A. and Wolinsky, A. (1985) 'The Nash Bargaining Solution in Economic Modelling', *Rand Journal of Economics*, vol. 17, no. 2, pp. 176–88.

Birdsall, N. and Behrman, J. R. (1983) 'Does Geographical Aggregation Cause Overestimates of the Return to Schooling?' (Washington, DC: The World Bank, DEDPH).

Birdsall, N. and Fox, M. L. (1985) 'Why Males Earn More: Location and Training of Brazilian Schoolteachers', *Economic Development and Cultural Change*, vol. 33, no. 3 (April), pp. 533–56.

Birdsall, N. and Sabot, R. (eds) (1991) *Unfair Advantage: Labor Market Discrimination in Developing Countries* (The World Bank).

Bishop, R. L. (1963) 'Game Theoretic Analyses of Bargaining', *Quarterly Journal of Economics*, vol. 77, no. 4, pp. 559–602.

Bishop, R. L. (1964) 'A Zeuthen–Hicks Theory of Bargaining', *Econometrica*, vol. 32, no. 3, pp. 410–17.

Blanchard, O. J. and Summers, L. (1986) 'Hysteresis and the European Unemployment Problem', *NBER Macroeconomics Annual*, vol. 1, pp. 15–17.

Blanchard, O. J. and Summers, L. H. (1988) 'Hysteresis and the European Unemployment Problem', in R. B. Cross (ed.), *Unemployment, Hysteresis, and the Natural Rate Hypothesis* (Oxford: Basil Blackwell), pp. 306–64.

Blanchflower, D. (1986) 'What Effects Do Unions Have on Relative Wages in Great Britain?', *British Journal of Industrial Relations*, vol. 24, no. 2, pp. 195–204.

Blau, F. D. (1984) 'Occupational Segregation and Labor Market Discrimination', in B. F. Reskin (ed.), *Sex Segregation in the Workplace: Trends, Explanations, Remedies* (Washington, DC: National Academy Press), pp. 11–26.

Blaug, M. (1970) *An Introduction to The Economics of Education* (Harmondsworth: Penguin).

Blaug, M. (1976) 'The Empirical Status on Human Capital Theory: A Slightly Jaundiced Survey', *Journal of Economic Literature*, vol. 14 (September), pp. 827–55.

Blinder, A. S. (1973) 'Wage Discrimination: Reduced Form and Structural Estimates', *Journal of Human Resources*, vol. 8, no. 4, pp. 436–55.

Blinder, A. S. (1974) *Toward an Economic Theory of Income Distribution* (Cambridge, Mass.: MIT Press).

Blinder, A. S. (1976) 'On Dogmatism in Human Capital Theory', *Journal of Human Resources*, vol. 6 (Winter), pp. 8–22.

Bloom, G. F. (1941) 'A Reconsideration of the Theory of Exploitation', *Quarterly Journal of Economics*, vol. 55, no. 2, pp. 413–42.

Bluestone, B., Murphy, W. and Stevenson, M. (1973) 'Low Wages and the Working Poor' (Ann Arbor: University of Michigan–Wayne State University, Institute of Labor and Industrial Relations).

Blundell, R. and Walker, I. (1982) 'Modelling the Joint Determination of Household Labour Supplies and Commodity Demands', *Economic Journal*, vol. 92, no. 366, pp. 351–64.

Booth, A. (1983) 'A Reconsideration of Trade Union Growth in the UK', *British Journal of Industrial Relations*, vol. 21, no. 3, pp. 377–91.

Booth, A. (1984) 'A Public Choice Model of Trade Union Behaviour and Membership', *Economic Journal*, vol. 94, no. 376, pp. 883–98.

Borooah, V. K. and Lee, K. C. (1988) 'The Effect of Changes in Britain's Industrial Structure on Female Relative Pay and Employment', *Economic Journal*, vol. 98.

Bowen, W. A. and Finegan, T. A. (1969) *The Economics of Labor Force Participation* (Princeton, NJ: Princeton University Press).

Bowles, S. (1970) 'Aggregation of Labor Inputs in the Economics of Growth and Planning: Experiments with a Two-Level CES Function', *Journal of Political Economy*, vol. 78, pp. 68–81.

Bowles, S. and Gintis, S. (1975) 'The Problem with Human Capital Theory: A Marxian Critique', *American Economic Review*, Papers and Proceedings, vol. 65, no. 2, pp. 74–82.

Brechling, F. (1965) 'The Relationship Between Output and Employment in British Manufacturing Industries', *Review of Economic Studies*, vol. 32, no. 3, pp. 187–216.

Briscoe, G. and Peel, D. A. (1975) 'The Specification of the Short-Run Employment Function', *Oxford Bulletin of Economics and Statistics*, vol. 37, no. 2, pp. 115–42.

Bronfenbrenner, M. (1939) 'The Economics of Collective Bargaining', *Quarterly Journal of Economics*, vol. 53, pp. 535–61.

Bronfenbrenner, M. (1956) 'Potential Monopsony in Labor Markets', *Industrial and Labor Relations Review*, vol. 9, pp. 577–88.

Bronfenbrenner, M. (1961) 'Notes on the Elasticity of Derived Demand', *Oxford Economic Papers*, vol. 13, no. 3, pp. 254–61.

Bronfenbrenner, M. (1971) *Income Distribution Theory* (Chicago: Aldine).

Brown, J. A. C. (1976) 'The Mathematical and Statistical Theory of Income Distribution', in A. B. Atkinson (ed.), *The Personal Distribution of Incomes* (London: George Allen & Unwin).

Brown, A. J. (1976) '*UV* Analysis', in G. D. N. Worswick (ed.), *The Concept and Measurement of Involuntary Unemployment* (London: Allen & Unwin), pp. 134–45.

Brown, C. V. (1983) *Taxation and the Incentive to Work*, 2nd edn (Oxford: Oxford University Press).

Brown, C. V., Levin, E. and Ulph, D. T. (1976) 'Estimation of Labour Hours Supplied by Married Male Workers in Great Britain', *Scottish Journal of Political Economy*, vol. 23, no. 3, pp. 261–77.

Brown, R. S., Moon, M. and Zoloth, B. S. (1980) 'Incorporating Occupational Attainment in Studies of Male–Female Earnings Differentials', *Journal of Human Resources*, vol. 15, no. 1, pp. 3–28.

Brown, W. and Wadhwani, S. (1990) 'The Economic Effects of Industrial Relations Legislation Since 1979', *National Institute Economic Review* (Feb.), pp. 57–70.

Bruno, M. (1986) 'Aggregate Supply and Demand Factors in OECD Unemployment: An Update', *Economica*, vol. 53 (Supplement), pp. S35–S52.

Bruno, M. and Sachs, J. D. (1985) *Economics of Worldwide Stagflation* (Cambridge, Mass.: Harvard University Press).

Burkitt, B. (1975) *Trade Unions and Wages* (London: Bradford University Press in association with Crosby Lockwood Staples).

Burkitt, B. and Bowers, D. (1978) 'The Determination of the Rate of Change of Unionisation in the United Kingdom, 1924–1966', *Applied Economics*, vol. 10, no. 2, pp. 161–72.

Bustillo, I. (1989) 'Female Educational Attainment in Latin America: A Survey', (Washington, DC: The World Bank) (PHREE/89/16).

Byers, J. D. (1976) 'The Supply of Labour', in D. F. Heathfield (ed.), *Topics in Applied Macroeconomics*, (London: Macmillan), pp. 69–90.

Cain, G. (1966) *Married Women in the Labor Force: An Economic Analysis* (Chicago: University of Chicago Press).

Cain, G. G. (1976) 'The Challenge of Segmented Labor Market Theory to Orthodox Theory', *Journal of Economic Literature*, vol. 14 (December), pp. 1215–57.

Cain, G. G. (1986) 'The Economic Analysis of Labor Market Discrimination: A Survey', in O. Ashenfelter and R. Layard (eds), *Handbook of Labour Economics* (Amsterdam: North-Holland).

Calvo, G. A. (1979) 'Quasi-Walrasian Theory of Unemployment', *American Economic Review*, vol. 69, no. 2, pp. 102–7.

Cannan, E. (1914) *Wealth* (London: P. S. King & Son).

Card, D. (1986) 'An Empirical Model of Wage Indexation Provisions in Union Contracts', *Journal of Political Economy*, vol. 94 (Supplement), pp. S144–75.

Carlin, W. and Soskice, D. (1990) *Macroeconomics and the Wage Bargain* (Oxford: Oxford University Press).

Carline, C., Pissarides, A. Siebert, W. S. and Sloane, P. J. (1985) *Labour Economics* (London: Longman).

Carnoy, M. (1980) 'Segmented Labor Markets', in UNESCO (ed.), *Education, Work and Employment Vol. II* (Paris: International Institute for Educational Planning).

Carruth, A. A. and Disney, R. (1988) 'Where Have 2 Million Trade Union Members Gone?', *Economica*, vol. 55, no. 217, pp. 1–19.

Carruth, A. A. and Oswald, A. J. (1985) 'Miners' Wages in Post-War Britain: An Application of a Model of Trade Union Behaviour', *Economic Journal*, vol. 95, no. 380, pp. 1003–20.

Carruth, A. A. and Oswald, A. J. (1986) 'On Union Preferences and Labour Market Models: Insiders and Outsiders' (Centre for Labour Economics, London School of Economics), Discussion Paper No. 256. Subsequently pub-

lished in *Economic Journal*, vol. 97, no. 387, pp. 431–45.
Carruth, A. A., Oswald, A. J. and Findlay, L. (1986) 'A Test of a Model of Union Behaviour: The Coal and Steel Industries in Britain', *Oxford Bulletin of Economics and Statistics*, vol. 48, no. 1, pp. 1–18.
Cartter, A. M. (1959) *Theory of Wages and Employment* (Homewood, Ill.: Irwin).
Cassel, G. (1918) *The Theory of Social Economy* (London: T. Fisher Unwin).
Catto, G., Goodchild, A. and Hughes, P. (1970) 'Higher Education and Employment' (London: Department of Employment).
Chamberlain, N. W. (1951) *Collective Bargaining* (New York: McGraw-Hill).
Chen, L., Hug, E. and D'Souza, S. (1981) 'Sex Bias in the Family Allocation of Food and Health Care in Rural Bangladesh', *Population and Development Review*, vol. 7, no. 1, pp. 55–70.
Chiang, A. C. (1984) *Fundamental Methods of Mathematical Economics*, 3rd edn (London: McGraw-Hill).
Chiplin, B. and Sloane, P. J. (1976) *Sex Discrimination in the Labour Market* (London: Macmillan).
Chiplin, B. and Sloane, P. J. (1988) 'The Effect of Britain's Anti-Discriminatory Legislation on Relative Pay and Employment: A Comment', *Economic Journal*, vol. 98, pp. 833–38.
Chiplin, B., Curran, M. M. and Parsley, C. J. (1980) 'Relative Female Earnings in Britain and the Impact of Legislation', in P. J. Sloane (ed.), *Women and Low Pay* (London: Macmillan).
Cigno, A. (1990) 'Home Production and the Allocation of Time', in D. Sapsford and Z. Tzannatos (eds), *Current Issues in Labour Economics* (London: Macmillan), pp. 7–32.
Clark, J. B. (1900) *The Distribution of Wealth* (New York: Macmillan).
Clark, K. B. and Summers, L. H. (1982) 'Labor Force Participation: Timing and Persistence', *Review of Economic Studies*, vol. 49, no. 5 (special issue), pp. 825–44.
Clegg, H. A. (1972) *The System of Industrial Relations in Great Britain*, 2nd edn (Oxford: Blackwell).
Coddington, A. (1968) *Theories of the Bargaining Process* (London: Allen & Unwin).
Coder, J., Rainwater, L. and Smeeding, T. (1988) *LIS Information Guide* (Working Paper No. 7) (Luxembourg: Walferdange).
Coder, J., Rainwater, L. and Smeeding, T. (1989) 'Inequality Among Children and Elderly in Ten Modern Nations: The United States in an International Context', *American Economic Review*, vol. 79 (Papers and Proceedings), pp. 320–324.
Cogan, J. (1980) 'Married Women's Labor Supply: A Comparison of Alternative Estimates', in J. P. Smith (ed.), *Female Labor Supply: Theory and Estimation* (Princeton, N.J.: Princeton University Press), pp. 90–118.
Collet, C. E. (1891) 'Women's Work in Leeds', *Economic Journal*, vol. 1, pp. 460–73.
Comay, Y., Melnik, A. and Subotnik, A. (1974) 'Bargaining Yield Curves and

Wage Settlements: An Empirical Analysis', *Journal of Political Economy*, vol. 82, no. 2, pp. 303–13.
Coombs, P. H. (1968) *The World Educational Crisis: A System Analysis* (New York: Oxford University Press).
Corry, B. A. and Laidler, D. E. W. (1967) 'The Phillips Relation: A Theoretical Explanation', *Economica*, new series, vol. 34, no. 134, pp. 189–97.
Corry, B. A. and Roberts, J. A. (1970) 'Activity Rules and Unemployment: The Experience of the United Kingdom, 1951–1966', *Applied Economics*, vol. 2, no. 3, pp. 179–201.
Corry, B. A. and Roberts, J. A. (1974) 'Activity Rates and Unemployment: The UK experience: Some Further Results', *Applied Economics*, vol. 6, no. 1, pp. 1–21.
Cripps, T. F. and Tarling, R. J. (1974) 'An Analysis of the Duration of Male Unemployment in Great Britain, 1932–73', *Economic Journal*, vol. 84, no. 334, pp. 289–316.
Cross, J. G. (1969) *The Economics of Bargaining* (London: Basic Books).
Cross, R. and Allen, A. (1988) 'On the History of Hysteresis', in R. Cross (ed.) *Unemployment, Hysteresis and the Natural Rate Hypothesis* (Oxford: Basil Blackwell), pp. 26–40.
Crossley, J. R. (1973) 'A Mixed Strategy for Labour Economists', *Scottish Journal of Political Economy*, vol. 20, no. 3, pp. 211–38.
Cubbin, J. and Foley, K. (1977) 'The Extent of Benefit-Induced Unemployment in Great Britain: Some New Evidence', *Oxford Economic Papers*, vol. 29, no. 1, pp. 128–40.
Davis, H. B. (1941) 'The Theory of Union Growth', *Quarterly Journal of Economics*, vol. 55, no. 3, pp. 611–37.
Deaton, D. (1982) 'Employers' Demand for Labour', in J. Creedy and B. Thomas (eds), *The Economics of Labour* (London: Butterworths, pp. 14–41).
Debeauvais, M. and Psacharopoulos, G. (1985) 'Forecasting the Needs for Qualified Manpower: Towards and Evaluation', in R. V. Youdi and K. Hinchliffe (eds), *Forecasting Skilled Manpower Needs: The Experience of Eleven Countries* (Paris: UNESCO (International Institute for Educational Studies)).
DeFina, R. H. (1983) 'Unions, Relative Wages and Economic Efficiency', *Journal of Labor Economics*, vol. 1, no. 4, pp. 408–29.
de Menil, G. (1971) *Bargaining: Monopoly Power versus Union Power* (Cambridge, Mass.: MIT Press).
Demery, D. and McNabb, R. (1978) 'The Effects of Demand on the Union Relative Wage Effect in the United Kingdom', *British Journal of Industrial Relations*, vol. 16, no. 3, pp. 303–8.
Demsetz, H. (1965) 'Minorities in the Labor Market', *North Carolina Law Review*, vol. 43, pp. 271–97.
Denison, E. F. (1962) 'The Sources of Economic Growth in the United States and Alternatives Before Us', Supplementary Paper No. 13 (New York: Committee for Economic Development).
Denison, E. F. (1967) *Why Growth Rates Differ: Post-War Experience in Nine*

Western Countries (Washington, DC: The Brookings Institution).

Dernburg, T. and Strand, K. (1966) 'Hidden Unemployment, 1953–62: A Quantitative Analysis by Age and Sex', *American Economic Review*, vol. 56, no. 1, pp. 71–95.

Dertouzos, J. N. and Pencavel, J. H. (1981) 'Wage and Employment Determination under Trade Unionism', *Journal of Political Economy*, vol. 89, no. 6, pp. 1162–81.

Desai, M. (1975) 'The Phillips Curve: A Revisionist Interpretation', *Economica*, new series, vol. 42, no. 165, pp. 1–19.

Dex, S. (1986) *The Costs of Discriminating: A Review of the Literature*, Research and Planning Unit Paper No. 39, Home Office.

Dex, S. and Shaw, L. B. (1986) *British and American Women at Work: Do Equal Employment Opportunities Matter?* (London: Macmillan).

Dex, S. and Sloane, P. (1988) 'Detecting and Removing Discrimination at the Market Place', *Journal of Economic Surveys*, vol. 2, no. 1, pp. 1–28.

Diewert, W. E. (1974) 'Applications of Duality Theory', in M. Intriligator (ed.), *Frontiers of Quantitative Economics*, vol. 2 (Amsterdam: North-Holland), pp. 106–71.

Doeringer, P. and Piore, M. J. (1971) *Internal Labor Markets and Manpower Analysis* (Lexington, Mass.: Heath Lexington).

Dolton, O. J. and Makepeace, G. H. (1987) 'Interpreting Sample Selection Effects', *Economic Letters*, vol. 24, no. 4, pp. 373–9.

Domar, E. D. (1946) 'Capital Expansion, Rate of Growth, and Employment', *Econometrica*, vol. 14, pp. 137–47.

Donovan, Lord (1968) *Report of the Royal Commission on Trade Unions and Employers' Associations, 1965–1968*, chaired by Lord Donovan, Cmnd 3623 (London: HMSO).

Dooley, M. D. (1982) 'Labor Supply and Fertility of Married Women: An Analysis with Grouped and Individual Data from the 1970 U.S. Census', *Journal of Human Resources*, vol. 17, no. 4, pp. 499–532.

Dougherty, C. R. S. (1972) 'Estimates of Labor Aggregation Functions', *Journal of Political Economy*, vol. 80, no. 6, pp. 1101–19.

Dougherty, C. R. S. (1985) 'Manpower Forecasting and Manpower Development Planning in the United Kingdom', in R. V. Youdi and K. Hinchliffe (eds), *Forecasting Skilled Manpower Needs: The Experience of Eleven Countries* (Paris: UNESCO (International Institute for Educational Studies)).

Dougherty, C. R. S. and Jimenez, E. (1991) 'The Specification of Earnings Functions: Tests and Implications', *Economics of Education Review*, vol. 10, no. 2, pp. 85–98.

Dougherty, C. R. S. and Selowsky, M. (1973) 'Measuring the Effects of the Misallocation of Labor', *Review of Economics and Statistics*, vol. 55, no. 3, pp. 386–90.

Douglas, P. H. (1939) *The Theory of Wages* (New York: Macmillan).

Duncan, G. M. and Leigh, D. E. (1985) 'The Endogeneity of Union Status: An Empirical Test', *Journal of Labor Economics*, vol. 3, no. 3, pp. 385–402.

Dunlop, J. T. (1944) *Wage Determination under Trade Unions* (New York: Macmillan).

Easterlin, R. (1981) 'Why Isn't the Whole World Developed?', *Journal of Economic History*, vol. 41, no. 1, pp. 1–19.

Eberts, R. W. and Stone, J. A. (1986) 'On the Contract Curve: A Test of Alternative Models of Collective Bargaining', *Journal of Labor Economics*, vol. 4, no. 1, pp. 66–81.

Edgeworth, F. Y. (1881) *Mathematical Psychics* (London: Kegan Paul).

Edgeworth, F. Y. (1922) 'Equal Pay to Men and Women for Equal Work', *Economic Journal*, vol. 32, pp. 431–57.

Edwards, R. C. (1979) *Contested Terrain: The Transformation of the Workplace in the Twentieth Century* (New York: Basic Books).

Ehrenberg, R. G. and Schwarz, J. L. (1986) 'Public-Sector Labor Markets', in O. Ashenfelter and R. Layard (eds), *Handbook of Labor Economics* (Amsterdam: North-Holland), pp. 1219–59.

Ehrenberg, R. G. and Smith, R. S. (1991) *Modern Labor Economics*, 4th edn (New York: HarperCollins).

Elsheikh, F. and Bain, G. S. (1978) 'Trade Union Growth: A Reply', *British Journal of Industrial Relations*, vol. 26, no. 1, pp. 99–101.

Elsheikh, F. and Bain, G. S. (1979) 'The Determination of the Rate of Change of Unionisation in the UK: A Comment and Further Analysis', *Applied Economics*, vol. 11, no. 4, pp. 451–63.

England, P. (1982) 'The Failure of Human Capital Theory to Explain Occupational Segregation by Sex', *Journal of Human Resources*, vol. 17, no. 3, pp. 358–70.

Ermisch, J. (1988) 'An Economic Perspective on Household Modelling', in N. Keilman, A. Kuijsten and A. Vossen (eds), *Modelling Household Formation and Dissolution* (Oxford: Clarendon Press), pp. 23–40.

Ermisch, J. F. and Wright, R. E. (1990) 'Entry to Lone Parenthood: Analysis of Marital Dissolution', Discussion Paper in Economics No. 9/90 (University of London: Birkbeck College).

Fair, R. C. (1969) *The Short-Run Demand for Workers and Hours* (Amsterdam: North-Holland).

Fair, R. C. and Jaffee, D. (1972) 'Methods for Estimating Markets in Disequilibrium', *Econometrica*, vol. 40, no. 3, pp. 497–514.

Fallon, P. and Verry, D. (1988) *The Economics of Labour Markets* (Oxford: Philip Alan).

Farber, H. S. (1978) 'Individual Preferences and Union Wage Determination: The Case of the United Mine Workers', *Journal of Political Economy*, vol. 86, no. 5, pp. 932–42.

Fawcett, M. (1892) 'Mr. Sidney Webb's Article on Women's Wages', *Economic Journal*, vol. 2, pp. 173–6.

Fawcett, M. (1917) 'The Position of Women in Economic Life', in W. H. Dawson (ed.), *After War Problems* (London: Allen & Unwin), pp. 191–215.

Fawcett, M. (1918) 'Equal Pay for Equal Work', *Economic Journal*, vol. 28, pp. 1–6.

Feldstein, M. S. (1968) 'Estimating the Supply Curve of Working Hours', *Oxford Economic Papers*, new series, vol. 20, no. 1, pp. 74–80.

Fellner, W. J. (1951) *Competition Among the Few* (New York: Knopf).

Ferguson, C. E. (1972) *Microeconomic Theory*, 3rd edn (Homewood, Ill.: Irwin).
Ferguson, C. E. and Gould, J. P. (1975) *Microeconomic Theory*, 4th edn (Homewood, Ill.: Irwin).
Finegan, T. A. (1962) 'Hours of Work in the United States: A Cross Sectional Analysis', *Journal of Political Economy*, vol. 70, no. 5, pp. 452–70.
Fiorito, F. and Greer, C. (1982) 'Determinants of US Unionism: Past Research and Future Needs', *Industrial Relations*, vol. 21, no. 1, pp. 1–32.
Fisher, I. (1926) 'A Statistical Relation Between Unemployment and Price Changes', *International Labour Review*, vol. 13, no. 6, pp. 785–92; reprinted as 'I Discovered the Phillips Curve', *Journal of Political Economy*, vol. 81, no. 2 (1972), pp. 496–502.
Fisher, M. R. (1971) *The Economic Analysis of Labour* (London: Weidenfeld & Nicolson).
Florence, P. S. (1931) 'A Statistical Contribution to the Theory of Women's Wages', *Economic Journal*, vol. 41, pp. 19–37.
Foldes, L. (1964), 'A Determinate Model of Bilateral Monopoly', *Economica*, new series, vol. 31, no. 1, pp. 117–31.
Freeman, R. (1980) 'The Exit-Voice Tradeoff in the Labor Market: Unionism, Job Tenure, Quits and Separations', *Quarterly Journal of Economics*, vol. 94, no. 4, pp. 643–73.
Freeman, R. (1988) 'Contraction and Expansion: The Divergence of Private Sector and Public Sector Unionism in the United States', *Journal of Economic Perspectives*, vol. 2, no. 2, pp. 63–88.
Freeman, R. and Medoff, J. L. (1979) 'The Two Faces of Unionism', *The Public Interest*, vol. 57 (Fall), pp. 69–73.
Freeman, R. and Medoff, J. L. (1984) *What Do Unions Do?* (New York: Basic Books).
Friedman, M. (1951) 'Some Comments on the Significance of Labor Unions for Economic Policy', in D. McCord Wright (ed.), *The Impact of the Union* (New York: Harcourt Brace), pp. 204–34.
Friedman, M. (1957) *A Theory of the Consumption Function* (Princeton, NJ: National Bureau of Economic Research).
Friedman, M. (1962) *Price Theory: A Provisional Text*, revised edn (Chicago: Aldine).
Friedman, M. (1968) 'The Role of Monetary Policy', *American Economic Review*, vol. 58, no. 1, pp. 1–17.
Friedman, M. (1975) *Unemployment versus Inflation*, with a British commentary by D. E. W. Laidler (London: Institute of Economic Affairs, Occasional Paper, No. 44).
Friedman, M. (1976) *Price Theory* (Chicago: Aldine).
Friedman, M. and Kuznets, S. (1945) *Income from Independent Professional Practice* (New York: National Bureau of Economic Research).
Frisch, H. (1977) 'Inflation Theory, 1963–75: A "Second Generation" Survey', *Journal of Economic Literature*, vol. 15, no. 4, pp. 1289–1317.
Ghez, G. R. and Becker, G. S. (1975) *The Allocation of Time and Goods over the Life Cycle* (New York: Columbia University Press).

Gibrat, R. (1931) *Les Inegalités Economiques* (Paris: Librairie du Recueil Sirey).

Gilbert, C. L. (1976) 'The Original Phillips Curve Estimates', *Economica*, new series, vol. 43, no. 169, pp. 51–7.

Gilman, H. J. (1965) 'Economic Discrimination and Unemployment', *American Economic Review*, vol. 55, pp. 1077–96.

Goldstein, M. (1972) 'The Trade-Off Between Inflation and Unemployment: A Survey of the Econometric Evidence for Selected Countries', *International Monetary Fund Staff Papers*, vol. 19, no. 3, pp. 647–95.

Gordon, D. M. (1972) *Theories of Poverty and Underemployment* (Lexington, Mass.: D. C. Heath).

Gordon, D. (1974) 'A Neo-classical Theory of Keynesian Unemployment', *Economic Inquiry*, vol. 12, no. 4, pp. 431–59.

Gordon, D. M., Edwards, R. and Reich, M. (1982) *Segmented Work, Divided Workers: The Historical Transformation of Labour in the United States* (Cambridge: Cambridge University Press).

Gordon, R. A. (1975) 'Wages, Prices and Unemployment, 1900–1970', *Industrial Relations*, vol. 14, no. 3, pp. 273–301.

Gordon, R. J. (1987) 'Why US Wage and Employment Behaviour Differs from that in Britain and Japan', *Economic Journal*, vol. 92, no. 365, pp. 13–44.

Grandjean, B. D. (1981) 'Review of Mincer's *Schooling, Experience and Earnings*', *American Journal of Sociology*, vol. 86, pp. 1057–73.

Gravelle, H. and Rees, R. (1992) *Microeconomics*, 2nd edn (London: Longman).

Greene, W. (1990) *Econometric Analysis* (New York: Collier Macmillan).

Greenhalgh, C. (1977) 'A Labour Supply Function for Married Women in Great Britain', *Economica*, new series, vol. 44, no. 175, pp. 249–65.

Greenhalgh, C. (1980) 'Male–Female Wage Differentials in Great Britain: Is Marriage an Equal Opportunity?', *Economic Journal*, vol. 90, no. 360, pp. 651–75.

Gregory, R. G. and Duncan, R. C. (1981) 'Segmented Labour Market Theories and the Australian Experience of Equal Pay for Women', *Journal of Post Keynesian Economics*, vol. 3, no. 3, pp. 403–28.

Griliches, Z. (1977) 'Estimating the Returns to Schooling: Some Econometric Problems', *Econometrica*, vol. 45, no. 1, pp. 1–22.

Griliches, Z. and Mason, W. M. (1972) 'Education, Income and Ability', in T. W. Schultz (ed.), *Investment in Education: The Equity Efficiency Quandary* (Chicago: Chicago University Press).

Gronau, R. (1973) 'The Intrafamily Allocation of Time: The Value of Housewives' Time', *American Economic Review*, vol. 63, no. 4, pp. 634–51.

Gronau, R. (1974) 'Wage Comparisons – A Selectivity Bias', *Journal of Political Economy*, vol. 82, no. 6, pp. 1119–43.

Gronau, R. (1982) 'Sex-Related Wage Differentials and Women's Interrupted Labor Careers: The Chicken and Egg Question' (Cambridge, Mass.: National Bureau of Economic Research), Working Paper No. 1002.

Gunderson, M. (1989) 'Male–Female Wage Differentials and Policy Responses', *Journal of Economic Literature*, vol. 27, no. 1, pp. 46–117.

Hall, S. and Henry, S. G. B. (1987) 'Wage Models', *National Institute Economic Review*, pp. 70–5.
Hall, S. and Henry, B. (1988) 'The Disequilibrium Approach to Modelling the Labour Market', *Modelling the Labour Market* (London: Chapman & Hall), pp. 49–69.
Hamermesh, D. (1986) 'The Demand for Labour in the Long Run', in O. Ashenfelter and R. Layard (eds), *Handbook of Labor Economics* (New York and Amsterdam: North-Holland).
Hansen, B. (1970) 'Excess Demand, Unemployment, Vacancies and Wages', *Quarterly Journal of Economics*, vol. 84, no. 334, pp. 1–23.
Hansen, W. L. (1963) 'Total and Private Rates of Return to Investment in Schooling', *Journal of Political Economy*, vol. 81, pp. 128–41.
Haque, N. (1984) *Work Status Choice and the Distribution of Family Earnings* (Santa Monica, Calif.: Rand Corporation).
Harman, A. (1969) *Interrelationship Between Procreation and Other Family Decision-Making* (Santa Monica, Calif.: Rand Corporation).
Harrod, R. F. (1939) 'An Essay on Dynamic Theory', *Economic Journal*, vol. 49, pp. 14–33.
Harsanyi, J. C. (1956) 'Approaches to the Bargaining Problem Before and After the Theory of Games: A Critical Discussion of Zeuthen's, Hicks' and Nash's theories', *Econometrica*, vol. 24, no. 2, pp. 144–57.
Hart, O. D. (1983) 'Optimal Labor Contracts Under Asymmetric Information: An Introduction', *Review of Economic Studies*, vol. 50, no. 160, pp. 3–35.
Hart, O. D. and Holmstrom, B. (1986) 'The Theory of Contracts', in T. Bewley (ed.), *Advances in Economic Theory* (Cambridge: Cambridge University Press).
Hart, R. A. (1984) *The Economics of Non-Wage Labour Costs* (London: Allen and Unwin).
Hart, R. A., Bell, D. N. F., Frees, R., Kawasaki, S. and Woodbury, S. A. (1988) *Trends in Non-Wage Labour Costs and their Effects on Employment* (Brussels: Commission of the European Communities).
Hashimoto, M. and Kochin, L. (1980) 'A Bias in the Statistical Estimation of the Effects of Discrimination', *Economic Enquiry*, vol. 18, no. 3, pp. 478–86.
Haveman, R. and Wolfe, B. (1984) 'Education and Economic Well Being', in E. Dean (ed.), *Education and Economic Productivity* (Cambridge, Mass.: Harper & Row), pp. 19–55.
Hazledine, T. (1981) 'Employment Functions and the Demand for Labour in the Short-Run', in Z. Hornstein, J. Grice and A. Webb (eds), *The Economics of the Labour Market* (London: HMSO), pp. 147–81.
Heckman, J. J. (1974) 'Shadow Prices, Market Wages and Labor Supply', *Econometrica*, vol. 42, no. 4, pp. 679–94.
Heckman, J. J. (1979) 'Sample Selection as a Specification Error', *Econometrica*, vol. 47, no. 1, pp. 153–61.
Heckman, J. J. and Hotz, J. (1986) 'An Investigation of the Labor Market Earnings of Panamanian Males: Evaluating Sources of Inequality', *Journal of Human Resources*, vol. 21, no. 4, pp. 507–42.
Heckman, J. J. and MaCurdy, T. (1980) 'A Life Cycle Model of Female Labor

Supply', *Review of Economic Studies*, vol. 47, no. 1, pp. 47–74.
Heckman, J. J. and MaCurdy, T. (1982) 'Corrigendum on a Life Cycle Model of Female Labor Supply', *Review of Economic Studies*, vol. 49, no. 4, pp. 659–60.
Heckman, J. J. and Willis, R. J. (1977) 'A Beta-Logistic Model for the Analysis of Sequential Labor Force Participation of Married Women', *Journal of Political Economy*, vol. 85, no. 1, pp. 27–58.
Henderson, J. M. and Quandt, R. E. (1980) *Micro-Economic Theory: A Mathematical Approach*, 3rd edn (London: McGraw-Hill).
Henry, S. G. B., Sawyer, M. C. and Smith, P. (1976) 'Models of Inflation in the United Kingdom: An Evaluation', *National Institute Economic Review*, no. 77, pp. 60–71.
Hepple, B. A. (1984) *Equal Pay and the Industrial Tribunals* (Oxford: Martin Robertson).
Herrick, B. and Kindleberger, C. P. (1983) *Economic Development*, 4th edn (London: McGraw-Hill).
Hey, J. (1979) *Uncertainty in Microeconomics* (Oxford: Martin Robertson).
Hicks, J. R. (1932) *The Theory of Wages* (London: Macmillan).
Hicks, J. R. (1963) *The Theory of Wages*, 2nd edn (London: Macmillan).
Hicks, J. R. (1976) 'Marshall's Third Rule: A Further Comment', *Oxford Economic Papers*, vol. 13, no. 3, pp. 262–5.
Hicks, N. (1980) 'Economic Growth and Human Resources', Staff Working Paper No. 408 (Washington, DC: The World Bank).
Hirsch, B. T. and Addison, J. T. (1986) *The Economic Analysis of Unions* (London: Allen & Unwin).
Hodson, R. (1983) *Workers' Earnings and Corporate Economic Structure* (New York: Academic Press).
Holden, K., Peel, D. and Thompson, J. L. (1985) *Expectations: Theory and Evidence* (London: Macmillan).
Holmstrom, B. (1981) 'Contractual Models of the Labor Market', *American Economic Review (Papers and Proceedings)*, vol. 71, pp. 318–30.
Hood, W. and Rees, R. (1974) 'Inter-industry Wage Levels in United Kingdom Manufacturing', *Manchester School*, vol. 42, no. 2, pp. 171–85.
Hornstein, Z., Grice, J. and Webb, A. (eds) (1982) *The Economics of the Labour Market* (London: HMSO).
Hughes, J. J. and Perlman, R. (1984) *The Economics of Unemployment* (Brighton: Wheatsheaf).
Hunter, L. C. (1970) 'Some Problems in the Theory of Labour Supply', *Scottish Journal of Political Economy*, vol. 17, no. 1, pp. 39–59.
Iglesias, F. H. and Riboud, M. (1985) 'Trends in Labor Force Participation of Spanish Women: An Interpretive Essay', *Journal of Labor Economics*, vol. 3, no. 1 (Part 2), pp. S201–S217.
Jackson, D., Turner, H. A. and Wilkinson, F. (1972) *Do Trade Unions Cause Inflation?* (Cambridge: Cambridge University Press).
Johnson, G. E. (1975) 'Economic Analysis of Trade Unionism', *American Economic Review (Papers and Proceedings)*, vol. 65, no. 2, pp. 23–8.
Johnson, H. G. and Mieszkowski, P. (1970) 'The Effects of Unionisation on the

Distribution of Income: A General Equilibrium Approach', *Quarterly Journal of Economics*, vol. 84, no. 4, pp. 539–61.

Johnston, J. and Timbrell, M. (1973) 'Empirical Tests of a Bargaining Theory of Wage Rate Determination', *Manchester School*, vol. 41, no. 2, pp. 141–67.

Jones, F. L. (1983) 'On Decomposing the Wage Gap: A Critical Comment on Blinder's Method', *Journal of Human Resources*, vol. XVIII, no. I, pp. 126–30.

Joseph, G. (1983) *Women at Work: The British Experience* (Oxford: Philip Alan).

Joshi, H. and Newell, M. L. (1987) 'Pay Differences Between Men and Women: Longitudinal Evidence from the 1946 Cohort', Discussion Paper No. 156 (London: Centre for Economic Policy Research).

Junankar, P. (1981) 'An Econometric Analysis of Unemployment in Great Britain, 1952–75', *Oxford Economic Papers*, vol. 33, no. 3, pp. 387–400.

Kalachcck, E. and Rainco, F. (1976) 'The Structure of Wage Differences Among Mature Male Workers', *Journal of Human Resources*, vol. 6 (Fall), pp. 484–506.

Kaldor, N. (1956) 'Alternative Theories of Distribution', Review of Economic Studies', vol. 23, pp. 83–100.

Kalecki, M. (April 1945) 'On the Gibrat Distribution', *Econometrica*, vol. 13, no. 2, pp. 161–170.

Kallenberg, A. L. (ed.) (1983) *Capital, Labor and Work: Structural Determinants of Work-Related Inequalities*, Special Issue of *Work and Occupations*, vol. 10, no. 3.

Kapteyen, J. C. (1903) *Skew Frequency Curves in Biology and Statistics* (Nordhobb).

Katz, E. and Ziderman, A. (1990) 'Investment in General Training: The Role of Information', *Economic Journal*, vol. 100, no. 403, pp. 1147–1158.

Keeley, M. C. (1981) *Labor Supply and Public Policy: A Critical Review* (New York: Academic Press).

Kerr, C. (1954) 'The Balkanization of Labor Markets', in E. W. Bakke *et al.* (eds), *Labor Mobility and Economic Opportunity* (New York: Wiley), pp. 92–110.

Keynes, J. M. (1936) *The General Theory of Employment, Interest and Money* (London: Macmillan).

Keynes, J. M. (1939) 'Relative Movements in Real Wages and Output', Economic Journal, vol. 49, no. 193, pp. 34–51.

Kiefer, N. and Neumann, G. (1979) 'An Empirical Job Search Model With a Test of the Constant Reservation Wage Hypothesis', *Journal of Political Economy*, vol. 87, no. 1, pp. 69–82.

Killingsworth, M. K. (1983) *Labor Supply* (Cambridge: Cambridge University Press).

Killingsworth, M. R. (1986) 'Female Labour Supply: A Survey', in O. Ashenfelter and R. Layard (eds), *Handbook of Labor Economics* (New York and Amsterdam: North-Holland).

Killingsworth, M. R. (1990) *The Economics of Comparable Work* (Kalamazoo, Mich.: W. E. Upjohn Institute for Employment Research).

Killingsworth, M. R. and Heckman, J. J. (1986) 'Female Labor Supply: A Survey', in O. Ashenfelter and R. Layard (eds), *Handbook of Labor Economics* (Amsterdam: North-Holland), pp. 103–204.

King, J. (1972) *Labour Economics* (London: Macmillan).

King, J. E. (1990) *Labour Economics*, 2nd edn (London: Macmillan).

Knight, K. G. (1987) *Unemployment: An Economic Analysis* (London: Croom Helm).

Knight, J. B. and Sabot, R. (1982) 'Labor Market Discrimination in Tanzania', *Journal of Development Studies*, vol. 19, no. 1, pp. 67–87.

La Belle, T. J. (1986) *Nonformal Education in Latin America and the Caribbean. Stability, Reform or Revolution?* (New York: Praeger).

Lancaster, T. (1979) Econometric Methods for the Duration of Unemployment', *Econometrica*, vol. 47, no. 4, pp. 939–56.

Layard, R. and Mincer, J. (eds) (1985) 'Trends in Women's Work, Education, and Family Building', *Journal of Labor Economics*, vol. 3, no. 1 (Part 2).

Layard, R. and Nickell, S. (1985) 'The Causes of British Unemployment', *National Institute Economic Review*, no. 111, pp. 62–85.

Layard, R. and Nickell, S. (1986) 'Unemployment in Britain', *Economica*, vol. 53 (Supplement on Unemployment), pp. S121–S169.

Lazear, E. (1980) 'Family Background and Optimal Schooling Decisions', *Review of Economics and Statistics*, vol. 62, no. 1, pp. 42–51.

Lazear, E. (1981) 'Agency, Earnings Profiles, Productivity and Hours Restrictions', *American Economic Review*, vol. 71 (September), pp. 275–96.

Lee, L. F. (1978) 'Unionism and Wage Rates: A Simultaneous Equations Model with Qualitative and Limited Dependent Variables', *International Economic Review*, vol. 19, no. 2, pp. 415–33.

Lee, L. F. (1982) 'Some Approaches to the Correction of Selectivity Bias', *Review of Economic Studies*, vol. 49, no. 3, pp. 355–72.

Leibenstein, H. (1957) 'The Theory of Underemployment in Backward Economies', *Journal of Political Economy*, vol. 65, no. 1, pp. 91–103.

Leontief, W. (1946) 'The Pure Theory of the Guaranteed Annual Wage Contract', *Journal of Political Economy*, vol. 54, no. 1, pp. 76–9.

Lester, R. A. (1946) 'Shortcomings of Marginal Analysis for Wage–Employment Problems', *American Economic Review*, vol. 36, no. 1, pp. 63–82.

Levine, V. and Moock, P. R. (1984) 'Labor Force Experience and Earnings: Women and Children', *Economics of Education Review*, vol. 3, no. 3, pp. 183–94.

Lewis, H. G. (1957) 'Hours of Work and Hours of Leisure', in *Proceedings of the Ninth Annual Meeting of the Industrial Relations Research Association*, ed. L. Reed Trip (Madison, Wisc.: Industrial Relations Research Association), pp. 196–206; reprinted in J. F. Burton *et al.* (eds), *Readings in Labor Market Analysis* (London: Holt, Rinehart & Winston, 1971).

Lewis, H. G. (1963) *Unionism and Relative Wages in the United States* (Chicago: Chicago University Press).

Lewis, H. G. (1963a) 'Relative Employment Effects of Unionism', in *Proceed-*

ings of the Sixteenth Annual Meeting of the Industrial Relations Research Association (Madison, Wisconsin: Industrial Relations Research Association), pp. 104–15.

Lewis, H. G. (1983) 'Union Relative Wage Effects: A Survey of Macro Estimates', *Journal of Labor Economics*, vol. 1, no. 1, pp. 1–27.

Lewis, H. G. (1986) 'Union Relative Wage Effects', in Ashenfelter, O. and Layard, R. (eds), *Handbook of Labour Economics* (New York and Amsterdam: North-Holland).

Lindbeck, A. and Snower, D. (1986) 'Wage-Setting, Unemployment and Insider–Outsider Relations', *American Economic Review*, vol. 76 (Papers and Proceedings), pp. 235–9.

Lindbeck, A. and Snower, D. (1987) 'Union Activity, Unemployment Persistence, and Wage–Employment Ratchets', *European Economic Review (Proceedings)*, vol. 31, pp. 157 67.

Lindbeck, A. and Snower, D. (1988) *The Insider–Outsider Theory of Unemployment and Employment* (Cambridge, Mass.: MIT Press).

Lindbeck, A. and Snower, D. (1988a) 'Cooperation, Harassment and Involuntary Unemployment: An Insider–Outsider Approach', *American Economic Review*, vol. 78, no. 1, pp. 167–88.

Linder, S. B. (1970) *The Harried Leisure Class* (New York: Columbia University Press).

Lippman, S. and McCall, J. (1976) 'The Economics of Job Search: A Survey, Parts I and II', *Economic Inquiry*, vol. 14, nos 2 and 3, pp. 155–89 and 347–68.

Lipsey, R. G. (1960) 'The Relationship Between Unemployment and the Rate of Change of Money Wage Rates in the UK, 1862–1957: A Further Analysis', *Economica*, new series, vol. 27, no. 105, pp. 1–31.

Lipsey, R. G. (1965) 'Structural and Deficient-Demand Unemployment Reconsidered', in A. M. Ross (ed.), *Employment Policy and the Labour Market* (Berkeley, Cal.: University of California Press), pp. 210–55.

Lipsey, R. G. (1989) *An Introduction to Positive Economics*, 7th edn (London: Weidenfeld & Nicolson).

Little, R. J. A. (1985) 'A Note About Models for Selectivity Bias', *Econometrica*, vol. 53, no. 6, pp. 1469–74.

Lloyd, C. B. and B. T. Niemi (1979) *The Economics of Sex Differentials* (New York: Columbia University Press).

Loucks, W. N. and Whitney, W. G. (1973) *Comparative Economic Systems*, International Edition (New York: Harper & Row).

Love, J. and Williams, T. D. (1990) 'Financing University Education: Oasis or Mirage?' *Royal Bank of Scotland Review*, no. 165, pp. 16–35.

Lucas, R. E. and Rapping, L. (1969) 'Real Wages, Employment and Inflation', *Journal of Political Economy*, vol. 77, no. 5, pp. 751–4.

Luce, R. D. and Raiffa, H. (1957) *Games and Decisions* (New York: Wiley).

Lundahl, M. and Wadensjo, E. (1984) *Unequal Treatment: A Study in the Neo-Classical Theory of Discrimination* (London: Croom Helm).

Lydall (1968), *The Structure of Earnings* (London: Oxford University Press).

Lydall, H. F. (1976) 'Theories of the Distribution of Earnings', in A. B. Atkinson (ed.) *The personal Distribution of Income* (Boulder, Colo.: Westview Press.)

Machlup, F. (1946) 'Marginal Analysis and Empirical Research', *American Economic Review*, vol. 36, no. 3, pp. 519–54.

MaCurdy, T. (1981) 'An Empirical Model of Labor Supply in a Life-Cycle Setting', *Journal of Political Economy*, vol. 89, no. 6, pp. 1059–85.

MaCurdy, T. and Pencavel, J. (1986) 'Testing Between Competing Models of Wage and Employment Setting in Unionised Labour Markets', *Journal of Political Economy*, vol. 94 (Supplement), pp. S3-S40.

McDonald, I. M. and Solow, R. M. (1981) 'Wage Bargaining and Employment', *American Economic Review*, vol. 71, no. 4, pp. 896–908.

MacKay, D. I., Boddy, D., Brack, J., Diack, J. A. and Jones, N. (1971) *Labour Markets under Different Employment Conditions* (London: Allen & Unwin).

McKenna, C. (1986) 'Theories of Individual Search Behaviour', *Bulletin of Economic Research*, vol. 38, no. 3, pp. 189–207.

McKenna, C. (1987) 'Models of Search Market Equilibrium', in J. Hey and P. Lambert (eds), *Surveys in the Economics of Uncertainty* (Oxford: Basil Blackwell), pp. 110–23.

McKenna, C. (1990) 'The Theory of Search in Labour Markets', in D. Sapsford and Z. Tzannatos (eds), *Current Issues in Labour Economics* (London: Macmillan), pp. 33–62.

McNabb, R. (1977) 'The Labour Force Participation of Married Women', *Manchester School*, vol. 45, no. 3, pp. 221–35.

McNabb, R. and Ryan, P. (1990) 'Segmented Labour Markets', in D. Sapsford and Z. Tzannatos (eds), *Currrent Issues in Labour Economics* (London: Macmillan), pp. 151–76.

Madden, J. F. (1973) *The Economics of Sex Discrimination* (Lexington, Mass.: D. C. Heath).

Main, B. G. M. and Elias, P. (1987) 'Women Returning to Paid Employment', *International Review of Applied Economics*, vol. 1, no. 1, pp. 86–108.

Maki, D. and Spindler, Z. A. (1975) 'The Effect of Unemployment Compensation on the Rate of Unemployment in Great Britain', *Oxford Economic Papers*, vol. 27, no. 3, pp. 440–54.

Malcomson, J. (1981) 'Unemployment and the Efficiency Wage Hypothesis', *Economic Journal*, vol. 91, no. 364, pp. 848–66.

Malkiel, B. G. and Malkiel, J. A. (1973) 'Male–Female Pay Differentials in Professional Employment', *American Economic Review*, vol. 63, no. 4, pp. 693–705.

Manning, A. (1987) 'An Integration of Trade Union Models in a Sequential Bargaining Framework', *Economic Journal*, vol. 97, no. 385, pp. 121–39.

Marris, R. (1982) *Economic Growth in Cross Section* (Department of Economics, Birkbeck College, University of London).

Marshall, A. (1890) *Principles of Economics*, 8th edn (London: Macmillan).

Marshall, F. R., Cartter, A. M. and King, A. G. (1976) *Labor Economics: Wages, Employment, and Trade Unionism*, 3rd edn (Homewood, Ill.: Irwin).

Marshall, R. (1974) 'The Economics of Racial Discrimination: A Survey', *Journal of Economic Literature*, vol. 12, pp. 849–71.
Martin, J. and Roberts, C. (1984) *Women and Employment: A Lifetime Perspective* (London: HMSO).
Martorell, R., Leslie, J. and Moock, P. (1984) 'Characteristics and Determinants of Child Nutritional Status in Nepal', *American Journal of Clinical Nutrition*, vol. 39, no. 1, pp. 74–86.
Maurice, S. C. (1975), 'On the Importance of Being Unimportant: An Analysis of the Paradox in Marshall's Third Rule of Derived Demand', *Economica*, new series, vol. 42, no. 168, pp. 385–93.
Mayhew, K. and Addison, J. (1983) 'Discrimination in the Labour Market', in G. S. Bain (ed.), *Industrial Relations in Britain* (Oxford: Basil Blackwell).
Mayhew, K. and Turnbull, P. (1989) 'Models of Union Behaviour: A Critique of Recent Literature', in R. Drago and R. Perlman (eds), *Microeconomic Issues in Labour Economics: New Approaches* (London: Harvester Wheatsheaf), pp. 105–29.
Melnik, A. and Comay, Y. (1972) 'The Effect of Bargaining Strategies in Strike Situations', *Western Economic Journal*, vol. 10, no. 4, pp. 370–5.
Metcalf, D. (1977) 'Unions, Incomes Policy and Relative Earnings in Great Britain', *British Journal of Industrial Relations*, vol. 15, no. 2, pp. 157–75.
Metcalf, D., and Richardson, R. (1986) 'Labour', in M. J. Artis (ed.), *The UK Economy: A Manual of Applied Economics*, 11th edn (London: Weidenfeld & Nicolson), pp. 266–332.
Miller, P. W. (1987) 'The Wage Effect of Occupational Segregation of Women in Britain', *Economic Journal*, vol. 97, no. 388, pp. 885–96.
Mincer, J. (1958) 'Investment in Human Capital and Personal Income Distribution', *Journal of Political Economy*, vol. 66, no. 4, pp. 281–302.
Mincer, J. (1962) 'Labor Force Participation of Married Women: A Study of Labor Supply', in H. G. Lewis (ed.), *Aspects of Labor Economics* (Princeton, NJ: Princeton University Press), pp. 63–97.
Mincer, J. (1966) 'Labor-Force Participation and Unemployment: A Review of Recent Evidence', in R. A. Gordon and M. S. Gordon (eds), *Prosperity and Unemployment* (New York: Wiley), pp. 73–112.
Mincer, J. (1974) *Schooling, Experience and Earnings* (National Bureau of Economic Research, New York: Columbia University Press).
Mincer, J. and Ofek, H. (1974) 'Family Investments in Human Capital: Earnings of Women', *Journal of Political Economy*, vol. 82, no. 2 (Part 2), pp. S76–S108.
Mincer, J. and Polachek, S. (1974) 'Family Investments in Human Capital: Earnings of Women', *Journal of Political Economy*, vol. 82, pp. S76–S108.
Minford, P. (1983) *Unemployment: Cause and Cure* (with Davies, D. H., Peel, M. J. and Sprague, A.) (Oxford: Basil Blackwell).
Mitchell, D. J. B. (1972) 'Union Wage Policies: The Ross–Dunlop Debate Re-opened', *Industrial Relations*, vol. 11, no. 1, pp. 46–61.
Mitchell, D. J. B. (1980) *Unions, Wages and Inflation* (Washington, DC: Brookings Institution).
Morgan, J. N. (1985) 'Using Survey Data from the University of Michigan's

Survey Research Centre', *American Economic Review*, Papers and Proceedings, vol. 65, no. 2, pp. 250–256.

Mortensen, D. (1986) 'Job Search and Labor Market Analysis', in D. Ashenfelter and R. Layard (eds), *Handbook of Labor Economics*, vol. 2 (Amsterdam: Elsevier/North-Holland), pp. 849–919.

Moser, C. and Layard, R. (1964) 'Planning The Scale of Higher Education in Britain: Some Statistical Problems', *Journal of the Royal Statistical Society*, Series A, Volume 127, Part 4.

Mulvey, C. (1976) 'Collective Agreements and Relative Earnings in UK Manufacturing in 1973', *Economica*, vol. 43, no. 172, pp. 419–27.

Mulvey, C. (1978) *The Economic Analysis of Trade Unions* (Oxford: Martin Robertson).

Muth, J. F. (1961) 'Rational Expectations and the Theory of Price Movements', *Econometrica*, vol. 29, no. 3, pp. 315–35.

Myrdal, G. (1944) *An American Dilemma: The Negro Problem and Modern Democracy* (New York: Harper & Row).

Nadiri, M. I. (1972) 'International Studies of Total Factor Productivity: A Brief Survey', *Review of Income and Wealth*, vol. 18, no. 2 (June), pp. 129–54.

Nakamura, A., Nakamura, N. and Cullen, D. (1979) 'Job Opportunities, the Offered Wage, and the Labor Supply of Married Women', *American Economic Review*, vol. 69, no. 5, pp. 787–805.

Narendranathan, W., Nickell, S. and Stern, J. (1985) 'Unemployment Benefit Revisited', *Economic Journal*, vol. 95, no. 378, pp. 307–29.

Nash, J. F. (1950) 'The Bargaining Problem', *Econometrica*, vol. 18, no. 2, pp. 155–62.

Nash, J. F. (1953) 'Two-Person Co-operative Games', *Econometrica*, vol. 21, no. 1, pp. 120–40.

Nelson, F. (1984) 'Efficiency of the Two-Step Estimator for Models With Endogenous Sample Selection', *Journal of Econometrics*, vol. 24, no. 1 (supplement), pp. 181–96.

Nickell, S. J. (1977) 'Trade Unions and the Position of Women in the Industrial Wage Structure', *British Journal of Industrial Relations*, vol. 15, no. 2, pp. 192–210.

Nickell, S. (1979) 'The Effect of Unemployment and Related Benefits on the Duration of Unemployment', *Economic Journal*, vol. 89, no. 353, pp. 34–49.

Nickell, S. (1979a) 'Estimating the Probability of Leaving Unemployment', *Econometrica*, vol. 47, no. 15, pp. 1249–66.

Nickell, S. J. (1980) 'A Picture of Male Unemployment in Britain', *Economic Journal*, vol. 90, no. 360, pp. 776–95.

Nickell, S. (1984) 'A Review of *Unemployment: cause and cure* by P. Minford', *Economic Journal*, vol. 94, no. 376, pp. 946–53.

Nickell, S. (1987) 'Why is Wage Inflation in Britain So High?', *Oxford Bulletin of Economics and Statistics*, vol. 49, no. 1, pp. 103–28.

Nickell, S. (1990) 'Unemployment: A Survey', *Economic Journal*, vol. 100, no. 401, pp. 391–439.

Nickell, S. and Andrews, M. (1983) 'Unions, Real Wages and Employment in

Britain, 1951–79', *Oxford Economic Papers*, vol. 35, no. 1, pp. 183–206.

Oaxaca, R. (1973) 'Male–Female Wage Differentials in Urban Labor Markets', *International Economic Review*, vol. 14, no. 1, pp. 693–709.

Oi, W. (1962) 'Labor as a Quasi-Fixed Factor', *Journal of Political Economy*, vol. 70, no. 6, pp. 538–55.

Olsen, R. J. (1980) 'A Least Squares Correction for Selectivity Bias', *Econometrica*, vol. 48, no. 7, pp. 1815–20.

Oppenheimer, V. (1974) *The Female Labor Force in the United States: Demographic and Economic Factors Governing its Growth and Changing Composition* (Berkeley: University of California Press).

Orazem, P. F., Mattila, J. P. and Yu, R. C. (1989) 'An Index Number Approach to the Measurement of Wage Differentials by Sex', *Journal of Human Resources*, vol. 25, no. 1, Winter, pp.125–136.

Oswald, A. J. (1982) 'The Microeconomic Theory of the Trade Union', *Economic Journal*, vol. 92, no. 367, pp. 576–95.

Oswald, A. J. (1985) 'The Economic Theory of the Trade Union: An Introductory Survey', *Scandinavian Journal of Economics*, vol. 87, no. 2, pp. 160–93.

Oswald, A. J. (1987) 'Efficient Contracts Are on the Labour Demand Curve: Theory and Facts' (Centre for Labour Economics, London School of Economics), Discussion Paper No. 284.

Oswald, A. J. and Turnbull, P. (1985) 'Pay and Employment Determination in Britain: What Are Labour Contracts Really Like?', *Oxford Review of Economic Policy*, vol. 1, pp. 80–97.

Oulton, W. N. (1974) 'The Distribution of Education and the Distribution of Earnings', *Economica*, vol. 41, no. 164, pp. 387–402.

Pareto, V. (1895) 'La Legge della Domanda', *Giornale Degli Economisti*, vol. 2, (ser. 2).

Pareto, V. (1896) *La Courbe de la Repartition de la Richess*, (Lausanne: Viret-Genton).

Pareto, V. (1987) *Cours d'Economie Politique* (Geneva: Librairie Droz).

Parnes, H. S. (1964) *Planning Education for Economic and Social Development* (Paris: Organisation for Economic Cooperation and Development).

Parsley, C. J. (1980) 'Labour Unions and Wages: A Survey', *Journal of Economic Literature*, vol. 18, no. 1, pp. 1–31.

Paul, J. J. (1985) 'Basic Concepts and Methods Used in Forecasting Skilled-Manpower Requirements in France', in R. V. Youdi and K. Hinchliffe (eds.), *Forecasting Manpower Needs: The Experience of Eleven Countries* (Paris: UNESCO (International Institute for Educational Studies)).

Peel, D. A. (1972) 'The Kinked Demand Curve: The Demand for Labour', *Recherches économiques de Louvain*, no. 3, pp. 267–74.

Pelling, H. (1971) *A History of British Trade Unionism*, 2nd edn (Harmondsworth: Penguin).

Pen, J. (1952) 'A General Theory of Bargaining', *American Economic Review*, vol. 42, no. 1, pp. 24–42.

Pen, J. (1959) *The Wage Rate under Collective Bargaining*, trans. by T. S. Preston (Cambridge, Mass.: Harvard University Press).

Pen, J. (1971) *Income Distribution* (Harmondsworth: Penguin).

Pencavel, J. H. (1974) 'Relative Wages and Trade Unions in the United Kingdom', *Economica*, new series, vol. 41, no. 162, pp. 194–210.

Pencavel, J. H. (1984) 'The Trade-Off Between Wages and Employment in Trade Union Objectives', *Quarterly Journal of Economics*, vol. 99, no. 2, pp. 215–32.

Pencavel, J. H. (1986) 'Labor Supply of Men: A Survey', in O. Ashenfelter and R. Layard (eds), *Handbook of Labor Economics* (New York and Amsterdam: North-Holland).

Perlman, R. (1969) *Labor Theory* (London: Wiley).

Pesaran, M. H. (1991) 'Expectations in Economics', in D. Greenaway, M. Bleaney and I. M. T. Stewart (eds), *Companion to Contemporary Economic Thought* (London: Routledge), pp. 161–83.

Phelps, E. S. (1968) 'Money Wage Dynamics and Labor Market Equilibrium', *Journal of Political Economy*, vol. 74, no. 4, pp. 678–711.

Phelps, E. S. (1972) 'The Statistical Theory of Racism and Sexism', *American Economic Review*, vol. 62, no. 4, pp. 659–61.

Phelps-Brown, E. H. (1968) *The Inequality of Pay* (Oxford: Oxford University Press).

Phillips, A. W. (1958) 'The Relationship Between Unemployment and the Rate of Change of Money Wage Rates in the UK, 1861–1957', *Economica*, new series, vol. 25, no. 100, pp. 283–99.

Pickering, G. M. and Pickering, J. E. (1985) *Contemporary Economic Systems: A Comparative View*, 2nd edn (St. Paul: West Publish Company).

Pigou, A. C. (1905) *Principles and Methods of Industrial Peace* (London: Macmillan).

Pigou, A. C. (1952) *Essays in Economics* (London: Macmillan).

Pike, M. (1982) 'Segregation by Sex, Earnings Differentials and Equal Pay: An Application of the Crowding Model to U.K. Data', *Applied Economics*, vol. 14, no. 5, pp. 503–14.

Pike, M. (1985) 'The Employment Response to Equal Pay Legislation', *Oxford Economic Papers*, vol. 37, pp. 304–18.

Piore, M. J. (1975) 'Notes for a Theory of Labor Market Stratification', in R. C. Edwards, M. Reich and D. M. Gordon (eds), *Labor Market Segmentation* (Lexington, Mass.: D. C. Heath), pp. 125–50.

Piore, M. J. (1979) *Unemployment and Inflation: Institutionalist and Structuralist Views* (White Plains, NY: M. E. Sharp).

Piore, M. J. (1983) 'Labor Market Segmentation: To What Paradigm Does it Belong?', *American Economics Association Papers and Proceedings*, vol. 73 (May), pp. 249–53.

Pissarides, C. (1978) 'The Role of Relative Wages and the Excess Demand in the Sectoral Flow of Labour', *Review of Economic Studies*, vol. 45, no. 141, pp. 453–468.

Pissarides, C. (1985) 'Job Search and the Functioning of Labour Markets', in D. Carline, C. Pissarides, W. Siebert and P. Sloane (eds), *Labour Economics* (London: Longman), pp. 159–85.

Polachek, S. W. (1975) 'Potential Biases in Measuring Male–Female Discrimination', *Journal of Human Resources*, vol. 10, no. 2, pp. 205–29.

Psacharopoulos, G. (1975) *Earnings and Education in OECD Countries* (Paris: Organisation for Economic Cooperation and Development).
Psacharopoulos, G. (1984) 'The Contribution of Education to Economic Growth: International Comparisons', in J. W. Kendrick (ed.), *International Comparisons of Productivity and Causes of Slowdown* (Cambridge Mass.: American Enterprise Institute/Ballinger Publishing Company), pp. 335–360.
Psacharopoulos, G. (1985) 'Returns to Education: A Further International Update and Implications', *Journal of Human Resources*, vol. 14, no. 4, pp. 584–604.
Psacharopoulos, G. (1987) 'To Vocationalize or Not to Vocationalize? That is the Curriculum Question', *International Review of Education*, vol. 33, no. 2, pp. 187–211.
Psacharopoulos, G. (1988) 'The Contribution of Education to Economic Growth: International Comparison', in J. W. Kendrick (ed.), *International Comparisons of Productivity and Causes of the Slowdown* (Cambridge, Mass.: American Enterprise Institute/Ballinger Publishing Company), pp. 335–59.
Psacharopoulos, G. and Hinchliffe, M. (1972) 'Further Evidence on the Elasticity of Substitution Between Different Types of Educated Labor', *Journal of Political Economy*, vol. 80, no. 4, pp. 786–92.
Psacharopoulos, G. and Layard, R. (1979) 'Human Capital and Earnings: British Evidence and a Critique', *Review of Economic Studies*, vol. 46, no. 3, pp. 485–503.
Psacharopoulos, G. and Tzannatos, Z. (1989) 'Female Labor Force Participation: An International Perspective', *The World Bank Research Observer*, vol. 4, no. 2, pp. 187–202.
Psacharopoulos, G. and Tzannatos, Z. (1991) 'Female Labor Force Participation and Education', in G. Psacharopoulos (ed.), *Essays on Poverty, Equity and Growth* (Pergamon Press for the World Bank).
Psacharopoulos, G. and Tzannatos, Z. (1992a) *Women's Employment and Pay in Latin America: Overview and Methodology* (Washington, DC: The World Bank).
Psacharopoulos, G. and Tzannatos, Z. (eds) (1992b) *Case Studies on Women's Employment and Pay in Latin America* (Washington, DC: The World Bank).
Raff, D. and Summers, L. (1987) 'Did Henry Ford Pay Efficiency Wages?', *Journal of Labor Economics*, vol. 5 (Supplement), pp. S57–S86.
Raisian, J. (1983) 'Contracts, Job Experience and Cyclical Labor Market Adjustment', *Journal of Labor Economics*, vol. 1, no. 2, pp. 152–70.
Rathbone, E. (1917) 'The Remuneration of Women's Services', *Economic Journal*, vol. 27, pp. 55–68.
Reder, M. (1952) 'The Theory of Union Wage Policy', *Review of Economics and Statistics*, vol. 34, no. 1, pp. 34–55.
Reder, M. W. (1960) 'Job Scarcity and the Nature of Union Power', *Industrial and Labor Relations Review*, vol. 13, no. 3, pp. 349–62.
Reder, M. W. (1965) 'Unions and Wages: The Problems of Measurement', *Journal of Political Economy*, vol. 63, no. 2, pp. 188–96.
Reder, M. (1988) 'The Rise and Fall of Unions: The Public Sector and the

Private', *Journal of Economic Perspectives*, vol. 2, no. 2, pp. 89–110.
Rees, A. (1963) 'The Effects of Unions on Resource Allocation', *Journal of Law and Economics*, vol. 6, pp. 69–78.
Rees, A. (1973) *The Economics of Work and Pay* (New York: Harper & Row).
Rees, A. and Schultz, G. (1970) *Workers and Wages in an Urban Labor Market* (Chicago: University of Chicago Press).
Reich, M. (1981) *Racial Inequality: A Political Economic Analysis* (Princeton, NJ: Princeton University Press).
Reynolds, L. G. (1978) *Labor Economics and Labor Relations*, 7th edn (Englewood Cliffs, NJ: Prentice-Hall).
Richardson, R. (1977) 'Review article, 'Trade union growth', *British Journal of Industrial Relations*, vol. 15, no. 2, pp. 279–82.
Richardson, R. (1978) 'Trade Union Growth: A Rejoinder', *British Journal of Industrial Relations*, vol. 26, no. 1, pp. 103–5.
Robbins, L. (1930) 'On the Elasticity of Demand for Income in Terms of Effort', *Economica*, vol. 10, no. 29, pp. 123–9.
Roberts, D. R. (1956) 'A General Theory of Executive Compensation Based on Statistically Tested Propositions', *Quarterly Journal of Economics*, vol. 70 (May), pp. 270–294.
Robinson, D. (ed.) (1970) *Local Labour Markets and Wage Structures* (London: Gower).
Robinson, J. (1933) *The Economics of Imperfect Competition* (London: Macmillan).
Roemer, J. E. (1979) 'Divide and Conquer: Microfoundations of a Marxian Theory of Wage Discrimination', *Bell Journal of Economics*, vol. 10, pp. 695–705.
Rosen, H. S. (1969) 'On Interindustry Wage and Hours Structure', *Journal of Political Economy*, vol. 77, no. 2, pp. 249–73.
Rosen, H. S. (1976) 'Taxes in a Labor Supply Model with Joint Wage-Hours Determination', *Econometrica*, vol. 44, no. 3, pp. 485–507.
Rosen, S. (1969) 'Trade Union Power, Threat Effects and the Extent of Organisation', *Review of Economic Studies*, vol. 36, no. 106, pp. 185–96.
Rosen, S. (1970) 'Unionism and the Occupational Wage Structure in the United States', *International Economic Review*, vol. 11, no. 2, pp. 269–86.
Rosen S. (1985) 'Implicit Contracts: A Survey', *Journal of Economic Literature*, vol. 23, pp. 1144–75.
Rosen, H. S. and Quandt, R. E. (1978) 'Estimation of a Disequilibrium Aggregate Labour Market', *Review of Economics and Statistics*, vol. 60, no. 3, pp. 341–9.
Ross, A. M. (1948) *Trade Union Wage Policy* (Berkeley, Calif.: University of California Press).
Rossi, A. S. (ed.) (1970) *Mill, J. S. and Mill, H. T.: on Sex Equality* (Chicago: University of Chicago Press).
Rubery, J. (ed.) (1988) *Women and the Recession* (London: Routledge).
Rubinstein, A. (1982) 'Perfect Equilibrium in a Bargaining Model', *Econometrica*, vol. 50, no. 1, pp. 97–110.
Sahn, D. and Alderman, H. (1988) 'The Effects of Human Capital on Wages

and the Determinants of Labor Supply in a Developing Country', *Journal of Development Economics*, vol. 28, no. 2, pp. 157–73.
Salop, J. and Salop, S. (1976) 'Self-Selection and Turnover in the Labour Market', *Quarterly Journal of Economics*, vol. 91 (November), pp. 619–27.
Salop, S. C. (1979) 'A Model of the Natural Rate of Unemployment', *American Economic Review*, vol. 69, no. 1, pp. 117–25.
Samuelson, P. A. (1954) 'Some Psychological Aspects of Mathematics in Economics', *Review of Economics and Statistics*, vol. 36, no. 4, pp. 380–386.
Santomero, A. and Seater, J. J. (1978) 'The Inflation–Unemployment Trade-off: A Critique of the Literature', *Journal of Economic Literature*, vol. 16, no. 2, pp. 499–544.
Sapsford, D. R. (1979) 'The Theory of Bargaining: A Selective Survey with Particular Reference to Union–Employer Negotiations and the Occurrence of Strikes', *Economic and Social Research Institute, Memorandum Series*, no. 132.
Sapsford, D. (1981) *Labour Market Economics* (London: Allen & Unwin).
Sapsford, D. (1981a) 'Productivity Growth in the UK: A Reconsideration', *Applied Economics*, vol. 13, no. 4, pp. 499–511.
Sapsford, D. (1982) 'The Theory of Bargaining and Strike Activity', *International Journal of Social Economics*, vol. 9, no. 2, pp. 3–31.
Sapsford, D. (1984) 'The Determinants of Trade Union Growth in the Republic of Ireland: An Econometric Investigation', *Economic and Social Review*, vol. 15, no. 4, pp. 305–23.
Sapsford, D. (1986) 'Some Further Evidence on the Role of Profits in Union Growth Equations', *Applied Economics*, vol. 17, no. 3, pp. 27–36.
Sapsford, D. (1990) 'Strikes: Models and Evidence', in D. Sapsford and Z. Tzannatos (eds), *Current Issues in Labour Economics* (London: Macmillan), pp. 126–50.
Sapsford, D. (1991) 'The Labour Market: Unemployment and Search Theory', in D. Greenaway, M. Bleaney and I. M. T. Stewart (eds), *Companion to Contemporary Economic Thought* (London: Routledge), pp. 461–81.
Sapsford, D. and Tzannatos, Z. (eds) (1990) *Current Issues in Labour Economics* (London: Macmillan).
Saraydar, E. (1965) 'Zeuthen's Theory of Bargaining: A Note', *Econometrica*, vol. 33, no. 4, pp. 802–13.
Sargan, J. D. (1964) 'Wages and Prices in the United Kingdom: A Study in Econometric Methodology', in P. E. Hart, G. Mills and J. K. Whitaker (eds), *Econometric Analysis for National Economic Planning* (London: Butterworths), pp. 25–54.
Sawyer, M. (1979) 'The Effects of Unemployment Compensation on the Rate of Unemployment in Great Britain: A Comment', *Oxford Economic Papers*, vol. 31, no. 1, pp. 135–46.
Sargan, J. D. (1980) 'A Model of Wage–Price Inflation', *Review of Economic Studies*, vol. 47, pp. 97–112.
Schiller, B. R. and Weiss, R. (1979) 'Frontier Production Function', *Econometric Reviews*, vol. 4, pp. 289–328.

Schmidt, P. (1978) 'Estimation of a Simultaneous Equations Model with Jointly Dependent Continuous and Qualitative Variables: The Union–Earnings Question Revisited', *International Economic Review*, vol. 19, no. 2, pp. 453–65.

Schmidt, P. and Strauss, R. P. (1976) 'The Effects of Unions on Earnings and Earnings on Unions: A Mixed Logit Approach', *International Economic Review*, vol. 17, no. 1, pp. 204–12.

Schultz, R. W. (1961) 'Education and Economic Growth', in N. B. Henry (ed.), *Social Forces Influencing American Education* (Chicago: University of Chicago Press for the National Society for the Study of Education), pp. 46–88.

Schultz, T. P. (1982) 'Women's Work and Their Status: Rural Indian Evidence of the Labor Market and Environment Effects on Sex Differences in Childhood Mortality', in R. Anker, M. Buvinic and N. Youssef (eds), *Women's Roles and Population Trends in the Third World* (London: Croom Helm), pp. 202–38.

Schultz, T. P. (1989) 'Returns to Women's Education' (Washington, DC: The World Bank) (PHRWD/89/001).

Schultz, T. W. (1984) 'A Comment on Education and Economic Growth', in J. W. Kendrick (ed.), *International Comparisons of Productivity and Causes of the Slowdown* (Cambridge, Mass.: American Enterprise Institute/ Ballinger Publishing Company), pp. 357–60.

Selowsky, M. (1979) *Who Benefits From Government Expenditure: A Case Study of Colombia* (Oxford: Oxford University Press).

Shackle, G. L. S. (1957) 'The Nature of the Bargaining Process', in J. T. Dunlop (ed.), *The Theory of Wage Determination* (London: Macmillan), pp. 292–314.

Shapiro, D. M. and Stelcner, M. (1986) 'Public–Private Sector Earnings Differentials in Canada, 1970–1980' (Concordia University, Montreal: Department of Economics), Working Paper No. 1986–3.

Shapiro, C. and Stiglitz, J. (1984) 'Equilibrium Unemployment as a Worker Discipline Device', *American Economic Review*, vol. 74, no. 3, pp. 433–44.

Shaw, G. K. (1984) *Rational Expectations: An Elementary Exposition* (Brighton: Wheatsheaf; New York: St Martin's Press).

Shaw, G. K. (1989) 'Expectations in Macroeconomics', in D. Greenaway (ed.), *Current Issues in Macroeconomics* (London: Macmillan), pp. 22–44.

Sheffrin, S. M. (1983) *Rational Expectations* (Cambridge: Cambridge University Press).

Sheflin, N. L., Troy, L. and Koeller, L. T. (1981) 'Structural Stability in Models of American Trade Union Growth', *Quarterly Journal of Economics*, vol. 96, no. 1, pp. 77–88.

Shubik, M. (1959) *Strategy and Market Structure* (New York: Wiley).

Siebert, W. S. (1985) 'Developments in the Economics of Human Capital', in D. Carline, C. A. Pissarides, W. S. Siebert and P. J. Sloane (eds), *Labour Economics* (London: Longman), pp. 5–77.

Siebert, W. S. (1989) 'Comparable Worth: An Evaluation', mimeograph (University of Birmingham: Institute of Economic and Business Studies).

Siebert, W. S. and Addison, J. T. (1991) 'Internal Labour Markets: Causes and Consequences', *Oxford Review of Economic Policy*, vol. 7, no. 1, Spring, pp. 76–92.

Simon, H. (1957) 'The Compensation of Executives', *Sociometry*, vol. 20, pp. 32–35.

Sinclair, P. (1987) *Unemployment: Economic Theory and Evidence* (Oxford: Basil Blackwell).

Sloane, P. J. (1985) 'Discrimination in the Labour Market', in D. Carline, C. A. Pissarides, W. S. Siebert and P. J. Sloane (eds), *Labour Economics* (London: Longman), pp. 78–157.

Smith, A. (1776) *The Wealth of Nations* (London: Strahan & Cadell, 1776; reprinted London: Everyman's Library, 1977).

Smith, S. P. (1977) *Equal Pay in the Public Sector: Fact or Fantasy?* (Princeton NJ: Princeton University Press).

Sobel, I. (1982) 'Human Capital and Institutionalist Theories of the Labor Market: Rivals or Compliments?', *Journal of Economic Issues*, vol. 16 (March), pp. 255–72.

Solow, R. (1979) 'Another Possible Source of Wage Stickiness', *Journal of Macroeconomics*, vol. 1, no. 1, pp. 79–82.

Solow, R. (1985) 'Insiders and Outsiders in Wage Determination', *Scandinavian Journal of Economics*, vol. 87, no. 2, pp. 411–28.

Sorenson, A. B. (1983) 'Sociological Research on the Labor Market: Conceptual and Methodological Issues', *Work on Occupations*, vol. 10 (August), pp. 261–87.

Sowell, T. (1981) *Markets and Minorities* (Oxford: Basil Blackwell).

Spence, M. A. (1974) *Market Signalling: Informational Transfer in Hiring and Related Screening Processes* (Cambridge, Mass.: Harvard University Press).

Stafford, F. P. (1968) 'Concentration and Labor Earnings: Comment', *American Economic Review*, vol. 58, no. 1, pp. 174–81.

Stelcner, M., and Breslaw, J. (1985) 'Income Taxes and Labor Supply of Married Women in Quebec', *Southern Economic Journal*, vol. 51, no. 4, pp. 1053–72.

Stewart, M. B. (1983) 'Relative Earnings and Individual Union Membership in the United Kingdom', *Economica*, vol. 50, no. 198, pp. 111–25.

Stewart, M. B. and Greenhalgh, C. A. (1984) 'Work History Patterns and Occupational Attainment of Women', *Economic Journal*, vol. 94, pp. 493–519.

Stigler, G. (1961) 'The Economics of Information', *Journal of Political Economy*, vol. 69, no. 3, pp. 213–25.

Stigler, G. (1962) 'Information in the Labor Market', *Journal of Political Economy*, vol. 70, no. 5 (Part 2).

Stiglitz, J. (1974) 'Wage Determination and Unemployment in LDC's: The Labor Turnover Model', *Quarterly Journal of Economics*, vol. 88, no. 1, pp. 194–227.

Stiglitz, J. E. (1985) 'Equilibrium Wage Distributions', *Economic Journal*, vol. 95, no. 379, pp. 595–618.

Stolzenberg, R. M. (1978) 'Bringing the Boss Back In: Employer Size, Employee

Schooling and Socio-economic Achievement', *American Sociological Review*, vol. 43, pp. 813–28.

Sumner, M. T. and Ward, R. (1983) 'The Reappearing Phillips Curve', *Oxford Economic Papers*, vol. 35 (special issue on unemployment), pp. 152–66.

Swidinsky, R. (1976) 'Strike Settlement and Economic Activity: An Empirical Analysis', *Relations Industrielles*, vol. 31, no. 2, pp. 209–23.

Taubman, P. J. and Wales, T. (1973) *Higher Education and Earnings: College as an Investment and a Screening Device* (New York: McGraw-Hill).

Taylor, J. (1974) *Unemployment and Wage Inflation with Special Reference to Britain and the USA* (London: Longman).

Taylor, J. B. (1979) 'Staggered Wage Setting in a Macro Model', *American Economic Review (Papers and Proceedings)*, vol. 68, pp. 108–13.

Taylor, J. B. (1980) 'Aggregate Dynamics and Staggered Contracts', *Journal of Political Economy*, vol. 88, no. 1, pp. 1–23.

Tella, A. (1964) 'The Relation of Labor Force to Employment', *Industrial and Labor Relations Review*, vol. 17, no. 3, pp. 454–69.

Tella, A. (1965) 'Labor Force Sensitivity to Employment by Age, Sex', *Industrial Relations*, vol. 4, no. 2, pp. 69–83.

Thatcher, A. R. (1976) 'The New Earnings Survey and the Distribution of Earnings', in A. B. Atkinson (ed.), *The Personal Distribution of Incomes*, (London: George Allen & Unwin).

Thirlwall, A. P. (1969) 'Types of Unemployment: With Special Reference to "Non-Demand-Deficient" Unemployment in Great Britain', *Scottish Journal of Political Economy*, vol. 16, no. 1, pp. 20–49.

Throop, A. W. (1968) 'The Union–Non-Union Wage Differential and Cost-Push Inflation', *American Economic Review*, vol. 58, no. 1, pp. 79–99.

Thurow, L. (1969) *Poverty and Discrimination* (Washington, DC: The Brookings Institution).

Thurow, L. C. (1975) *Generating Inequality* (New York: Basic Books).

Tilak, J. B. G. (1987) *The Economics of Inequality in Education* (New Delhi: Sage).

Tinbergen, J. (1975) 'Income Distribution' (Amsterdam: North Holland).

Tinbergen, J. and Bos, H. C. (1965) 'A Planning Model for the Educational Requirements of Economic Development', in *OECD Econometric Models of Education* (Paris: OECD).

Todaro, M. P. (1989) *Economic Development in the Third World*, 4th edn (London: Longman).

Treble, J. (1984) 'Does the Union/Non-Union Differential Exist?', *Manchester School*, vol. 52, no. 2, pp. 160–170.

Turnbull, P. (1988) 'Industrial Relations and the Seniority Model of Union Behaviour', *Oxford Bulletin of Economics and Statistics*, vol. 50, no. 1, pp. 53–70.

Turnbull, P. (1989) 'Trade Unions and Productivity: Opening the Harvard "Black Boxes"', *Journal of Labor Research*, vol. 12, no. 2, pp. 35–50.

Turnbull, P. and Sapsford, D. (1992) 'A Sea of Discontent: The Tides of Organised and "Unorganised" Conflict on the Docks', *Sociology*, vol. 26, no. 2, pp. 291–309.

Turner, H. A. (1962) *Trade Union Growth, Structure and Policy* (London: Allen & Unwin).
Tzannatos, Z. (1986) 'Female Discrimination in Britain: Has the State Unshackled the Market?', *Economic Affairs*, vol. 7, no. 2, pp. 26–9.
Tzannatos, Z. (1987a) 'Equal Pay in Greece and Britain', *Industrial Relations Journal*, vol. 18, no. 4 (1984), pp. 275–83.
Tzannatos, Z. (1987b) 'A General Equilibrium Model of Discrimination and Its Effects on Incomes', *Scottish Journal of Political Economy*, vol. 34, no. 1, pp.19–36.
Tzannatos, Z. (1987c) 'The Greek Labour Market: Current Perspectives and Future Prospects', *Greek Economic Review*, vol. 9, no. 2, pp. 224–38.
Tzannatos, Z. (1988a) 'The Long Run Effects of the Sex Integration of the British Labour Market', *Journal of Economic Studies*, vol. 15, no. 1, pp. 5–18.
Tzannatos, Z. (1988b) 'The Distribution of Earnings in Britain', *Developments in Economics*, vol. 4, pp. 43–63.
Tzannatos, Z. (1989) 'Female Wages and Equal Pay in Greece', *Journal of Modern Greek Studies*, vol. 7, pp. 155–169.
Tzannatos, Z. (1991) 'Reverse Discrimination in Higher Education: Does It Reduce Inequality and at What Cost to the Poor?', *International Journal of Educational Development*, vol. 11, no. 3, pp. 177–92.
Tzannatos, Z. and Zabalza, A. (1984) 'The Anatomy of the Rise of British Female Relative Wages in the 1970s: Evidence from the New Earnings Survey', *British Journal of Industrial Relations*, vol. 22, no. 2, pp. 177–94.
Tzannatos, Z. and Zabalza, A. (1985) 'The Effect of Sex Discrimination Legislation on the Variability of Female Employment in Britain', *Applied Economics*, vol. 17, pp. 1117–34.
Tzannatos, Z. and Symons, J. (1989) 'An Economic Approach to Fertility in Britain Since 1860', *Journal of Population Economics*, vol. 2, no. 2 (1989), pp. 121–38.
Ullman, L. (1955) 'Marshall and Friedman on Union Strength', *Review of Economics and Statistics*, vol. 37, no. 4, pp. 384–401.
Ulph, A. and Ulph, D. (1990) 'Union Bargaining: A Survey of Recent Work', in D. Sapsford and Z. Tzannatos (eds), *Current Issues in Labour Economics* (London: Macmillan), pp. 85–125.
Varian, H. R. (1978) *Microeconomic Analysis* (New York: Norton).
Varoufakis, Y. and Sapsford, D. (1990) 'A Real Target Model of Wage Inflation with Variable Union Power', *Applied Economics*, vol. 22, no. 8, pp. 1103–17.
Visaria, P. M. (1971) 'The Sex Ratio of the Population of India, 1961.' Census of India vol. 1, Monograph no. 10 (New Delhi: Office of the Registrar General of India).
Wabe, S. and Leech, D. (1978) 'Relative Earnings in UK Manufacturing: A Reconsideration of the Evidence, *Economic Journal*, vol. 88, no. 350, pp. 296–313.
Wachter, M. L. (1972) 'A Labor Supply Model for Secondary Workers', *Review of Economics and Statistics*, vol. 54, no. 2, pp. 141–51.

Wachter, M. L. (1974) 'A New Approach to Equilibrium Labor Force', *Economica*, new series, vol. 41, no. 161, pp. 35–51.

Wales, T. and Woodland, A. D. (1980) 'Sample Selectivity and the Estimation of Labor Supply Functions', *International Economic Review*, vol. 21, no. 2, pp. 437–68.

Wallis, K., Andrews, M. J., Bell, D. N. F., Fisher, P. G. and Whitley, J. D. (1984) *Models of the UK Economy* (Oxford University Press).

Walton, R. E. and McKersie, R. B. (1965) *A Behavioral Theory of Labor Negotiations* (New York: McGraw-Hill).

Webb, B. (1919) *The Wages of Men and Women: Why Should They be Equal?* (London: Fabian Society and Allen & Unwin).

Webb, S. (1891) 'The Alleged Differences in the Wages Paid to Men and Women for Similar Work', *Economic Journal*, vol. 1, pp. 635–62.

Webb, S. and Webb, B. (1920) *The History of Trade Unionism*, revised edn (London: Longmans Green).

Weiniger, O. (1906) *Sex and Character* (London: Heineman).

Weiss, L. W. (1966) 'Concentration and Labor Earnings', *American Economic Review*, vol. 56, no. 1, pp. 96–117.

Weiss, A. (1980) 'Job Queues and Layoffs in Labor Markets with Flexible Wages', *Journal of Political Economy*, vol. 88, no. 3, pp. 526–38.

Weiss, A. (1990) *Efficiency Wages: Models of Unemployment, Layoffs, and Wage Dispersion* (Oxford: Clarendon Press).

Weiss, Y. and Gronau, R. (1981) 'Expected Interruptions in Labor Force Participation and Sex-related Differences in Earnings Growth', *Review of Economic Studies*, vol. 58, pp. 607–19.

Welch, F. (1966) 'Measurement of the Quality of Schooling', *American Economic Review*, vol. 56, no. 2, pp. 311–27.

Wickens, M. R. (1974) 'Towards a theory of the labour market', *Economica*, new series, vol. 41, no. 163, pp. 278–94.

Willis, R. J. (1986) 'Wage Determinants: A Survey and Reinterpretation of Human Capital Earnings', in O. Ashenfelter and R. Layard (eds), *Handbook of Labor Economics* (Amsterdam: North-Holland), pp. 525–601.

Willis, R. J. and Rosen, S. (1979) 'Education and Self-Selection', *Journal of Political Economy*, vol. 87, no. 5 (Part 2), pp. S7–S36.

Wolpin, K. (1977) 'Education and Screening', *American Economic Review*, vol. 67, no. 5 (December), pp. 949–58.

Wright, R. E. and Ermisch, J. F. (1991) 'Gender Discrimination in the British Labour Market: A Reassessment', *Economic Journal*, vol. 101, no. 406, pp. 508–22.

Yellen, J. (1984) 'Efficiency Wage Models of Unemployment', *American Economic Review (Papers and Proceedings)*, vol. 74, pp. 200–5.

Yfantopoulos, J. (1991) *An Assessment of the European Communities Household Panel on the Base of the National Feasibility Studies* (Luxembourg: EUROSTAT, Doc. HI 12/91).

Youdi, R. V. and Hinchliffe, K. (eds) (1985) *Forecasting Skilled Manpower Needs: The Experience of Eleven Countries* (Paris: UNESCO (International Institute for Educational Studies)).

Zabalza, A. and Arrufat, J. L. (1985) 'The Extent of Sex Discrimination in Britain', in A. Zabalza and Z. Tzannatos (eds), *Women and Equal Pay: The Effects of Legislation on Female Employment and Wages in Britain* (Cambridge: Cambridge University Press), pp. 70–96.

Zabalza, A. and Tzannatos, Z. (1985a) *Women and Equal Pay: The Effects of Legislation on Female Employment and Wages in Britain* (Cambridge: Cambridge University Press).

Zabalza, A. and Tzannatos, Z. (1985b) 'The Effect of Britain's Sex Anti-Discriminatory Legislation on Relative Pay and Employment', *Economic Journal*, vol. 95, pp. 679–99.

Zabalza, A. and Tzannatos, Z. (1988) 'Reply to the Comments on the Effects of Britain's Anti-Discriminatory Legislation on Relative Pay and Employment', *Economic Journal*, vol. 98, pp. 839–43.

Zeuthen, F. (1930) *Problems of Monopoly and Economic Warfare* (London: Routledge).

Zymelman, M. (1980a) *Occupational Structure of Industries* (Washington, DC: The World Bank (Education Department)).

Zymelman, M. (1980b) *Forecasting Manpower Demand* (Washington DC: The World Bank (Education Department)).

Index